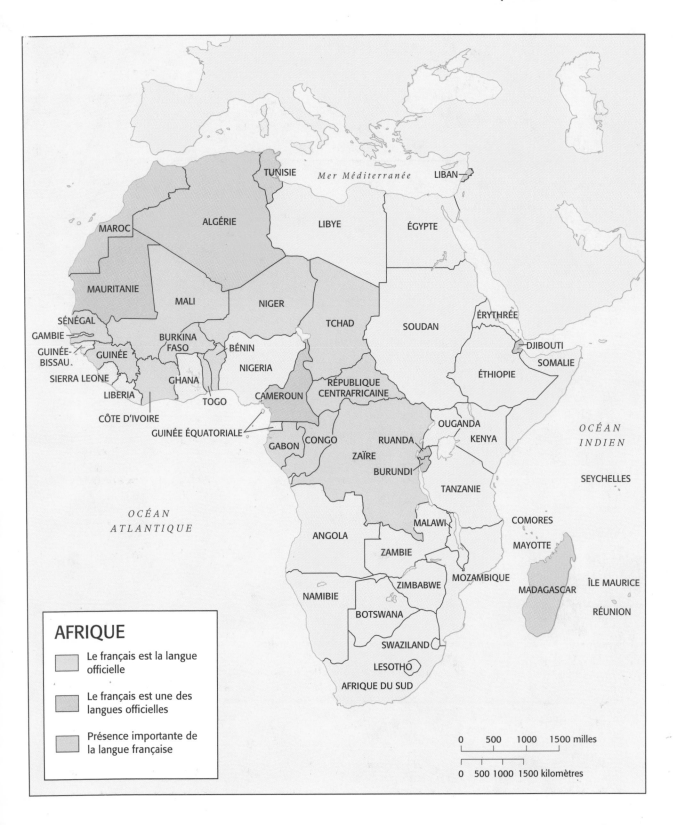

W9-API-549

AFRIQUE

Mer Méditerranée

LIBAN

OCÉAN ATLANTIQUE

OCÉAN INDIEN

TUNISIE
MAROC
ALGÉRIE
LIBYE
ÉGYPTE
MAURITANIE
MALI
NIGER
TCHAD
SOUDAN
ÉRYTHRÉE
SÉNÉGAL
GAMBIE
GUINÉE-BISSAU
GUINÉE
BURKINA FASO
BÉNIN
NIGERIA
DJIBOUTI
SOMALIE
SIERRA LEONE
GHANA
ÉTHIOPIE
LIBERIA
TOGO
CÔTE D'IVOIRE
CAMEROUN
RÉPUBLIQUE CENTRAFRICAINE
GUINÉE ÉQUATORIALE
GABON
CONGO
RUANDA
OUGANDA
KENYA
ZAÏRE
BURUNDI
TANZANIE
SEYCHELLES
MALAWI
COMORES
ANGOLA
MAYOTTE
ZAMBIE
MOZAMBIQUE
ZIMBABWE
ÎLE MAURICE
NAMIBIE
MADAGASCAR
RÉUNION
BOTSWANA
SWAZILAND
LESOTHO
AFRIQUE DU SUD

AFRIQUE

Le français est la langue officielle

Le français est une des langues officielles

Présence importante de la langue française

0   500   1000   1500 milles

0   500 1000 1500 kilomètres

Rapports

Rapports

Fourth Edition

Language, Culture, Communication

Joel Walz
UNIVERSITY OF GEORGIA

Jean-Pierre Piriou
UNIVERSITY OF GEORGIA

Houghton Mifflin Company   BOSTON   NEW YORK

Senior Sponsoring Editor: E. Kristina Baer
Development Editor: Cécile Strugnell
Senior Project Editor: Rosemary R. Jaffe
Senior Production/Design Coordinator: Carol Merrigan
Director of Manufacturing: Michael O'Dea
Marketing Manager: Elaine Uzan Leary

Cover design by Harold Burch, Harold Burch Design, New York City.

Credits for text, illustrations, realia, and photographs are found following the Index at the end of the book.

Printed in the U.S.A.

Library of Congress Catalog Card Number: 96-76970

Student Text ISBN: 0-669-41645-2

Instructor's Annotated Edition ISBN: 0-669-41646-0

    4 5 6 7 8 9-VH-00 99

Table des matières

Preface

Rapports, Fourth Edition, is a complete first-year French program for college and university students. It promotes the active command of spoken French without neglecting the development of your listening, reading, and writing skills. Because *Rapports* focuses on the practical use of French for communication in context, it also emphasizes the everyday life and cultures of the French and of French speakers in other francophone countries.

The Text

Rapports consists of a brief preliminary chapter and eighteen chapters. After every three chapters, there is a review section with oral and written exercises for class work and interactive activities for pair and small group work.

The preliminary chapter enables you to begin talking in French with your fellow students on the very first day of class. In this chapter, you will learn greetings, leave-takings, and basic information about French pronunciation, and you will be introduced to the francophone world through a reading in English.

Each subsequent chapter contains the following features:

1. **Chapter Opener** The first page of each chapter introduces you to the theme, topics, and structures you will study.

   A. **Theme** Each chapter is centered around a theme. The chapter theme will be evident in the opening dialogue, vocabulary, language exercises and activities, functional / situational phrases, and the cultural reading. A unifying theme enhances your ability to understand and learn the language.

   B. **Objectives** The first page of each chapter also sets forth the learning objectives for the chapter according to the textbook's three goals: *Language,* or the structures and vocabulary you will learn; *Culture,* information on the French-speaking world that provides an authentic context; and *Communication,* the notions, functions, and situational language that you will use to express yourself.

2. **Commençons** This section provides samples of everyday language, cultural information, active vocabulary related to the chapter's theme, and information on pronunciation. All these will help you integrate the structures you will be learning so that you can communicate in French.

   A. **Dialogue** Each chapter opens with a dialogue or other type of communication such as a phone conversation, a postcard, a formal letter, a poem, or a fable. The setting for each text is a situation that you might encounter or one that is typical of college-age people in francophone countries. **Etudions le dialogue** provides questions on the content of the opening text. A **Mots clés** section follows, listing all new active vocabulary from the dialogue or text. Three icons refer you to other components of the program. A video icon ▢ indicates that video clips are provided

for each chapter on the accompanying videocassette. A CD-ROM icon
⊙ indicates that the dialogue or text is used as the basis for interactive
learning activities on the CD-ROM. A cassette icon ▭ indicates that the
dialogue or text is recorded on the *Cassette Program* that accompanies
the *Laboratory Manual*. The WWW symbol that appears with most
chapter openers and elsewhere in the chapter means that additional information relating to the content can be accessed through the *Rapports*
Web site.

B. **Faisons connaissance**   This section presents cultural information in English that will help you understand the interaction in the dialogue. It is thematically related to the rest of the chapter and especially to the reading
passage in the **Lecture culturelle** at the end of the chapter.

C. **Enrichissons notre vocabulaire**   Active vocabulary appears here in draw-
ings and in conversational exchanges. The vocabulary will recur throughout the chapter in grammar exercises and activities and in the *Workbook / Laboratory Manual. Rapports* has tightly controlled vocabulary
with active words appearing only in the dialogue, **Faisons connaissance,**
Enrichissons, and grammar presentations when they pertain to the structure being taught. All other sections contain only passive vocabulary,
which your teacher may ask you to learn.

D. **Prononciation**   This section offers detailed, yet simple explanations of
the major features of French pronunciation along with exercises. You
may go over the exercises in class or practice them in the language laboratory since they are recorded on the *Cassette Program* (as the cassette
icon indicates).

3. **Grammaire**   The grammar sections present structures that you can be ex-
pected to handle and use actively. The clear presentations in English allow
you to prepare the lesson before coming to class and thus spend more class
time using the language than talking about it.

A. **Usage statement**   Each presentation begins with a short explanation in
English of *why* you would need to know the structure in order to communicate in French.

B. **Explanation**   The structure is explained in a clear fashion with numerous
examples, which often come from the dialogue.

C. **Ce qu'ils disent**   Spoken French is not exactly like the more formal language taught in textbooks. While you should learn a fairly formal style,
these explanations will help you to understand what you will hear in a
French-speaking country.

D. **L'orthographe**   This section describes the features of the French language
that appear only in writing, since written French sometimes differs from
spoken French.

E. **Attention**   This section points out elements of the language that cause
trouble for non-native speakers or that are easy to forget.

F. **Language / Langue**   The first group of exercises for each grammar point
carries this name (the names as well as directions to all exercises, changes

from English to French as of Chapter 7). These exercises are all meaningful; that is, you must understand the French to produce the correct answer. Virtually all of these exercises also have a short context that unifies the items so that you practice each structure in an everyday situation.

G. **Culture**   For every point of grammar taught, *Rapports,* Fourth Edition, has at least one activity based on cultural similarities and differences between the United States and francophone cultures. You must understand not only the language but also the culture to produce a correct answer. The activities reflect a wide range of content involving everything from famous artists and historical figures to how French speakers conduct their daily lives. You will not know some of the information at first, but you can create sentences that seem logical, and your teacher will guide you to the correct answers.

H. **Communication**   Every grammar point is also followed by a number of activities that allow you to express your own ideas and experiences. The formats always provide suggestions to get you started, but they also encourage originality. The personal questions revolve around a context, which helps you interact with your teacher and classmates in a natural conversation.

4. **Communiquons**   This section introduces a notion, a function, or a situation that is important to communication. A short paragraph in English introduces the topic. Then, you learn various common phrases so you can express your thoughts appropriately in French. The **Expressions** and dialogue or **Interaction** that follows illustrates authentic usage of the phrases presented, and the communication activities allow you to practice, using the new expressions in other contexts. A CD-ROM icon indicates that this dialogue will be used as a trigger for more interactive activities on the CD-ROM.

5. **Lecture culturelle**   Each chapter concludes with a reading passage on a topic related to the cultural theme introduced in the **Commençons** section. The pre-reading section will give you background information, and its activities will help you develop skills so that you can read French more proficiently. The post-reading activities will check your comprehension of the reading passage and will enable you to discuss what you have learned in terms of your own life.

6. **Vocabulaire**   At the end of the chapter, a list of all the active vocabulary in the chapter will help you review the new words you have learned.

End-of-Text Reference Materials

1. Appendices include the International Phonetic Alphabet, the French names of and prepositions used with the fifty American states and the provinces of Canada, supplemental grammar points, and verb conjugation charts.

2. The French-English vocabulary lists all active and passive vocabulary in *Rapports,* Fourth Edition. The English-French vocabulary lists all active words and expressions. Each entry in the vocabularies is followed by a reference indicating the chapter in which it first appears.

3. An index provides ready access to all grammatical structures, vocabulary topics, and pronunciation points presented in the textbook.

The *Rapports* Web Site

A Web site created specifically for users of *Rapports* has more than 150 links to the French-speaking world available to you. Using the World Wide Web is useful for expanding one's knowledge of the French-speaking world, obtaining up-to-date information, and increasing reading skills. We have referenced sites every time we found one corresponding to the content of this book. In order to make use of this feature, you should do the following: Look for the symbol **WWW** in your book; then visit the Houghton Mifflin College Division's site at **http://www.hmco.com/college/languages/Home.html.** When you are on the *Rapports* Resource Center site, read the introduction, or scroll down to the Table of Contents. You can then click on the chapter in *Rapports,* Fourth Edition, that you are currently studying, which will display all the links to sites that correspond to the content of that chapter. Clicking on any underlined words in a contrasting color will connect you with that site. These Web sites will allow you to do such things as see the latest fashions from Paris, study the itinerary of the next Tour de France, plan a subway trip, find out what is on TV in France or Canada, or read the morning paper in French!

The Workbook / Laboratory Manual and Cassette Program

The *Workbook / Laboratory Manual* is fully integrated with *Rapports,* Fourth Edition, to further develop your writing, speaking, and listening skills. The *Workbook* section offers a variety of exercises that require you to write in French using the structures and vocabulary of the corresponding textbook chapter. Each *Workbook* section concludes with **Ecrivons,** a section devoted to directed compositions and open-ended, personalized writing assignments. The *Laboratory* section guides you through the *Cassette Program,* providing pronunciation explanations and exercises and cues for all of the listening-and-speaking and listening-and-writing activities that accompany each chapter. The *Workbook / Laboratory Manual* also provides workbook exercises and laboratory activities for the review sections, which appear after every three chapters.

The *Cassette Program* provides you with forty to fifty minutes of listening material for each textbook chapter and additional listening activities for each review section. The textbook dialogues and pronunciation exercises are recorded. They are followed by a series of listening-and-speaking and listening-and-writing activities for each grammar point. Each chapter concludes with a dictation and a global listening comprehension activity tied thematically to the content of the corresponding textbook chapter.

At the end of the *Workbook / Laboratory Manual,* you will find answers to all exercises and activities that have a fixed response, including the **Dictée** and the **Compréhension.** Check these answers as you complete an activity to be aware of any errors you have made. Whenever you have questions that require a personalized response, you will see the comment "Answers will vary." In those cases, your teacher will have to grade your work. Also, watch for "Possible answers." Your response could be just as correct as the ones given; check with your teacher if you are not sure. Having answer keys will allow you to work independently, to obtain immediate feedback, and to do more than the minimum assignments your teacher gives.

CD-ROM

The *Rapports* CD-ROM incorporates dialogues, vocabulary, and readings from each chapter as source material. This fun, interactive tool provides pronunciation practice, on-line grammar notes, word and phrase meanings, supplemental exercises, and quizzes and self-tests to help you prepare for exams. Four types of activities with sound, voice recordability, scoring, and beat-the-clock options make learning French enjoyable.

Videocassette and Video Manual

This sixty-minute video is divided into modules that present authentic materials related to the cultural theme and / or vocabulary of each textbook chapter. These include television ads, short documentaries, and other materials from French television. The accompanying *Video Manual* contains the complete videoscript followed by activity sheets for each video clip.

Acknowledgments

The authors would like to express their appreciation to the Houghton Mifflin editorial staff for their support in the development and production of this revision. We are particularly grateful to Denise St. Jean who initiated this revision, and to Cécile Strugnell, Development Editor, and Rosemary R. Jaffe, Senior Project Editor, who helped us to complete it. Our thanks also to Eileen LeVan, who revised the *Testing Program* for this edition.

In addition, we would especially like to thank Valérie Boulanger, Ph.D. candidate in Linguistics at the University of Georgia, for compiling the end vocabularies, including the chapter codes that users have found so helpful. Her specialization in lexicography served us well in this respect. We could not have completed this revision without frequent contacts in France, especially with Jean-Claude Pfeffer and his family, Shane Fowler, and Daphne McConnell. We received documents and information from colleagues and students, in particular from Jennifer Higdon, Teri Hernández, Denis Jamet, Andy Wallis, Michael Lindsey, Kristin Bruno, and Raymond Cormier. Our apologies to whomever we have forgotten to mention.

We would also like to thank the following reviewers, who have all used *Rapports* in the past and who have made interesting and useful comments for this revision.

Catherine Jolivet, Southwest Missouri State University, MO
Peter Rogers, Loyola University, New Orleans, LA
Philip Grant, University of Central Florida, Orlando, FL
Megan Conway, Louisiana State University in Shreveport, LA

JOEL WALZ

JEAN-PIERRE PIRIOU

Rapports

Bonjour!

Chapitre préliminaire

Bonjour, Amélie!
Ça va?

Objectives

Language
Idiomatic expressions • Some basic information on pronunciation

Culture
How people greet and take leave of each other • The French-speaking world

Communication
Greetings and leave-takings

Commençons

Stéphane et Amélie ▭

STÉPHANE:	Bonjour!
AMÉLIE:	Salut! Ça va?
STÉPHANE:	Oui, ça va bien. Et toi?
AMÉLIE:	Ça va, merci.
STÉPHANE:	Je m'appelle Stéphane. Et toi?
AMÉLIE:	Amélie.

Laurent et Madame Dumas

MME DUMAS:	Bonjour, Laurent.
LAURENT:	Bonjour, Madame. Comment allez-vous?
MME DUMAS:	Je vais bien, merci. Et vous?
LAURENT:	Très bien, merci.

Mots clés

Bonjour!	*Hello! / Good morning!*	**Je m'appelle...**	*My name is . . .*
Salut!	*Hi!*	**Madame**	*Mrs.; ma'am*
Ça va?	*How's it going?*	**Comment allez-vous?**	*How are you?*
oui	*yes*		
Ça va bien.	*Fine.*	**Je vais bien.**	*I'm fine.*
Et toi?	*And you?*	**Et vous?**	*And you?*
Merci.	*Thank you.*	**Très bien.**	*Very well.*

Faisons connaissance

The way people greet each other varies from culture to culture and depends on how well they know each other. When French people meet, they always make physical contact. Friends and business associates exchange a brief handclasp (**une poignée de main**) not only upon being introduced, but also upon seeing each other for the first time each day, and again upon parting. In France, women shake hands as often as men.

Bonjour, Stéphane!
Ça va?

When two French people who are relatives or good friends see each other, they may embrace lightly and kiss on both cheeks (**faire une bise à…**). It is not unusual for French men to greet each other this way, especially if they are related or if they are celebrating an important occasion. In a French family, all children, no matter how old, will kiss both parents before leaving for the day or going to bed.

Relationships also influence the kind of language people use in greeting each other. For example, in the dialogue, two friends of the same age say «**Salut, ça va?**», but a young person would say to an adult: «**Bonjour, comment allez-vous?**». In general, French people are more formal than Americans, and they are less likely to act casually with new acquaintances.

Enrichissons notre vocabulaire

Faisons connaissance! *(Let's get to know each other!)*

Au revoir.	*Good-bye.*
Bonsoir.	*Hello / Good evening.*
A bientôt.	*See you soon.*
A plus tard.	*See you later.*
A tout à l'heure.	*See you later.*

—Comment ça va?	*How's it going?*
—Pas mal.	*Not bad.*
—Comme ci, comme ça.	*So-so.*
Quoi de neuf?	*What's up?*
monsieur	*Mister; sir*
mademoiselle	*Miss*

Communication

Using the expressions you have just learned in the dialogue, greet the student next to you, introduce yourself, and ask how things are going.

Prononciation   Some basic information

A. Although French and English use the same alphabet, the combinations of letters and the sounds that they represent can be very different. Each language contains some sounds that do not exist in the other. French has no *th* sound as in *thank,* no *ch* sound as in *children.* English has no **u** sound, as in **une,** no **r** sound as in **merci.**

B. Both languages have words containing letters that are not pronounced.

French: tar*d*, alle*z*, Madam*e*
English: *i*sland, *k*nife, ni*gh*t

C. In French, as in English, one letter or one combination of letters can be pronounced more than one way.

French: *c*omme, mer*c*i
English: *c*all, *c*ircle

D. In French, as in English, one sound can be written more than one way.

French: *ç*a, *s*alut, mer*c*i, profe*ss*eur
English: con*qu*er, *k*itchen, *ch*aracter

Lecture culturelle

Le français dans le monde   www

The word **francophonie** refers to the use of the French language, and the expression **le monde francophone** (the French-speaking world) designates all the countries in the world where French is spoken. Only about half of the people who use French daily live in France. The others
5 are scattered all over the world, in Europe, North and South America, Asia, and

Réunion de chefs d'Etat
francophones

Africa. Altogether, almost 106 million people speak French, and for more than
67 million of them, it is their mother tongue.

   The French language derives from Latin, and its introduction into different
areas of the world occurred at various times in history. In 1534, the Age of Dis-
10 covery brought Jacques Cartier to Canada, where French is now the official language of over 7 million **Québécois.** Numerous French-speaking communities are
also found in the eastern provinces and as far west as Manitoba. It also brought
La Salle to Louisiana, where there are still a quarter of a million speakers of
French. Later, when slave trading became a profitable enterprise, the French in-
15 fluence spread over West Africa and the Antilles. In the nineteenth century,
France evolved as a colonial power in Africa, the Near East, and Southeast Asia.
The French colonial empire began to crumble in 1954 with the loss of Vietnam
and continued to dissolve as one country after another declared its independence
from France in the sixties. France has retained control of a certain number of
20 lands overseas known as **DOM (départements d'outre-mer)** and **TOM (territoires d'outre-mer).** The **DOM** include **la Martinique, la Guadeloupe, la
Guyane,** and **la Réunion,** while the **TOM** consist of **la Nouvelle-Calédonie,
Wallis-et-Futuna, la Polynésie française,** and **les Terres australes et antarctiques
françaises. Saint-Pierre-et-Miquelon** and **Mayotte** have a separate status in rela-
25 tion to France as **Collectivités territoriales.** The **DOM** and **TOM** elect represen-
tatives to the parliament in Paris and are represented by a minister in the French
government.

   You can find maps of the different parts of the French-speaking world on
the inside front and back covers of this book.

Vocabulaire

Noms / Pronoms

madame	Mrs. / Ms. / ma'am	poignée de main	handshake
mademoiselle	Miss / Ms.	toi	you
monsieur	Mr. / sir	vous	you

Adjectifs / Adverbes

bien	well	très bien	very well
très	very		

Expressions

à bientôt	see you soon	et	and
à plus tard	see you later	et toi	and you
à tout à l'heure	see you later	et vous	and you
au revoir	good-bye	faire une bise à…	to kiss (someone)
bonjour	good morning / hello	Je m'appelle…	My name is . . .
bonsoir	good evening / hello	Je vais bien.	I'm fine.
Ça va?	How are you?	merci	thank you
Ça va bien.	I'm fine.	oui	yes
comme ci, comme ça	so-so	pas mal	not bad
Comment allez-vous?	How do you do?	Quoi de neuf?	What's new?
Comment ça va?	How are you?	Salut.	Hi.

La vie universitaire

 Commençons

 Grammaire

 Communiquons

 Lecture culturelle

 Vocabulaire

En cours

Objectives

Language

Vocabulary for the classroom • The International Phonetic Alphabet, the French alphabet, accent marks, and punctuation • Nouns and definite articles • Subject pronouns • **-er** verbs • Yes-or-no questions • Numbers from 0 to 20

Culture

University life

Communication

Managing a brief conversation • Naming things • Describing actions • Asking questions • Doing math problems

Commençons

A l'université, en cours d'anglais

LE PROFESSEUR:	Commençons! Mademoiselle, comment vous appelez-vous?
L'ÉTUDIANTE:	Je m'appelle Patricia Keller.
LE PROFESSEUR:	Alors, vous parlez bien anglais, n'est-ce pas?
PATRICIA:	Non, juste un peu.
LE PROFESSEUR:	Eh bien, ouvrez votre livre page neuf et lisez le dialogue. *(A la classe)* Ecoutez et répétez ensemble après Patricia.

Etudions le dialogue

1. Repeat the dialogue after your teacher.
2. Read the dialogue with another classmate.
3. Ask one of your classmates to act out the dialogue with you in front of the class.

Mots clés

à l'université *(f.)*	*at the university*	**Eh bien**	*Well then*
en cours *(m.)*	*in class*	**Ouvrez votre livre.**	*Open your book*
anglais *(m.)*	*English*	**page**	*page*
professeur	*teacher*	**neuf**	*nine*
Commençons! (commencer)	*Let's begin!*	**lisez (lire)**	*read*
Comment vous appelez-vous?	*What's your name?*	**dialogue**	*dialogue*
étudiant, -e *(m., f.)*	*student*	**à**	*to*
Alors...	*Then . . .*	**classe**	*class*
parlez (parler)	*speak*	**écoutez (écouter)**	*listen (to)*
n'est-ce pas?	*don't you?*	**répétez (répéter)**	*repeat*
non	*no*	**ensemble**	*together*
juste un peu	*just a little bit*	**après**	*after*

Faisons connaissance   www

French universities are state-supported. Since 1968, new universities have been created in many French cities. However, in Paris and in other major cities, the universities are so big that they are divided and have numbers. For example, the former **Sorbonne** is now **Paris IV**. In addition to having numbers, many universities also have names. For instance, **Lyon III** is also called **l'université Jean**

La Sorbonne

Moulin, whereas **Montpellier III** is known as **l'université Paul Valéry.** Students use the term **la fac,** an abbreviation of **la faculté,** to refer to the university or any of its schools, such as **la faculté de Médecine** *(School of Medicine)* or **la faculté des Lettres et des Sciences humaines** *(College of Arts and Humanities).*

Most French students go to the university nearest to their home and continue to live with their families. Students who cannot return home every night often have to rent a room from individuals because universities cannot provide housing for everyone who needs it. This also helps explain why there is little campus life. Students often go to cafés between classes and when classes are over to meet friends or simply study. Traditionally, one can stay in a café for an unlimited period of time without having to place another order. Near universities, however, a sign may indicate that orders will be taken again every two hours.

Enrichissons notre vocabulaire

Voilà la salle de classe. *(Here is the classroom.)*

le tableau
la craie
le bureau de Madame Dumas
la clé
la chaise le stylo le cahier les livres
la porte la fenêtre
le cadeau
le crayon

la carte

l'alphabet *(m.)*

l'affiche *(f.)*

le sac à dos

Expressions utiles pour le cours de français *(Useful expressions for French class)*

Continuez la leçon.
Continue the lesson.

Commencez ici et répétez **avec** Patricia.
Start here and repeat with Patricia.

Commencez l'examen *(m.)* / vos devoirs *(m.)*.
Start the test / your homework.

Lisez de la page quatre **à** la page cinq et **répondez aux** questions.
Read from page four to page five and answer the questions.

Faites l'exercice A.
Do exercise A.

Parlez beaucoup en classe, mais **en** français!
Speak a lot in class, but in French!

—**Qu'est-ce que c'est?**
What is this?

—**C'est** le bureau de Madame Dumas.
It's Mrs. Dumas's desk.

—**Ce sont** les livres de français.
They're the French books.

—**Comment dit-on** «good-bye» à Paris / au Québec?
How do you say "good-bye" in Paris / in Quebec?

—**Je ne sais pas.**
I don't know.

—A Paris, **on dit** «au revoir», mais au Québec, on dit «bonjour». | *In Paris, **you say** "au revoir," but in Quebec, you say "bonjour."*

—**Qu'est-ce que** «salut» **veut dire**? | *What does "salut" mean?*
—**Cela** veut dire «hi». | *It means "hi."*

—**Voici** le livre de français. | *Here is the French book.*
—Merci. | *Thank you.*
—**Il n'y a pas de quoi. / De rien.** | *Don't mention it. / You're welcome.*

Prononciation   The International Phonetic Alphabet

The International Phonetic Alphabet (IPA), which is used in the **Prononciation** sections of this book, simplifies learning new words because each written symbol represents one specific sound. The International Phonetic Alphabet appears in Appendix I.

The French alphabet

A. The French alphabet is the same as the English, but the names of the letters differ. The following chart gives the letters, the IPA symbols showing the pronunciation of each letter, and a short, imaginary word to help you remember the names.

a	/ a /	ah	j	/ ʒi /	ji	s	/ ɛs /	esse
b	/ be /	bé	k	/ ka /	ka	t	/ te /	té
c	/ se /	sé	l	/ ɛl /	elle	u	/ y /	u
d	/ de /	dé	m	/ ɛm /	emme	v	/ ve /	vé
e	/ ø /	euh	n	/ ɛn /	enne	w	/ du blø ve /	double vé
f	/ ɛf /	ef	o	/ o /	oh	x	/ iks /	iks
g	/ ʒe /	jé	p	/ pe /	pé	y	/ i gʀɛk /	i grec
h	/ aʃ /	ache	q	/ ky /	ku	z	/ zɛd /	zed
i	/ i /	i	r	/ ɛʀ /	erre			

B. The letters **k** and **w** are rare in French and occur only in words borrowed directly from other languages. Examples are le **week**-end, le **wagon**, le **kiosque**.

C. The letter **h** is always silent. Words that start with **h** sound as though they start with the vowel that follows. Two examples are **homme** / ɔm / and **hôtel** / o tɛl /.

Accent marks and punctuation

A. French has a system of written accent marks that are as important as the dot of an **i** or the cross of a **t**. Be sure to learn accents as part of the spelling of words.

accent	name		example
´	l'accent aigu	*acute accent*	poignée
`	l'accent grave	*grave accent*	très
^	l'accent circonflexe	*circumflex accent*	hôtel
¸	la cédille	*cedilla*	français
¨	le tréma	*dieresis*	Noël

B. Accents can indicate pronunciation.

commençons / kɔ mã sɔ̃ /
classe, café / klas /, / ka fe /

C. Accents can differentiate words.

a	*has*	ou	*or*
à	*to*	où	*where*

You will not, however, see accents on capital letters. For example, you will see **à Paris**, but **A Paris**.

D. French uses almost the same punctuation marks as English; only quotation marks look different.

.	le point	*period*
,	la virgule	*comma*
-	le trait d'union	*hyphen*
'	l'apostrophe	*apostrophe*
«»	les guillemets	*quotation marks*

E. To spell words aloud in French, say the letter and any accent mark it may have immediately after it. If the word has a double consonant, say **deux** *(two)* before the letter that is doubled. A *capital* letter is **majuscule** and a *small* letter is **minuscule**.

ça **c** cédille **a**   accent **a** deux **c e n t**
café **c a f e** accent aigu   René **r** majuscule **e n e** accent aigu

Exercices

A. Repeat the French alphabet after your teacher.

B. In French, spell your full name, your mother's maiden name, and the name of the street where you live.

C. Team up with a classmate and ask each other to spell words from the dialogue. When giving the words, be sure your pronunciation is correct. When spelling the words, be sure to remember accents.

Grammaire

I. Nouns and definite articles

You use nouns to name people, places, and things.

A. In French, all nouns, whether they represent living or nonliving things, are either masculine or feminine. Nouns referring to male human beings are generally masculine. Nouns referring to female human beings are generally feminine.

B. An article almost always accompanies a noun in French. The article indicates the gender (masculine or feminine) and the number (singular or plural) of the noun. A masculine noun is introduced by a masculine article. A feminine noun is introduced by a feminine article. French has four forms that may correspond to the English definite article *the*.

definite articles		
	singular	*plural*
masculine	**le** dialogue	**les** dialogues
	l'étudiant	**les** étudiants
feminine	**la** porte	**les** portes
	l'étudiante	**les** étudiantes

C. Le / lø / is used with masculine singular nouns that begin with a consonant.

le stylo	*pen*	**le** crayon	*pencil*
le café	*sidewalk café; coffee*	**le** français	*French (language)*

D. La / la / is used with feminine singular nouns that begin with a consonant.

la radio	*radio*	**la** leçon	*lesson*
la télévision	*television*	**la** classe	*class*

E. L' is used with all singular nouns that begin with a vowel sound.

l'ami *(m.)*	/ la mi /	*friend*	**l'**hôtel *(m.)*	/ lo tɛl /	*hotel*
l'amie *(f.)*	/ la mi /	*friend*	**l'**enfant *(m. or f.)*	/ lã fã /	*child*

F. Les is used with plural nouns, masculine and feminine. It is pronounced / le / before a consonant and / lez / before a vowel sound.

les livres *(m.)*	/ le livʀ /	*books*
les femmes *(f.)*	/ le fam /	*women*
les hommes *(m.)*	/ le zɔm /	*men*
les amies *(f.)*	/ le za mi /	*friends*

Ce qu'ils disent

You are no doubt aware that people do not always use a language the way grammar books (or textbooks) describe it. For example, English has the verb *going to,* but most people say "gonna." To help you bridge the gap between written and spoken French, this section, **Ce qu'ils disent** *(What people say),* will appear throughout this book.

In conversations, French people often shorten words. Two that you have just seen are **la télévision,** which becomes **la télé** (often written **la TV**), and **le professeur,** which is shortened to **le prof.** While you must use the masculine **le professeur** for male and female teachers, both **le prof** and **la prof** exist.

L'orthographe

As with English, there are numerous differences in French between what you say and what you write. This section, **L'orthographe** *(Spelling),* will appear throughout the book to explain forms that are present only when you write in French.

1. In French, the plural of most nouns is formed by adding an **s** to the singular noun. If the noun already ends in **s,** the singular and the plural are the same.

le disque	les disques	*records*
la leçon	les leçons	*lessons*
le cours	les cours	*classes*
l'autobus	les autobus	*buses*

2. The letter **x** is used for the plural of words ending in **-eau.**

le cadeau	les cadeaux	*gifts*
le bureau	les bureaux	*desks, offices*
le tableau	les tableaux	*chalkboards*

Attention!

Notice the similarity between **classe** and *class.* French and English words that are alike in sound, spelling, and meaning are *cognates.* There are, however, French words that are similar in spelling to English words but that differ in meaning. These are **faux amis,** or *false friends.* An example is **comment,** which means *how.*

Language

A. Les pluriels. Make the following nouns plural.

1. l'enfant   3. le stylo   5. l'ami   7. l'étudiante
2. la carte   4. le disque   6. la clé   8. l'affiche

B. Les singuliers. Make the following nouns singular.

1. les cours   3. les femmes   5. les exercices   7. les livres
2. les radios   4. les étudiants   6. les hommes   8. les amies

C. Les articles définis. Use the correct definite article with the following nouns. (Watch for the plural marker **s** or **x**.)

1. fenêtre   4. hommes   7. bureaux   10. amies
2. disques   5. crayon   8. alphabet   11. leçon
3. classe   6. ami   9. stylos   12. femmes

Culture   WWW

D. L'hypermarché. An **hypermarché** is a huge store that combines a supermarket and a discount store, such as Kmart, under one roof. Two well-known French chains are **Carrefour** and **Mammouth**. Indicate whether or not you think the following items are available for sale in an **hypermarché** by adding a definite article and **Oui** or **Non**.

MODEL: livres *Les livres? Oui.*
    étudiants *Les étudiants? Non!*

1. cartes   3. disques   5. affiches   7. crayons
2. bises   4. enfants   6. cours   8. livres

Communication

E. La salle de classe. Divide into pairs. Take turns pointing to classroom or personal objects and asking, **Qu'est-ce que c'est?** Your partner will answer with **C'est,** a definite article, and a noun.

MODEL: Student 1: (Pointing to the window) *Qu'est-ce que c'est?*
    Student 2: *C'est la fenêtre.*

F. Les objets. Team up with a classmate to study the nouns you have learned. When giving the French word, use the definite article.

MODEL: Student 1: *Comment dit-on «book»?*
    Student 2: *On dit «le livre».*

Then choose a French word and ask for the English equivalent.

MODEL: Student 1: *Qu'est-ce que «le stylo» veut dire?*
    Student 2: *Cela veut dire «pen».*

II.   Subject pronouns and -er verbs

A.   Subject pronouns

> You use pronouns to avoid repeating the names of people and things when the meaning is clear.

1. Subject pronouns replace noun subjects.

Paul chante. → **Il** chante.	***Paul** sings.* → ***He** sings.*
Paul et Marie étudient. →	***Paul and Marie** study.* →
Ils étudient.	***They** study.*

subject pronouns			
je	*I*	nous	*we*
tu	*you*	vous	*you*
il	*he*	ils	*they (m.)*
elle	*she*	elles	*they (f.)*
on	*one, we, you, they*		

2. Note that there are two French forms for *you*: **tu** and **vous**. **Tu** is the singular, informal form. Use **tu** to address a person that you know well, such as a friend or a relative, or a child.

Tu parles français?	*Do **you** speak French?*

Vous can be singular or plural. Use **vous** to speak to one person you do not know well, or are unsure how to address, or wish to treat with respect. Also use **vous** to speak to more than one person, regardless of your relationship.

Vous parlez anglais, Madame?	*Do **you** speak English, ma'am?*
Philippe et Isabelle, **vous**	*Philippe and Isabelle, are **you***
écoutez le professeur?	*listening to the teacher?*

Ce qu'ils disent

In the last few years, the French people have relaxed their constraints on the use of **tu**. Business associates who would have used **vous** in the past are now more likely to use **tu** with each other. As a foreigner, you should still use **vous** with native speakers until they use **tu** with you. It is generally acceptable, however, to use **tu** with another student.

In other parts of the French-speaking world, particularly Louisiana, rules for the **tu–vous** distinction are even more relaxed, with **tu** used for individuals and **vous** for more than one person.

3. There is no specific word in French for *it*. Since all nouns have a gender, **il** refers to masculine nouns and **elle** refers to feminine nouns.

4. **Elles** refers to two or more females or feminine nouns.

Marie et Amélie? **Elles** travaillent bien.	*Marie and Amélie? **They** work hard.*
La porte et la fenêtre? **Elles** ferment mal.	*The door and the window? **They** close badly.*

5. **Ils** refers to two or more males or masculine nouns. **Ils** also refers to a combined group of males and females or masculine and feminine nouns.

Les étudiants? **Ils** écoutent en cours.	*The students? **They** listen in class.*
La carte et le livre? **Ils** sont ici.	*The map and the book? **They** are here.*

6. There is one impersonal subject pronoun in French: **on**. It is used in a general sense and has at least four English equivalents: *we, one, they, people.*

Ici **on** parle français.	*Here **we** speak French.*
	*Here **one** speaks French.*
	*Here **they** speak French.*
	*Here **people** speak French.*

Ce qu'ils disent

In conversational French, the pronoun **on** usually replaces **nous**.

On regarde la télévision?	*Shall **we** watch television?*
On commence!	***Let's** begin!*

B.   -er Verbs

You use verbs to describe actions or states of being.

1. French verbs are classified by the ending of the infinitive. The infinitive consists of a stem (like **chant**) and an ending (like **-er**). The largest group of French verbs has an infinitive that ends in **-er,** like **chanter**.

		infinitive: chanter *(to sing)*
	singular	
1st person	je **chante**	*I sing, I am singing, I do sing*
2nd person	tu **chantes**	*you sing, you are singing, you do sing*
3rd person	il **chante**	*he sings, he is singing, he does sing*
	elle **chante**	*she sings, she is singing, she does sing*
	on **chante**	*one sings, one is singing, one does sing*
	plural	
1st person	nous **chantons**	*we sing, we are singing, we do sing*
2nd person	vous **chantez**	*you sing, you are singing, you do sing*
3rd person	ils **chantent**	*they sing, they are singing, they do sing*
	elles **chantent**	*they sing, they are singing, they do sing*

2. The present tense in French corresponds to three English forms as shown in the preceding verb chart.

> En général, ils **chantent** bien, mais ce soir ils **chantent** mal.
>
> *Generally, they **sing** well, but tonight they **are singing** badly.*

3. Conjugated **-er** verbs have only three pronunciations. The singular forms and the third-person plural forms (**ils / elles**) are pronounced alike. The listener must know from the context whether / il ʃɑ̃t / is singular or plural.

je	/ ʃɑ̃t /	nous	/ ʃɑ̃ tɔ̃ /
tu	/ ʃɑ̃t /	vous	/ ʃɑ̃ te /
il	/ ʃɑ̃t /	ils	/ ʃɑ̃t /
elle	/ ʃɑ̃t /	elles	/ ʃɑ̃t /

4. When a verb starts with a vowel sound, **je** becomes **j'**, the letter **n** of **on** is pronounced, and the final **s** of all plural subject pronouns is pronounced.

J'invite.	/ ʒɛ̃ vit /	Vous invitez.	/ vu zɛ̃ vi te /
On invite.	/ ɔ̃ nɛ̃ vit /	Ils invitent.	/ il zɛ̃ vit /
Nous invitons.	/ nu zɛ̃ vi tɔ̃ /	Elles invitent.	/ ɛl zɛ̃ vit /

L'orthographe

1. All regular -er verbs are conjugated the same way. Written present-tense endings for -er verbs are: -e, -es, -e, -ons, -ez, -ent.

2. In written French, verbs that end in -ger add an e before the -ons ending (nous mangeons). Verbs that end in -cer add a cédille to the c before the -ons ending (nous commençons). These small changes preserve the "soft" sounds of the g and c.

Mots clés *Common and useful* -er *verbs*

adorer	*to love; to adore*	fermer	*to close*
aimer	*to like*	fumer	*to smoke*
arriver	*to arrive*	habiter	*to live (in a place)*
commencer	*to begin*	inviter	*to invite*
continuer	*to continue*	jouer	*to play*
danser	*to dance*	manger	*to eat*
demander	*to ask (for)*	montrer	*to show*
donner	*to give*	parler	*to speak*
écouter	*to listen*	regarder	*to watch*
étudier	*to study*	terminer	*to end*
expliquer	*to explain*	travailler	*to work*

Language

A. **En cours.** Make complete sentences about the following classmates with each group of words provided.

MODEL: Pierre / aimer / université
Pierre aime l'université.

1. Je / écouter / professeur
2. Stéphane / arriver / avec Marie
3. Nous / commencer / examen
4. étudiants / étudier / français
5. Hélène et Chantal / travailler / ensemble
6. Vous / terminer / devoirs

Culture   WWW

B. **Le Crazy Horse.** The **Crazy Horse Saloon** is a famous Parisian nightclub. Guess what people do there by using the verbs below with either **Oui** or **Non.**

MODEL: danser *On danse? Oui.*
étudier le français *On étudie le français? Non!*

1. fumer
2. manger
3. parler
4. travailler
5. regarder les hommes et les femmes
6. écouter la radio
7. regarder la télé
8. jouer

Communication

C. **J'aime ça!** Make a list of five statements about yourself using the **-er** verbs and other vocabulary you have learned. Share your list with a classmate to find differences and similarities.

> MODEL: *J'aime les enfants. Je chante bien. Je danse mal. Je regarde la télévision. J'étudie le français.*

D. **Questions personnelles.** A l'université.

1. Le professeur de français explique bien la leçon?
2. Vous parlez français?
3. Vous étudiez beaucoup?
4. Les étudiants travaillent bien ici?
5. Vous écoutez bien le professeur?
6. Vous aimez les cours à l'université?

Carte Bleue Visa. Elle parle toutes les langues.

III. Yes-or-no questions

> You use yes-or-no questions to find out information.

A. One of three basic ways to ask a yes-or-no question in French is to use intonation. This means that you make your voice rise, rather than fall, at the end of a sentence.

Statement:	Il travaille ici.	*He works here.*
Question:	Il travaille ici?	*He works here?*

B. You can add the phrase **Est-ce que** to the beginning of a sentence.

Statement:	Cécile parle bien.	*Cécile speaks well.*
Question:	Est-ce que Cécile parle bien?	*Does Cécile speak well?*

When the subject of a sentence begins with a vowel, the **e** of **que** is not pronounced and is replaced with an apostrophe.

Est-ce **qu'il** regarde la télévision?   *Is he watching television?*
Est-ce **qu'on** parle français ici?   *Is French spoken here?*

C. You can add the phrase **n'est-ce pas?** to the end of a sentence.

Statement:	Je joue bien.	*I play well.*
Question:	Je joue bien, n'est-ce pas?	*I play well, don't I?*
Statement:	Elle parle français.	*She speaks French.*
Question:	Elle parle français, n'est-ce pas?	*She speaks French, doesn't she?*

Ce qu'ils disent

In conversation, rising intonation is the most frequently used type of question. The expression **n'est-ce pas?** is used often, to be sure that the other person is listening.

J'explique bien la situation, n'est-ce pas?	*I'm explaining the situation well, aren't I?*
Oui, très bien.	*Yes, very well.*

Language

A. Incrédule. Since you do not believe everything you hear, ask for a clarification of each of the following sentences, using yes-or-no questions.

MODEL: Patricia aime le français.
  Patricia aime le français?
  Est-ce que Patricia aime le français?
  Patricia aime le français, n'est-ce pas?

1. Les enfants étudient la carte.
2. Le prof ferme la porte.
3. Les étudiants fument beaucoup.
4. Tu aimes danser.
5. Jean et Marie habitent ici.
6. On écoute beaucoup la radio.

B. Conversations interrompues. You are circulating from group to group at a party and you overhear several conversations. Ask the question that elicited the following answers. Be sure to use the correct pronoun. You have a choice as to which question form to use.

MODEL: Oui, je travaille après le cours.
  Tu travailles après le cours?
  Est-ce que tu travailles après le cours?
  Tu travailles après le cours, n'est-ce pas?

1. Oui, elles aiment la radio.
2. Oui, tu parles bien.
3. Oui, je chante bien.
4. Oui, vous mangez beaucoup.
5. Oui, on parle anglais ici.
6. Oui, elles jouent ensemble.

Culture

C. **Interview.** You are going to interview someone about the francophone world. Ask questions using **on** with the following expressions.

1. aimer les Américains
2. fumer beaucoup
3. regarder beaucoup la télé
4. aimer faire la bise
5. étudiants / travailler beaucoup
6. parler anglais à Paris
7. manger bien
8. parler français au Québec

Communication

D. *Tu ou vous*? Remember that in asking questions, you must indicate your relationship with the person to whom you are speaking by choosing between **tu** and **vous.** Use the following expressions to ask questions of your classmates and your teacher.

1. regarder beaucoup la télé?
2. aimer les étudiants?
3. adorer les enfants?
4. fumer?
5. aimer danser?
6. travailler beaucoup?

E. **Questions personnelles.** Prepare five questions using -er verbs from the list on page 19. Interview a classmate in a small group or in front of the class.

IV. Numbers from 0 to 20

0 zéro	6 six	11 onze	16 seize
1 un	7 sept	12 douze	17 dix-sept
2 deux	8 huit	13 treize	18 dix-huit
3 trois	9 neuf	14 quatorze	19 dix-neuf
4 quatre	10 dix	15 quinze	20 vingt
5 cinq			

A. Numbers can be used alone, as in telephone numbers, or they can be used with nouns, for example, **trois livres.** When used with nouns, many numbers require pronunciation changes. You will study this in Chapter 4.

B. To express math problems, use the following:

Combien font deux **et** trois?	*How **much** are two **and** three?*
ou	*or*
Combien font deux **plus** trois? Deux plus trois font cinq.	*How **much** are two **and** three?* *Two and three are five.*
Combien font vingt **moins** six? Vingt moins six font quatorze.	*How much is twenty **minus** six?* *Twenty minus six is fourteen.*
Combien font quatre **multiplié par** trois? Quatre multiplié par trois font douze.	*How much is four **multiplied by** three?* *Four multiplied by three is twelve.*
Combien font seize **divisé par** quatre? Seize divisé par quatre font quatre.	*How much is sixteen **divided by** four?* *Sixteen divided by four is four.*

Language

A. Comptons! Count in French, continuing each series of numbers started below.

1. 1, 2, 3 . . . 20
2. 2, 4, 6 . . . 20
3. 1, 3, 5 . . . 19
4. 20, 19, 18 . . . 0
5. 20, 18, 16 . . . 0
6. 19, 17, 15 . . . 1

B. Calculons! Do the following math problems in French.

1. $12 + 3 =$
2. $11 + 2 =$
3. $2 \times 2 =$
4. $15 \div 3 =$
5. $1 + 5 =$
6. $16 - 2 =$
7. $3 \times 5 =$
8. $20 \div 2 =$
9. $9 + 8 =$
10. $5 - 5 =$
11. $4 \times 4 =$
12. $18 \div 3 =$
13. $2 + 17 =$
14. $20 - 1 =$
15. $6 \times 3 =$
16. $10 \div 2 =$

Culture   WWW

C. Au Québec. In Quebec, people say telephone numbers one digit at a time. Read the numbers for the following places you might have to call while in Quebec.

1. la Banque nationale du Canada   (416) 867-5000
2. la Bibliothèque nationale du Québec   (514) 873-4553
3. le Musée du Québec   (418) 643-4173
4. *Le Devoir*   (514) 842-9645
5. l'Hôpital général de Montréal   (514) 937-6011
6. l'Université du Québec   (418) 657-3551

Communication

D. Les maths. Divide into pairs and ask each other math problems, the answers to which range from 0 to 20.

MODEL: Student 1: *Combien font sept et deux?*
            Student 2: *Sept et deux font neuf.*

            Student 1: *Combien font cinq multiplié par deux?*
            Student 2: *Cinq multiplié par deux font dix.*

E. Votre numéro. Read aloud your Social Security number, and your classmates will write it. Then ask one of them to verify your number by reading it aloud.

Communiquons

Commencer et terminer les conversations

The way people greet each other and manage conversations varies from culture to culture. An important consideration is the degree of familiarity between the speaker and the person being greeted. In France, people greet acquaintances (**les connaissances**) and business associates with a few words and a handshake. Good friends and relatives may embrace lightly and kiss on both cheeks (**faire la bise**). Formal situations require a word of greeting (e.g., **Bonjour**) and the title **Monsieur, Madame,** or **Mademoiselle,** but no last name.

Small talk in French involves topics similar to those of American conversations: the speakers' health, their recent activities, and the weather. Like English speakers, French speakers use a variety of expressions to end a conversation. However, the expressions **Salut!** and **Bonsoir!** can be used for both arrival and departure. In Quebec, **Bonjour** is also used in this way.

Expressions

> ▶ **On commence les conversations avec les amis / les connaissances.**

Salut!	*Hi!*
Tiens!	*Hey!*
Dis donc!	*Say!*

> ▶ **On commence les conversations avec les personnes importantes.**

Bonjour, Monsieur / Messieurs.	*Good morning / afternoon, sir / gentlemen.*
Bonjour, Madame / Mesdames.	*Good morning / afternoon, ma'am / ladies.*
Bonsoir, Mademoiselle / Mesdemoiselles.	*Good evening, miss / ladies.*

> ▶ **On commence les conversations avec les inconnus** *(strangers).*

Pardon, Monsieur.	*Pardon / Excuse me, sir.*
Excusez-moi, Madame.	*Excuse me, ma'am.*
Pardonnez-moi, Mademoiselle.	*Pardon me, miss.*

> ▶ **On continue les conversations.**

Ça va? / Comment ça va? / Ça va bien?	*How's it going?*
Comment allez-vous?	*How are you?*
Qu'est-ce que tu deviens?	*What are you up to?*
Qu'est-ce que vous faites?	*What are you doing?*
Quoi de neuf?	*What's new?*
Il fait chaud!	*It's hot!*
Il fait froid!	*It's cold!*

► **On termine les conversations.**

A bientôt.	*See you soon.*
A ce soir.	*See you this evening.*
A demain.	*See you tomorrow.*
A la prochaine.	*See you next time.*
A tout à l'heure.	*See you a little later.*
Bonne nuit.	*Good night. (when one is going to bed)*
Bonsoir.	*Good evening. / Good night.*
Salut.	*So long.*
Au revoir.	*Good-bye.*

Interaction *Marie rencontre* (meets) *Monsieur Dupont.*

MARIE: Bonjour, Monsieur!

M. DUPONT: Bonjour, Marie. Comment ça va?

MARIE: Ça va, merci. Et vous?

M. DUPONT: Pas mal. Qu'est-ce que vous faites?

MARIE: J'étudie l'anglais à l'université.

M. DUPONT: Très bien. A la prochaine!

Activités

A. What would the person mentioned in the following situations be most likely to say?

1. Jacques is kissing his mother good night.
2. Patricia has just run into a friend on campus.
3. Philippe and his English teacher arrive at the classroom at the same time.
4. Cécile is leaving class, but she will see her classmates the next day.
5. Anne and Marie are going to different classes, but they have plans to study together later in the afternoon.
6. The school year is over, and you may not see your friends for several months.
7. You stop someone on the street to ask directions.
8. Marc is leaving the room, but he will be back in an hour.

B. Greet the student next to you.

C. Go to the front of the class with a classmate. Greet each other and say good-bye.

D. Write a short dialogue with a classmate involving two friends who run into each other, and then present it in front of the class.

Lecture culturelle

Avant la lecture

French and American universities and university life (**la vie universitaire**) differ widely. Unlike their American counterparts, French students take a comprehensive examination at the end of secondary school. The two-thirds who pass are entitled to attend one of the numerous French universities, almost all of which are public. Tuition is practically free, and with the appropriate background students may select any field they wish.

Despite the increase in the number of suburban universities, French universities are principally located in large cities. Because they are often in the center of town, they do not have a campus as is common in the United States; there are no open, grassy areas or student unions to serve as gathering places.

Activité

Skim the reading passage to find the following information:

1. the name of the examination students take at the end of high school
2. what high school students and college students are called
3. where students live while attending the university

L'université française

En France, le «college» n'existe pas. A la fin° de l'école secondaire°, on passe° le baccalauréat (le «bac», le «bachot»), un examen très complet, et on entre à l'université.

A l'université, on n'est plus élève°, on est étudiant. On commence les cours
5 en octobre et on termine en mai. Les examens sont en juin. Quand on échoue°, on peut repasser° en septembre.

En France, l'université ressemble à la «graduate school» américaine. Généralement les étudiants n'habitent pas sur° le campus. Ils habitent en famille ou ils louent une chambre en ville°. Les activités extra-universitaires ne sont pas très
10 nombreuses°. Les «sororities» et «fraternities», et le football américain n'existent pas.

A la... *At the end / * école... *high school / takes*

n'est... *is no longer a pupil*
fails
retake

on
louent... *rent a room in town / numerous*

La cour de la Sorbonne

Après la lecture

Questions sur le texte

1. Qu'est-ce que c'est que *(What is)* le bac?
2. Quand *(When)* est-ce que l'année universitaire commence en France? Et aux Etats-Unis?
3. Quand est-ce qu'elle finit?
4. Quand est-ce que les étudiants passent les examens en France?
5. Généralement, est-ce que les étudiants habitent sur le campus en France?

Activité

Using the reading selection, make a list in French of differences (**différences**) and similarities (**similarités**) between university life in France and in the United States.

Vocabulaire

Noms / Pronoms

affiche	poster	fac	university / school
alphabet	alphabet	faculté	university / school
ami(e)	friend	femme	woman
anglais	English	fenêtre	window
autobus	bus	français	French
bureau	desk	homme	man
cadeau	present	hôtel	hotel
café	cafe	il	he / it
cahier	notebook	ils	they
carte	map	je	I
cela	this	leçon	lesson
chaise	chair	livre	book
classe	classroom	nous	we
clé	key	on	one / we / they
cours	class / course	page	page
craie	chalk	porte	door
crayon	pencil	professeur	teacher / professor
devoirs	homework	question	question
dialogue	dialogue	radio	radio
disque	record	sac à dos	backpack
elle	she / it	salle de classe	classroom
elles	they	stylo	pen
enfant	child	tableau	board
étudiant	student	télévision	television
examen	exam	tu	you
exercise	exercise	université	university

Verbes

adorer	to adore	fumer	to smoke
aimer	to like / to love	habiter	to live
arriver	to arrive	inviter	to invite
chanter	to sing	jouer	to play
commencer	to begin	manger	to eat
continuer	to continue	montrer	to show
danser	to dance	ouvrir	to open
demander	to ask (for)	parler	to speak / to talk
donner	to give	regarder	to look
écouter	to listen	répéter	to repeat
étudier	to study	terminer	to end
expliquer	to explain	travailler	to work
fermer	to close		

Adjectifs / Adverbes

alors	then	multiplié	multiplied
beaucoup	much	neuf	nine
cinq	five	non	no
combien	how much	onze	eleven
deux	two	plus	more
divisé	divided	quatorze	fourteen
dix	ten	quatre	four
dix-huit	eighteen	quinze	fifteen
dix-neuf	nineteen	seize	sixteen
dix-sept	seventeen	sept	seven
douze	twelve	six	six
ensemble	together	treize	thirteen
huit	eight	trois	three
ici	here	un, une	one
le, la, l', les	the	vingt	twenty
mais	but	zéro	zero
moins	less		

Expressions

à	at, in	faites	do
après	after	Il n'y a pas de quoi.	Don't mention it. / You're welcome.
avec	with		
ce soir	tonight	je ne sais pas	I don't know
c'est, ce sont	it is, they are	juste un peu	just a little
Combien font... ?	How much is . . . ?	lisez	read
Comment dit-on... ?	How do you say . . . ?	n'est-ce pas?	isn't it so?
Comment vous appelez-vous?	What's your name?	ou	or
		Ouvrez votre livre.	Open your book.
de	of / from	par	by
de rien	not at all	Qu'est-ce que _____ veut dire?	What does _____ mean?
eh bien	well then		
en cours	in class	Qu'est-ce que c'est?	What is it?
en français	in French	répondez à / aux	answer
en général	in general	voici	here is
est-ce que...	is / are / does / do	voilà	there is

Chapitre 2

La famille et les amis

Commençons

Grammaire

Communiquons

Lecture culturelle

Vocabulaire

Dans un parc à Paris

Objectives

Language

Vocabulary for the family, friends, pastimes, and likes and dislikes • Word stress • Negation • **Etre** • Vocabulary for occupations and nationalities • Descriptive adjectives • Numbers from 21 to 69 • Ordinal numbers

Culture

Family life • Pastimes • Introducing people

Communication

Describing people and things • Counting • Making introductions

Commençons

Au café

WWW

Gilles et Laure, deux étudiants, sont au café.

GILLES: Tiens, voilà Monique!

LAURE: Oui, elle est avec Jacques.

GILLES: C'est le dernier petit ami?

LAURE: Oui, il est sympathique et studieux.

GILLES: Et Monique, elle n'est pas studieuse?

LAURE: Si, elle est toujours première. Ils étudient l'anglais ensemble.

GILLES: L'anglais? Tu es certaine?

LAURE: Oui, quand ils ne sont pas au café!

Devant une boîte

Des jeunes gens sont devant une boîte.

MONIQUE: Où est la sœur de Patrick?

LAURE: Chantal? Elle arrive avec un copain américain.

CHANTAL: Salut! *(Elle embrasse Monique et Laure.)* Voici Jim. Il est étudiant avec Patrick; ils sont ensemble en philo à la fac.

JIM: Enchanté. Je suis très heureux de passer la soirée avec vous. *(A Chantal)* Ton frère n'est pas là?

MONIQUE: Si. Il gare la voiture.

CHANTAL: Il est toujours en retard. Entrons sans lui.

Etudions les dialogues

A. Au café

1. Est-ce que Monique est la petite amie de Gilles?
2. Elle est studieuse, n'est-ce pas? Et Jacques?
3. Est-ce que Jacques est toujours premier? *always first*
4. Jacques et Monique étudient le français, n'est-ce pas?

B. Devant une boîte

1. Est-ce que Monique est la sœur de Patrick?
2. Jim est américain, n'est-ce pas?
3. Jim et Patrick sont en philo?
4. Patrick gare la voiture, n'est-ce pas?

Mots clés

sont (être)	*are*	premier, -ère	*first*
au	*at*	es (être)	*are*
Tiens!	*Hey!*	certain, -e	*certain*
C'est (être)	*It's*	quand	*when*
le dernier, la dernière	*the latest*	ne… pas	*not*
petit ami / petite amie	*boyfriend / girlfriend*	devant	*in front of*
sympathique	*nice*	boîte	*(night)club*
studieux, -euse	*studious*	des jeunes gens	*some young people*
Si.	*Yes, of course.*	où	*where*
toujours	*always*		

Sympa (handwritten note next to "sympathique")

sœur	*sister*	soirée	*evening*
copain *(m.)* / copine *(f.)*	*friend*	ton frère *(m.)*	*your brother*
américain, -e	*American*	là	*here*
embrasse (embrasser)	*kisses*	gare (garer)	*is parking*
philo(sophie) *(f.)*	*philosophy*	voiture	*car*
Enchanté, -e.	*Delighted.*	en retard	*late*
suis (être)	*am*	Entrons (entrer)	*Let's go in*
heureux, -se	*happy*	sans	*without*
passer	*to spend*	lui	*him*

Faisons connaissance

In general, French families are much closer than American families. Many people remain in the areas where they were brought up as children, and families are not scattered all over the country as in the United States. Even after they are married, people continue to visit their parents regularly. The main meal on Sunday still provides an opportunity for family members to get together. The French calendar also has many holidays that constitute occasions for family reunions. In addition, it is not unusual for parents, married children, and sometimes grandparents to plan their summer vacations together.

Having friends is very important to French people. They tend, however, to have fewer friends than Americans do, because in their view, friendships take longer to get established and are not as casual as some relationships among Americans. The French still make a distinction between an acquaintance (**une connaissance**) and a friend (**un[e] ami[e]**). This is also true in the business world, where doing business with someone does not automatically turn the person into a friend. Most of the time, that person remains a business acquaintance (**une relation d'affaires**).

Un dîner en famille

Enrichissons notre vocabulaire

La famille de Marie *(Marie's family)*

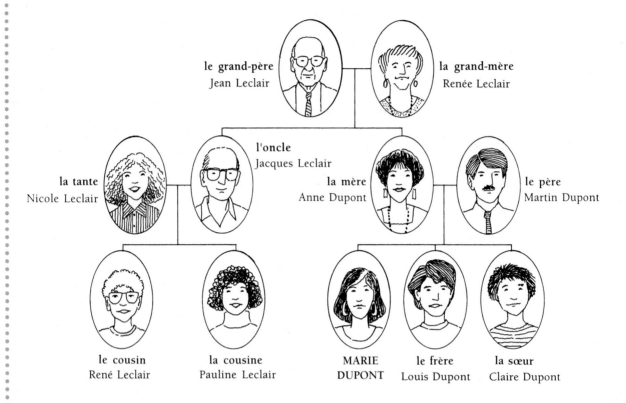

le grand-père		la grand-mère
Jean Leclair		Renée Leclair

l'oncle
Jacques Leclair

la tante		la mère		le père
Nicole Leclair		Anne Dupont		Martin Dupont

le cousin	la cousine	MARIE	le frère	la sœur
René Leclair	Pauline Leclair	DUPONT	Louis Dupont	Claire Dupont

la femme	*the wife*	le beau-père	*the stepfather / the father-in-law*
le mari	*the husband*	la belle-mère	*the stepmother / the mother-in-law*
les parents	*the parents*	les enfants	*the children*
les grands-parents	*the grandparents*	les petits-enfants	*the grandchildren*
le fils	*the son*	le neveu	*the nephew*
la fille	*the daughter*	la nièce	*the niece*

Les amis *(The friends)*

le / la camarade de chambre	*the roommate*
le / la camarade de cours	*the classmate*
la fille	*the girl*
le garçon	*the boy*

Quelques distractions favorites *(A few favorite pastimes)*

l'art *(m.)* moderne	*modern art*
le rock	*rock 'n' roll*
le jazz	*jazz*
la musique classique	*classical music*
les sports *(m.)*	*sports*
les matchs *(m.)* de football	*soccer games*
les films *(m.)* à la télé	*films on TV*

J'aime / Je déteste *(I like / I dislike)*

aimer / aimer **faire**	*to love / to like **to do***
aimer **bien**	*to like*
aimer **mieux**	*to prefer*
apprécier	*to appreciate*
désirer	*to want*
détester / détester faire	*to hate / to hate to do*

—**Qu'est-ce que** tu aimes / aimes faire?   ***What** do you like / like to do?*

—J'adore **fréquenter** les **boîtes de nuit**.   *I love **to go to nightclubs**.*

—**Moi aussi,** je fréquente souvent les **clubs** *(m.).*   ***Me too,** I often go to **nightclubs**.*

—Qu'est-ce que tu détestes?   *What do you hate?*

—Je déteste l'**hypocrisie** *(f.)* / l'**intolérance** *(f.).*   *I hate **hypocrisy** / **intolerance**.*

—J'aime mieux la **sincérité**.   *I prefer **sincerity**.*

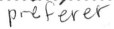
préférer

Prononciation   Word stress in French

A. Learners of English as a foreign language often have difficulty putting stress on the proper syllables. Some words, such as *record* or *present*, can vary in pronunciation according to their meaning. Words can even vary according to region. For example, one says *laboratory* in England and *laboratory* in the United States. In French, however, all syllables receive the same stress except the last, which has a somewhat longer vowel.

Notice the difference in stress as you repeat the following pairs of English and French words after your teacher.

English	French
ex*am*ine	ex*amine*
*mer*chandise	marchan*dise*
a*part*ment	apparte*ment*

B. In French, each syllable has the same stress, and vowels maintain the same pronunciation throughout the word. This is not the case in English. For example, *Alabama* has the same written vowel throughout, but in its unaccented syllables (the second and the fourth), the vowel sound is reduced to / ə /, the "uh" sound. In French, vowel quality does not change.

Note the difference in the sound and quality of the italicized vowels as you repeat the following pairs of English and French words after your teacher.

English	French
uni*v*ersity	uni*v*ersité
tel*e*vision	télé*v*ision
labor*a*tory	labor*a*toire

Exercice

Read the following sentences aloud, taking care to put equal stress on all syllables.

1. Je regarde la télévision.
2. Paul examine l'itinéraire.
3. Nous visitons le laboratoire.
4. Elle expédie les marchandises.
5. La police occupe l'appartement.
6. Le professeur est intelligent.

Grammaire

I. Negation

You use the negative to indicate that something is not true or does not occur.

A. To make a statement negative in French, place the words **ne... pas** around the conjugated verb.

Est-ce qu'ils sont au café?	*Are they at the café?*
Non, ils **ne** sont **pas** au café.	*No, they aren't at the café.*

B. If there are two consecutive verbs, you still place the **ne... pas** around the conjugated verb to make the statement negative.

Ils aiment travailler ensemble?	*Do they like to work together?*
Non, ils **n'**aiment **pas** travailler ensemble.	*No they **don't** like to work together.*

C. If the verb begins with a vowel sound, you do not pronounce the **e** of **ne**, and you write **n'**.

Elle **n'**est pas studieuse.	*She isn't studious.*
Tu **n'**es pas étudiant.	*You aren't a student.*

Even before a consonant, the **e** of **ne** is rarely pronounced.

Vous n͟e parlez pas bien.	*You don't speak well.*
Je n͟e ferme pas la fenêtre.	*I am not closing the window.*

The pronunciation of the **s** of **pas** before a vowel is optional.

Ils ne sont pas‿au café. ⎫	
Ils ne sont pas / au café. ⎭	*They aren't at the café.*

Ce qu'ils disent

In casual conversation, the French leave out the **ne** of the negation. This is particularly the case with young people. However, they would never write that way, and you must always use **ne** to maintain an appropriate style.

Speaking	Writing
On mange pas beaucoup.	On **ne** mange pas beaucoup.
Il écoute pas la radio.	Il **n'**écoute pas la radio.
C'est pas un stylo.	Ce **n'**est pas un stylo.

Language

A. **Mais non!** You think your friend Robert is always wrong. Contradict every sentence he says.

MODEL: Nadine joue avec les enfants.
Nadine ne joue pas avec les enfants.

1. Je danse avec les sœurs de Louise.
2. Le frère de Jean parle beaucoup.
3. Les parents de Michelle adorent la musique.
4. Tu apprécies l'art moderne.
5. Vous travaillez bien.
6. Marthe et Jean mangent souvent.

Culture

B. **En France?** Answer the following questions based on your knowledge of life in France.

1. On parle anglais avec les copains?
2. Les femmes travaillent?
3. Les Français fument beaucoup de cigares?
4. Ils détestent la musique américaine?
5. Les parents voyagent avec les enfants?
6. Les Français fréquentent les cafés?

Communication

C. **En famille.** Complete the following statements as they apply to your family and you. If your answer is negative, give your own alternative or use one of the suggestions in parentheses.

MODEL: J'aime l'art. (la musique)
Non, je n'aime pas l'art. J'aime la musique.

1. Je travaille mal. (bien / beaucoup / souvent)
2. J'apprécie l'intolérance. (l'hypocrisie / la sincérité)
3. Mes *(My)* parents aiment le rock. (jouer / danser)
4. Mes frères / sœurs adorent étudier. (les sports / les cafés)
5. Ma *(My)* famille et moi, nous regardons les matchs de football. (écouter la radio / fréquenter les clubs)
6. Ma famille déteste mes copains. (adorer / apprécier)

D. **C'est vrai?** Divide into groups of three or four and find someone who can answer truthfully each of the following questions in the negative.

1. Tu chantes bien?
2. Tu écoutes souvent la radio?
3. Tu fumes?
4. Tu travailles beaucoup?

5. Tu fréquentes les clubs?
6. Tu aimes regarder les films à la télé?

CHAMPAGNE
POMMERY
CRÉER POMMERY C'EST TOUT UN ART.

II. Etre / Etre and occupation or nationality

> You use **être** to indicate a state of being or to describe something.

A. Etre

1. **Etre** is an irregular verb, so you must memorize its forms.

être	(to be)			
je **suis**	/ ʒø sɥi /	*I am*	nous **sommes** / nu sɔm /	*we are*
tu es	/ ty ɛ /	*you are*	vous êtes / vu zɛt /	*you are*
il est	/ i lɛ /	*he is*	ils **sont** / il sɔ̃ /	*they are*
elle est	/ ɛ lɛ /	*she is*	elles **sont** / ɛl sɔ̃ /	*they are*
on est	/ ɔ̃ nɛ /	*we are*		

2. The final written consonant of each form of *être* is usually not pronounced. When the verb occurs before a vowel, however, the **t** of the third-person forms is pronounced.

Elle est étudiante.   *She is a student.*
Ils sont en philo.   *They are philosophy majors.*

3. The other final consonants may be pronounced and linked before vowels, but it is not necessary.

Je suis étudiant.
Je suis / étudiant.   *I am a student.*

Tu es américaine.
Tu es / américaine.   *You are American.*

B. Etre with occupation or nationality

1. When **être** is used with occupation or nationality, no article is used—the noun or adjective follows the verb directly.

Marie **est médecin.**   *Marie **is a doctor.*** (noun)
Christian **est allemand.**   *Christian **is German.*** (adjective)

L'orthographe

Note that adjectives of nationality are not capitalized in French. When used as nouns, however, they are capitalized.

Il invite trois **Français.**   *He is inviting three **French people.***

Les **Canadiens** travaillent beaucoup.   ***Canadians** work a lot.*

---

2. Some occupations have one form for both the masculine and feminine.

Mme Dupont est **professeur.**   *Mrs. Dupont is **a teacher.***
L'auteur est aussi **actrice.**   *The author is also **an actress.***

Mots clés   Professions and nationalities

Les professions (f.)

l'acteur (m.),	l'avocat (m.),	l'ingénieur (m.)	le président,
l'actrice (f.)	l'avocate (f.)	le / la journaliste	la présidente
l'agent de police (m.)	*lawyer*	le médecin	le programmeur,
l'architecte (m.)	le diplomate	*doctor*	la programmeuse
l'artiste (m. or f.)	l'économiste (m.)	le musicien,	le / la secrétaire
l'auteur (m.)	l'écrivain (m.)	la musicienne	

Les nationalités (f.)

allemand, allemande	anglais, anglaise	espagnol, espagnole	français, française
German	canadien, canadienne	*Spanish*	italien, italienne
américain, américaine			

Ce qu'ils disent

1. In very informal conversation, the **u** of **tu** is often dropped with the verb **être.** This may occur in sentences in which the **ne** of the negative is also dropped.

   T'es certain?   *Are you sure?*
   T'es pas anglais!   *You aren't English!*

2. In Quebec, French speakers have invented the feminine form **écrivaine** because there are so many active women writers there. The **Québécois** in general are more relaxed about vocabulary than the French; one also sees **auteure** and **professeure.**

Language

A. **Les professions.** What do the following people do? Use the correct form of être.

   MODEL: Je / étudiant(e)
            Je suis étudiant(e).

   1. L'oncle de Jean / musicien
   2. Les cousines de Patricia / profs
   3. Vous / diplomate
   4. Nous / étudiants
   5. Elle / agent de police
   6. La nièce de Robert / journaliste

Culture

B. **Des célébrités françaises.** Identify the professions of the following famous French-speaking people.

MODEL: Debussy
          Il est musicien.

1. Gérard Depardieu *actor*
2. l'Inspecteur Clouseau *police*
3. Le Corbusier *architect*
4. Gauguin et Van Gogh *artist*

5. Catherine Deneuve *actor*
6. Jacques Chirac *president*
7. Gustave Eiffel *architect ingenieur*
8. Dumas père et Dumas fils *auteur*

C. **Familles célèbres.** With a partner, try to match the following people with their famous French-speaking family members, living or dead.

MODEL: La fille de Victor Hugo?
          C'est Adèle H.

1. Le mari de Joséphine? *c*
2. La femme de Louis XVI? *f*
3. Le père de Louis IX
   (Saint Louis)? *e*
4. La copine de Sartre? *a*
5. La femme de Louis Malle? *b*
6. L'ex-femme de Roger Vadim? *b d*

a. Simone de Beauvoir
b. Jane Fonda
c. Napoléon
d. Candice Bergen
e. Louis VIII
f. Marie-Antoinette

Communication

D. **Les célébrités.** Can you think of famous people with the following occupations and nationalities? Work in groups of three or four to see which group can find the most names within the time limit given by your teacher.

MODEL: Student 1: *Qui* (Who) *est acteur?*
          Student 2: *Alain Delon est acteur.*

actrice	français(e)	espagnol(e)	anglais(e)
médecin	américain(e)	diplomate	journaliste
artiste	avocat	étudiant(e)	auteur
canadien(ne)	italien(ne)	musicien(ne)	agent de police

E. **Mes connaissances.** Ask each other the following questions about people you know. Be sure to answer in complete sentences, and honestly!

1. Le professeur est français?
2. Est-ce que le président est intelligent? Et le vice-président?
3. Les parents de votre *(your)* copain / copine sont sympathiques?
4. Les camarades de cours sont américains?
5. Est-ce que vous êtes studieux (-euse)?
6. Vous êtes toujours premier (-ère)?

III. Descriptive adjectives

You use adjectives to describe people and things.

A. In French, adjectives are usually placed *after* the noun, and they may vary in pronunciation or spelling or both, to agree in gender and number with the nouns they describe.

B. Singular and plural forms

1. Most adjectives add a written **-s** to form the plural. The pronunciation does not change.

L'étudiant **intelligent** travaille beaucoup.	The **intelligent** student works a lot.
Les étudiants **intelligents** travaillent beaucoup.	**Intelligent** students work a lot.
Elle n'est pas **studieuse?**	She isn't **studious?**
Elles ne sont pas **studieuses.**	They aren't **studious.**

2. Masculine adjectives that end in a written **-s** or **-x** do not have a different plural form.

Le professeur **français** est **ambitieux.**	The **French** professor is **ambitious.**
Les professeurs **français** sont **ambitieux.**	The **French** professors are **ambitious.**

3. To describe a mixed group of masculine and feminine nouns, use the masculine plural form of the adjective.

Marie et Pierre ne sont pas **italiens.**	*Marie and Pierre are not **Italian.***

C. Masculine and feminine forms

1. Masculine singular adjectives that end in a silent **-e** do not change in pronunciation or spelling in the feminine.

Le garçon est **sympathique.**	The boy is **nice.**
La fille est **sympathique.**	The girl is **nice.**

Some adjectives that have the same masculine and feminine forms are as follows:

agréable *pleasant*	inutile *useless*	riche
désagréable	magnifique	simple
difficile	malade *sick*	sincère
facile *easy*	optimiste	stupide
fantastique	pauvre *poor*	sympathique nice, fun
formidable *great*	pessimiste	timide
hypocrite	possible	utile *useful*
impossible	rapide	

2. Masculine singular adjectives that end in a pronounced vowel or a pronounced consonant are spelled differently in the feminine, although they are pronounced the same.

José est **espagnol**.	*José is **Spanish.***
Maria est **espagnole**.	*Maria is **Spanish.***

Some adjectives that change in spelling but not in pronunciation are as follows:

compliqué,		impoli, impolie	*impolite*
compliquée	*complicated*	poli, polie	*polite*
espagnol, espagnole		seul, seule	*alone*
fatigué, fatiguée	*tired*	vrai, vraie	*true*
fermé, fermée	*closed*		

3. Many adjectives end in a silent consonant in the masculine. To form their feminine, add a written -e and pronounce the consonant.

Le livre **français** est magnifique.	*The **French** book is great.*
La musique **française** est magnifique.	***French** music is great.*

Some adjectives that end in a silent consonant in the masculine are as follows:

absent, absente		indépendant, indépendante	
anglais, anglaise		intelligent, intelligente	
charmant, charmante	charming	intéressant, intéressante	
chaud, chaude	*hot*	laid, laide	*ugly*
compétent, compétente		mauvais, mauvaise	*bad (quality)*
content, contente	*happy*	méchant, méchante	*bad (character)*
fascinant, fascinante			
français, française		ouvert, ouverte	*open*
froid, froide	*cold*	présent, présente	
incompétent, incompétente		prudent, prudente	*careful*

4. Some adjectives end in a nasal vowel in the masculine. To create their feminine forms, add a written -e. If the masculine ends in -en, however, double the -n before adding the -e. In both cases, the vowel loses its nasality and the -n is pronounced.

Il n'est pas **italien**, mais **américain**.	*He's not **Italian**, but **American.***
Elle n'est pas **italienne**, mais **américaine**.	*She's not **Italian**, but **American.***

Some adjectives of this type are as follows:

-ne	-nne
américain, américaine	ancien, ancienne *old*
certain, certaine	canadien, canadienne
féminin, féminine	italien, italienne
masculin, masculine	parisien, parisienne
mexicain, mexicaine	

Ce qu'ils disent

One of the adjectives used most frequently in conversations is **bien**, which means *good*, *great*, or *fine*. It is invariable; that is, it never changes in pronunciation or spelling.

L'hôtel est **bien**!	*It's a **good** hotel.*
Ses copains sont **bien**.	*His friends are **great**.*

---

5. To form the feminine of adjectives that end in **-eux**, add the sound **/ z /** and change the **-x** to **-se**.

Le garçon est **paresseux**.	*The boy is **lazy**.*
La fille est **paresseuse**.	*The girl is **lazy**.*

Some adjectives ending in **-eux, -euse** are as follows:

affectueux,	**généreux, généreuse**
affectueuse *affectionate*	**heureux, heureuse** *happy*
affreux, affreuse *terrible*	**malheureux,**
ambitieux, ambitieuse	**malheureuse** *unhappy*
courageux, courageuse	**paresseux, paresseuse** *lazy*
dangereux, dangereuse	**sérieux, sérieuse**
ennuyeux, ennuyeuse *boring*	**studieux, studieuse**

L'orthographe

Two quick rules of thumb that will work for spelling most French adjectives are as follows:

Plural: Add an **-s** to any letter except **s** or **x**.
Feminine: Add an **-e** to any letter except unaccented **e**, **x**, or **en**.

Language

A. Les descriptions. Describe the following people with the definite article and the adjective provided.

MODEL: étudiant / français   *l'étudiant français*

1. actrice / formidable
2. étudiante / intelligent
3. auteur / ennuyeux
4. enfant / paresseux
5. hommes / fatigué
6. femmes / indépendant

B. **C'est comment?** Describe the following people and things with the verb **être** and the correct form of the adjective provided.

MODEL: garçons / fatigué   *Les garçons sont fatigués.*

1. musique / affreux
2. filles / sympathique
3. livres / facile
4. Ils / malade
5. professeurs / intéressant
6. Nous / fatigué   *(two possibilities)*
7. Je / américain   *(two possibilities)*
8. Vous / poli   *(four possibilities)*

Culture

C. **L'Amérique.** Describe what you believe are traditional French attitudes toward Americans and American culture, using the following nouns and adjectives.

MODEL: les Américains: agréable / désagréable
     Les Américains sont agréables.

1. Les Américains: sympathique / froid
2. la musique: ennuyeux / fantastique
3. la télévision: fascinant / affreux
4. le café: mauvais / formidable
5. les présidents: compétent / incompétent
6. la politique *(politics)*: prudent / dangereux

Communication

D. **Les qualités.** Use the adjectives listed below to describe the following people and things. You may also provide your own adjectives if you prefer. Find a classmate who disagrees with you.

MODEL: *Les journalistes sont ambitieux et intelligents.*

sincère	ennuyeux	inutile	charmant
hypocrite	ambitieux	fantastique	intelligent
formidable	paresseux	fatigué	heureux
compliqué	utile	méchant	malheureux

1. secrétaires
2. professeurs
3. rock
4. télévision
5. université
6. Français
7. médecins
8. président
9. femmes
10. hommes
11. étudiants
12. Je

E. **Vos préférences.** Tell your preferences by choosing one item from each of the columns and adding any necessary words. Work with a classmate to find a consensus.

MODEL: *J'aime les hommes intelligents.*
     Je n'aime pas les enfants méchants.

A	B	C	
J'aime	femmes	désagréable	généreux
Je n'aime pas	hommes	compétent	stupide
	familles	incompétent	sérieux
	médecins	charmant	sympathique
	étudiants	impoli	sincère
	Français *(pl.)*	intelligent	méchant
			???

IV. Numbers from 21 to 69 / Ordinal numbers

You use cardinal numbers to count or quantify *(one, two, three . . .)* and ordinal numbers *(first, second, third . . .)* to rank people or things.

A. A few of the cardinal numbers from 20 to 69 are as follows:

20 vingt	30 trente	40 quarante
21 vingt et un	31 trente et un	41 quarante et un
22 vingt-deux	32 trente-deux	44 quarante-quatre
23 vingt-trois	36 trente-six	47 quarante-sept

50 cinquante	60 soixante
51 cinquante et un	61 soixante et un
55 cinquante-cinq	67 soixante-sept
58 cinquante-huit	69 soixante-neuf

1. **Et** is used with the numbers 21, 31, 41, 51, and 61; the **t** of **et** is never pronounced.

2. The succeeding numbers are hyphenated.

3. The **t** of **vingt** is pronounced from 21 to 29.

4. In **soixante** (/ swa sãt /), the **x** is pronounced / s /.

5. Except for **un / une,** numbers do not agree in either number or gender with the nouns they modify.

Quatre garçons habitent ensemble.	*Four boys live together.*
Voilà **neuf** filles.	*There are **nine** girls.*
but: **vingt et une** pages	*twenty-one pages*

B. Ordinal numbers

1. To form ordinal numbers, in most cases simply add the suffix **-ième** to the cardinal number.

cardinal	ordinal	
deux	**deuxième**	*second*
trois	**troisième**	*third*
dix-sept	**dix-septième**	*seventeenth*
vingt	**vingtième**	*twentieth*
vingt et un	**vingt et unième**	*twenty-first*

C'est le **troisième** médecin de la famille.	*He / She is the **third** doctor in the family.*
Nous terminons le **quatrième** exercice.	*We are finishing the **fourth** exercise.*

2. Three exceptions are as follows:

cardinal	ordinal
un, une	**premier, première**
cinq	**cinquième**
neuf	**neuvième**

In addition, for **deuxième** an alternate form, **second / seconde**, is used.

L'orthographe

1. If the cardinal number ends in -e, you must drop the written -e before adding the **-ième** suffix.

cardinal	ordinal
onze	**onzième**
trente	**trentième**
cinquante-quatre	**cinquante-quatrième**

2. Ordinal numbers may be abbreviated as follows:

premier → 1er première → 1ère

cinquième → 5ème or 5e vingtième → 20ème or 20^{e}

Language

A. Comptons! Count in French.

1. 30, 31, 32... 40
2. 21, 24, 27... 69
3. 25, 26, 27... 35
4. 20, 22, 24... 68
5. 21, 23, 25... 69
6. 60, 59, 58... 50

B. Calculons! Do the following problems in French.

1. $10 + 11 =$
2. $14 + 16 =$
3. $47 - 19 =$
4. $15 + 16 =$
5. $21 - 12 =$
6. $18 + 22 =$
7. $30 + 15 =$
8. $20 + 29 =$
9. $24 + 27 =$
10. $19 + 33 =$
11. $40 - 22 =$
12. $55 - 34 =$

Culture   WWW

C. Au lycée. The French count years of schooling in reverse order of the American system. The *sixth grade* is **la sixième**, but *seventh grade* is **la cinquième**. Give the French equivalent of the following grades. (The *senior year* is called **la terminale**.)

1. sixth grade
2. seventh grade
3. eighth grade
4. freshman
5. sophomore
6. junior

D. **Au téléphone.** You are in Paris and want to plan your visits to the following places in advance. Read the names and numbers to your hotel switchboard operator.

1. Air Canada   01. 43. 20. 14. 15
2. le Centre Georges Pompidou
   01. 45. 08. 25. 00
3. Notre-Dame   01. 40. 33. 22. 63
4. la tour Eiffel   01. 47. 05. 44. 13

5. La Tour d'Argent
   01. 43. 44. 32. 19
6. Le Moulin Rouge
   01. 42. 64. 33. 69

Communication

E. **Les priorités.** Rank the following things according to how important they are to you. Use the phrases **En premier:...**, **En deuxième:...**, and so on, to do so. Find a classmate who agrees with you and one who disagrees.

les amis	la famille	la nationalité
être riche	la profession	être heureux (-euse)

Communiquons

Faire les présentations

The basic rules of politeness that exist in the United States are also observed in France. You must introduce people who do not know each other, and you must pay attention to the style of language you use. To introduce someone who is older than you, use one of the following formal expressions. For friends and relatives, one of the informal expressions is appropriate.

Expressions

> ▶ **On présente les adultes.**

Monsieur / Madame / Mademoiselle, je voudrais vous présenter Marie.

Sir / Ma'am / Miss, I would like you to meet Marie.

Permettez-moi de vous présenter Marie.

Allow me to introduce Marie to you.

Enchanté, Monsieur / Madame / Mademoiselle.

Pleased to meet you, sir / ma'am / miss.

Très heureux (-euse) (de faire votre connaissance).

A pleasure (to meet you).

▶ **On présente les amis.**

Robert, je voudrais te présenter Marie.	*Robert, I'd like you to meet Marie.*
Robert, je te présente Marie.	*Robert, this is Marie.*
Robert, voilà Marie.	*Robert, this is Marie.*
Salut, Marie.	*Hi, Marie.*
Bonjour, Marie, ça va?	*Hello, Marie, how are you?*

Interaction

Solange et son père rencontrent un professeur sur le campus.

SOLANGE:	Bonjour, M. Renaud!
M. RENAUD:	Bonjour, Solange. Comment allez-vous?
SOLANGE:	Très bien. Je voudrais vous présenter mon père.
M. RENAUD:	Enchanté, Monsieur.
LE PÈRE DE SOLANGE:	Très heureux.

Je voudrais vous présenter mon ami!

Activités

A. What would you say to introduce the following people?

1. your roommate and your
    teacher

3. your parents and your
    faculty advisor

2. your roommate and an old
    friend from high school

4. your sister and someone in
    your class

B. Divide into groups of three and practice introducing your classmates to each
other.

Lecture culturelle

Avant la lecture

According to a recent poll of the **INSEE (Institut national de la statistique et des
études économiques)**, the birth rate is dropping in France, and a typical French
family has only 1.65 children. The number of divorces, which tripled between
1970 and 1985, is now stable, but a divorce still occurs in 41 out of each 100
marriages.

French people today get married later than they used to. In general, men wait until they are 27, while the average age for women is 25. However, many couples live together before getting married.

Activité

Skim the reading passage for the following information:

1. Find five descriptive adjectives, and tell which ones are cognates and which are not.
2. Find three things that have a great influence on the upbringing of French children outside their families.

La famille française

L'éducation° d'un enfant est le résultat d'une série d'influences extérieures comme l'école°, les médias et les copains. Mais en France, la famille, et surtout° les parents, constitue encore° l'influence la plus° importante. Les enfants observent leurs° parents et ils développent leur concep-
5 tion de la vie°.

Cependant°, la vie familiale est différente. Dans la majorité des familles, les grands-parents n'habitent plus° avec leurs enfants et leurs petits-enfants. De plus°, le développement de l'union libre°, le nombre important des divorces et la réduction du nombre des naissances° jouent un rôle essentiel dans l'éducation
10 des enfants français.

Malgré° tous les changements°, les années quatre-vingt° et quatre-vingt-dix signalent une amélioration° des relations entre les générations. Les parents et les enfants sont très affectueux et ils communiquent facilement°. Pour la majorité des enfants, la famille constitue toujours° un refuge.

upbringing
comme... *such as school*
particularly / still / the most
their
life
However
n'... *no longer live*
De... *Furthermore /* **union...** *living together / births*
In spite of / changes / **Les...** *the 1980s / improvement*
easily
still

On joue avec les enfants.

Après la lecture

Questions sur le texte

1. Est-ce que l'école, les médias et les copains sont les influences les plus importantes sur les enfants?
2. Les grands-parents habitent toujours avec leurs enfants et petits-enfants?
3. Est-ce que les années quatre-vingt signalent une différence dans les relations familiales?
4. Aujourd'hui, qu'est-ce que la famille est pour les enfants?

Activités

A. Using the reading selection, make a list in French of differences (**différences**) and similarities (**ressemblances**) between family life in France and in the United States.

B. List the people you like and do not like to go to when you have problems.

    MODEL: *J'aime parler avec mes copains.*
              Je n'aime pas parler de mes problèmes avec mes grands-parents.

C. In your family, who are your favorite people? Why?

    MODEL: *J'aime ma sœur; elle est fantastique.*
              J'aime bien mon cousin; il est très intelligent.

Vocabulaire

Noms / Pronoms

acteur	actor	copine	friend (female)
actrice	actress	cousin(e)	cousin
agent de police	policeman	diplomate	diplomat
architecte	architect	distraction	entertainment
artiste	artist	économiste	economist
auteur	author	écrivain(e)	writer
avocat	lawyer	famille	family
beau-père	stepfather / father-in-law	femme	wife
belle-mère	stepmother / mother-in-law	fille	girl / daughter
		film	film
		fils	son
boîte	club	football	soccer
boîte de nuit	nightclub	frère	brother
camarade de chambre	roommate	garçon	boy
camarade de cours	classmate	grand-mère	grandmother
club	club / nightclub	grand-père	grandfather
connaissance	acquaintance	grands-parents	grandparents
copain	friend (male)	hypocrisie	hypocrisy

ingénieur	engineer	petit(e) ami(e)	boyfriend / girlfriend
intolérance	intolerance	petits-enfants	grandchildren
jazz	jazz	philosophie	philosophy
jeunes gens	young people	président(e)	president
journaliste	journalist	profession	profession
lui	him	programmeur	computer programmer
mari	husband	relation d'affaires	business acquaintance
médecin	doctor	rock	rock
mère	mother	secrétaire	secretary
moi	me / I	sincérité	sincerity
musicien	musician	sœur	sister
nationalité	nationality	soirée	evening
neveu	nephew	sports	sports
nièce	niece	tante	aunt
oncle	uncle	télé	TV
parents	parents	voiture	car
père	father		

Verbes

apprécier	to appreciate	être	to be
désirer	to desire / to wish	fréquenter	to go to / go out with
détester	to hate	garer	to park
embrasser	to kiss	passer	to spend (time)
entrer	to enter / go in		

Adjectifs / Adverbes

absent	absent	le dernier	the latest
affectueux	affectionate	désagréable	unpleasant
affreux	horrible	deuxième	second
agréable	pleasant	difficile	difficult
allemand	German	dix-septième	seventeenth
ambitieux	ambitious	enchanté	delighted
américain	American	ennuyeux	boring
ancien	old / former	espagnol	Spanish
aussi	also	facile	easy
bien	nice	fantastique	fantastic
canadien	Canadian	fascinant	fascinating
certain	certain / some	fatigué	tired
charmant	charming	favori	favorite
chaud	hot	féminin	feminine
cinquante	fifty	fermé	closed
cinquième	fifth	formidable	sensational / terrific
classique	classical	froid	cold
compétent	competent	généreux	generous
compliqué	complicated	heureux	happy
content	happy	hypocrite	hypocritical
courageux	courageous	impoli	impolite
dangereux	dangerous	impossible	impossible

incompétent	incompetent	prudent	careful
indépendant	independent	quand	when
intelligent	intelligent	quarante	forty
intéressant	interesting	quatrième	fourth
inutile	useless	quelque	some
italien	Italian	rapide	fast
là	there	riche	rich
laid	ugly	second	second
magnifique	magnificent	sérieux	serious
malade	sick	seul	alone
malheureux	unhappy	si	yes
masculin	masculine	simple	simple
mauvais	bad	sincère	sincere
méchant	mean, bad	soixante	sixty
mexicain	Mexican	souvent	often
ne… pas	not	studieux	studious
neuvième	ninth	stupide	stupid
onzième	eleventh	sympathique	nice
optimiste	optimistic	timide	shy
où	where	ton	your
ouvert	open	toujours	always
paresseux	lazy	trente	thirty
parisien	Parisian	trentième	thirtieth
pauvre	poor	troisième	third
pessimiste	pessimistic	utile	useful
premier	first	vingtième	twentieth
présent	present	vrai	true

Expressions

aimer bien	to like / to be fond of	détester faire	to hate doing
aimer faire	to enjoy doing	devant	in front of
aimer mieux	to prefer	en retard	late
art moderne	modern art	sans	without
au	at	Tiens!	Hey!

Au restaurant

 Commençons

 Grammaire

 Communiquons

 Lecture culturelle

 Vocabulaire

On va manger
un couscous

Objectives

Language

Vocabulary for beverages and food • Silent consonants • Indefinite and partitive articles • The verb **avoir** and idiomatic expressions • Use of articles • The imperative

Culture

French restaurants • North African food • Traditional meals in France

Communication

Ordering food • Making commands and requests • Expressing quantity

Commençons

A La Goulette

www

Sylvie, programmeuse à IBM, et Maude, journaliste à Elle, *sont dans un restaurant tunisien à Paris. Elles regardent la carte.*

LE GARÇON:	Bonsoir. Vous désirez?
SYLVIE:	Je voudrais un apéritif. Vous avez du Martini? *(Brand)*
LE GARÇON:	Oui, mademoiselle. Du rouge ou du blanc?
SYLVIE:	Du rouge, s'il vous plaît.
LE GARÇON:	Mademoiselle aussi?
MAUDE:	Non, merci.
SYLVIE:	J'ai faim ce soir. Je voudrais un couscous au mouton.
LE GARÇON:	Vous aussi, mademoiselle?
MAUDE:	Non, je ne mange pas de viande. Je voudrais un couscous aux légumes.
LE GARÇON:	Qu'est-ce que vous prenez comme boisson?
SYLVIE:	*(What)* Apportez de l'eau minérale et un pichet de vin rouge, s'il vous plaît.
LE GARÇON:	Très bien. J'apporte l'apéritif tout de suite.

Etudions le dialogue

1. La Goulette est un restaurant anglais?
2. Maude aime l'apéritif?
3. Est-ce que Sylvie et Maude demandent du vin blanc?
4. Est-ce que Sylvie a faim ce soir?
5. Maude mange un couscous au mouton aussi?
6. Le garçon est poli *(polite)* ou impoli?

10, rue Christine, Paris 6e
Métro Odéon - Saint-Michel
☎ 326-13-45

vous propose

sa cuisine *Tunisienne*
typique *et Française*

Restaurant Oriental, sympa! et pas cher...
le Grand Texel

Mots clés

dans	in	au	with/in the
le restaurant	restaurant	mouton *(m.)*	mutton
l tunisien(ne)	Tunisian	de	any
la carte	menu	viande *(f.)*	meat
le garçon	waiter	aux	with
je voudrais	I would like	légumes *(m.)*	vegetables
? une apéritif	before-dinner drink	prenez (prendre)	take
avez (avoir)	have	comme	for
du	any	boisson *(f.)*	drink
rouge	red	apportez (apporter)	bring
blanc	white	eau minérale *(f.)*	mineral water
s'il vous plaît	please	*le* pichet	pitcher
J'ai faim. (avoir faim)	I am hungry.	*le* vin *(m.)*	wine
ce soir	this evening	tout de suite	immediately
des couscous	couscous		

Faisons connaissance

WWW

France offers a variety of restaurants that range from very elegant and expensive establishments to little **bistrots** or **cafés** where people can go for a simple meal. Fast-food places have become popular, and McDonald's is a presence in all major French cities. Unlike its American counterpart, however, McDonald's does serve wine and beer.

Le fast-food en France

Restaurants featuring foreign cooking are also very popular in France. Because of France's ties to its former colonies in North Africa, Tunisian, Algerian, and Moroccan specialties are particularly well liked. Couscous is a typical Arab dish made with a wheat product called semolina (**la semoule**), which resembles rice somewhat. On top of the grain one puts a vegetable stew and a choice of meat. Mutton, lamb chops, or chicken are the usual choices.

Traditionally, Arabs do not drink alcohol, but North African restaurants in France do serve it. An **apéritif** usually contains alcohol and is drunk before meals to increase one's appetite. **Un pichet** would be the house wine, which is less expensive than bottled wine. Many French people order mineral water in restaurants; they rarely drink tap water.

Menus are posted in the windows of restaurants. Patrons often have a choice of ordering individual items from **la carte** or a three- or four-course meal from **le menu.** Many choose the latter because the fixed price (**prix fixe**) usually includes the tip (**service compris**) and often a beverage. The selection normally offers an appetizer (**le hors-d'œuvre**), a main course (**le plat principal**), a vegetable, and a choice of cheese, fruit, or dessert.

Enrichissons notre vocabulaire

Des boissons *(Drinks)*

du thé de l'eau du café du coca

du vin du lait de la bière du jus de fruit

De la nourriture *(Food)*

du poisson
du jambon
de la **viande**
de la **salade**
du poulet
de la **glace**
du **fromage**
des **légumes**
des fruits
de la soupe
du **beurre**
un **hamburger**
du **pain**
un gâteau · du **gâteau**
des **frites**

Quelques expressions utiles *(Some useful expressions)*

il boit nous buvons ils boivent

boire: je **bois**, tu **bois**; vous **buvez**	*to drink: I drink, you drink, you drink*
commander	*to order*
consommer	*to consume*
déjeuner	*to have lunch*
dîner	*to eat dinner or supper, to dine*
goûter	*to taste (a food), to have a snack*
préparer	*to prepare*
recommander	*to recommend*

Je prends
tu prends
il prend
nous prenons
vous prenez
ils prennent

—Comment **trouvez**-vous le couscous à La Goulette?
*How do you **like** the couscous at La Goulette?*

—Il est **délicieux**; c'est le **plat** préféré de Sylvie.
*It is **delicious**; it is Sylvie's favorite dish.*

—**Quelle sorte de cuisine** est-ce qu'elle aime?
What kind of cooking does she like?

—La cuisine tunisienne.
Tunisian cooking.

Prononciation   Silent consonants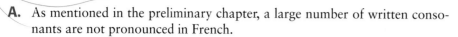

A. As mentioned in the preliminary chapter, a large number of written consonants are not pronounced in French.

Il es̸t paresseux̸.   *He is lazy.*
Jacques̸ e̸t Gilles̸ étudien̸t   *Jacques and Gilles are studying*
   l'anglais̸.   *English.*

B. Final written consonants are rarely pronounced.

Nous̸ ne travaillon̸s̸ pas̸.   *We aren't working.*
Les̸ livres̸ sont ennuyeux̸.   *The books are boring.*

There are, however, exceptions to this rule.

Mar*c* apporte un apériti*f*.   *Marc is bringing a drink.*
I*l* travaille seu*l*.   *He works alone.*

C. In general, a final silent **e** shows that the preceding consonant is pronounced.

Ell*e* regar*d*e la car*t*e.   *She is looking at the menu.*
Jean̸ est présen̸t; Jea*nn*e est   *Jean is present; Jeanne is*
   absen*t*e.   *absent.*

Remember that the final silent **e** marks the difference between masculine and feminine nouns and adjectives such as **étudiant / étudiante** and **froid / froide**.

Exercice

Read the following sentences aloud, paying particular attention to silent consonants.

1. Les trois Français étudient l'anglais.
2. Nous sommes très contents.
3. Jean est méchant et il n'est pas heureux.
4. Elles dansent avec le fils de Monsieur Legrand.
5. Tu es paresseux et tu n'études pas.
6. Mon amie canadienne est médecin.

Grammaire

I.   Indefinite and partitive articles

You use indefinite and partitive articles with names of people, things, and ideas to indicate something not specific or previously mentioned.

As mentioned in Chapter 1, an article almost always accompanies a noun in French. The most frequently used articles in French are *nondefinite*—they stand for a person, thing, or idea that is not specific and not defined.

There are two types of nondefinite articles because in French, as in English, there is a distinction between nouns that can be counted *(count nouns)*, and those that cannot *(mass nouns)*. *Indefinite articles* are used with count nouns. *Partitive articles* are used with mass nouns.

A. Indefinite articles

indefinite articles				
	singular		*plural*	
masculine	un	} *a, an*	des	} *some*
feminine	une		des	

1. Indefinite articles refer to one unspecified object or person or to an unspecified group of *countable* objects or persons.

Elles sont dans **un** restaurant tunisien.	*They are in a Tunisian restaurant.*
Je commande **des** fruits comme dessert.	*I order fruit for dessert.*

2. The indefinite articles **un** and **une** correspond to the English *a* or *an*. The masculine singular indefinite article is **un,** pronounced / ɛ̃ / before a consonant and / ɛ̃n / before a vowel.

un bureau	/ ɛ̃ by ʀo /	*a desk, an office*
un mur	/ ɛ̃ myʀ /	*a wall*
un stylo	/ ɛ̃ sti lo /	*a pen*
un élève	/ ɛ̃ ne lɛv /	*a (male) student*

3. The feminine singular indefinite article is **une,** always pronounced / yn /.

une carte	/ yn kaʀt /	*a map, a card, a menu*
une école	/ y ne kɔl /	*a school*
une élève	/ y ne lɛv /	*a (female) student*
une photo	/ yn fo to /	*a photograph*

4. The plural indefinite article is **des,** pronounced / de / before consonants and / dez / before vowel sounds.

des chaises *(f.)*	*(some) chairs*
des examens *(m.)*	*(some) exams*

B. Partitive articles

partitive articles		
before masculine, singular nouns	**du**	
before feminine, singular nouns	**de la**	some, any
before singular nouns beginning with a vowel	**de l'**	

1. Partitive articles refer to an unspecified portion, or *part*, of an object that is measurable but not countable, such as water, wine, or meat. **Du, de la,** and **de l'** may be expressed in English as *some* or *any*, or may not be expressed at all.

Je désire **du** vin.	*I want wine.*
	or:
	*I want **some** wine.*
Elle mange **de la** tarte.	*She is eating pie.*
	or:
	*She is eating **some** pie.*
Apportez **de l'**eau minérale!	*Bring **some** mineral water!*

2. The masculine partitive article for mass nouns—those that are not counted—is **du,** pronounced / dy /.

du chocolat	*hot chocolate, chocolate candy*
du gâteau	*cake*
du sel	*salt*
du sucre	*sugar*

3. The feminine partitive article for mass nouns is **de la.**

de la confiture	*jam*
de la farine	*flour*
de la moutarde	*mustard*
de la crème	*cream*

4. The singular partitive article **de l'** is used with masculine or feminine mass nouns that start with a vowel sound.

de l'agneau *(m.)*	*lamb*
de l'alcool *(m.)*	*alcohol*
de l'argent *(m.)*	*money*
de l'huile *(f.)*	*oil*

5. When referring to a countable unit of a mass noun, such as *a bottle* of beer, *a loaf* of bread, or *two cups* of coffee, the indefinite article is used.

Mass		**Count**	
de la bière	*(some) beer*	**une** bière	*a bottle of beer*
du café	*(some) coffee*	**un** café	*a cup of coffee*
du couscous	*(some) couscous*	**un** couscous	*a meal of couscous*
du gâteau	*(some) cake*	**un** gâteau	*a cake*
du pain	*(some) bread*	**un** pain	*a (loaf of) bread*
de la pizza	*(some) pizza*	**une** pizza	*a pizza*

Attention!

In negative sentences, all indefinite and partitive articles change to **de** (**d'** before a vowel sound), except when the verb is **être**.

Elle mange **de la** viande.	Elle **ne** mange **pas de** viande.
Vous avez **des** disques?	Vous **n'**avez **pas de** disques?
J'ai **un** stylo.	Je **n'** ai **pas de** stylo.

but:

C'est **un** stylo.	Ce **n'**est **pas un** stylo.
Le Martini **est un** apéritif.	Le Perrier **n'**est **pas un** apéritif.

Language

A. **Des noms.** Identify the following nouns as primarily count nouns or mass nouns and provide an indefinite or partitive article as appropriate.

1. stylo   4. homme   7. sucre   10. élève
2. crayon   5. photo   8. moutarde   11. fille
3. lait   6. crème   9. eau   12. sel

B. **Au supermarché.** You are going to a supermarket and have begun a list of what you need. Finish your list by adding the correct partitive or indefinite article.

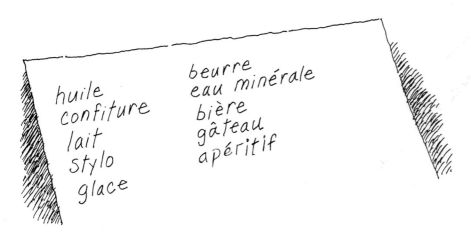

huile
confiture
lait
stylo
glace

beurre
eau minérale
bière
gâteau
apéritif

C. Je suis désagréable! You are very unpleasant today! Contradict the following statements.

MODEL: J'invite des copains.
Je n'invite pas de copains.

1. Marc commande du fromage.
2. Ils demandent du vin.
3. Le mouton est un légume.
4. Nous invitons des amis.
5. Je mange de la viande.
6. Catherine prépare de la salade.
7. Tu bois un coca.
8. Le couscous est un apéritif.

Culture   WWW

D. A l'épicerie. In a neighborhood grocery store in France (**une épicerie**), you may have to ask the grocer to get your supplies. What do you have on your shopping list for a party you are giving this weekend for French friends?

MODEL: *Je voudrais du pain, du beurre et du lait.*

E. Qu'est-ce qu'ils vendent? What do the following companies headquartered in French-speaking countries sell? Can you think of others?

MODEL: Chanel? *Ils vendent du parfum.* (They sell perfume.)

1. Mouton Cadet?
2. Labatt?
3. Evian?
4. Larousse?
5. Nestlé?
6. Knorr?
7. Martini?
8. La Vache qui rit?
9. Godiva?
10. Bic?

Communication

F. Answer the following questions, using any of the suggested words below or your own ideas.

intéressant	ennuyeux	anglais	gâteau
simple	sérieux	formidable	vin
difficile	américain	de jazz	thé
fantastique	français	de rock	lait

MODEL: Quelle sorte de livres est-ce que tu aimes regarder?
J'aime regarder des livres intéressants.

1. Qu'est-ce qu'on trouve dans votre *(your)* frigidaire?
2. Quelle sorte de boissons est-ce que vous buvez?
3. Qu'est-ce que vous aimez manger?
4. Quelle sorte de films est-ce que vous regardez à la télé?
5. Quelle sorte de disques est-ce que vous écoutez?

G. Interview a classmate to find out what he or she likes to eat.

MODEL: Student 1:   *Est-ce que tu aimes manger de la tarte?*
           Student 2:   *Non, je ne mange pas de tarte.*

           Student 1:   *Est-ce que tu bois du thé?*
           Student 2:   *Oui, je bois du thé.*

II.   The irregular verb avoir / Expressions with avoir

You use **avoir** to state possession and to describe certain conditions.

A.   Avoir

1.   **Avoir** is an irregular verb, and you must memorize its forms.

avoir		*(to have)*			
j' **ai**	/ ʒe /	*I have*	nous **avons**	/ nu za vɔ̃ /	*we have*
tu **as**	/ ty a /	*you have*	vous **avez**	/ vu za ve /	*you have*
il **a**	/ i la /	*he has*	ils **ont**	/ il zɔ̃ /	*they have*
elle **a**	/ ɛ la /	*she has*	elles **ont**	/ ɛl zɔ̃ /	*they have*
on **a**	/ ɔ̃ na /	*we have*			

2.   The final **s** of **nous, vous, ils,** and **elles** is pronounced / z / and the **n** of **on** is pronounced / n / in the affirmative because the verb forms start with a vowel sound. The **s** of **sont** *(they are)* is pronounced as / s /: **ils sont** → / il sɔ̃ /.

3.   Before a vowel sound, **je** becomes **j'** and **ne** becomes **n'**.

> J'ai du talent.   *I have talent.*
> Je **n'**ai pas de patience.   *I don't have any patience.*

B.   Expressions with avoir

Avoir is used in several idiomatic expressions.

Elle a chaud; ils ont froid.	*She is hot; they are cold.*
Je ne mange pas; je **n'ai pas faim.**	*I'm not eating; **I'm not hungry.***
Elle désire de l'eau; elle a soif.	*She wants some water; **she's thirsty.***
Vous n'avez pas raison, vous avez tort!	*You aren't right; you are wrong!*
—Quel âge avez-vous?	*How old are you?*
—J'ai dix-huit ans.	*I'm eighteen.*
Il y a une carte dans la classe.	*There's a map in the classroom.*
Il **n'y a pas** de vin.	*There isn't any wine.*

Attention!

Voilà is used to point out something; **il y a** merely indicates existence. Both take singular or plural objects.

Voilà le père de Luc!	*There's Luc's father! (over there)*
Voilà des touristes américains!	*There are some American tourists.*
Il y a du sucre dans le café?	*There is sugar in the coffee?*
Il y a des légumes dans un couscous.	*There are vegetables in a couscous.*

Mots clés *Expressions with* **avoir**

avoir faim	*to be hungry*	avoir tort	*to be wrong*
avoir soif	*to be thirsty*	avoir ____ ans	*to be ____ years old*
avoir chaud	*to be hot*	il y a	*there is, there are*
avoir froid	*to be cold*	il n'y a pas	*there isn't, there aren't*
avoir raison	*to be right*		

Ce qu'ils disent

You saw in Chapter 2 that the **u** of **tu** often disappears in informal conversation when the verb is **être**. The same is true with **avoir**.

T'as froid?	*Are you cold?*
T'as pas faim?	*Aren't you hungry?*

Language

A. Les copains. Chantal is talking to her friends about other people. Make complete sentences by adding any necessary words.

1. Ils / avoir / souvent / tort
2. Tu / ne / avoir / pas / faim?
3. Les enfants de Jacques / avoir / clé
4. On / ne / avoir / pas / froid
5. Tu / avoir / raison
6. Je / ne / avoir / pas / frère
7. Vous / ne / avoir / pas / 21 / ans?
8. Jeanne / avoir / amis

B. J'ai, je n'ai pas. Name three things that you have with you, three things a classmate has with him or her, and one thing you do not have with you.

MODEL: *J'ai un stylo, deux crayons et des livres.*
Anne et Jacqueline ont de l'argent, des photos et un sac à dos.
Je n'ai pas de nourriture.

Culture

C. En cours. Look at the photograph of a French classroom on page 7, and state what there is and is not to be found.

MODEL: *Il y a des étudiants.*
Il n'y a pas de café.

Communication

D. **Mes amis.** Describe the kind of friends you have, using the suggestions provided below or your own ideas.

MODEL: *J'ai des amis sympathiques.*

intéressant	intelligent	ennuyeux	studieux
bien	paresseux	sympathique	???

E. **Des célébrités.** Name famous people who have the following things. Can you think of someone who does not have them? See if you agree with your classmates.

MODEL: du talent? *Paul Simon a du talent.*
 Michael Bolton n'a pas de talent.

1. de l'argent?
2. un restaurant?
3. beaucoup d'ex-femmes?
4. beaucoup d'ex-maris?
5. beaucoup d'enfants?
6. des étudiants intelligents?

F. **Questionnaire.** Find out more about your classmates by asking them questions using the following expressions.

1. avoir froid ou chaud?
2. avoir soif ou faim?
3. avoir des frères ou des sœurs?
4. avoir quel âge?
5. avoir souvent raison ou tort?
6. avoir de la patience?

G. **Questions personnelles.** Parlez de vous!

1. Vous avez souvent faim? Qu'est-ce que vous mangez?
2. Quelle boisson est-ce que vous commandez quand vous avez soif?
3. Quel âge avez-vous? Quel est l'âge idéal?
4. Est-ce que vous avez du talent? Quelle sorte? *(What kind?)*
5. Est-ce que vous avez de l'argent? Qu'est-ce que vous désirez avoir?
6. Vous désirez avoir des enfants? Combien de garçons et combien de filles?

III. Use of articles

You must always use articles with nouns, which name people, things, and ideas. The type of article you use determines the nature of the noun (specific or general, previously mentioned or not).

Now that you have learned the definite, indefinite, and partitive articles, it is essential to know when to use each kind.

A. Use of definite articles

1. Definite articles refer to one specific person or thing.

Elles regardent **la** carte.	*They are looking at **the** menu. (a specific menu)*
Tu as **le** livre?	*Do you have **the** book? (referring to a book just mentioned)*

2. They also refer to all of a given item in a generalized sense.

Les enfants aiment **le** chocolat.	*Children like chocolate. (in general)*
Je déteste **la** bière.	*I hate beer. (all beer)*

Verbs that lend themselves to use in a generalized sense include **aimer, aimer mieux, adorer, apprécier, détester.**

B. Use of indefinite and partitive articles

1. Indefinite articles refer to a person or thing not previously mentioned.

Tu as **un** stylo?	*Do you have **a** pen? (any pen)*
Elles sont dans **un** restaurant tunisien.	*They are in **a** Tunisian restaurant. (an unspecified Tunisian restaurant)*

2. Partitive articles refer to an unspecified portion, or part, of an object that is measurable but not countable.

Apportez **de** l'eau minérale.	*Bring **some** mineral water. (not all of it)*
Jacques n'a pas **de** talent.	*Jacques doesn't have **any** talent. (none at all)*

Many verbs almost always imply a portion of an item and therefore take a partitive article. These include **consommer, demander, désirer, boire, manger,** and the expression **je voudrais.**

3. In the negative, all indefinite and partitive articles become **de** or **d',** but definite articles do not change.

—Vous buvez **du** lait.	—Tu aimes **le** café?
—Non, je **ne** bois **pas de** lait.	—Non, je **n'**aime **pas le** café.

Attention!

Translating into English will *not* help you choose the proper article. In French, you must decide whether the item is considered in a general or specific sense or as a portion. For example, compare the following sentences:

*I like **wine**.* → J'aime **le** vin.
*I want **wine**.* → Je voudrais **du** vin.

4. If you modify a noun with an adverb of quantity, use only the preposition
    de (**d'** before a vowel).

Il n'a pas **assez de** talent.	*He doesn't have **enough** talent.*
Elle a **beaucoup de** devoirs.	*She has **a lot of** homework.*
Moins de sel, s'il vous plaît!	***Less** salt, please.*
Je voudrais **un peu de** crème.	*I would like **a little** cream.*
Nous avons **peu d'**argent.	*We have **little** money.*
Un peu plus de café, Madame?	***A little more** coffee, ma'am?*
Elle a **trop de** poisson.	*She has **too much** fish.*

trop de poisson

beaucoup de devoirs

pas assez de talent

Mots clés

assez de	*enough*	**(un) peu de**	*(a) little*
beaucoup de	*many, a lot*	**plus de**	*more*
moins de	*less*	**trop de**	*too many, too much*

Language

A. Mais non! Contradict the following statements.

1. Il déteste la bière.
2. Ils mangent un couscous.
3. Tu aimes le pain français?
4. Nous avons du gâteau.
5. Christine et Michel
    demandent de la soupe.
6. Anne-Marie a de la salade.

B. Les préférences. Make complete sentences, adding any necessary words to
indicate what the following people like.

1. Catherine / désirer / fromage
2. Je / demander / mouton
3. Elles / adorer / glace
4. enfants / détester / légumes
5. Vous / ne / apprécier / pas / vin français
6. Tu / ne / bois / pas / eau

Culture   **WWW**

C. **Les végétariens.** Some French people are extremely conscious about eating healthy foods, and some do not eat meat (**végétariens**) or do not eat anything of animal origin, such as fish, eggs, or milk (**végétaliens**). State their habits by making complete sentences from the words below.

MODEL: commander / fruits
                  Ils commandent des fruits.

1. aimer / agneau
2. manger / beaucoup / légumes
3. détester / poulet
4. adorer / pain
5. désirer / salade
6. avoir / faim!

D. **Dînons dans un restaurant élégant.** Eating habits vary widely from one culture to another. Below is a list of eight items frequently associated with eating. Using the verb **avoir,** guess which ones you would have with dinner at a nice restaurant and which ones the restaurant would not have.

MODEL: eau   *Ils ont de l'eau.*
                «French dressing»   *Ils n'ont pas de «French dressing».*

1. thé froid
2. salade après la viande
3. café au lait
4. coca
5. plat avec du sel et du sucre
6. fruits comme dessert
7. lait comme boisson
8. tarte

Communication

E. **J'ai ça!** State whether or not you have the following.

sœur	enfants	camarade de	carte de
radio	disques	chambre	France
frère	stylo	amis français	voiture

F. **Mes préférences.** Tell whether you would like more or less / fewer of the following items using **plus de** or **moins de.**

1. argent
2. devoirs
3. camarades de chambre
4. cours
5. exercices
6. amies
7. français en classe
8. étudiants sur le campus

G. **Mes qualités.** Using expressions of quantity, tell to what degree you have the following qualities.

MODEL: *Je n'ai pas assez de patience.*

patience	talent	courage
ambition	énergie	tact
imagination	prestige	intelligence

H. **Mes opinions.** Express your opinions on the following subjects by completing the sentences in a logical manner.

1. Je n'aime pas…
2. J'apprécie…
3. Le professeur n'a pas…
4. Mon restaurant préféré prépare…
5. Je mange…
6. Les Français aiment…
7. Ma mère adore…
8. Mon frère / Ma sœur a…

I. Questions personnelles. A table!

1. Qu'est-ce que vous mangez quand vous avez faim?
2. Qu'est-ce que vous buvez quand vous avez très soif?
3. Qu'est-ce que vous aimez comme boisson?
4. Qu'est-ce que vous détestez? appréciez?
5. Vous préparez le dîner? Qu'est-ce que vous aimez préparer?
6. Est-ce que vous êtes végétarien(ne)? Pourquoi *(why)* ou pourquoi pas?

IV. The imperative

You use the imperative to give orders, advice, or suggestions.

A. Forms

1. To form the imperative, you simply drop the pronoun subject, except in the **tu** form in which the final **s** of the present indicative is also dropped.

   Indicative: **Vous apportez** un pichet de vin rouge.
   Imperative: **Apportez** un pichet de vin rouge.

   Indicative: **Vous invitez** des étudiants.
   Imperative: **Invitez** des étudiants.

   Indicative: **Tu manges** du pain.
   Imperative: **Mange** du pain.

2. There is also an imperative in the **nous** form. Equivalent to the English *Let's . . .* , it is used to suggest something.

   Parlons!   *Let's talk!*
   Travaillons ensemble. *Let's work together.*

3. The negative imperative is formed with **ne... pas** like the other verb forms you have learned.

   Ne regarde pas la télévision.   *Don't watch television.*
   Ne parlez pas en classe.   *Don't talk in class.*
   Ne mangez pas de sel.   *Don't eat salt.*

B. Irregular verbs in the imperative

The imperative forms of **être** and **avoir** are irregular.

Sois	/ swa /		**Aie**	/ e /	
Soyons	/ swa jɔ̃ /	*Be*	**Ayons**	/ e jɔ̃ /	*Have*
Soyez	/ swa je /		**Ayez**	/ e je /	

   Sois prudent!   *Be careful!*
   Ne **soyez** pas méchante!   *Don't be mean!*
   Ayez de la patience!   *Have patience!*

C. Politeness

In French, as in English, one normally adds *please* to the imperative for politeness. There are two such forms in French.

Ouvrez la porte, **s'il vous plaît.**	*Open the door, **please**. (formal)*
Ferme la fenêtre, **s'il te plaît.**	*Close the window, **please**. (familiar)*

Ce qu'ils disent

The imperative is increasingly used only as a written form, often in advertising. In conversations, the French will often give directions in declarative sentences.

Vous commencez ici.	*Begin here.*
Tu donnes l'argent au garçon.	*Give the money to the waiter.*

Language

A. Des ordres. Give commands with the following expressions and address them to the people indicated, being polite in doing so.

MODEL: *(to your classmate)* parler avec le professeur
           Parle avec le professeur.

1. *(to your brother)* danser avec Jacqueline
2. *(to your teacher)* fermer la porte
3. *(to a group of friends)* préparer un couscous
4. *(to your roommate)* étudier beaucoup
5. *(to your family, including yourself)* écouter la radio
6. *(to your classmates)* travailler ensemble

Culture

B. **En vacances!** A large proportion of the French population goes on vacation around August 1, creating throughout the country enormous traffic jams and dangerous driving conditions, often due to driver fatigue. On the radio, you hear advice constantly about what to do to be a safe driver. Form sentences in the imperative to give this type of advice, and do not forget to use the negative when appropriate.

1. consommer / alcool
2. être / prudent *Soyez*
3. avoir / patience
4. manger beaucoup
5. consommer souvent / café
6. être «macho»
7. étudier / carte
8. demander / apéritifs au café

Communication

C. **Des conseils.** In pairs, one student will read a statement, and the other will give advice. Use the imperative of the verbs listed below or those of your own choosing in your sentences.

MODEL: J'ai chaud.
Ouvre la fenêtre.

étudier   manger   fermer   inviter   boire   écouter

1. J'ai faim.
2. La leçon est difficile.
3. J'ai soif.
4. Nous avons froid.
5. Je suis seul.
6. J'adore le rock.

D. **Je suis stressé(e)!** Give advice to your classmates as to what they should do to relax and have a good time. You may refer to the following list for ideas, but feel free to add your own ideas.

MODEL: *Mangez de la glace. Ne travaillez pas.*

écouter les disques de...
regarder... à la télévision
manger...
(ne... pas) étudier...

inviter...
parler avec...
boire...
(ne... pas) travailler

Communiquons

Exprimer des quantités

Being able to express quantity in French is very useful because these expressions apply to a variety of situations such as shopping for food and talking about people and objects. You have already learned adverbs of quantity; you can also use adjectives and nouns.

Expressions

▶ **On utilise des noms de quantité.**

As with adverbs of quantity, the preposition **de** (**d'**) is used after nouns of quantity; no article is used.

Ils commandent une bouteille de vin.	*They're ordering a bottle of wine.*
Un kilo de farine, s'il vous plaît!	*A kilo (2.2 pounds) of flour, please!*
Je voudrais un litre d'eau minérale.	*I would like a liter of mineral water.*
Elle désire une livre de beurre.	*She wants a pound of butter.*
Le garçon apporte une tasse de thé.	*The waiter is bringing a cup of tea.*
Sylvie commande un verre de vin rouge.	*Sylvie is ordering a glass of red wine.*
Tu manges une tranche de pizza?	*You are eating a slice of pizza?*
L'enfant demande un morceau de gâteau.	*The child is asking for a piece of cake.*

▶ **On utilise des adjectifs de quantité.**

The adjectives **plusieurs** and **quelques** do not take the preposition **de**.

Il y a plusieurs cartes dans la salle de classe.	*There are several maps in the classroom.*
Marie invite quelques amis.	*Marie is inviting a few friends.*

Interaction   *Jacques et Monique sont au café.*

LE GARÇON: Vous désirez?

MONIQUE: Une tasse de thé et un verre de vin blanc.

LE GARÇON: Tout de suite.

Activités

A. **La quantité.** Match up the words of quantity in the left column with the foods in the right. There are several possibilities for each one, especially if you make some nouns plural.

1. beaucoup *a lot, many*
2. tasse *cup*
3. verre *glass*
4. tranche *slice*
5. un kilo *2.2 pounds*
6. litre *liter*
7. trop *too many, much*
8. plusieurs *several*
9. assez *enough*
10. quelques *ante*

a. poisson
b. gâteau
c. pain
d. café
e. eau minérale *(1)*
f. couscous
g. apéritifs *before-dinner drink*
h. coca
i. beurre *butter*
j. bière

B. **La santé.** Are you eating better for your health? Use the expressions of quantity and the foods below to indicate any changes you have made in your diet.

of – de

MODEL: *Je mange moins de sel et beaucoup de fruits.*

moins de   plus de   ne... pas
peu de   beaucoup *a lot*   ne... pas beaucoup

1. café
2. viande
3. chocolat
4. eau
5. sucre
6. légumes

7. poisson
8. poulet
9. crème
10. frites
11. huile
12. vin

Lecture culturelle

Avant la lecture

French cuisine is celebrated all over the world. In France, a meal is a ritual most people follow scrupulously. There are unwritten "rules" to observe, things that one does or does not do. For instance, salad comes with almost every meal, but usually *after* the meat and the vegetables, not with them. Many French people consider a meal without cheese incomplete. One always serves red wine with cheese, which comes after the meal but before dessert. A French proverb says that a meal without wine and cheese is like a day without sunshine.

Activités

A. What specialties of French cooking do you know? Do you know what goes into traditional French cooking that makes it French?

B. What courses are served during a formal dinner? In what order are they served in the United States?

De la cuisine
provençale

C. Do you know any words for food that come from French? (**crêpes, quiche**)

D. Try to guess what would follow these statements about French cooking. Then see if you can find the answers in the reading.

1. The French use butter and cream, but not . . .
2. Heavy cooking is being replaced by . . .
3. The three meals each day are . . .
4. Between lunch and dinner, children have . . .
5. Popular foreign restaurants in France might include . . .

Les Français et la cuisine   www

*L*es Français aiment la cuisine fine°. En France, la gastronomie° est une tradition ancienne et les spécialités régionales sont très appréciées. Dans la cuisine française, on utilise généralement du beurre et de la crème, mais peu d'huile. On mange presque° toujours de la salade et du
5 fromage, et on boit du vin et de l'eau minérale ou naturelle. Bien manger reste° important, mais les habitudes° changent. Avec la cuisine minceur°, on élimine le beurre et la crème et on réduit° les calories.

Depuis° plusieurs années, les spécialistes ont remarqué que les Français qui mangent plus et boivent° plus de vin que les Américains ont moins° de pro-
10 blèmes cardiaques causés par le cholestérol. On attribue cela au vin, principalement au rouge qui, en quantité raisonnable, semble avoir des effets positifs sur la santé°.

Chaque° jour, on prépare trois repas°: le petit déjeuner°, le déjeuner et le dîner. Souvent°, quand les enfants rentrent de l'école°, ils goûtent°: ils mangent
15 du chocolat, du pain et du beurre, des petits gâteaux°, avec du coca, du café au lait ou du chocolat chaud.

Les Français aiment aussi manger dans des restaurants étrangers°—chinois, italiens, vietnamiens, nord-africains, etc. Quand on préfère manger rapidement, on a les fast-food avec les McDonald's et les Burger King!

cuisine... *refined cooking /
gourmet cooking*

almost

Bien... *To eat well remains*
habits / **cuisine...** *low-
calorie cooking* / *reduces*

For
drink / *fewer*

health
Each / *meals* / *breakfast*
Often / **rentrent...** *return
from school* / *snack* /
petits... *cookies*

foreign

Après la lecture

Questions sur le texte

1. Quelle sorte de cuisine est-ce que les Français aiment?
2. En général, est-ce qu'on utilise de l'huile en France? Qu'est-ce qu'on utilise?
3. Qu'est-ce qu'on prend comme boisson en France?
4. Qu'est-ce que la cuisine minceur remplace?
5. Qu'est-ce qui contribue à une bonne santé en France?
6. Quels sont les trois repas de chaque jour?
7. Qu'est-ce que les enfants français mangent quand ils ont faim après l'école?
8. Quelles sortes de restaurants étrangers est-ce que les Français fréquentent?

Activité

Study the recipe below and try it out at home.

Quiche Lorraine (4 pers)

ALLUMEZ LE FOUR (8).

METTEZ DANS UN BOL
1 TASSE DE FARINE
3 *cuillères à soupe* DE BEURRE
3 *cuillères à soupe* D'EAU
3 *pincées* DE SEL.
PÉTRISSEZ POUR FAIRE UNE PATE.
ÉTENDEZ-LA AVEC LE ROULEAU.
GARNISSEZ-EN UN MOULE PLAT.
AU FOUR.

COUPEZ 6 TRANCHES DE BACON.

en 24 carrés

DANS UN GRAND BOL
CASSEZ 2 ŒUFS.
AJOUTEZ 2 *pincées* DE SEL
3/4 DE TASSE DE CRÈME FRAÎCHE
ET 4 *cuillères à soupe* DE FROMAGE RAPÉ.
BATTEZ BIEN AVEC UNE FOURCHETTE.

SORTEZ LE MOULE DU FOUR.
RANGEZ DEDANS
les carrés DE BACON.
VERSEZ DESSUS
LE CONTENU DU BOL.
AU FOUR 20 MINUTES.

allumez *turn on* / **four** *oven*

mettez *put*

pincées *pinches*
pétrissez *knead* / **pâte** *dough* / **étendez** *spread* / **rouleau** *rolling pin* / **garnissez** *fill* / **moule plat** *flat dish*

cassez *break*

crème fraîche *whipped cream* / **rapé** *grated*

sortez *take out*
rangez *place*

versez *pour*
contenu *contents*

Vocabulaire

Noms / Pronoms

âge	age	huile	oil
agneau	lamb	jambon	ham
alcool	alcohol	jus de fruit	fruit juice
an	year	lait	milk
apéritif	before-dinner drink	légumes	vegetables
argent	money	menu	menu
beurre	butter	merguez	merguez *(sausage)*
bière	beer	moutarde	mustard
bistrot	café / restaurant	mouton	mutton
café	coffee	mur	wall
carte	menu	nourriture	food
chocolat	chocolate	pain	bread
coca	cola	photo	photo
confiture	jam	pichet	pitcher
couscous	couscous	pizza	pizza
crème	cream	plat	dish
cuisine	cooking	plat principal	main course
eau	water	poisson	fish
eau minérale	mineral water	poulet	chicken
école	school	prix fixe	fixed price *(menu)*
école secondaire	secondary school	restaurant	restaurant
élève	pupil	salade	salad
farine	flour	sel	salt
frites	French fries	semoule	semolina
fromage	cheese	soir	evening
fruit	fruit *(in general)*	soupe	soup
garçon	waiter	sucre	sugar
gâteau	cake	tarte	tart
glace	ice cream	thé	tea
hamburger	hamburger	viande	meat
hors-d'œuvre	appetizer	vin	wine

Verbes

apporter	to bring	dîner	to have dinner
avoir	to have	goûter	to have an afternoon snack
bois	drink	préparer	to prepare
buvez	drink	recommander	to recommend
commander	to order	trouver	to find
consommer	to consume		
déjeuner	to have lunch		

Adjectifs / Adverbes

assez de	enough of	préféré	favorite
autant de	as much as	rouge	red
blanc	white ⟨m⟩	trop	too much / too many
délicieux	delicious	tunisien	Tunisian
peu	little		

Expressions

avoir _____ an(s)	to be _____ old	Comment trouvez-vous... ?	How do you like . . . ?
avoir chaud	to be hot	dans	in
avoir de la patience	to be patient	il y a	there is, there are
avoir du talent	to have talent	je voudrais	I would like
avoir faim	to be hungry	quelle sorte de	what kind of
avoir froid	to be cold	service compris	tip included
avoir raison	to be right	s'il te plaît	please
avoir soif	to be thirsty	s'il vous plaît	please
avoir tort	to be wrong	tout de suite	right away
comme	like		

Chapitres 1 à 3

Révision A

Class work

A. Rewrite the following sentences using the cues in parentheses. Make any necessary changes.

MODEL: Il est studieux. (Elles…)
Elles sont studieuses.

Les gens *(People)*

1. Nous sommes généreux. (Madeleine…)
2. Tu as froid. (… fatigué.)
3. Vous invitez des Américains? (Luc et Jeanne… Canadienne?)
4. Ils sont tunisiens? (Marie… ?)
5. Je suis malade. (… chaud.)
6. Nous sommes sérieux. (Claire, tu…)

Les boissons

7. Vous buvez du thé? (Tu… bière?)
8. J'aime les jus de fruit. (… demander…)
9. Il a soif. (Marc et Marie…)
10. Jean-Pierre n'aime pas le vin. (… commander… coca.)

Les possessions

11. Un sac à dos est utile. (… cartes…)
12. Nous adorons les enfants. (… avoir…)
13. Tu as une affiche? (Nous… plusieurs…)
14. Elles écoutent des disques. (… avoir… radio.)

B. **La nourriture.** Answer the following questions using the cues provided.

MODEL: Vous avez des légumes? (Non,…)
Non, je n'ai pas de légumes.

1. Qu'est-ce que vous mangez? (Nous… frites.)
2. Vous avez des gâteaux? (Non,…)
3. Qu'est-ce que tu détestes? (… poisson.)
4. Vous aimez le couscous? (Oui, nous…)
5. Jeanne et Sylvie ont faim? (Non,… soif.)
6. Est-ce qu'elles aiment le coca? (Oui,… demander…)
7. Qu'est-ce que Paulette prépare? (… mouton et… beaucoup… légumes.)
8. Est-ce que tu bois de la bière? (Non,… détester… alcool.)
9. Est-ce qu'il y a du lait? (Non,…)

10. Vous aimez la cuisine française? (Non,… aimer mieux… américain…)
11. Vous mangez de la soupe? (Non, nous… aimer mieux… salade.)
12. Est-ce que les enfants mangent assez? (Non,… et… malade…)
13. Tu désires de la crème? (Non,… beurre,… vin et… huile.)
14. Quand est-ce que vous demandez du chocolat? (… avoir froid…)

C. Create a complete sentence with each group of words below, making appropriate changes and adding any necessary words.

MODEL: étudiants / aimer / musique
Les étudiants aiment la musique.

A table! *(Let's eat!)*

1. enfants / adorer / glace
2. crème / et / sel / être / mauvais
3. On / avoir / eau / chaud?
4. Paul / ne… pas / manger / fromage
5. garçon / préparer / quelques / boissons

Les gens

6. La sœur de Philippe / avoir / talent
7. Vous / avoir / tort / Monsieur
8. Françoise et Marc / avoir / disques / américain
9. Est-ce que / elle / avoir / raison?
10. Robert / être / bien!

En cours

11. Nous / commencer / leçon / intéressant
12. Fermer / porte / s'il te plaît!
13. Ecouter / s'il vous plaît!
14. étudiant / avoir / examens / difficile

D. Complete the following sentences according to your opinion.

1. J'adore…
2. Je déteste…
3. Les Américains aiment…
4. Je voudrais…
5. Quand j'ai soif, je…
6. Quand je suis malade, je…
7. Je ne suis pas…
8. Le professeur est…

E. Translate the following sentences into French.

Bavardage *(Gossip)*

1. She likes a lawyer.
2. They watch football games.
3. Does he smoke a lot?
4. No, but he is lazy.
5. They are happy when they are together.

A la cuisine *(In the kitchen)*

6. Let's make *(préparer)* a cake!
7. You don't have any sugar?
8. We want butter and milk.
9. They hate milk and cream.
10. They are wrong. They are delicious!

F. Do the following math problems in French.

1. $5 + 7 =$ 5. $6 + 45 =$ 9. $3 \times 4 =$ 13. $11 \times 3 =$
2. $15 + 16 =$ 6. $13 + 14 =$ 10. $15 \times 3 =$ 14. $7 \times 3 =$
3. $51 - 27 =$ 7. $49 - 10 =$ 11. $48 \div 3 =$ 15. $42 \div 7$
4. $69 - 8 =$ 8. $41 - 12 =$ 12. $66 \div 2 =$ 16. $39 \div 3 =$

G. **Questions personnelles.** Qui êtes-vous?

1. Vous êtes optimiste? pessimiste? sincère? hypocrite?
2. Est-ce que vous avez beaucoup d'amis dans le cours de français?
3. Quelle sorte d'amis est-ce que vous avez?
4. Qu'est-ce que vous mangez quand vous avez faim?
5. Quelles boissons est-ce que vous aimez?
6. Est-ce que vous travaillez beaucoup? Vous avez assez de devoirs?
7. Est-ce que vous avez des frères et sœurs? Combien?
8. Vous désirez être avocat(e)? ingénieur? journaliste? ???

Pair and small group work

A. With a partner, practice spelling in French. Select ten words that you have learned thus far. Then, take turns spelling them to each other and guessing what each other's words are.

B. Say a word in English to your partner and ask for its French equivalent. Then, say a French noun, and your partner will make a sentence using the noun with the correct definite, indefinite, or partitive article.

C. In groups of three or four, count from 1 to 20 in French, continuing around the group so that each person must give the next number. Then count, taking turns, from 20 to 40 by odd numbers and from 40 to 60 by even numbers.

D. With a partner, play the role of two people who disagree with each other. If one of you makes an affirmative statement, the other makes it negative and vice versa.

MODEL: Student 1:   *J'ai du vin.*
          Student 2:   *Je n'ai pas de vin.*

          Student 1:   *Tu aimes faire la cuisine.*
          Student 2:   *Tu n'aimes pas faire la cuisine.*

E. In groups of four students, take turns describing yourself, using three adjectives. Then describe one of your classmates without naming him or her, and have the members of the group guess whom you are describing.

F. In groups of three or four students, take turns giving one or two students commands that they can carry out.

G. Interview your classmates to find out the following information. Be prepared to report your findings to the class.

1. what they are like
2. what their likes and dislikes are
3. what they do every day and on weekends (**Le week-end...**)

H. Create a brief dialogue based on the following drawing.

Les voyages

 Commençons

 Grammaire

 Communiquons

 Lecture culturelle

 Vocabulaire

Le port de Nice

Objectives

Language

Vocabulary for travel and vacations • **Enchaînements** and **liaisons** • **A** and **de** with definite articles • Place names • **Aller** and **futur proche** • Articles and prepositions with place names • Numbers from 70 to 1,000,000,000

Culture

Travel in France • Vacations

Communication

Finding a hotel • Expressing future time • Counting • Asking directions

Commençons

A Nice, au Syndicat d'Initiative   WWW

Robert et Eric, deux étudiants américains, rentrent de Corse et voyagent sur la Côte d'Azur. Ils arrivent à Nice et ils cherchent un hôtel près de la plage. Ils sont maintenant au Syndicat d'Initiative, où ils demandent des renseignements.

L'HÔTESSE: Bonjour, Messieurs.

ÉRIC: Bonjour, Mademoiselle. Nous cherchons une chambre dans un hôtel près de la mer.

L'HÔTESSE: A côté de la plage, cela va être difficile!

ROBERT: Pourquoi?

L'HÔTESSE: Parce que les hôtels sont chers et parce qu'ils sont tous pleins aujourd'hui. Mais il y a de la place en ville. C'est près des restaurants et des cinémas; ce n'est pas loin du Casino et il faut dix minutes pour aller à la plage.

ROBERT: S'il n'y a pas de chambres au bord de la mer, nous n'allons pas rester à Nice. Nous allons visiter l'Italie. Est-ce que vous avez une liste des hôtels de San Remo?

L'HÔTESSE: Ah, non, pas du tout! Nous n'avons pas de renseignements sur l'Italie, mais vous avez une agence de voyages au coin de la rue.

ÉRIC   Où ça?

L'HÔTESSE: Là-bas, Monsieur. A côté de l'église.

ROBERT: Merci mille fois. Au revoir.

L'HÔTESSE: Au revoir, Messieurs.

Etudions le dialogue

1. Où sont Robert et Eric?
2. Qu'est-ce qu'ils cherchent?
3. Ils désirent être loin de la plage, n'est-ce pas?
4. Est-ce qu'il y a de la place au bord de la mer?
5. Qu'est-ce qu'il y a en ville?
6. Où est-ce que Robert et Eric vont aller s'ils ne restent pas à Nice?

Mots clés

Syndicat d'Initiative (m.)	Tourist Office	mais	but
rentrent de (rentrer de)	come back from	de la place	room
Corse (f.)	Corsica	en ville	downtown
voyagent (voyager)	are traveling	cinémas (m.)	movie theaters
sur	on	loin du Casino	far from the Casino
Côte d'Azur	French Riviera	il faut	it takes · necessary
cherchent (chercher)	are looking for	minutes (f.)	minutes
près de	near	pour aller à	to go to
plage	beach	s' (si)	if
maintenant	now	au bord de la mer	at the seashore
renseignements (m.)	information	rester	to stay
hôtesse (f.)	hostess	visiter	to go to
Messieurs	gentlemen	Italie (f.)	Italy
chambre	room	liste	list
mer	sea	ah, non	of course not
à côté de	next to	pas du tout	not at all
va être (aller être)	is going to be	agence de voyages	travel agency
pourquoi	why	au coin de	at the corner of
parce que	because	rue	street
chers (cher, -ère)	expensive	Où ça?	Whereabout?
tous	all	là-bas	over there
pleins	full	église (f.)	church
aujourd'hui	today	Merci mille fois.	Thanks a million.

Faisons connaissance

Upon arrival in a French city or town, the useful thing to do is to go to the **Syndicat d'Initiative,** where you will get information about points of interest and a list of hotels arranged by categories. If you wish, someone at the **Syndicat** will call hotels for you to check for vacancies. There you can also find out about other areas in France you may wish to visit. Because the service is run by the French government, it does not include information about other countries.

Nice is the largest city on **la Côte d'Azur,** one of the principal vacation areas of France. You may also have heard of Cannes because of its international film festival in May. Saint-Tropez was made famous in the 1950s as the playground of Brigitte Bardot and other screen personalities. The tiny country of Monaco is also wedged into the Mediterranean coast to the east of Nice. San Remo, an Italian city, is farther along the coast.

While **la Côte d'Azur** is known throughout the world for its splendid beaches, Americans are often surprised to find many of them covered with smooth stones (**les galets**) rather than with sand.

Sur la Côte d'Azur

Enrichissons notre vocabulaire

En ville *(In the city)*

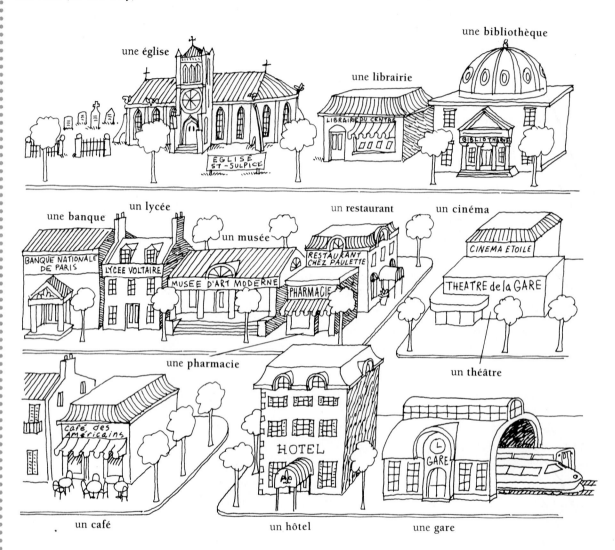

D'autres endroits *(m.)* *(Other places)*

un appartement	*apartment*	un parc	*park*
un arrêt d'autobus	*bus stop*	un parking	*parking lot*
		une piscine	*a swimming pool*
un bureau de poste	*post office*	une résidence universitaire	*dormitory*
un centre commercial	*shopping center*	un restau-U (restaurant universitaire)	*university restaurant*
un laboratoire	*a laboratory*		
un magasin	*store*	un stade	*a stadium*
une maison	*house*	une usine	*a factory*

Prononciation   Enchaînements et liaisons   [o ▬ o]

A. In spoken French, words flow together very smoothly. When a word begins with a vowel sound, French speakers pronounce the last consonant of the preceding word as if it were the first letter of the next word. This is **enchaînement.**

avec elle	/ avɛ kɛl /	il a	/ i la /
sept étudiants	/ sɛ te ty djɑ̃ /	elle est	/ ɛ lɛ /

Practice **enchaînements** by repeating the following expressions after your teacher.

neuf étudiantes / elle habite / il invite / cinq acteurs / l'artiste intelligent / le professeur intéressant

B. There is a separate category of **enchaînement** in which a written final consonant that is normally not pronounced must be sounded because a vowel sound follows it. Notice the difference in the pronunciation of: **nous travaillons** / nu tʀa va jɔ̃ / and **nous habitons** / nu za bi tɔ̃ /.

The **s** of **nous** in **nous habitons** must be pronounced because the verb begins with the vowel sound / a /. This is **liaison.** It is limited to closely linked word groups (pronoun subject–verb, adjective–noun), and most often involves the / z / sound.

Listen carefully and repeat the following paired words after your teacher, paying particular attention to the **liaisons.**

No liaison	Liaison	No liaison	Liaison
un livre	un ami	nous dansons	nous invitons
deux clés	deux amies	ils sont	ils ont
trois cafés	trois hôtesses	des légumes	des hôtels
six portes	six étudiants	les filles	les enfants
dix cartes	dix hommes	en France	en Amérique

Exercice

Practice reading these sentences aloud, while concentrating on the **enchaînements** and **liaisons.**

1. Les Américains habitent en Amérique.
2. Nous étudions avec un professeur intéressant.
3. Vous avez une opinion d'elle?
4. Les enfants sont intelligents.
5. Ils invitent des amis sympathiques.
6. Elle donne un examen aux étudiants.

Grammaire

To   from (handwritten)

I. A and de with definite articles

You use **à** to indicate location or direction and **de** to indicate origin or possession.

A. Two very common French prepositions are **à** *(to, in, at,* or *into)* and **de** *(from* or *of).*

Cécile habite **à** Paris.	Elle est **de** New York.
Ils arrivent **à** Nice.	J'ai le stylo **de** Robert.

B. **A** and **de** are often used with the definite articles **l'** and **la.**

Elle travaille **à l'**université.	C'est le livre **de l'**étudiant.
Ils sont **à la** maison.	Quel est le prix **de la** chambre?

C. When **à** and **de** come before the definite articles **le** or **les,** the two words form a contraction.

à + le = **au**	de + le = **du**
à + les = **aux**	de + les = **des**

Ils sont **au** Syndicat d'Initiative.	Il est **du** Canada.
Je donne la glace **aux** enfants.	Elles ont les cahiers **des** étudiants.

Note that the **x** of **aux** and the **s** of **des** are pronounced / z / in front of a vowel sound, just like the **s** of **les.**

Attention!

The preposition **de** in combination with the definite articles has the same forms as the partitive articles and the plural indefinite article, which you learned in Chapter 3, but, unlike them, the preposition **de** never changes in the negative.

Indefinite article:

J'ai **des** enfants.	*I have (**some**) children.*
Je **n'**ai **pas d'**enfants.	*I **don't** have (**any**) children.*

Preposition **de** and the definite article **les:**

Je parle **des** enfants.	*I'm talking **about the** children.*
Je **ne** parle **pas des** enfants.	*I'm **not** talking **about the** children.*

D. The preposition **de** is part of some prepositional expressions, subject to the same rules regarding contractions.

Ils cherchent un hôtel **près de** la mer.
Ils trouvent un hôtel **en face de** l'agence de voyages.
Ce n'est pas **loin du** Casino.
C'est **près des** restaurants.

Mots clés

Prepositions with de

à côté de	*next to*	loin de	*far (from)*
au coin de	*at the corner of*	près de	*near*
en face de	*across from*		

Other common prepositions that do not take de

chez	*at the home of*	entre	*between*
dans	*in*	sous	*under*
derrière	*behind*	sur	*on*
devant	*in front of*		

Language

A. **A la résidence.** Someone is calling your floor in the dorm, but everyone is out. Tell the caller where everyone is by forming complete sentences.

1. Marie / travailler / librairie
2. Marc / étudier / bibliothèque
3. Jacques et Jean / être / centre commercial
4. Monique / manger / restau-U
5. Jeanne et Chantal / être / près / cinéma
6. Je / être / dans / chambre de Paul

B. **Où ça?** Describe the activities and locations of the people below, using an item from each of the four columns provided.

MODEL: Je / être / à / université
Je suis à l'université.

A	B	C	D
Les étudiants	travailler	à	bibliothèque
Je	habiter	de	cinéma
Vous	être	derrière	maison
Luc	étudier	à côté de	appartement
Mes amis	manger	devant	étudiants
Nous	parler	loin de	théâtre
agents de police		sous	université
Mes parents		sur	magasin
		près de	parc

C. Using the map in **Enrichissons notre vocabulaire,** give the locations of the following places.

MODEL: Café des Américains / musée
Le Café des Américains est près du musée.

1. cinéma Etoile / théâtre de la Gare
2. église Saint-Sulpice / Café des Américains
3. gare / hôtel
4. pharmacie / restaurant Chez Paulette

5. musée / pharmacie
6. librairie / église / bibliothèque
7. banque / lycée
8. restaurant Chez Paulette / cinéma Etoile

Culture

D. Visitons Paris. Identify where various landmarks in Paris are located by adding **être** and a preposition to the places listed below. For help, refer to the map of Paris on page 193.

MODEL: Le parc des Expositions / le palais des Sports
Le parc des Expositions est derrière le palais des Sports.

1. La tour Eiffel / le palais de Chaillot
2. Le Louvre / la Seine
3. Notre-Dame / le Palais de Justice
4. la gare Montparnasse / le Sacré-Cœur
5. L'Arc de Triomphe / la place Charles-de-Gaulle
6. La place de la Concorde / l'avenue des Champs-Elysées et les Tuileries

a. près de
b. à côté de
c. entre
d. sur
e. en face de
f. loin de

Communication

E. Nos activités. Interview two classmates and find out where they do the following things:

MODEL: étudier?   *J'étudie dans ma chambre.*

1. jouer
2. terminer les devoirs
3. dîner
4. travailler
5. regarder la télé
6. aimer danser

F. Questions personnelles. Votre ville *(Your town)*

1. Vous êtes de New York?
2. Où est-ce que vous habitez? C'est près de… ?
3. Qu'est-ce qu'il y a dans la ville où vous habitez?
4. Dans la ville où vous habitez, où est le musée? la gare? Où sont les cinémas? les cafés? les restaurants?
5. Vous aimez bien un restaurant? Où est-ce qu'il est?
6. Qu'est-ce que vous aimez à l'université où vous étudiez?

II.   Aller / The futur proche

You use **aller** to express the idea of going somewhere, to talk about health, or to express an action or a state in the future.

A. Forms of aller

1. **Aller** is an irregular verb, and you must memorize its forms.

aller *(to go)*	
je **vais**	nous **allons**
tu **vas**	vous **allez**
il / elle / on **va**	ils / elles **vont**

2. **Aller** is almost never used alone as it can be in English *(I'm going!)*. It is often followed by expressions that indicate manner or direction.

Nous **allons en** France.
Je **vais au** café **avec** Marie.
Est-ce que vous **allez au** théâtre?

Pour étudier, elle **va à la** bibliothèque.

3. The formation of the imperative of **aller** is regular: **va, allons, allez.**

Allons au cinéma.

Ne va pas avec Jean.

4. You have already learned some idiomatic expressions with **aller**. Those and some other common expressions are listed below.

—**Comment ça va? Ça va?**
—**Ça va. Ça va bien.**

—**Comment allez-vous?**
—**Je vais bien.**

On y va?
Allez-y! Vas-y!
Allons-y!

Shall we go?
Go ahead!
Let's go!

B. The futur proche

1. One very frequent use of **aller** is to express an action in the future by using a conjugated form of **aller** + an *infinitive*. This construction is similar to the English *to be going* + an *infinitive* and is called the **futur proche** (near future). The main action is expressed by the infinitive, which directly follows the conjugated verb **aller**.

Nous **allons visiter** l'Italie.

Je **vais travailler** demain.

2. To make negative sentences with the **futur proche,** you simply place **ne... pas** around the conjugated form of **aller.**

—Tu **vas regarder** la télévision?
—Non, je **ne vais pas regarder** la télévision.

3. The **futur proche** is frequently used with expressions of time.

maintenant	*now*	demain	*tomorrow*
aujourd'hui	*today*	demain matin	*tomorrow morning*
ce matin	*this morning*	demain soir	*tomorrow evening*
cet après-midi	*this afternoon*	tous les jours	*every day*
ce soir	*tonight*		

le week-end prochain	*next weekend*
la semaine prochaine	*next week*
l'année prochaine	*next year*

Language

A. **Nos destinations.** Say where the following people are going today, using the cues provided and the verb **aller**.

MODEL: Paul / cinéma   *Paul va au cinéma.*

1. Tu / université
2. Nous / arrêt d'autobus
3. Mes amis / librairie
4. Je / bureau de poste
5. Vous / centre commercial
6. Françoise / maison

B. **Au futur.** Tell what will happen to the following people in the future by changing the sentences from the present tense to the **futur proche**.

MODEL: Il arrive fatigué.
     Il va arriver fatigué.

1. Je travaille en ville.
2. Elle est ingénieur.
3. Ils invitent des amis.
4. Jacques a chaud.
5. Est-ce que vous habitez ici?
6. Nous aimons le restaurant.
7. Tu vas au Canada.
8. Elles mangent un couscous.

Culture

C. **A l'Office de tourisme.** This office, located on the **Champs-Elysées** in Paris, gives tourist advice. Pretend you are working there by matching the interests of various tourists on the left with places to go on the right.

MODEL: la poésie   musée Victor-Hugo
     Allez au musée Victor-Hugo.

1. l'impressionnisme
2. l'art classique
3. l'art moderne
4. le cubisme
5. la sculpture
6. le Moyen Age *(Middle Ages)*

a. musée Cluny
b. musée Rodin
c. musée d'Orsay
d. le Louvre
e. musée Picasso
f. le Centre Pompidou

D. **En France ou aux Etats-Unis?** Form complete sentences, then state whether the action is more typical in France or in the U.S.

1. Les touristes / aller / gare pour changer de l'argent.
2. On / aller / café parce qu'on a soif.
3. Vous / aller / gare pour dîner.
4. Les enfants / aller / pharmacie pour manger une glace.
5. Les étudiants / aller / café pour étudier.
6. Tu / aller / librairie / parce que tu désires avoir un tee-shirt.

Communication

E. **Vos préférences.** Answer the following questions.

1. Où est-ce que vous allez aujourd'hui pour étudier? pour manger? pour regarder un film?
2. Où est-ce que vous allez pour dîner? pour danser? pour parler?
3. Vous allez regarder la télévision ce soir? écouter la radio? aller à l'église le week-end prochain?
4. L'année prochaine, est-ce que vous allez étudier le français?

F. **Mes camarades.** Ask a classmate if he or she is going to do the following things. Afterwards, present a summary to the class.

1. travailler à la maison cet après-midi?
2. aller dans une boîte ce soir?
3. rester à la résidence demain matin?
4. déjeuner chez des amis le week-end prochain?
5. être malade le jour de l'examen final?
6. trouver une profession intéressante?

G. **Mon professeur.** Ask your professor if he or she is going to do the following things.

1. donner des devoirs pour demain?
2. donner un examen facile la semaine prochaine?
3. préparer un couscous en classe?
4. être agréable ou désagréable?
5. aller à la mer l'année prochaine?
6. visiter la France?

III. Articles and prepositions with place names

> You use articles, prepositions, and place names to indicate geographical location or destination.

A. Unlike English, French does not make a distinction between going *to* or being *in* a place. Instead, the correct preposition depends on the type of place name.

1. Use **à**, meaning *to* or *in*, with cities.

   Nous n'allons pas rester **à Nice**.   Robert est **à New York**.
   A Madrid on dîne à 22 heures.   Gilles rentre à Québec.

2. Use **en**, meaning *to* or *in*, with feminine countries, all continents, and countries whose names begin with a vowel. (Most countries whose names end in a written **e** are feminine.)

   Vous allez étudier **en France.**
   Nous allons aller **en Italie.**
   Ils désirent voyager **en Russie.**
   En Asie, on parle français.
   Le diplomate va voyager **en Israël, en Iraq,** et **en Iran.**

3. Use **au** (*pl.* **aux**), meaning *to* or *in*, with countries that are masculine. (Masculine countries have names that end in letters other than **e**, with the exceptions of **le Mexique, le Mozambique,** and **le Zaïre**.)

   Ils désirent voyager **au Canada.**
   Nous sommes **aux Etats-Unis.**
   Au Portugal on trouve des universités très anciennes.

B. To express *from*, use **du** with masculine singular countries, **des** with plural countries, and **de** without an article for feminine countries and cities. Some verbs often followed by **de** are **arriver, être, rentrer,** and **aller.**

> Il est **du** Canada, mais elle est **des** Etats-Unis.
> Mes parents rentrent **de** Paris la semaine prochaine.
> Nous allons aller **de** Grande-Bretagne en Belgique.

C. Use the definite article when the country is not a location but the subject or the object of the verb.

> Nous allons visiter **la France.**　　　J'adore **le Québec.**
> **La Chine** est en Asie.　　　Cherche **le Zaïre** sur la carte!

Mots clés　Cities, continents, and countries

Des villes

		Des continents	
Bruxelles	Mexico	**l'Afrique**	**l'Asie**
Genève	Moscou	**l'Amérique du Nord**	**l'Europe**
Lisbonne	La Nouvelle-Orléans	**l'Amérique du Sud**	
Londres	Varsovie *Warsaw*		

Des pays féminins

l'Algérie		**la Grande-Bretagne**	*Great Britain*
l'Allemagne	*Germany*	**la Grèce**	
l'Angleterre	*England*	**la Hollande**	
l'Australie		**l'Irlande**	
l'Autriche	*Austria*	**l'Italie**	
la Belgique		**la Norvège**	*Norway*
la Chine		**la Pologne**	
la Côte d'Ivoire		**la Russie**	
l'Espagne		**la Suède**	*Sweden*
la Finlande		**la Suisse**	*Switzerland*
la France		**la Tunisie**	

Des pays masculins

le Brésil		**le Mozambique**	
le Canada[1]		**les Pays-Bas**	*the Netherlands*
le Danemark		**le Portugal**	
les Etats-Unis[1]	*U.S.A.*	**le Sénégal**	
le Japon		**le Tchad**	*Chad*
le Maroc	*Morocco*	**le Zaïre**	
le Mexique			

---

1. Articles and prepositions used with states of the United States and provinces of Canada are found in Appendix II.

Attention!

If you are not expressing *to* or *in* a place, no preposition is necessary, but the definite article *must* be used with most countries. Do not use an article with cities unless the city name already contains an article, such as **La Nouvelle-Orléans** or **La Havane**.

L'Italie est un pays fascinant.
Ils adorent **la Chine**.
Paris a des restaurants fantastiques.
Je vais visiter **La Nouvelle-Orléans** pour écouter du jazz.

CONSULATS A LA MARTINIQUE

ALLEMAGNE: M. Bernard Hayot. Société SODICAR. 97232 Acajou-Lamentin. Tél. 50 37 56/50 38 39.
BELGIQUE: M. Delavigne. Ets COTTREL, Z.I. de la Lézarde. Tél. 51 21 64.
DANEMARK: M. Meyer. 72–74, rue Victor-Hugo. Tél. 71 61 04.
ESPAGNE: M. Philippe Lachenez-Heude. Maison Duquesne. Avenue des Arawacks 97232 Le Lamentin. Tél. 71 30 78/75 03 12.
HAITI: M. Georges Colimon. 10, rue Galliéni 97200 Fort-de-France. Tél. 70 32 15.
ITALIE: M. Nicolas Landi. 28, bd Allègre. Tél. 70 54 75.
NORVEGE: M. Emile Hayot. Garage Mercedes. Acajou. 97232 Lamentin. Tél. 50 37 55.
PAYS-BAS: M. Jean-Pierre Dormoy. 34, rue Ernest-Deproge. 97200 Fort-de-France. Tél. 63 04 94/73 31 61.
SUEDE: M. Jacques Huygues-Despointes. BP 579 Kerlys, Garage Peugeot 97200 Fort-de-France. Tél. 63 54 54.
SUISSE: M. Patrick de la Houssaye. Z.I. de la Jambette. 97232 Lamentin. Tél. 50 12 43.
VENEZUELA: M. Paul Verna. 1 km 400 Route de Didier. Tél. 63 34 16.
GRANDE-BRETAGNE: Mme Jane-Alison Ernoult. Entreprise Serge Ernoult–Route du Phare. Fort-de-France. Tél. 61 56 30/61 58 70/61 46 34.
CHAMBRE .5DE COMMERCE ET D'INDUSTRIE: Rue Ernest Deproge, Fort-de-France. Tél. 55 28 00.

Language

A. **Où sont-ils?** Form a sentence to describe where the people below are, based on the following model.

MODEL: Yves: Paris, France
Yves est à Paris, en France.

1. Carlo: Rome, Italie
2. Maria: Mexico, Mexique
3. Tom: Washington, Etats-Unis
4. Mamadou: Dakar, Sénégal
5. Rachel: Tel-Aviv, Israël
6. Robert et Line: Bruxelles, Belgique
7. Paul et Claire: Montréal, Canada
8. Fatima: Casablanca, Maroc

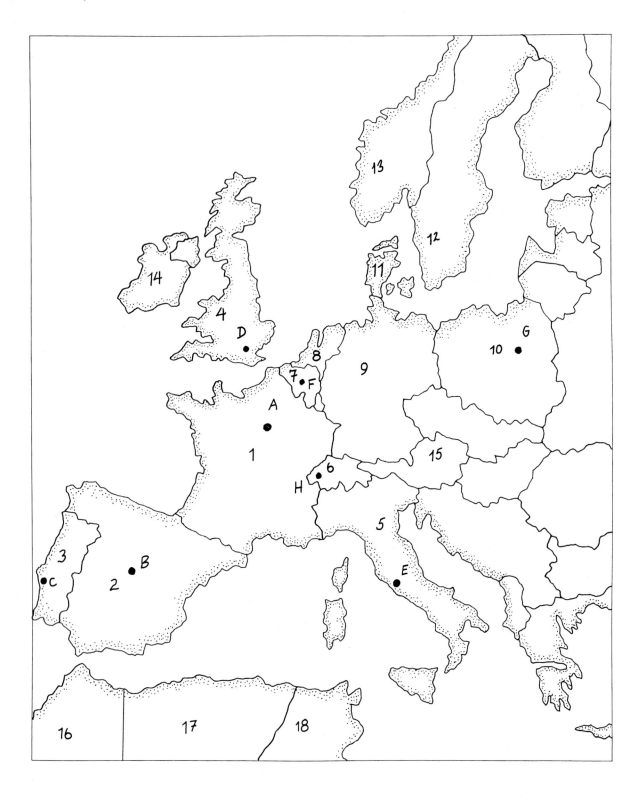

B. Un peu de géo. Identify the following countries by what continent they are on.

MODEL: *La France est en Europe.*

1. Mexique   3. Chine   5. Brésil   7. Portugal
2. Angleterre   4. Zaïre   6. Tchad   8. Japon

Culture

C. Voyages à l'étranger. Cars crossing borders in Europe often have an oval sticker on the back that indicates the country where the car is registered. Name the country of the drivers of cars with the following stickers.

MODEL: F *Elle est de France.*

1. D   3. I   5. CH   7. E
2. B   4. DK   6. A   8. GB

Communication

D. Où sommes-nous? In pairs, try to identify where you are, as another student chooses a number for a country or a letter for a city from the map of Europe on page 98.

MODEL: Student 1: *1*
Student 2: *Nous sommes en France.*

Student 1: *B*
Student 2: *Nous sommes à Madrid.*

E. Voyage en Europe. With a classmate, plan a trip through Europe using the map on page 98. Then read your itinerary.

MODEL: *J'arrive à Paris. Je visite la France. Après, je vais en Suisse et en Italie. Je continue le voyage en Autriche et je termine à Berlin.*

F. Un voyage idéal. Interview a classmate to find out the information below.

1. Où est-ce que vous désirez aller en Afrique? en Europe?
2. Quelles *(Which)* villes et quels pays est-ce que vous désirez visiter?
3. Où est-ce que la vie *(life)* est agréable? désagréable? Pourquoi?
4. Quels pays est-ce que vous recommandez aux Américains? Pourquoi?

IV. Numbers from 70 to 1,000,000,000

70	soixante-dix	74	soixante-quatorze
71	soixante et onze	75	soixante-quinze
72	soixante-douze	76	soixante-seize
73	soixante-treize	77	soixante-dix-sept

78	soixante-dix-huit	97	quatre-vingt-dix-sept
79	soixante-dix-neuf	98	quatre-vingt-dix-huit
80	quatre-vingts	99	quatre-vingt-dix-neuf
81	quatre-vingt-un	100	cent
82	quatre-vingt-deux	101	cent un
83	quatre-vingt-trois	108	cent huit
84	quatre-vingt-quatre	172	cent soixante-douze
85	quatre-vingt-cinq	199	cent quatre-vingt-dix-neuf
86	quatre-vingt-six	200	deux cents
87	quatre-vingt-sept	231	deux cent trente et un
88	quatre-vingt-huit	284	deux cent quatre-vingt-quatre
89	quatre-vingt-neuf	300	trois cents
90	quatre-vingt-dix	400	quatre cents
91	quatre-vingt-onze	701	sept cent un
92	quatre-vingt-douze	1.000	mille
93	quatre-vingt-treize	3.200	trois mille deux cents
94	quatre-vingt-quatorze	1.000.000	un million
95	quatre-vingt-quinze	1.000.000.000	un milliard
96	quatre-vingt-seize		

A. Note that **et** is used with 21, 31, 41, 51, 61, and 71 (**vingt et un, trente et un,...**), but not with 81, 91, and 101 (**quatre-vingt-un, quatre-vingt-onze, cent un**).

B. **Cent** and **mille** are *never* preceded by **un**, but **un million** and **un milliard** *(one billion)* must be.

　　100　cent
　　1005　mille cinq
　　1.500.000　un million cinq cent mille
　　1.003.800.000　un milliard trois millions huit cent mille

C. When counting in millions or billions, you must use the preposition **de (d')** before a noun. However, when **million** or **milliard** is followed by a number, the preposition is dropped.

un million d'habitants	*one million inhabitants*
quatre milliards de francs	*four billion francs*
deux millions cinq cent mille dollars	*two million five hundred thousand dollars*

D. To express a distance, use the preposition **à**. For distances from one place to another, use **être à... de**. Distances would typically be in **mètres (m)** or **kilomètres (km)**.

　　Jacques habite à 100 m de chez moi.
　　Le centre commercial est à 2 km d'ici.
　　Marseille est à 778 km de Paris.

ANGLETERRE

PAYS-BAS

⊛ AMSTERDAM
● LA HAYE

ALLEMAGNE

LA MANCHE

⊛ BRUXELLES

● Lille

BELGIQUE

LUXEMBOURG

● Amiens

● Le Havre
● Rouen
● Caen

la Seine

LUXEMBOURG
⊛ LUXEMBOURG

● Brest

PARIS
⊛
● Versailles

● Reims

la Meuse

la Marne

la Moselle

● Nancy

● Strasbourg

le Rhin

● Rennes

● Chartres

● Le Mans

la Loire

● Angers

● Orléans

FRANCE

● Nantes

● Tours

● Dijon

LES VOSGES

● Besançon

⊛ BERNE

● La Rochelle

LE JURA

SUISSE

L' OCÉAN

ATLANTIQUE

● Limoges

la Saône

● Genève

● Clermont-Ferrand

● Lyon

● Annecy

● Bordeaux

la Dordogne

le Rhône

● Grenoble

ITALIE

la Garonne

LE MASSIF CENTRAL

LES ALPES

● Biarritz

● Toulouse

● Avignon

● Nice

LES PYRÉNÉES

● Montpellier

● Cannes

MONACO

● Marseille

ANDORRE

● Perpignan

● Toulon

CORSE

ESPAGNE

LA MER MÉDITERRANÉE

0   100   200 Km.

Ajaccio ●

L'orthographe

1. **Quatre-vingts** and multiples of **cent** take an **s** when they are not followed by another number. When they are followed by another number, there is no **s**.

quatre-vingts	quatre-vingt-cinq
deux cents	deux cent trente-quatre
quatre cents	quatre cent dix

2. **Mille** never takes an **s**.

   Mille, deux mille, trois mille...

3. Note that French uses a period to mark thousands, not a comma as in English. (Some French publications, however, mark thousands by leaving a space between digits: 1 000.) Decimals are the opposite: two and five-tenths (2.5 in English) is **2,5** in French (**deux virgule cinq**).

Language

A. Des numéros. Say the following numbers in French.

1. 71	4. 99	7. 151	10. 500
2. 81	5. 100	8. 274	11. 544
3. 89	6. 102	9. 391	12. 1.000

B. Say the following numbers in French.

1. 1.000	3. 2.000	5. 16.552	7. 1.000.000
2. 1.600	4. 10.000	6. 200.000	8. 100.000.000

Culture

C. Au Québec. Give the distances in kilometers to the following destinations in French-speaking Canada.

MODEL: New York—Montréal 613
New York est à six cent treize kilomètres de Montréal.

1. Montréal—Québec 270
2. Chicoutimi—Rivière-du-Loup 182
3. Gaspé—Rivière-du-Loup 499
4. Sherbrooke—Victoriaville 97
5. Trois-Rivières—Chicoutimi 367
6. Québec—Ville-Marie 918

D. Les musées les plus visités. Below are the most visited museums in France for 1990. Put them in order of most to least frequently visited by reading the name and the number of visitors.

le musée Picasso	340 000 *4*	le Louvre	3 400 000 *1*
l'Orangerie	254 000 *6*	Fontainebleau	291 000 *5*
le musée d'Orsay	2 000 000 *3*	Versailles	2 500 000 *2*

[handwritten: trois millions quatre cents mille]

Tirage du mercredi 89-08-16		

9 12 13 32 34 35 | no complémentaire **47**

	GAGNANTS	LOTS
Prochain tirage:	6/6	0	1 909 130,60 $
Samedi 89-08-19	5/6 +	4	180 306,70 $
	5/6	229	2 408,40 $
Prochain gros lot:	4/6	13 417	79,00 $
4 300 000,00 $	3/6	273 009	10,00 $
approx.		

Ventes totales: **15 494 672,00 $**

Les modalités d'encaissement des billets gagnants paraissent au verso des billets. En cas de disparité entre cette liste et la liste officielle, cette dernière a priorité.

WWW

E. **La loterie.** Answer the following questions about the results of a lottery drawing based on the newspaper report above.

1. Où est cette (this) loterie? *a Quebec*
2. Quels numéros gagnent (win)? *9 12*
3. Combien est-ce qu'on gagne avec les six numéros?
4. Combien de personnes ont quatre numéros?
5. Combien de personnes gagnent dix dollars?
6. Combien d'argent est-ce qu'on va gagner la prochaine fois (time)?

F. **Les salaires en France.** As in the United States, men in France earn more than women. In groups of three, one student will say a year from the chart below, a second will give the average salary for men, the third the salary for women.

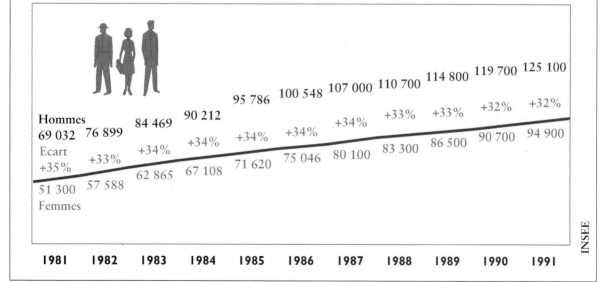

Les hommes gagnent un tiers de plus que les femmes

Evolution des salaires nets moyens annuels (en francs) et de l'écart (en %) selon le sexe

Hommes
69 032 76 899 84 469 90 212 95 786 100 548 107 000 110 700 114 800 119 700 125 100

Ecart
+35% +33% +34% +34% +34% +34% +34% +33% +33% +32% +32%

51 300 57 588 62 865 67 108 71 620 75 046 80 100 83 300 86 500 90 700 94 900
Femmes

1981   1982   1983   1984   1985   1986   1987   1988   1989   1990   1991

INSEE

Communication

G. **Votre numéro de téléphone.** Give your phone number to the class. In France, you would read the first three digits as a whole number and break the other number into a pair of two-digit numbers.

MODEL: 549-8859
cinq cent quarante-neuf, quatre-vingt-huit, cinquante-neuf

H. **On n'est pas des numéros.** Choose a partner to ask and answer the following questions with complete French sentences.

1. Quel âge a le professeur?
2. Quel âge a le président des Etats-Unis?
3. Combien d'étudiants est-ce qu'il y a à la résidence? à l'université?
4. Combien de pages est-ce qu'il y a dans le livre de français?
5. Vous habitez à quelle distance de l'université? de vos parents?
6. Combien d'étudiants vont aux matchs de football?

Communiquons

Demander son chemin

When traveling in a new place, one must be able to ask for directions (**demander son chemin**) and understand them. In this situation, you need to know how to get someone's attention on the street and then ask for directions politely. Most French people are used to seeing tourists and are glad to help.

One custom of giving directions is very different in Europe. While Americans judge distances in cities by blocks, the French generally estimate the distance in meters. A meter is about three inches longer than a yard.

Pardon, Messieurs, je cherche une banque.

Expressions ●

> ### ► On demande son chemin.

S'il vous plaît, pourriez-vous me dire où se trouve la gare?	Could you please tell me where the train station is located?
Excusez-moi, pourriez-vous m'indiquer une banque?	Excuse me, could you show me a bank?
Pardon, où se trouve le bureau de poste?	Pardon me, where is the post office?

> ### ► On indique le chemin.

Tournez à droite à 200 mètres d'ici.	Turn right 200 meters from here.
Vous tournez à gauche au coin de la rue.	You turn left at the corner.
Ensuite, continuez jusqu'à la rue Pascal.	Then, continue until Pascal Street.
Là, vous allez tout droit.	There, you go straight ahead.
Traversez la rue.	Cross the street.

> ### ► On regarde une carte de la francophonie.

La Tunisie est à l'est de l'Algérie.	Tunisia is east of Algeria.
Le Sénégal est au sud de la Mauritanie.	Senegal is south of Mauritania.
Le Gabon est à l'ouest du Congo.	Gabon is west of the Congo.
Le Cameroun est au nord du Zaïre.	Cameroon is north of Zaire.

Interaction *Robert cherche la gare.*

ROBERT: Pardon, Monsieur…

UN PASSANT°: Oui? *passer-by*

ROBERT: Pourriez-vous me dire où se trouve la gare?

UN PASSANT: Oui, mais c'est loin!

ROBERT: Mais, j'ai un train dans vingt minutes!

UN PASSANT: Alors, traversez cette rue, allez jusqu'au coin là-bas, et tournez à droite. Ensuite continuez jusqu'au coin de la rue Montaigne, à 400 mètres. Là, vous tournez à gauche et vous avez la gare en face de vous. across

ROBERT: Merci beaucoup, Monsieur.

UN PASSANT: Je vous en prie.° *Don't mention it.*

Activités

A. **Votre campus.** Answer the following questions about your campus.

1. Comment est-ce que vous allez de la bibliothèque au restau-U?
2. Comment est-ce que vous allez de la salle de classe à la librairie?
3. Pour aller de la salle de classe à la résidence, on va tout droit? Expliquez.
4. Le parking des étudiants est à quelle distance de la classe? Le parking des professeurs est loin ou près de la classe?

B. **Jeu de rôles.** With a classmate, prepare and act out the following situations in front of the class.

1. You are a French tourist who becomes lost in an American college town while looking for a local tourist attraction. Your partner is a French-speaking American who gives you directions to the landmark you are seeking.
2. You are an American tourist visiting the French town pictured in **Enrichissons notre vocabulaire** (p. 88). Using the map, decide where you are in the town and choose a destination that you would like to visit. Your partner will play the role of the town resident whom you stop on the street to ask for directions to your chosen destination.

Lecture culturelle

Avant la lecture   WWW

Throughout its history, France has been divided into large geographical regions called **provinces.** Some, like **Provence, Côte d'Azur,** and **Bretagne,** are very well known for their tourist attractions. Also, the population of France has traditionally been divided into two groups: the people from Paris (**les Parisiens**) and the people from **la province** (**les provinciaux**). Even though the rivalry between the two is decreasing, mainly because of efforts to decentralize the country and to move some of its administration from Paris to **la province,** to refer to someone as a **provincial** is still considered an insult.

Next to **Côte d'Azur, Provence** is probably the French province that attracts the greatest number of foreign tourists. Many have purchased land and houses where they spend extended vacations, and some have even moved there permanently. One of them, Peter Mayle, an Englishman, left England with his family and settled in a little village in Provence. His books about Provence became instant bestsellers and enhanced the reputation of the region.

Un champ de lavande

Activités

A. Answer the following questions to prepare yourself for the reading.

1. Choose a region in the United States that you know very well, and describe its appeal for tourists.
2. Prepare a list of American specialties with the regions they come from (lobster from Maine, peaches from Georgia, and so on).
3. The **jeu de boules** is a game played all over France, but it is more closely associated with the south of France. Do you know games or activities associated with certain areas of the United States? Name a few and describe them.

B. The following words, which you will see in the reading, are closely related to English words. What do you think they mean?

Nouns	**Adjectives**
les couleurs	bleu
un peintre	typiques
la menthe	renommée
les histoires	
la spécialité	

Impressions de Provence

Quand on regarde le paysage°, on cligne des yeux° à cause de la lumière°. Le ciel° est bleu, presque violet. On retrouve° toutes les belles couleurs de Provence dans les tableaux° de peintres comme Van Gogh, Gauguin et Picasso. Il y a des arbres° typiques comme l'olivier°, le
5 cyprès° et la vigne°, et les collines° provençales sentent bon° la lavande°, le romarin° et la menthe.

landscape / cligne... blink
light / sky / encounters
paintings
trees / olive tree
cypress / vineyards / hills /
   sent... smell good /
   lavender / rosemary

L'été° il fait très chaud, et on aime faire la sieste°. Mais il y a aussi le vent°, le mistral: il souffle° très fort°, parfois° sept à huit jours, mais il balaie° tous les nuages° sur son passage.

10 En fin de journée°, quand il fait moins chaud, les gens se retrouvent° sur la place du village, à l'ombre° des grands platanes°. Ils discutent° assis° sur une chaise; ils racontent° des histoires; ils font des parties de boules°; et le touriste de passage° entend° des mots et des expressions inconnus° dans d'autres régions. On s'appelle° «fada», cest-à-dire «un peu fou°», mais c'est gentil° et personne ne 15 se fâche°.

Enfin°, en Provence, chaque ville a sa spécialité de fruits et de légumes. Cavaillon a ses melons, Carpentras est fière° de ses tomates et Châteauneuf-du-Pape est renommée pour son vin. La Provence est une région très touristique comme la Côte d'Azur, la Bretagne et beaucoup d'autres provinces françaises.

*summer / **faire…** take a nap / wind / blows / strongly / sometimes / sweeps / clouds / **En fin…** At the end of the day / **se…** meet / shade / plane trees / chat / seated / tell / bowling games / **de…** passing / hears / unknown / calls / slightly crazy / nice / **se…** gets mad*
Finally
proud

Après la lecture

Questions sur le texte

1. Pourquoi est-ce qu'on cligne des yeux en Provence?
2. Où est-ce qu'on retrouve les couleurs de Provence?
3. Quels arbres sont typiques de Provence?
4. Quel temps est-ce qu'il fait en Provence?
5. Qu'est-ce que les gens font en fin de journée?
6. Que signifie le mot «fada»?
7. Quelle est la spécialité de Carpentras?
8. Nommez *(Name)* d'autres provinces françaises.

Activités

A. Regardez une carte de France et préparez un itinéraire touristique en Provence.
B. Choisissez une autre province française et décrivez cette province. Utilisez «Impressions de Provence» comme modèle.
C. Préparez une liste d'autres spécialités de provinces françaises (la choucroute en Alsace, le camembert en Normandie, etc.).

Vocabulaire

Noms / Pronoms

Afrique	Africa	**année**	year
agence de voyages	travel agency	**appartement**	apartment
Algérie	Algeria	**après-midi**	afternoon
Allemagne	Germany	**arrêt d'autobus**	bus stop
Amérique du Nord	North America	**Asie**	Asia
Amérique du Sud	South America	**Autriche**	Austria
Angleterre	England	**banque**	bank

Belgique	Belgium	Maroc	Morocco
bibliothèque	library	matin	morning
Brésil	Brazil	*la* mer	sea
Bruxelles	Brussels	messieurs	gentlemen
bureau de poste	post office	Mexico	Mexico City
Canada	Canada	Mexique	Mexico
casino	casino	milliard	billion
centre commercial	shopping center	million	million
chambre	bedroom	minute	minute
Chine	China	Moscou	Moscow
cinéma	cinema	Mozambique	Mozambique
continent	continent	musée	museum
Corse	Corsica	Norvège	Norway
Côte d'Azur	Riviera	parc	park
Côte d'Ivoire	Côte d'Ivoire	parking	parking lot
Danemark	Denmark	pays	country
église	church	Pays-Bas	Netherlands
endroit	place	pharmacie	drugstore
Espagne	Spain	piscine	swimming pool
Etats-Unis	United States	place	square
Europe	Europe	plage	beach
Finlande	Finland	Pologne	Poland
France	France	Portugal	Portugal
galet	smooth stone	renseignement	information
gare	train station	résidence universitaire	dorm
Genève	Geneva	restau-U	university cafeteria
Grande-Bretagne	Great Britain	rue	street
Grèce	Greece	Russie	Russia
Hollande	Holland	semaine	week
hôtesse	hostess	Sénégal	Senegal
Irlande	Ireland	stade	stadium
Italie	Italy	Suède	Sweden
Japon	Japan	Suisse	Switzerland
laboratoire	laboratory	Syndicat d'Initiative	Tourist Office
La Havane	Havana	Tchad	Chad
La Nouvelle-Orléans	New Orleans	théâtre	theater
librairie	bookstore	Tunisie	Tunisia
Lisbonne	Lisbon	*l'* usine	factory
liste	list	Varsovie	Warsaw
Londres	London	ville	city / town
lycée	high school	voyage	trip
magasin	store	week-end	weekend
maison	house	Zaïre	Zaire

Verbes

aller	to go	rester	to stay / remain
chercher	to look for	visiter	to visit
rentrer	to go back	voyager	to travel

Adjectifs / Adverbes

aujourd'hui	today	mille	thousand
autre	other	plein	full
cent	hundred	pourquoi	why
cher	expensive	prochain	next
demain	tomorrow	si	if
demain matin	tomorrow morning	sous	under
demain soir	tomorrow evening	sur	on
là-bas	over there	tous	all
maintenant	now		

Expressions

à côté de	next to	entre	between
Ah non!	Oh no!	il faut	it is necessary
allez-y	go ahead	loin de	far from
allons-y	let's go	merci mille fois	thanks a million
au bord de	along / by	Où ça?	Whereabout?
au coin de	at the corner of	parce que	because
chez	at / at the home of	pas du tout	not at all
derrière	behind	(de la) place	room
en	in	pour	to / in order to
en face de	across from	près de	near
en ville	downtown	tous les jours	every day

Chapitre 5

Le monde francophone

 Commençons

 Grammaire

 Communiquons

 Lecture culturelle

 Vocabulaire

A Fort-de-France en Martinique

Objectives

Language

Vocabulary for clothing and colors • Vowel tension • **Faire** and expressions using **faire** • **Passé composé** • Possessive adjectives • Stressed pronouns

Culture

The French-speaking world

Communication

Talking about common activities • Describing past events • Expressing ownership • Giving and getting information

Commençons

Lise et Gaëtan Morin font leurs bagages. www

Lise et Gaëtan sont québécois. Ils habitent à Montréal et, tous les ans en hiver, ils font un voyage en Martinique.

GAËTAN: Est-ce que tu as fait les valises?

LISE: Oui, mais je n'ai pas terminé les bagages à main; et toi, est-ce que tu as fait toutes tes courses?

GAËTAN: Bien sûr. Tu as pensé à mon short blanc et à mon tee-shirt de l'université de Montréal?

LISE: Si tu portes quelque chose comme cela, tu vas avoir l'air du parfait touriste!

GAËTAN: Tu as raison; ce n'est pas une bonne idée. Je vais faire des achats à Fort-de-France.

LISE: Moi aussi. Leurs maillots de bain sont super.

GAËTAN: Ça y est! Nous sommes prêts, mais où sont mes lunettes de soleil?

LISE: Dans la poche de ton veston. Fais attention; n'oublie rien!

Etudions le dialogue

1. Est-ce que Lise et Gaëtan sont français? Où est-ce qu'ils habitent?
2. Pourquoi est-ce qu'ils font leurs bagages?
3. Pourquoi Lise n'aime pas le short blanc et le tee-shirt de Gaëtan?
4. Qu'est-ce que Gaëtan va faire à Fort-de-France?
5. Qu'est-ce que Lise aime aux Antilles? Pourquoi?
6. Qu'est-ce que Gaëtan cherche?

Mots clés

font leurs bagages (m.) (faire ses bagages)	pack their luggage	avoir l'air parfait (e)	to look like perfect
québécois	from Quebec	touriste (m., f.)	tourist
tous les ans	every year	bonne (bon)	good
l' hiver (m.)	winter	idée (f.)	idea
font un voyage (faire un voyage)	take a trip	faire des achats (m.) moi	to go shopping purchase I
as fait les valises (f.) (faire les valises)	packed the suitcases	maillots de bain (m.) super	bathing suits terrific
bagages à main	hand luggage	Ça y est! Ci et	That's it!
toi	you	prêts prêt	ready
as fait toutes tes courses (f.) (faire des courses)	did all your errands	mes	my
		lunettes de soleil (f.)	sunglasses
Bien sûr.	Of course.	poche	pocket
as pensé à (penser à)	thought of	ton	your
mon (m.)	my	veston	sports coat jacket
short	shorts	Fais attention. (faire attention)	Be careful.
tee-shirt	T-shirt		
portes (porter)	wear – carry	N'oublie rien. (oublier)	Don't forget anything.
quelque chose	something		

en automne – autumn
en été – summer
au printemps – spring

un prêt – alone

Faisons connaissance

French is the native language of more than seven million Canadians and the official language of Quebec. Montreal is the second largest French-speaking city in the world. It has a large, cosmopolitan population and exhibits cultural features of English- and French-speaking communities and many other ethnic groups. It is often the site of international meetings and events and in 1976 hosted the Summer Olympics.

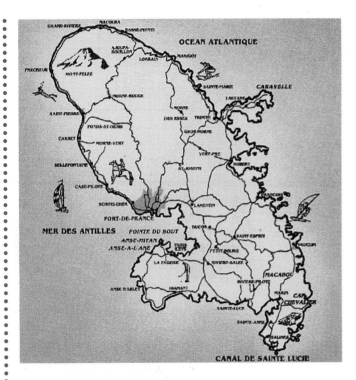

La Martinique

The people of Quebec love to travel, and because of the long winters, many take a vacation in a warmer climate. Some of their favorite places are the state of Florida and two French **départements** in the Caribbean, Guadeloupe and Martinique.

Discovered in 1495 by Christopher Columbus, the island of Martinique is part of the **Petites Antilles,** and it has always been a part of France except for two short periods when it was occupied by English-speaking people. Fort-de-France is its administrative, commercial, and cultural center. With its mild climate all year round and its beautiful sandy beaches, the island attracts many European and Quebecois tourists. As in Guadeloupe, French is spoken in Martinique, but **le créole** is another language spoken by the natives.

Enrichissons notre vocabulaire

Les vêtements *(m.) (Clothing)*

les bottes *(f.)*	*the boots*	le manteau	*the coat*
le chapeau	*the hat*	le parapluie	*the umbrella*
le costume	*the suit*	le pull	*the sweater*
l'écharpe *(f.)*	*the scarf*	la robe de chambre	*the robe*
l'imperméable *(m.)*	*the raincoat*	les tennis *(m.)*	*the tennis shoes*

[handwritten: une tailleur - women suit]

[handwritten: des chaussures - shoes / souliers - prom shoes]

le chemisier

la cravate

la chemise

la robe

les jeans (m.)

les chaussettes (f.)

la jupe

le pantalon

les chaussures (f.)

Combien est-ce a couter — How much does it cost
couter — cost

Quelques expressions utiles (*Useful expressions*)

Quel polo est-ce que vous allez acheter?

Combien coûte le pyjama / la chemise de nuit?

Quelles vestes / ceintures est-ce que Christine
va emporter?

Quels gants est-ce que Lise porte?

Which polo shirt are you going to buy?

How much are the pajamas / the nightgown?

*Which jackets / belts is Christine
going to take?*

Which gloves is Lise wearing?

robe de chambre — bathrobe

Les couleurs (*f.*) (*Colors*)

orange

bleu / bleue

gris / grise

poupre
violette) purple
raison
lilas

vert / verte

jaune / jaune

Rose — pink

marron
(chestnut) brun / brune

noir / noire

aqua marine — turquoise

blanc / blanche

rouge / rouge

emeraude

—De quelle couleur est la jupe?

—Elle est bleue.

What color is the skirt?

It is blue.

Prononciation   Vowel tension   `○━○`

French vowels are pronounced with much more tension of the muscles in the tongue, lips, and jaw than English vowels. The gliding of one vowel sound into another is common in English, and the sound produced is called a *diphthong*. You must avoid tongue movement when pronouncing French vowel sounds, so that each is distinct.

Repeat the following English and French word pairs after your teacher, being careful to avoid any unwanted movement when pronouncing the French words.

English	French	English	French
see	si	day	des
D	dit	Fay	fait
boo	bout	foe	faut
do	doux	low	l'eau

Exercices

A. Repeat the following words after your teacher, paying attention to vowel tension.

	/ i /	/ u /	/ e /	/ o /
1.	si	où	et	l'eau
2.	dit	bout	des	beau
3.	Guy	cou	les	faut
4.	J	fou	mes	mot
5.	oui	vous	été	tôt

B. Read the following sentences, taking care to keep your muscles tense when you pronounce the vowels.

1. Vous travaillez au café?
2. Sylvie étudie le français.
3. Hervé va aller au musée.
4. Les Anglais vont visiter l'université.
5. Le bureau est à côté du tableau.
6. J'ai oublié mon idée.
7. Vous allez téléphoner cet après-midi?
8. Nous aimons le café de Colombie.

Grammaire

I. The verb faire

You use the verb **faire** to describe many activities and to ask other people what they are doing.

---

faire *(to do, make)*

je **fais**	nous **faisons**
tu **fais**	vous **faites**
il / elle / on **fait**	ils / elles **font**

Imperative: **fais, faisons, faites**

All singular forms are pronounced alike: / fɛ /. The **nous** form is pronounced / fø zɔ̃ /.

Il ne **fait** pas de devoirs.   **Faisons** la cuisine ensemble!

Mots clés   *Common expressions* with **faire**

A la maison

faire la cuisine	*to cook*	**faire la grasse matinée**	*to sleep late*
des crêpes *(f.)*	*crepes*	**faire la lessive**	*to do the washing*
une omelette	*omelet*	**faire le ménage**	*to do housework*
un sandwich	*sandwich*	**faire un régime**	*to be on a diet*
des pâtes *(f.)*	*noodles*	**faire la vaisselle**	*to do the dishes*

A l'université

faire attention à	*to pay attention to*	**faire la queue**	*to wait in line*
faire des devoirs	*to do homework*	**faire du sport**	*to play sports*

En ville

faire les bagages *(m.)* / **la valise**	*to pack one's bags / a suitcase*
faire des courses *(f.)*	*to go shopping, to do errands*
faire une promenade / **un tour**	*to go for a walk*
faire un voyage	*to take a trip*

A l'extérieur *(Outside)*

The verb **faire** is also used with the impersonal pronoun **il** to talk about the weather.

Quel temps fait-il? *What's the weather like?*

Il fait beau.	*It is nice.*	**Il fait chaud.**	*It is warm.*
Il fait mauvais.	*The weather is bad.*	**Il fait froid.**	*It is cold.*

Attention!

As in English, the answer to a question using **faire** often has a different verb.

—Qu'est-ce que vous **faites** ce soir?
—Je **vais regarder** la télévision.

Language

A. **Des activités.** Indicate what people are doing or asking about by filling in the blanks with the appropriate form of **faire.**

1. Nous _____ des devoirs.
2. Il _____ la vaisselle.
3. Il va _____ un tour en ville.
4. Est-ce que vous _____ les bagages de Paul?
5. Tu _____ la grasse matinée?
6. On a faim; *faire* des sandwichs!

B. **Interview.** You are being interviewed to find out about life in your home. Answer the following questions, using the cues provided.

1. Vous aimez faire des promenades?   (Oui, nous...)
2. Qu'est-ce que vous aimez faire le week-end?   (... des courses.)
3. Est-ce que les enfants font attention?   (Oui, mais Jacqueline ne...)
4. Vous faites la cuisine?   (Oui,... ce soir.)
5. Qu'est-ce que vous préparez?   (Nous... faire... omelette.)
6. Est-ce que vous faites la vaisselle?   (Non,... détester...) *faire.*

Culture

C. **Des gens célèbres.** Look at the list below. What do these French-speaking people do for a living? Can you think of other famous people and name their professions?

MODEL: *Agnès Varda fait des films.*

1. Guy Forget et Yannick Noah	a.	la cuisine
2. Justin Wilson et Paul Prudhomme	b.	des films
	c.	du cinéma
3. Jean-Claude Killy	d.	de la politique
4. Julie Delpy et Isabelle Huppert	e.	du ski
5. Claude Chabrol	f.	du tennis
6. Jacques Chirac		

D. **Les vêtements.** Match the clothes and accessories in the left column with the famous French designers that specialize in them in the right column, using the verb **faire.**

MODEL: maillots de bain   Rasurel   WWW
          Rasurel fait des maillots de bain.

1. écharpes	a.	Yves Saint-Laurent
2. lunettes de soleil	b.	Bally et Charles Jourdan
3. robes	c.	Lacoste
4. costumes pour hommes	d.	Hermès
5. chaussures	e.	Vuarnet
6. polos	f.	Christian Dior et Guy Laroche

Communication

E. Mes projets. What are your plans for next weekend? Indicate your activities for each time slot, using the suggestions provided or your own ideas.

[handwritten: faire]
[handwritten: morn]
[handwritten: after noon]
[handwritten: evenin]

des devoirs   la grasse matinée   aller danser
la cuisine   aller au cinéma   regarder la
des courses   travailler à la   télévision
une promenade *walk*   bibliothèque

1. vendredi soir *(Friday night)*   3. samedi soir *(Saturday night)*
2. samedi *(Saturday)*   4. dimanche *(Sunday)*

F. Une interview. Interview a classmate to find out the following information.

[handwritten: passé comp / present]

1. où il / elle fait des courses
2. où il / elle fait des promenades
3. s'il / si elle fait la cuisine / le ménage
4. s'il / si elle va faire un régime
5. quand il / elle aime faire le ménage
6. s'il / si elle fait attention au professeur / aux agents de police

II. The passé composé

> You use the **passé composé** to tell what happened in the past.

A. The **passé composé** refers to actions or events that the speaker views as completed in the past. To form the **passé composé,** use the present indicative forms of **avoir** and the past participle of the main verb.

travailler *(to work)*	
j' **ai travaillé**	nous **avons travaillé**
tu **as travaillé**	vous **avez travaillé**
il / elle / on **a travaillé**	ils / elles **ont travaillé**

J'ai tout **terminé** ce matin.   Tu **as acheté** un pantalon bleu?

B. To form the past participle of **-er** verbs, drop the **-er** of the infinitive and add **é** as in **travailler** → **travaillé.** (The pronunciation does not change.)

C. The **passé composé** has several English equivalents. For example, **elle a chanté** could be *she sang, she has sung,* or *she did sing.*

Elle a chanté la semaine dernière.   *She sang last week.*
Elle a chanté trois fois.   *She has sung three times.*
Elle a chanté?   *Did she sing?*

D. In the negative, place the **ne... pas** around the auxiliary verb **avoir**.

    Il **n'a pas** porté de costume.   Je **n'ai pas** trouvé les gants.

E. To ask a question in the **passé composé**, use the forms you learned in Chapter 1:

    Elle a fait du sport?
    Est-ce que tu as terminé les bagages à main?
    Tu as fait tous les achats, **n'est-ce pas?**

F. Many verbs have irregular past participles. Here are the ones for the verbs that you have studied so far.

avoir → eu	Il **a eu** une idée.	*He **had** an idea.*
être → été	Elle **a été** malade.	*She **has been** sick.*
faire → fait	Tu **as fait** la lessive?	***Did** you **do** the wash?*

G. Generally, expressions of time are placed either at the end or at the beginning of the sentence. Some frequent expressions indicating past time are the following:

hier	*yesterday*	le mois dernier	*last month*
récemment	*recently*	l'été dernier	*last summer*
le week-end dernier	*last weekend*	l'année dernière	*last year*
la semaine dernière	*last week*		

    J'ai fait une promenade **hier.**
    Hier il a fait le ménage pendant trente minutes.
    Le week-end dernier nous avons fait la grasse matinée.

In contrast, many frequently used adverbs precede the past participle.

beaucoup	*a lot*	peu	*little*	souvent	*often*
bien	*well*	mal	*poorly, badly*	toujours	*always*
déjà	*already*	pas encore	*not yet*	trop	*too much, too many*

    —Vous avez **déjà** acheté des vêtements de plage?
    —Non, je n'ai **pas encore** été au magasin.

    —Ils ont **bien** dîné?
    —Oui, mais ils ont **trop** mangé.

Language

A. **Un voyage.** Replace the infinitive with the **passé composé** in the following sentences.

1. Jean-Paul (faire) un voyage en Grande-Bretagne avec Christine.
2. Pierre (donner) un cadeau à Jean-Paul.
3. —Tu (être) content du cadeau?
4. —Nous (trouver) le livre sur l'Angleterre formidable.
5. Nous (visiter) Paris aussi.

6. —Tu (manger) un couscous?

7. —On ne... pas (trouver) cela mauvais.

8. Il (faire) froid en Angleterre.

B. **Pas du tout!** Change the following sentences to the negative to state that people did *not* do the following things.

1. Nous avons fait le ménage.
2. Il a beaucoup aimé le livre.
3. Michelle a trouvé l'hôtel.
4. Gaston a fait attention au prof.
5. Elles ont cherché une chambre.
6. On a souvent invité des amis.

C. **Des activités.** Make complete sentences to show what happened at the times in column **A** by using these expressions with words from columns **B** and **C**.

A	B	C
hier	je	acheter une jupe
le week-end dernier	mes amis	faire froid
récemment	mes parents	avoir chaud
la semaine dernière	le professeur	visiter un parc
l'année dernière	il	être fatigué(e)(s)
l'été dernier - last summer???		???

Culture

D. **Des célébrités.** What did the following French-speaking people do to become famous?

MODEL: *François Mitterrand a été président de la République française.*

1. Marie Curie
2. Louis Pasteur
3. Edith Piaf
4. Jean Chrétien
5. Gustave Eiffel
6. Jacques Villeneuve
7. Léopold Senghor
8. Simone Signoret

a. être premier aux 500 miles d'Indianapolis
b. être président du Sénégal et membre de l'Académie française
c. avoir le prix Nobel de physique et de chimie
d. développer des vaccins
e. être ingénieur
f. avoir un Oscar
g. être Premier ministre du Canada
h. chanter «La Vie en rose»

Communication

E. **Ma journée.** Tell your classmates one thing you did yesterday. Then, tell them something you did not do last week that you should have. Use the suggestions provided or your own responses.

MODEL: *Hier j'ai fait la lessive. La semaine dernière je n'ai pas préparé la leçon.*

préparer la leçon
manger au restau-U
parler à mes parents
faire le ménage

faire la lessive
écouter les professeurs
terminer les exercices
étudier à la bibliothèque

F. **Discussion.** Divide into small groups and find out what your partners did or did not do last summer. Report your findings to the class. Some possible answers are listed below.

MODEL: *L'été dernier, Robert a étudié le français et il a visité la Floride.*

travailler à...	faire un voyage...
visiter l'état de...	inviter des amis à...
acheter...	parler au téléphone avec...
étudier...	???

G. **Questions personnelles.** Mes activités récentes.

1. Où avez-vous été récemment?
2. Est-ce que vous avez acheté des vêtements? De quelle couleur?
3. Combien est-ce qu'ils ont coûté?
4. Est-ce que vous avez invité un(e) ami(e) à la maison?
5. Qu'est-ce que vous avez fait ensemble?
6. Quel pays est-ce que vous avez déjà visité?
7. Vous avez parlé avec une personne célèbre *(famous)*? Qui?
8. Quel film est-ce que vous avez regardé à la télévision récemment?

III.   Possessive adjectives

You use possessive adjectives to show ownership.

A. In English, possessive adjectives show the ownership of an object (*my* coat) or of a quality (*your* honesty). They also show relationship: *his* girlfriend / *her* boyfriend.

In French, these adjectives show not only the possessor but also indicate the number (singular or plural) of the object or quality possessed. They can also show the gender (masculine or feminine) of the thing possessed.

mon pull	*my sweater* (**pull** is *m.* + *sing.*)
ma ceinture	*my belt* (**ceinture** is *f.* + *sing.*)
mes bottes	*my boots* (**bottes** is *pl.*)

B. The written forms are as follows:

		singular		
person	*English equivalent*	*masculine*	*feminine*	*plural*
1st singular	*my*	mon	ma	mes
2nd singular	*your*	ton	ta	tes
3rd singular	*his, her its, one's*	son	sa	ses

		plural		
person	*English equivalent*	*masculine*	*feminine*	*plural*
1st plural	*our*		**notre**	**nos**
2nd plural	*your*		**votre**	**vos**
3rd plural	*their*		**leur**	**leurs**

[handwritten margin note: m, f, pL / le livres / mon livres (m)]

French identifies the gender of the item possessed, not the gender of the person who owns the item(s).

—C'est l'imperméable de Marie?
—Oui, c'est **son** imperméable.
—C'est l'imperméable de Jacques?
—Oui, c'est **son** imperméable.

—C'est la robe de chambre de Lise?
—Oui, c'est **sa** robe de chambre.
—C'est la robe de chambre de Robert?
—Oui, c'est **sa** robe de chambre.

Attention!

1. The adjectives **ma, ta,** and **sa** are not used before a vowel. You must use **mon, ton,** and **son,** even if the word is feminine.

   Vous êtes **son** étudiante?   Voilà **son** amie.

   Therefore, **ton enfant** may refer to a male or female child.

2. To identify the possessor, use **c'est** (for the singular) or **ce sont** (for plurals) as the subject of the sentence.

   —Mme Morin, **c'est** votre manteau?
   —Oui, **c'est** mon manteau.

   —**Ce sont** les chaussures de Jean?
   —Oui, **ce sont** ses chaussures.

C. The pronunciation of possessive adjectives changes according to whether the following noun starts with a consonant or a vowel sound.

1. The only final written consonant that is always pronounced is the **r** of **leur.** The pronunciation of all other possessive adjectives changes before a vowel sound.

   Où est **leur argent?**   / lœ ʀaʀ ʒɑ̃ /   Voici **leur valise.**   / lœʀ va liz /

2. The **n** of **mon, ton, son** and the **s** of **mes, tes, ses, nos, vos, leurs** are pronounced before a vowel sound because of **liaison.**

Liaison		No liaison	
leurs enfants	/ lœʀ zɑ̃ fɑ̃ /	leurs classes	/ lœʀ klas /
mon écharpe	/ mɔ̃ ne ʃaʀp /	mon frère	/ mɔ̃ fʀɛʀ /

3. The final **e** in **notre** and **votre** is not pronounced before a vowel; the adjective and noun should be pronounced as one word.

> notre appartement / nɔ tra par tø mã /   votre école / vɔ trø kɔl /

4. Remember that **ma, ta,** and **sa** change the most: they become **mon, ton,** and **son** when the following noun begins with a vowel sound.

Ce qu'ils disent

In conversation, the **-re** of **notre** and **votre** is often dropped when it occurs before a consonant.

> Notre voiture est rouge. / nɔt vwa tyr /
>
> Ils ont votre sac. / vɔt sak /
>
> *but:* C'est votre imperméable? / vɔ trɛ̃ pɛr me abl /

Language

A. **En cours.** Replace the italicized words with each of the suggested subjects and change the possessive adjective to reflect the new subject.

1. *Il a* demandé son cahier. (je)
2. *Pierre a* trouvé son stylo. (Ils)
3. *Elles* ont parlé à leurs amis. (Vous)
4. *J'ai* oublié mon sac à dos. (Tu)
5. *Vous avez* fait vos devoirs? (Elles)
6. *Elle* a expliqué ses idées. (Nous)

B. **Faisons la lessive!** Your friends did a load of laundry, but they washed everything together, so confusion reigns as they sort out the wash. Answer their questions using possessive adjectives and the cues provided.

MODEL: C'est le chemisier de Micheline?   *Oui, c'est son chemisier.*

1. C'est la chemise de Jacques? (Oui,...)
2. Tu as trouvé les chaussettes de Monique? (...sont ici.)
3. Où est la jupe de Jeanne? (Voici...)
4. Tu cherches le pyjama de mon frère? (Oui,...)
5. Est-ce que c'est le jean de Pierre? (Oui,...)
6. Tu as la robe de Chantal? (Oui,...)

C. **A la douane.** A customs agent is going through your suitcase. Answer her questions according to the cues provided.

1. Est-ce que vous avez vos bagages à main? (Oui,...)
2. Vous êtes avec vos amis? (Non,... famille.)
3. Ce sont vos vêtements? (Oui,...)
4. Où est-ce que vous avez trouvé votre jean et vos chemises? (... à Kmart.)
5. Qu'est-ce qu'il y a dans vos chaussures? (... chaussettes.)
6. Vous avez fait votre lessive récemment? (Oui,... la semaine dernière.)

AIR CANADA
Téléphonez à Air Canada ou à votre agent de voyages pour des renseignements concernant nos tours-vacances.

Culture

D. **Les préférences.** Try to guess the preferences of French people in the categories below.

MODEL: Vacances préférées des Français?
a. Italie b. Espagne c. Suisse
Leurs vacances préférées sont en Espagne.

1. Boisson préférée avec le dîner?
   a. eau   b. vin   c. bière
2. Activité préférée pour les jeunes?
   a. faire du sport   b. jouer   c. regarder la télé
3. Musique préférée des jeunes?
   a. le rock   b. le reggae   c. le rap
4. Films préférés des Français?
   a. films comiques   b. films d'amour   c. films d'aventure
5. Sport préféré des jeunes?
   a. la gymnastique   b. le tennis   c. le football
6. Et avec qui est-ce que les jeunes parlent de leurs problèmes?
   a. frère ou sœur   b. amis   c. mère

Communication

E. **Une décision importante.** You are stranded on a desert island. With a classmate, consult the following list and decide what three items you want to have with you.

MODEL: *Je voudrais avoir ma radio, mon short et mes tee-shirts.*

disques	petit(e) ami(e)	bière préférée
jean	parents	livre de français
cravates	professeurs	lunettes de soleil
radio	maillot de bain	???

F. **Ma famille.** Describe the members of your family, according to the ideas below. Present your description to the class.

MODEL: *Mon frère est sympathique.*
           Mes cousins habitent à New York.

Où est-ce qu'ils habitent?	Qu'est-ce qu'ils aiment?
Où est-ce qu'ils travaillent?	Qu'est-ce qu'ils détestent?
Quel âge est-ce qu'ils ont?	Où est-ce qu'ils aiment aller?

G. **Questions personnelles.** A l'université ou chez moi?

1. Où est-ce que vos parents habitent?
2. De quelle couleur est leur maison?
3. Où est votre résidence universitaire ou votre appartement?
4. Vous faites vos devoirs là ou à la bibliothèque?
5. Vous aimez mieux faire votre lessive en ville ou chez vos parents?
6. Qu'est-ce qu'il y a sur votre bureau?
7. Quand vous n'étudiez pas, qu'est-ce que vous faites avec vos ami(e)s?
8. Quel est votre restaurant préféré? Et le restaurant préféré de vos ami(e)s?

IV. Stressed pronouns

> You use stressed pronouns to talk about people when it is clear whom you are talking about.

	stressed pronouns	
person	*singular*	*plural*
1st	**moi** I, me	**nous** *we, us*
2nd	**toi** you	**vous** *you*
3rd	**lui** *(m.)* *he, him*	**eux** *(m.)* *they, them*
	elle *(f.)* *she, her*	**elles** *(f.)* *they, them*

A. Stressed pronouns are used without a verb, in order to ask or answer a question with one word, or in a compound subject when separated from the verb.

Et **toi?** Tu as fait tes courses?

—Qui aime le vin?
—**Moi!**

Elle et **toi,** vous n'allez pas acheter cela!

B. Stressed pronouns are also used after a preposition.

—Tu vas travailler avec **nous?**	—Est-ce qu'ils sont en retard?
—Non, je travaille avec **elle.**	—Oui, le professeur a commencé sans **eux.**

C. Stressed pronouns can show ownership when used with the expression **être à**. To ask to whom something belongs, use **A qui est... ?** or **A qui sont... ?**

A qui est le polo rouge?	*Whose red shirt is this?*
Il **est à moi.**	*It's mine.*
Elles **sont à vous,** les bottes?	*The boots are yours?*
Non, elles **sont à Lucie.**	*No, they're Lucie's.*

D. You also use stressed pronouns to put emphasis on a subject pronoun.

1. In French, you cannot simply emphasize a word by putting stress on it as you can in English (*I don't care!*). To emphasize a word in French, you use a stressed pronoun to repeat the subject.

> —J'adore les vêtements de Madonna.
> —**Moi,** je n'aime pas ses chemisiers.

> —Elles sont riches, **elles.**
> —Pas du tout! Elles sont professeurs.

2. This structure also allows you to contrast people:

> **Lui,** il est médecin; **elle,** avocate.

Note that a stressed pronoun can come at the beginning or the end of a sentence, and that the intonation rises at the comma. If you want to emphasize a noun, however, the stressed pronoun must follow it.

> Les Canadiens, **eux,** ils sont sympathiques.

3. Another way to emphasize a subject pronoun is to use the stressed pronoun followed by **-même(s)**. This is the equivalent of *-self* in English.

> —Est-ce que vous avez fait votre robe **vous-même?**
> —Oui, la semaine dernière.

> —Vous mangez au restaurant?
> —Non, nous faisons la cuisine **nous-mêmes.**

Ce qu'ils disent

1. Stressed pronouns appear very frequently in conversation.

> **Lui,** Jacques, il est studieux.

2. The pronoun **moi** may appear unexpectedly to mean *in my opinion.*

> **Moi,** j'aime le sucre dans mon café.
> **Moi,** pas du tout.

3. Since **on** frequently replaces **nous** as a subject pronoun, you will hear the stressed pronoun **nous** used with it.

> On travaille beaucoup, **nous!**

Language

A. **Les possessions.** The following sentences all show possession with posses-sive adjectives. Change them by using the expression **être à.**

MODEL: C'est mon livre.   *Il est à moi.*

1. Ce sont leurs valises.
2. C'est ton costume.
3. Ce sont vos disques.
4. C'est la robe de Sylvie.
5. C'est mon argent.
6. Ce sont nos tennis.
7. C'est la maison des Morin.
8. C'est le pyjama de l'enfant.

B. **Des opinions.** Daniel has very strong opinions about everything. How would he make the subjects of the following sentences more emphatic?

MODEL: Elle ne va pas au cinéma.

    Elle, elle ne va pas au cinéma. / Elle ne va pas au cinéma, elle.

1. Mes amis sont très intelligents.
2. Je déteste faire des courses.
3. Nous allons acheter des vêtements formidables.
4. Mes sœurs ont du talent.
5. Tu ne travailles pas beaucoup.
6. Vous n'habitez pas une maison magnifique.

Culture

C. **Les préférences.** American and French tastes are sometimes different, some-times similar. Form sentences from the elements below and add stressed pro-nouns to indicate preferences.

MODEL: le lait avec le dîner

    Nous, nous aimons le lait; les Français, eux, ils aiment
       mieux l'eau.

1. aimer porter un jean
2. (ne… pas) aimer les westerns
3. avoir beaucoup d'amis
4. faire des promenades en voiture
5. commander de l'eau naturelle au restaurant
6. aimer acheter beaucoup de vêtements
7. (ne… pas) faire souvent la bise
8. (ne… pas) manger souvent du fromage

D. **Les vêtements.** You are staying with a French family, and you discover that the son / daughter is the same size as you. Using the size comparison chart on the next page, make plans for a shopping trip by converting your sizes for the clothing listed below.

MODELS: *(for women) Les robes? Moi, je porte un 8, elle, un 36.*
       (for men) Les costumes? Moi, je porte un 36, lui, un 38.

Les femmes	**Les hommes**
1. Les robes	1. Les costumes
2. Les collants *(pantyhose)*	2. Les chemises
3. Les chaussures	3. Les chaussures
4. Les chemisiers	4. Les tricots *(knitted wear)*

TABLE DE COMPARAISON DE TAILLES

Robes, chemisiers et tricots femmes.

F	36	38	40	42	44	46	48
GB	10	12	14	16	18	20	22
USA	8	10	12	14	16	18	20

Bas et collants femmes.

F	1	2	3	4	5
USA	8½	9	9½	10	10½

Chaussures femmes.

F	35½	36	36½	37	37½	38	39
GB	3	3½	4	4½	5	5½	6
USA	4	4½	5	5½	6	6½	7½

Chaussures hommes.

F	39	40	41	42	43	44	45
GB	5½	6½	7	8	8½	9½	10½
USA	6	7	7½	8½	9	10	11

Costumes hommes.

F	36	38	40	42	44	46	48
GB	35	36	37	38	39	40	42
USA	35	36	37	38	39	40	42

Chemises hommes.

F	36	37	38	39	40	41	42
USA	14	14½	15	15½	16	16½	17

Tricots hommes.

F	36	38	40	42	44	46
GB	46	48	51	54	56	59
USA	46	48	51	54	56	59

Communication

E. **Moi et eux.** Think about a person or a group of people who do the following things and people who do not. Express the contrast using stressed pronouns.

MODEL: parler français
Moi, je parle français; mon camarade de chambre, lui, il parle anglais.

1. avoir du talent
2. parler espagnol
3. aimer le vin
4. chanter bien
5. faire bien la cuisine
6. porter des vêtements super

F. **Cherchez la réponse!** Question your classmates to find out the following information.

MODEL: Qui a acheté un tee-shirt récemment?
Robert, lui, il a acheté un tee-shirt.

1. Qui a des chaussures rouges?
2. Qui a deux frères?
3. Qui a visité l'Europe?
4. Qui habite une maison blanche?
5. Qui adore la cuisine mexicaine?
6. Qui a fait la grasse matinée aujourd'hui?

G. **Questions personnelles.** Et vous?

1. Vous habitez chez vos parents?
2. Vous parlez français avec votre professeur?
3. Est-ce que le professeur parle français avec vous?
4. Vous allez au cinéma seul(e) ou avec vos amis?
5. Est-ce que vos camarades aiment étudier avec vous?
6. Est-ce que vous pensez souvent à vos parents?

Communiquons

Demander des renseignements

In Chapter 4 you learned how to ask for and give directions. There are many other types of information that you will have to ask for when traveling through or living in a French-speaking country. You will also have to clarify the meaning of what you hear and want to say, participate in basic conversations, and understand questions and provide information when it is asked of you.

Où est-ce qu'on trouve les maillots de bain?

Expressions

> ▶ **En ville on demande...**
>
> | | |
> |---|---|
> | —Comment vous appelez-vous? | *What's your name?* |
> | —Je m'appelle Chantal Laforge. | *My name is Chantal Laforge.* |
> | | |
> | —Comment allez-vous? / Comment ça va? / Ça va? | *How are you?* |
> | —Je vais bien. / Ça va. | *I'm fine.* |

—Quelle heure est-il?

—A quelle heure est-ce que l'autobus arrive?

—Il arrive à trois heures.

—Quel temps fait-il / va-t-il faire?

What time is it?

At what time does the bus arrive?

It arrives at 3:00.

What's the weather like / going to be like?

▶ **En cours on demande…**

—Comment dit-on *coat* en français?

—On dit «manteau».

—Qu'est-ce que ça veut dire?

—Que veut dire «chaussures»?

—Ça veut dire «*shoes*».

—Que veut dire l'expression «à tout à l'heure»?

—Ça veut dire «*see you soon*».

How do you say coat *in French?*

You say "manteau."

What does that mean?

What does chaussures *mean?*

It means "shoes."

What does the expression à tout à l'heure *mean?*

It means "see you soon."

▶ **Au magasin on demande…**

—Est-ce que vous avez des gants?

—Oui, là-bas, au fond, Monsieur.

—C'est combien?

—C'est 125 francs.

—Combien coûte l'écharpe bleue?

—Elle coûte 89 francs.

—Combien coûtent les pulls là-bas?

—Le pull rouge coûte 430 francs et les blancs 520.

Do you have gloves?

Yes, over there, in the back, sir.

How much is it?

It's 125 francs.

How much is the blue scarf?

It's 89 francs.

How much are the sweaters over there?

The red sweater costs 430 francs, and the white ones 520.

▶ **Chez les amis on demande…**

—Quoi de neuf?

—Pas grand-chose!

—Qu'est-ce qui se passe?

—Qu'est-ce qui s'est passé?

—Rien d'important.

—Qu'est-ce qu'il y a?

—Qu'est-ce qui ne va pas?

—Frédéric est malade.

What's new?

Not much.

What's going on?

What happened?

Nothing much.

What is the matter?

What's wrong?

Fred is sick.

Interaction   *Une touriste entre dans une boutique.*   (⊙)

L'EMPLOYÉE:	Vous désirez, Madame?
LA TOURISTE:	Vous avez des robes de chambre?
L'EMPLOYÉE:	Oui, de quelle couleur?
LA TOURISTE:	Noire, de préférence°.
L'EMPLOYÉE:	Regardez; ça vous plaît°?
LA TOURISTE:	Oui, c'est combien?
L'EMPLOYÉE:	670 francs en solde°.

de... *preferably*

ça... *do you like it?*

en... *on sale*

Activités

A. Interviews. Interview a classmate to find out the following information:

1. son nom
2. son âge
3. son adresse
4. où il ou elle habite

B. Voyage au Québec. You are traveling in Quebec. Play the following roles with a classmate.

1. You are in Pollack's department store in Quebec and are looking for an article of clothing that you do not see.
2. You see an interesting person while going for a walk on the Terrasse Dufferin in Quebec City and want to start up a conversation with him / her.
3. You run into an old friend you haven't seen for several years.
4. You are reading the menu in the dining room of the Reine Elisabeth Hotel in Montreal, and you come across the name of a dish with which you are not familiar.
5. You want to go on a cruise on the Saint Lawrence (Saint-Laurent) but you are unsure of what weather to expect.
6. You are in the lobby of your hotel, and you see a little boy crying.

Lecture culturelle

Avant la lecture   WWW

Although the adjective **francophone** appeared in *Le Grand Larousse de la langue française* as early as 1930, the noun **francophonie** was not found in French dictionaries until the sixties and seventies. This happened because it took a long time before a consensus on a definition could be reached. For many years, different people gave the term different connotations even though they agreed on a very broad meaning. However, after the first summit meeting of **francophone** heads of state held in Versailles in February 1986, the definition of the word became clearer. All parties recognized that **francophonie** had several meanings; in addition to the linguistic characteristic of people who all speak French, it took on a geographical meaning to designate the countries where French was spoken and a cultural meaning applying to communities in which people shared common values.

Activités

A. Where is English spoken in the world? Are the reasons that so many people speak English the same as the reasons people speak French? Does English sound the same everywhere?

B. French immigrants have had a strong influence in North America. What cities do you know that have French names? What family names do you know that have a French origin?

C. Guess the meanings of the following words that appear in the reading. The words in the left column are near cognates. Those in the right column are related to English words that come from the same word families.

occupé	célèbre *(celebrity)*
nombreuses	diable *(diabolic)*
langues	jour *(journal)*
esclaves	conservé *(conservation)*
emploient	monde *(mundane)*
nom	travail *(travail)*
	nouvelle *(novel)*
	vie *(vital)*

La francophonie

*L*a France, la Belgique, et la Suisse ne sont pas les seuls pays francophones. On parle français dans beaucoup de pays et sur plusieurs° continents. En Amérique du Nord, on utilise le français tous *several*
les jours au Québec, en Nouvelle-Angleterre et en Louisiane; mais il y a aussi des
5   francophones dans l'Ontario et dans les provinces de l'ouest du Canada. Dans les Caraïbes, et en Amérique du Sud, le français est parlé en Haïti, en Martinique, en Guadeloupe et en Guyane. Sur le continent africain, de nombreux pays, comme le Maroc, la Côte d'Ivoire et le Sénégal, ont conservé° l'usage de la   *kept*
langue française.
10   Après la France, c'est au Québec qu'il y a le plus de francophones. Plus de sept millions de Québécois emploient le français à l'école ou à l'université, dans leur travail et en famille. En Louisiane, on trouve trois langues à côté de l'anglais. Certains° parlent le «français grammatical», une variété du français   *Some*
standard. Quelques descendants d'esclaves emploient encore° un créole similaire   *still*
15   à la langue parlée en Haïti, et les descendants des Québécois chassés° du Canada   *forced out*
au dix-huitième siècle° parlent le «cadien», une autre variété de français.   *century*
Dans les pays francophones africains, même si on parle des langues africaines comme le ouolof et le bambara dans la vie de tous les jours, le français est

étudié à l'école, et il reste° la langue de l'administration et la langue littéraire   *remains*
20   principale. Ainsi°, plus de cent millions de personnes° parlent le français comme   *Thus / people*
langue maternelle ou comme langue officielle. Régulièrement, il y a des réunions
des chefs d'Etats francophones et la francophonie joue° un rôle politique et   *plays*
économique important dans le monde.

Après la lecture

Questions sur le texte

1. Où est-ce qu'on parle français en Europe? En Amérique du Nord?
   En Afrique?
2. Est-ce que les Québécois parlent souvent français? Où?
3. Où est-ce qu'on parle français aux Etats-Unis?
4. Le ouolof et le bambara sont-ils une variété du français?
5. Combien de personnes parlent français dans le monde?

Activité

The following famous people were associated with the French-speaking world.
Can you match the person with the modern name of the country?

1. le Dr. Albert Schweitzer   a. le Zaïre (l'ancien [*former*]
2. le Dr. David Livingstone et   Congo belge)
   Sir Henry M. Stanley   b. la Guyane (l'île du Diable)
3. Papillon   c. le Gabon
4. Jean-Jacques Rousseau   d. le Canada (Québec)
5. Georges Simenon   e. la Belgique
6. Lucien Bouchard   f. la Suisse

Vocabulaire

Noms / Pronoms

achats	purchases	jean	jeans
bagages	luggage	jupe	skirt
bagages à main	hand luggage	lunettes de soleil	sunglasses
botte	boot	maillot de bain	bathing suit
ceinture	belt	manteau	coat
chapeau	hat	mois	month
chaussettes	socks	omelette	omelet
chaussures	shoes	pantalon	pants
chemise	shirt	parapluie	umbrella
chemise de nuit	nightgown	pâtes	noodles
chemisier	blouse	Petites Antilles	Lesser Antilles
costume	suit	poche	pocket
couleur	color	polo	polo shirt
courses	errands	pull	pullover
cravate	tie	pyjama	pajamas
créole	Creole	robe	dress
crêpe	crepe	robe de chambre	robe
département	department (administrative division)	sandwich	sandwich
		short	shorts
		tee-shirt	T-shirt
écharpe	scarf	tennis	tennis
elle	her	touriste	tourist
été	summer	valise	suitcase
eux	them	veste	coat / jacket
gant	glove	veston	coat
hiver	winter	vêtements	clothes
idée	idea	voyage organisé	tour
imperméable	raincoat		

Verbes

acheter	to buy	oublier	to forget
coûter	to cost	penser à	to think about
emporter	to take	porter	to wear
faire	to do / to make		

Adjectifs / Adverbes

bleu	blue	peu	little
bon(ne)	good	prêt	ready
brun	brown	québécois	from Quebec
déjà	already	quel	what / which
gris	gray	récemment	recently
hier	yesterday	rien	nothing
jaune	yellow	sa	his / her / its
leur(s)	their	ses	his / her / its
ma	my	son	his / her / its
même	same	super	super
mes	my	ta	your
mon	my	tes	your
noir	black	trop	too
nos	our	vert	green
notre	our	vos	your
parfait	perfect	votre	your

Expressions

à l'extérieur	outside	faire la lessive	to do the laundry
avoir l'air	to look like	faire la queue	to stand in line
bien sûr	of course	faire la vaisselle	to do the dishes
Ça y est!	That's it!	faire le ménage	to clean
être à	to belong to	faire les bagages	to pack
faire attention	to pay attention	faire les valises	to pack the suitcases
faire beau	to be nice weather	faire mauvais	to be bad weather
faire chaud	to be hot	faire un régime	to be on a diet
faire des courses	to run errands	faire un tour	to go for a walk
faire des devoirs	to do homework	faire un voyage	to take a trip
faire du sport	to play sports	faire une promenade	to go for a walk
faire froid	to be cold	pas encore	not yet
faire la cuisine	to cook	quelque chose	something
faire la grasse matinée	to sleep late	tous les ans	every year

6

Chapitre

Les transports

Commençons

Grammaire

Communiquons

Lecture culturelle

Vocabulaire

L'Eurostar

Objectives

Language

Vocabulary for means of transportation • The sounds / y /, / u / and / ɥ / •
Passé composé with **être** • Inversion and interrogative adverbs • **-re** verbs •
Telling time

Culture

Subway system of Paris • The 24-hour clock • **L'Eurotunnel**

Communication

Expressing how to get places • Talking about events in the past • Asking
questions • Telling time

Commençons

Dans le métro 🔲 ⊙   WWW

Un soir, Chantal a retrouvé ses amis Hélène et Richard à la station Nation. Ils ont décidé d'aller à un concert de rock au Palais Omnisport de Bercy.

CHANTAL: Salut, les copains! J'attends depuis longtemps, moi!

HÉLÈNE: Salut, Chantal! On a un gros problème. Richard a oublié nos billets dans la poche de son imperméable.

RICHARD: On a changé à Gare du Nord et quand je suis descendu, j'ai laissé mon imper sur la banquette.

HÉLÈNE: Nous sommes allés au bout de la ligne pour rien. Heureusement, le bureau des objets trouvés est ouvert le soir.

CHANTAL: C'est au métro Plaisance. Allons-y!

Au bureau des objets trouvés

Les trois jeunes gens sont arrivés au bureau et ils parlent avec l'employé.

L'EMPLOYÉ: C'est à qui?

HÉLÈNE: C'est à nous. Est-ce qu'on a rapporté un imperméable?

L'EMPLOYÉ: Comment est-il?

RICHARD: Il est beige avec une ceinture.

L'EMPLOYÉ: Est-ce qu'il est avec les manteaux là-bas?

RICHARD: Oui, justement.

L'employé donne l'imperméable à Richard. Richard cherche dans la poche et trouve les billets.

RICHARD: Quelle chance! Voilà les billets. Il est huit heures et on a encore le temps de prendre un pot avant le début du concert.

Etudions les dialogues

A. Dans le métro

     1.   Où est Chantal?
     2.   Qu'est-ce qu'elle va faire avec ses amis?
     3.   Quelle sorte de problème est-ce que Richard et Hélène ont?
     4.   Où est-ce que Richard a laissé son imperméable?

B. Au bureau des objets trouvés

     1.   Les trois amis, avec qui parlent-ils au bureau des objets trouvés?
     2.   Comment est l'imperméable de Richard?
     3.   Est-ce que l'employé a l'imperméable?
     4.   Est-ce que les billets sont toujours dans la poche de l'imperméable?

Mots clés

métro	*subway*	laissé (laisser)	*left*
retrouvé (retrouver)	*met*	imper	*raincoat*
station	*metro stop*	banquette	*seat*
ont décidé d' (décider de)	*decided*	allés (aller)	*went*
concert	*concert*	bout	*end*
attends (attendre)	*waited*	ligne	*line*
depuis longtemps	*for a long time*	pour rien	*for nothing*
gros(-se)	*big*	heureusement	*fortunately*
problème	*problem*	bureau des objets trouvés	*lost and found*
billets *(m.)*	*tickets*	Allons-y!	*Let's go!*
changé (changer)	*changed*	Quelle chance!	*What luck!*
employé *(m.)*	*employee*	huit heures	*eight o'clock*
C'est à qui?	*Whose turn is it?*	encore	*still*
rapporté (rapporter)	*brought back*	temps	*time*
Comment est-il?	*What is it like?*	prendre un pot	*to have a drink*
beige	*beige*	avant	*before*
justement	*as a matter of fact*	début	*beginning*
descendu (descendre)	*got off*		

Faisons connaissance

The **métro** in Paris is a system of one hundred miles of rails connected with the **RER (Réseau Express Régional)**, a network of suburban lines. It is not only a very efficient system of transportation, it is also one of the easiest to use. Thanks to the numerous **correspondances** (stations where you can change lines), the **métro** is the fastest way to get from one point to another in Paris. Because you

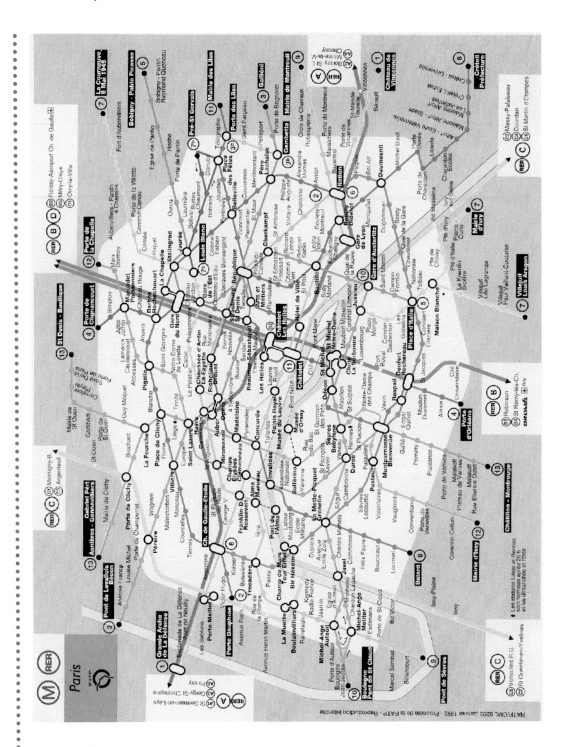

go any distance on one ticket, travel is very inexpensive. Rather than buy one ticket (**un ticket**) at a time, it is more economical to buy a booklet (**un carnet**) of ten tickets or a **carte orange,** which permits unlimited travel for specified periods of time. All of these are also valid on the bus system.

Work is constantly being done to enlarge and improve the **métro.** The old rails have been replaced, and most trains now run on rubber tires rather than on metal wheels. Some **stations** (**Louvre**, **Franklin Roosevelt**, and **Chaussée d'Antin**) are quite artistically decorated. Other stations (**Opéra**) are true commercial centers with many underground shops. Of course, the traditional accordion and guitar players performing for tips are still seen in the **métro**. In the near future, tickets will be replaced by cards with chips similar to the *Télécartes* currently used to make phone calls.

Enrichissons notre vocabulaire

Les transports (*m.*) *(Forms of transportation)*

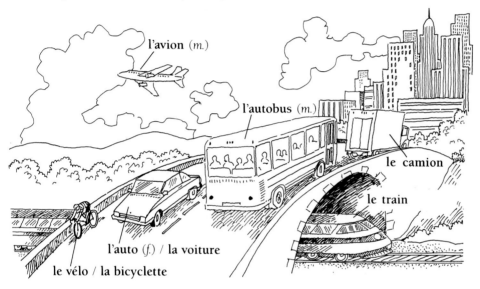

l'avion (*m.*)

l'autobus (*m.*)

le camion

le train

l'auto (*f.*) / la voiture

le vélo / la bicyclette

Comment est-ce qu'on voyage? *(How does one travel?)*

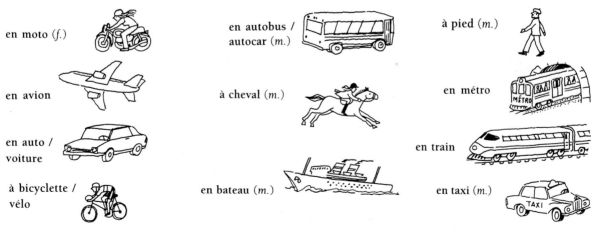

en moto (*f.*)

en autobus / autocar (*m.*)

à pied (*m.*)

en avion

à cheval (*m.*)

en métro

en auto / voiture

en train

à bicyclette / vélo

en bateau (*m.*)

en taxi (*m.*)

Est-ce qu'on va aller en ville en auto?
Non, **faisons du stop!**

Are we going to go to town by car?
*No, let's **hitchhike**!*

Prononciation   The sounds / y /, / u / and / ɥ /   ☐▭☐

A. You have already encountered the sound / y / several times in words such as **tu** and **du**. It is always represented in writing by the letter **u** and must not be confused with the sound / u /, written **ou** (**nous, vous**). The / y / sound is produced with the tongue forward in the mouth and lips rounded. The easiest way to say it is to pronounce the / i / sound (as in **si**) and then round your lips without moving your tongue.

Repeat the following pairs of words, which differ only in lip rounding.

/ i / (unrounded)	/ y / (rounded)
si	su
dit	du
fit	fut
J	jus
qui	Q
rit	rue

Repeat these pairs, which differ only in tongue position, after your teacher.

/ u / (back)	/ y / (front)
où	U
bout	bu
nous	nu
sous	su
tout	tu
vous	vu

B. When the / y / sound is followed by another vowel sound, it is pronounced in a shorter fashion, but still with the lips rounded and the tongue forward. Many English speakers attempting to pronounce **lui** (/ lɥi /) say / lwi / instead, which is understood as **Louis**.

Practice the / ɥ / sound, called a *semi-vowel,* by repeating the following words after your teacher.

> lui / cuisine / je suis / huit / huile / ennuyeux / affectueux / tout de suite / la Suisse

Exercice

Read the following sentences aloud, paying particular attention to the vowel sounds / y / and / ɥ /.

1. Je suis curieux.
2. Tu étudies avec lui?
3. Lucie trouve vos chaussures ridicules.
4. Ils sont étudiants à l'université de Tours.
5. Luc a eu huit amis chez lui.
6. Je suis allé avec lui au Portugal.

Grammaire

I. The passé composé with être

You use the **passé composé** to tell what happened in the past.

A. In the last chapter, you learned the formation of the **passé composé** using the conjugated form of **avoir** and the past participle.

> **Chantal a retrouvé ses amis.**

B. There are about twenty verbs in French that use **être** and not **avoir** as the auxiliary verb in the formation of the **passé composé**. The verb **aller** is one of them; you will learn it and five other **être** verbs in this section.

passé composé of **aller**	
je **suis allé(e)**	nous **sommes allé(e)s**
tu **es allé(e)**	vous **êtes allé(e)(s)**
il **est allé**	ils **sont allés**
elle **est allée**	elles **sont allées**
on **est allé(e)(s)**	

Nous **sommes allés** au bout de la ligne.

Mots clés	*Some common verbs conjugated* with **être**	
	infinitives	*past participles*
aller	*to go*	allé
arriver	*to arrive*	arrivé
monter	*to get on; to go up*	monté
naître	*to be born*	né
rentrer	*to return*	rentré
rester	*to stay*	resté

Les trois jeunes gens **sont arrivés** au bureau.
Il **est rentré** chez lui et **est monté** dans sa chambre.
Ma mère **est née** aux Etats-Unis.

L'orthographe

1. Note that, unlike verbs conjugated with **avoir**, verbs conjugated with **être** show agreement in number and gender between the subject and the past participle. This can lead to a number of forms with the same subject. You must use the correct agreement when writing to make your meaning clear.

Vous êtes **allé** au café?	*(if you are talking to a man)*
Vous êtes **allée** au café?	*(if you are talking to a woman)*
Vous êtes **allés** au café?	*(if you are talking to a group of men or of men and women)*
Vous êtes **allées** au café?	*(if you are talking to a group of women)*

2. The agreement of the past participle with the verbs listed above never causes a change in pronunciation: **Vous êtes arrivé** and **Vous êtes arrivées** are pronounced alike.

Attention!

With **aller** and **arriver** there is almost always a **liaison** with three forms of **être: suis, est,** and **sont.**

Je suis_allée à Québec.
Il est_arrivé en autobus.
Elles sont_arrivées de Paris.

Language

A. Mon retour. Chantal has just returned from vacation. Change her sentences to the **passé composé.**

1. Je rentre de mes vacances en France.
2. Nous arrivons à Paris en autocar.
3. Nous restons quinze jours.
4. Je montre mes photos à mes amis.
5. Vous allez souvent en France?
6. Chantal est contente de ses vacances!

B. Leurs activités. Describe the activities of the following people by replacing the italicized words with each of the suggested phrases.

1. Jacqueline *est allée au musée.* (visiter une église / monter à la tour Eiffel / dîner au restaurant / rentrer à l'hôtel en taxi)
2. Georges *n'a pas trouvé son parapluie.* (chercher chez lui / aller au bureau des objets trouvés / rentrer chez lui)
3. Est-ce que tu *es arrivé en retard?* (faire tes devoirs / rester à la bibliothèque / avoir beaucoup à faire / rentrer à bicyclette ou en moto)

Culture

C. Personnages célèbres. Match the famous French people with what they did.

1. Jacques Cartier   a. aller jusqu'en Espagne
2. Charles de Gaulle   b. naître en Pologne
3. Napoléon   c. arriver au Canada en 1534
4. Marie Curie   d. naître en Corse
5. Charlemagne   e. monter en avion en 1890
6. Clément Ader   f. rester en Angleterre

D. Les trains en France. France is a world leader in public transportation. Form sentences with the words that follow and indicate what the French have already done (**... déjà...**) and have not yet done (**ne... pas encore...**) with trains.

MODEL: aller à 300 km/h
On est déjà allé à trois cents kilomètres à l'heure.

1. monter de Lyon à Paris en deux heures
2. aller en Angleterre
3. préparer des dîners élégants
4. aller à Nice et rentrer à Paris dans la journée *(day)*
5. arriver de Madrid à la gare du Nord
6. aller au sommet du mont Blanc

Communication

E. Les vacances de mon professeur. You spied on your French teacher the last time he or she was in Paris. Make a report using the following questions as a guide.

Il / Elle... rester à l'hôtel? monter à la tour Eiffel?
acheter des souvenirs? aller en métro à Pigalle?
oublier son passeport à la banque? visiter des musées?
fréquenter les bars? consommer trop de vin?
ne (n')... pas rentrer à l'hôtel?

F. Nos activités. Tell what you, your friends, and your family did at the times given below. Add original sentences to develop a complete picture.

1. Hier, je (j')... aller à la bibliothèque? acheter... ? faire mon français? arriver en classe en retard? rester chez moi?
2. Le week-end dernier, mes amis... faire un tour en auto? aller au parc? monter à cheval? rentrer chez eux? faire du sport?
3. L'été dernier, mes parents et moi, nous... aller en vacances? rester en ville? monter en avion? voyager.... ? faire beaucoup de promenades?

G. **Questions personnelles.** Vos activités récentes. Pretend you are interviewing a person on the street for a French news report and make a summary for your audience.

1. Où est-ce que vous êtes allé(e) le week-end dernier? Comment?
2. Qu'est-ce que vous avez fait?
3. Combien de temps êtes-vous resté(e) là-bas?
4. Vous êtes rentré(e) chez vos parents récemment? Quand?
5. Est-ce que vous êtes resté(e) chez vous hier?
6. Est-ce que vous êtes arrivé(e) en retard ce matin? Pourquoi?

II. Inversion and interrogative adverbs

You use interrogative adverbs to ask questions when you are seeking specific information. Inversion adds a more formal style to your questions.

A. Questions with inversion

1. In Chapter 1 you learned three ways of asking a question in French: *rising intonation*, **Est-ce que**, and **n'est-ce pas**. Another way to form a question is through *inversion*, in which you invert the pronoun subject and the verb.

    Vous travaillez ici?   **Travaillez-vous** ici?
    Ils font un régime?   **Font-ils** un régime?

2. When the subject is a noun, you add a pronoun subject of the same number and gender, in the inverted position.

    Les Français font du sport?   **Les Français font-ils** du sport?
    Jacques et Marie vont au cinéma   **Jacques et Marie vont-ils** au
      ce soir?   cinéma ce soir?

3. In the third-person singular, you must add a **t** between hyphens for all forms of verbs not ending in a written **t**.

    Parle-t-on français ici?   *but:*
    A-t-il chaud?
    Ecoute-t-elle la radio?   Etienne **est-il** arrivé à pied?

4. Inversion is usually avoided when **je** is the subject. Use **Est-ce que** instead.

> **Est-ce que je** suis en retard?　　　**Est-ce que j'**ai bien fait?

5. When there are two verbs in a sentence, as in the **futur proche** and the **passé composé,** you invert the conjugated verb and the pronoun.

> **Allons-nous faire** du stop?　　　**A-t-elle visité** la Martinique?

6. In the negative interrogative, the **ne... pas** surrounds both the conjugated verb and the pronoun subject.

> **Ne va-t-il pas faire** la vaisselle?　　　Les gens **ne sont-ils pas rentrés?**

7. You must pay attention to the style you use when asking questions. The most formal type would be one with inversion.

> **Y a-t-il** une pharmacie près d'ici?

The next most formal is the use of **Est-ce que.**

> **Est-ce qu'**il y a une pharmacie près d'ici?

The most informal is the use of rising intonation.

> Il y a une pharmacie près d'ici?

B.　Inversion with interrogative adverbs

1. Inversion is frequently used with interrogative adverbs.

> **Combien de** frères **as-tu?**　　　**Pourquoi n'êtes-vous pas arrivés**
> **Comment vont-ils** à Québec?　　　ensemble?
> **Où faites-vous** du sport?　　　**Quand vont-elles** au restaurant?

Mots clés	*Interrogative adverbs*		
Combien de?	*How much?, How many?*	**Pourquoi?**	*Why?*
Comment?	*How?*	**Quand?**	*When?*
Où?	*Where?*	ici	here

2. Inversion is common with **où,** and the repetition of the pronoun subject is not necessary with the present tense.

> **Où** se trouve le bureau des objets trouvés?
> **Où** habitent les Morin?

Ce qu'ils disent

1. Inversion is very common in English (*Is he studying? What is he studying?*), but in French, it shows a more formal style. In conversation, rising intonation and **est-ce que** are more common.

2. In a very familiar style, the French do use interrogative adverbs without inversion or **est-ce que**. They also place all the interrogative adverbs except **pourquoi** at the end of the sentence. Be aware, however, that these two structures may be too informal for many situations you will encounter.

Où tu vas?
Comment il est, ton imper?
Tu as combien de frères?

Tu arrives quand?
C'est combien?
Pourquoi vous n'allez pas au restaurant?

Language

A. On va au concert. Change the following questions with **est-ce que** to the inverted form to make them more formal.

1. Est-ce que tu vas au concert ce soir?
2. Est-ce que Monique a invité ses amis?
3. Où est-ce que nous allons aller après?
4. Comment est-ce qu'on va aller en ville?
5. Quand est-ce que vous allez arriver ici?
6. Pourquoi est-ce que vos amis ne sont pas encore arrivés?

B. Un procès. You are a district attorney and are charged with eliciting the following information during a trial. What questions would you ask?

1. Oui, Je suis né aux Etats-Unis.
2. J'habite à New York.
3. Je suis allé au cinéma l'apres-midi.
4. Parce que j'aime le cinéma!
5. Un billet coûte huit dollars.
6. J'ai trouvé le film ennuyeux.

Culture

C. Jean-Paul et sa famille. You have just made friends with Jean-Paul, and he has invited you home to meet his family. Ask questions to find out the information listed below. Make two sets of questions, one in an informal style for Jean-Paul, and the other in a more formal style to ask Jean-Paul's parents about him.

MODEL: aimer / télévision
(*à Jean-Paul*) *Tu aimes la télé?*
(*à ses parents*) *Jean-Paul aime-t-il la télévision?*

1. Où / naître
2. Combien / frères / sœurs
3. Pourquoi / étudier l'anglais
4. Comment / aller en cours
5. Quand / arriver à la fac
6. Où / aller en vacances

j'attends

tu descends

il entend

nous perdons

vous perdez patience

ils rendent

je rends visite à

tu réponds à

il vend

...nversion, ask questions to elicit
...ort to the class.

...rquoi il / elle est à l'université
...ment il / elle va en classe
... / elle est allé(e) en vacances

...1?
...près le travail?

...cela?
...lic? Comment sont vos

...ing.

...verbs with infinitives ending in **-re** drop the **-re** and add the following endings:

attendre *(to wait for)*	
j' **attends**	nous **attendons**
tu **attends**	vous **attendez**
il/ elle / on **attend**	ils / elles **attendent**
Passé composé: il **a attendu**	

Mots clés

attendre	*to wait for*	rendre	*to give back, to return*
descendre	*to go down, come down; to get off*	rendre visite à	*to visit (a person)*
entendre	*to hear*	répondre à	*to answer*
perdre	*to lose*	vendre	*to sell*
perdre patience	*to lose patience*		

Où est-ce qu'on **vend** des vêtements?
Les étudiants **attendent** leur professeur.

B. The final **d** of the third-person singular of **-re** verbs has a / t / sound with inversion, so using **-t-** is not necessary.

    Répond-il à ta lettre?

C. The imperative of **-re** verbs is regular; the **s** is not deleted from the **tu** form.

    Descendons maintenant!   **Attendez** à la station.
    Ne **perds** pas ton imper!

D. The past participle is formed by dropping **-re** and adding **u.**

    J'ai **perdu** mon vélo.   Il a **vendu** sa maison.

E. **Descendre** is conjugated with **être** in the **passé composé.**

    Nous sommes **descendus** à Juan-les-Pins.

Attention!

The différence in pronunciation between the singular and plural third-person forms in the present tense is the / d / sound. You must make an extra effort to pronounce this sound when using the plural form of the verb to distinguish it clearly from the singular form.

il perd   / il pɛr /   ils perdent   / il pɛʀd /
elle rend   / ɛl rã /   elles rendent   / ɛl ʀãd /

Language

A. **La journée de François.** Tell what François and his friends are doing by conjugating the verbs in the following sentences.

    1.   François (attendre) ses amis ici.
    2.   Ils (descendre) en ville ensemble.
    3.   François (vendre) des chaussures dans un magasin.
    4.   Moi, je (perdre) patience quand il est en retard.
    5.   Le soir, nous (rendre visite) à un ami malade.
    6.   Notre ami (entendre) nos questions, mais il (ne... pas répondre).

B. **A l'aéroport.** Complete the following paragraph by adding the appropriate form of **-re** verbs.

Je suis à l'aéroport Charles-de-Gaulle à Roissy, près de Paris.
J(e) _____ l'avion pour New York. J(e) _____ mon imperméable et je demande à un employé où est le bureau des objets trouvés. Il _____ :
«_____ . Vous allez le trouver en face du magasin où on _____ des vêtements.» J(e) _____ et je vois un autre employé. «Pardon, Monsieur.
J(e) _____ mon imperméable. L'a-t-on trouvé?» Il ne _____ pas et j(e) _____ patience.

Culture

C. **Qui a perdu?** In the following famous confrontations with French people, tell who lost.

MODEL: Jacques Chirac / François Mitterrand en 1988
              Jacques Chirac a perdu en 1988.

    1.   les Anglais / Guillaume le Conquérant en 1066
    2.   les Français / les Anglais dans la guerre de Sept Ans

3. Danton / Robespierre pendant la Révolution
4. Les Français / les Prussiens en 1871
5. les Allemands / les résistants en 1945
6. Lionel Jospin / Jacques Chirac en 1995

Communication

D. J'ai perdu la tête! Interview a classmate to discuss something each of you lost recently. Use the following questions to prepare a report to the class.

Qu'est-ce que vous avez perdu récemment? votre transistor? votre stylo? vos clés? votre portefeuille? votre argent? votre calculette? votre livre de français? Pendant combien de temps l'avez-vous cherché? Où? Vous avez perdu patience?

E. Questions personelles. Vos habitudes.

1. Chez vous, qui répond au téléphone?
2. Quand est-ce que vous ne répondez pas?
3. Qu'est-ce que vous n'aimez pas entendre?
4. Faites-vous du sport? Dans quel sport perdez-vous souvent?
5. A qui désirez-vous rendre visite?
6. Vous rendez vos livres à la bibliothèque toujours à temps?
7. Qu'est-ce que vous avez vendu récemment?
8. Qui perd patience avec vous?

IV. Telling time

A. To ask about and tell time in French, use the following expressions.

Quelle heure est-il?	*What time is it?*
Il est une heure.	*It is one o'clock.*
Il est deux heures.	*It is two o'clock.*

B. To express minutes after the hour until the half hour, you add the minutes or the following expressions:

Il est **trois heures dix.**	*It is ten after three.*
Il est **six heures et quart.**	*It is a quarter after six.* / *It is six fifteen.*
Il est **sept heures et demie.**	*It is half past seven.* / *It is seven thirty.*

C. To express time falling within thirty minutes of the next hour, you subtract the time from the hour.

Il est **huit heures moins vingt.**	*It is seven forty.* / *It is twenty to eight.*
Il est **onze heures moins cinq.**	*It is ten fifty-five.* / *It is five to eleven.*
Il est **neuf heures mois le quart.**	*It is eight forty-five.* / *It is a quarter to nine.*

D. There are special terms for *noon* and *midnight*.

Il est **midi.**	*It is noon.*
Il est **minuit.**	*It is midnight.*

> ### L'orthographe
>
> 1. Because **heure** is feminine, **demie** following **heure** is also feminine: **une heure et demie.**
> 2. **Midi** and **minuit** are masculine, so **demi** does not take a final **e** with either term: **midi et demi, minuit et demi.**
> 3. **Demi(e)** is never plural: **trois heures et demie.**
> 4. When writing a time in numbers, the French separate the hours and minutes with an **h** or a period, not a colon.
>
> 2 h 30   **deux heures et demie**   5.10   **cinq heures dix**

E. To express A.M. and P.M. in French, use **du matin** (from midnight to noon), **de l'après-midi** (from noon until about six), and **du soir** (from about six until midnight).

Il est trois heures **du matin.**	*It is 3 A.M.*
Il est quatre heures et demie **de l'après-midi.**	*It is 4:30 P.M.*
Il est onze heures **du soir.**	*It is 11 P.M.*

F. To express other time relationships, use the following expressions:

à *at, to*	**jusqu'à** *until*	**à l'heure** *on time*
de *from*	**en avance** *early*	**en retard** *late*
entre *between*		

—**A** quelle heure est-ce que vous dînez?	*At what time do you have dinner?*
—Je dîne **à** six heures et quart.	*I have dinner at 6:15.*
Je suis en cours **de** huit heures **à** trois heures.	*I'm in class from 8 to 3.*
J'étudie **jusqu'à** minuit.	*I study until midnight.*
Nous regardons la télé **entre** sept et dix heures.	*We watch TV between 7 and 10.*
—Arrivent-ils **en avance?**	*Do they arrive early?*
—Non, elle, elle est toujours **à l'heure**; lui, il est toujours **en retard.**	*No, she is always on time; he is always late.*

Language

A. **L'heure.** Quelle heure est-il?

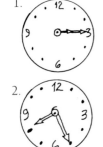

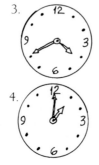

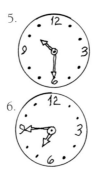

B. **Robert est paresseux!** Robert and Marianne go out together, but Robert is always fifteen minutes late. If Marianne arrives at the following times, when does Robert arrive?

1. 11:00 A.M.
2. 12:00 P.M.
3. 8:15 P.M.
4. 11:45 P.M.
5. 3:30 P.M.
6. 10:20 P.M.

Culture

C. **Allons au cinéma.** You have only two days in Paris and must make the most of your time if you want to fit in a movie. To arrive exactly at the beginning of the film (**à deux heures et demie de l'après-midi**), count back to see when you must leave the hotel.

1. le film commence (2 h 30)
2. le début de la séance (15 minutes)
3. descendre du métro, aller à pied jusqu'au cinéma (6 minutes)
4. correspondance, deuxième métro (12 minutes)
5. monter dans le métro, aller à Châtelet (12 minutes)
6. aller de l'hôtel à la station de métro (15 minutes)

Communication

D. **Dans ma ville.** Tell at what time of day these things occur on your campus or in town.

1. Les premiers cours de la journée commencent à…
2. Moi, j'ai des cours entre… et…
3. Les films commencent à…
4. Les matchs de football américain sont à…
5. Les bars vendent de l'alcool jusqu'à…
6. Les cafés sont ouverts jusqu'à…

E. **Questions personnelles.** Mon emploi du temps (*schedule*).

1. A quelle heure est-ce que vous arrivez en cours?
2. Arrivez-vous en avance ou en retard?
3. Jusqu'à quelle heure est-ce que vous êtes à l'université?
4. A quelle heure est-ce que vous dînez?
5. Jusqu'à quelle heure est-ce que vous étudiez le soir?
6. Vous parlez au téléphone / regardez la télé jusqu'à quelle heure?

Communiquons

Utiliser l'heure officielle

The way that you just learned to tell time is called **l'heure conventionnelle,** and it is used primarily in informal conversations. In more formal situations such as those involving train or plane schedules, store hours, television schedules, and times of appointments, you will need to use **l'heure officielle,** which is based upon the twenty-four-hour clock.

In official time, times from midnight to noon are expressed as **zéro heure** to **douze heures**. To express a time from noon to midnight, continue counting the hours from twelve to twenty-four. Official time never uses the expressions **et quart, demi(e),** or **moins le quart.** You simply count the total number of minutes past the hour and use **quinze, trente,** and **quarante-cinq** respectively.

Expressions

▶ **On donne l'heure de minuit à midi.**

Le train arrive à six heures.	*The train arrives at 6 A.M.*
La classe commence à huit heures.	*The class begins at 8 A.M.*
Le camion arrive à onze heures quinze.	*The truck arrives at 11:15 A.M.*
J'attends l'autocar de neuf heures trente.	*I'm waiting for the 9:30 bus.*

▶ **On donne l'heure de midi à minuit.**

J'arrive à treize heures.	*I am arriving at 1 P.M.*
Le restau-U ferme à vingt et une heures.	*The university restaurant closes at 9 P.M.*
Le film commence à dix-neuf heures quarante-cinq.	*The film starts at 7:45 P.M.*
Le parc ferme à vingt-quatre heures.	*The park closes at midnight.*

Interaction *M. Robert va acheter un billet de train pour Marseille.*

M. ROBERT: Pardon, Monsieur, à quelle heure est le prochain train pour Marseille?

L'EMPLOYÉ: Il y a un express° à quatorze heures cinq et un rapide° à quinze heures trente.

local / express

M. ROBERT: A quelle heure arrivent-ils?

L'EMPLOYÉ: L'express à une heure dix, mais le rapide à zéro heure vingt-cinq.

M. ROBERT: L'express arrive après le rapide?

L'EMPLOYÉ: Oui, le rapide a moins d'arrêts.

Activités

A. **L'heure officielle.** Convert the following times in the conversational style to the more formal style (**l'heure officielle**).

1. deux heures du matin
2. trois heures et quart du matin
3. onze heures et demie du matin

4. midi vingt-cinq
5. une heure moins le quart de l'après-midi
6. quatre heures cinq de l'après-midi
7. neuf heures moins dix du soir
8. minuit moins le quart

B. L'heure conventionnelle. Convert the following official times to the conversational style. Do not forget to indicate whether it is A.M. or P.M.

1. trois heures	4. quatorze heures quarante
2. cinq heures quinze	5. vingt-deux heures dix
3. douze heures trente	6. zéro heure quinze

C. Le tunnel sous la Manche. Consult the schedule for the Chunnel train to answer the questions below. Note that England is one hour behind France.

1. Où est-ce qu'on va à Paris pour avoir un train pour Londres?
2. Le train numéro 9011 arrive à Londres à quelle heure?
3. Vous arrivez à quelle gare?
4. Il faut combien de temps pour aller de Paris à Londres?
5. Le train numéro 9113 passe par quelle ville?
6. Vous êtes à Lille l'après-midi, et vous désirez aller à Bruxelles. Par quel train allez-vous?   WWW

PARIS-LONDRES		**DU LUNDI AU SAMEDI**						**DIMANCHE**					
Train No	8007	8011	8027	9043	9047	9051	9055	9011	9027	9043	9047	9051	9059
Paris-Nord	07.13	08.10	12.12	16.06	17.09	18.18	19.08	08.07	12.12	16.06	17.09	18.18	20.11
Calais-Fréthun	08.39	-	-	-	-	-	-	09.36	-	-	-	-	-
Londres-Waterloo	09.20*	10.13	14.13	18.09	19.09	20.13	21.13	10.26	14.30	18.09	19.09	20.13	22.09

★ 08.13 le samedi

Calais - Fréthun n'est pas desservi par Eurostar au départ de Paris.

Eurostar 9043   Circule à partir du 3 avril : uniquement les vendredis et dimanches, sauf les 16 et 30 avril, les 7 et 26 mai ; circule en outre le 24 mai.

Eurostar 9051   Du 27 février au 2 avril : circule uniquement les vendredis et dimanches ; à partir du 3 avril : circule tous les jours.

LONDRES-PARIS		**DU LUNDI AU SAMEDI**						**DIMANCHE**					
Train No	9006	9010	9028	9042	9044	9048	9052	9018	9028	9038	9044	9048	9052
Londres-Waterloo	07.23	08.23	12.53	16.23	16.48	17.48*	18.53	10.10	12.53	15.23	16.53	17.53	18.53
Calais-Fréthun	-	-	-	-	-	-	-	-	-	-	20.28	-	-
Paris-Nord	11.24	12.24	16.54	20.23	20.57	21.57	22.52	14.22	16.54	19.24	20.57	21.57	22.52

★ 17.53 le samedi

Eurostar 9044   Circule uniquement les vendredis et dimanches sauf le 14 avril ; circule en outre le 13 avril.

Eurostar 9052   Du 27 février au 2 avril : circule uniquement les dimanches ; à partir du 3 avril : circule tous les jours.

Eurostar 9038   Circule à partir du 3 avril : uniquement les dimanches sauf les 16 et 30 avril, les 7 et 25 mai.

BRUXELLES-LONDRES	**DU LUNDI AU SAMEDI**			**DIMANCHE**		
Train No	9113	9133	9157	9121	9141	9161
Bruxelles-Midi	07.31	12.31	18.26	09.28	14.26	19.28
Lille-Europe	08.44	-	19.39	10.41	-	20.41
Londres-Waterloo	09.43	14.43	20.39	11.43	16.39	21.39

LONDRES-BRUXELLES	**DU LUNDI AU SAMEDI**			**DIMANCHE**		
Train No	9110	9132	9152	9116	9138	9152
Londres-Waterloo	06.57	12.27	17.15*	08.14	13.10	17.27
Lille-Europe	09.57	-	20.28	11.27	-	20.28
Bruxelles-Midi	11.08	16.44	21.39	12.38	17.38	21.39

★17.27 le samedi

Attention! –Les 8 et 25 mai, les horaires d'Eurostar sont ceux du dimanche.
   –Les horaires des 9, 11, 15, 16, 17 avril et 1er mai sont susceptibles d'être légèrement modifiés : renseignez-vous en gare ou auprès de votre agence de voyages.
   –Vous devez enregistrer au plus tard 20 mn avant le départ du train.
   –Les horaires sont indiqués en heure locale.

Lecture culturelle

Avant la lecture

WWW

Linking France and England near Calais and Folkestone, the Channel Tunnel has two single-track rail tunnels and a service tunnel. A shuttle train carries cars and passengers, and freight and passenger trains use the same tunnels. The total traveling time varies between thirty-five minutes and one hour depending on whether you are traveling by car or by train. The system operates seven days a week, and shuttles leave so frequently that there is no need to arrive at the terminal a long time ahead. Tickets can be purchased in advance at any travel agency or they can be bought at the ticket booth.

Two kinds of shuttles are available: a heavy-goods shuttle with partially open cars that transport trucks, and a passenger-vehicle shuttle, the length of eight soccer fields, that accommodates cars, buses, and motorcycles. Motorists can either remain in their cars or move about the air-conditioned shuttle.

L'Eurotunnel

Activités

A. Try to imagine various reasons why some English people on one side, and some French people on the other, may not be happy to see England and France linked by a tunnel.

B. Scan the following reading to find the verbs used in the **passé composé**. Separate the instances of a **passé composé** with **être** and the examples of a **passé composé** with **avoir**.

L'Eurotunnel: L'Angleterre n'est plus° une île°

n'... no more / island

*P*our Shakespeare, l'Angleterre était «Cette pierre° précieuse sertie dans l'argent de la mer°». Cette splendide isolation est maintenant finie. La frontière maritime entre l'Angleterre et la France, entre l'Angleterre et le Continent, a disparu. Tout le monde° n'est pas content et
5 beaucoup d'Anglais pensent comme leur Premier ministre, Lord Palmerston, qui s'est opposé à un projet de tunnel en 1858 parce qu'un tunnel raccourcirait° «une distance que nous trouvons déjà trop courte°». Cependant, une attirance° mutuelle unit les Français et les Anglais et le développement du tourisme entre les deux pays le prouve°.

10 Aujourd'hui, vous montez à bord de l'Eurostar, un superbe TGV° jaune et noir, à la gare du Nord, Paris. Le train quitte la capitale française à sept heures. Après un copieux petit déjeuner, l'Eurotunnel est en vue vers° huit heures et demie. Quelques minutes de traversée°, et le Kent constitue votre premier contact avec la Grande-Bretagne. A 160 kilomètres/heure°, l'Eurostar vous
15 emmène° au cœur° de Londres. Vous entrez dans la nouvelle gare de Waterloo quand Big Ben sonne° neuf heures. Le voyage a duré° trois heures dans des conditions de confort fantastiques. Mais avec le décalage horaire° entre les deux pays, vous êtes au centre de la capitale britannique à l'ouverture° des bureaux° et des magasins.

stone
sertie... set in the silver sea

everybody

would shorten
short / attraction

le... proves it
train à grande vitesse *(bullet train)*
around
crossing
160... 100 miles per hour
takes / heart
rings / lasted
décalage... *time difference*
opening / offices

Après la lecture

Questions sur le texte

1. A quoi est-ce que Shakespeare a comparé l'Angleterre?
2. Pourquoi est-ce que la majorité des Français et des Anglais sont satisfaits de l'Eurotunnel?
3. Il faut combien de temps pour aller de Paris à Londres avec l'Eurostar?
4. A quelle vitesse *(speed)* est-ce que le train va?
5. A quelle heure est-ce que les bureaux et les magasins ouvrent à Londres?

Activités

A. In the reading passage, you came across an abbreviation, **TGV**. French people use many abbreviations and acronyms, which are common in daily speech. Look at the following list of corresponding abbreviations and acronyms in French and in English. Try to match them.

French	English
1. ONU	a. AIDS
2. OTAN	b. SPCA
3. TVA	c. UFO
4. SIDA	d. UN
5. OVNI	e. VAT
6. SPA	f. NATO

B. Débats en classe.

1. Les avantages des voyages en train *vs* les avantages des voyages en avion.
2. Avantages et inconvénients des transports publics et des voitures personnelles.

C. Comment est-ce qu'on va de Paris à Londres si *(if)* on n'utilise pas l'Euro-tunnel? Expliquez ou racontez.

Vocabulaire

Noms / Pronoms

auto	car	heure	hour / time
autocar	bus	imper	raincoat
avion	airplane	ligne	line
banquette	seat	métro	subway
bateau	boat	midi	noon
bicyclette	bicycle	minuit	midnight
billet	ticket	moto	motorcycle
bout	end	pot	drink
bureau des objets trouvés	lost and found	problème	problem
camion	truck	quart	quarter
carnet	book of tickets	station	stop
carte orange	orange card	taxi	taxi
chance	luck	temps	time / weather
concert	concert	ticket	ticket
correspondance	connection	train	train
début	beginning	transport	transportation
employé	employee	vélo	bicycle

Verbes

attendre	to wait for	perdre	to lose
changer	to change	rapporter	to bring back
décider	to decide	rendre	to give back / to return (something)
descendre	to get off / to go down / to come down	rentrer	to return
entendre	to hear	répondre à	to answer
laisser	to leave	retrouver	to find again
monter	to get on / to go up	vendre	to sell
naître	to be born		

Adjectifs / Adverbes

beige	beige	heureusement	fortunately
combien de?	how much? / how many?	justement	as a matter of fact
comment	how	longtemps	for a long time
demi(e)	half	où?	where?
encore	still	pourquoi?	why?
gros(se)	big	quand?	when?

Expressions

à cheval	on horseback	en avance	early
à l'heure	on time	en retard	late
à pied	on foot	faire du stop	to hitchhike
Allons-y!	Let's go!	jusqu'à	until
avant	before	perdre patience	to lose patience
C'est à qui?	Whose turn is it?	pour rien	for nothing
de l'après-midi	P.M.	prendre un pot	to have a drink
depuis	since	Quelle chance!	What luck!
du matin	A.M.	rendre visite à	to visit (a person)
du soir	P.M.		

Class Work

A. Rewrite the following sentences using the cues in parentheses and making any necessary changes.

MODEL: Marie étudie le français.   (L'année prochaine…)
L'année prochaine Marie va étudier le français.

Des activités

1. Nous attendons l'autobus.   (Hier,…)
2. J'ai un examen aujourd'hui.   (Demain…)
3. Lise fait une promenade en auto le week-end?   (Les garçons… auto-stop… le week-end dernier?)
4. Christine a fait des courses en ville.   (Nous ne… pas… souvent…)
5. Nous allons à la bibliothèque cet après-midi.   (… hier.)
6. Les enfants écoutent-ils leurs parents?   (Isabelle… ?)
7. Vous rendez un livre?   (… demain matin?)
8. Mes sœurs étudient beaucoup.   (La semaine dernière…)

En voyage

9. Claire passe un mois au Sénégal.   (… l'été prochain.)
10. Il fait froid ici.   (Le mois dernier… Europe.)
11. Les étudiants ne restent pas chez eux en été.   (Paul… l'été dernier.)
12. Il fait un voyage en Amérique.   (Vous… déjà…)

B. Answer the following questions using the cues provided.

MODEL: Où allez-vous?   (… université.)
Je vais à l'université.

Les possessions

1. C'est votre imper?   (Oui,…)
2. Il donne des cadeaux à Mme Morin?   (Non,… frère.)
3. Ton jean est français?   (Non,… Etats-Unis.)
4. As-tu acheté une cravate bleue?   (Non,… verte.)
5. C'est ta jupe?   (Non,… ma mère.)
6. Où as-tu trouvé tes chemises?   (… Angleterre.)

D'autres activités

7. Où Pierre fait-il un voyage en été?   (descendre… Mexique.)
8. Où étudiez-vous le soir?   (… bibliothèque.)
9. Est-ce que Sylvie visite la France?   (Non,… Tunisie.)

10. Où allez-vous?   (… parc.)
11. Qu'est-ce que Jean va faire?   (… vendre… voiture.)
12. Tu as des amis en France?   (Non, mais… Maroc.)

C. Make complete sentences with each group of words below, adding any necessary words.

MODEL: Je / faire / promenade
          Je fais une promenade.

Dans ma ville

1. Quand / mon / parents / aller / cinéma?
2. Tu / passer / vacances / ici?
3. Où / on / faire / lessive?
4. Marie / entendre / voitures / hier soir
5. On / faire / promenades / parc
6. Mon / fille / naître / minuit

Qu'est-ce qu'on a fait?

7. Pourquoi / Eric / rester chez lui / hier?
8. Jacques / monter / dans / voiture / et faire / tour
9. Nous / faire / ménage / hier matin
10. Elle / chercher / parapluie / sœur / et / perdre / patience
11. Nous / ne / être / pas / restaurant / récemment
12. Chantal / chercher / ceinture / pour / son / jupe / blanc

D. Fill in the blanks when necessary with the appropriate article or preposition.

MODEL: … Rome est… Italie.
          Rome est en Italie.

1. … Canada est un pays magnifique.
2. … Madrid est une ville intéressante.
3. J'ai visité… Dakar,… Sénégal.
4. Avez-vous passé vos vacances… Japon?
5. … Etats-Unis, les villes sont très grandes.
6. … Florence, il y a beaucoup de musées.
7. … Abidjan est… Côte d'Ivoire.
8. … été prochain, mes parents vont visiter… Mexique.
9. … Italie est un pays fantastique.
10. Je suis allé au concert… semaine dernière.
11. Je vais rendre visite… mon professeur… 4 h.
12. Marc adore répondre… questions.

E. Translate the following sentences into French.

1. Where is my book?
2. It is on your table.
3. Yesterday, your mother visited my school.
4. She likes our teacher a lot.
5. Their friends have my car.
6. They lost their bicycles.
7. Her dorm is far from her parents' house.
8. She hates living at their house.

F. In French, read aloud or write the following numbers.

1.	71	6.	321	11.	1.000	16.	259.500
2.	81	7.	554	12.	1.433	17.	1.000.000
3.	95	8.	742	13.	1.982	18.	3.000.000
4.	100	9.	891	14.	2.600	19.	10.500.000
5.	214	10.	961	15.	10.971	20.	324.657.895

Pair and small group work

A. Form groups of three or four students, and find out the birthdays of everyone in your group.

B. Work with a partner to practice the **futur proche** and the **passé composé**. Take turns making statements in the **futur proche** and having your partner repeat your statements in the **passé composé**. Use the following verbs:

aller	inviter	acheter	descendre
oublier	rester	visiter	rendre
faire	manger	rentrer	perdre
monter	étudier	arriver	attendre

C. Write a number on a slip of paper starting with one digit and adding a digit each time (**7, 17, 175...**). Your partner will read your number aloud, and then you will reverse roles. Continue until one of you makes a mistake.

D. In groups of three or four, take turns identifying objects that belong to you, and point them out to your classmates using the expression **C'est...** or **Ce sont...** and possessive adjectives.

MODEL: *C'est mon stylo. Ce sont mes chaussures.*

E. Using the **Est-ce que** form or inversion and the verbs **avoir** and **être**, ask a question about your partner's feelings or present state of mind.

MODEL: Student 1: *Est-ce que tu as chaud?* or *As-tu chaud?*
Student 2: *Oui, j'ai chaud.*

F. With a classmate, make up a schedule of your daily activities. What things do you do at different times?

MODEL: *Notre premier cours commence à neuf heures, mais elle déjeune à midi et je déjeune à une heure.*

G. Interview a classmate about the following subjects. Prepare a report of your findings for the class.

1. Qu'est-ce que tu as fait le week-end dernier?
2. Comment va-t-on chez toi?
3. Où fais-tu tes courses? ta lessive?
4. Qu'est-ce que tu aimes?
5. Quel pays as-tu visité? Où désires-tu aller?
6. Aimes-tu faire la cuisine? Quelle est ta spécialité?
7. Où es-tu allé hier? Pourquoi?
8. Fais-tu toujours tes devoirs? Pourquoi ou pourquoi pas?

Chapitre 7 Au téléphone

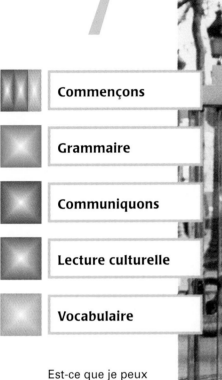

- **Commençons**
- **Grammaire**
- **Communiquons**
- **Lecture culturelle**
- **Vocabulaire**

Est-ce que je peux parler à Elisabeth?

Objectives

Language

Vocabulary for common possessions • Nasal vowels • Interrogative and demonstrative adjectives • **-ir** verbs • Interrogative pronouns • **Pouvoir** and **vouloir**

Culture

The French telephone system • The **Minitel**

Communication

Using the telephone • Talking about one's possessions

Commençons

C'est une erreur!

Le téléphone sonne chez Elisabeth Cambon.

UNE VOIX
FÉMININE: Allô, 45.26.88.46, j'écoute.

BENJAMIN: Allô, est-ce que je peux parler à Elisabeth, s'il vous plaît?

LA VOIX: Qui est à l'appareil?

BENJAMIN: Benjamin Ducaud.

LA VOIX: Ne quittez pas, je vais voir si elle est là.

Après une ou deux minutes...

LA VOIX: Allô, je suis désolée; elle est dans sa chambre et elle dort. Voulez-vous laisser un message?

BENJAMIN: *(Il réfléchit.)* Je voudrais savoir si elle peut sortir avec moi ce soir. Est-ce que je peux rappeler plus tard?

LA VOIX: Non, ce n'est pas la peine de téléphoner, Elisabeth n'est pas libre. Au revoir.

BENJAMIN: Ne coupe pas! Elisabeth, c'est toi? Pourquoi est-ce que tu ne veux pas sortir avec moi?

Etudions le dialogue

1. A qui est-ce que Benjamin veut parler?
2. Pourquoi est-ce qu'il ne peut pas parler à Elisabeth?
3. Quel message veut-il laisser?
4. Qu'est-ce qu'il veut faire plus tard?
5. Pourquoi est-ce que ce n'est pas la peine?
6. A qui est-ce que Benjamin parle au téléphone?

Mots clés

erreur	*wrong number*	voulez (vouloir)	*want*
téléphone	*telephone*	message	*message*
sonne (sonner)	*rings*	réfléchit (réfléchir)	*thinks*
voix	*voice*	savoir	*know*
Allô.	*Hello.*	peut (pouvoir)	*can*
J'écoute.	*Go ahead.*	sortir	*go out*
peux (pouvoir)	*may*	rappeler	*call back*
Qui est à l'appareil?	*Who's calling?*	plus tard	*later*
Ne quittez pas.	*Hold on.*	ce n'est pas la peine	*it's no use*
voir	*to see*	téléphoner (à)	*to phone*
désolée	*sorry*	libre	*free*
chambre	*bedroom*	Ne coupe pas.	*Don't hang up.*
dort (dormir)	*is sleeping*		

Allô! C'est toi, Nicole?

Faisons connaissance WWW

In France the telephone system is run by **France Télécom,** an agency that administers one of the most sophisticated telephone systems in the world. One can call anywhere in France or the rest of the world in a matter of seconds, even from public phone booths. Since over 90% of the population now have a phone, the French use the telephone much more than in the past. Their use of it, however, still tends to be more conservative than that of Americans. The French often do not have as many phones in a home as Americans do.

To make a phone call, some people still go to a post office (**bureau de poste**) or a tobacco shop (**bureau de tabac**), where prior to the modernization of the phone system over the last twenty years, one traditionally went to use a phone. Today, however, with the installation of numerous phone booths (**cabines téléphoniques**) on the streets, in metro stations and other public places, the French can make a phone call from almost anywhere. French people also use car phones and cellular phones a lot.

Enrichissons notre vocabulaire

Mes affaires (f.) (My things)

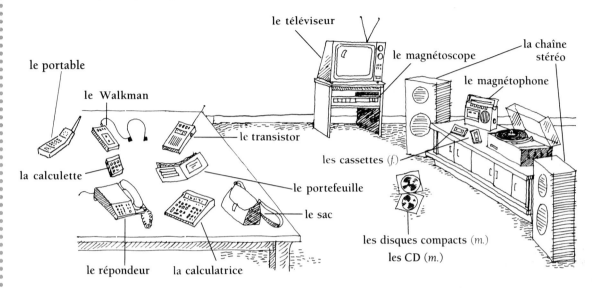

le téléviseur

le magnétoscope

la chaîne stéréo

le magnétophone

le portable

le Walkman

le transistor

les cassettes (f.)

la calculette

le portefeuille

le sac

les disques compacts (m.)
les CD (m.)

le répondeur   la calculatrice

Quelques expressions utiles

—Maman, je peux **allumer** la télé? — *Mom, can I **turn on** the TV?*

—**Range** ta chambre **d'abord!** — ***Pick up** your room **first!***

—Où est-ce que je **branche** le lecteur laser? — *Where do I **plug in** the CD player?*

—Ce n'est pas **nécessaire;** il marche avec des **piles** (f.). — *It's not **necessary;** it **works** with **batteries.***

Prononciation   Nasal vowels

French has three vowel sounds that are nasalized. This means that air is allowed to pass into the nasal cavity and vibrate. If you pinch your nose and say the words **vin** and **va,** you will feel the vibrations as you say **vin,** but not **va.**

Repeat the following words, which are grouped according to the nasal vowel sound they contain, after your teacher.

/ ã / (Your lips are slightly rounded, your tongue back.)
an / dans / gant / quand / sans / blanc / banque / chantez / changez / cent deux / je danse / il demande

/ ɔ̃ / (Your lips are more rounded, your tongue farther back.)
on / blond / ton / non / son / ils vont / ils font / elles sont / faisons / travaillons / nous avons / mon

/ ɛ̃ / (Your lips are spread, your tongue forward.)
pain / cinq / vin / bien / impossible / important / loin / Alain / sympathique

Exercices

A. Repeat the following words after your teacher, paying particular attention to the nasal vowels.

> allons / faisons / mes enfants / à demain / en France / invite / bonjour / sa maison / continuons / magasin / canadien / mexicain / examen / tu manges / pardon

B. Repeat each sentence after your teacher, paying particular attention to the nasal vowels.

1. Chantal danse bien.
2. Combien de garçons allons-nous inviter?
3. Les Américains sont-ils sympathiques?
4. Jean et Alain vont partir en vacances en Angleterre.
5. Mes enfants vont répondre aux questions.
6. Elles ont trouvé un restaurant mexicain fantastique.

Grammaire

I. Interrogative and demonstrative adjectives

> You use interrogative adjectives to ask someone to make a choice and demonstrative adjectives to point out or choose.

A. Interrogative adjectives

1. In French, interrogative adjectives (*what?* or *which?* in English) ask for a choice. Like other French adjectives, they agree in gender and number with the nouns they modify. Either inversion or **est-ce que** is used with **quel.**

	singular	*plural*
masculine	**quel**	**quels**
feminine	**quelle**	**quelles**

> **Quel** répondeur avez-vous vendu?   Vous attendez avec **quels** amis?
> A **quelle** heure est-elle arrivée?   **Quelles** sont vos cassettes préférées?

2. The plural **quels** and **quelles** call for a **liaison obligatoire.**

> Quels‿artistes est-ce que tu apprécies?
> Quelles‿universités vont-ils visiter?

B. Demonstrative adjectives

1. French uses several forms of **ce** as demonstrative adjectives. They are equivalent to *this, that, these,* and *those* in English.

	singular	*plural*
masculine	ce, cet	ces
feminine	cette	ces

2. **Cet** is a special form of **ce** used with masculine singular adjectives or nouns beginning with a vowel sound.

   Cet autocar va à Marseille.   A-t-elle invité **cet au**tre homme?

3. All the singular forms in the table above can mean *this* or *that,* and **ces** can mean *these* or *those.* The distinction between *this* and *that* and between *these* and *those* is rarely necessary in French.

   —Quel Walkman recommandez-vous?
   —**Ce** Walkman marche bien.

   —Quand est-ce que vous allez arriver chez nous?
   —**Cet** après-midi.

   —Tu aimes **ces** CD?
   —Quels CD?

   When a distinction in meaning is necessary, you add **-ci** to the noun to express *this* or *these* and **-là** to express *that* or *those.*

   —**Cette calculette-ci** est à toi?   —Vous désirez?
   —Non, elle est à mon frère.   —Montrez-moi **ce téléviseur-là.**

Langue

A. **Questions et réponses.** Employez un adjectif interrogatif et un adjectif démonstratif avec les mots suivants *(following).*

   MODÈLE: cassette   *Quelle cassette? Cette cassette.*

   1. idées   4. trains   7. examen
   2. saison   5. chaînes stéréo 8. autobus
   3. magnétoscope   6. hôtel   9. piles

B. **Suivons** *(Let's follow)* **M. et Mme Ducharme à un restaurant.** Formez des phrases complètes en employant *(using)* les mots donnés et en faisant *(making)* tous les changements nécessaires.

   1. Tu / penser / quel / restaurant?
   2. Tu / ne… pas / laisser / ce / imper / ici?
   3. hôtesse / ne… pas / recommander / restaurant-là
   4. quel / heure / nous / dîner?
   5. Quel / viande / et / quel / légume / nous / commander / soir?
   6. Aller / chercher / le / garçon; / ce / boissons / ne… pas / être / à nous

C. **Les Dupont font une promenade.** Répondez aux questions suivantes en employant les mots entre parenthèses et des adjectifs démonstratifs.

1. Est-ce qu'on va au parc ce matin?   (Non,... après-midi)
2. Jacques a-t-il son parapluie?   (Non,... porter... imper)
3. Est-ce que Louise va porter cette robe?   (Oui, et... chaussures aussi)
4. Qu'est-ce que Pierre a oublié?   (... transistor...)
5. Michel va rester à la maison pour faire la cuisine?   (Non,... soir)
6. Est-ce que j'ai mon sac?   (Non,... sac... être à moi!)

Quel Président? Avec quelle majorité?
Quel Premier Ministre?
Dissolution ou non de l'Assemblée Nationale?
Le dimanche 8 mai à partir de 20 h 00
et le lundi 9 mai dès 6 h 30 du matin,
les journalistes de France-Inter, de France-Info et L'Express
et leurs invités politiques vous apporteront
des éléments de réponses aux questions
que vous vous posez.

Culture   WWW

D. **Les Français et leurs affaires.** La liste suivante donne les pourcentages d'équipement audio-visuel qu'on trouve dans une famille française. Demandez à un(e) partenaire le pourcentage pour chaque objet.

Téléviseur en noir et blanc 7,3	Magnétoscope 60
Téléviseur en couleurs 91,6	Transistor 89,2
Téléphone 95,6	Walkman 60
Minitel 28	CDs 26
Magnétophone 40	Chaîne stéréo 71

MODÈLE: Quel pourcentage des familles a une voiture?   77%.

Communication

E. **Questionnaire.** Formez des questions avec les mots suivants. Posez ces questions à un(e) camarade et préparez un résumé des réponses pour les autres.

A	B		C
Quel	appartement	musée	habites-tu?
Quelle	disque compact	pays	aimes-tu mieux?
Quels	ville	villes	vas-tu visiter?
Quelles	film	café	fréquentes-tu?
	cours	cinéma	
	artistes	boîtes	

F. **Poursuite triviale.** Répondez aux questions suivantes avec un adjectif démonstratif si vous savez *(know)* la réponse!

MODÈLE: Quelle femme a été pilote dans les années trente?
Cette femme est Amelia Earhart.

1. Quelle actrice a joué le rôle de Scarlett O'Hara?
2. Quels journalistes ont été célèbres *(famous)* après Watergate?
3. Quelle a été la première université fondée aux Etats-Unis?
4. Quel explorateur français est arrivé au Canada en 1534?
5. Quel président a acheté la Louisiane?
6. Les Américains n'ont pas élu *(elected)* quel président?

G. **Questions personnelles.** Vos préférences.

1. Dans quels restaurants est-ce que vous aimez manger?
2. Quelle cuisine aimez-vous?
3. Quel vin aimez-vous beaucoup?
4. Quelle boisson aimez-vous en été? en hiver?
5. Quelle sorte de musique aimez-vous écouter dans les boîtes?
6. A quelle heure est-ce que vous rentrez de ces boîtes?

II. -ir verbs

> You use verbs to describe actions or activities.

In Chapter 1 you learned that French verbs are categorized according to the infinitive ending. In addition to **-er** and **-re** verbs, there is a group ending in **-ir.** There are two distinct conjugations for this group.

A. -ir verbs conjugated like finir

Note the **-iss-** in the plural forms.

---

finir   *(to finish)*

---

je **finis**	nous **finissons**
tu **finis**	vous **finissez**
il / elle / on **finit**	ils / elles **finissent**

Mots clés   *Verbs conjugated like* **finir**

choisir	*to choose*	**réfléchir à**	*to think (about), consider*
désobéir à	*to disobey*	**réussir (à)**	*to succeed; to pass*
obéir à	*to obey*		*(an exam)*
punir	*to punish*	**rougir**	*to blush*

Je **finis** mes cours à dix-sept heures.
Elle va **choisir** une chaîne stéréo pour son frère.
M. Dupont ne **punit** pas ses enfants.
Elles **réussissent** toujours aux examens.

1. The imperative of this group of **-ir** verbs is regular: you simply delete the subject.

  Finis tes devoirs.   **Obéissez** à vos parents!

2. To form the past participle, drop the **r** of the infinitive.

  —Vous avez **choisi** votre dessert?
  —Non, nous n'avons pas **fini** notre fromage.

  —Pourquoi est-ce qu'ils ont **puni** leur fils?
  —Parce qu'il a **désobéi**.

3. Note that **obéir**, **désobéir**, and **réfléchir** must take the preposition **à** before a following noun. With **réussir**, however, **à** is optional.

  J'obéis toujours à mes parents.
  Ne **désobéissez** pas à l'agent de police.
  Je n'aime pas **réfléchir aux** problèmes difficiles.

Langue

A. **Des décisions.** Formez des phrases complètes avec les mots donnés. Faites les changements nécessaires.

1. Je / finir / ce / livre
2. Qu'est-ce que / tu / choisir / comme cours?
3. Tu / ne... / réfléchir / pas / quand / tu / étudier
4. parents / punir / enfants / quand / ils / désobéir
5. Il / ne... pas / réussir / examen
6. Tu / finir / ménage / demain

B. Conversations à la résidence. Refaites *(Redo)* les phrases suivantes en employant les mots donnés.

1. *Nous* finissons nos devoirs.   (Je...)
2. *Marc* ne va pas *finir* son examen ce matin.   (Vous... réussir...)
3. *Luc* obéit à *l'agent*.   (Nous... agents)
4. *Vous* finissez à huit heures?   (Jacqueline...)
5. *Ce soir,* je vais choisir le restau.   (Hier soir,...)
6. *Jean* rougit souvent en cours.   (Jean et Marie...)

B. -ir verbs conjugated like servir

Note that you drop the last consonant of the infinitive stem in the singular forms of the present tense.

servir *(to serve)*	
je **sers**	nous **servons**
tu **sers**	vous **servez**
il / elle / on **sert**	ils / elles **servent**

Mots clés   *Verbs conjugated like* servir

dormir *to sleep*	je dors, nous dormons	**sentir** *to smell, to feel*	je sens, nous sentons
mentir *to lie*	je mens, nous mentons	**sortir** *to go out*	je sors, nous sortons
partir *to leave*	je pars, nous partons		

Je **sors** avec des amis après les cours.
Ce fruit **sent** mauvais.
Nous **allons dormir** tard ce week-end.
Elles **partent** aujourd'hui.
Tu **ne vas pas mentir** à ton frère.

---

1. The imperative of this group of **-ir** verbs is also regular.

   Servons du café à nos amis.   Ne **mentez** pas à vos parents.

2. To form the past participle, drop the **r** of the infinitive.

   Je n'ai pas **dormi** cette nuit.   Ils n'ont pas **servi** de vin.

3. The **passé composé** of **partir** and **sortir** take **être**, so the subject and past participle must agree.

   Elles sont **parties** hier.   Nous sommes **sortis** mardi soir.

Langue

C. **Les Français.** Formez des phrases complètes avec les mots donnés. Faites les changements nécessaires.

1. Les Français / servir / souvent / vin
2. Ils / partir / en vacances / à la plage
3. On / aimer / sortir / le week-end
4. enfants / dormir / huit heures
5. Les Français / réfléchir / beaucoup
6. Un jeune Français / ne… pas / mentir / parents

D. **M. et Mme Morin interrogent leur fils.** Mettez les phrases suivantes au présent.

1. Tu vas sortir avec Marie ce soir?
2. Tu vas dormir cet après-midi?
3. Tu ne vas pas partir en retard?
4. Elle va servir un dîner?
5. Qu'est-ce que tu vas choisir si le dîner ne sent pas bon?
6. Tu ne vas pas mentir si tu n'aimes pas sa cuisine?

Culture

E. **La France ou les Etats-Unis?** Formez des phrases avec les mots donnés et dites *(say)* si l'activité est typique des Français ou des Américains.

MODÈLE: On / servir / salade / avant / repas
   On sert la salade avant le repas. C'est typique des Américains.

1. Les jeunes gens / sortir / en groupes, / pas à deux
2. On / rougir / vite / devant la nudité
3. Les élèves / réussir / moins souvent au lycée
4. On / choisir / les restaurants avec un livre
5. Les parents / servir / vin aux enfants
6. Les gens / partir en vacances / en même temps

Communication

F. **A mon avis.** Est-ce que les phrases suivantes sont vraies *(true)* ou fausses *(false)*? Si elles sont fausses, corrigez-les *(correct them)*.

1. Je dors cinq heures tous les jours.
2. Mes amis choisissent des cours difficiles.
3. Je ne mens pas à mes parents.
4. Les étudiants réfléchissent quand ils font leurs devoirs.
5. Mes amis ne servent pas d'alcool.
6. Quand je fais la cuisine, cela sent toujours bon.

G. **Finissons nos phrases.** Complétez les phrases suivantes.

1. Je réussis à mes examens quand…
2. Nous sommes partis en vacances…
3. Comme restaurant, mes parents aiment choisir…
4. Je rougis toujours quand…
5. Le week-end, je dors jusqu'à…
6. Je voudrais sortir avec…

H. **Que choisissez-vous?** Répondez selon le modèle suivant et justifiez vos réponses.

MODÈLE: un restaurant chinois ou américain
Moi, je choisis un restaurant chinois parce que j'adore cette cuisine.

1. un concert de musique classique ou un match de football
2. des vacances chez vos parents ou à la plage
3. du coca ou de la bière
4. un autocar ou votre voiture pour un voyage
5. la radio ou la télévision
6. une profession intéressante ou bien payée

I. **Questions personnelles.** Ma vie à l'université.

1. A quelle heure partez-vous pour vos cours le matin?
2. Réussissez-vous toujours à vos examens? Et votre camarade de chambre?
3. Avez-vous rougi en cours? Quand?
4. Comment est-ce que votre professeur punit la classe quand les étudiants ne préparent pas la leçon?
5. Jusqu'à quelle heure dormez-vous le week-end?
6. Vous sortez beaucoup? Qu'est-ce que vous faites le week-end quand vous ne sortez pas?

1. VOUS AVEZ DÉCIDÉ DE PRENDRE LE TRAIN. VOUS CHOISISSEZ VOTRE HORAIRE EN PÉRIODE BLEUE OU BLANCHE, VOUS VOYAGEREZ PLUS CONFORTABLEMENT...

III. Interrogative pronouns

> You use interrogative pronouns to find out specific information about people and things.

In French, the form of an interrogative pronoun depends on whether the pronoun is the subject or the object of the verb. As in English, the form also varies according to whether you are asking about a person *(Who? Whom?)* or a thing *(What?)*.

A. Persons

1. To ask about a person as the subject of a verb *(Who?)*, use **Qui est-ce qui** or **Qui.**

   —**Qui est-ce qui** a faim?   —**Qui** a téléphoné?
   —Moi!   —Benjamin.

2. If the person is an object of the verb *(Whom?)*, use **Qui est-ce que** or **Qui** with inversion.

   —**Qui est-ce que** vous admirez?   —**Qui est-ce que** tu as invité?
     Qui admirez-vous?   **Qui** as-tu invité?
   —J'admire mes parents.   —J'ai invité mes amis.

3. If the person is the object of a preposition *(Whom?)*, use the preposition plus **qui est-ce que** or **qui** with inversion.

   —**Avec qui est-ce qu'**ils ont joué?   —**A qui est-ce que** tu as parlé?
     Avec qui ont-ils joué?   **A qui** as-tu parlé?
   —Avec leurs enfants.   —J'ai parlé à la secrétaire.

B. Things

1. To ask about a thing as the object of a verb *(What?)*, use **Qu'est-ce que** or **Que** with inversion.

   —**Qu'est-ce que** vos frères   —**Qu'est-ce que** c'est?
     cherchent?   —C'est un téléphone portable.
   —Ils cherchent leurs clés.

   —**Qu'est-ce que** vous avez choisi?
     Qu'avez-vous choisi?
   —J'ai choisi un magnétoscope allemand.

2. A thing can be the subject of a sentence. In this case, the only interrogative pronoun that can be used is **Qu'est-ce qui** *(What?)*. This pronoun is often used with **arriver** *(to happen)* and **rester** *(to be left over; to remain)*.

   —**Qu'est-ce qui** est arrivé?   —**Qu'est-ce qui** reste?
   —Mes parents sont partis.   —Un peu de coca.

3. If a thing is the object of a preposition *(What?)*, use **quoi,** which is followed by **est-ce que** or inversion.

—De **quoi** est-ce qu'ils parlent? —A **quoi** est-ce que tu penses?
 De **quoi** parlent-ils? A **quoi** penses-tu?
—Ils parlent de leurs affaires. —A mes vacances!

C. Summary

	persons (who? whom?)	*things (what?)*
subject of verb	**Qui** *or* **Qui est-ce qui**	**Qu'est-ce qui**
object of verb	**qui** + inversion *or* **qui est-ce que**	**que** + inversion *or* **qu'est-ce que**
object of prep.	Prep. + **qui** + inversion *or* Prep. + **qui est-ce que**	Prep. + **quoi** + inversion *or* Prep. + **quoi est-ce que**

Langue

A. **Interview avec des Français.** Vous allez interviewer des Français. Traduisez les questions suivantes en français.

1. What do you do?
2. What do you like to talk about?
3. What happened at your home last night?
4. What have you bought recently?
5. Whom do you phone often?
6. What does your family watch on TV?

B. **Des questions.** Complétez les phrases suivantes avec un pronom interrogatif approprié *(appropriate).*

1. ___ a mangé ma glace?
2. A ___ avez-vous donné l'argent?
3. ___ est arrivé ce matin?
4. Avec ___ a-t-on fait des crêpes?
5. ___ il y a dans la chambre?
6. ___ ont-ils regardé?

C. **Interview avec des étudiants.** Trouvez les questions qui ont provoqué les réponses en italique *(italics).*

1. Nous sommes *étudiants.*
2. Nous étudions *l'anglais.*
3. *Marie et Jacqueline* sont absentes aujourd'hui.
4. *La résidence* est agréable.
5. Je vais téléphoner à *mon ami Luc* ce soir.
6. Luc va acheter *un téléviseur.*

Culture

D. **Des célébrités francophones.** En utilisant les mots de la colonne de gauche *(left column)*, trouvez des questions qui décrivent *(describe)* les gens célèbres de la colonne de droite *(right)*.

1. chanter bien	a. Catherine Deneuve
2. danser bien	b. Paul Prudhomme et Justin Wilson
3. encourager les femmes	
4. faire du cinéma	c. Simone de Beauvoir
5. recommander un parfum	d. Bertrand Blier
6. donner des leçons de cuisine	e. Joséphine Baker
	f. Céline Dion

E. **Des statistiques.** Trouvez les questions qui correspondent aux renseignements en italique, et posez *(ask)* ces questions à un(e) camarade de classe.

MODÈLE: *Les Portugais* sont les immigrés les plus nombreux en France.
Qui sont les immigrés les plus nombreux en France?

1. 72% des parents français donnent *de l'argent de poche* à leurs enfants. (141 francs par mois en moyenne [*on average*])
2. 83% des Français ont de la sympathie *pour les Américains.*
3. Les Français regardent *la télévision* une heure et quarante-cinq minutes par jour.
4. *Les vêtements* représentent les achats les plus fréquents des jeunes Français (25%).
5. 50,7% des Français ne consomment pas *d'alcool.*
6. En France, il est possible de payer une contravention *(traffic ticket)* directement *à l'agent de police.*

Communication

F. **Enquête.** Formez des groupes et posez des questions en utilisant des pronoms interrogatifs. Consultez les verbes donnés et inventez des questions originales. Informez vos camarades de cours des résultats.

MODÈLE: *Qui admires-tu?*
Qu'est-ce que tu as à la maison?

aimer bien	détester
porter en cours demain	ne... pas faire cette semaine
téléphoner à	manger
oublier	regarder... à la télévision
faire bien	aller faire ce week-end

G. **Questions personnelles.** Votre passé.

1. Qu'est-ce que vous avez fait l'été dernier?
2. Avec qui est-ce que vous avez fait un voyage?
3. Pour qui est-ce que vous avez voté en 1996?
4. De quoi avez-vous parlé avec vos amis le week-end dernier?
5. A qui avez-vous téléphoné?
6. Qui avez-vous invité chez vous cette semaine?
7. Qui a fait le ménage chez vous récemment? Cette année?
8. Qu'est-ce qui est arrivé d'intéressant ce mois-ci?

IV. Pouvoir **and vouloir**

> You use **pouvoir** to express ability or permission and **vouloir** to indicate a desire.

A. Pouvoir

1. **Pouvoir** *(to be able, can, may, to be allowed to)* is an irregular verb, so you must learn its forms.

je **peux**	nous **pouvons**
tu **peux**	vous **pouvez**
il / elle / on **peut**	ils / elles **peuvent**

2. **Pouvoir** is often followed by another verb in the infinitive.

—Est-ce que je **peux parler** à Elisabeth?
—**Pouvez**-vous **rappeler** plus tard?

—Est-ce que ton frère **peut partir** aujourd'hui?
—Non, tu **peux attendre** demain?

3. The past participle of **pouvoir** is **pu.**

—Qu'est-ce que vous avez?   —Vous avez **pu** parler à
—Je n'ai pas **pu** dormir.   Elisabeth?
                                        —Non, elle est sortie.

B. Vouloir

1. **Vouloir** *(to want)* is also irregular and must be memorized.

je **veux**	nous **voulons**
tu **veux**	vous **voulez**
il / elle / on **veut**	ils / elles **veulent**

2. Like **pouvoir, vouloir** is frequently used with an infinitive.

—Tu **veux finir** mon dessert?
—Non, je ne **peux** pas.

3. The past participle of **vouloir** is **voulu.**

—Ils n'ont pas **voulu** partir le matin?
—Non, ils ont préféré faire la grasse matinée.

4. You have already seen the expression **je voudrais,** which is a form of **vouloir** used to say *I want* politely.

> **Je voudrais** parler au médecin.
> **Je voudrais** du café, s'il vous plaît.

5. The expression **vouloir bien** means *to be willing.*

> —Tu veux sortir ce soir?
> —Oui, je **veux bien.**

Attention!

Pouvoir and **vouloir** share a similar pronunciation.

1. The vowel sounds are the same.

je peux / je veux	/ ʒə pø /, / ʒə vø /
nous pouvons / nous voulons	/ nu pu vɔ̃ /, / nu vu lɔ̃ /
ils peuvent / ils veulent	/ il pœv /, / il vœl /

2. Although the third-person vowels are written **eu,** the vowel sound changes from the singular to the plural. You must open your mouth wider to pronounce the sound for **eu** in the plural.

il peut, ils peuvent	/ il pø /, / il pœv /
il veut, ils veulent	/ il vø /, / il vœl /

Langue

A. **Jacques est difficile!** Dans les phrases suivantes, remplacez **vouloir** par **pouvoir** et vice versa.

1. Jacques ne veut pas aller en cours.
2. Vous ne pouvez pas téléphoner demain, Jacques?
3. Il n'a pas voulu parler.
4. Nous ne pouvons pas inviter des amis chez lui!
5. Ils veulent bien écouter la radio.
6. Je n'ai pas pu rester chez Jacques.

B. **Elodie et sa famille.** Formez des phrases complètes avec les mots donnés. Faites les changements nécessaires.

1. Elodie / ne… pas / pouvoir / sortir avec nous / parce que / parents / ne… pas / vouloir
2. week-end / dernier / ils / vouloir / aller / mer / ensemble
3. La semaine prochaine / ils / pouvoir / aller en ville
4. Elodie / ne… pas / vouloir / ranger / sa chambre
5. Les parents d'Elodie / vouloir / inviter / son amie Juliette
6. Juliette / ne… pas / pouvoir / rester / chez eux

Culture   **WWW**

C. **Les élections en France.** Formez des phrases avec les mots donnés. Si une phrase est fausse, corrigez-la.

1. Les Français / pouvoir / choisir / entre plusieurs candidats
2. Ils / pouvoir / voter / deux fois *(twice)* pour un candidat

3. En France, on / vouloir / communistes dans l'administration
4. Les Français / pouvoir / voter pour le président seulement *(only)* en novembre
5. On / pouvoir / voter à dix-huit ans
6. Les Français / vouloir / voter

Communication

D. **Vos préférences.** Qu'est-ce que vous voulez faire et qu'est-ce que vous ne voulez pas faire? Utilisez les suggestions données ou vos propres idées.

MODÈLE: *Je voudrais manger de la glace.*
Je ne veux pas aller au parc.

téléphoner à	travailler le week-end
écouter mon Walkman	dormir jusqu'à midi demain
aller à la plage	acheter un lecteur laser
avoir une chaîne stéréo	sortir au restaurant avec mes amis

E. **Je ne peux pas.** Regardez les listes des activités et des excuses ci-dessous *(below)*. Pourquoi ne faites-vous pas chaque activité? Choisissez ou inventez une excuse.

MODÈLE: *Je ne peux pas parler français aujourd'hui parce que j'ai mal dormi hier soir.*

Activités	**Excuses**
étudier ce soir	être fatigué(e), paresseux (-euse)
aller en cours	vouloir écouter mes disques
faire le ménage	dormir mal hier soir
parler français	préparer un examen important
???	???

F. **Mes activités d'hier.** Qu'est-ce que vous avez pu faire hier et qu'est-ce que vous avez voulu faire? Employez les suggestions données ou inventez des réponses originales.

MODÈLE: *Hier, j'ai pu terminer mes devoirs.*
J'ai voulu aller à la plage hier.

parler à un(e) ami(e)	oublier mes devoirs
aller en cours	acheter un vêtement
rester à la maison	téléphoner à mes parents
faire des courses	ranger mes affaires

G. **Questions personnelles.** Votre avenir.

1. Qu'est-ce que vous voulez pour votre anniversaire?
2. Où pouvez-vous aller pour vos vacances d'été?
3. Pour qui voulez-vous voter en 2000?
4. Quelle profession voulez-vous avoir?
5. Où est-ce que vous voulez habiter?
6. Combien d'enfants voulez-vous avoir?

Communiquons

Donner un coup de téléphone

www

To make a telephone call in France, you can find a phone in post offices and some cafés, and, of course, there are telephone booths on the streets and in public buildings such as train stations. There had been a serious problem of vandalism of public phone booths, but it was solved with the introduction of the **télécarte**. This card has a set price encoded in a computer chip, and each time it is used, the phone electronically subtracts the cost of the call until the entire value is used up. You can buy a **télécarte** at all post offices and **bureaux de tabac.**

Telephone numbers in France became ten digits in late 1996. For example, the number for the **bureau des objets trouvés** for the metro system is **01.45.31.82.10,** which is read **zéro un, quarante-cinq, trente et un, quatre-vingt-deux, dix.**

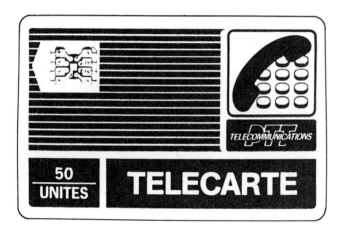

Expressions

▶ **On donne un coup de téléphone.**

Elisabeth donne / passe un coup de téléphone / un coup de fil.

Elisabeth is making a phone call.

Elle cherche le numéro de téléphone dans l'annuaire / le bottin / le Minitel.

She looks up the phone number in the phone book / the Minitel.

Elle compose / fait le numéro des renseignements.

She dials the number for information.

Elle utilise un numéro vert.

She is using a toll-free number.

Le téléphone sonne.

The phone rings.

On décroche le téléphone.

Someone picks up the phone.

► **On commence la conversation.**

Allô!	*Hello!*
Qui est à l'appareil?	*Who's calling?*
C'est de la part de qui?	*May I say who's calling?*
Est-ce que je pourrais parler à Mlle Leclerc?	*May I speak to Ms. Leclerc?*
Poste 325.	*Extension 325.*
Ne quittez pas.	*Hold the line.*
Un instant, je vous prie.	*One moment, please.*

► **On finit la communication.**

La ligne est occupée.	*The line is busy.*
Il / Elle n'est pas là.	*He / She isn't in.*
Il / Elle est sorti(e).	*He / She has gone / stepped out.*
Pouvez-vous rappeler dans une heure?	*Can you call back in an hour?*
Elisabeth raccroche.	*Elisabeth hangs up.*

Interaction   *Jacques téléphone à son ami François Morin.*

MME MORIN: Allô!

JACQUES: Bonjour, Madame. Est-ce que je pourrais parler à François?

MME MORIN: C'est de la part de qui?

JACQUES: C'est Jacques Calvet.

MME MORIN: Ne quittez pas, Monsieur.

Une minute plus tard

MME MORIN: Il n'est pas là. Pouvez-vous rappeler dans une heure?

JACQUES: Bien sûr. Merci, Madame.

MME MORIN: Merci et au revoir.

JACQUES: Au revoir.

Activités

A. Le téléphone. Répondez aux questions suivantes.

1. Avez-vous le téléphone? Est-ce que le téléphone est essentiel? Pourquoi?
2. Quel est votre numéro de téléphone? le numéro de la police? des renseignements?
3. En France, comment trouve-t-on un numéro de téléphone?
4. Vous êtes en France et vous voulez téléphoner à vos parents aux Etats-Unis. Que faites-vous?
5. Avez-vous utilisé un téléphone portable? C'est utile?
6. Vous aimez les répondeurs? Sont-ils indispensables?

B. Jeux de rôles. Avec un(e) camarade, inventez des dialogues adaptés aux situations suivantes.

1. Call for an appointment (**un rendez-vous**) with the doctor.
2. Call someone and ask him / her to go to the movies with you.
3. Call the train station to find out the schedule for trains from Paris to Bordeaux.
4. Call information for a phone number.
5. Call the lost and found office of your hotel to ask about your wallet, which you left in your room.
6. Call a restaurant to find out about their menu and hours.

Lecture culturelle

Avant la lecture

WWW

Today France has one of the best telephone systems in the world. The phone company has always been nationalized and is now operated by **France Télécom,** an agency created on January 1, 1991, and placed under the **ministre de l'Industrie, des Postes et Télécommunications, et du Commerce extérieur.**

Au Minitel

A unique feature of the telephone system is the **Minitel,** a small computer terminal plugged into one's phone line and designed to replace the paper phone book (**l'annuaire** or **le bottin**). The people who invented the **Minitel** had the ingenious idea of supplying it for free and offering an introductory monthly rate for using it. Now the French type in codes to get phone numbers, train schedules, horoscopes, video games, or hundreds of other services.

Today, about 28% of French households have a **Minitel.** There are more than 6.5 million sets throughout the country, and it is estimated that each one is used for an average of ninety minutes a month. The highly successful service is not without its critics, however. Some are shocked at the content of the personal message services, and some run up huge telephone bills because they use their **Minitels** too much.

Activités

A. You have a brand-new, sophisticated product to market. How would you get people to use it?

B. If you had a computer hooked up to phone lines, what services would you like to have? Number the following in order of importance to you, and add others you can imagine.

___ telephone numbers	___ sports results
___ weather forecast	___ horoscope
___ news	___ personal messages
___ ???	___ ???

C. It is easier to guess the meaning of new words if you know frequently used prefixes and suffixes. Study the definitions below and find the words in the reading passage that use the prefixes and suffixes given.

prefixes	suffixes
co = ensemble	**-ologue** = une personne qui *(who)* étudie
mini = petit	
télé = de loin	**-scope** = regarder
pseudo = faux	

Le Minitel   WWW

e compagnon indispensable de tous les «branchés°», le Minitel est un paradis où jeux° et messages personnels coexistent avec les annuaires télématiques° et les services utilitaires.

Le mot **Minitel** est la contraction de «mini» et «télématique». Imaginez un
5 petit écran° avec un clavier à touches° branché sur votre téléphone. Imaginez toute la France à votre portée°. Maintenant, il n'est pas nécessaire de sortir: on fait un numéro et on peut converser avec tout le monde.

L'idée est simple: France Télécom offre d'installer de petits terminaux dans les maisons françaises où il y a le téléphone. Ces terminaux servent d'annuaire
10 téléphonique informatisé° et remplacent les vieux° bottins en papier. Pour chercher le numéro d'une personne, on tape° son nom° et le nom de sa ville. Immédiatement, tous les gens de la même localité avec le même nom passent sur l'écran, et vous pouvez choisir votre correspondant.

cool people
games
computerized

petit... *small screen /*
clavier... *keyboard /*
reach

computerized / old
types / name

sur minitel:
■ 24 h sur 24
Pour sélectionner une école correspondant à vos desiderata, et recevoir sa documentation grâce au service lecteur
ACCÈS AU SERVICE:

3615 CIDE

Les Écoles se présentent sur Minitel.

INFORMATIONS

C.I.D.E.
CENTRE D'INFORMATION ET
DE DOCUMENTATION SUR L'ENSEIGNEMENT
1, rue de Choiseul, 75002 Paris
Tél.: **(1) 42 96 16 68**

Avec un Minitel, on peut consulter son horoscope, son compte en banque°, *bank account*
15 la météo, un médecin, un vétérinaire, un psychiatre et même un sexologue. Le
Minitel donne aussi des nouvelles° et remplace les journaux écrits°. Si on veut *news / written*
faire des courses sans quitter la maison, on tape le code «Télémarket» et on peut
acheter du beurre ou une bouteille° d'huile par exemple. *bottle*

Il ne faut pas oublier non plus° les messages personnels échangés la nuit par *either*
20 beaucoup d'abonnés. Les gens utilisent généralement un pseudonyme et par-
ticipent aux «messageries roses°». *messageries... adult mes-*
sages / matter
L'affaire° Minitel est très sérieuse. La France, avant tous les autres pays a
expérimenté avec la télématique de masse. Entreprises°, grandes banques, ser- *Companies*
vices publics et créateurs de programmes spéciaux pour Minitel ne veulent pas
25 manquer une occasion°. *manquer... miss an oppor-*
tunity

(Adapté de l'article «Le Minitel», Vol. 9, No. 5 du *Journal Français d'Amérique.*
Reprinted by permission)

Après la lecture

Questions sur le texte

1. Décrivez le Minitel.
2. Qui distribue le Minitel?
3. Qui peut avoir un Minitel?

4. Pour chercher un numéro, que faites-vous?
5. Quels sont les autres services?
6. Qu'est-ce que «les messageries roses»?

Activités

A. Répondez aux questions suivantes.

1. Voulez-vous avoir un Minitel chez vous? Pourquoi ou pourquoi pas?
2. Quels services sont utiles pour vous?
3. Quel est le montant *(cost)* de votre facture téléphonique? Est-ce peu ou beaucoup?
4. Pourquoi est-ce que le Minitel existe en France et pas aux Etats-Unis?

B. Regardez l'extrait du *Minitel Magazine* et répondez aux questions basées sur l'extrait.

1. A quoi sert le programme **Anglatel**?
2. Si on réussit bien, qu'est-ce qu'on peut gagner *(win)*?
3. Quand est-ce qu'on peut faire un stage *(training course)* d'anglais à Avignon ou à Aix-en-Provence?
4. Comment peut-on pratiquer sa prononciation?

36.15 + ANGLATEL

Au préalable, donner son pseudo et sa date de naissance, indispensable pour le suivi pédagogique.

INStructions

Faites les leçons et exercices, *Anglatel* vous indiquera si vous avez donné la bonne réponse. *Anglatel* comptabilisera et mémorisera vos points ; en cours d'exercice, la touche « guide » permet d'être assisté. Vous pouvez aussi pratiquer votre prononciation en lisant à haute voix la réponse correcte.

ABOnnements

Accès par le 36.14 à tarifs préférentiels.

ANGlatel lessons

Les différents niveaux (begining, pre-intermediate, intermediate, post-intermediate, pre-advanced, advanced) et les domaines (grammar, vocabulary, usage, pronunciation, reading comprehension, dialogues, idioms, etc).

DANgerous scoop

Le premier feuilleton d'aventure sur minitel.

SPEak with the professor

De 18 h 00 à 20 h 00 le lundi, mardi, mercredi et jeudi, salon « Anglatel » avec un professeur anglophone du Centre franco-américain de Provence.

BOOkshop

Consultation d'une liste de livres en anglais.

STAges d'anglais

Présentation des stages intensifs à Avignon et Aix-en-Provence, en juillet et août prochains.

SEE the top-scores

Les meilleurs scores réalisés par les usagers du service ; un aller/retour Paris-New York-Paris a été gagné par une personne en 1986.

MAIl-box

Boîtes aux lettres pour écrire aux profs du Centre.

TRIp to the USA

Conditions de participation au concours du meilleur score de l'année (1er prix : un voyage aux USA).

NEWs from the center

Présentation des activités du Centre franco-américain d'Aix-en-Provence.

FERnand Nathan

Informations de « Speakeasy Publications » (cassettes et journaux pour tous niveaux).

AUPair aux USA

Présentation de « Au pair in America », programme d'échanges culturels destiné aux jeunes européennes parlant anglais.

Vocabulaire

Noms / Pronoms

affaires	possessions	pile	battery
bureau de tabac	tobacco shop	portable	cellular phone
cabine téléphonique	phone booth	portefeuille	wallet
calculatrice	calculator	que	which, that
calculette	pocket calculator	qui	who
cassette	cassette	qu'est-ce que	what
CD	CD	qu'est-ce qui	what
chaîne stéréo	stereo system	qui est-ce que	whom
courrier électronique	e-mail	qui est-ce qui	who
disque compact	compact disk	quoi	what
erreur	wrong number	répondeur	answering machine
expression	expression	sac	purse
lecteur de disques compacts	CD player	téléphone	telephone
		téléviseur	TV set
magnétophone	tape recorder	voix	voice
magnétoscope	VCR	Walkman	Walkman
message	message		

Verbes

allumer	to turn on	rappeler	to call back
arriver	to arrive	réfléchir	to think about
brancher	to plug in	rester	to stay
choisir	to choose	réussir	to succeed / to pass (a test)
couper	to disconnect	rougir	to blush
désobéir	to disobey	savoir	to know
dormir	to sleep	se passer	to happen
finir	to finish	sentir	to feel
marcher	to function / to work	servir à	to be used for
mentir	to lie	sonner	to ring
obéir	to obey	sortir	to go out
partir	to leave	téléphoner	to telephone
pouvoir	can, may	voir	to see
punir	to punish	vouloir	to want
ranger	to put away, to clean up		

Adjectifs / Adverbes

ce, cette, cet	this	libre	free
ces	these / those	nécessaire	necessary
d'abord	first	plus tard	later
désolé	sorry	quel, quelle, quels, quelles	what / which
encore	still		

Expressions

à qui	to whom	Ne coupe pas.	Don't hang up.
Allô, j'écoute.	Hello.	Ne quittez pas.	Hold on.
ce n'est pas la peine	it's not worth the trouble	Qui est à l'appareil?	Who's speaking?
		vouloir bien	to be willing

Chapitre 8

Chapitre

Paris

 Commençons

 Grammaire

 Communiquons

 Lecture culturelle

 Vocabulaire

Notre-Dame et un bateau-mouche

Objectives

Language

Vocabulary for the computer and the post office • Oral vowels and nasal consonants • The weather • **Suivre** and **suivre des cours** • Direct object pronouns: Third person • **Voir**

Culture

Paris and its monuments • Studying in France • The post office

Communication

Talking about the weather • Discussing classes and course work • Using the post office

Commençons

Deux cartes postales

Roger Diallo est un étudiant sénégalais. Il est à Paris, et il va suivre des cours à la Sorbonne pendant l'année. Deux semaines après son arrivée, il passe le week-end à la campagne et il fait une carte postale à ses parents.

Paris, le 12 octobre

Mes chers parents,

Je suis arrivé le 15 septembre. Il a fait très chaud pendant deux semaines, mais maintenant il fait beau. Puisque les cours n'ont pas encore commencé, je visite la capitale et ses monuments avec mes amis français. Hier, nous sommes allés au musée d'Orsay et je l'ai trouvé impressionnant. L'autre jour, nous avons visité la Conciergerie, la Sainte-Chapelle et Notre-Dame. Si nous avons le temps la semaine prochaine, nous allons aller à la tour Eiffel et à l'Arc de Triomphe.

Tout va bien, mais j'ai déjà dépensé beaucoup d'argent! Donnez-moi de vos nouvelles.

Affectueux baisers,
Roger

Quinze jours plus tard, juste avant la rentrée, il expédie une autre carte à sa sœur, Monique.

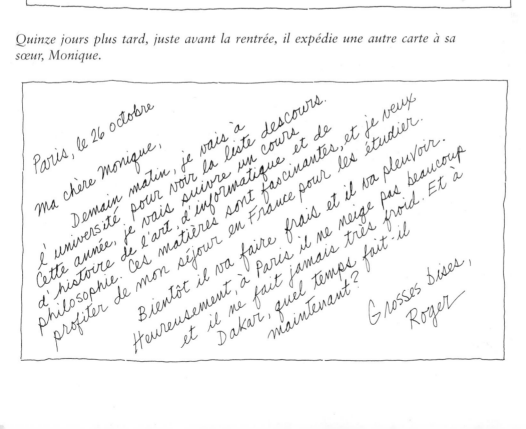

Paris, le 26 octobre

Ma chère Monique,

Demain matin, je vais à l'université pour voir la liste des cours. Cette année, je vais suivre un cours d'histoire de l'art, d'informatique et de philosophie. Ces matières sont fascinantes, et je veux profiter de mon séjour en France pour les étudier.

Bientôt il va faire frais et il va pleuvoir. Heureusement, à Paris il ne neige pas beaucoup et il ne fait jamais très froid. Et à Dakar, quel temps fait-il maintenant?

Grosses bises,
Roger

Etudions les cartes postales

1. Quand Roger est-il arrivé en France?
2. Quel temps fait-il en France?
3. Avec qui Roger visite-t-il Paris?
4. Quels monuments veut-il visiter?
5. A qui expédie-t-il la deuxième carte postale?
6. Quels cours Roger va-t-il suivre cette année?

Mots clés

cartes postales	*postcards*	affectueux baisers	*hugs and kisses*
sénégalais	*Senegalese*	juste	*just*
suivre des cours	*to take courses*	rentrée	*start of classes*
pendant	*during*	expédie (expédier)	*sends*
arrivée *(f.)*	*arrival*	chère	*dear*
campagne	*countryside*	histoire *(f.)* de l'art	*art history*
chers	*dear*	informatique *(f.)*	*computer science*
puisque	*since*	matières *(f.)*	*subjects*
ne... pas encore	*not yet*	profiter de	*take advantage*
capitale	*capital*	séjour	*stay*
monuments *(m.)*	*monuments*	bientôt	*soon*
l'	*it*	Il va faire frais.	*It is going to be cool.*
impressionnant	*impressive*	pleuvoir	*to rain*
avons le temps (avoir le temps)	*have the time*	Il ne neige pas. (neiger)	*It doesn't snow.*
tout	*all*	ne... jamais	*never*
ai dépensé (dépenser)	*have spent*	Quel temps fait-il?	*What's the weather like?*
Donnez-moi de vos nouvelles.	*Let me hear from you.*	grosses bises	*love and kisses*

Faisons connaissance

www

Paris, the capital of France, is one of the most beautiful cities in the world and is renowned for its monuments, modern and historical, which millions of tourists come to visit each year. The **musée d'Orsay** is an art museum that opened in late 1986 in what used to be a train station, **la gare d'Orsay.** The museum houses a

Musée
d'Orsay

Informations générales

Musée d'Orsay
62, rue de Lille
75007 Paris
tél. 45 49 48 14

répondeur
informations
générales : 45 49 11 11

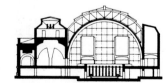

Entrée principale : 1, rue de Bellechasse.
Entrée des Grandes expositions du M'O :
place Henry-de-Montherlant (sur le quai).
Entrée du restaurant après la fermeture
du Musée : 62 bis, rue de Lille.

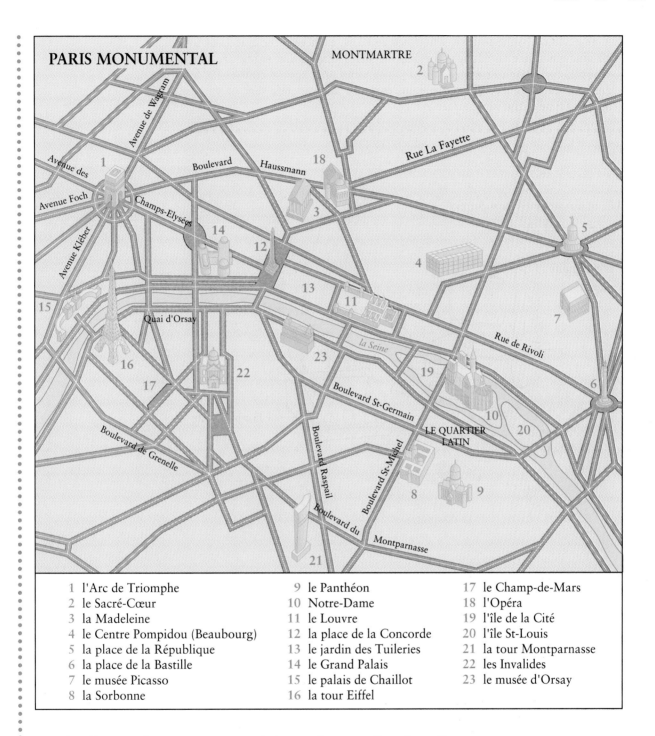

PARIS MONUMENTAL

MONTMARTRE

1 l'Arc de Triomphe	9 le Panthéon	17 le Champ-de-Mars
2 le Sacré-Cœur	10 Notre-Dame	18 l'Opéra
3 la Madeleine	11 le Louvre	19 l'île de la Cité
4 le Centre Pompidou (Beaubourg)	12 la place de la Concorde	20 l'île St-Louis
5 la place de la République	13 le jardin des Tuileries	21 la tour Montparnasse
6 la place de la Bastille	14 le Grand Palais	22 les Invalides
7 le musée Picasso	15 le palais de Chaillot	23 le musée d'Orsay
8 la Sorbonne	16 la tour Eiffel	

superb collection of over 4,000 pieces of nineteenth-century French art. It now attracts a large number of visitors (4 million in its first year) and has received great critical acclaim. The **Conciergerie,** the **Sainte-Chapelle,** and **Notre-Dame** cathedral, magnificent examples of Gothic art, are all located on the **île de la Cité** and surrounded by the river **Seine.** Nearby is the **Quartier latin,** so named because at the **Sorbonne,** the original university of Paris, classes were once conducted in Latin.

In addition to the tourists who flock to Paris, each year thousands of foreign students come to France. Among the main centers for study are Paris, Grenoble, and Aix-en-Provence, but all universities offer special courses for foreigners to learn French. These programs may last an academic year or varying lengths of time in the summer.

Enrichissons notre vocabulaire

Un ordinateur *(A computer)*

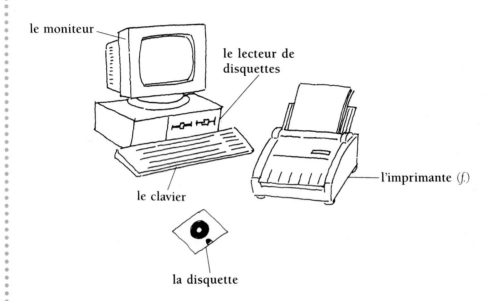

le moniteur

le lecteur de disquettes

le clavier

l'imprimante (f.)

la disquette

Faites-vous de l'informatique? *(Are you studying computer science?)*

—Qu'est-ce que tu penses du **matériel** IBM?	*What do you think of IBM **hardware**?*
—C'est formidable! J'ai acheté deux **logiciels**.	*It's fantastic! I bought two **software programs**.*
—Quelles sortes?	*What kind?*
—J'ai un **traitement de texte** pour mes **notes** et mes devoirs **écrits** et un **tableur**.	*I have a **word processor** for my **notes** and my **written** work, and a **spreadsheet**.*
—Avec mon **modem**, je peux consulter mon **courrier électronique** et le **réseau Internet**.	*With my **modem**, I can check my **e-mail** and the **Internet**.*
—Tu as **rencontré** des problèmes?	*Have you **met** with any problems?*

—Non, et je vais **gagner** de l'argent si je **tape** les devoirs de mes amis.

No, and I am going to **earn** money if I **type** my friends' papers.

—Est-ce que je peux **emprunter** ton matériel et tes logiciels?

May I **borrow** your equipment and your software?

—Non, je **ne** les **prête jamais;** je les **utilise tout le temps.**

No, I **never lend** them; I **use** them **all the time.**

Au bureau de poste (At the post office)

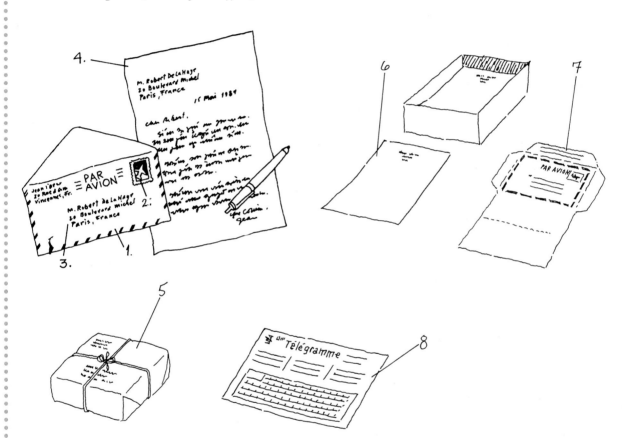

1. une **enveloppe**
2. un **timbre**
3. l'**adresse** (f.)
4. une **lettre**
5. un **paquet** / un **colis**
6. du **papier à lettres**
7. un **aérogramme**
8. un **télégramme**

Le **facteur:** Bonjour, Madame.

The **mailman:** Good morning, ma'am.

Mme Legrain: Vous avez du **courrier** pour moi?

Mme Legrain: Do you have any **mail** for me?

Le facteur: Oui, une lettre **recommandée** et un **mandat.**

The mailman: Yes, a **registered** letter and a **money order.**

Mme Legrain: Tenez, merci beaucoup.

Mme Legrain: There, thanks a lot.

Prononciation   Oral vowels and nasal consonants   [○━○]

A. In Chapter 7, you learned the pronunciation of the three nasal vowels in French: / ɛ̃ / (**pain**), / ɑ̃ / (**lent**), and / ɔ̃ / (**ton**). With nasal vowels, you never pronounce the letter **n** or **m** that accompanies the written vowel.

    The masculine forms of the following adjectives end in a nasal vowel, so the **n** is not pronounced. The **n** must be pronounced in the feminine, however, so the preceding vowel is oral instead of nasal.

Masculine	Feminine
améric**ain**	améric**ain**e
canadi**en**	canadi**en**ne
itali**en**	itali**en**ne

B. The **n** or **m** must be pronounced if it is doubled (**sommes**) or followed by a vowel (**téléphone**).

Pronounce the following words and indicate whether the underlined vowels in boldface are oral or nasal.

    je d**o**nne / t**on** stylo / bi**en** / **en** ville / s**o**nne / **a**nnée / v**in** / mat**in** / **i**nutile / t**i**mbre / le m**o**niteur / **i**mpressi**o**nn**a**nt

Exercices

A. Pronounce the following pairs of words after your teacher, making a clear distinction between the oral and nasal vowels.

1. Jean / Jeanne
2. an / année
3. matin / matinée
4. plein / pleine
5. un / une
6. vietnamien / vietnamienne
7. gens / jeune
8. brun / brune

B. Read the following sentences aloud, taking care not to nasalize vowels before pronounced **n** and **m**.

1. Les usines anciennes consomment beaucoup d'énergie.
2. Elle aime un homme ambitieux.
3. Tiens! Etienne déjeune avec une Canadienne.
4. Anne et Micheline vont emprunter mon traitement de texte.
5. Jean et Jeanne ont acheté un ordinateur.
6. Yvonne expédie un télégramme à Lisbonne.

Grammaire

I. The weather (La météo)   WWW

A. In Chapter 5 you learned that the verb **faire** is often used to describe the weather.

Quel temps fait-il?

Il **fait** beau.	Il **fait** chaud.
Il **fait** mauvais.	Il **fait** froid.

There are other descriptions of the weather that contain **faire**:

Il fait **du vent.**   Il fait **du brouillard.**

Il fait **du soleil.**   Il fait **de l'orage.**

Il fait **frais.**	*It is cool.*
Il fait **bon.**	*It is nice.*
Il fait **une chaleur insupportable!**	*The heat is unbearable!*

B. In addition to **faire**, there are other verbs and terms used to describe weather:

être: **Le ciel est couvert.**	*The sky is overcast. / It's cloudy.*
neiger: **Il neige.**	to snow: *It is snowing.*
pleuvoir: **Il pleut.**	to rain: *It is raining.*
Il y a des **nuages** *(m.)*.	*There are clouds.*
Il y a des **éclairs** *(m.)* et du **tonnerre.**	*There is lightning and thunder.*
Il y a déjà beaucoup de **neige** *(f.)*.	*There is already a lot of snow.*
Nous avons eu beaucoup de **pluie** *(f.)* cette année.	*We've had a lot of rain this year.*

C. The following examples show how weather expressions are used in other tenses.

Passé composé

Il **a fait** très chaud pendant deux semaines.
Le week-end dernier, il **a plu** mais il **n'a pas neigé.**

Futur proche

Il **va faire frais** et il **va pleuvoir.**
Il **va neiger** la semaine prochaine.

Attention!

1. **Il fait beau** is used for general weather conditions *(warm, sunny)*, while **il fait bon** refers to temperature and can refer to a room indoors.

   Il fait bon dans cette chambre.

2. **Chaud** and **froid** can be used with three different verbs, depending on what is being described.

weather (**faire**):	Il **fait chaud.** Il **fait froid.**
people (**avoir**):	J'ai **chaud.** Robert **a froid.**
things (**être**):	Cette eau **est chaude.** Ma bière n'**est** pas assez **froide.**

Langue

A. **Quel temps fait-il?** Faites deux phrases pour chaque dessin *(each drawing)*.

B. **La météo.** Refaites les phrases suivantes en employant les mots entre parenthèses.

1. Quel temps fait-il?   (… hier?)
2. Il pleut.   (… hier.)
3. Il neige beaucoup.   (L'année dernière…)
4. Il ne fait pas froid.   (… demain.)
5. Il fait de l'orage.   (Le week-end dernier…)
6. Il va faire du brouillard.   (… hier matin.)

C. **Le climat en Europe.** Caractérisez le climat des pays suivants en faisant des phrases complètes avec les mots donnés.

1. pleuvoir / beaucoup / Angleterre
2. neiger / beaucoup / Suisse
3. faire / soleil / Italie
4. Espagne / faire / chaud
5. faire / brouillard / Irlande
6. Norvège / faire / froid

Culture

D. **Les prévisions de la météo.** Regardez la carte météorologique ci-dessous *(below)* et répondez aux questions.

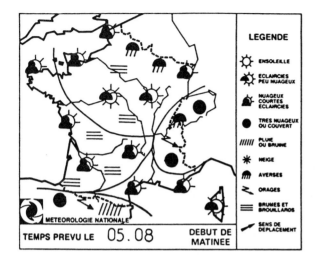

La carte

1. Est-ce qu'il va faire du soleil en France?
2. Quel temps va-t-il faire dans les Alpes?
3. Va-t-il faire beau sur une des plages en France?

La liste des villes

4. Dans combien de villes est-ce qu'il a plu?
5. Est-ce qu'il a neigé?
6. Il a fait très froid à Tokyo?

Communication

E. **En vacances.** Vos camarades partent en vacances. Suggérez des activités pour les différentes conditions météorologiques.

MODÈLE: quand il fait bon
Quand il fait bon, faites une promenade!

1. quand il pleut
2. quand il neige
3. quand il fait mauvais
4. quand il fait du soleil
5. quand il fait de l'orage
6. quand il fait très froid

F. **Les prévisions de la météo.** Choisissez un(e) camarade et préparez ensemble un bulletin météorologique *(weather report)* pour une des situations suivantes.

1. votre ville cet après-midi
2. votre ville l'hiver dernier
3. votre région ce week-end
4. San Diego en hiver
5. le Sénégal
6. Montréal en hiver

G. **Questions personnelles.** Votre temps préféré.

1. Etes-vous content(e) quand il fait froid? quand il fait chaud?
2. Aimez-vous faire une promenade quand il pleut?
3. Quel temps a-t-il fait le week-end dernier? Qu'est-ce que vous avez fait?
4. Quel temps voulez-vous avoir pour vos prochaines vacances?
5. Où est-ce qu'on trouve un climat idéal?
6. Avez-vous visité une ville uniquement pour son climat?

II.   Suivre / Suivre des cours   www

You use **suivre** to express the idea of *to follow (to follow a person; to follow an idea)* and to talk about taking an academic course.

A.   Suivre

suivre *(to follow)*	
je **suis**	nous **suivons**
tu **suis**	vous **suivez**
il / elle / on **suit**	ils / elles **suivent**
Passé composé: il **a suivi**	

Nous allons **suivre** cette auto.
Suivez-moi, s'il vous plaît.
Vous **suivez** ce prof?

B.   Suivre des cours

1. **Suivre** is often used with academic subjects (**suivre des cours, suivre un cours de...**) to express *to take a course or courses.*

   Il va **suivre des cours** à la Sorbonne.
   J'ai **suivi des cours** d'informatique.

   The following vocabulary can be used to talk about the school year: **un trimestre** *(a quarter),* **un semestre** *(a semester),* and **l'année scolaire** *(the school year).*

2. There are three ways to state the subjects you study.

suivre un cours de (d'):	Mon ami **suit un cours** d'histoire.
faire du (de la, des, de l'):	Moi, je **fais de la** physique mais j'aime mieux la psychologie.
étudier le (la, les):	Ma sœur **étudie** le latin et le grec.

Attention!

You must be sure to use the correct article with each verb.

1. **Suivre un cours** takes only the preposition **de**, not an article.

2. **Faire** takes only the articles **du, de la, de l', des.**

3. **Etudier** takes only the definite articles **le, la, l', les.**

Mots clés **Academic subjects**

l'anthropologie *(f.)*	les langues étrangères	*foreign languages*
l'architecture *(f.)*	l'allemand *(m.)*	le grec
l'art *(m.)*	l'anglais *(m.)*	l'italien *(m.)*
la biologie	l'arabe *(m.)*	le japonais
la chimie *chemistry*	le chinois	le latin
le droit *law*	l'espagnol *(m.)*	le russe
l'éducation physique *(f.)*	le français	
la géographie	la médecine	
la géologie	la musique	
la gestion *management*	la philosophie	
l'histoire *(f.)*	la physique	
l'informatique *(f.)*	la psychologie	
le journalisme	les sciences économiques *(f.)*	
la littérature	les sciences politiques *(f.)*	
les mathématiques *(f.)*	la sociologie	

Note that all languages are masculine and all sciences are feminine.

Ce qu'ils disent

1. When French students talk about the subjects that they study, they often use abbreviations. Most of them end in **o**.

philo philosophie		**psycho** psychologie	
sciences éco sciences économiques		**socio** sociologie	
sciences po sciences politiques		**les maths** mathématiques	

2. To indicate their majors, students use the verb **être** with the preposition **en**.

   Je **suis en socio** à la fac.   *I'm a sociology major at the university.*

Langue

A. Des présentations. Faites des phrases en remplaçant les mots en italique par les mots entre parenthèses.

MODÈLE: Il fait du français.   (étudier)
         Il étudie le français.

1. Luc *étudie* le japonais.   (suivre un cours)
2. Je *fais* du droit.   (étudier)
3. Nous *allons suivre un cours* d'histoire.   (faire)
4. Tu *vas étudier* la géologie.   (suivre un cours)
5. Mon camarade de chambre *a fait* du chinois.   (suivre un cours)
6. Julie et Kevin *ont étudié* la physique.   (être en)

B. Les études de Juliette. Faites une phrase complète avec les mots donnés.

1. Juliette / suivre / cours / informatique / Etats-Unis
2. semestre dernier / elle / étudier / grec / et / latin
3. Sa sœur / être / sciences économiques
4. année prochaine / elles / suivre / cours / psychologie?
5. Non, elles / ne… pas / étudier / sciences
6. trimestre prochain / Juliette / faire / informatique

Culture

C. Au collège. Un «collège» est l'équivalent d'un *junior high school* aux Etats-Unis. Ci-dessous vous avez l'emploi du temps *(schedule)* de Caroline, une élève de cinquième qui habite à Lyon. Décrivez son emploi du temps en répondant aux questions à la page 203.

		LUNDI	SALLE	MARDI	SALLE	MERCREDI	SALLE	JEUDI	SALLE	VENDREDI	SALLE	
8H.15												
MATIN	I	maths	15	Sciences Naturelles 1h 30	50	maths	16	Histoire Géo	62	Français	10	I
	II	Anglais	26			Dessin	18	Enseignement religieux	23	Soutien de Français ou Hist-Géo	10 62	II
	III	musique	13	Sciences Physiques 1h 30	2	Français	36	Français	39	Hist-Géo	62	III
12H.15	IV					Français	36					IV
13H.30												
SOIR	V	Instruction Civique	62	Technologie	At			Soutien de maths		maths	27	V
	VI	Sport		Technologie	At			Anglais		Soutien d'Anglais	26	VI
15H.30	VII	sport		Français	9			Sport		Anglais	26	VII

1. Qu'est-ce que Caroline étudie le lundi matin?
2. Quand fait-elle du sport?
3. Dans quelle salle de classe a-t-elle son instruction civique?
4. Suit-elle un cours de philosophie?
5. Quelle langue étrangère Caroline étudie-t-elle? Combien d'heures par semaine?
6. Quand est-ce qu'elle n'a pas de cours?

Communication

D. De la littérature. Votre camarade de chambre a un livre d'un des auteurs suivants. Quelle langue étudie-t-il / elle?

MODÈLE: Dante *Il / Elle fait de l'italien.*
Il / Elle étudie l'italien.

1. Cervantes
2. Goethe
3. Jules César
4. Simone de Beauvoir
5. Homère
6. Confucius
7. Tolstoï
8. Emily Brontë

E. Questions personnelles. Vos études.

1. Quels cours suivez-vous ce trimestre / ce semestre?
2. Qu'est-ce que vous allez étudier la prochaine année scolaire?
3. Faites-vous des sciences cette année?
4. Quels cours aimez-vous / détestez-vous?
5. Quel cours est trop difficile pour vous?
6. Qu'est-ce que vous faites quand vous n'allez pas aux cours?

III.   Direct object pronouns: Third person

You use direct object pronouns to refer to someone or something already mentioned in a conversation.

A.   Direct objects

1. In English, a direct object receives the action of the verb directly. In the following sentences, the words in boldface type are direct objects.

He is buying **the apple**.

I like **your ideas**.

They are going to meet **Joe** at school.

We saw **Jane** at the movies.

2. A direct object can be a person, an object, or an idea. It answers the question *whom?* or *what?* Direct object pronouns replace nouns that have already been mentioned.

"Where is the jacket?"
"He is buying **it**."

"What do you think of his ideas?"
"I like **them**."

"Are they going to get Joe?"
"Yes, they are going to get **him**."

"Has anyone seen Mary?"
"I saw **her**."

B. Third-person direct object pronouns

French also has direct objects. They may be replaced by direct object pronouns that are placed *before* the verb in an affirmative or negative present-tense statement.

Roger visite **la capitale.** → Roger **la** visite.
Il trouve **le musée** impressionnant. → Il **le** trouve impressionnant.
Il aime **l'informatique.** → Il **l'**aime.
Il suit **ses cours** à la Sorbonne. → Il **les** suit à la Sorbonne.

The following chart summarizes the third-person direct object pronouns.

	singular	*plural*
masculine	**le, l'** *him, it*	
		les *them*
feminine	**la, l'** *her, it*	

Attention!

Remember that every French noun has a gender, so *it* is expressed by either **le** or **la**, depending on the noun for which it stands. Both **le** and **la** become **l'** before a vowel, while the silent **s** of **les** becomes the sound / z / with a *liaison*.

—Vous faites du russe?
—Je **l'**étudie, mais je ne **le** parle pas.

—Pourquoi parle-t-il aux Dupont?
—Il **les** invite chez lui.

C. Position of direct object pronouns

1. As you have just seen, the direct object pronoun precedes the verb in an affirmative or negative present tense statement.

   —Vous avez **beaucoup d'argent?**
   —Non, je **le** dépense tout de suite.

   —Vous avez utilisé **ce logiciel?**
   —Oui, mais je ne **le** trouve pas intéressant.

2. The same is true of questions, including inversion.

   —Voilà **notre étudiant sénégalais!**
   —**L'**avez-vous en cours ce trimestre?

   —Où est **la lettre de Bernard?**
   —Est-ce que vous **la** voulez maintenant?

3. In any *helping verb plus infinitive* construction, the direct object pronoun precedes the infinitive, that is, the verb of which the pronoun is a direct object.

> —Il a **beaucoup de devoirs?**
> —Oui, mais il ne peut pas **les** faire.

> —Tu as **mes aérogrammes?**
> —Non, je vais **les** apporter demain.

4. In the **passé composé**, the pronoun precedes the auxiliary verb **avoir**.

> —Tu vas suivre **un cours** sur Corneille?
> —Non, je **l'**ai déjà étudié.

> —Avez-vous **votre Walkman?**
> —Non, je **l'**ai laissé chez moi.

L'orthographe

1. In the **passé composé**, the past participle must agree in gender and in number with a direct object pronoun that precedes it. This does not change the pronunciation of most past participles.

> —Tu as acheté **cette voiture?**
> —Non, je **l'**ai empruntée à un ami.

> —Où as-tu trouvé **ces chaussures?**
> —Je **les** ai trouvées à Montréal.

2. You have learned only one past participle whose masculine and feminine forms can be *audibly* distinguished: **faire** (**fait / faite**).

> —Est-ce que je peux faire **la vaisselle?**
> —Non, nous **l'**avons déjà faite.

> —Ils vont faire **leurs courses** cet après-midi?
> —Non, ils **les** ont faites ce matin.

Langue

A. **Changeons des phrases.** Mettez les phrases suivantes au **passé composé** et au **futur proche.**

1. Nous les empruntons tous les jours.
2. Vous la suivez.
3. Il la laisse à la gare.
4. Les porte-t-on aujourd'hui?
5. Est-ce que vous l'invitez?
6. Je la regarde le soir.

B. **Qu'est-ce qu'on fait?** Remplacez les compléments d'objet direct *(direct objects)* par un pronom dans les phrases suivantes.

1. J'utilise mon ordinateur.
2. Julie emprunte-t-elle ton logiciel?
3. Jacques a fini son livre.
4. Tu vas inviter Sylvie et Monique?
5. Vous n'avez pas étudié l'allemand?
6. Henri n'aime pas prêter son imprimante.

Culture

C. **Les Français et la télévision.** Répondez aux questions suivantes en employant un pronom complément d'objet direct.

1. Est-ce que les Français regardent beaucoup la télévision?
2. Aiment-ils regarder la télé l'après-midi?
3. Ils aiment Jerry Lewis?
4. Ils aiment les westerns?
5. Est-ce qu'ils apprécient les jeux télévisés *(game shows)*?
6. Ils mangent et regardent la télé en même temps?

Communication

D. **Conversations interrompues.** Vous entendez *(hear)* la dernière partie d'une conversation. Dans chaque situation, imaginez le sujet de cette conversation.

MODÈLE: Je ne peux pas la faire.
    Tu ne peux pas faire la vaisselle?

1. Pouvez-vous l'expédier?
2. Il ne va pas les inviter.
3. Tu ne l'as pas préparée?
4. Nous ne l'avons pas étudié.
5. Je ne les ai pas trouvés.
6. Je n'aime pas le faire.

E. **Interviews.** Posez des questions à vos camarades avec les éléments donnés ci-dessous. Ils / Elles vont répondre en employant des pronoms.

MODÈLE: Etudiant(e) 1: *Vas-tu préparer ton dîner ce soir?*
    Etudiant(e) 2: *Oui, je vais le préparer. / Non, je ne vais pas le préparer.*

aller	consulter le médecin
désirer	acheter un ordinateur
pouvoir	expédier une lettre à tes grands-parents
vouloir	étudier l'arabe ou le chinois
	écouter tes parents
	expliquer tes absences
	faire la cuisine chez toi
	montrer tes photos
	oublier ton passé
	préparer ton dîner ce soir
	finir tes cours cette année
	choisir ton / ta camarade de chambre pour l'année prochaine
	suivre le cours du même professeur le trimestre prochain

F. **Votre vie à l'université.** En petits groupes, préparez des réponses aux questions suivantes. Employez des pronoms et informez vos camarades de cours des résultats.

1. As-tu étudié la musique? l'informatique?
2. Aimes-tu tes cours ce trimestre?
3. Vas-tu étudier le français le trimestre prochain?
4. Où fais-tu tes devoirs?
5. Utilises-tu ton ordinateur pour faire tes devoirs?
6. Où expédies-tu ton courrier?

G. Vos opinions. Dites *(Tell)* comment vous trouvez les personnes suivantes. Utilisez les adjectifs donnés.

super	formidable	charmant	bien
ennuyeux	insupportable	affreux (-se)	pas mal

MODÈLE: *Newt Gingrich? Je le trouve ennuyeux.*

1. Michael Bolton
2. Jim Carrey
3. Mary-Kate et Ashley Olsen
4. Madonna
5. Fabio
6. Roseanne
7. Yanni
8. Pauly Shore

H. Questions personnelles. La vie moderne. Employez des pronoms compléments d'objet direct dans vos réponses.

1. Aimez-vous le jazz? le rock? le rap?
2. Quand écoutez-vous cette musique?
3. Votre camarade de chambre prête ses logiciels? ses vêtements?
4. Appréciez-vous l'art moderne?
5. Avez-vous étudié l'informatique?
6. Avez-vous utilisé les ordinateurs de votre université? Pourquoi?

IV. Voir

You use the verb **voir** to indicate seeing as well as understanding.

voir *(to see)*	
je **vois**	nous **voyons**
tu **vois**	vous **voyez**
il / elle / on **voit**	ils / elles **voient**

Passé composé: il **a vu**
Imperative: **vois / voyons / voyez**

—**Avez**-vous **vu** mon sac?
—Oui, nous l'**avons vu** dans ta chambre.

—Tu **as vu** mes cartes postales?
—Non, je ne les **ai** pas **vues**.

A. The singular forms and the third-person plural (**voient**) have the same pronunciation, / vwa /.

—Son père a 82 ans! Comment va-t-il?
—Pas mal, mais il ne **voit** pas bien.

—Ils ne sont pas contents!
—Ils ne **voient** pas pourquoi tu es toujours en retard.

Attention!

1. The expression **aller voir** means *to visit* and is used with people. **Visiter** can only be used with places.

> Quand j'**ai visité** Paris l'année dernière, je **suis allé voir** des amis.

2. **Voir un film** is used for movie theaters. For films on television, use **regarder**.

> Ils ne veulent pas **regarder** ce film parce qu'ils l'**ont** déjà **vu** au cinéma.

B. Other verbs conjugated like **voir** are **prévoir** *(to foresee)* and **revoir** *(to see again* or *to review)*.

> Il n'**a** pas **prévu** cela.
> Elle va **revoir** ses leçons.

Ce qu'ils disent

The imperative form **Voyons!** changes meaning according to the speaker's tone of voice. With the simple declarative intonation, it means *Let's see*, as when someone is looking for something or trying to think of something. With a slightly exasperated intonation, it means *Come on!*

> Voyons. Où est-ce que j'ai laissé mon parapluie?
> Voyons! Tu n'es pas sérieux!

Langue

A. Voyage en Europe. Faites des questions avec les mots donnés.

1. Qu'est-ce que / tu / voir / en France / été dernier?
2. Tu / revoir / amis parisiens?
3. amis / prévoir / une visite d'une semaine?
4. Vous / voir / bon film / ensemble?
5. On / prévoir / un / été / très chaud / n'est-ce pas?
6. Tu / vouloir / revoir / Paris?

B. Après les vacances. Répondez aux questions suivantes en employant des pronoms à la place des compléments d'objet direct.

1. A-t-on bien prévu *la météo* pour tes vacances?
2. Tu as revu *ta petite amie?*
3. Tes amis ont revu *leurs parents?*
4. Tu n'as pas vu *le dernier film d'Isabelle Adjani?*
5. Est-ce que je vais voir *tes photos de vacances?*
6. Est-ce que nous allons revoir *nos leçons de français* maintenant?

Culture   WWW

C. **Visitons Paris.** Vous allez visiter Paris avec votre famille. Expliquez-leur quels monuments on voit des sites donnés ci-dessous. Utilisez le plan de Paris à la page 193 pour préparer vos réponses.

MODÈLE: le boulevard Saint-Michel
Du boulevard Saint-Michel on voit le Panthéon.

1. le boulevard Montparnasse
2. le quai d'Orsay
3. la Seine
4. le boulevard Haussmann
5. le palais de Chaillot
6. le jardin des Tuileries

Communication

D. **Votre avenir** *(future)*. Qu'est-ce que vous voyez dans votre futur? Utilisez les suggestions suivantes et votre imagination pour interviewer un(e) camarade de cours.

MODÈLE: *Je vois cinq enfants, une profession fascinante et beaucoup d'argent.*

une maison blanche   une profession intéressante
une voiture de sport   des enfants intelligents
un appartement à Nice   des vacances à Tahiti
une femme / un mari riche   un yacht aux Antilles

E. **Au revoir!** Qui voulez-vous revoir ou ne pas revoir? Qu'est-ce que vous voulez revoir ou ne pas revoir? Cherchez en classe les étudiants qui ont les mêmes opinions que vous.

MODÈLE: *Je ne veux pas revoir mon professeur d'éducation physique.*
Je veux revoir le film Casablanca.

film   villes
ami(es)   chanteurs (-euses)
professeur(s)   émissions de télévision *(TV shows)*

F. **Questions personnelles.** Vos activités.

1. Avez-vous vu vos parents récemment? Quand?
2. Allez-vous voir un film ce week-end? Quel film?
3. Est-ce qu'on voit souvent des films français dans votre ville?
4. Vous avez passé des vacances avec votre famille? Qu'est-ce que vous avez vu ensemble?
5. Qu'est-ce qu'on peut voir dans votre ville?
6. Qu'est-ce qu'on voit de la fenêtre de votre chambre?

Communiquons

Aller au bureau de poste

The post office (**le bureau de poste, la poste** or **les PTT**) is an institution in France that every visitor should know because it plays so many roles. You not only mail things there but also make phone calls. The French use the post office even for some banking needs, such as a checking account (**un compte-chèque postal** or **CCP**).

Expressions

> ▶ **On expédie le courrier.**

C'est combien pour envoyer une lettre aux Etats-Unis?	*How much is it to send a letter to the United States?*
Par avion, ça coûte quatre francs trente les cinq grammes.	*Air mail is four francs and thirty centimes for five grams.*
Je voudrais acheter un timbre à trois francs.	*I would like to buy a three-franc stamp.*

▶ On donne un coup de téléphone.

Je voudrais téléphoner avec
préavis à un ami à Lyon.

*I would like to make a
person-to-person call to a
friend in Lyon.*

L'étudiant va téléphoner à ses
parents aux Etats-Unis en
P.C.V.

*The student is going to call his
parents in the U.S. collect.*

Allez dans la cabine numéro
onze, Mademoiselle.

Go into booth #11, miss.

Je désire faire un appel
interurbain / international.

*I want to make a long-distance /
international call.*

▶ On utilise la poste restante.

En France on peut recevoir
son courrier à la poste
restante.

*In France, you can receive mail
at general delivery.*

Le préposé demande toujours
une pièce d'identité.

*The employee always asks for
an ID.*

Il faut payer la surtaxe.

You must pay a charge.

Interaction *Un étudiant américain va au bureau de poste.* ⊙

L'ÉTUDIANT: Est-ce que vous avez une lettre pour moi? Ma famille l'a
envoyée à la poste restante.

LA PRÉPOSÉE: Oui, s'ils ont bien indiqué ce bureau. Je vais chercher. Vous
avez une pièce d'identité avec photo? Et il va y avoir une petite
surtaxe à payer.

L'ÉTUDIANT: D'accord°. Et est-ce que vous pouvez me donner un numéro de   *O.K.*
téléphone?

LA PRÉPOSÉE: Ah, non, Monsieur, mais vous avez le Minitel dans le hall à
gauche°.   *left*

Activités

A. Votre correspondance. Répondez aux questions suivantes.

1. Si vous allez en Europe, à qui allez-vous envoyer des cartes postales?
   des lettres?
2. Vous avez déjà envoyé des cartes postales? Avec une photo de quoi?
3. Avez-vous téléphoné d'un téléphone public? A qui? Comment avez-
   vous payé?
4. Où pouvez-vous recevoir du courrier en France? Et aux Etats-Unis?
   Est-ce que la poste restante est utile?

B. **Jeu de rôles.** Jouez les scènes suivantes avec un(e) camarade de cours.

1. Vous voulez envoyer des cartes postales dans plusieurs pays.
2. Vous voulez téléphoner à vos parents, mais vous n'avez pas d'argent.
3. Vous pensez avoir une lettre à la poste restante, mais l'employé ne peut pas la trouver.
4. Vous voulez envoyer un télégramme.

Lecture culturelle

Avant la lecture

From one year to the next, Paris undergoes important transformations, and even tourists who visit the French capital regularly find that changes have occurred since their last trip. Recently, people have discovered the glass pyramid of the **Louvre,** the new opera house on the **place de la Bastille,** the dome of the **Invalides** and the **Génie de la Bastille,** both glistening with the new gold leaf that was spread upon them for the celebration of the **bicentenaire de la Révolution.** But they also find that the number of fast-food establishments is steadily growing along the **Champs-Elysées,** which is one of the world's most famous avenues.

More recently, new architectural projects have developed in the eastern part of the city. The **quartier de la Villette** now has a new park which Parisians have already adopted. Anyone who enjoys strolling about the streets in **Belleville** or walking along the banks of the old **canal Saint-Martin** should hurry before promoters start tearing down all the old buildings to replace them with offices and luxury apartments.

Activités

A. Select a major American city that you visit frequently and identify the important changes that you have noticed from one trip to the next.

B. On the map of Paris on page 193, find as many as possible of the sites mentioned in the postcards at the beginning of the chapter, in the preceding **Avant la lecture** paragraphs, and in the following **Lecture culturelle.**

C. Scan the following reading passage and find ten nouns that refer to parts of a city or structures that one would find in a city (e.g., **rue, parc,** etc.).

Paris change   WWW

*L*es vieux° quartiers parisiens changent et ceux qui les connaissent° et les aiment depuis toujours doivent se dépêcher° d'aller les revoir parce qu'ils risquent de perdre bientôt cette originalité appréciée par des générations de Parisiens et de touristes.

5   Regardez Montmartre par exemple. La Butte a toujours beaucoup de visiteurs et elle attire° de plus en plus d'artistes. Mais la Ville de Paris qui est op-

old / ceux... those who know them / doivent... must hurry

attracts

Place du Tertre et le Sacré-Cœur

posée à cette prolifération, a décidé qu'ils doivent limiter leurs activités à la place du Tertre.

Allez à Belleville, le quartier où Edith Piaf est née et a grandi°. Quel change-
10 ment! Il y a maintenant un étranger sur cinq résidents et lentement, des im-
meubles° modernes remplacent les vieux. Des Arabes, des Africains, des Antil-
lais et des Asiatiques habitent là depuis longtemps, et leurs magasins et leurs
restaurants remplissent° les rues de parfums exotiques. Bientôt tout cela va
disparaître°.

15 A la Villette, le nouveau° parc est terminé. C'est le plus grand espace vert
construit dans la capitale depuis dix ans. Cependant, en même temps, d'autres
espaces verts disparaissent. La construction de parkings souterrains° est souvent
la cause de la disparition° d'arbres parfois centenaires°.

Et la Bastille? Est-ce qu'elle va résister? Elle a gardé son côté° un peu anar-
20 chique; elle offre toujours beaucoup de cafés, de restaurants et de boîtes, mais on
démolit les vieux immeubles et on les remplace par des immeubles à grand
standing°. On a placé beaucoup d'espoir° sur le nouvel° Opéra pour donner au
quartier une certaine respectabilité.

Beaucoup de Parisiens et de touristes étrangers voient toutes ces transfor-
25 mations avec regret, mais même° si Paris change de caractère, elle reste la Ville
Lumière°, l'endroit où tout le monde rêve° d'aller.

grew up

buildings

fill

disappear

new

underground
removal / arbres... trees sometimes one hundred years old / aspect

deluxe / hope / new

even
City of Light / dreams

(Adapté de l'article «Paris», Vol. 13, No. 10 du *Journal Français d'Amérique.*
Reprinted by permission.)

Après la lecture

Questions sur le texte

1. Est-ce que Paris reste toujours Paris?
2. Est-ce que les artistes vont continuer à fréquenter toutes les rues de Montmartre?
3. Qu'est-ce qui donne aux rues de Belleville un caractère original?
4. Pourquoi les Parisiens aiment-ils aller dans le quartier de la Villette?
5. Est-ce que le nouvel Opéra de la Bastille a changé le quartier?
6. Avec tous ces changements, est-ce qu'on ne va plus aimer Paris?

Activités

A. Make a list of famous Parisian sites and monuments that you know and that have not been mentioned in this chapter.

B. With the help of the information about Paris provided in this chapter, prepare your ideal itinerary of a one-day visit of the French capital.

Vocabulaire

Noms / Pronoms

adresse	address	employée	clerk *(female)*
aérogramme	aerogram	enveloppe	envelope
année scolaire	school year	étranger	foreign
anthropologie	anthropology	facteur	mailman
architecture	architecture	géographie	geography
arrivée	arrival	géologie	geology
art	art	gestion	management
baiser	kiss	grec	Greek
biologie	biology	guichet	window
bise	kiss	histoire	history
campagne	countryside	histoire de l'art	art history
capitale	capital	imprimante	printer
carte postale	postcard	informatique	computer science
chaleur	heat	japonais	Japanese
chimie	chemistry	journalisme	journalism
ciel	sky	langue	language
clavier	keyboard	latin	Latin
colis	package	le, l', la, les	him, her, it, them
courrier	mail	lecteur de disquettes	disk drive
courrier électronique	e-mail	lettre	letter
dame	lady	littérature	literature
disquette	diskette	logiciel	software
droit	law	mandat	money order
éclair	lightning	match de football	soccer game
éducation physique	physical education	matériel	hardware

mathématiques	math	psychologie	psychology
matière	subject	rentrée	beginning of school year
médecine	medicine		
météo	forecast	réseau Internet	Internet
modem	modem	sciences économiques	economics
moniteur	monitor	sciences politiques	political science
monument	monument	séjour	stay
musique classique	classical music	semestre	semester
neige	snow	sociologie	sociology
notes	grades	tableur	spread sheet
nouvelles	news	télégramme	telegram
nuage	cloud	temps	weather
ordinateur	computer	timbre	stamp
papier à lettres	stationery	tonnerre	thunder
paquet	parcel	traitement de texte	word processor
physique	physics	trimestre	quarter
pluie	rain		

Verbes

dépenser	to spend	profiter de	to take advantage of
emprunter	to borrow	rencontrer	to meet
expédier	to mail	revoir	to see again
gagner	to win	suivre	to take (courses) / to follow
neiger	to snow		
pleuvoir	to rain	taper	to type
prêter	to lend	utiliser	to use
prévoir	to foresee		

Adjectifs / Adverbes

bientôt	soon	insupportable	unbearable
cher, chère, chers	dear	ne... jamais	never
couvert	overcast	ne... pas encore	not yet
écrit	written	recommandé	registered
exactement	exactly	sénégalais	Senegalese
impressionnant	impressive	tout	every

Expressions

affectueux baisers	love	faire du soleil	to be sunny
grosses bises	hugs and kisses	faire du vent	to be windy
Donnez-moi de vos nouvelles.	Let me hear from you.	faire frais	to be cool
		juste avant	just before
faire bon	to be nice	pendant	during / for
faire de l'orage	to be stormy	puisque	since
faire des économies	to save	tout le temps	all the time
faire du brouillard	to be foggy	Voyons!	Let's see. / Come on!

Chapitre **9**

La cuisine

 Commençons

 Grammaire

 Communiquons

 Lecture culturelle

 Vocabulaire

Elle choisit des fruits.

Objectives

Language

Vocabulary for food and meals • The consonant / R / • Prenominal adjectives •
The calendar • Indirect object pronouns: Third person • **Prendre**

Culture

Meals • **Les marchés en plein air** • Paul Bocuse

Communication

Describing people and things • Talking about food and meals

Commençons

Au marché d'Antibes

WWW

*Anne Bryan passe ses vacances à Juan-les-Pins chez de bons amis de ses parents,
M. et Mme Leconte. Aujourd'hui, c'est jeudi et c'est le jour du marché à Antibes.
Mme Leconte va faire ses provisions et Nathalie, la fille des Leconte, a invité
Anne à passer la matinée au marché.*

NATHALIE: Commençons par les marchands de poissons et de fruits de mer!
Tu peux prendre des photos si tu veux.

ANNE: Regarde tous ces gros poissons. Et les crevettes! Comme elles sont
petites!

NATHALIE: Allons où ils vendent les fromages. Veux-tu apprendre leurs noms?

ANNE: C'est impossible, il y a trop de variétés. Est-ce qu'on peut vraiment manger un fromage différent tous les jours de l'année?

NATHALIE: Bien sûr. Est-ce que tu aimes les olives? Moi, je les mange comme
des bonbons. Ici, c'est le coin de la viande. Tu vois, ça, ce sont des
lapins.

ANNE: Je n'aime pas voir cela. Et les poulets, on leur a laissé la tête et les
pattes!

NATHALIE: Ça, là-bas, c'est un gigot. Maman va servir cela dimanche; j'espère
que tu es contente.

ANNE: Ma pauvre Nathalie, je ne mange jamais de viande; je suis
végétarienne!

Etudions le dialogue

1. Où Anne passe-t-elle ses vacances?
2. Qu'est-ce que Nathalie et Anne vont faire?
3. Pourquoi Anne ne veut-elle pas apprendre les noms des fromages?
4. Pourquoi Anne n'aime-t-elle pas voir les poulets?
5. Qu'est-ce que les parents de Nathalie vont servir dimanche?
6. Pourquoi Anne ne mange-t-elle pas de viande?

Mots clés

marché	*market*	variétés *(f.)*	*varieties*
vacances *(f.)*	*vacation*	vraiment	*truly*
bon(-ne)	*good*	différent	*different*
jeudi	*Thursday*	olives *(f.)*	*olives*
matinée	*morning*	bonbons *(m.)*	*candy*
faire ses provisions	*to do her shopping*	coin	*area*
marchands *(m.)*	*merchants*	ça	*that*
fruits de mer *(m.)*	*shellfish*	lapins *(m.)*	*rabbits*
prendre	*take*	leur	*them*
crevettes *(f.)*	*shrimp*	tête	*head*
comme	*how*	pattes *(f.)*	*paws*
petit(e)	*small*	gigot	*leg of lamb*
vendent (vendre)	*sell*	espère que (espérer que)	*hope that*
apprendre	*to learn*	végétarien(-ne)	*vegetarian*
noms *(m.)*	*names*		

Faisons connaissance

Many French towns and villages are renowned for their open-air markets (**marchés en plein air**). They usually take place once a week and last from seven in the morning to one or two in the afternoon. **Le jour du marché** is always an important event for local people and tourists alike.

The **marché** is held on a square often named **la place du Marché,** and merchants are lined up in rows of temporary booths covered with a canopy in case of rain. The **marché** is principally a food market where people enjoy buying fresh vegetables and fruit that farmers bring and sell directly to the consumers. Although it is not as common as it used to be, it is still possible to buy live chickens and rabbits in some markets.

Southern markets, like the one in Antibes, are very picturesque. The smell of olive oil and spices used in **provençal** cooking fills the air. Other ingredients that characterize the cuisine of southern France, such as garlic, anchovies, and green and red peppers, are available in abundance at open-air booths.

Des fruits de mer

   Another enjoyable experience at open-air markets is the opportunity to taste various foods. For instance, before buying cheese, it is perfectly all right to sample several varieties. This is also true with other products such as **pâtés, saucissons,** and other foods available at the delicatessen.

Enrichissons notre vocabulaire

Les repas *(Meals)*

le petit déjeuner	*breakfast*
le déjeuner	*lunch*
le dîner	*dinner*

Des hors-d'œuvre *(Appetizers)*

des carottes râpées	*grated carrots*	une salade de tomates	*a sliced tomato salad*
des crudités	*raw vegetables*	une salade de concombres	*a sliced cucumber salad*
un œuf, des œufs	*eggs*	du saucisson	*salami*
du pâté	*pâté*		

Des plats principaux *(Main dishes)*

du bœuf	*beef*	du porc	*pork*
un rosbif	*roast beef*	une côtelette de porc	*a pork chop*
un bifteck	*a steak*	un rôti de porc	*a pork roast*
un filet de sole	*a filet of sole*	du veau	*veal*
une truite	*a trout*	une escalope de veau	*a veal cutlet*

Des légumes *(Vegetables)*

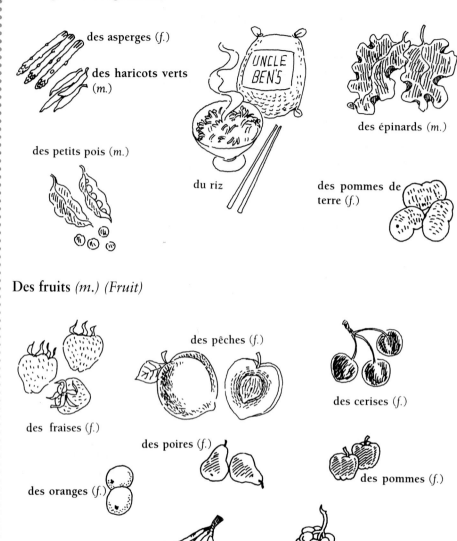

des asperges (f.)

des haricots verts (m.)

des petits pois (m.)

du riz

des épinards (m.)

des pommes de terre (f.)

Des fruits *(m.) (Fruit)*

des pêches (f.)

des cerises (f.)

des fraises (f.)

des poires (f.)

des pommes (f.)

des oranges (f.)

des bananes (f.)

du raisin

Prononciation   The French / ʀ / sound

To pronounce the French / ʀ / sound, tuck in the tip of your tongue behind your lower teeth, and curve the back of your tongue toward the back of the roof of your mouth. The words **gaz** (/ gaz /) and **rase** (/ ʀaz /) are almost identical, except that with the / g / sound, the back of your tongue touches the roof of your mouth, while with the / ʀ / sound, there is a small gap that causes friction.

Exercices

A. Practice the / R / sound preceded by a consonant in the following words by repeating them after your teacher.

> crème / cravate / grand / grammaire / groupe / crêpe / crevettes / crudités

B. Practice the / R / sound in the middle of the following words by repeating them after your teacher.

> Marie / admirer / africain / agréable / heureux / parapluie / différent / marché

C. Practice the / R / sound at the end of the following words by repeating them after your teacher.

> alors / lecture / lettre / mer / milliard / sur / porc / leur

D. Practice the / R / sound at the beginning of the following words by repeating them after your teacher.

> radio / rapide / regarder / regretter / rentrer / repas / riz / rosbif

E. Repeat the following sentences after your teacher, paying particular attention to the / R / sound.

1. Brigitte travaille au restaurant.
2. Il va faire du brouillard à Londres.
3. Marie a perdu son portefeuille dans le parc.
4. Christine et son mari apprécient l'art moderne.
5. Beaucoup d'Américains vont avoir froid cet hiver.
6. La librairie ferme à trois heures et quart.

Grammaire

I. Prenominal adjectives

> You use adjectives to describe people and things.

A. As you learned in Chapter 2, an adjective agrees in gender and number with the noun it modifies, and it usually follows the noun.

> Mes parents ont préparé un repas **délicieux** hier soir.
> On peut manger un fromage **différent** tous les jours.

There is, however, a group of frequently used adjectives that must precede the noun. The chart on page 222 gives the most common ones.

> Regarde tous ces **gros** poissons.   Ce sont de **petites** crevettes.

	singular	plural		
masculine	**feminine**	**masculine**	**feminine**	**meaning**
ancien	ancienne	anciens	anciennes	*former, old*
autre	autre	autres	autres	*other*
beau	belle	beaux	belles	*beautiful, handsome*
bon	bonne	bons	bonnes	*good*
cher	chère	chers	chères	*dear, expensive*
dernier	dernière	derniers	dernières	*last*
grand	grande	grands	grandes	*big, great*
gros	grosse	gros	grosses	*big*
jeune	jeune	jeunes	jeunes	*young*
joli	jolie	jolis	jolies	*pretty*
mauvais	mauvaise	mauvais	mauvaises	*bad*
nouveau	nouvelle	nouveaux	nouvelles	*new*
pauvre	pauvre	pauvres	pauvres	*poor*
petit	petite	petits	petites	*small, little*
premier	première	premiers	premières	*first*
propre	propre	propres	propres	*own, clean*
vieux	vieille	vieux	vieilles	*old*

B. Because these adjectives precede the noun, **liaison** is obligatory when the noun begins with a vowel sound.

> J'ai téléphoné à un **bon** ami.
> Les Wright ont fait le **premier** avion.
> Elle a invité ses **bons** amis.

C. Because of **liaison**, there are some irregular adjective forms. Before masculine singular nouns that begin with a vowel, you will find:

beau → **bel**	Le Concorde est un **bel** avion.
nouveau → **nouvel**	La classe a commencé un **nouvel** exercice.
vieux → **vieil**	Il a vu un **vieil** ami.

It will help you to remember that when a masculine singular noun begins with a vowel sound, the preceding adjective sounds like its feminine form. For example, in the following phrases, **bon** and **bonne** and **vieil** and **vieille** are pronounced the same.

un **bon** étudiant, une **bonne**   un **vieil** ami, une **vieille** amie
étudiante

D. A few adjectives may come either before or after the noun, but they change meaning according to their position.

un **ancien** professeur	a **former** teacher
une église **ancienne**	an **old** church
la **dernière** semaine	the **last** week (of a series)
la semaine **dernière**	**last** week
un **pauvre** homme	a **poor** man (unfortunate)
un homme **pauvre**	a **poor** man (no money)
ma **propre** voiture	my **own** car
une voiture **propre**	a **clean** car
un **cher** ami	a **dear** friend
un cadeau **cher**	an **expensive** gift

E. Adjectives can be used alone as nouns.

Les **pauvres** ne mangent pas bien.
Les **jeunes** vont aller voir les **vieux**.

Attention!

1. Whenever the indefinite article **des** is followed by an adjective, it becomes **de**.

Ils vendent **des** cerises.   Ils vendent **de belles** cerises.
Ce sont **des** amis.   Ce sont **de vieux** amis.

   but: Ce sont **des marchands** désagréables.

2. In **liaison**, the masculine form of **grand** is pronounced with a / t / sound, and the masculine form of **gros** and other adjectives ending in **s** (**anciens, pauvres**, etc.) are pronounced with a / z / sound.

   un grand‿appartement, un grand‿homme
   un gros‿oeuf, les gros‿avions
   de bons‿amis, de belles‿olives

Langue

A. En ville. Donnez le contraire de l'adjectif en italique dans les phrases suivantes.

MODÈLE: J'ai une *petite* voiture.
            J'ai une grande voiture.

1. Il habite un *petit* appartement.
2. C'est un *bon* restaurant.
3. Ces *jeunes* employés travaillent beaucoup.
4. Je n'ai pas vu tes *dernières* photos de la ville.
5. Est-ce que c'est un *nouvel* hôtel?
6. Il a acheté une cravate *laide* dans ce magasin.

B. **Mon ami arrive.** Ajoutez la forme appropriée des adjectifs entre parenthèses aux noms en italique dans les phrases suivantes. Faites attention à la place de l'adjectif.

MODÈLE: Nous avons voyagé dans un *avion.* (gros)
  Nous avons voyagé dans un gros avion.

1. Un *ami* arrive de New York. (bon)
2. Nous avons visité des *églises.* (joli)
3. Nous avons parlé avec des *enfants.* (petit)
4. Avez-vous trouvé un *appartement* pour votre ami? (beau)
5. Il a déjà invité des *amis.* (sympathique)
6. Est-ce qu'il y a beaucoup d'*écoles* près d'ici? (bon)

Culture

C. **En France ou aux Etats-Unis?** Formez des phrases avec les mots donnés et dites *(tell)* si la phrase décrit *(describes)* la France ou les Etats-Unis.

1. On / aimer / gros / voitures
2. jeune / gens / pouvoir / avoir / voiture / à seize ans
3. vieux / personnes / habiter / avec / leur / enfants
4. On / avoir / grand / universités / dans / petit / villes
5. On / prendre / bon / petit / déjeuner / tous les matins
6. «18» / être / très / bon / note
7. On / pouvoir / acheter / joli / petit / tartes / délicieux
8. nouveau / trains / être / rapide
9. On / vendre / son / propre / affaires / devant / son / maison
10. Un / ancien / maire *(mayor)* / être / président

Communication

D. **Votre vie à l'université.** Donnez votre opinion en répondant aux questions suivantes. Commencez vos réponses avec «C'est... » ou «Ce sont... ».

MODÈLE: Votre cours de français est facile ou difficile?
  C'est un cours facile.

1. Votre université est grande ou petite?
2. La cuisine du restaurant universitaire est délicieuse ou affreuse?
3. L'idée d'étudier l'informatique est bonne ou mauvaise?
4. Vos vêtements sont nouveaux ou vieux?
5. Votre professeur est jeune ou vieux?
6. Vos réponses en cours sont bonnes ou mauvaises? intelligentes ou stupides?

E. **Vos achats.** Qu'est-ce que vous avez acheté récemment? Qu'est-ce que vous avez depuis longtemps? Utilisez la liste suivante ou vos propres idées.

MODÈLE: *J'ai un nouveau vélo. J'ai une vieille voiture.*

appartement	cravate	imperméable	sac à dos
pantalon	auto	Walkman	robe
bicyclette	chaussures	chaîne stéréo	magnétophone
calculatrice	magnétoscope	cassette	répondeur

F. **Questions personnelles.** Vos préférences.

1. Quels restaurants aimez-vous mieux? (simples ou chers?)
2. Quelles sortes d'amis avez-vous? (bons? sincères?)
3. Quelles sortes de villes voulez-vous visiter? (vieilles ou modernes?)
4. Quelle sorte de maison habitez-vous? (petite? grande? blanche?)
5. Quelles autos aimez-vous? (petites? grandes? économiques? chères?)
6. Quelle sorte de musique écoutez-vous? (classique? moderne?)

II. Le calendrier   www

> You use vocabulary related to the calendar to situate events in time.

A. Les jours de la semaine (The days of the week)

lundi	*Monday*	vendredi	*Friday*
mardi	*Tuesday*	samedi	*Saturday*
mercredi	*Wednesday*	dimanche	*Sunday*
jeudi	*Thursday*		

1. On the French calendar, the week begins with Monday (**lundi**), not Sunday (**dimanche**). Note that in French, another way of saying *one week* (**une semaine**) is **huit jours. Quinze jours** is *two weeks*, but after that you say **trois semaines** and **quatre semaines** (**un mois**).

2. Do not use a preposition to express the English *on* a day of the week.

    Je vais aller au bureau lundi.   *I'm going to the office on Monday.*

3. All of the days of the week are masculine nouns. They take the article **le** only to indicate a habitual action or repeated occurrence. In English, this is expressed by a plural.

    Le bureau est ouvert **le jeudi soir.**   *The office is open on **Thursday evenings.***

    Nous allons **au marché le mardi.**   *We go to the market on **Tuesdays.***

4. You can use **prochain** and **dernier** with the days of the week.

    Il y a un concert jeudi **prochain.**
    Ils n'ont pas travaillé mardi **dernier.**

B. Les mois de l'année (The months of the year)

janvier	*January*	mai	*May*	septembre	*September*
février	*February*	juin	*June*	octobre	*October*
mars	*March*	juillet	*July*	novembre	*November*
avril	*April*	août	*August*	décembre	*December*

1. August (**août**) has two acceptable pronunciations, / u / and / ut /.

2. To say *in* a month, you use **en** plus the month or **au mois de.**

    Les Français ne travaillent pas **en août.**
    Je vais aller en vacances **au mois de juin.**

3. Days of the week and months of the year are not capitalized in French.

C.　Les quatre saisons (The four seasons)

le printemps　*spring*　　　　l'automne *(m.)*　*fall*
l'été *(m.)*　*summer*　　　　l'hiver *(m.)*　*winter*

J'aime faire des promenades **au printemps.**
Je ne suis pas de cours **en été.**
Je vais aux matchs de football américain **en automne.**
Je reste chez moi **en hiver.**

D.　La date

1.　To ask the date, you say:

　　Quelle est la date aujourd'hui? *or* **Quel jour sommes-nous?**

2.　To express a date in French, use a combination of the definite article **le,** the number, and then the month.

　　La Saint-Valentin est **le 14 février.**
　　En Belgique, la fête nationale c'est **le 21 juillet.**

3.　Cardinal numbers, which you have already learned, are always used in dates, except for the first day of the month, **le premier.**

　　Le premier mai est la fête du Travail en Europe.

4.　If you wish to add the day of the week to a date, you may place it before or after the article.

　　le jeudi 12 décembre　　　　**dimanche, le 1ᵉʳ novembre**

E.　Les années (Years)

1.　In French, there are two ways of expressing calendar years. Start with **mil** (a special spelling of **mille** used for years) and count in hundreds. You may also simply count in hundreds:

　　1963　**mil neuf cent** soixante-trois or **dix-neuf cent** soixante-trois

2.　When only the year is given, the preposition **en** is used.

　　Il a visité la Chine **en** 1981.

　　but: Il est arrivé en Chine **le** 22 juin 1981.

Attention!

1.　The e of **le** is not dropped before numbers that begin with a vowel.

　　le huit février　　　　　　**le** onze novembre

2.　No prepositions are used with days of the month or with **week-end.**

　　Ils vont partir le 4 octobre.　　　Elles travaillent beaucoup le
　　　　　　　　　　　　　　　　　week-end.

3.　When dates are abbreviated, the day is always given before the month.

　　10-3-94　→　le 10 mars 1994　　　2-6-95　→　le 2 juin 1995

Langue

A. Des dates. Lisez les dates suivantes en français.

1. January 1, 1918
2. March 10, 1929
3. April 23, 1776
4. Thursday, August 1, 1881
5. Friday, September 30, 1993
6. Saturday, December 25, 1996

B. Leurs projets. Qu'est-ce que les amis de Robert vont faire? Lisez les phrases suivantes en ajoutant *(adding)* un mot si c'est nécessaire.

1. Le copain de Robert va acheter une voiture _____ printemps.
2. Paul veut revoir l'Angleterre _____ été.
3. Sylvie va inviter Luc _____ dimanche prochain.
4. Les parents de Sylvie ne travaillent pas _____ samedi.
5. Leurs vacances commencent _____ juillet.
6. Robert dîne toujours au restaurant _____ vendredi.

Culture

C. Examen d'histoire. Choisissez la date qui convient *(that is appropriate)* pour chaque événement *(each event)* dans l'histoire de France.

1. Jeanne d'Arc brûlée *(burned)*
2. L'édit de Nantes
3. Naissance *(Birth)* de Louis XIV
4. Libération de la Bastille
5. Marie-Antoinette guillotinée
6. Napoléon couronné *(crowned)*

a. 14-7-1789
b. 30-5-1431
c. 5-9-1638
d. 16-10-1793
e. 13-4-1598
f. 2-12-1804

D. Les fêtes. Les Américains et les francophones ont souvent les mêmes fêtes, mais plusieurs fêtes ne sont pas le même jour. Comparez les fêtes en formant des phrases avec les mots donnés.

1. les Américains / les Français: avoir la fête du Travail en septembre / en mai
2. les Américains / les Canadiens: avoir *Thanksgiving* en novembre / en octobre
3. les Américains / les Français: aller en vacances en été / en août
4. les Américains / les Suisses: avoir leur fête nationale en juillet / en août
5. En janvier, les Américains / les Français: avoir la fête de Martin Luther King, Jr. / l'Epiphanie
6. Le 15 août, les Américains / les Français: travailler / ne... pas travailler (c'est l'Assomption.)

Communication

E. Mes activités. Parlez de vos activités en ajoutant les jours, les mois ou les saisons.

MODÈLE: Je n'étudie pas...
Je n'étudie pas le dimanche.

1. J'aime aller danser...
2. Mes parents vont à l'église...
3. J'aime faire mes provisions...
4. Je regarde toujours la télévision...
5. Je fais mes courses...
6. Je vais en vacances...

F. **Votre agenda.** Remplissez *(Fill in)* l'agenda avec une activité pour six jours différents. Ensuite *(Then)*, demandez à un(e) camarade de cours quelles choses *(things)* il / elle a faites et les dates de ces activités.

Exemples

passer mon dernier examen	aller chez le médecin
faire mes provisions	préparer un bon dîner
voir mes parents	acheter des bonbons pour…
expédier un colis	utiliser un ordinateur

L	M	Me	J	V	S	D
				1	2	3
4	5	6	7	8	9	10
11	12	13	14	15	16	17

G. **Questions personnelles.** Votre agenda.

1. Qu'est-ce que vous allez faire l'été prochain?
2. Qu'est-ce que vous avez fait samedi dernier?
3. Quel mois est votre anniversaire *(birthday)*?
4. Quand est-ce que vous faites du sport? Quel sport?
5. Allez-vous suivre un cours cet été? Quel cours?
6. Qui est-ce que vous voulez voir dimanche?
7. Quelle est votre saison préférée? Pourquoi?
8. Quel est votre jour préféré? Pourquoi?

III. Indirect object pronouns: Third person

You use indirect object pronouns to refer to people and things already mentioned in a conversation that receive the action of the verb.

A. Introduction

In Chapter 8 you learned direct object pronouns, which receive the action of the verb (**La clé? Je l'ai perdue.**). An indirect object indicates *to whom* or *to what* this action is directed.

He sold the car *to John.*	*or*	He sold the car *to him.*
He sold *John* the car.	*or*	He sold *him* the car.

In these examples, *John* is the indirect object, since the action of selling the car is directed to him. The examples also show that the indirect object noun, *John*, may be replaced with an indirect object pronoun, *him*.

B. Third-person indirect object pronouns

	singular	*plural*
masculine *feminine*	lui	leur

1. A pronoun can also replace the indirect object noun in French. The masculine and feminine singular form, **lui**, means *(to) him / (to) her.*

    L'étudiant répond **au professeur?** → L'étudiant **lui** répond?
    Sylvie rend les CD **à son amie.** → Sylvie **lui** rend les CD.

    The masculine and feminine plural form, **leur**, means *(to) them.*

    On a demandé **aux enfants** leur nom. → On **leur** a demandé leur nom.
    Elle téléphone **à ses copines.** → Elle **leur** téléphone.

2. Indirect objects are somewhat easier to identify in French than in English because an indirect object noun is almost always preceded by the preposition **à**.

    Il a vendu des bonbons **à Jean-Paul.** → Il **lui** a vendu des bonbons.

C. Position of indirect object pronouns

1. The position of indirect object pronouns is the same as that of direct object pronouns: they precede the verb from which the action is directed.

Present	**Passé composé**
Je **leur** apporte des fraises.	Nous ne **leur** avons pas téléphoné hier.
Luc ne **lui** prête pas son auto.	Elle **lui** a montré les lapins au marché.

2. Past participles do not agree with preceding indirect objects, as they do with preceding direct objects.

    A qui ont-elles donné la pomme?
    Elles l'ont donnée au professeur.

    but: Elles lui ont donné la pomme.

3. Indirect object pronouns follow helping verbs.

    Il va **leur** servir des crudités.   Vous ne pouvez pas **lui** répondre?

4. In negative commands, indirect object pronouns precede the verb.

    Ne **lui** téléphonez pas   Ne **leur** montrez pas ma lettre.
    maintenant.

5. The position of pronouns is irregular in affirmative commands. Both direct and indirect object pronouns are placed after the verb and joined with a hyphen.

> **Regarde-le!** **Apportez-lui** une pêche.
> **Vendez-les** tout de suite! **Servons-leur** du riz avec les crevettes.

Mots clés **Verbs that may take indirect objects**

acheter	obéir
apporter / rapporter	parler
commander	passer
demander	poser une question *to ask a question*
désobéir	préparer
donner	présenter *to introduce*
emprunter / prêter	recommander
expédier	rendre
expliquer	répéter
faire mal	répondre
indiquer *to indicate*	ressembler *to resemble*
laisser	servir
mentir	téléphoner
montrer	vendre

Attention!

French verbs do not always take the same kind of object as their English equivalents. Translating will not always help determine whether a direct object pronoun or an indirect object pronoun should be used.

1. **Attendre, chercher, demander, écouter,** and **regarder** take a direct object in French, but are followed by a preposition in English.

> Je cherche **le métro.** → Je **le** cherche.
> Il a demandé **cette poire.** → Il **l'**a demandée.
> Nous allons écouter **la radio.** → Nous allons **l'**écouter.
> J'ai regardé **ses poissons.** → Je **les** ai regardés.

2. **Obéir à, désobéir à, téléphoner à, rendre visite à, répondre à,** and **ressembler à** take indirect objects in French but take direct objects in English.

> Ils ont obéi **à l'agent de police.** → Ils **lui** ont obéi.
> Téléphone **à Jacques.** → Téléphone-**lui.**
> Elle ressemble **à sa mère.** → Elle **lui** ressemble.

Langue

A. **A la résidence.** Répondez aux questions suivantes en utilisant des pronoms compléments d'objet indirect.

1. Est-ce que Jacques a rendu ses devoirs à son prof? (Oui,...)
2. Vous ne servez pas de bière à vos amis? (Non,... cocas.)
3. Tu ne veux pas parler aux autres? (Si,...)

4. On va servir des repas aux pauvres? (Oui,...)
5. Paul a-t-il téléphoné à son copain? (Non,...)
6. Peux-tu demander l'adresse à Jacqueline? (Oui,...)

B. **Vous avez invité Monique hier soir?** Refaites les phrases suivantes selon les indications entre parenthèses.

1. Vous lui servez du bifteck et des haricots verts? (... hier soir)
2. Je lui ai montré mon ordinateur. (... vendre... nouveau...)
3. Ne lui demandez pas de sortir samedi prochain! *(make affirmative)*
4. Elle ressemble *à ses parents*. *(use a pronoun)*
5. Je lui présente mes amis. (Le week-end prochain...)
6. Nous lui donnons un beau cadeau. *(give a command)*

Culture

C. **Les pourboires.** A qui est-ce qu'on donne un pourboire *(tip)* en France? Est-ce qu'on le donne toujours, jamais, ou uniquement pour un service spécial?

MODÈLE: garçon de café
On ne lui donne jamais de pourboire. (Le service est compris.)

1. le marchand
2. l'ouvreuse *(usher)*
3. le facteur
4. le médecin
5. les agents de police
6. les hôtesses du Syndicat d'Initiative
7. les chauffeurs de taxi
8. les garçons de restaurant

Communication

D. **Une nouvelle connaissance.** Vous avez vu un très bel homme / une très belle femme et vous voulez le / la revoir. Qu'est-ce que vous pouvez faire pour arranger un rendez-vous? Utilisez les suggestions données ou vos propres idées.

MODÈLE: *Je lui demande son nom.*

parler après la classe
téléphoner ce soir
demander s'il / si elle veut sortir
inviter chez moi
donner mon adresse

présenter mes amis
parler de son avenir *(future)*
servir...
montrer mes timbres
???

E. **Qui voyez-vous?** Voyez-vous souvent les personnes suivantes? Leur téléphonez-vous? Tous les combien *(How often)*? Utilisez les suggestions données ou vos propres idées.

MODÈLE: votre frère
Je ne le vois pas souvent, mais je lui téléphone toutes les semaines.

vos amis
vos parents
votre frère / sœur
votre petit(e) ami(e)
vos grands-parents
votre camarade de chambre
votre professeur

tous les jours / mois / ans
toutes les heures / semaines
une / deux / trois fois
    par jour / semaine / mois
souvent / pas souvent
rarement
ne... jamais

F. **Des conseils.** Que pouvez-vous dire *(say)* à vos amis dans les trois situations suivantes? Trouvez un(e) partenaire et créez *(create)* de bons conseils.

1. Ils ont un invité *(guest)* important.

MODÈLE: présenter vos amis *Présentez-lui vos amis.*

> servir une boisson / montrer votre appartement / ne... pas demander leur âge / ne... pas laisser seul / parler du temps

2. Leur professeur les a invités à dîner.

> apporter un cadeau / demander comment il (elle) va / admirer ton prof pour son travail / ne... pas demander d'argent / ne... pas expliquer vos absences / ne... pas parler de l'examen final

3. Ils vont visiter le campus avec des étudiants de première année.

> montrer la librairie / le laboratoire, etc. / ne... pas recommander le restaurant universitaire / parler des cours faciles / ne... pas inviter dans les bars / ne... pas vendre de billets pour la bibliothèque

G. **Questions personnelles: Vos habitudes.** Utilisez des pronoms compléments d'objet indirect dans vos réponses.

1. Avez-vous téléphoné à vos parents samedi ou dimanche? Pourquoi?
2. Qu'est-ce que vous allez demander au Père Noël *(Santa Claus)* cette année?
3. Prêtez-vous votre voiture à vos amis? vos CD? vos vêtements?
4. A qui vendez-vous vos livres?
5. Qu'est-ce que vous servez à vos amis quand ils dînent chez vous?
6. Qu'est-ce que vous allez apporter à vos professeurs le dernier jour de cours?

IV. Prendre

> You use the verb **prendre** to express the idea *to take* and, when referring to food or drink, to express *to have* or *to eat*.

prendre	*(to take; to have [food])*		
je **prends**	/ prã /	nous **prenons**	/ prø nɔ̃ /
tu **prends**	/ prã /	vous **prenez**	/ prø ne /
il / elle / on **prend**	/ prã /	ils / elles **prennent**	/ prɛn /

Passé composé: il **a pris**

A. Although its infinitive ends in **-re, prendre** is not conjugated like the **-re** verbs you learned in Chapter 6. In the present tense, **prendre** differs in the plural forms, resulting in three different vowel sounds: / pʀɑ̃ /, / pʀø nɔ̃ /, and / pʀɛn /.

> On **prend** le métro pour aller au marché.
> Nous **prenons** quel autobus?
> Ils ne **prennent** pas le train vendredi?

B. The verb **prendre** can also mean *to have* or *to eat* when used with foods and drinks, replacing **manger.** It *must* be used with the names of meals.

> Je ne **prends** pas de porc. Qu'est-ce que tu **prends?**
> Ils ne **prennent** pas de petit déjeuner.
> On **prend** le dîner à huit heures.

C. The past participle of **prendre** is **pris.** The feminine form is **prise,** and the **s** in it is pronounced.

> Nous **avons pris** des poires.   Cette **photo?** Je ne **l'ai** pas **prise.**

D. Apprendre *(to learn)* and **comprendre** *(to understand)* are conjugated like **prendre.**

> —Est-ce que tu **comprends** le français?
> —Oui, je **l'ai appris** à l'école.

While **apprendre** means *to learn (how to),* **apprendre à** + *a person* means *to teach.* This expression can be followed by a direct object noun or, for the subject taught, **à** plus an infinitive.

> Il apprend l'italien **aux** étudiants.
> Il apprend **aux** étudiants **à** parler italien.

Attention!

Since the letter **d** has a / t / sound in **liaison,** there is no need to add -t- with inversion of the third-person singular form of **prendre** and verbs conjugated like it.

> **Prend-elle** l'avion ce matin?
> **Apprend-il** le japonais?

Langue

A. A l'université. Substituez le verbe entre parenthèses dans les phrases suivantes.

1. On entend l'arabe à l'université?   (apprendre)
2. On vend des livres de chinois à la librairie.   (prendre)
3. Est-ce que vous avez emprunté mon livre de maths?   (prendre)
4. Etudiez l'allemand!   (apprendre)
5. Nous rendons les notes de Jean-Paul.   (ne... pas comprendre)
6. Je parle très bien l'italien.   (comprendre)

B. **Interview avec une étudiante américaine.** Répondez aux questions suivantes avec les mots donnés. Remplacez les compléments d'objet direct en italique par des pronoms.

MODÈLE: Avez-vous pris *votre voiture* ce matin? (Oui,...)
Oui, je l'ai prise.

1. Les étudiants comprennent-ils *leurs leçons?* (Non, ils...)
2. Peuvent-ils apprendre *le japonais?*
3. Et vous, apprenez-vous *le chinois?* (Non,...)
4. Comprenez-vous *l'informatique?* (Non,...)
5. Avez-vous pris *votre petit déjeuner* ce matin? (Non,... plus tard.)
6. Avez-vous pris *l'autobus* récemment? (Oui, la semaine dernière...)

Culture

C. **Les habitudes gastronomiques des Français.** Les habitudes des Français sont différentes de celles *(those)* des Américains quand il est question de manger. Formez des phrases avec les mots donnés, et si la phrase ne représente pas la réalité en France, ajoutez *(add)* ne... pas.

1. Français / prendre / café au lait / au dîner
2. Français / prendre / toujours / asperges / froid
3. En France / on / aller / restaurant / pour / prendre / petit déjeuner
4. On / prendre / œufs / au petit déjeuner
5. On / prendre / dîner / à six heures du soir
6. Beaucoup de Français / prendre / fruit / comme dessert
7. On / prendre / vin rouge / avec / rosbif
8. On / prendre / salade / après / dîner

Communication

D. **A table!** Décrivez *(Describe)* vos repas typiques en utilisant les suggestions suivantes ou vos propres idées. Précisez *(Specify)* l'heure, les plats et les boissons.

MODÈLE: *A midi je prends un sandwich et un coca.*

Les plats

riz	glace	pizza
bifteck	asperges	frites
veau	fromage	œufs
gâteau	salade	sandwich

Les boissons

eau	café	vin
eau minérale	thé	coca
bière	lait	jus de fruit

E. **Jeu de rôles.** Vous allez dîner au restaurant. Avec un(e) camarade, jouez une des scènes suivantes.

1. Vous êtes végétariens.
2. Votre camarade est au régime, mais vous avez très faim.
3. Vous êtes snobs.
4. Vous êtes pauvre, mais votre camarade veut dépenser beaucoup d'argent.

F. **Questions personnelles.** Vos études.

1. Quelles langues comprenez-vous? Et dans votre famille?
2. Qu'est-ce que vous apprenez à l'université?
3. Qu'est-ce que vous avez pris ce matin avant vos cours?
4. Que prenez-vous avant un examen?
5. Après vos cours, qu'est-ce que vous aimez prendre avec vos amis?
6. Qu'est-ce que vous avez appris à votre frère / à votre sœur / à votre ami(e)?

Communiquons

Prendre les repas

French people usually have three complete meals a day. Breakfast is very light, consisting of **café au lait** (half coffee, half hot milk) or tea and bread or **croissants.** Lunch is much more substantial, often consisting of meat, vegetables, cheese, and wine. The French have traditionally taken a two-hour lunch break to go home or to a restaurant while offices, banks, and stores closed. This tradition

Au bistrot

is rapidly changing. Lunch breaks are shorter, fast-food restaurants have gained in popularity, and more and more businesses stay open during the lunch hour.

The French usually eat dinner at home and often begin as late as 8 P.M. «**A table!**» signals to everyone that a meal is ready. The first course, **les hors-d'œuvre,** can be cold cuts (**de la charcuterie**) or **des crudités,** for instance. Then the **plat principal** is served. Normally meat or fish, it is accompanied by vegetables. The last part of the meal consists of salad, cheese, and fruit or dessert.

There are many differences in eating habits between France and America. In France, you should keep both hands on the table rather than keeping one on your lap. At informal dinners in France, bread does not have a special plate, but is put directly on the table. You generally do not put butter on bread, but you do on radishes! Milk and hot beverages are not drunk with meals. Plates are changed several times during the meal, but some people wipe them with a piece of bread. Finally, French people, like all Europeans, eat with the fork in their left hand.

Expressions

▶ **On met le couvert.** *(One sets the table.)*

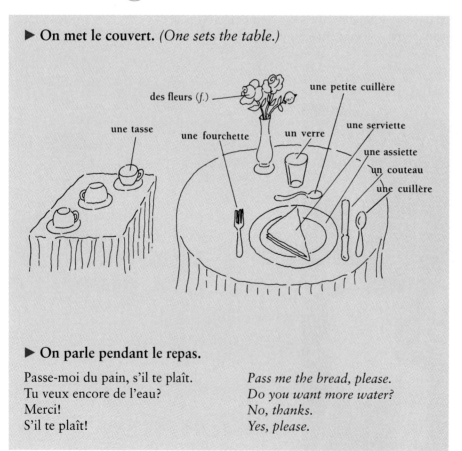

▶ **On parle pendant le repas.**

Passe-moi du pain, s'il te plaît.	*Pass me the bread, please.*
Tu veux encore de l'eau?	*Do you want more water?*
Merci!	*No, thanks.*
S'il te plaît!	*Yes, please.*

▶ **On est au restaurant.**

Le maître d'hôtel leur montre leur table.	*The maître d' shows them to their table.*
Ils veulent voir la carte des vins.	*They want to see the wine list.*
Le garçon / La serveuse explique la carte et le menu.	*The waiter / The waitress explains the menu and the list of fixed-priced meals.*
Le plat du jour est délicieux.	*Today's special is delicious.*
On apporte l'addition.	*They bring the check.*
Ils donnent un pourboire au garçon.	*They give the waiter a tip.*
Boisson et service en sus.	*Drinks and tip are extra.*
Service compris.	*The tip is included.*
Payez à la caisse.	*Pay the cashier.*

Interaction

M. Marchand téléphone au restaurant Jamin pour réserver une table.

LE MAÎTRE D'HÔTEL:	Allô, le restaurant Jamin.
M. MARCHAND:	Bonjour, je voudrais réserver une table pour quatre ce soir.
LE MAÎTRE D'HÔTEL:	Attendez voir… Non, ce soir, nous sommes complets°. Mais je veux bien prendre votre nom. Nous allons peut-être° avoir une annulation°.
M. MARCHAND:	Et demain soir?
LE MAÎTRE D'HÔTEL:	Oui, à quelle heure?
M. MARCHAND:	Vingt heures trente?
LE MAÎTRE D'HÔTEL:	C'est noté°. C'est à quel nom?
M. MARCHAND:	Monsieur Marchand.
LE MAÎTRE D'HÔTEL:	C'est convenu°. A demain soir.
M. MARCHAND:	A demain.

booked

perhaps / cancellation

C'est… I've got it.

C'est… All right

Activités

A. Votre spécialité. Expliquez comment vous préparez votre spécialité. Donnez votre recette *(recipe)* préférée à la classe.

MODÈLE: *Je prends du sucre, de la farine…*

B. On a faim. En petits groupes, demandez à vos camarades quels plats ils aiment et quels plats ils détestent. Ensuite, préparez un repas idéal et un repas affreux selon vos préférences et échangez vos idées avec vos camarades de cours.

C. **Jeu de rôles.** Jouez les scènes suivantes avec un(e) camarade de cours.

1. Vous êtes dans un restaurant et vous commandez un repas.
2. Vous téléphonez à votre restaurant préféré pour réserver une table.
3. Vous demandez au garçon / à la serveuse pourquoi votre repas est si *(so)* cher / froid / mauvais. (Choisissez!)

Lecture culturelle

Avant la lecture

From time to time, French people love to eat in one of the twenty or so restaurants that are considered the very best in the country and are known by everyone, even by people who never had a chance to eat in one of them. In France, most restaurants are listed in the *Guide Michelin,* an absolute necessity for anyone who travels in France. When you look up a restaurant, you find out immediately whether it was awarded stars (one, two, or three). The three-star rating is reserved for outstanding restaurants—the twenty or so mentioned above. Restaurants are rated periodically, and if one happens to lose its third star because the quality is deemed to have dropped, it becomes a national issue that is discussed on television and in the newspapers.

For some people, the opportunity to eat in a three-star restaurant is the experience of a lifetime. One must remember that it is impossible to have such a meal for less than $150!

Chez Bocuse

Paul Bocuse

Activités

A. Can you think of the names of restaurants in one of the major American cities that everyone would immediately recognize?

B. What would you want to know about a restaurant before going there?

C. Can you remember a memorable meal you had in a very fancy restaurant in the United States or abroad? What specialities did you have?

Paul Bocuse, cuisinier° et philosophe WWW

           chef

C'est à Collonges-au-Mont-d'Or, dans la banlieue° de Lyon que se trouve° le Restaurant Paul Bocuse, symbole de la gastronomie française. A 70 ans, Paul Bocuse est aussi célèbre° qu'un acteur de cinéma, qu'une vedette° de la chanson° ou qu'un homme politique, et son
5 restaurant qui a reçu° sa troisième étoile° Michelin en 1965 a maintenant une réputation mondiale°.

    En 1996, Paul Bocuse a publié un livre, *La Bonne Chère°*. Dans la première partie il parle du métier° de cuisinier et il consacre° la deuxième partie à la dié-tétique qui est responsable de profonds° changements dans la gastronomie. A
10 l'occasion de ses 70 ans, il a donné une série d'interviews où il décrit° la gastro-nomie comme un véritable humanisme. Pour lui, «recevoir° quelqu'un, c'est se charger° de son bonheur° pendant tout le temps qu'il est sous votre toit°». Cet humanisme n'affecte pas seulement l'hôte°, il s'exprime° dans une convivialité avec les amis et les camarades qui fait d'une profession une confrérie°. Enfin, le
15 message de Paul Bocuse est orienté vers le futur, les jeunes. Pour lui, «le devoir° d'un cuisinier est de transmettre à la génération qui le remplacera° le savoir-faire°, mais aussi les enrichissements°, les mots nouveaux».

    Pour la France, Paul Bocuse et son restaurant trois étoiles sont des ambas-sadeurs extraordinaires, tout comme° Christian Dior et sa haute couture°, Guer-
20 lain et ses parfums, Moët et Chandon et son champagne.

suburb
se... is located
famous
star / song
received / star
worldwide
La... Good Food
profession / devotes
profound
describes
to host
to be responsible / happi-
    ness / roof / guest / ex-
    presses itself / fraternity
duty
will replace
know-how / improvements
tout... just like / designer
    clothes

Après la lecture

Questions sur le texte

1. Qui est Paul Bocuse?
2. Pourquoi son restaurant est-il spécial?
3. De quoi est-ce qu'il parle dans *La Bonne Chère*?
4. Pour lui, qu'est-ce que la gastronomie?
5. Les cuisiniers forment une «confrérie». Expliquez cela.
6. Quelle est la responsabilité d'un cuisinier?

Activitiés

A. A la bibliothèque, consultez le *Guide Michelin* rouge et cherchez d'autres restaurants trois étoiles en France.

B. Préparez une liste de produits français qui sont d'autres «ambassadeurs extraordinaires», et une liste d'«ambassadeurs extraordinaires» de la culture américaine.

C. Est-ce que vous connaissez d'autres métiers qui sont plus que des professions et qui sont de véritables confréries?

Vocabulaire

Noms/Pronoms

année	year	dîner	dinner
août	August	épinards	spinach
asperges	asparagus	escalope	cutlet
automne	fall	été	summer
avril	April	fête du Travail	Labor Day
banane	banana	Fête nationale	Independence Day
bifteck	steak	février	February
bœuf	beef	filet	filet
bonbon	candy	fraise	strawberry
ça	that	fruits de mer	shellfish
calendrier	calendar	gigot	leg of lamb
carottes râpées	grated carrots	haricots verts	green beans
cerise	cherry	hiver	winter
coin	corner / area	janvier	January
concombre	cucumber	jeudi	Thursday
côtelette	chop	jour	day
crevette	shrimp	juillet	July
crudités	raw vegetables	juin	June
date	date	lapin	rabbit
décembre	December	leur	them
déjeuner	lunch	lui	her / him
dimanche	Sunday	lundi	Monday

mai	May	pomme de terre	potato
marchand	merchant	porc	pork
mardi	Tuesday	printemps	spring
marché en plein air	open-air market	raisin	grape
mars	March	repas	meal
matinée	morning	riz	rice
mercredi	Wednesday	rosbif	roast beef
moi	me	rôti	roast
mois	month	Saint-Valentin	St. Valentine's Day
nom	name	saison	season
novembre	November	samedi	Saturday
octobre	October	saucisson	salami
œuf	egg	semaine	week
olive	olive	septembre	September
orange	orange	sole	sole
pâté	pâté	tête	head
pattes	feet (animals)	tomate	tomato
pêche	peach	truite	trout
petit déjeuner	breakfast	vacances	vacation
petits pois	peas	variété	variety
poire	pear	veau	veal
pomme	apple	vendredi	Friday

Verbes

apprendre	to learn / to teach	prendre	to take / to have
comprendre	to understand	présenter	to introduce
espérer	to hope	ressembler	to look like
indiquer	to indicate		

Adjectifs / Adverbes

beau	beautiful / nice	petit	small
bon	good	propre	clean, own
différent	different	provençal	from Provence
grand	big / tall	végétarien	vegetarian
jeune	young	vieux	old
joli	pretty	vraiment	truly
nouveau	new		

Expressions

tout comme	like
faire ses provisions	to do one's shopping
poser une question	to ask a question

Tous ensemble!

A. Refaites les phrases suivantes selon les indications entre parenthèses.

En cours

1. Il finit ses cours à onze heures.   (Elles... midi.)
2. Elle a suivi un cours d'informatique.   (... faire...)
3. Je ne comprends pas pourquoi ils dorment en classe.   (Nous... il...)
4. Elle explique ce dialogue aux étudiants.   (... apprendre ... leçon...)
5. Ils font de l'italien.   (... étudier...)

Au café

6. Ils finissent cette bière froide.   (... servir... bon...)
7. Elle présente ses vieux amis à son fils.   (... ami... fille.)
8. Nous allons voir nos copains mardi.   (... mardi dernier.)
9. Je prends du café quand il fait froid.   (Ils... pleuvoir.)
10. Demain nous allons voir nos amis anglais ici.   (Hier... bon...)

B. Répondez aux questions suivantes en employant les mots entre parenthèses.

En ville

1. Quel temps va-t-il faire demain?   (... chaud et... pleuvoir.)
2. J'ai soif. Qu'est-ce que je peux prendre?   (Prendre... eau!)
3. Qui choisit les films quand vous allez au cinéma?   (Nos parents...)
4. Est-ce que vous êtes descendu en voiture?   (Non,... prendre... taxi... parce que... brouillard.)
5. Quels fruits voulez-vous?   (... choisir... pêches et... poires.)

Chez vous

6. Est-ce que tes parents ont un répondeur?   (Non... répondre eux-mêmes.)
7. Avez-vous donné de l'argent aux enfants?   (Non... petit cadeau.)
8. Vous avez fait vos provisions?   (Non...)
9. Va-t-il voir les filles?   (Non... dimanche dernier.)
10. Quelle sorte de vêtements a-t-il choisis?   (... beau...)

C. Formez des phrases complètes en employant les mots donnés.

En famille

1. Ce / homme / ressembler / mère
2. Que / vous / voir / fenêtre?
3. Mes sœurs / sortir / souvent, / mais / elles / ne... pas / dormir assez
4. Qui / pouvoir / fermer / ce / porte?
5. Je / servir / thé / chaud / mon / père / hiver

Les études

6. Quel / cours / vous / choisir?
7. Nous / réussir / examen / maths / semaine / prochain?
8. Elle / vouloir / acheter / nouveau / ordinateur
9. Nous / faire / sciences économiques / automne
10. Ce / femmes / étudier / langues / étranger

D. Répondez aux questions suivantes selon les indications entre parenthèses et en remplaçant les mots en italique par des pronoms compléments.

1. Vous avez parlé *à vos amis?* (Oui,…)
2. Avez-vous vu *son magnétophone?* (Non,… pas encore…)
3. Elle apprend l'anglais *aux enfants?* (Non,… le français.)
4. Est-ce que Christine veut acheter *cette robe?* (Non,… détester.)
5. Nous allons inviter *les Ouellette* cette semaine? (Non,… octobre)
6. Tu vas téléphoner *à Mme Ouellette?* (Non,… voir au bureau et… parler à midi.)
7. Est-ce qu'on fait *la vaisselle* maintenant? (Non,… demain.)
8. Est-ce que j'ai perdu *mon livre de français?* (Non,… oublier chez toi.)

E. Complétez les phrases suivantes logiquement *(logically)*.

1. Le dimanche à six heures, je…
2. Ce cours est…
3. En cours, nous ne pouvons pas…
4. Mes amis ne veulent pas…
5. Quand il pleut,…
6. Ce trimestre, je suis des cours…
7. De ma chambre, on peut voir…
8. Je ressemble à…

F. Questions personnelles

1. Quand vous mangez au restaurant, qu'est-ce que vous aimez prendre?
2. A quelle heure prenez-vous votre petit déjeuner?
3. Qu'est-ce que vous voulez apprendre?
4. Quel cours suivez-vous ce trimestre / semestre?
5. Quelles langues étrangères comprenez-vous?
6. A qui téléphonez-vous souvent?
7. Dans votre famille, qui désobéit souvent?
8. Où aimez-vous aller quand vous sortez?

Entre nous!

A. Avec un(e) camarade de cours, parlez de vos études le trimestre (semestre) dernier, ce trimestre (semestre), et le trimestre (semestre) prochain.

B. Interviewez un(e) camarade de cours sur ses rapports avec son / sa camarade de chambre. Utilisez les questions suivantes et des questions originales.

Vous l'aimez / le détestez?
Vous lui téléphonez souvent?
Vous lui donnez des cadeaux?
Vous lui prêtez des vêtements?
Vous l'écoutez toujours?
Vous lui avez présenté votre famille?
Vous l'avez invité(e) chez vous?

C. Quels bons films avez-vous vus? Choisissez un film et racontez-le à vos camarades de cours, mais ne leur donnez pas le titre *(title)*. Ils vont le deviner *(guess)*.

D. Avec un(e) autre étudiant(e), préparez un voyage pour le week-end prochain. Avec qui et comment allez-vous voyager? Qu'est-ce que vous voulez visiter? Qui est-ce que vous voulez voir?

E. En groupes de trois ou quatre personnes, faites des interviews pour connaître les réponses aux questions suivantes.

1. Qu'est-ce que tu voudrais apprendre à faire?
2. Où peux-tu aller pour l'apprendre?
3. Qu'est-ce que tu peux apprendre à une autre personne?
4. A qui veux-tu apprendre quelque chose?

F. **Jeu de rôles.** Jouez les scènes suivantes.

1. Vous sortez avec un(e) ami(e). Choisissez un restaurant et un film à voir.
2. Un(e) camarade de cours téléphone et il / elle veut sortir avec vous. Vous ne l'aimez pas. Trouvez des excuses.
3. Vous êtes journaliste et vous interviewez une célébrité.
4. Vous êtes au marché en plein air et vous achetez vos provisions.

Chapitre 10

En voiture

Commençons

Grammaire

Communiquons

Lecture culturelle

Vocabulaire

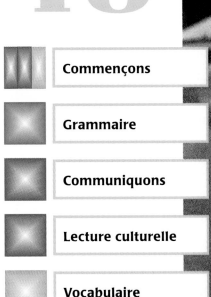

Une Laguna

Objectives

Language

Vocabulary for the car • The mid vowels / e / and / ɛ / • **Savoir** and **connaître** •
Review of the **passé composé** • The imperfect • **Venir** and verbs conjugated like
venir • **Venir de**

Culture

La Belgique • Renting a car • **La 2 CV**

Communication

Talking about whom and what you know • Describing past events and
conditions • Driving a car

Commençons

On loue une voiture.   WWW

Trois étudiants américains font un voyage en Europe pendant les grandes va-
cances. Ils viennent d'arriver à l'aéroport de Zaventem à Bruxelles et ils sont
allés au bureau de la compagnie de location de voitures Avis.

L'EMPLOYÉE: Bonjour, vous avez besoin d'une voiture?

JANE: Oui, nous l'avons réservée aux Etats-Unis et nous l'avons payée.

L'EMPLOYÉE: Très bien. Mais vous savez, il faut régler la T.V.A. en Belgique quand vous rendez la voiture.

JANE: Nous ne savions pas cela quand nous l'avons louée. Est-ce qu'il y a d'autres frais?

L'EMPLOYÉE: L'assurance tous risques est en plus. Elle n'est pas obligatoire, mais si vous ne connaissez pas bien les habitudes des chauffeurs européens, elle est presque indispensable.

JANE: Oui, d'accord. Je vais payer avec ma carte de crédit. Est-ce que la voiture est automatique?

L'EMPLOYÉE: Oui. C'est une Renault Laguna. Tenez, voilà les papiers à signer et les clés.

LA CARTE CLE WIZARD,

LA LOCATION EN UN TEMPS RECORD

DEMANDE (ou MODIFICATION) DE CARTE-CLÉ WIZARD

Cette carte vous est délivrée gratuitement

Veuillez compléter en lettres capitales.
Si vous demandez une modification de votre carte Clé-Wizard, notez votre numéro Wizard ci-dessous ainsi que les éléments à corriger.

☐ Demande   ☐ Modification carte Clé-Wizard N° _____

Veuillez indiquer le mode de paiement que vous préférez en cochant la case appropriée et en reportant, le cas échéant, le numéro de votre carte de crédit.

☐ AMERICAN EXPRESS   ☐ DINERS CLUB   ☐ CARTE BLEUE

☐ EUROCARD   ☐ AUTRE   ☐ PAIEMENT COMPTANT

Numéro ⌊_⌊_⌊_⌊_⌊_⌊_⌊_⌊_⌊_⌊_⌊_⌊_⌋

Etudions le dialogue

1. Que font les trois étudiants américains à l'aéroport de Bruxelles?
2. Est-ce qu'ils ont déjà réservé une voiture? Où?
3. En Belgique, qu'est-ce qu'on paye en plus du prix de la location?
4. Quand paye-t-on la T.V.A.?
5. Quand est-il prudent de prendre une assurance tous risques?
6. Quelle sorte de voiture Jane et ses amis ont-ils louée?

Mots clés

loue (louer)	*are renting*	**en plus**	*extra*
grandes vacances *(f.)*	*summer vacation*	**obligatoire**	*required*
viennent d' (venir de)	*have just*	**connaissez (connaître)**	*know*
aéroport *(m.)*	*airport*	**habitudes** *(f.)*	*habits*
compagnie de location	*rental company*	**chauffeurs** *(m.)*	*drivers*
avez besoin de	*need*	**européens**	*European*
(**avoir besoin de**)		**presque**	*almost*
réservée	*reserved*	**indispensable**	*indispensable*
payée	*paid for*	**d'accord**	*O.K.*
régler	*pay*	**carte de crédit**	*credit card*
T.V.A. (taxe à la valeur ajoutée)	*value-added tax*	**automatique**	*automatic (transmission)*
frais *(m.)*	*costs*	**Tenez.**	*Here.*
assurance tous risques *(f.)*	*full collision insurance*	**papiers** *(m.)*	*documents*
		signer	*sign*

Faisons connaissance

Renting a car is an excellent, if expensive, way to see Europe. One reason that rentals are expensive is the **T.V.A.** This is a tax that many European countries add to purchases; it can be 33% of the total cost, or even more for luxury items. Another major expense in renting a car is additional insurance coverage. The deductible on standard coverage is quite high, making **assurance tous risques** a good idea for renters. In general, you must be at least 21 years old to rent a car in Europe; you must also produce a valid driver's license and a major credit card.

For many years, Belgium has been a popular point of arrival for American tourists who visit Europe. Sabena, the government-operated airline, was among the first European airlines to establish gateways in major American cities and to offer competitive transatlantic fares. Belgium also has a lot to offer to tourists.

Le soir sur la Grand-Place à Bruxelles

Cities like Brussels (**Bruxelles**), Ghent (**Gand**), Bruges, and Liège contain historical treasures. Brussels is also very well known for its fine cuisine and for the luxury shops that line its **avenue Louise,** which is often compared to the **Champs-Elysées.**

Enrichissons notre vocabulaire

Une auto *(A car)*

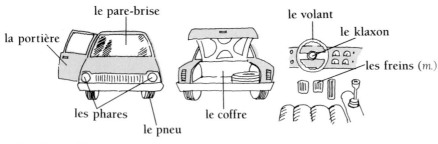

les places *(f.)*	*seats*		
le siège avant	*front seat*	le siège arrière	*back seat*

La circulation *(Traffic)*

conduire	*to drive*	tomber en	*to have a*
démarrer	*to start*	panne	*breakdown*
un embouteillage	*a traffic jam*	une voiture	*a brand-new*
réparer	*to repair*	neuve	*car*
stationner	*to park*	une voiture	*a secondhand*
		d'occasion	*car*

Un accident *(An accident)*

la ceinture de sécurité	*seatbelt*
freiner	*to brake*
les gendarmes *(m.)*	*police officers*
le permis de conduire	*the driver's license*
la priorité à droite	*the right of way*
rouler à... kilomètres à l'heure	*to go . . . kilometers per hour*

Prononciation   The mid vowels / e / and / ɛ /

A. French has three pairs of mid vowels, so called because the mouth is neither fully open as with the / a / sound nor closed as with the / i / sound. With all three pairs, it is important to note whether a consonant sound follows the vowel sound.

B. The mid vowel sound / ɛ / is often followed by a consonant. It is pronounced with the mouth slightly open and the tongue forward.

Practice the / ɛ / sound by repeating the following words after your teacher.

> treize / faire / laisse / cette / faites / laide / Bruxelles

C. The mid vowel sound / e / is extremely tense, so you must be careful not to move your tongue or jaw when pronouncing it.

Repeat the following pairs of words after your teacher.

English	French
say	ses
day	des
bay	B

D. In French, a consonant sound never follows the / e / sound at the end of a word. Usual spellings for the / e / sound are **-é, -ez,** and **-er.** The letters **z** and **r** are silent.

Practice the / e / sound by repeating the following words after your teacher.

> allé / vous arrivez / réserver / sécurité / tenez / payée

Exercices

A. Repeat the following pairs of words after your teacher.

/ e /   / ɛ /

1. les   laisse
2. B   bête
3. mes   mère

B. Now, practice the / e / and / ɛ / sounds in words of several syllables. Be sure to avoid diphthongizing the final / e / .

céder / chercher / acceptez / préféré / fermer / préparer

C. Read the following sentences aloud, keeping all vowels very tense.

1. Daniel fait des crêpes pour la fête de sa mère.
2. Cet employé a déjà fermé la fenêtre.
3. Visitez le musée près du café.
4. Merci pour ce verre de lait frais.
5. Elle est née en janvier l'année dernière.
6. Préférez-vous aller danser ou rester chez vous?

Grammaire

I. Savoir and connaître

You use **connaître** and **savoir** to indicate that you know someone or something.

A. Forms

savoir	connaître
Present: je **sais**	je **connais**
tu **sais**	tu **connais**
il / elle / on **sait**	il / elle / on **connaît**
nous **savons**	nous **connaissons**
vous **savez**	vous **connaissez**
ils / elles **savent**	ils / elles **connaissent**
Passé composé: elle **a su**	il **a connu**

B. Uses

Savoir and **connaître** are not often interchangeable.

1. **Savoir** means *to know a fact, to know very well,* or *to know how to do something.* Never use it to mean *to know people.*

> Je ne **sais** pas réparer cette voiture.
> Elle ne **sait** pas quelle sorte d'auto nous avons.
> Mais vous **savez**, il faut régler la T.V.A. en Belgique.

Ce qu'ils disent

In conversation, the French often drop the **ne** of **Je ne sais pas.** The je and **sais** combine to become / ʃe pa /.

—Quelle heure est-il?
—J'sais pas.

---

2. **Connaître** means *to know, to be acquainted with,* or *to be familiar with.* Always use it to mean *to know people* or *places.*

> Je ne **connais** pas ce professeur.
> **Connais**-tu Bruxelles?

3. Another verb conjugated like **connaître** is **reconnaître,** *to recognize.*

> Il l'a vu mais il ne l'**a** pas **reconnu.**
> **Reconnaissez**-vous cette photo?

Mots clés   *Words often used with* **savoir** *and* **connaître**

Connaître

les étrangers *(f.)*	*foreigners*	quelqu'un	*somebody*
les gens *(m.)*	*people*	le roman	*novel*
la loi	*law*		

Savoir ou connaître

la chanson	*song*	la règle	*rule*
le numéro de téléphone	*phone number*	la réponse	*answer*
le poème	*poem*		

---

4. In some cases, both **savoir** and **connaître** can be used in similar sentences, but the meaning will then be different.

Connaissez-vous cette chanson?	*Do you **know** that song? (Are you familiar with. . .)*
Savez-vous cette chanson?	*Do you **know** that song? (Do you know the words. . .)*

Attention!

1. When implying knowledge rather than the presence or absence of an impediment, use **savoir**—not **pouvoir. Savoir** is the French equivalent of the verb *can* in English.

Elle **ne sait pas** chanter.	*She can't sing. (That is, she has a poor voice.)*
Elle **ne peut pas** chanter.	*She can't sing. (She has a sore throat.)*
Je **ne sais pas** conduire.	*I can't drive. (That is, I never learned.)*
Je **ne peux pas** conduire.	*I can't drive. (My car is in the shop.)*

2. The conjunction **que** introduces a fact; the verb **savoir** may precede it, but not **connaître.**

> Ont-ils **su** que tu n'as pas 21 ans?
> Je ne **connais** pas le professeur, mais je **sais** qu'il est sérieux.

Langue

A. Notre prof. Complétez les phrases suivantes avec la forme correcte du verbe **savoir** ou **connaître,** selon le cas.

1. _____-tu le nom de notre prof?
2. Oui, mais je ne _____ pas où il est né.
3. Nos camarades ne _____ pas qu'il est prof.
4. Où est-ce qu'il _____ sa femme? —Je ne _____ pas!
5. Il ne _____ pas parler italien.
6. Nous _____ ses enfants.
7. Est-ce que tu _____ ses livres?
8. Non, mais je _____ qu'ils sont difficiles.

B. Robert a changé. Traduisez les phrases suivantes.

1. I saw Robert, but I didn't recognize him.
2. He has changed, but I don't know why.
3. Can he play music with us?
4. We know he is working this afternoon.
5. Can he go out tonight?
6. He knows a good Italian restaurant near here.

Culture

C. Des livres français. Quel livre peut-on consulter pour connaître la France? Choisissez entre **savoir** et **connaître** dans vos réponses.

MODÈLE: *L'Argus*
> *On consulte* L'Argus *pour savoir combien coûte une voiture d'occasion.*

1.	le *Larousse*	a.	de bons restaurants
2.	le *Guide Michelin*	b.	comment conjuguer un verbe
3.	le *Quid*	c.	des définitions
4.	Le *Bon Usage*	d.	une règle de grammaire
5.	le *Bescherelle*	e.	des statistiques
6.	*Rapports*	f.	parler français

Communication

D. **Connaissez-vous… ?** Circulez parmi *(among)* vos camarades de cours pour trouver une réponse affirmative à chaque question ci-dessous.

MODÈLE: des villes   *Oui, je connais Londres.*

1. des villes loin d'ici
2. une autre culture
3. des gens célèbres *(famous)*
4. de bons films
5. un très mauvais restaurant
6. de bons poèmes
7. un pays européen
8. des professeurs ennuyeux

E. **Interview.** Formez des questions avec **Sais-tu, Connais-tu** ou **Peux-tu** et une des expressions ci-dessous. Utilisez vos questions pour interviewer un(e) camarade de cours; ensuite *(then)*, communiquez ses réponses aux autres.

danser
faire la cuisine
réciter un poème
des gens en France
une chanson récente
jouer du piano ici

parler une langue étrangère
un numéro de téléphone important
stationner une grosse voiture
dîner chez moi ce soir
reconnaître toutes les voitures américaines

F. **Questions personnelles.** Vos connaissances.

1. Où avez-vous connu votre petit(e) ami(e)? votre camarade de chambre?
2. Connaissez-vous des poèmes français? Quels poèmes?
3. Savez-vous votre numéro de Sécurité sociale (sans vérifier)?
4. Qui n'avez-vous pas reconnu récemment? Avez-vous été embarrassé(e)?
5. Qui connaissez-vous le mieux *(the best)?*
6. Savez-vous réparer une voiture? Quels problèmes savez-vous résoudre *(solve)?*

II.   Le passé composé (review)

You use the **passé composé** to relate events in the past.

A.   The passé composé with avoir

1. In most cases, you form the **passé composé** with the present tense of **avoir** and the past participle of the verb. The past participle is based on the infinitive.

Infinitive	Past participle
chanter	chanté
choisir	choisi
répondre	répondu

2. You have also learned several irregular past participles.

apprendre	**appris**	pouvoir	**pu**
avoir	**eu**	prendre	**pris**
comprendre	**compris**	reconnaître	**reconnu**
connaître	**connu**	savoir	**su**
être	**été**	suivre	**suivi**
faire	**fait**	voir	**vu**
pleuvoir	**plu**	vouloir	**voulu**

3. Remember that in the **passé composé** with **avoir** construction, the past participle agrees with the direct object that *precedes* the verb.

—Quelle **robe** avez-vous choisie?
—J'ai choisi une **robe** rouge.

—Vous avez loué quelle voiture?
—La rouge. Nous l'avons réservée et nous l'avons payée.

B. The passé composé with être

1. As you learned in Chapter 6, a small group of verbs forms the **passé composé** with the conjugated form of **être** and the past participle. Most of these are verbs of motion.

Mots clés	*Verbs conjugated with* être *in the* passé composé	
Infinitive		**Past participle**
aller	*to go*	allé
arriver	*to arrive*	arrivé
descendre	*to go down*	descendu
*devenir	*to become*	devenu
entrer (dans)	*to go in*	entré
monter	*to climb, go up*	monté
mourir	*to die*	mort
naître	*to be born*	né
partir	*to leave*	parti
passer (par)	*to pass (by)*	passé
rentrer	*to return; to run into*	rentré
rester	*to stay*	resté
retourner	*to return*	retourné
*revenir	*to come back*	revenu
sortir	*to leave*	sorti
tomber	*to fall*	tombé
*venir	*to come*	venu

---

*Verbs you will study later in this chapter.

2. Remember that past participles of verbs conjugated with **être** agree in gender and number with their subjects.

> **Ils** sont allés au bureau de la compagnie.
> Quand **elle** est entrée, **elle** est tombée.

Attention!

1. In spoken French, you hear past participle agreement with only one verb that takes **être**. That verb is **mourir.**

> Il **est mort** (/ i lɛ mɔʀ /) en 1967, et elle **est morte**
> (/ ɛ lɛ mɔʀt /) en 1970.

2. **Passer** can mean *to spend (time), to take (an exam),* or *to pass (something).* When it takes a direct object, it forms the **passé composé** with **avoir.**

> J'**ai passé** trois jours à Paris.   *I **spent** three days in Paris.*
> Elle lui **a passé** le pain.   *She **passed** him / her the bread.*

When the verb indicates motion, it cannot have a direct object, so it forms the **passé composé** with **être.**

> Des amis **sont passés** chez moi   *Some friends **came by** my house*
>   hier soir.   *last night.*
> Elle **est passée par** Marseille.   *She **went by** Marseille.*

3. **Retourner** indicates motion and is therefore conjugated with **être.**

> Elle **est retournée** à la résidence.   *She **returned** to the dorm.*

The French equivalent of *to return (an object),* **rendre,** is conjugated with **avoir.**

> Elles **ont rendu** le parapluie.   *They **returned** the umbrella.*

Langue

A. Les vacances de Marie-Claire et de sa famille. Formez des phrases avec les mots donnés.

1. Tu / faire / voyage / agréable?
2. Oui, / nous / aller / Belgique
3. Combien de temps / vous / rester / là-bas?
4. Nous / passer / une semaine / Bruxelles
5. Quand / vous / rentrer?
6. Jeudi dernier. / Nous / passer / par / Montréal

B. Conversation au téléphone. Répondez aux questions suivantes en employant les mots entre parenthèses.

1. Est-ce que Pierre est à la maison? (Non... partir avec son frère)
2. Font-ils un voyage? (Oui,... aller à la plage)
3. Pourquoi n'ont-ils pas pris ta voiture? (Elle ne marche pas; je... avoir... un accident)
4. Quand est-ce qu'on va voir tes parents? (... arriver hier soir)
5. Ton père est-il vieux? (Oui... naître en 1930)
6. Ils ont déjà vu l'appartement de Pierre? (Oui,... passer le voir le mois dernier)

Culture

C. **Des personnages historiques célèbres.** Identifiez les personnages historiques dans la colonne de gauche en formant une phrase avec les expressions de la colonne de droite.

MODÈLE: Rimbaud / partir pour l'Afrique
Rimbaud est parti pour l'Afrique.

1. de Gaulle
2. Napoléon
3. LaSalle
4. Camus
5. George Sand
6. Jean Genet

a. sortir de prison / devenir auteur
b. partir à Majorque avec Chopin
c. mourir dans un accident de voiture en 1960
d. descendre jusqu'en Louisiane en 1682
e. naître sur une île *(island)* / mourir sur une autre île
f. entrer dans le débat politique au Québec en 1967

Communication

D. **Des biographies.** Séparez-vous en petits groupes et interviewez vos camarades. Utilisez les expressions suivantes.

naître en quelle année? où?
arriver quand à l'université?
rentrer avant minuit samedi?
étudier le français au lycée?
aller au cinéma récemment?

étudier ou sortir le week-end dernier?
connaître votre petit(e) ami(e) où?
???

E. **Hier.** Interviewez un(e) camarade de cours au sujet de sa journée d'hier. Utilisez les possibilités données ci-dessous ou vos propres idées. Ensuite, présentez un résumé à la classe.

prendre le petit déjeuner à... heures
partir pour...
prendre l'autobus / ta voiture
attendre tes amis à...
aller à ton cours de...
répondre à... questions
déjeuner avec...

voir...
rentrer chez toi à... heures
regarder la télévision l'après-midi
faire des courses à...
monter dans ta chambre à...
téléphoner à...
???

F. **Questions personnelles.** Vos activités extraordinaires.

1. Où êtes-vous allé(e) plusieurs fois *(several times)* en vacances? Pourquoi?
2. Etes-vous déjà resté(e) seul(e) chez vous tout un week-end? Qu'est-ce que vous avez fait?
3. Etes-vous né(e) le même jour qu'une célébrité? Quelle célébrité?
4. Etes-vous descendu(e) en Amérique du Sud? Quels pays avez-vous visités?
5. Vous êtes allé(e) à New York? Par où êtes-vous passé(e)?
6. A quel monument très haut *(high)* êtes-vous monté(e)? La tour Eiffel? Le monument à George Washington?

III. The imperfect

You use the imperfect when you are describing conditions in the past.

A. Formation of the imperfect

1. In addition to the **passé composé,** French has another past tense—**l'imparfait** (the imperfect). Its forms are based on the first-person plural (**nous** form) of the present tense: you drop the **-ons** and add the following endings.

parler (parlons)	finir (finissons)
je parlais	je finissais
tu parlais	tu finissais
il / elle / on parlait	il / elle / on finissait
nous parlions	nous finissions
vous parliez	vous finissiez
ils / elles parlaient	ils / elles finissaient

partir (partons)	descendre (descendons)
je partais	je descendais
tu partais	tu descendais
il / elle / on partait	il / elle / on descendait
nous partions	nous descendions
vous partiez	vous descendiez
ils / elles partaient	ils / elles descendaient

2. The imperfect of **il pleut** is **il pleuvait.**

Attention!

Because the imperfect tense is based on the first-person plural of the present tense, you must keep the pronunciation of the stem. Be careful especially with je **faisais** (/ fø zɛ /) and **tu prenais** (/ prø nɛ /). Note that the first vowel of each verb has the same sound as **je peux** (/ ʒø pø /).

L'orthographe

1. Because four imperfect endings begin with the letter **a**, verbs ending in -**cer** and -**ger** undergo spelling changes in those forms. For infinitives ending in -**cer**, the **c** becomes **ç** before **a** or **o**. For verbs ending in -**ger**, the **g** becomes **ge** whenever the ending begins with an **a** or an **o**:

    commen*cer* → commen*çons* → commen*çais*
    man*ger* → man*geons* → man*geais*

2. Verbs with infinitives ending in -**ier** (**apprécier, étudier, expédier, oublier**) will have two i's in the **nous** and **vous** forms.

    Nous étudi*ions* la gestion.
    Vous appréci*iez* les chauffeurs prudents.

B. The imperfect of être

Etre has an irregular stem, **ét-**.

être	
j' étais	nous étions
tu étais	vous étiez
il / elle / on était	ils / elles étaient

C. Differences between the imperfect and the passé composé

1. The difference between these two tenses depends on your perception of the action:

    Passé composé: Events: What happened or what happened next?

    Quand j'**ai vu** l'enfant, j'**ai freiné**.
    Quand elle avait onze ans, elle **est allée** au Canada.
    Il **a perdu** son permis de conduire parce qu'il **a eu** un accident.

    Imparfait: Circumstances: What were the conditions?

Il **pleuvait** quand je suis sorti.	*It **was raining** when I went out.*
En 1962, nous **habitions** en Belgique.	*In 1962, we **lived** in Belgium.*
Quand j'**étais** petit, j'**allais** à l'école en autobus.	*When I **was** young, I **used to go** to school on the bus.*

2. Two actions of one person going on at the same time cannot both be in the **passé composé**. The **imparfait** shows the conditions, and the **passé composé** indicates the events.

Circumstance	Event
Je **prenais** le petit déjeuner	quand **j'ai entendu** le téléphone.
Il **était** minuit	quand Christine **est rentrée**.
Il y **avait** trop de gens chez Yves	et **il est parti**.

D. Because the difference between the **imparfait** and the **passé composé** does not exist in English, English speakers must sometimes use different verbs to establish the distinction.

Il **connaissait** la femme.	*He **knew** the woman.*
Il **a connu** la femme.	*He **met** the woman.*
Elle **savait** la réponse.	*She **knew** the answer.*
Elle **a su** la réponse.	*She **found out** the answer.*
Je ne **voulais** pas le faire.	*I **didn't want** to do it.*
Je n'**ai** pas **voulu** le faire.	*I **refused** to do it.*

Langue

A. Mes habitudes. Mettez le paragraphe suivant à l'imparfait. Commencez avec **L'année dernière,...**

Le dimanche, nous faisons la grasse matinée. Je prends mon petit déjeuner très tard et je sors. Je fais une promenade et je rentre à la maison. L'après-midi, je regarde la télé ou j'écoute des disques. Ma femme téléphone à ses parents et elle leur parle de nos enfants. Nous ne travaillons pas beaucoup le dimanche!

B. Monique et ses copines rentrent. Dans le paragraphe suivant, mettez les verbes au passé composé ou à l'imparfait, selon le cas. Faites les changements nécessaires.

Le week-end dernier, Monique et nous _____ (visiter) la ville où nous _____ (habiter) quand nous _____ (avoir) dix ans. Nous _____ (chercher) nos anciennes maisons et nous _____ (voir) beaucoup de vieux amis aussi. Nous _____ (avoir) froid quand nous _____ (retourner) à Montfort et nous _____ (prendre) une boisson chaude. Quand Monique _____ (partir), nous _____ (être) malheureuses. Je lui _____ (téléphoner) après qu'elle _____ (arriver) chez elle. Quand elle _____ (entendre) le téléphone, elle _____ (savoir) que c' _____ (être) moi. Elle _____ (vouloir) parler longtemps, mais moi, j' _____ (avoir) des courses à faire.

C. A la gare. Mettez les verbes du paragraphe suivant au passé composé ou à l'imparfait, selon le cas.

Samedi dernier, il _____ (pleuvoir) et il _____ (faire) du brouillard. Nous _____ (arriver) à la gare à sept heures. Nous _____ (être) en avance car le train pour Paris _____ (aller) partir à huit heures. Mes parents _____ (avoir) froid et ils _____ (ne... pas vouloir) rester. Nous _____ (aller) au restaurant et nous _____ (prendre) un café bien chaud. A huit heures moins cinq, le train _____ (entrer) en gare et il y _____ (avoir) beaucoup de gens. Nous _____ (monter) et nous _____ (trouver) trois places ensemble. Le train _____ (partir). Nous _____ (être) contents de rentrer.

Culture   WWW

D. **La France d'autrefois** *(of the past).* Qu'est-ce qui a changé en France et qu'est-ce qui n'a pas changé?

MODÈLE: parler deux langues
On ne parlait pas deux langues, mais beaucoup de Français parlent deux langues maintenant.

1. manger beaucoup à midi
2. regarder peu la télé
3. avoir des colonies en Afrique
4. divorcer peu
5. avoir un mauvais système téléphonique
6. utiliser peu le téléphone
7. avoir beaucoup d'enfants
8. consommer du coca

Communication

E. **Ma jeunesse.** Quand vous étiez petit(e), que faisiez-vous pour embêter *(annoy)* les gens? Utilisez les suggestions données ou vos propres idées.

manger du chewing gum   porter des vêtements bizarres
rentrer après dîner   manger des insectes
désobéir   écouter un transistor
étudier peu   ???

F. **Quelles étaient les circonstances?** Décrivez le temps, les personnes, les émotions, les lieux, etc., pour les activités suivantes.

1. Votre plus long voyage en voiture
2. Un accident que vous avez eu
3. Un voyage en avion
4. La première fois que vous êtes sorti(e) avec un garçon / une fille
5. Le moment le plus embarrassant de votre vie *(life)*
6. Des vacances que vous n'allez jamais oublier

G. **Questions personnelles.** Votre passé.

1. Quand vous étiez petit(e), qu'est-ce que vous aimiez faire? Est-ce que vous étiez bon(ne) élève?
2. Qui admiriez-vous?
3. Quand vous alliez au lycée, où habitiez-vous?
4. Que faisiez-vous que *(that)* vous ne faites pas maintenant?
5. Quel âge aviez-vous quand vous êtes entré(e) à l'université?
6. Qui voyiez-vous souvent l'année dernière que *(whom)* vous ne voyez pas maintenant?

IV. Venir / Verbs conjugated like venir / Venir de + *infinitive*

You use the verb **venir** to express the idea of coming or to express a recent action.

A. Venir

venir *(to come)*	
Présent: je **viens**	nous **venons**
tu **viens**	vous **venez**
il / elle / on **vient**	ils / elles **viennent**
Passé composé: il **est venu**	

Tu **viens** chez nous ce soir?
Ils vont **venir** demain.

Je **suis venu** à huit heures.
Elle **venait** toujours avec une amie.

B. Verbs conjugated like venir

1. A number of verbs are conjugated like **venir** in the present tense.

appartenir à *to belong to*	Ce transistor ne lui **appartient** pas.
contenir *to contain*	Mon *Guide Michelin* **contient** les renseignements nécessaires.
devenir *to become*	Tu **deviens** impossible!
obtenir *to obtain*	Elle **obtient** son permis.
retenir *to hold back, to remember*	Je ne **retiens** pas les dates.
revenir *to come back*	Vous **revenez** le week-end prochain?
tenir *to hold, to keep*	Tu **tiens** l'enfant?
tenir à + *noun* *to be fond of*	Ils **tiennent** à leur vieille voiture.
tenir à + *verb* *to be anxious to, to insist on*	Nous **tenons** à partir tout de suite.
tenir de *to take after*	Elle **tient** de son père.

2. Like **venir, devenir** and **revenir** use **être** in the **passé composé**. All other verbs conjugated like **venir** use **avoir** in the **passé composé**.

    Il **est devenu** méchant.
    Elles **sont revenues** ensemble.

    Elle **a tenu** à réparer sa voiture elle-même.
    Il n'a pas **obtenu** son permis de conduire.

Attention!

1. **Devenir** is often used in the expression **Qu'est-ce que tu deviens?**, meaning *What are you up to?* In the **passé composé**, **Qu'est-ce qu'il est devenu?** means *Whatever became of him?* Like **être, devenir** does not take an article with professions that are not modified by adjectives.

    Elle est devenue **professeur**.　　　*She became a **teacher.***

2. The verb **tenir** is used in the expressions **Tenez!** and **Tiens!,** which mean *Say! Here!*

    Tenez! Voilà vos papiers.
    Tiens! Je n'ai pas mon permis de conduire!

C. Venir de + *infinitive*

The construction **venir de** + *infinitive* represents the **passé immédiat** and is used in two tenses: the present and the imperfect.

1. In the present tense, a conjugated form of **venir de** + *infinitive* indicates a recently completed action and is equivalent to the English *have just* + *past participle*.

Je **viens d'**avoir un accident.	*I've **just had** an accident.*
Ils **viennent d'**arriver à l'aéroport.	*They've **just arrived** at the airport.*

2. In the imperfect tense, a conjugated form of **venir de** + *infinitive* indicates an action that was completed just before another past action, which is expressed in the **passé composé**. In this case, the French **venir de** + *infinitive* is equivalent to the English *had just* + *past participle*.

Il **venait d'**arriver quand je suis rentré.	*He **had just** arrived when I got home.*
Nous **venions d'**ouvrir la porte quand le téléphone a sonné.	*We **had just** opened the door when the telephone rang.*

Langue

A. Promenade en auto. Faites des phrases complètes avec les mots suivants.

1. Ton / voiture / contenir / combien / personnes?
2. Six, / si / on / ne... pas / tenir / beaucoup de place
3. Marc / venir / arriver / et nous / tenir / l'emprunter!
4. Marc, / qu'est-ce que / tu / devenir?
5. Je / venir / obtenir / permis de conduire!
6. Alors, / venir / avec nous / et prendre / volant!

B. Chez moi. On téléphone pour parler avec les membres de votre famille. Mettez les phrases suivantes au passé immédiat en employant **venir de** au présent ou à l'imparfait, selon le cas.

1. Mon père part.
2. Ma sœur descend de sa chambre.
3. Robert finissait son dîner quand ma mère est arrivée.
4. Ma mère monte.
5. Elle finit son fromage.
6. Je faisais la vaisselle quand le téléphone a sonné.

Culture

C. Les anciennes colonies. A quel pays européen est-ce que les pays africains suivants appartenaient avant leur indépendance?

MODÈLE: Le Cameroun appartenait à la France et à la Grande-Bretagne.

1.	Le Zaïre	a.	la Hollande
2.	l'Algérie	b.	le Portugal
3.	le Mozambique	c.	l'Italie
4.	le Nigeria	d.	la Belgique
5.	l'Ethiopie	e.	la Grande-Bretagne
6.	l'Afrique du Sud	f.	la France

Communication

D. Un objet précieux. A quoi tenez-vous? Quel objet aimez-vous beaucoup? Décrivez cet objet et expliquez pourquoi vous l'aimez beaucoup.

un vêtement (de vieilles   des livres anciens
  chaussures?)   un cadeau d'un(e) petit(e) ami(e)
une belle photo (de votre   un poème
  famille?)   ???

E. Mes activités récentes. Séparez-vous en petits groupes et répondez à la question «**Qu'est-ce que vous avez fait récemment?**» Employez **venir de** et utilisez les suggestions données ou vos propres idées.

prendre le petit déjeuner   parler avec un(e) camarade
obtenir une bonne note en...   arriver sur le campus
réussir à un examen de...   sortir de mon cours de...
rentrer de...   avoir un accident
finir un coca   ???

F. Questions personnelles. Interviewez un(e) camarade de cours et présentez un résumé de ses réponses à la classe.

1. Vous et vos amis, vous allez partir ce week-end? Quand revenez-vous?
2. Avez-vous obtenu une bonne note? Quand? Dans quelle matière?
3. Venez-vous toujours en cours? Pourquoi pas?
4. A quelles organisations appartenez-vous?
5. De qui tenez-vous?
6. Que voulez-vous devenir?

Communiquons

Connaître le code de la route   www

In order to drive in France, you must be eighteen years old and take private lessons from an **auto-école.** The French driver's license is very difficult to obtain, but, once you have it, you never need to renew it. An American wishing to drive in France would do well to obtain an international driver's license before going and to become familiar with French traffic regulations (**le code de la route**).

The basic driving rules in France are the same as in North America for the most part, but there are some differences. For example, the right of way is usually given to the vehicle on the right unless otherwise indicated. In addition, to reduce noise in cities, it is forbidden to honk. Instead, drivers signal with high beams (**faire un appel de phares**) to warn others. To reduce casualties, the use of seat belts is mandatory and children under twelve are forbidden from riding in the front seat. Americans generally find French drivers very aggressive, so it is wise to be cautious when driving in France.

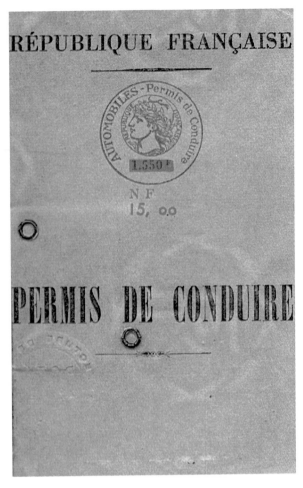

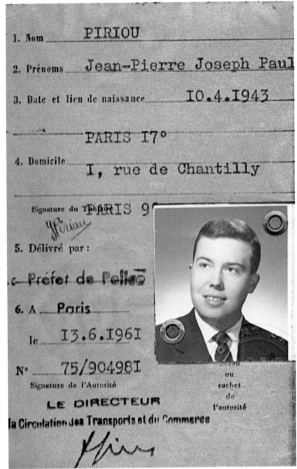

A new campaign to reduce drunken driving involves selling individual blood-alcohol tests, called **un éthylotest**, in drug stores and cafés for use on a voluntary basis.

Expressions

▶ **On conduit sa voiture.**

Ce chauffeur fait du 100 kilomètres à l'heure.	*That driver is going 62 miles per hour.*
Ce chauffard a brûlé le feu.	*That reckless driver ran the red light.*
Ne doublez pas ici!	*Don't pass here!*
Cette auto a beaucoup de passagers (-ères) / occupants (-es).	*This car has a lot of passengers.*
J'ai pris le volant.	*I got behind the wheel.*

▶ **On entretient** *(maintains)* **sa voiture.**

J'ai besoin de prendre de l'essence / de l'huile.	*I need to get some gas / oil.*
Faites le plein, s'il vous plaît.	*Fill it up, please.*
Le garagiste vérifie les pneus / l'huile.	*The mechanic is checking the tires / the oil.*
Le mécanicien travaille à la station-service.	*The mechanic works at the gas station.*

Interaction   *M. Lafont fait le plein.*

M. LAFONT:	Le plein de super°, s'il vous plaît.	*premium*
LA POMPISTE°:	D'accord. Je vérifie l'huile?	*attendant*
M. LAFONT:	Oui, et le pneu arrière droit°.	**arrière...** *right rear*
LA POMPISTE:	Vous allez loin?	
M. LAFONT:	Oui, nous allons à Aix. C'est à combien d'ici?	
LA POMPISTE:	Eh bien, par l'autoroute, il faut compter° trois heures.	*plan on*

Elle fait le plein.

Activités

A. En France, on utilise **les panneaux routiers** *(road signs)* **internationaux.** Identifiez les panneaux correspondant aux définitions suivantes.

1. stop
2. stationnement interdit *(forbidden)*
3. chaussée glissante *(slippery)*
4. défense de *(forbidden)* tourner à droite
5. sens *(way)* unique
6. défense de doubler
7. vitesse *(speed)* limitée à cent kilomètres
8. sens interdit

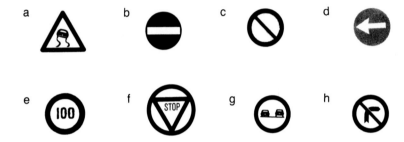

B. Répondez aux questions suivantes.

1. En général, roulez-vous vite? Du combien faites-vous sur l'autoroute *(interstate)*? En ville?
2. Brûlez-vous souvent les feux? Pourquoi?
3. Etes-vous un chauffard? A quelles lois désobéissez-vous souvent?
4. Aimez-vous mieux prendre le volant ou être passager (-ère)? Pourquoi?
5. Avez-vous déjà fait du stop? Pour aller où? Est-ce une bonne idée?
6. Où stationnez-vous à l'université? C'est près de votre salle de cours?
7. Etes-vous tombé(e) en panne? Dans quelles circonstances?
8. Quelle station-service fréquentez-vous? Pourquoi? Connaissez-vous un(e) bon(ne) mécanicien(ne)?
9. Que faites-vous à votre voiture avant de partir en vacances? Faites une liste.

consommation - consumption - consumo	
5 l/100 km	= 56,5 mi/gal
10 l/100 km	= 28,2 mi/gal
15 l/100 km	= 18,8 mi/gal
20 l/100 km	= 14,1 mi/gal
20 mi/gal	= 14,1 l/100 km
30 mi/gal	= 9,4 l/100 km
40 mi/gal	= 7,1 l/100 km
50 mi/gal	= 5,6 l/100 km

Lecture culturelle

Avant la lecture

French people have always been fascinated with cars. Today, three families out of four own an automobile, one out of three of these is an import, and the average yearly operating cost is $5,333. Lately, the French have been buying either small or big cars; the sales of medium-sized cars have dropped considerably. As in the United States, four-wheel drive vehicles are very popular; they are known as **les 4 × 4 (les quatre-quatre).**

In spite of the high price of gasoline, insurance premiums, and the cost of the **vignette,** a sticker that must be purchased once a year from the government, French people continue to drive a lot, causing serious traffic problems on the roads and in the cities. It is estimated that each car owner drives an average of 8,680 miles per year, an impressive amount given the size of France.

Activités

A. Name five American cars that are extremely popular today because they are very economical, and indicate how many miles per gallon they use, both on the highway and in a city.

B. What cars do you know that have typified a style of life?

C. Look at the picture of the French car, called a **2 CV,** on page 268. What do you think the reading passage will tell you about the car?

La dernière 2 CV   www

*O*n a marqué la fin° d'une époque° quand la dernière «Deuche» est sortie de l'usine Citroën de Malgualde au Portugal.

L'agonie a commencé quand on a fermé l'usine de Levallois, près de Paris, où on la fabriquait° depuis longtemps. Commercialisée à 876 exem-
5 plaires° en 1949, on a vendu la célèbre° «2 pattes°» à plus de° 7 millions d'exemplaires dans le monde entier° pendant une carrière record de 41 ans.

A l'automne 1935, les ingénieurs d'André Citroën ont reçu pour mission de concevoir° une voiture capable de transporter deux personnes et 50 kilo-grammes de pommes de terre à 60 kilomètres à l'heure°, en consommant seule-
10 ment 3 litres au cent°. Il a fallu attendre° après la Seconde Guerre° mondiale pour voir la voiture sortir.

A l'origine, on avait prévu un toit en toile qui permettait° à une personne de monter dans la voiture et de garder un chapeau haut-de-forme° sur la tête. La voiture avait seulement un phare, à gauche°, car c'était tout ce que° le code de la
15 route demandait. Quand on voulait tourner°, comme° il n'y avait pas de cligno-tant°, il fallait tendre le bras° par la moitié° de la vitre° qui était relevable°.

end / era

manufactured
units / famous / 2 legs /
over / monde… whole
world

devise
à… at 37 mph
3… 3 liters per 100 km /
a… was necessary to
wait / Guerre… World
War / un… a canvas roof
that allowed / garder…
keep a top hat / on the
left / tout… all that / turn
/ since / turn signal / ten-
dre… stretch one's arm /
half / window / était…
could be lifted

Finalement, le 7 octobre 1948, on a montré pour la première fois° au public la nouvelle voiture. Le succès a été immédiat, et dès° 1950, il fallait° attendre six ans entre le moment de la commande° et le moment de la livraison°. La produc-
20 tion a culminé en 1966 avec 168.384 unités pour l'année.

time
starting in / one had to
order / delivery

C'est l'époque de la gloire de cette voiture que les Allemands, les Hollandais et les Scandinaves baptisaient «le vilain petit canard°». La «Deuche» passait partout°, et on pouvait la réparer facilement. On raconte l'histoire d'un journa-liste qui, tombé en panne dans un désert, a été dépanné° quand on a mis des ba-
25 nanes dans le carter°.

vilain... *ugly little duck*
everywhere
rescued
gear box

Pendant ses dernières années, la «Deuche» est devenue plus confortable. Elle était plus rapide et on ne gelait° plus dedans° en hiver. Même embour-geoisée°, elle continuait à être un symbole, et avec sa disparition°, les 35–60 ans ont enterré° une partie de leur jeunesse°.

froze / inside
gentrified / disappearance
buried / youth

(Adapté de l'article «La dernière 2CV», *Journal Français d'Amérique*, Vol. 12, No. 17. Reprinted by permission.)

Une Deuche

Après la lecture

Questions sur le texte

1. Qu'est-ce que la dernière «Deuche» a annoncé?
2. Quand est-ce qu'on a compris que la 2 CV était condamnée?
3. Combien de 2 CV a-t-on vendu pendant 41 ans?
4. En 1935, quelle sorte de voiture est-ce que les ingénieurs de Citroën devaient fabriquer?
5. Pourquoi avait-elle un toit en toile?
6. Combien de phares avait-elle?
7. Qu'est-ce qui montre que la voiture était un succès?
8. Comment est-ce que les Allemands appelaient la 2 CV?

Activités

A. Using popular French magazines, such as *Paris-Match*, *Le Point*, or *L'Express*, look up ads for popular French cars. Try to identify three models for the following makes: *Renault*, *Peugeot*, and *Citroën*, and make a list of the parts of the car mentioned in each ad.

B. Avez-vous déjà eu un accident de voiture? Qu'est-ce qui est arrivé?

1. Qui avait tort / raison?
2. Est-ce que les gendarmes sont venus?
3. Le conducteur était ivre *(drunk)*?
4. Une personne a été blessée *(hurt)*?
5. Est-ce que la voiture marchait encore?
6. ???

C. Débats en classe

1. La voiture: un luxe ou une nécessité?
2. Les voitures électriques sont-elles possibles?
3. Les voitures personnelles ou les transports publics?
4. Solutions au problème des chauffards?

A Noël, la Panda dans vos souliers !.. ... et payez à Pâques !

PANDA PLUS
Moteur Fire 4 CV + Essuie-glace AR + Lunette thermique + Feu de recul + Feu de brouillard + Appuis-tête AV + Dossiers AV réglables + Stripping AR.

36 900 F
A.M. 88. Prix au 17.09.87

1re mensualité à 120 jours, pour toute commande d'un modèle de la gamme Panda passée en décembre 87. Exemple de crédit pour 10 000 F : sur 48 mois remboursables en 45 mensualités de 340,85 F (perceptions forfaitaires comprises et hors assurance). T.E.G. 17,94 %. Coût total du crédit 5 338,25 F hors assurance. Coût total de l'opération 15 338,25 F hors assurance. Sous réserve d'acceptation du dossier par FIAT CREDIT FRANCE

FIAT

Vocabulaire

Noms / Pronoms

accident	accident	chanson	song
aéroport	airport	chauffeur	driver
assurance tous risques	full collision insurance	circulation	traffic
carte de crédit	credit card	coffre	trunk
ceinture de sécurité	seat belt	compagnie de location	rental agency

embouteillage	traffic jam	phare	headlight
étranger	foreigner	places	seats
frais	expenses	pneu	tire
frein	brake	poème	poem
gendarme	policeman	portière	door (car)
gens	people	quelqu'un	someone
habitude	habit	règle	rule
kilomètre	kilometer	réponse	answer
klaxon	horn	roman	novel
location	rental	siège arrière	back seat
loi	law	siège avant	front seat
numéro de téléphone	phone number	T.V.A.	V.A.T. (value added tax)
papiers	I.D.	vacances (grandes)	summer vacation
pare-brise	windshield	voiture d'occasion	used car
permis de conduire	driver's license	voiture neuve	new car

Verbes

appartenir à	to belong to	réserver	to reserve
avoir besoin de	to need	retenir	to hold back / to remember
conduire	to drive		
connaître	to know	retourner	to return
contenir	to contain	revenir	to come back
démarrer	to start	rouler à… km à l'heure	to go … miles per hour
devenir	to become	savoir	to know
freiner	to brake	signer	to sign
louer	to rent	stationner	to park
mourir	to die	tenir	to hold
obtenir	to obtain	tenir à	to be fond of
passer par	to pass by	tenir de	to take after
payer	to pay	tomber	to fall
reconnaître	to recognize	venir	to come
régler	to pay	venir de	to have just
réparer	to repair		

Adjectifs / Adverbes

automatique	automatic	neuf	new
étranger	foreign	obligatoire	compulsory
européen	European	presque	almost
indispensable	indispensable	quelqu'un	somebody

Expressions

d'accord	all right	priorité à droite	right of way on the right
d'occasion	used	tomber en panne	to break down
en plus	in addition		

La télé

Chapitre **11**

Commençons

Grammaire

Communiquons

Lecture culturelle

Vocabulaire

Interview pour
la télévision

Objectives

Language

Vocabulary for social problems, happiness, television • The vowel sounds / o /
and / ɔ / • Direct and indirect object pronouns (first and second persons) • The
subjunctive of regular verbs and of **avoir** and être • Uses of the subjunctive

Culture

Opinion polls • Preoccupations of society • French television

Communication

Discussing social issues • Expressing emotion, wishes, doubt, and judgment •
Expressing opinions and uncertainty

Commençons

Une interview avec Simone Trudeau   WWW

Simone Trudeau est journaliste à FR1. Elle prépare un reportage sur les opinions des Français sur les grands problèmes de la vie contemporaine dans le monde. Elle discute avec Claude, 25 ans, cadre dans un grand magasin parisien, et avec Marc, 20 ans, étudiant en sciences politiques.

SIMONE: Qu'est-ce qui vous préoccupe le plus?

CLAUDE: Je suis contente que vous nous posiez cette question, mais j'ai peur qu'il ne soit pas facile de répondre. Il semble que la qualité de la vie soit le plus important.

MARC: Absolument! Selon moi, les gens ont peur qu'il y ait un désastre écologique et ils ne pensent pas qu'on réussisse à rendre la société plus juste.

SIMONE: Je suis surprise que vous ne me parliez pas de l'importance de l'argent et du succès!

CLAUDE: Tous les sondages d'opinion que je consulte montrent que la santé et le bonheur viennent avant le compte en banque et le travail pour un grand nombre de Français.

SIMONE: Je vous remercie pour votre franchise. N'oubliez pas de regarder le Journal de 20 heures demain soir.

Etudions le dialogue

1. Sur quoi est-ce que Simone Trudeau fait un reportage?
2. Qui sont Claude et Marc?
3. Qu'est-ce qui préoccupe Claude?
4. Selon Marc, de quoi les gens ont-ils peur?
5. Pourquoi est-ce que Simone est surprise?
6. Qu'est-ce qui est plus important que l'argent et le succès pour Claude?

Mots clés

interview	*interview*	selon	*according to*
reportage	*feature story*	il y ait (avoir)	*there might be*
opinions *(f.)*	*opinions*	désastre	*disaster*
vie	*life*	écologique	*ecological*
contemporaine	*contemporary*	rendre la société	*make society more*
monde	*world*	plus juste	*just*
discute (discuter)	*is discussing*	surprise	*surprised*
cadre *(m.)*	*middle-level*	importance	*importance*
	manager	succès	*success*
grand magasin	*department store*	sondages *(m.)*	*opinion polls*
préoccupe	*preoccupies*	d'opinion	
(préoccuper)		consulte (consulter)	*consult*
le plus	*the most*	santé	*health*
j'ai peur que	*I'm afraid that*	bonheur	*happiness*
(avoir peur)		compte en banque	*bank account*
soit (être)	*is*	travail	*work*
Il semble	*It seems*	nombre	*number*
qualité	*quality*	remercie (remercier)	*thank*
important	*important*	franchise	*candor*
absolument	*absolutely*	Journal	*news*

Faisons connaissance   www

French people are avid readers of public opinion polls. These appear regularly in French newspapers and magazines and vary in content from the serious (national politics) to the frivolous (reactions to an American soap opera in *Paris-Match*). The French take polls so seriously that it is forbidden to publish the results of political polls immediately before an election.

On French television, many programs are devoted to round tables (**des tables rondes**) where journalists and personalities discuss the latest contemporary issues. During an election year, it is not unusual for all the channels to present such round tables several times a week. Amazingly, the viewers rarely seem to object.

D'après un sondage I.P.S.O.S.-« J.D.D. », 5 % seulement des personnes interrogées accepteraient des « contributions à but politique »

ARGENT ET POLITIQUE

58 % DES FRANÇAIS REFUSENT DE FINANCER LES PARTIS

Marc's fears reflect the opinions of a majority of his fellow citizens. In a recent poll, people ranked the following problems as sources of worry:

WWW

Problèmes	% des réponses affirmatives
le **sida** *AIDS*	93,7
le **chômage** *unemployment*	93,3
la **drogue** *drugs*	91,1
la **pollution**	87,6
la **sécurité, la délinquance**	86,4

Enrichissons notre vocabulaire

Le bonheur *(Happiness)*

—Qu'est-ce qu'**il te faut** pour être heureux?	*What do **you need** in order to be happy?*
—Il me **faut** de l'argent; je suis **matérialiste**.	*I **need** money; I'm **materialistic**.*
—Nous avons besoin de **justice** (*f.*) et de **paix** (*f.*).	*We need **justice** and **peace**.*
—Qu'est-ce que le bonheur pour vous?	*What is happiness for you?*
—L'**amour** (*m.*) de ma famille.	***Love** of my family.*
—La sécurité d'un **emploi**.	***Job** security.*
—L'**égalité** (*f.*) dans la société.	***Equality in society.***
—Des vacances à la **montagne**.	*A vacation in the **mountains**.*

Les grands problèmes sociaux *(Major social problems)*

—Qu'est-ce qui vous **préoccupe**?	*What worries you?*
—La **criminalité** me **fait peur**.	*Crime scares me.*
—Le **trafic** des drogues.	*Drug **trafficking**.*
—La **politique**.	*Politics.*
—La possibilité d'une **guerre nucléaire**.	*The possibility of **nuclear war**.*
—L'**inflation** (*f.*).	*Inflation.*
—Les **sans-logis** (*m.*) / **sans-abris** (*m.*) / **SDF**	*The homeless.*
—Les **sans-papiers**	*Undocumented aliens*

Les petits inconvénients *(Annoyances)*

—Qu'est-ce qui t'**embête** le plus?	*What **annoys** you the most?*
—Beaucoup de **choses** *(f.)!*	*Many **things**!*
—Je ne peux pas **supporter** mes **voisins** *(m.)*. Ils **font du bruit**.	*I can't **stand my neighbors**. They **make noise**.*
—L'**incertitude** *(f.)* de l'**avenir** *(m.)*.	*The **uncertainty** of the **future**.*
—Mes parents n'**arrêtent** pas de me donner des **conseils** *(m.)*.	*My parents don't **stop** giving me advice.*

La télé *(TV)*

les actualités *(f.)*	*news*	un feuilleton	*series*
la chaîne	*channel*	un jeu télévisé	*game show*
la chaîne câblée / le câble	*cable channel*	le programme	*schedule*
		la publicité	*commercials*
un dessin animé	*cartoon*	une série	*series*
les émissions *(f.)*	*shows*		
une émission de variétés	*variety show*		

Prononciation   The vowel sounds / o / and / ɔ /   🔊

A. The vowel sounds / o / and / ɔ / are pronounced with the tongue back and the lips very rounded. As with the sounds / e / and / ɛ /, the tongue is neither high nor low.

Repeat the following English and French word pairs after your teacher.

English	French		English	French
bow	beau		dough	dos
foe	faux		oh	eau

B. The / ɔ / sound is the same as the / o / sound, except that in the former, the mouth is held more open. You use the / o / sound when the word ends in a vowel sound. The / ɔ / sound is used when a pronounced consonant follows it.

Repeat the following pairs of words after your teacher.

/ o /	/ ɔ /	/ o /	/ ɔ /
beau	bonne	tôt	tort
faux	fort	trop	drogues
nos	notre	pot	poche

C. The spellings **au** and ô are almost always pronounced / o /, not / ɔ /. If the consonant that follows is a / z / sound, you also use / o /.

Repeat the following pairs of words after your teacher.

/ ɔ /	/ o /	/ ɔ /	/ o /
notre	autre	école	Côte d'Azur
botte	Claude	note	chose
pomme	pauvre	comme	cause

Exercice

Read the following sentences aloud, paying particular attention to the open / ɔ / sound and the closed / o / sound.

1. Robert veut un beau chapeau.
2. Donne-moi le téléphone!
3. A l'automne, nous faisons de bonnes promenades.
4. Paulette propose des choses idiotes.
5. Le chômage et la drogue me préoccupent.
6. Et comme fromage? —Du Roquefort!

Grammaire

I. Direct and indirect object pronouns: First and second persons

You use these pronouns to refer to yourself or to the person or people to whom or about whom you are speaking.

A. Direct and indirect object pronouns: First and second persons

	singular	plural
1st person	me	nous
2nd person	te	vous

You studied third-person direct object pronouns (**le, la, l'**, and **les**) in Chapter 8 and indirect object pronouns (**lui** and **leur**) in Chapter 9. In contrast, first- and second-person object pronouns do not vary in form from direct to indirect objects. Also note that **me** and **te** become **m'** and **t'** before a vowel.

Pronouns as direct objects

Tu **m'**as vu à la télévision?
Est-ce que ces problèmes **te** préoccupent beaucoup?
On ne **nous** consulte jamais quand on fait un sondage d'opinion.
Qu'est-ce qui **vous** embête le plus?

Pronouns as indirect objects

Vous **me** parlez de quelque chose d'important.
Le journaliste **t'**a posé des questions?
Tu **nous** fais peur.
Elle **vous** donne ses opinions?

B. Placement of pronouns

First- and second-person object pronouns are placed in the same position as third-person object pronouns:

1. directly before the conjugated verb in the present, imperfect, and **passé composé** tenses:

    Vous **me** posez cette question?
    Marc **me** parlait quand Sylvie **nous** a vus.

2. in front of the infinitive when there is a helping verb:

    Elle ne veut pas **vous** embêter mais est-ce qu'elle peut **vous** parler maintenant?
    Cette réponse va **vous** rendre très heureux.

3. in front of the verb in the negative imperative:

    Ne **me** parlez pas de l'importance de l'argent!
    Ne **nous** fais pas peur!

4. after the verb in the affirmative imperative and linked to the verb with a hyphen:

> Posez-**nous** des questions!

The pronoun **me** becomes **moi** in the affirmative imperative.

> Ne **me** donnez pas votre opinion → Donnez-**moi** votre opinion!
> Ne **me** laissez pas seul. → Laissez-**moi** seul.

Attention!

The distinction between direct and indirect object pronouns with **me, te, nous,** and **vous** is important only when determining past participle agreement in the **passé composé.** Only preceding *direct* object pronouns agree when the auxiliary verb is **avoir.**

Direct objects	Indirect objects
Elle **nous** a regardés.	On **vous** a téléphoné?
Je **vous** ai **vus** au cinéma.	Elle ne **nous** a pas **obéi.**

Langue

A. **La jalousie.** Pierre a vu sa petite amie Julie en ville et il est très jaloux *(jealous)*. Jouez le rôle de Julie et répondez aux questions de Pierre en employant les mots entre parenthèses.

1. Je t'ai vue au café avec Robert?   (Oui, tu...)
2. Il t'a commandé une boisson?   (Oui,... coca.)
3. Est-ce que vous m'avez vu?   (Non, nous...)
4. Est-ce qu'il t'a parlé longtemps?   (Oui,...)
5. Est-ce qu'il va te téléphoner?   (Non,...)
6. Est-ce qu'il t'a donné son numéro de téléphone?   (Non,...)
7. Est-ce que vous allez m'inviter demain?   (Non,...)
8. Est-ce que tu m'aimes?   (Non,... ne... pas pouvoir supporter.)

B. **Au téléphone.** Votre sœur parle au téléphone. Imaginez des questions pour les réponses suivantes.

MODÈLE: Oui, il m'aime.
Est-ce que Paul t'aime?

1. Oui, elle m'a parlé hier soir.
2. Oui, elles vont nous inviter.
3. Non, ils ne peuvent pas te comprendre.
4. Oui, je t'ai présenté mon nouveau petit ami.
5. Non, nous ne vous avons pas oubliées.
6. Oui, apporte-moi tes photos.

Culture

C. **En famille.** Indiquez des différences culturelles entre votre famille américaine (vos parents et vous) et les familles françaises (les parents français et leurs enfants) en formant des phrases avec les mots donnés. Attention! Il y a aussi des similarités!

MODÈLE: souhaiter *(wish)* une bonne fête *(saint's day)*
Mes parents ne m'ont jamais souhaité une bonne fête.
Les parents français leur souhaitent une bonne fête tous les ans.

1. donner de l'argent
2. punir souvent
3. téléphoner tous les jours
4. voir tous les dimanches
5. servir du vin quand on était jeune(s)
6. embrasser tous les soirs avant de dormir

Communication

D. **Une rencontre.** Vous rencontrez un garçon / une fille charmant(e) dans une boîte. Imaginez la conversation. Utilisez les suggestions données ou vos propres idées.

Est-ce que je vous ai déjà rencontré(e)?
Comment vous appelez-vous?
Vous venez souvent ici?
Je peux vous offrir une boisson?
Tu me donnes ton numéro de téléphone?
Tu veux me laisser ton adresse?
Je peux passer te voir?
Je peux t'embrasser?

E. **Votre journée d'hier.** Vous êtes condamné(e) *(condemned)* et vous allez mourir demain matin. Qu'est-ce que vous demandez à la dernière minute?

MODÈLE: donner du champagne   *Donnez-moi du champagne.*
laisser seul   *Ne me laissez pas seul.*

servir un bon dîner	parler
donner des cigarettes	faire un gâteau
prêter une Bible	montrer un film de…
apporter du vin	oublier
laisser partir	faire mal
écouter: «Je suis innocent!»	donner la clé

F. **Questions personnelles.** La famille et les amis.

1. Qu'est-ce que le Père Noël vous a apporté l'année dernière?
2. Qui vous téléphone souvent?
3. Qui est passé vous voir récemment?
4. Qui est-ce qui vous fait les repas?
5. Qu'est-ce qui vous rend heureux (-euse)? furieux (-euse)?
6. Qui est-ce qui ne peut pas vous supporter?

II. The subjunctive of regular verbs and of avoir and être

> Until now, you have been using the indicative mood (**le présent, l'imparfait,** and **le passé composé**) to express facts and the imperative mood to express commands and requests. You use the subjunctive mood to express feelings, such as emotion, wishes, doubt, and judgment.

A. Introduction

Even though the subjunctive is used more frequently in French, it also exists in English:

I wish *that* he *were* home now.

As in English, the subjunctive in French is used mostly in subordinate clauses following a main clause. Both clauses are linked by **que** (that).

Emotion:	Je suis contente **que** vous nous **posiez** cette question.
Wishing:	Je voudrais **que** vous me **parliez** de cela.
Doubt:	Les gens ne pensent pas **qu'**on **rende** la société plus juste.
Judgment:	Il semble **que** la qualité de la vie vous **préoccupe** le plus.

B. Forms of the present subjunctive

1. The subjunctive endings are the same for the four groups of regular verbs you know. They are added to the stem of the third-person plural (**ils / elles** form) of the present indicative.

chanter (chant~~ent~~)	partir (part~~ent~~)
que je **chante**	que je **parte**
que tu **chantes**	que tu **partes**
qu'il / elle / on **chante**	qu'il / elle / on **parte**
que nous **chantions**	que nous **partions**
que vous **chantiez**	que vous **partiez**
qu'ils / elles **chantent**	qu'ils / elles **partent**

finir (finiss~~ent~~)	vendre (vend~~ent~~)
que je **finisse**	que je **vende**
que tu **finisses**	que tu **vendes**
qu'il / elle / on **finisse**	qu'il / elle / on **vende**
que nous **finissions**	que nous **vendions**
que vous **finissiez**	que vous **vendiez**
qu'ils / elles **finissent**	qu'ils / elles **vendent**

Attention!

Adding a written -e to the stem of **-ir** and **-re** verbs causes the final consonant to be pronounced:

dormir	→	dorm-	→	qu'il **dorme**
sortir	→	sort-	→	que tu **sortes**
attendre	→	attend-	→	qu'on **attende**
descendre	→	descend-	→	que tu **descendes**

2. Even though they are irregular in the present indicative, **connaître** and **suivre** are regular in the present subjunctive.

| connaître | → | connaiss- | → | que je **connaisse** |
| suivre | → | suiv- | → | que tu **suives** |

C. The subjunctive of avoir and être

Two irregular verbs in the subjunctive are **avoir** and **être**. You will learn other irregular verbs in the subjunctive in Chapter 12.

avoir	être
que j' **aie**	que je **sois**
que tu **aies**	que tu **sois**
qu'il / elle / on **ait**	qu'il / elle / on **soit**
que nous **ayons**	que nous **soyons**
que vous **ayez**	que vous **soyez**
qu'ils / elles **aient**	qu'ils / elles **soient**

Les gens ont peur qu'il y **ait** un désastre écologique.
Il semble que la qualité de la vie **soit** très importante.

Attention!

The **nous** and **vous** forms of the subjunctive of **avoir** are pronounced with the / e / sound: **nous ayons** / nu ze jɔ̃ /, **vous ayez** / vu ze je /.

Langue

A. Des substitutions. Remplacez les verbes en italique par les verbes donnés dans les phrases suivantes.

1. Je veux que vous *restiez*. (répondre, partir, réussir, parler, obéir, étudier)
2. Il faut que nous *chantions* ici. (travailler, dormir, finir, attendre, descendre, être)
3. Nous désirons que tu *finisses*. (écouter, ne pas fumer, partir, finir, avoir de la patience, être à l'heure)

B. **Le succès.** Formez des phrases complètes avec les mots donnés.

1. Vous / vouloir / que / nous / être / heureux?
2. Vos parents / désirer / que / vous / trouver / travail
3. Mon père / ne... pas vouloir / que / je / avoir / trop / argent
4. Il faut / que / tu / réussir / dans / avenir
5. Nous / aimer mieux / que / vous / étudier / université
6. Mon prof / ne... pas vouloir / que / je / perdre / mon / temps

Culture

C. **Connaître un pays.** Vos amis veulent visiter un pays où on parle français. Qu'est-ce qu'ils peuvent faire pour connaître la culture de ce pays? Quels conseils pouvez-vous leur donner? Commencez avec **Il faut que vous...** et choisissez la meilleure *(best)* réponse.

1. rester...
   a. dans un petit hôtel   b. dans un grand hôtel   c. avec une famille

2. aimer...
   a. parler avec des gens   b. observer les gens
   c. expliquer des traditions américaines

3. fréquenter...
   a. les musées   b. les cafés   c. les parcs

4. utiliser...
   a. le métro   b. des taxis   c. les autobus

5. passer... dans le pays.
   a. une semaine   b. un mois   c. une année

6. avoir...
   a. beaucoup de patience   b. beaucoup d'argent
   c. beaucoup de temps

7. voyager entre les villes...
   a. en voiture   b. en train   c. en auto-stop

8. étudier
   a. leur langue   b. leur art   c. leur politique

Communication

D. **Pour réussir.** Pour être un(e) bon(ne) étudiant(e), qu'est-ce qu'il faut faire?

MODÈLE: étudier beaucoup
       Il faut que nous étudiions beaucoup.

écouter le professeur	finir tous les devoirs
passer beaucoup de temps à la bibliothèque	réussir aux examens
être studieux (-euse)	ne... pas sortir le soir
regarder des jeux télévisés tout le temps	répondre à toutes les questions
dormir peu	réfléchir beaucoup
	???

E. **Cher monsieur.** Vous allez composer une lettre au Président des Etats-Unis pour lui donner des conseils. Utilisez les suggestions données ou vos propres idées.

MODÈLE: m'inviter à la Maison-Blanche
Je voudrais que vous m'invitiez à la Maison-Blanche.

ne... pas oublier les pauvres
dépenser moins d'argent
écouter les femmes
voyager en autobus
avoir moins de vacances
répondre aux questions des
    journalistes

être plus patient avec les
    sénateurs
encourager les gens sans travail
penser aux problèmes des
    sans-papiers
ne... pas manger trop de
    hamburgers

F. **Questions personnelles.** Vos problèmes.

1. Est-ce qu'il faut que vous passiez un examen cette semaine? Dans quelle matière?
2. Combien d'heures faut-il que vous étudiiez?
3. Est-ce qu'il est important qu'un professeur soit sévère? Pourquoi ou pourquoi pas?
4. Est-ce que votre petit(e) ami(e) veut que vous sortiez avec elle / lui trop souvent?
5. Est-ce qu'il est préférable que vous gagniez beaucoup d'argent ou que vous soyez heureux (-euse)?
6. De quoi avez-vous peur?

III. Uses of the subjunctive

The verb in the main clause of a sentence determines whether you will use the indicative or the subjunctive in the subordinate clause. The indicative is used most frequently; it follows verbs indicating facts or certainty.

Ils **savent** que vous **êtes** préoccupé.
Les sondages **montrent** que le bonheur **vient** avant l'argent.

The subjunctive occurs in subordinate clauses after verbs of emotion, wishing, doubt, and uncertainty, and some impersonal expressions implying judgment.

Attention!

Note that the subjunctive is used only if the subject in the subordinate clause is different from the subject of the main clause. If the subjects in both clauses are the same, the infinitive is used.

J'ai peur qu'**elle** ait froid cet hiver.	*I'm afraid (that) **she**'ll be cold this winter.*
J'ai peur d'**avoir** froid cet hiver.	*I'm afraid that I'll be cold this winter.*

A. Emotion

The subjunctive mood is used in subordinate clauses starting with **que** after verbs and expressions of emotion.

> Je **suis contente que vous nous posiez** cette question.
> J'**ai peur qu'il ne soit** pas facile de répondre.
> Je **suis surprise que vous ne me parliez** pas d'argent.

Mots clés   **Expressions of emotion**

avoir peur	*to be afraid*	être heureux (-euse)	*to be happy*
être content(e)	*to be happy*		
être désolé(e)	*to be sorry*	être surpris(e)	*to be surprised*
être étonné(e)	*to be surprised*	être triste	*to be sad*
être furieux (-euse)	*to be angry*	regretter	*to be sorry*

If the subject of the main clause does not change, use **de** plus an infinitive with all of the expressions listed above.

> J'ai peur **de** conduire.   Elle regrette **de** ne pas pouvoir venir.

B. Wishing

The subjunctive is used in clauses starting with **que** after verbs expressing wishes, desire, preference, and other impositions of will.

> Elle **veut que nous arrivions** à l'heure.
> Tu **aimes mieux que je choisisse** le restaurant?
> Nous **souhaitons que vous passiez** une bonne soirée.

Mots clés   **Verbs and expressions of will, wishing, and desire**

aimer mieux	*to prefer*	souhaiter	*to wish*
avoir envie (de)	*to feel like*	vouloir	*to want*
désirer	*to want*		

If the subject of the main clause does not change, use an infinitive with all of the verbs listed above, except **avoir envie**, which takes **de**.

> J'aime mieux conduire.   Marc a envie **de** dormir.   Elle veut partir.

C. Doubt and uncertainty

The subjunctive is also used after verbs and expressions of doubt or uncertainty.

> Je **ne pense pas** que **nous ayons** envie de beaucoup de choses.
> Elle **n'est pas sûre** qu'il **soit** là.

Mots clés   Verbs and expressions of doubt and uncertainty

douter	*to doubt*
ne... pas penser	*not to think*
ne... pas être sûr (de)	*not to be sure, to be unsure*
ne... pas être certain (de)	*not to be certain, to be uncertain*
ne... pas trouver	*not to think / find*

If the subject of the main clause does not change, use an infinitive with **penser** and **de** plus an infinitive with **sûr** and **certain**. Sentences with **trouver** must have a change of subject.

> Ils ne pensent pas pouvoir téléphoner.   Il n'est pas sûr **de** réussir.

Attention!

1. Because they imply certainty, **penser**, **trouver**, and **être sûr** in the affirmative are followed by a verb in the indicative.

    > Elle **pense** qu'il **est** beau.   *but:*   Elle **ne pense pas** qu'il **soit** intelligent.

2. The verb **savoir** is always followed by a verb in the indicative.

    > Je **sais** que **vous êtes** italien.   Je **ne savais pas** que **vous étiez** cadre.

3. Several other verbs that you have learned, including **apprendre**, **décider**, **es-pérer**, **expliquer**, **indiquer**, **montrer**, **oublier**, and **répondre**, do not imply doubt. They are therefore followed by a verb in the indicative.

    > Le journaliste **a expliqué** que le Président ne **peut** pas venir.
    > N'**oublie** pas que nous **avons** du chômage.

D.   Impersonal expressions of judgment

The subjunctive is used in the subordinate clause after expressions with no specific subject, that is, without a reference to any particular person or thing, if they express a judgment or opinion on the speaker's part.

> Il **semble** que la qualité de la vie **soit** le plus important.
> Il **faut** que nous **rendions** la société plus juste.

Mots clés   Impersonal expressions implying opinion or personal judgment

Il est bon que	*It is good that*	**Il est possible /**	*It is possible /*
Il est dommage que	*It's too bad that*	**impossible que**	*impossible that*
Il est faux que	*It is untrue that*	**Il est préférable que**	*It is preferable that*
Il est important que	*It is important that*	**Il est rare que**	*It is rare that*
Il est juste / injuste que	*It is fair / unfair that*	**Il est temps que**	*It is time that*
		Il est nécessaire que	*It is necessary that*

The expressions above take **de** with an infinitive when no specific subject is expressed.   **Il est bon de faire ça.**

Il faut que	*It is necessary that*
Il semble que	*It seems that*
Il vaut mieux que	*It is better that*

The expressions above are followed directly by an infinitive when no specific subject is expressed.   **Il faut partir.**

Il est peu probable que	*It is unlikely that*
Il se peut que	*It may be that / Perhaps / It's possible that*

The expressions above always require a specific subject and cannot be used with an infinitive.

Attention!

The following verbs and expressions imply certainty in the speaker's mind and do *not* take the subjunctive.

Il est certain / sûr que	*It is certain / sure that*
Il est évident que	*It is obvious that*
Il est probable que	*It is probable that*
Il est vrai que	*It is true that*

Il est **certain que** vous n'obéissez pas.
Il est **probable que** Marc est très fatigué.

Langue

A. **En vacances.** Formez des phrases complètes avec les mots donnés.

1. Je / souhaiter / vous / passer / bon / vacances
2. Elle / penser / nous / partir / demain
3. Ils / avoir peur / il y a / orage
4. Tu / aimer mieux / je / être / gare / sept heures?
5. Nous / être surpris / tu / avoir / quinze / jour / de vacances
6. Il / être / certain / elles / sortir / des Etats-Unis

B. **Il faut suivre ses propres conseils!** Changez les phrases suivantes pour indiquer que la première personne pense à elle-même!

MODÈLE: Jacqueline veut qu'on parte maintenant.
Jacqueline veut partir maintenant.

1. Robert aime que nous passions chez ses amis.
2. Marie a envie que tu sortes ce soir.
3. Claire est contente que nous ayons de bonnes notes.

4. Alain aime mieux que nous pensions à l'avenir
5. Yves n'est pas sûr qu'ils partent tout de suite.
6. Chantal veut que vous ayez de la patience.

C. **Les problèmes sociaux.** Dans les phrases suivantes, remplacez les mots en italique par les mots entre parenthèses. Attention au deuxième verbe!

1. Ils *pensent* que le sida est un désastre.   (… avoir peur…)
2. Il est *vrai* que nous perdons patience avec les SDF.   (… dommage…)
3. Il est *peu probable* que nous ayons une guerre nucléaire.
   (… possible…)
4. Ils *expliquent* que nous ne réfléchissons pas assez aux problèmes de pauvres.   (… regretter…)
5. Je *doute* qu'ils aient faim.   (… apprendre…)
6. Il est *évident* qu'il y a trop de criminalité.   (… certain…)

Culture

D. **Connaître un pays.** Vos amis ont décidé de visiter un pays francophone, et ils veulent connaître cette culture. Donnez-leur des conseils. Faites des phrases avec les mots donnés; ensuite *(then)*, mettez les phrases dans l'ordre du plus important au moins important.

MODÈLE: Il est bon / préparer votre voyage en avance
Il est bon que vous prépariez votre voyage en avance.

1. Il faut / goûter tous les vins
2. Il est important / choisir un bon guide
3. Il est évident / avoir besoin de parler leur langue
4. Il faut / parler avec beaucoup de gens
5. Il vaut mieux / manger avec une famille
6. Il est certain / aller chercher un bon café

Communication

E. **Mes opinions.** Donnez votre opinion des sujets suivants en employant «Je pense que… » ou «Je ne pense pas que… ».

1. l'Amérique:
   a. Les Américains sont sympathiques.
   b. Ils parlent beaucoup de langues.
   c. Ils ne pensent pas à l'avenir.
   d. Ils sont préoccupés par l'argent.

2. les parents:
   a. Ils sont très sévères.
   b. Ils perdent souvent patience.
   c. Ils aiment mes amis.
   d. Ils ont toujours raison.

3. les grandes villes:
   a. Il y a trop de bruit.
   b. La pollution est un problème.
   c. Les habitants sont sympathiques.
   d. On dort bien en ville.

4. mes amis:
   a. Ils sont ennuyeux.
   b. Ils ont du talent.
   c. Ils réfléchissent aux problèmes importants.
   d. Ils sont préoccupés.

F. **Des solutions.** Avec un partenaire, complétez les phrases avec une bonne solution aux situations suivantes. Ensuite, demandez aux autres groupes, s'ils ont les mêmes idées.

1. Vous avez un examen demain matin. Il vaut mieux que vous...
   a. étudier ce soir
   b. écouter des disques
   c. sortir avec des amis
   d. ???

2. Votre frère veut sortir avec une jolie fille. Il vaut mieux qu'il...
   a. lui téléphoner à trois heures du matin
   b. l'inviter chez lui
   c. lui parler en français
   d. ???

3. Vos amis veulent aller en France cet été. Il vaut mieux qu'ils...
   a. travailler le week-end
   b. dépenser beaucoup d'argent
   c. partir maintenant
   d. ???

4. Les restaurants sont fermés et vous avez faim. Il est probable que vous...
   a. demander un sandwich à vos voisins
   b. préparer quelque chose à la maison
   c. attendre le petit déjeuner
   d. ???

5. Votre grand-mère veut venir vous voir mais une amie vous a déjà invité(e). Il vaut mieux que vous...
   a. attendre votre grand-mère chez vous
   b. expliquer le problème à votre grand-mère
   c. partir tout de suite
   d. ???

G. **Mes réactions.** Dans les situations suivantes, êtes-vous content(e) ou pas content(e)?

MODÈLE: Le professeur est sévère.
   Je suis désolé(e) que le professeur soit sévère.

1. Nous étudions le subjonctif.
2. Le professeur me choisit pour répondre à la question.
3. Nous donnons de l'argent aux pays pauvres.
4. Mon français (n')est (pas) très bon.
5. Il y a du chômage.
6. J'ai une voiture.

H. **Questions personnelles.** Votre personnalité.

1. Avez-vous peur d'obtenir une mauvaise note? Dans quel cours?
2. Pensez-vous savoir parler français? Avec qui voulez-vous parler?
3. Est-ce qu'il est possible que vous changiez de personnalité?
4. De quoi avez-vous envie?
5. Quand êtes-vous furieux (-euse)?
6. Qu'est-ce que vous regrettez?
7. Etes-vous sûr(e) que vos études soient importantes?
8. Est-il vrai que vous pensiez aux autres?

Communiquons

Exprimer l'imprécision

In English, when people are unsure of a person's name or simply wish to speak quickly without stopping to think of an exact name, they use a variety of expressions such as *What's-his-name* or *Mr. / Mrs. So-and-So*. These expressions of imprecision also exist for talking about places and things. French has similar expressions, and you will find them useful for getting your ideas across in situations where you are not sure of the precise terms to use for designating certain people, places, and things.

**pour tous
ou pour quelques-uns ? ▪**

ENQUÊTE

Madame, Monsieur,
Il est toujours 4 heures de l'après-midi quelque part.

*Paris, Tokyo, Londres, New York, Hong-Kong:
notre champ d'action est à l'échelle du monde.
Présent dans plus de 50 pays, opérant sur tous les
marchés, multipliant les alliances, Paribas est
l'une des grandes institutions bancaires et finan-
cières internationales. Il y a toujours quelque part
une porte de Paribas grande ouverte sur le monde.*

PARIBAS

Paribas Actionnariat, 3 rue d'Antin 75002 Paris · Tél. : (1) 42 98 17 88 · Minitel : 36 15 Eco A2.

Expressions

▶ **On parle des gens.**

1. Use **on** as the subject when you cannot name a specific person.

On nous a pris notre magnétoscope.	*They took our VCR.*
On a sonné à la porte.	*They rang the doorbell.*

2. Use **quelqu'un** to express the idea of *someone*. When used with an adjective, **quelqu'un** is followed by **de (d')** and a masculine adjective.

Quelqu'un m'a déjà posé cette question.	*Somebody already asked me that question.*
J'ai vu quelqu'un dans l'auto.	*I saw somebody in the car.*
Il a rencontré quelqu'un d'important.	*He met someone important.*

3. To express *Mr. So-and-So* and *Mrs. So-and-So*, use **Monsieur Untel** and **Madame Unetelle.** When you have forgotten a person's name, or when you do not want to be bothered saying it, use the names **Machin, Machin-Chouette** *(What's-his-name)* or **Chose.**

Madame Unetelle est déjà partie.	*Mrs. So-and-So has already left.*
Machin-Chouette m'a téléphoné.	*What's-his-name phoned.*

▶ On parle des endroits.

Use **quelque part** *(somewhere)*, **un coin** *(spot)*, or **un endroit** *(a place)* to talk about an unspecified place.

Les enfants sont allés quelque part.	*The kids went somewhere.*
Ils ont laissé mon parapluie dans un coin.	*They left my umbrella in some spot.*

▶ On parle des choses.

1. Use **quelque chose** *(something)* to indicate a thing that cannot be specified. **Quelque chose** is always masculine and takes **de (d')** before an adjective.

Quelque chose a fait du bruit.	*Something made a noise.*
Je voudrais quelque chose pour ma mère.	*I'd like something for my mother.*
Vous me parlez de quelque chose d'important.	*You are talking to me about something important.*

2. There are several familiar French expressions that mean a *gadget*, a *thingamajig*, or a *doohickey*.

J'ai besoin d'un bidule pour ouvrir le coffre!	*I need a thingamajig to open the trunk.*
Je parle d'un engin pour réparer ma voiture.	*I'm talking about a doohickey for repairing my car.*
Qu'est-ce que c'est que ce machin?	*What's that gadget?*
Je cherche un truc pour réparer ma bicyclette.	*I'm looking for a gadget to repair my bicycle.*

3. Use **une chose** *(a thing)* for abstract nouns or ideas.

Le bonheur pour moi, c'est une chose simple.	*Happiness for me is a simple thing.*
Je voudrais vous expliquer une chose sérieuse.	*I would like to explain a serious thing to you.*

Interaction   *Simon va acheter un cadeau pour son frère.*

SIMON: Je cherche quelque chose de pas trop cher.

L'EMPLOYÉ: C'est pour quelqu'un de quel âge?

SIMON: Vingt-trois ans. Il aime les machins électroniques.

L'EMPLOYÉ: J'ai un truc pour prévoir l'avenir. Je viens de le poser° quelque   *set down*
             part.

SIMON: Non, j'aime mieux les bidules amusants.

L'EMPLOYÉ: On va en avoir beaucoup à la fin de la semaine.

SIMON: D'accord. Je vais revenir samedi.

Activités

A. Refaites le paragraphe suivant en remplaçant les mots en italique par des ex-
    pressions d'incertitude.

> Un *homme* m'a téléphoné hier soir. C'était *Robert Ducroc.* Il voulait
> emprunter *ma voiture* parce qu'il avait des problèmes *en ville* et *les gens*
> ne voulaient pas l'aider à réparer sa voiture. *Une femme* lui a prêté de
> l'argent pour téléphoner *d'un café* près de l'hôtel. Je n'avais pas envie de
> sortir et je lui ai demandé d'aller voir *Mme Fantaisie* à l'hôtel.

B. Répondez aux questions suivantes.

1. Avez-vous déjà rencontré quelqu'un de célèbre? Qui?
2. Etes-vous allé(e) quelque part le week-end dernier?
3. Avez-vous visité un joli coin? Où?
4. Avez-vous fait quelque chose d'intéressant récemment?
5. Est-ce qu'on vous a invité(e) quelque part ce week-end?
6. Est-ce que quelqu'un va passer vous voir ce soir? Qui?

Lecture culturelle

Avant la lecture   WWW

Although they were once all nationalized, some French TV channels are now independent. They get their revenue from an annual tax on TV sets (**la redevance**)
and from ever more frequent commercials, which are grouped together and interrupt shows less frequently than in the United States. One channel, **Canal +**
(**Canal Plus**), requires a converter box and a monthly fee, much like movie channels on American TV. In many families, evening schedules follow television programming. One very popular show is **Les Guignols de l'Info,** featured on **Canal
+**. It is a political satire: the characters are puppets with each representing an

easily recognizable French political figure. To enjoy the show, one must be very familiar with contemporary French political life.

The number of American TV shows broadcast on French TV and dubbed in French continues to increase. With so many channels competing for air time, producers have found it cheaper to buy American programs than to make their own. Some examples are *Beverly Hills 90210, Melrose Place,* and *Sauvé par le gong (Saved by the Bell)*. The French also copy American game shows, as with *La Roue de la fortune, Une Famille en or (Family Feud),* and *Pyramide*.

Top 20 des meilleures audiences

Nº	Chaine	Date	Heure	Durée	Emission	Aud	4 ans et + Pm	Nombre
1	TF1	Jeu 27 avr 95	20:58	01:40	Sér. Julie Lescaut	23,8	55	12 295 080
2	TF1	Lun 27 mar 95	20:53	01:32	Sér. Navarro	23,5	52	12 140 100
3	TF1	Lun 27 fév 95	20:53	01:32	Sér. Navarro	23,0	51	11 881 800
4	TF1	Lun 30 jan 95	19:58	00:41	TF1 20 heures (Patrick Poivre d'Arvor)*	22,9	48	11 830 140
5	TF1	Jeu 23 nov 95	20:57	01:38	Sér. Julie Lescaut	22,8	50	11 778 480
6	2	Mer 12 avr 95	20:58	01:20	Tvf. Une nana pas comme les autres	22,7	52	11 726 820
7	TF1	Dim 19 nov 95	20:48	01:54	Film: L'arme fatale III	21,9	51	11 313 540
8	TF1	Lun 13 nov 95	20:53	01:33	Sér. Columbo	21,6	49	11 158 560
-	2	Mer 29 nov 95	20:51	01:31	Sér. L'instit	21,6	49	11 158 560
10	TF1	Mer 07 mar 95	20:24	00:29	Face à la une (Valéry Giscard d'Estaing)	21,3	45	11 003 580
11	TF1	Jeu 02 mar 95	20:16	00:33	Face à la une (Bernard Tapie)	21,2	45	10 951 920
-	2	Dim 10 déc 95	20:16	00:29	Invité Spécial (Alain Juppé)	21,2	42	10 951 920
-	TF1	Jeu 30 mar 95	20:49	01:39	Sér. Julie Lescaut	21,2	47	10 951 920
14	TF1	Mer 19 avr 95	20:28	01:49	Foot: Ligue des Champions	20,8	45	10 745 280
-	TF1	Sam 28 jan 95	20:52	01:54	Les grosses têtes	20,8	54	10 745 280
16	TF1	Lun 06 mar 95	20:30	00:15	Face à la une (Raymond Barre)	20,7	43	10 633 620
-	TF1	Lun 30 jan 95	20:54	01:30	Sér. Navarro	20,7	46	10 693 620
18	TF1	Mer 05 avr 95	20:28	01:51	Foot: Ligue des Champions	20,5	46	10 530 300
-	TF1	Jeu 07 déc 95	20:56	01:32	Sér. Navarro	20,5	45	10 530 300
20	TF1	Lun 10 avr 95	20:53	01:29	Sér. Navarro	20,4	45	10 538 640

Fictions   Informations   Films   Divertissements   Sports

(*) Seule la plus forte audience a été retenue.   (+) Individus de 4 ans et plus

Activités

Examinez le «Top 20 des Meilleures Audiences» ci-dessus, et répondez aux questions suivantes.

1. Quel genre d'émissions est-ce que les téléspectateurs français préfèrent?
2. Est-ce que les gens s'intéressent beaucoup aux nouvelles à la télévision?
3. Quelle série américaine est-ce que les Français aiment?
4. Quel sport semble être populaire à la télévision?
5. Quelles sont les heures préférées des Français pour regarder la télévision?

La Télévision à la Carte

F1, la première chaîne de télévision en Europe, est la première chaîne de télévision française qui s'est investie dans des projets d'autoroutes de l'information°. C'est en février 1996 que TF1 a présenté son système de *video on demand,* «La Télévision à la Carte» à l'occasion d'un forum *information superhighway*
5 sur «Les Autoroutes de l'Information» organisé par le Ministère français à la Poste, aux Télécommunications et à l'Espace. Ce système offre aux téléspectateurs une variété de services interactifs (films, actualités, magazines, etc.) parmi lesquels° ils choisissent la séquence vidéo qu'ils veulent regarder. Une fois sélec- **parmi...** *among which* tionnée, cette séquence apparaît instantanément sur leur téléviseur. Avec sa
10 télécommande°, le téléspectateur peut contrôler la vidéo comme sur un mag- *remote control* nétoscope (retour en arrière, pause, avance rapide).

Le premier service de vidéo à la demande a été expérimenté dans un hôtel. De sa chambre, le client peut consulter les produits audiovisuels classiques (films, magazines, sports) et se renseigner° sur les services proposés par l'hôtel, *obtain information*
15 et aussi sur la vie locale (tourisme, spectacles, musées). La particularité de ce service est d'offrir de l'information à la demande°, c'est-à-dire le dernier journal *on demand* télévisé, dans la langue de son choix°, quelques minutes après sa diffusion°. *choice / broadcast*

Cette nouvelle forme de télévision offre, à une ville par exemple, des moyens° pour diffuser l'information qui n'existaient pas avant. Dans le do- *means*
20 maine° de l'éducation, on peut concevoir la création d'une bibliothèque interac- *area* tive de ressources multimédia, par exemple. Pour le tourisme, cela peut être la production d'un système de présentations multimédia pour présenter la ville. Mais il y a aussi beaucoup d'autres applications qui vont se développer dans l'avenir.
25 TF1 est non seulement° la première chaîne française et européenne; avec **non...** *not only* son système de «Télévision à la Carte», elle est aussi à la pointe° des nouvelles *cutting edge* technologies.

Après la lecture

Questions sur le texte

1. Qu'est-ce que «La Télévision à la Carte» signifie?
2. Quels sont les avantages de ce service?
3. Où est-ce qu'on a testé ce système?
4. Qu'est-ce que ce service permet de faire dans le domaine de l'éducation?
5. Pensez-vous que «La Télévision à la Carte» marque la fin des magnéto-scopes? Expliquez.

Activités

A. Pouvez-vous penser à d'autres applications de «La Télévision à la Carte» qui ne sont pas évoquées dans le texte?

B. En petits groupes, préparez un «Top 10 des Meilleures Audiences» à la télévision américaine à votre avis.

C. Organisez un débat sur les avantages et les désavantages de censurer la télévision pour les jeunes.

Vocabulaire

Noms / Pronoms

actualités	news	journal	TV news
amour	love	justice	justice
avenir	future	monde	world
bonheur	happiness	montagne	mountain
bruit	noise	nombre	number
câble	cable	opinion	opinion
cadre	middle manager	paix	peace
chaîne	station	politique	politics
chaîne câblée	cable station	pollution	pollution
chômage	unemployment	possibilité	possibility
chose	thing	programme	program
compte en banque	bank account	publicité	ads
conseil	advice	qualité	quality
criminalité	crime	reportage	report
délinquance	delinquency	sans-abris	homeless
désastre	disaster	sans-logis	homeless
dessin animé	cartoon	sans-papiers	undocumented aliens
drogue	illegal drug	santé	health
égalité	equality	SDF	homeless
émission	program	série	series
emploi	job	sécurité	security
feuilleton	series	sida	AIDS
franchise	frankness	société	society
grand magasin	department store	sondage d'opinion	opinion poll
guerre nucléaire	nuclear war	succès	success
importance	importance	table ronde	round table
incertitude	uncertainty	trafic	(drug) traffic
inconvénient	inconvenient	travail	work
inflation	inflation	variétés	variety shows
interview	interview	vie	life
jeu télévisé	game show	voisin	neighbor

Verbes

arrêter	to stop
consulter	to consult
discuter	to discuss
douter	to doubt
embêter	to bother
éviter	to avoid
préoccuper	to preoccupy

regretter	to regret / to be sorry
remercier	to thank
rendre	to give back / to make
sembler	to seem
souhaiter	to wish
supporter	to tolerate

Adjectifs / Adverbes

absolument	absolutely
contemporain	contemporary
écologique	ecological
étonné	amazed
furieux	furious
important	important

matérialiste	materialistic
selon	according
social	social
sûr	certain
surpris	surprised
triste	sad

Expressions

avoir envie	to feel like
avoir peur	to be afraid
faire du bruit	to make noise
faire peur	to scare
il est bon	it's good
il est dommage	it's too bad
il est évident	it's obvious
il est faux	it's false
il est important	it's important
il est injuste	it's unfair
il est juste	it's fair
il est nécessaire	it's necessary

il est peu probable	it's unlikely
il est préférable	it's preferable
il est probable	it's likely
il est rare	it's rare
il est sûr	it's certain
il est temps	it's time
il faut que	it's necessary
il se peut	it's likely
il semble	it appears
il vaut mieux	it's better
le plus	the most

Chapitre 12
Les achats

Commençons

Grammaire

Communiquons

Lecture culturelle

Vocabulaire

Aux Galeries
Lafayette, à Paris

Objectives

Language

Vocabulary for stores and shops • The vowel sounds / ø / and / œ / • **Boire,
recevoir, devoir** • Irregular verbs in the subjunctive • Negatives

Culture

Shopping and stores • Money • Spending habits of the French

Communication

Expressing emotions, wishes, opinions, doubts, and judgments • Expressing
negative statements • Making purchases

Commençons

A la charcuterie

Sophie et Annick louent un appartement au centre-ville. A midi, elles mangent au restau-U, mais le soir, comme elles ne rentrent jamais de bonne heure, elles aiment acheter des plats cuisinés dans une charcuterie et les emporter chez elles pour dîner.

LE CHARCUTIER: Bonjour, Mesdemoiselles, vous désirez?

ANNICK: Vous n'avez plus de pâté de foie?

LE CHARCUTIER: Si, nous avons reçu notre commande ce matin. Voulez-vous que j'aille le chercher?

SOPHIE: Je ne sais pas; il vaut peut-être mieux que nous prenions autre chose.

LE CHARCUTIER: J'ai de la très bonne choucroute garnie. Vous devriez l'essayer.

ANNICK: Tiens! C'est une idée. Qu'est-ce que vous nous conseillez de boire avec cela?

SOPHIE: Tu sais bien qu'avec la choucroute, il faut qu'on boive du vin blanc sec ou de la bière.

ANNICK: Très bien. Donnez-nous 500 grammes de choucroute et une bouteille de Riesling.

Une charcuterie

LE CHARCUTIER:　Voilà, Mademoiselle!

SOPHIE:　Combien je vous dois?

LE CHARCUTIER:　Quatre-vingt-dix-neuf francs.

Etudions le dialogue

1. Est-ce que Sophie et Annick habitent à la campagne?
2. Qu'est-ce qu'elles aiment faire quand elles ne rentrent pas de bonne heure?
3. Est-ce que le charcutier a du pâté de foie?
4. Qu'est-ce qu'il recommande aussi?
5. Quelle sorte de vin va bien avec la choucroute?
6. Qu'est-ce qu'il est possible de boire aussi?

Mots clés

charcuterie	*pork butcher's shop*	autre chose	*something else*
centre-ville	*downtown*	choucroute garnie	*sauerkraut and assorted*
de bonne heure	*early*		*meat*
plats cuisinés *(m.)*	*prepared dishes*	devriez (devoir)	*ought*
charcutier	*pork butcher*	essayer	*to try*
Mesdemoiselles	*ladies*	conseillez (conseiller)	*advise*
n'... plus	*not . . . any more*	boire	*to drink*
pâté de foie *(m.)*	*liver pâté*	boive (boire)	*drink*
reçu (recevoir)	*received*	sec	*dry*
commande *(f.)*	*order*	grammes *(m.)*	*grams*
que j'aille (aller)	*me to go*	bouteille	*bottle*
peut-être	*perhaps*	dois (devoir)	*owe*
prenions (prendre)	*take*	francs *(m.)*	*francs*

Faisons connaissance　　　　　　　　　WWW

Although supermarkets (**supermarchés** [*m.*]) are very popular in France, many people continue to buy food at specialty stores. They go to a neighborhood store at least once a day to pick up freshly baked bread, dairy products, or items they need for just one meal. **La charcuterie** specializes in pork products such as ham, sausages, and **pâté**. It also sells prepared dishes such as **hors-d'œuvre**, salads, and ready-to-eat foods that the shopper can warm up just before dinner. Bakeries are also specialized. You go to a **boulangerie** *(f.)* to buy bread and to a **pâtisserie** *(f.)* for pastries.

French people also go to gigantic supermarkets called **hypermarchés** *(m.).* Items that they commonly purchase include canned goods (**des conserves** [*f.*]), frozen foods (**des produits surgelés**), cleaning products, paper goods, and cases of beverages such as beer and mineral water. They also buy articles of clothing, furniture, and other items found in department stores (**les grands magasins**). In

Paris, the **Galeries Lafayette** and the **Printemps** are among the most popular department stores. They have branches in large cities throughout France.

Enrichissons notre vocabulaire

Les boutiques *(Shops)*

| une bijouterie | une boucherie | une crémerie | une épicerie |

un magasin
d'articles de sports   un magasin de
chaussures   une papeterie   une poissonnerie

la brasserie	*the café-restaurant*
le magasin de disques	*the record store*
la teinturerie	*the dry cleaner's*

Les commerçants *(Shopkeepers)*

le boulanger / la boulangère	*the baker*
le boucher / la bouchère	*the butcher*
le pâtissier / la pâtissière	*the pastry maker*
l'épicier / l'épicière	*the grocer*
le poissonnier / la poissonnière	*the fishmonger*
le marchand de... / la marchande de...	*the person who sells . . .*
le / la buraliste	*the tobacconist*
le / la fleuriste	*the florist*

Dans un magasin *(In a store)*

le vendeur / la vendeuse	*the salesperson*
le rayon	*the department*
la caisse	*the cashier's*
les soldes	*sales*
en solde	*on sale*
une remise de 10%	*a 10% discount*

Prononciation   The vowel sounds / ø / and / œ /

A. The third pair of mid vowels in French is / ø / and / œ /. The / ø / sound is pronounced with the mouth mostly closed, the tongue forward, and the lips rounded. It is represented by the letters **eu** and occurs in words such as **bleu** and **heureux**. The unaccented **e** in words such as **je, ne, ce,** and **que** approximates this sound.

B. The / ø / sound occurs when it is the last sound in a syllable. If the syllable ends in a consonant, you must pronounce the / œ / sound by opening your mouth slightly. The / œ / sound is also written **eu**, but it occurs only before a pronounced consonant in words such as **leur, veulent,** and **neuf.**

Repeat the following pairs of words after your teacher.

/ ø /	/ œ /		/ ø /	/ œ /
heureux	chauffeur		peu	peur
eux	heure		veut	veulent

C. There is only one frequent exception to the preceding rule. When the final consonant is the / z / sound, usually written **-se**, you keep the vowel sound / ø /. In the following lists, the adjectives in the right column have the same final vowel sound as those in the left column.

Repeat the following pairs of words after your teacher.

/ ø /	/ øz /		/ ø /	/ øz /
affreux	affreuse		courageux	courageuse
ambitieux	ambitieuse		délicieux	délicieuse
dangereux	dangereuse		généreux	généreuse

Exercice

Read the following sentences aloud, distinguishing between the closed / ø / sound and the open / œ / sound.

1. Je veux aller chez eux.
2. Elle a peur que tu ne sois pas à l'heure.
3. Ce vendeur ne peut pas supporter les chauffeurs furieux.
4. Cet acteur veut avoir deux répondeurs.
5. Le docteur peut venir à deux heures vingt-neuf.
6. Je suis heureuse que ma sœur soit ambitieuse et studieuse.

Grammaire

I. Boire / recevoir / devoir

> You use these verbs to express the actions of drinking and receiving and the state of having to do something, respectively.

A. The irregular French verbs **boire**, **recevoir**, and **devoir** have similar conjugations.

	boire *(to drink)*	recevoir *(to receive)*	devoir *(must, to have to, to be supposed to, to owe)*
présent:	je **bois** tu **bois** il / elle / on **boit** nous **buvons** vous **buvez** ils / elles **boivent**	je **reçois** tu **reçois** il / elle / on **reçoit** nous **recevons** vous **recevez** ils / elles **reçoivent**	je **dois** tu **dois** il / elle / on **doit** nous **devons** vous **devez** ils / elles **doivent**
passé composé:	j' **ai bu**	tu **as reçu**	il **a dû**
imparfait:	nous **buvions**	vous **receviez**	elles **devaient**

Qu'est-ce que vous nous conseillez de **boire?**
Nous **avons reçu** notre commande hier.
Vous **devez** partir maintenant?

B. **Devoir** is a frequently used verb and has many English equivalents.

1. When followed by an infinitive, **devoir** has several possible meanings:

Je **dois aller** chez le charcutier.	*I **have to** / **am supposed to** go to the pork butcher's.*
Elle **a dû aller** à l'épicerie.	*She **had to go** / **must have gone** to the grocery store.*
Nous **devions acheter** quelque chose au supermarché.	*We **were supposed to buy** something at the supermarket.*

2. **Devoir** + a verb in the infinitive can replace the expression **il faut que** + a verb in the subjunctive.

Il faut que tu réussisses à cet examen.	**Tu dois** réussir à cet examen.

3. **Devoir** accompanied by a noun or pronoun means *to owe*.

—C'est combien?	—Je **vous dois** combien?
—Vous **me devez** 95 F.	—C'est 75 francs.

4. **Devoir** is frequently used in the conditional mood to give advice, in which case it means *should* or *ought to*.

Tu **devrais** dormir huit heures.
Je **devrais** téléphoner à ma mère.
Vous **devriez** aller à la boulangerie avant sept heures.

Langue

A. **Connaissez-vous Jacqueline?** Formez des phrases complètes avec les mots donnés.

1. Quand / elle / être / petit / elle / ne… pas / boire / lait
2. Qu'est-ce que / elle / devoir / faire /aujourd'hui
3. Le week-end dernier / sa sœur / et / elle / devoir / rester / maison
4. Hier / Jacqueline / recevoir / lettre / de sa grand-mère
5. Est-ce que / son / parents / recevoir / souvent / son / amis?
6. Chez elle / on / ne… pas boire / souvent / alcool

B. **Conseils personnels.** Dans les phrases suivantes, remplacez **Il faut que** par la forme correcte du verbe **devoir**.

1. Il ne faut pas que je mente.
2. Il faut que vous finissiez votre travail.
3. Il faut que tu sois généreux.
4. Il faut que les gens connaissent leurs voisins.
5. Il faut que nous pensions aux sans-logis.
6. Il faut qu'on ait beaucoup de patience.

Culture   WWW

C. Les boissons traditionnelles. Qu'est-ce qu'on boit dans les régions francophones du monde? Faites des phrases en trouvant la bonne réponse dans la liste de possibilités.

du cidre	du vin blanc	du bourgogne
de la bière	du champagne	du rhum

1. Pour un anniversaire *(birthday)*, on…
2. A Dijon, les gens…
3. Avec les écrevisses *(crayfish)*, les Louisianais…
4. Avec une fondue, les Suisses…
5. En Bretagne, avec les crêpes, on…
6. Pour l'apéritif en Martinique, les gens…

D. Les achats. Pour connaître la France des petits commerçants, vous devez faire vos achats d'une certaine manière. Qu'est-ce qu'on doit faire dans les situations suivantes? Trouvez la conclusion à chaque phrase dans la colonne de droite et formez une phrase avec **devoir**.

MODÈLE: Pour acheter du pain / aller à une boulangerie
Pour acheter du pain, vous devez aller à une boulangerie.

1. Si un Français vous invite à dîner chez lui, vous…
2. Si on veut servir des truites, on…
3. Quand on a envie d'un fromage, on…
4. Si les Français ont besoin d'un stylo, ils…
5. Pour acheter un plat cuisiné, on…
6. Si vous voulez goûter une belle petite tarte, vous…

a. aller à la poissonnerie
b. chercher une papeterie
c. acheter des fleurs *(flowers)* ou des bonbons
d. trouver une pâtisserie
e. aller à la crémerie
f. aller à une charcuterie

Communication

E. Donnez des conseils. Vous êtes assistant(e) dans une résidence universitaire et des étudiants vous parlent des problèmes suivants. Qu'est-ce que vous devriez leur recommander de faire dans ces situations?

MODÈLE: J'ai un examen de français demain.
Tu devrais étudier les verbes.

1. Il pleut beaucoup.
2. Mon / Ma camarade de chambre est très malheureux (-euse).
3. Je dois beaucoup d'argent à un(e) ami(e).
4. Mon ami(e) boit / fume trop.
5. Mon / Ma camarade de chambre et moi, nous ne recevons jamais de lettres.
6. Les étudiants font trop de bruit à la résidence.

F. **Questions personnelles.** Vos habitudes.

1. Qu'est-ce que vous aimez boire le matin? à minuit?
2. Qu'est-ce que vous buvez quand vous avez très soif? Quand vous êtes fatigué(e)?
3. De qui recevez-vous souvent des colis? du courrier électronique?
4. Aimez-vous recevoir des amis chez vous ou aimez-vous mieux sortir?
5. A qui devez-vous de l'argent? un service *(favor)*? Pourquoi?
6. Qu'est-ce que vous devriez faire que vous n'allez pas faire ou que vous n'aimez pas faire?

II. Irregular verbs in the subjunctive

A. Verbs with one subjunctive stem

Some French verbs are irregular in the present subjunctive. In all forms, they use one stem.

faire (fass-)	
que je **fasse**	que nous **fassions**
que tu **fasses**	que vous **fassiez**
qu'il / elle / on **fasse**	qu'ils / elles **fassent**

The other verbs that are also irregular in the subjunctive and use one stem in their forms are **pouvoir** and **savoir.**

pouvoir: que je **puisse** / que nous **puissions**
savoir: que je **sache** / que nous **sachions**

Je suis étonnée qu'ils **puissent** venir.
Il faut qu'on **sache** les réponses.

PREMIÈRE. LE MAGAZINE QUI PARLE DES FILMS AVANT QU'ILS NE FASSENT PARLER D'EUX.

Tous les mois, Première porte un certain regard sur le cinéma. Celui du cœur. Tous les mois, Première démontre que les films ont la vedette : on parle de l'Ours, du Grand Bleu, de Camille Claudel (films dont Première a parlé bien avant tout le monde...) au même titre qu'on parle de De Niro ou d'Adjani. Mais Première, c'est aussi un regard en profondeur sur le cinéma. Des critiques, des portraits d'acteurs et de réalisateurs, des repérages sur les petits films qui méritent souvent qu'on en parle en grand, et bien sûr des exclusivités. Première, le magazine qui parle des films comme personne n'en parle.

B. Verbs with two subjunctive stems

1. Some verbs use both the **nous** and the **ils / elles** forms of the present indicative to create two different subjunctive stems—one for the **nous** and **vous** plural forms and one for the four other forms.

boire	
present indicative: ils **boivent** nous **buvons**	*subjunctive stems:* **boiv** **buv-**
que je **boive** que tu **boives** qu'il / elle / on **boive**	que nous **buvions** que vous **buviez** qu'ils / elles **boivent**

devoir	prendre	recevoir
stems: **doiv-,** **dev-**	*stems:* **prenn-,** **pren-**	*stems:* **reçoiv-,** **recev-**
que je **doive** que tu **doives** qu'il / elle / on **doive** que nous **devions** que vous **deviez** qu'ils / elles **doivent**	que je **prenne** que tu **prennes** qu'il / elle / on **prenne** que nous **prenions** que vous **preniez** qu'ils / elles **prennent**	que je **reçoive** que tu **reçoives** qu'il / elle / on **reçoive** que nous **recevions** que vous **receviez** qu'ils / elles **reçoivent**

venir	voir
stems: **vienn-, ven-**	*stems:* **voi-, voy-**
que je **vienne** que tu **viennes** qu'il / elle / on **vienne** que nous **venions** que vous **veniez** qu'ils / elles **viennent**	que je **voie** que tu **voies** qu'il / elle / on **voie** que nous **voyions** que vous **voyiez** qu'ils / elles **voient**

Il vaut mieux qu'on **boive** du vin blanc.
Il est temps que nous **recevions** du courrier.

2. The verbs that you have already learned that are conjugated like **prendre**, **venir**, and **voir** in the present indicative are conjugated like those respective verbs in the subjunctive.

apprendre:	que j'**apprenne** / que nous **apprenions**
comprendre:	que je **comprenne** / que nous **comprenions**
appartenir:	que j'**appartienne** / que nous **appartenions**
contenir:	qu'il **contienne**
devenir:	que je **devienne** / que nous **devenions**
obtenir:	que j'**obtienne** / que nous **obtenions**
retenir:	que je **retienne** / que nous **retenions**
revenir:	que je **revienne** / que nous **revenions**
tenir:	que je **tienne** / que nous **tenions**

3. The verbs **aller** and **vouloir** take one subjunctive stem from the **nous** form of the present indicative. It is used in the **nous** and **vous** forms of the subjunctive. The other subjunctive stem is irregular and is used in the other four forms.

aller	vouloir
stems: **aill-, all-**	*stems:* **veuill-, voul-**
que j' **aille**	que je **veuille**
que tu **ailles**	que tu **veuilles**
qu'il / elle / on **aille**	qu'il / elle / on **veuille**
que nous **allions**	que nous **voulions**
que vous **alliez**	que vous **vouliez**
qu'ils / elles **aillent**	qu'ils / elles **veuillent**

Voulez-vous que j'**aille** le chercher?
Il se peut qu'il **veuille** sortir ce soir.

C. Falloir and pleuvoir

1. The following verbal expressions are irregular in the subjunctive.

il faut → qu'il **faille**
il pleut → qu'il **pleuve**

Il est possible qu'il **faille** payer la TVA.
Je ne veux pas qu'il **pleuve** ce week-end.

2. In the indicative, **il faut** becomes **il a fallu** and **il fallait** in the past and **il va falloir** in the future.

Il **a fallu** que je prenne l'avion.
Il **fallait** que nous partions de bonne heure.
Il **va falloir** que tu fasses la vaisselle.

Langue

A. **Des substitutions.** Remplacez les mots en italique avec les expressions données.

1. Il a fallu que nous *travaillions beaucoup*.   (faire le ménage, aller à la charcuterie, boire de l'eau, voir ce film, retenir ces dates)
2. Elle a peur que vous *arriviez en retard*.   (vouloir rester longtemps, ne... pas prendre le dernier métro, devenir furieux, ne... pas pouvoir répondre, la voir)
3. Il va falloir qu'on *rentre*.   (aller à la charcuterie, faire des courses, recevoir ces gens, prendre un taxi, obtenir de bonnes notes)

B. **On va faire un pique-nique.** Formez des phrases complètes en employant les mots donnés.

1. Notre / amis / vouloir / nous / aller / faire un pique-nique / demain
2. Je / avoir peur / Roland / ne... pas vouloir / venir / avec nous
3. Nous / être certain / vous / pouvoir / arriver à l'heure
4. Paul / douter / faire / froid / demain
5. Nous / penser / il / pleuvoir
6. Elles / être / désolé / leurs amies / ne... pas venir
7. Marie / aimer mieux / nous / faire des courses / l'hypermarché
8. Il faut / vous / voir / ces plats!

C. **Mes projets.** Formez des phrases en utilisant des expressions dans les deux colonnes.

MODÈLE: *Il est possible que je fasse la grasse matinée ce week-end.*

Etes-vous désolé	apprendre à jouer de la musique
Je suis certain	aller au cinéma ce soir
Il faut	vouloir aller au concert
Je pense	faire la cuisine
Il est probable	pleuvoir cet après-midi
Nous sommes sûrs	voir un film anglais
Il vaut mieux	devoir de l'argent à la banque
Nous ne savions pas	recevoir des amis

Culture

D. **Les habitudes gastronomiques des Français.** Qu'est-ce que les Français ont l'habitude de faire quand ils mangent? Choisissez entre les deux possibilités dans la proposition *(clause)* principale pour former une phrase correcte.

MODÈLE: Il est probable / peu probable / / les Français / boire du vin blanc avec du fromage
   Il est peu probable que les Français boivent du vin blanc avec du fromage.

1. Il est rare / certain / / beaucoup de Français / prendre un fruit comme dessert
2. Il est vrai / faux / / les adultes en France / ne... pas boire beaucoup de lait
3. Il est probable / peu probable / / un Français / tenir à manger de la salade avant le repas

4. Il est rare / n'est pas rare / les Français / faire leurs provisions presque tous les jours

5. Il est sûr / peu probable / / la majorité des Français / prendre des œufs au petit déjeuner

6. Il semble / Il n'est pas sûr / / il faut être un homme pour devenir un grand chef de cuisine en France

Communication

E. **Quelles sont les possibilités?** Indiquez le degré de certitude des situations suivantes.

certain   probable   possible   peu probable   impossible

MODÈLE: Il pleut ce soir.
Il est possible qu'il pleuve ce soir.

1. Je vais en Europe cet été.
2. Les étudiants sont contents de ce cours.
3. Je deviens professeur de lycée.
4. Je bois trop de café.
5. Nous voulons aller en cours le samedi.
6. Mes amis peuvent me prêter de l'argent.

F. **Vos regrets.** Qu'est-ce que vous regrettez dans la vie? Choisissez vos réponses dans la liste suivante, ou exprimez vos propres regrets *(express your own regrets)*.

MODÈLE: Mes professeurs sont trop sérieux.
Je regrette que mes professeurs soient trop sérieux.

Mon voisin reçoit trop d'amis.
On doit passer des examens.
Notre classe ne va pas au laboratoire tous les jours.
Mon / Ma camarade de chambre fait trop de bruit.
Il y a un pâtissier en face de chez moi.
???

G. **Vrai ou faux?** Que pensez-vous des affirmations suivantes? Doutez-vous / êtes-vous sûr(e) qu'elles soient vraies? Interviewez un(e) camarade de cours pour voir si vous avez la même opinion.

MODÈLE: Le pâté fait un bon hors-d'œuvre.
Je suis sûr(e) que le pâté fait un bon hors-d'œuvre.

1. On doit abolir la peine capitale *(capital punishment)*.
2. On peut aller sur d'autres planètes.
3. Il y a une guerre nucléaire bientôt.
4. Nous allons connaître les causes du cancer au vingt et unième siècle *(century)*.
5. Certaines personnes prévoient l'avenir.
6. Nous ne tenons pas à notre passé.

H. **Questions personnelles.** Vos opinions.

1. Est-il important qu'on apprenne des langues étrangères?
2. Pensez-vous qu'on voie de bons films à la télévision? de bonnes émissions?
3. Est-il nécessaire que vous alliez en classe tous les jours? Pourquoi?
4. Est-il possible que vous vouliez travailler pendant les vacances?
5. A quel âge pensez-vous qu'on puisse boire de l'alcool?
6. Est-ce qu'il vaut mieux pour l'économie que vous fassiez vos courses aux hypermarchés ou chez les petits commerçants?

CLIMATURQUOISE®

Rien n'est trop beau!

———— NICE - SAINT-LAURENT-DU-VAR ————
Avenue Léon Béranger. 06700 St-Laurent-du-Var. Tél. 93.31.15.90
———————————— GENEVE ————————————
80, Rue de Lausanne. 1202 Genève. Tél. (022) 38.39.40

III. Negatives

You use negative expressions to state that people do not do certain things or that certain situations do not exist.

A. Forms

In addition to the general negative expression **ne... pas,** French has other negative expressions.

Affirmative	Negative
Ils prennent **quelque chose.**	Ils **ne** prennent **rien.**
*They are having **something.***	*They are **not** having **anything.***
Elle a **encore** de la patience.	Elle **n'**a **plus** de patience.
*She **still** has patience.*	*She does **not** have **any more** patience.*
Ils reçoivent des **gens / tout le monde.**	Ils ne reçoivent **personne.**
*They receive **people / everyone.***	*They do **not** receive **anybody.***
J'ai **beaucoup** d'argent.	Je **n'**ai **que** deux dollars.
*I have **a lot of** money.*	*I have **only** two dollars.*
Il va **souvent / toujours** en cours.	Il **ne** va **jamais** en cours.
*He **often / always** goes to class.*	*He **never** goes to class.*

Mots clés	Negative expressions
ne... jamais	*never, not ever*
ne... personne	*no one, nobody, not anyone*
ne... plus	*no longer, no more, not any longer, not any more*
ne... rien	*nothing, not anything*
ne... que	*only*

B. Position of negatives

1. The negative expressions **ne... jamais**, **ne... plus**, and **ne... rien** are used in exactly the same places in sentences as **ne... pas:** surrounding the conjugated verb and any object pronouns in declarative sentences and surrounding the verb and pronoun subject with inversion.

> Nous **n'**allons **plus** aller à cette bijouterie.
> Cette épicière **ne** m'a **jamais** servi!
> **N'**as-tu **rien** vu à la boutique?

2. The negative **ne... personne** surrounds the helping verb *and* the past participle in the **passé composé.** It surrounds the conjugated verb and the infinitive with double verbs.

> Nous **n'**avons reconnu **personne.**   Je **ne** veux oublier **personne.**

3. The **que** of **ne... que** immediately precedes the noun or preposition it modifies.

> Je n'ai pas de pâté; je **n'**ai **que** de la choucroute.
> Elles **n'**ont vu **qu'**un film français.
> Nous **n'**étudions **qu'**après les actualités.

4. **Rien** and **personne** can be the subject of a sentence. In this case, **ne** comes after them.

> Rien **n'**est arrivé.   *Nothing* happened.
> Personne **n'**est venu.   *No one came.*

5. **Jamais, personne,** and **rien** can be used alone as responses to statements or questions.

> Tu regardes les émissions de   —Jamais!
>   variété?
> Qui vous a invité?   —Personne!
> Qu'est-ce qu'il a commandé?   —Rien.

Attention!

1. Remember that the indefinite and partitive articles all become **de** in the negative. The only exception is **ne... que,** which does not require the article to change because it does not express complete negation.

> Ils ont toujours **des** idées; ils **n'**ont jamais **d'**argent.
> Je n'ai pas **de** dollars; je n'ai que **des** francs.

2. While it is possible to use two or more negative expressions in the same sentence, **pas** is never used with **jamais, plus, personne,** or **rien.**

Elle ne mange **plus rien** le matin.   *She no longer eats anything in the morning.*

Je ne vois **jamais plus personne.**   *I never see anyone anymore.*

3. To contradict a negative question or statement, use the word **si.**

—Vous **n'avez plus** de hors-d'œuvre?
—**Si,** j'ai encore du pâté.

Ce qu'ils disent

1. In conversations, French speakers often drop **ne** from the negation.

J'ai plus de patience.   Ils ont vu personne.

2. **Que** can also be used entirely by itself to mean *only.*

Que de l'eau, s'il vous plaît!

Langue

A. Eric n'est pas comme son ami Luc. Remplacez **Luc** par **Eric** et mettez les phrases suivantes à la forme négative.

MODÈLE: Luc fait beaucoup de choses. *Eric ne fait rien.*

1. Luc a encore du temps pour étudier.
2. Luc a perdu quelque chose.
3. Luc a rencontré des amis à la brasserie.
4. Luc va acheter quelque chose pour sa mère.
5. Luc aime toujours recevoir ses amis.
6. Luc téléphone à quelqu'un le samedi.

B. Interrogation. Répondez aux questions suivantes à la forme affirmative.

1. Tu ne manges jamais dans un parc?
2. Ton frère ne veut jamais m'inviter?
3. Tu n'es plus malheureux?
4. Personne ne te comprend?
5. Tes amis ne font rien?
6. Il n'y a personne chez toi?
7. Tu ne bois plus de vin?
8. Tu ne peux rien faire?

C. J'ai été difficile hier. Mettez les phrases suivantes au passé composé.

1. Je ne veux rien faire.
2. Je ne bois que de l'eau minérale.
3. Je ne fais jamais la vaisselle.
4. Je ne reçois personne chez moi.
5. Je ne suis jamais content.
6. Tu n'as plus peur de moi?

Culture

D. **Les magasins en France.** Qu'est-ce qu'on trouve dans les magasins suivants? Combinez les mots donnés pour former des phrases correctes en choisissant entre les mots entre parenthèses.

MODÈLE: trouver (souvent / jamais) / lait / boucherie
On ne trouve jamais de lait dans une boucherie.

1. (Tout le monde / Personne) / aller / pharmacie / pour acheter de la glace
2. On / aller / (souvent / jamais) / papeterie / pour acheter un stylo
3. Les charcutiers / vendre / (toujours / jamais) / poisson
4. (Les gens / Personne) / aller à l'hypermarché pour acheter des vêtements
5. Les buralistes / vendre / (toujours / jamais) / viande
6. Si on / ne chercher / que légumes, / on / trouver / (tout / rien) / dans une pâtisserie

E. **Les Français et la culture.** Un sondage du Ministère de la Culture montre combien de Français n'ont jamais participé aux activités suivantes. Faites des phrases en cherchant les pourcentages appropriés de la colonne de droite et les activités correspondantes dans la colonne de gauche.

MODÈLE: aller au zoo / 12%
Douze pourcent des Français ne sont jamais allés au zoo.

1.	aller au cinéma	a.	83%
2.	visiter un musée	b.	73%
3.	aller dans une discothèque	c.	39%
4.	voir une pièce de théâtre	d.	50%
	(play)	e.	19%
5.	assister à un concert de rock	f.	9%
6.	aller à l'opéra		

Communication

F. **Mes habitudes.** Qu'est-ce que vous faites **souvent, assez souvent** ou **de temps en temps** *(from time to time)*, et qu'est-ce que vous ne faites **jamais** ou **presque jamais**? Utilisez les suggestions données ou vos propres idées.

MODÈLE: étudier le samedi soir   *Je n'étudie jamais le samedi soir.*
manger du poisson   *Je mange du poisson de temps en temps.*

avoir faim l'après-midi   écouter de la musique classique
boire de l'alcool   fréquenter les pâtisseries
faire du sport   perdre mon temps
sortir avec un footballeur   ???

G. **Le snobisme.** Pour être snob, il ne faut faire ou utiliser que certaines choses. Qu'est-ce qu'on doit faire dans les situations suivantes? Préparez vos réponses avec un camarade de cours.

MODÈLE: servir / vin   *On ne sert que du vin français.*

1. porter / jean...
2. porter / chaussures...
3. aimer les... (autos)
4. sortir avec...
5. passer / vacances à...
6. faire des courses à...

MODÈLE: manger à   *Il ne faut jamais manger à McDonald's.*

7. fréquenter…   10. inviter…
8. porter…   11. passer ses vacances…
9. écouter des disques de…   12. utiliser…

H. Questions personnelles. Votre vie personnelle.

1. Est-ce que vous allez inviter quelqu'un à dîner? Quand?
2. Est-ce que vous servez toujours du lait?
3. Quand est-ce que vous ne faites rien?
4. Quand est-ce que vous ne voulez voir personne?
5. Est-ce que vous devez de l'argent à quelqu'un?
6. Qu'est-ce que vous n'avez jamais fait?

Communiquons

Parler d'argent

WWW

The monetary system in France is based on the franc. Francs are available as bills (**billets de banque**) in denominations of twenty, fifty, one hundred, two hundred, and five hundred francs and as coins (**pièces**) in denominations of one, two, five, ten, and twenty francs. In a **franc**, there are one hundred **centimes**, which are available only as coins in denominations of five, ten, twenty, and fifty **centimes**. Belgian and Swiss currencies are also called **francs**.

De l'argent français

In contrast to American banknotes, French bills vary both in size and color according to the denomination and depict famous artists and writers as well as heads of state. In addition, French banknotes have a white spot, which contains a watermark to prevent counterfeiting.

It is possible to obtain French currency in exchange for dollars at large banks in many American cities. In France, francs are available in traveler's checks (**les chèques de voyage**), but some stores will not accept them. The most advantageous way of changing money in France is at a bank. After hours, you can find currency exchanges (**les bureaux de change**) at airports and large train stations. You may also change money at many hotels and restaurants, but at lower rates. The latest development in currency exchange is the installation of machines similar to American automated teller machines that change money automatically.

Expressions   www

▶ On fait des achats.

C'est combien?	*How much is it?*
Je vous dois combien?	*How much do I owe you?*
Combien coûte ce stylo / coûtent ces stylos?	*How much does this pen / do these pens cost?*
Quel est le prix de cette cassette?	*What's the price of this cassette?*
Quel est le taux de change du dollar?	*What's the exchange rate for the dollar?*
Gardez la monnaie.	*Keep the change.*
Le vendeur fait de la monnaie.	*The sales clerk is making change.*
Je vous rends la monnaie, Monsieur.	*I'm giving you the change, sir.*
Je vous remercie.	*Thank you.*
On ne marchande pas dans cette boutique.	*One doesn't bargain / haggle in this shop.*
Ça coûte soixante-quinze centimes.	*That costs seventy-five centimes.*
Ce stylo coûte un franc cinquante (1,50 F).	*That pen costs one franc and fifty centimes.*
Le prix? C'est trois francs dix (3,10 F).	*The price? It's three francs and ten centimes.*

▶ On parle d'argent.

Mon père me donne de l'argent de poche chaque semaine.	*My father gives me an allowance every week.*
Il ne faut pas dépenser trop d'argent.	*One shouldn't spend too much money.*

J'économise / Je fais des économies.	*I'm saving my money.*
Je ne gaspille jamais mon argent.	*I never waste my money.*
Ce magnétoscope coûte cher.	*This VCR is expensive.*
Dix dollars pour cette chemise? C'est bon marché!	*Ten dollars for this shirt? That's cheap!*

Interaction   *Un client fait des achats à la papeterie.*

LE PAPETIER: Voilà vos enveloppes et votre stylo.

LE CLIENT: Merci, je vous dois combien?

LE PAPETIER: Trente-sept francs cinquante, s'il vous plaît.

LE CLIENT: Je suis désolé, monsieur, mais je n'ai qu'un billet de cinq cents francs.

LE PAPETIER: Cela ne fait rien.° Je vais vous rendre la monnaie… Trente-sept cinquante, trente-huit, quarante, cinquante, cent, trois cents, et cinq cents! Je vous remercie.

That doesn't matter.

Activités

A. Répondez aux questions suivantes.

1. Combien d'argent de poche recevez-vous chaque *(each)* mois?
2. Combien d'argent avez-vous sur vous en ce moment? Avez-vous la monnaie d'un dollar?
3. Avez-vous économisé de l'argent? Pourquoi? Qu'est-ce que vous avez fait pour avoir cet argent?
4. Qu'est-ce qui coûte trop cher? Qu'est-ce qui est bon marché?

B. Jouez les scènes suivantes avec un(e) camarade de cours.

1. Vous entrez dans une boulangerie pour acheter du pain et des croissants.
2. Vous voulez acheter un beau pantalon dans un marché aux puces *(flea market)* mais vous pensez qu'il coûte trop cher. Marchandez!
3. Dans un restaurant où vous venez de dîner, le garçon vous apporte l'addition *(check)*. Vous trouvez une erreur. Expliquez-la au garçon.
4. Vous avez une interview pour un travail. Demandez combien on va vous payer (**dollars de l'heure**). Est-ce que c'est assez?

Lecture culturelle

Avant la lecture

In the last twenty years, French attitudes toward spending money have changed radically. Because of inflation, changing habits, and the availability of new products, the French spend a much larger percentage of their income than before, and more of their money goes toward buying services, leaving less available for the purchase of durable goods (furniture, appliances, etc.).

Another interesting development in the way French people handle their money is their greater use of credit cards and checks. Cash transactions are now limited to small purchases in neighborhood stores. To pay for major purchases, a hotel or restaurant bill, and even gasoline, people routinely write checks or use

18^F95
DONT 20% GRATUIT
TARTE NORMANDE
SURGELEE
BROSSARD
576 g. Soit le kg : 32,90 F

28^F40
LE LOT
POISSON SAUCE CREVETTES SURGELE
VIVAGEL
2 x 400 g. Soit le kg : 35,50 F

a credit card. In addition, the French are ahead of North Americans in their use of electronic money. Using their **Minitel,** many French people perform a wide array of financial transactions from their homes without going to their bank.

Activités

A. What would be the major purchases for a family under the following categories? Make up your lists in French.

Durable goods	Non-durable goods
1.	1.
2.	2.
3.	3.

B. Close or exact cognates, such as **l'impression,** are easy to identify. See if you can guess the meanings of the following words found in the **Lecture culturelle** even though they differ from English by several letters.

dépenses	en fait	diminuent
maintenir	éphémères	courant
typique	assurances	logement

Les Français et l'argent

*C*omment les Français dépensent-ils leur argent? Que font-ils de leurs revenus° quand ils ont payé leurs impôts°? Ils n'ont que deux solutions: dépenser ou épargner°. Pendant longtemps, la majorité des gens a choisi de faire des économies, mais depuis les années 70, la crise 5 économique a forcé les Français à dépenser plus pour maintenir ou améliorer° leur niveau de vie°. En 1978, ils ne dépensaient que 82,5% de leurs revenus, mais maintenant, ce pourcentage est de 87%.

Quand on examine le budget d'une famille française typique, on a l'impression qu'ils mangent de moins en moins et qu'ils n'achètent plus de vêtements 10 pour pouvoir dépenser plus d'argent pour leur santé et pour leurs loisirs°. En fait, une analyse détaillée montre que les Français continuent à dépenser de plus en plus d'argent pour leur nourriture. Ils vont souvent au restaurant et la nourriture est très chère.

Dans un budget, l'examen de la part des biens durables (meubles°, 15 équipement ménager°, voiture, etc.) et de celle des dépenses plus éphémères (alimentation°, services) donne une idée de l'évolution du mode de vie° des Français.

On remarque aussi que les Français dépensent de plus en plus pour les achats de services. Une distinction entre les achats de produits manufacturés et 20 ceux de services (assurances, réparations°, coiffeur°) montre que les premiers diminuent et les seconds augmentent.

Comment les Français réussissent-ils à continuer d'améliorer leur niveau de vie et à acheter plus? Ils le font grâce° au crédit. Consommer avant de payer! Le principe est maintenant très courant en France. Le crédit permet aussi à la ma-25 jorité des gens de devenir propriétaires d'un logement°.

income / taxes
save

improve
niveau... *standard of living*

leisure

furniture
équipement... *appliances*
food / **mode...** *way of life*

repairs / hairdresser

thanks

apartment

• Bureau d'accueil • Interprètes
• Détaxe à l'exportation
• Défilés de mode hebdomadaires
• Bureau de change • Restaurants

GALERIES LAFAYETTE
40, Boulevard Haussmann, 75009 Paris.
Ouvert du lundi au samedi de 9 h 30 à 18 h 45.
Nocturne jusqu'à 21 h le jeudi.

Après un début assez lent dans les années 70, les Français sont maintenant plus de 10 millions à posséder au moins une carte de crédit, et la carte n'est plus considérée comme un privilège réservé aux hommes d'affaires° et aux cadres supérieurs°. La plupart des° Français la considère aujourd'hui comme un in-
30 strument utile et souvent indispensable. Aujourd'hui, ils l'utilisent pour acheter 25% des TV, 33% des magnétoscopes, 25% des lave-vaisselle°, et 25% des machines à laver.

hommes... *businessmen*
cadres... *upper-level managers* / La... *Most*
dishwashers

(Adapté de *Francoscopie* / Larousse)

Après la lecture

Questions sur le texte

1. Pourquoi est-ce que les Français dépensent plus d'argent depuis 1970?
2. Quel pourcentage de leurs revenus est-ce qu'ils économisaient en 1978? Et maintenant?
3. Pourquoi est-ce que les Français dépensent de plus en plus d'argent pour leur nourriture?
4. Combien de Français possèdent au moins une carte de crédit?
5. Qu'est-ce que les gens achètent en utilisant le crédit?

Activités

A. Regardez la liste suivante des dépenses des Français. Ajoutez les pourcentages qui *(which)* correspondent à votre situation maintenant. Et si vous aviez une famille?

Les dépenses	Les Français	Moi	Avec une famille
Alimentation	21,3%	_____	_____
Vêtements	6,2%	_____	_____
Logement	17,9%	_____	_____
Santé	13,5%	_____	_____
Transports	13,6%	_____	_____
Loisirs	6,4%	_____	_____

B. Répondez aux questions suivantes.

1. Avez-vous acheté des biens durables récemment? Quoi? Les avez-vous achetés à crédit?
2. Avez-vous des cartes de crédit? Combien? Est-ce un avantage ou un désavantage?
3. Que pensez-vous de la nécessité des biens suivants? Indiquez s'ils sont indispensables ou utiles ou si c'est un privilège de les avoir.

des meubles	un magnétoscope
une voiture	une machine à laver
un téléviseur	un lecteur de disques compacts
un ordinateur personnel	une chaîne stéréo

Vocabulaire

Noms / Pronoms

article de sport	sports item / sporting goods	**boulangerie**	bakery
bijouterie	jeweler's	**bouteille**	bottle
boucher (-ère)	butcher	**boutique**	shop
boucherie	butcher shop	**brasserie**	café-restaurant
boulanger (-ère)	baker	**buraliste**	tobacconist
		caisse	the cashier's

centre-ville	downtown	Mesdemoiselles	ladies
charcuterie	pork butcher's shop	papeterie	stationer's
charcutier (-ère)	pork butcher	pâté de foie	liver pâté
choucroute garnie	sauerkraut and assorted meat	pâtisserie	pastry shop
		pâtissier (-ère)	pastry maker
commande	order	plat cuisiné	prepared dish
commerçant	shopkeeper	poissonnerie	fish market
conserves	canned food	poissonnier (-ère)	fishmonger
crémerie	dairy store	produit	product
épicerie	grocery	rayon	department
épicier (-ère)	grocer	remise	discount
fleuriste	florist	soldes	sales
franc	franc	supermarché	supermarket
gramme	gram	teinturerie	dry cleaner's
hypermarché	giant supermarket	vendeur (-euse)	salesperson

Verbes

boire	to drink	essayer	to try
conseiller	to advise	falloir	must
devoir	must	recevoir	to receive

Adjectifs / Adverbes

ne... personne	nobody	ne... rien	nothing
ne... plus	no more	sec	dry
ne... que	only	surgelé	frozen

Expressions

autre chose	something else	peut-être	maybe
de bonne heure	early	tout le monde	everybody
en solde	on sale		

Chapitres 10 à 12

Révision **D**

Tous ensemble!

A. Répondez aux questions suivantes en employant les mots entre parenthèses.

Les amis

1. As-tu vu Françoise?   (Oui,... venir... hier)
2. Tu m'aimes?   (Oui,...)
3. Etes-vous étonnées que vos copains ne vous téléphonent jamais? (Oui,...)
4. Qui a appris à ton ami à utiliser le réseau internet?   (Personne...)
5. Est-ce que je peux te voir ce soir?   (Non, parler... demain)

Les activités

6. Est-ce que vous pouvez nous prêter votre auto?   (Oui,...)
7. Avez-vous peur qu'il fasse mauvais demain?   (Oui, je... pleuvoir)
8. Est-ce que vous venez me voir?   (Oui,...)
9. Est-il possible que vous partiez demain?   (Non, il faut que... partir aujourd'hui)
10. Est-ce que je vous ai vus à la boulangerie?   (Oui,...)

B. Refaites les phrases suivantes en utilisant les mots entre parenthèses.

Qu'est-ce qu'il y a?

1. Elle part à neuf heures et elle va à la charcuterie.   (Hier,...)
2. Quelque chose est arrivé au courrier.   (Rien...)
3. Je les vois quand ils sortent.   (... la semaine dernière.)
4. Il a attendu trois minutes.   (... ne... que...)
5. Elles apprend une langue étrangère?   (L'année dernière,...)

Des opinions

6. Je suis sûr qu'il ne veut pas venir.   (... furieux...)
7. Il ne faut pas qu'on oublie les sans-abris.   (... devoir...)
8. Je doute qu'ils soient pauvres.   (... penser...)
9. Es-tu sûr que nous ayons un désastre écologique un jour?   (Moi, je suis sûr...)
10. Je dois partir quand elle arrive.   (... hier.)

C. Faites des phrases complètes avec les mots donnés, en faisant les changements nécessaires.

Des activités

1. Jeanne / travailler / jamais / dans / boucherie
2. Hier / nous / descendre / en ville / avec / enfants
3. Paul / boire / jamais / eau
4. Hier soir / je / recevoir / personne
5. Tu / venir / répondre / téléphone?

La famille

6. Personne / devoir / rien / mes parents
7. Il / être / peu probable / tu / voir / ton / grands-parents
8. Quand / je / habiter / Québec / je / recevoir / souvent / cousins
9. Mon / sœurs / tenir / faire / promenade
10. Mes parents / ne... pas penser / guerre / être / possible

D. Complétez le paragraphe suivant avec la forme correcte des verbes donnés.

Le week-end dernier, Chantal et ses sœurs _____ (décider) d'aller au bord de la mer. Elle _____ (inviter) son petit ami Charles; il ne _____ (pouvoir) pas aller avec elles, mais il _____ (recommander) une belle plage près d'Arcachon.

Quand elles _____ (partir), il _____ (faire) du brouillard et il _____ (falloir) qu'elles _____ (faire) attention. Il _____ (être) cinq heures quand elles _____ (partir), mais dans la voiture personne ne _____ (dormir). Après deux heures, elles _____ (arriver) dans une petite ville. Il _____ (être) sept heures et tout le monde _____ (vouloir) continuer pour être à la mer avant les touristes. Mais Chantal _____ (être) fatiguée et elle _____ (vouloir) qu'on _____ (prendre) quelque chose. Elles _____ (chercher) un café ou un restaurant, mais comme il _____ (être) peu probable qu'elles _____ (pouvoir) trouver un café ouvert à cette heure, elles _____ (décider) de continuer.

Elles _____ (arriver) deux heures plus tard. Elles _____ (sortir) de la voiture et _____ (aller) sur la plage. Chantal _____ (comprendre) tout de suite pourquoi Charles aime cette plage: il n'y _____ (avoir) que des nudistes!

E. Complétez les phrases suivantes de manière logique.

1. Je ne pense pas que...
2. Il est probable que...
3. Mes parents veulent que...
4. A ma résidence, nous venons de...
5. Il ne faut pas que nous...
6. Je doute que mon professeur...
7. Hier, j'ai reçu...
8. Je suis sûr(e) que...
9. Les Américains pensent que...
10. Il se peut que...

Entre nous!

A. Interviewez un(e) camarade de cours et posez-lui les questions suivantes. Après, informez la classe des résultats.

1. Que veux-tu faire dans la vie?
2. Quelle sorte de travail as-tu déjà fait?
3. Où es-tu allé(e) le week-end dernier?

    4.   Qu'est-ce que tu as fait?

    5.   Qu'est-ce que tu ne fais jamais?

    6.   Qui te donne ton argent?

B. En petits groupes, interrogez vos camarades de cours sur leurs compétences. Qu'est-ce qu'ils savent faire? Quand est-ce qu'ils ne peuvent pas faire ces choses et pourquoi?

C. Racontez votre enfance *(childhood)* à un(e) camarade de cours. Employez les expressions suivantes ou vos propres idées.

jouer beaucoup	être méchant(e)
manger beaucoup de glace	dormir l'après-midi
regarder… à la télévision	???

D. En petits groupes, expliquez vos réactions aux situations suivantes. Utilisez les suggestions des deux colonnes ou d'autres expressions.

J'ai peur que	il y a un conflit international
Je pense que	le Président va à Moscou
Je ne pense pas que	le Canada veut coloniser les Etats-Unis
???	les jeunes peuvent influencer le gouvernement
	les athlètes russes ne sont pas compétitifs
	le Japon vend trop de voitures aux Etats-Unis
	l'inflation est un problème sérieux

E. Avec un(e) camarade de cours, faites une liste des activités que vous devez faire. Utilisez les suggestions suivantes ou vos propres idées.

étudier plus souvent?	faire une lettre à des amis?
téléphoner à mes parents?	aller à l'église?
dormir moins?	réparer ma voiture?

F. **Jeu de rôles.** Jouez les scènes suivantes avec un(e) camarade de cours.

    1.   Vous avez loué une voiture et vous la rendez à l'agence. Vous devez expliquer pourquoi vous êtes en retard.

    2.   Vous êtes journaliste. Interviewez trois personnes qui ont vu un accident de voiture.

    3.   Vous téléphonez au charcutier pour commander un dîner pour huit personnes. Quels plats voulez-vous servir?

    4.   Vous êtes dans un hypermarché et vous ne pouvez rien trouver. Demandez à un(e) employé(e) où vous pouvez trouver les choses que vous cherchez.

    5.   Vous cherchez du travail. Un(e) camarade de cours va prendre des renseignements sur votre identité (nom, âge, adresse…) et va vous poser des questions sur vos compétences.

    6.   Vous êtes journaliste et vous préparez un reportage sur les opinions des étudiants à votre université. Interrogez des camarades de cours pour voir s'ils sont optimistes ou pessimistes pour l'avenir. Qu'est-ce qui les préoccupe?

13

Chapitre

La santé

Le marathon de Paris

Commençons

Grammaire

Communiquons

Lecture culturelle

Vocabulaire

Objectives

Language
Vocabulary for parts of the body • Initial and final consonant sounds • Stem-changing verbs • Reflexive verbs in the present, **futur proche,** and infinitive • Reflexive verbs in the **passé composé** and imperative

Culture
Medical care in France • **Médecins sans Frontières**

Communication
Consulting a doctor • Discussing health • Describing one's daily routine

Commençons

Chez le médecin

Paul Prévot va consulter son médecin car il dort mal et il est très fatigué depuis deux semaines.

LE MÉDECIN: Bonjour, Paul. Qu'est-ce qui ne va pas?

PAUL: Depuis quinze jours je suis très fatigué et le soir, je m'endors très tard.

LE MÉDECIN: Est-ce que vous vous couchez de bonne heure? Est-ce que vous vous réveillez tôt le matin? Vous reposez-vous dans la journée?

PAUL: Je me couche généralement vers onze heures et je ne me lève jamais avant sept heures, mais je ne ferme pas l'œil de la nuit.

LE MÉDECIN: Déshabillez-vous. Je vais vous examiner mais je ne pense pas que cela soit sérieux.

L'examen terminé, le médecin appelle Paul dans son bureau.

PAUL: Alors, docteur, j'espère que ce n'est pas une maladie grave!

LE MÉDECIN: Je ne trouve rien. Il faut que vous vous détendiez davantage. Faites-vous de l'exercice régulièrement?

PAUL: Non, mais je me promène tous les soirs après dîner.

LE MÉDECIN: Très bien. Ne vous inquiétez pas, mais suivez mon conseil: évitez de boire du café avant de vous coucher, mais si cela ne va pas mieux, il va falloir qu'on vous fasse une prise de sang.

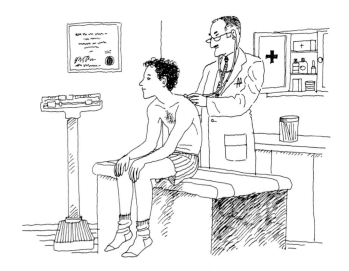

Etudions le dialogue

1. Pourquoi Paul Prévot va-t-il chez le médecin?
2. Combien d'heures est-ce qu'il dort?
3. Est-ce que le docteur pense que c'est grave?
4. Est-ce qu'il examine Paul?
5. Qu'est-ce que le docteur recommande?
6. Est-ce qu'il faut que Paul boive beaucoup de café?

Mots clés

consulter	*visit*	examiner	*to examine*
Qu'est-ce qui ne va pas?	*What's wrong?*	appelle (appeler)	*calls*
		maladie	*illness*
m'endors (s'endormir)	*fall asleep*	grave	*serious*
tard	*late*	vous détendiez (se détendre)	*relax*
vous vous couchez (se coucher)	*you go to bed*	davantage	*more*
vous vous réveillez (se réveiller)	*you wake up*	Faites-vous de l'exercice?	*Do you exercise?*
tôt	*early*	régulièrement	*regularly*
reposez-vous (se reposer)	*you rest*	me promène (se promener)	*go for a walk*
journée	*day*		
généralement	*generally*	bien	*well*
vers	*about, around*	Ne vous inquiétez pas. (s'inquiéter)	*Don't worry.*
me lève (se lever)	*get up*		
ne ferme pas l'œil de la nuit	*can't sleep a wink all night long*	évitez (éviter)	*avoid*
		ne va pas mieux (aller mieux)	*do not feel better*
Déshabillez-vous. (se déshabiller)	*Get undressed.*	prise de sang	*blood test*

Faisons connaissance

The medical profession remains a popular choice for young people in France, and medical students must go through a rigorous training that begins the year after high school. However, a surplus of physicians, particularly in the major urban centers, is beginning to create problems. Many physicians now have to compete for patients; their average income is decreasing; and the profession as a whole has lost some of its social prestige.

A la pharmacie

Many family doctors in France still follow the tradition of making house calls. A family would never go to a hospital first for an emergency—it would call the doctor. Many doctors work in their own homes and do not have secretarial help. French citizens and foreigners working in France are reimbursed by the social security system for 80 percent of their medical expenses.

In France, many people consult pharmacists rather than doctors for minor problems. A pharmacist can offer advice and sell medicines over the counter that might not be available in this country without a prescription. Pharmacies are numerous in French cities and are easily identifiable by the green cross (**la croix verte**) that hangs above the store. When a pharmacy is closed, there is always a sign hanging on the door with the address of the nearest **pharmacie de garde** or **pharmacie de nuit,** which is the pharmacy designated to stay open at night or on Sunday and holidays.

Enrichissons notre vocabulaire

Les parties du corps *(Parts of the body)*

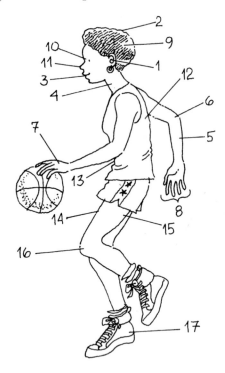

1. les oreilles *(f.)*	7. la main	12. le dos
2. la tête	8. les doigts *(m.)*	13. le ventre
3. la bouche	9. les cheveux *(m.)*	14. la jambe
4. la gorge	10. les yeux /	15. la cuisse
5. le bras	l'œil *(m.)*	16. le genou
6. le coude	11. le nez	17. le pied

La santé *(Health)*

être en bonne / mauvaise santé	*to be in good / bad health*
avoir bonne mine / mauvaise mine	*to look good / bad*
avoir mal à	*to hurt*
être malade	*to be ill*
avoir de la fièvre	*to have a fever*
se porter bien	*to be in good health*
être au régime / faire un régime	*to be on a diet / to follow a diet*
aller chez le dentiste	*to go to the dentist*
—Qu'est-ce qui te fait mal? / Où as-tu mal?	*Where does it hurt?*
—J'ai mal aux dents, *(f.)*, au cou, à l'épaule *(f.)*, à la cheville.	*My teeth, neck, shoulder, ankle hurt.*
—Tu es hypocondriaque!	*You're a hypochondriac!*

Prononciation   Initial and final consonant sounds

A. If you place your hand in front of your mouth and pronounce an English word starting with the / p /, / t /, or / k / sounds, you will feel a puff of air. This is *aspiration,* and you must avoid it in French when you pronounce such initial consonant sounds.

Listen carefully to your teacher and repeat the following pairs of words, trying to eliminate the aspiration in the French words.

English	French	English	French
Paul	Paul	two	tout
Paris	Paris	car	car

B. Final consonant sounds are stronger in French than in English. In French, it is very important to pronounce final consonant sounds clearly. As you know, some grammatical distinctions depend on the presence or absence of a final consonant sound in the oral form.

Gender: étudiant / e ty djã /, étudiante / e ty djãt /
Number: il descend / il dɛ sã /, ils descendent / il dɛ sãd /

Repeat the following pairs of words after your teacher, making the final consonant sound much stronger in French.

English	French	English	French
habit	habite	port	porte
bees	bise	long	longue
descend	descendent	mine	mine

Repeat the following words after your teacher, making sure to pronounce the final consonant sound clearly.

verte / sorte / verbe / servent / heureuse / tienne / sac / rendent / tête

Exercice

Read the following sentences aloud, avoiding the aspiration of initial consonant sounds and stressing final ones.

1. Le professeur pose une question intéressante.
2. Patrick passe l'été dans l'appartement de sa tante.
3. Au printemps, à Paris, les cafés sont pleins de monde.
4. Ces pays deviennent de plus en plus pauvres.
5. Un cours de psychologie demande beaucoup de travail.
6. Brigitte part faire des courses avec Monique.

Grammaire

I. Stem-changing verbs

You use verbs to describe actions or states of being.

A. Two groups of common **-er** verbs have stem changes in the **je, tu, il,** and **ils** forms of the present indicative. These are verbs that have é or e at the end of their stem, such as **préférer** and **acheter.**

préférer	acheter
je préfère	j' achète
tu préfères	tu achètes
il / elle / on préfère	il / elle / on achète
nous préférons	nous achetons
vous préférez	vous achetez
ils / elles préfèrent	ils / elles achètent

Mots clés *Some verbs conjugated like* **préférer** *and* **acheter**

préférer		acheter	
espérer	*to hope*	amener	*to bring*
inquiéter	*to worry*	emmener	*to take*
posséder	*to own*	enlever	*to take off / away*
répéter	*to repeat*	lever	*to raise*
sécher	*to dry*	promener	*to walk*
sécher un cours	*to cut class*		

Je **préfère** la cuisine vietnamienne. Qu'est-ce que vous **préférez?**
Eux, ils n'**achètent** jamais rien, mais nous, nous **achetons** souvent des vêtements.
Les maladies **inquiètent** beaucoup les Français.

B. Note that in the **je, tu, il,** and **ils** forms, the vowel at the end of the stem is pronounced as a more open / ɛ / sound, thus causing a change from é or e to an **accent grave** (è) before a pronounced final consonant.

préférer	→ je préfère	/ ʒø pre fɛʀ /
répéter	→ tu répètes	/ ty ʀe pɛt /
acheter	→ elles achètent	/ ɛl za ʃɛt /
lever	→ il lève	/ il lɛv /

L'orthographe

1. **Appeler** *(to call)* uses a double **l** instead of an **accent grave** to make the vowel sound / ɛ / before a final consonant. The **je, tu, il,** and **ils** forms of the present indicative show this stem change.

   j'appelle, ils appellent *but:* nous appelons

   Le médecin appelle Paul dans son bureau.

2. In the present indicative, only the **nous** and **vous** forms keep the same pronunciation and spelling as the infinitive because these forms end in a vowel sound and not in a consonant sound.

espérer	→ nous espérons	/ nu zɛ spe rɔ̃ /
acheter	→ vous achetez	/ vu za ʃte /

C. Since the present subjunctive has similar endings, the vowels change as in the indicative.

Il faut que je sèche	que j'enlève
que tu sèches	que tu enlèves
qu'on sèche	qu'il / elle / on enlève
que nous séchions	que nous enlevions
que vous séchiez	que vous enleviez
qu'ils sèchent	qu'ils / elles enlèvent

D. The past participle is pronounced like the infinitive; therefore, the vowels in the stem do not change.

espérer	→ espéré	lever → levé
posséder	→ possédé	appeler → appelé

E. Since the imperfect has a vowel ending in all forms of the verb, the vowel in the stem does not change.

Je **possédais** une voiture, mais je l'ai vendue.
Nous **appelions** Jacques quand il est arrivé.

Langue

A. En classe. Dans les phrases suivantes, mettez les verbes au singulier au pluriel et les verbes au pluriel au singulier.

1. Répétez le dialogue!
2. N'enlève pas tes chaussures en classe!
3. Nous possédons une bonne calculatrice.
4. J'espère qu'il va réussir.
5. Lève la main si tu sais la réponse.
6. Vous appelez son professeur?
7. Elle va sécher son cours d'espagnol.
8. Achète-lui un nouveau cahier.

B. Des substitutions. Substituez les expressions données dans les phrases suivantes.

1. Tu sèches tes cours? (préférer l'eau minérale, espérer gagner le match, enlever ton manteau, promener tes amis, inquiéter ta famille)
2. Elle appelait sa sœur. (posséder une bicyclette, espérer être heureuse, préférer aller au cinéma, répéter la question)
3. Je ne pense pas qu'elle achète une voiture. (emmener son ami, préférer mon dentiste, enlever son imperméable, appeler le docteur, amener les boissons)

Culture

C. Les distractions des Français. Choisissez la chose ou la personne que les Français préfèrent parmi *(among)* les trois possibilités.

MODÈLE: comme distraction: la télé / les livres / les sports
Les Français préfèrent la télé.

1. comme distraction: la radio / les cafés / le cinéma
2. comme lecture: *Télé 7 Jours / Paris-Match / L'Express*
3. à la télé: la fiction / les films / le journal / les sports
4. l'origine des films: les films français / les films américains / les films italiens
5. comme genre de film: les films d'amour / les films d'aventure / les films comiques
6. comme film américain: *E.T. l'Extra-terrestre / Les Dix Commandements / Le Livre de la jungle*

D. Le français québécois. Comment est-ce que les Québécois appellent les choses suivantes?

MODÈLE: un week-end? *Ils l'appellent «une fin de semaine».*

1. une voiture	a.	une vue
2. un dîner	b.	de la fesse
3. un match	c.	un char
4. du jambon	d.	un souper
5. de l'auto-stop	e.	une joute
6. un film	f.	du pouce

Communication

E. **Vivent les différences!** Etes-vous différent(e) de votre camarade de chambre? Choisissez entre les différentes possibilités. Suivez le modèle.

> MODÈLE: le jazz / la musique classique / le rock
> *Moi, je préfère la musique classique.*
> *Lui, il préfère le jazz.*

1. cinéma / théâtre / télévision
2. lait / thé / bière / vin
3. étudier / faire une promenade / aller danser / sécher les cours
4. la plage / les parcs / le centre-ville
5. avoir une profession bien payée / avoir une profession intéressante
6. parler de grands problèmes / parler de ses amis

F. **Les possessions.** Trouvez quelqu'un dans la classe qui possède les choses suivantes.

> MODÈLE: un vélo   *Je possède un vélo.*
> une calculette   *Marc possède une calculette.*

une auto jaune
un lecteur de disques compacts
des disques des Beatles
une carte du monde
un téléphone portable

un magnétoscope
un pantalon vert
une photo de famille
un Walkman
des chaussures rouges

G. **Questions personnelles.** L'avenir.

1. Qu'est-ce qui vous inquiète? L'avenir? Votre santé?
2. Qu'est-ce que vous allez pouvoir acheter dans dix ans que vous ne pouvez pas acheter maintenant?
3. Combien d'enfants espérez-vous avoir? Préférez-vous des garçons ou des filles?
4. Préférez-vous un beau mari / une belle femme ou un mari / une femme intelligent(e)?
5. Qu'est-ce que vos amis espèrent avoir un jour? Et vous?
6. Quelle erreur n'allez-vous jamais répéter?

II. Reflexive verbs: Present tense, futur proche, and the infinitive

Reflexive verbs in French describe an action that the subject performs upon itself.

A. Present tense

1. Reflexive verbs are conjugated with a reflexive pronoun, which represents the same person as the subject. Reflexive pronouns have the same position as the other object pronouns you have learned.

se coucher *(to go to bed)*	**s'amuser** *(to have a good time)*
je **me** couche	je **m'**amuse
tu **te** couches	tu **t'**amuses
il / elle / on **se** couche	il / elle / on **s'**amuse
nous **nous** couchons	nous **nous** amusons
vous **vous** couchez	vous **vous** amusez
ils / elles **se** couchent	ils / elles **s'**amusent

2. In the negative, the reflexive pronoun precedes the conjugated verb.

   Je **ne me lève jamais** avant sept heures.

3. With inversion in the interrogative, the reflexive pronoun precedes the conjugated verb.

   Vous réveillez-vous tôt le matin?
   Paul **se promène-t-il** tous les soirs?

Alors, on se promène en ville?

Mots clés Reflexive verbs

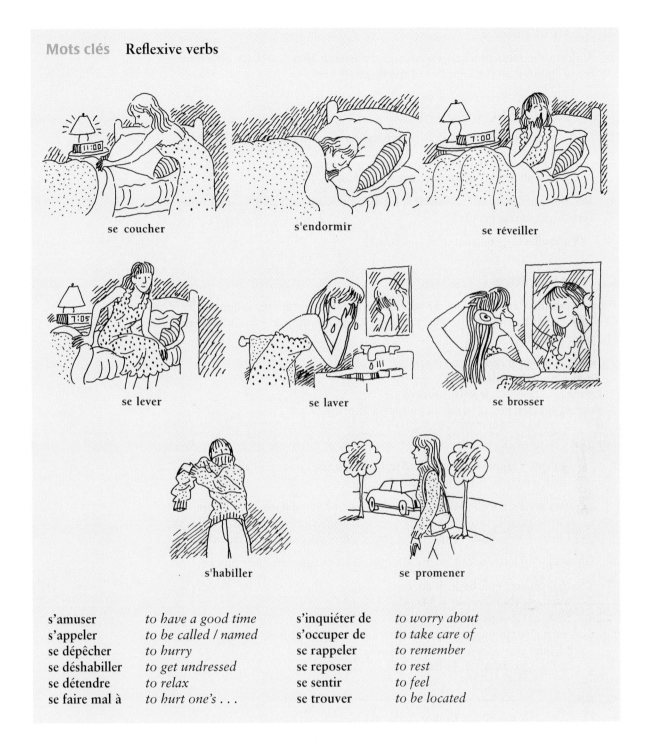

se coucher   s'endormir   se réveiller

se lever   se laver   se brosser

s'habiller   se promener

s'amuser	*to have a good time*	s'inquiéter de	*to worry about*
s'appeler	*to be called / named*	s'occuper de	*to take care of*
se dépêcher	*to hurry*	se rappeler	*to remember*
se déshabiller	*to get undressed*	se reposer	*to rest*
se détendre	*to relax*	se sentir	*to feel*
se faire mal à	*to hurt one's . . .*	se trouver	*to be located*

Attention!

Note that definite articles, not possessive adjectives, are used with parts of the body: ownership is understood!

Elle se brosse **les** dents.   Ils se lavent **les** mains.

B. Le futur proche

1. To form the **futur proche,** you conjugate the verb **aller** and place the reflexive pronoun with the infinitive of the reflexive verb.

> Nous **allons nous reposer** ce soir.
> Tu **vas t'amuser** ce week-end?

2. In the negative, place the negative expression around the conjugated verb.

> Je **ne vais pas m'occuper** de la lessive.
> Nous **n'allons pas nous dépêcher** maintenant.

3. The interrogative with inversion is formed the same way as it is with other verbs in the **futur proche:**

> **Vont-elles se promener** après les cours?

C. The Infinitive

With an infinitive construction, the reflexive pronoun precedes the infinitive. Reflexive pronouns must represent the same person as the subject, even if the verbs are not conjugated.

> Je ne peux pas **m'endormir.**
> **Tu** as besoin de **te détendre!**
> **Evitez** le café avant de **vous coucher.**
> Pour **m'amuser,** j'aime passer la journée à la plage.

Langue

A. **Une journée typique de Monique.** Mettez les phrases suivantes à la forme interrogative en utilisant l'inversion.

1. Ton amie s'appelle Monique.
2. Elle se réveille tôt.
3. Elle se lave tout de suite.
4. Elle s'habille dans sa chambre.
5. Elle s'occupe de son fils.
6. Son bureau se trouve en ville.

B. **Un week-end à Arcachon.** Mettez les phrases suivantes au futur proche.

1. Nous nous dépêchons de partir.   WWW
2. Yvette se promène sur la plage.
3. Je ne me lève pas tôt.
4. Vous ne vous inquiétez pas si Yves amène des copains?
5. Jacques ne s'occupe pas de la vaisselle.
6. Nous nous amusons là-bas.

Culture

C. **La France ou les Etats-Unis?** Formez des phrases complètes avec les mots donnés et dites si l'activité est plus typique des Français ou des Américains.

1. On / faire / bises / avant / se coucher
2. grands-mères / s'appeler / «Mamie»
3. On / pouvoir / se lever tard / 1er mai
4. Les personnes âgées / se promener / dans / centres commerciaux / pour leur santé

5. On / se déshabiller / sur / plage
6. On / se reposer / au déjeuner
7. Beaucoup de gens / s'inquiéter / leur poids *(weight)*
8. On / se promener / en auto / pour / se détendre

D. **Les provinces françaises.** Traditionnellement, la France est divisée en provinces. Dites *(Say)* dans quelle province on trouve les villes suivantes.

MODÈLE: Bordeaux   *Bordeaux se trouve en Aquitaine.*   WWW

1.	Dijon	a.	Provence
2.	Reims	b.	Normandie
3.	Brest	c.	Bretagne
4.	Rouen	d.	Bourgogne
5.	Marseille	e.	Alsace
6.	Strasbourg	f.	Champagne

Communication

E. **Une journée typique.** Racontez une journée typique dans votre vie. Ensuite, racontez une journée idéale. Si vous voulez, utilisez les mots de la liste suivante et un adverbe: **à... heure(s), tôt, tard, de bonne heure.**

se réveiller	se dépêcher	s'occuper de
se lever	partir pour les cours	se déshabiller
se laver	rentrer	se coucher
s'habiller	se reposer	???

F. **Mes habitudes.** Que faites-vous pour vous amuser? vous reposer? vous endormir? vous détendre? vous réveiller? Comparez vos réponses avec les réponses d'un(e) camarade de cours et présentez les similarités et les différences à la classe.

MODÈLE: *Pour me réveiller, je bois du café.*

G. **On s'inquiète.** Quand est-ce que les gens s'inquiètent? Répondez en utilisant un élément de chaque colonne avec l'expression **s'inquiéter quand.**

Je	rentrer tard
Mes parents	faire du stop
Mon petit ami	dépenser trop d'argent
Ma petite amie	sécher les cours
Mon professeur	ne pas répondre aux lettres
???	???

H. **Questions personnelles.** Réfléchissons!

1. Qu'est-ce que vous vous rappelez de votre enfance *(childhood)*?
2. Vous inquiétez-vous souvent? De quoi?
3. Préférez-vous vous coucher tôt ou tard et vous lever tôt ou tard?
4. Quand est-ce que vous vous sentez triste?
5. Où se trouve votre endroit préféré?
6. Qui doit s'occuper des pauvres?

III.   Reflexive verbs: Passé composé and imperative

You use reflexive verbs in the **passé composé** to describe personal actions in the past and in the imperative to give commands.

A.   Passé composé

All reflexive verbs are conjugated with **être** in the **passé composé.**

Je **me suis levé** à sept heures.   Tu ne **t'es pas couché** hier soir?
Il **s'est inquiété.**   **Vous êtes-vous** déjà **lavé?**

L'orthographe

1.   Unlike other verbs conjugated with **être** in the **passé composé,** the past participle agrees with the reflexive pronoun, which is usually a direct object and which is the same as the subject.

   Nous **nous** sommes habillé**s.**   Elle ne s'est pas dépêché**e.**

2.   There is no agreement with the past participle when a part of the body follows the verb.

   Elle s'est **lavé** les mains.   Nous nous sommes **brossé** les dents.

B.   The imperative

The reflexive pronoun follows the verb in the affirmative and precedes the verb in the negative.

Déshabillez-vous!   **Ne te couche pas** trop tard!
Dépêchons-nous!   **Ne vous inquiétez pas** trop!

Attention!

The pronoun **te** becomes **toi** when it *follows* the verb.

Ne **te** dépêche pas!   → Dépêche-**toi!**
Ne **t'**habille pas maintenant! → Habille-**toi** maintenant!

Langue

A.   **Notre journée d'hier.** Mettez les phrases suivantes au passé composé.

   1.   Nous nous levons tôt.
   2.   Vous vous réveillez avant sept heures?
   3.   Nous ne nous promenons pas avant le déjeuner.
   4.   Robert et Julie s'amusent après notre promenade.

5. Lise se repose avant le dîner.
6. Jean se dépêche pour dîner avec nous.
7. Tu ne t'endors pas de bonne heure?
8. Je me couche tard.

B. **Des conseils.** Mettez les phrases suivantes à l'impératif pour donner des conseils à vos amis.

1. Tu ne te lèves pas trop tard.
2. Vous vous dépêchez pour aller en classe.
3. Tu te reposes cet après-midi.
4. Nous nous amusons ce soir.
5. Tu ne t'endors pas au concert.
6. Vous vous déshabillez avant de vous coucher.
7. Nous ne nous détendons pas avant l'examen.
8. Vous ne vous couchez pas à deux heures du matin.

Culture

C. **Des Américains ou des Français?** Avec un nom comme **Robert** ou **Michelle,** on peut être français ou américain. Formez des phrases complètes au passé pour décrire *(describe)* les activités des personnes suivantes. Ensuite dites si la personne est américaine ou française, selon l'activité.

1. Michelle / téléphoner / sa copine / avant de se coucher
2. Robert / se laver / dans sa chambre
3. Michelle / s'habiller / très mal / pour aller en cours
4. Robert / prendre un somnifère *(sleeping pill)* / et il / s'endormir
5. Michelle / se sentir / très mal / quand elle / se réveiller / et / demander au médecin / venir chez elle
6. Robert / s'amuser / faire des crêpes / 2 février

Communication

D. **Expliquez-vous!** Trouvez des excuses ou des raisons pour les situations suivantes. Utilisez les suggestions données ou vos propres idées.

MODÈLE: Vous êtes très fatigué(e).
 Je n'ai pas pu m'endormir.

1. Vous arrivez en cours en retard.   (se lever tard / ne pas se dépêcher / se coucher à une heure / se faire mal au pied)
2. Un(e) camarade de classe n'a pas fait ses devoirs.   (s'amuser hier soir / s'endormir sur ses livres / se reposer après dîner / avoir mal aux yeux / emmener un ami chez le dentiste)
3. Votre ami(e) a l'air malheureux (-euse).   (s'inquiéter trop / ne pas se détendre assez / ne pas se reposer ce week-end)
4. Vos amis n'ont pas voulu vous recevoir.   (ne pas se laver / ne pas s'habiller / vouloir se promener en ville)

E. **Encore des conseils.** Quels conseils donnez-vous à quelqu'un pour les problèmes suivants? Si vous voulez, utilisez les verbes de la liste suivante et des adverbes: **moins, plus souvent, plus tôt, plus tard.**

se lever	se détendre	se réveiller
se coucher	s'amuser	s'endormir
se reposer	se promener	s'inquiéter

MODÈLE: Un ami ne veut pas aller en cours.
Promenons-nous!

1. Vos amis n'ont pas d'énergie.
2. Un(e) ami(e) est trop sérieux (-euse).
3. Vos ami(e)s veulent sortir avec vous.
4. Vos ami(e)s ont peur de ne pas réussir aux examens.
5. Vos parents n'ont pas le temps de prendre le petit déjeuner.
6. Votre camarade de chambre veut éviter les maladies.

F. **Hier.** Interrogez un(e) camarade de cours et ensuite racontez sa journée d'hier aux autres. Utilisez les mots de la liste d'activités et des adverbes de temps (**tôt, de bonne heure, tard**) ou indiquez l'heure.

se lever	rentrer
se laver	se reposer
s'habiller	dîner avec
prendre le petit déjeuner	se coucher
partir pour l'université	s'endormir
étudier à la bibliothèque	???

G. **Questions personnelles.** Le week-end dernier.

1. Est-ce que vous vous êtes réveillé(e) tôt le week-end dernier? A quelle heure?
2. A quelle heure vous êtes-vous levé(e) samedi? dimanche?
3. Vous êtes-vous détendu(e)? Comment?
4. Vos ami(e)s se sont-ils / se sont-elles bien amusé(e)s chez vous? Qu'est-ce que vous avez fait ensemble?
5. Comment est-ce que vous vous êtes habillé(e) dimanche?
6. De quoi est-ce que vous vous êtes occupé(e)?

Communiquons

Parler de sa santé

www

The French are extremely health-conscious. For several years, eating healthful foods has been a major concern and each French person averages about six visits to the doctor a year. In addition to traditional medical care, the French believe in homeopathy, visits to health spas, and a close relationship with their pharmacist. Health spas (**stations thermales**) are so widely accepted that Social Security will reimburse a stay that was ordered by a doctor and approved by an examining board. Seeking such care is called **faire une cure** and the patients, **curistes**. Some of these spas are known in the U.S. because they also bottle their water for export (**Vichy, Evian**). Using sea water for therapy is also popular and is called **thalassothérapie.**

One tradition that remains in France is to blame a general malaise on one's liver. Because of the rich foods and alcoholic beverages that they consume, the French still complain of the stereotypical **crise de foie.**

Centre de Thalassothérapie

thalgo la baule

Dispense des cures de Thalassothérapie classiques (Médicale, Remise en Forme, Diététique) ou spécifiques (Anti-tabac, Vithalgo, Thalgo Beauté) pour prévenir ou traiter Troubles Ostéo-articulaires, Affections Cardio-vasculaires, Stress, Surmenage, Surcharges pondérales...

Hébergement privilégié à l'Hotel ROYAL**** du Groupe Lucien BARRIERE relié directement au Centre, ainsi que nombreuses possibilités hôtelières, para-hôtelières et locatives.

Possibilités forfaits séminaires sur demande.

Expressions

▶ **On parle de la santé.**

Comment allez-vous?	*How are you?*
Je vais bien.	*I'm fine.*
Je ne vais pas bien.	*I'm not well.*
Comme ci, comme ça.	*So-so.*
Mes grands-parents sont en bonne santé.	*My grandparents are in good health.*
Je suis malade.	*I'm sick.*
Vous sentez-vous bien?	*Do you feel well?*
Non, je me sens un peu fatigué.	*No, I feel a little tired.*
A tes souhaits!	*Bless you!*

▶ **On indique où on a mal.**

Les enfants ont mal au ventre.	*The children have a stomachache.*
Elle s'est cassé le bras quand elle est tombée.	*She broke her arm when she fell.*
Il s'est fait mal au genou dans un accident.	*He hurt his knee in an accident.*
Je me suis foulé le poignet.	*I sprained my wrist.*

Interaction   *Monique va chez le médecin.* ⊙

LE MÉDECIN: Comment allez-vous, Monique?

MONIQUE: Pas très bien. Depuis deux jours j'ai mal partout°.   *everywhere*

LE MÉDECIN: Vous avez de la fièvre? Je vais prendre votre température.

MONIQUE: J'ai mal au dos et j'ai toujours froid. Et je commence à avoir mal à la gorge.

LE MÉDECIN: C'est sans doute une petite grippe°. Déshabillez-vous; je vais vous ausculter°.   *flu*
                                                                                              examine

Activités

A.   Où est-ce que les personnages historiques suivants ont eu mal?

   MODÈLE: Marie Antoinette?
             Elle a eu mal au cou.

   1. Van Gogh
   2. Le Cyclope
   3. Jesse James
   4. Socrate
   5. Isaac Newton
   6. Pinocchio
   7. Le Capitaine Crochet *(Hook)*
   8. Quasimodo

B.   Répondez aux questions suivantes.

   1. Comment allez-vous aujourd'hui?
   2. En général, êtes-vous en bonne ou en mauvaise santé?
   3. Avez-vous été malade récemment? Avez-vous consulté un médecin?
   4. Comment vous sentez-vous maintenant?
   5. Avez-vous souvent mal? Où?
   6. Est-ce que vous vous êtes déjà cassé quelque chose? Que faisiez-vous quand vous vous êtes fait mal?

C.   Avec un(e) camarade de cours, jouez les scènes suivantes.

   1. Vous êtes chez le médecin. Parlez-lui de vos problèmes de santé.
   2. Vous avez séché votre classe de français hier. Inventez une excuse médicale et présentez-la à votre professeur.
   3. Vous avez mal aux dents. Téléphonez chez le dentiste et prenez rendez-vous *(make an appointment)* avec lui / elle.
   4. Vous travaillez dans une station thermale. Ecoutez les problèmes de vos curistes et donnez-leur de bons conseils.

Lecture culturelle

Avant la lecture

The largest private philanthropic organization dedicated to providing medical services is called **Médecins sans Frontières** *(Doctors Without Borders)* and is headquartered in France. It was founded in 1971 as a response to medical emergencies in various parts of the world.

Medical personnel are asked to volunteer for up to six months at a time. Those staying on site for at least three months receive a salary. The organization goes to areas that have been hit by a disaster, either natural (floods, earthquakes) or man-made (war). The name of the organization comes from the fact that aid is provided to everyone who needs it, regardless of politics, religion, or race.

Activités

A. **Cognates.** It is often said that people who study foreign languages increase their vocabulary in their native language. What English words do you know that have the same origin as the following words that appear in the reading passage?

1. secours
2. belligérance
3. terre
4. urgence
5. exode
6. se poursuivent
7. dons
8. fournir

B. **Skimming.** Read the following passage without looking up any words. Then make two lists in English containing the following information.

1. types of disasters that cause medical problems
2. activities of **Médecins sans Frontières** in the field

Médecins sans Frontières   WWW

« *L*es Médecins sans Frontières apportent leur secours° à toutes les victimes de catastrophes naturelles, d'accidents collectifs et de situations de belligérance, sans aucune° discrimination de race, de politique, de religion ou de philosophie.»

help

any

5   (Extrait de la Charte de Médecins sans Frontières)

L'association Médecins sans Frontières (MSF) a été créée° le 20 décembre 1971 par deux groupes de médecins: les uns revenus de mission au Biafra avec la Croix-Rouge Internationale, les autres rentrés du Bangladesh après les inondations° causées en 1970 par un raz-de-marée°. Dès° le début, l'éthique de
10 l'organisation est affirmée dans sa charte: « soigner° de manière désintéressée et sans discrimination… ».

created

floods / tidal wave / From
to treat

Médecins sans
Frontières en Somalie

    Aujourd'hui les Médecins sans Frontières sont présents dans beaucoup de pays du monde. En se développant, l'association a augmenté° son aide médicale et a diversifié son rôle: interventions dans des situations diverses comme les con-
15 flits armés, les camps de réfugiés, les catastrophes naturelles et les régions sous-médicalisées.

    Quand un conflit éclate° dans un point du globe, les équipes° de Médecins sans Frontières, composées de chirurgiens°, d'anesthésistes, d'infirmières°, inter-viennent° très rapidement pour apporter les premiers soins° aux blessés°, dis-
20 tinguer les cas critiques et assurer le traitement médico-chirurgical souvent avec des moyens° rudimentaires. Il faut, par exemple, installer une salle d'opération dans une école, dans un parking ou sous une tente.

    Médecins sans Frontières a répondu au terrible problème des réfugiés. L'arrivée massive de milliers de personnes, souvent en mauvaise santé, dans des
25 régimes parfois° hostiles, pose des problèmes spécifiques: il faut développer rapidement des soins° curatifs, prévoir l'hygiène et l'assainissement° du camp, prévoir et enrayer° les épidémies favorisées par les mauvaises conditions sani-taires, éduquer la population et former des auxiliaires médicaux parmi les réfugiés.

30   L'intervention de Médecins sans Frontières est aussi cruciale dans le cas de catastrophes naturelles. Tremblement de terre° à Mexico, raz-de-marée au Bangladesh, inondations en Bolivie, éruption volcanique en Colombie, guerre civile en Bosnie et au Ruanda... sont des événements difficiles à prévoir. Ils de-mandent la mobilisation immédiate de chirurgiens et spécialistes en médecine
35 d'urgence°.

    Qui sont les Médecins sans Frontières? Médecins, infirmières, laborantins°, anesthésistes, sage-femmes°, chirurgiens,... sont aux avant-postes° des conflits et

increased

breaks out / teams
surgeons / nurses
intervene / first aid / injured

means

sometimes
treatments / disinfection
stem

Tremblement... *Earth-quake*

emergency
lab technicians
midwives / outposts

des cataclysmes. Désintéressés°, ils sont chaque° année sept cents à mettre leur   *Neutral / each*
professionnalisme au service d'autres hommes en détresse. Les compétences re-
40 quises° varient selon les postes, mais les diplômes, l'expérience professionnelle   *required*
sur le terrain, la bonne connaissance de langues étrangères sont les principaux
critères de recrutement.

Le financement de Médecins sans Frontières est assuré à 75% par des dons°   *gifts*
individuels. Cette autonomie financière est la garantie de l'indépendance morale
45 de l'organisation. Les autres 25% proviennent° des financements des pro-   *come from*
grammes médicaux spécifiques par des organisations internationales comme le
Haut Commissariat aux Réfugiés des Nations unies, par exemple.

Comme l'indique la charte de l'association, les Médecins sans Frontières
sont «anonymes et bénévoles°. Ils n'attendent de l'exercice de leur activité au-   *volunteer*
50 cune satisfaction personnelle ou collective. Ils mesurent les risques et les périls
des missions qu'ils accomplissent et ne réclameront°… aucune compensation   *will demand*
autre que celle que l'association sera en mesure de leur fournir°.»   *provide*

(Adapté d'une annonce de presse de Médecins sans Frontières)

URGENCE AU SOUDAN.
AIDEZ-NOUS ! »»

*Tous les malheurs s'abattent à la fois
sur un des pays
les plus pauvres du monde.*

Un million et demi de personnes sans abri dans ce
pays déjà meurtri par la guerre et la famine.
Les journaux , la radio, la télévision vous en parlent.
Mais la réalité est pire, avec les cris, les pleurs et
l'insoutenable silence, qui succède au désastre...

Les Médecins sans Frontières y sont.
La tâche est immense et les moyens
sont infimes.
Mais ils savent que vous êtes avec eux.
Merci infiniment.

Rony Brauman

R. BRAUMAN
Président de Médecins sans Frontières

*AGISSEZ
DES AUJOURD'HUI*

Après la lecture

Questions sur le texte

1. Pourquoi l'organisation s'appelle-t-elle « Médecins sans Frontières » ?
2. Dans quelles situations est-ce que les MSF interviennent ?
3. Comment sont composées les équipes de MSF ?
4. Quels problèmes existent dans les camps de réfugiés ?
5. Quelles catastrophes naturelles demandent l'aide des MSF ?
6. Quel genre de personnes sont les MSF ?
7. Qui paye pour les missions des MSF ?
8. Est-ce que les MSF sont bien payés ? Pourquoi font-ils cela ?

Activités

A. Où est-ce qu'on a eu les désastres suivants?

1. un tremblement de terre   a. Ethiopie
2. un raz-de-marée   b. Johnstown en Pennsylvanie
3. une inondation   c. Irlande
4. une éruption volcanique   d. San Francisco
5. une famine   e. Pompéi
6. un exode   f. Krakatoa

B. Répondez aux questions suivantes.

1. A quelle organisation américaine ou internationale est-ce que MSF ressemblent? Quelles sont les différences entre les deux?
2. Avez-vous envie d'appartenir à une organisation comme MSF? A quelles activités des MSF pouvez-vous participer? Avez-vous déjà aidé une société bénévole? A quelle organisation donnez-vous de l'argent?
3. Quels désastres récents ont nécessité une intervention médicale importante?
4. Est-ce que le gouvernement des Etats-Unis aide les autres pays «sans aucune discrimination» politique? Etes-vous pour ou contre cette idée?

Vocabulaire

Noms / Pronoms

bouche	mouth	gorge	throat
bras	arm	jambe	leg
cheveux	hair	journée	day
cheville	ankle	main	hand
corps	body	maladie	illness
cou	neck	nez	nose
coude	elbow	nuit	night
croix verte	green cross	œil	eye
cuisse	thigh	oreille	ear
dent	tooth	partie	part
dentiste	dentist	pharmacie de garde	emergency drugstore
doigt	finger	pharmacie de nuit	all-night drugstore
dos	back	pied	foot
épaule	shoulder	prise de sang	blood test
fièvre	fever	ventre	stomach
genou	knee	yeux	eyes

Verbes

amener	to bring	s'habiller	to get dressed
appeler	to call	s'inquiéter	to be worried
emmener	to take	s'occuper de	to take care of
enlever	to remove	se brosser	to brush
faire de l'exercice	to exercise	se coucher	to go to bed
éviter	to avoid	se dépêcher	to hurry
examiner	to examine	se déshabiller	to get undressed
inquiéter	to worry	se détendre	to relax
lever	to raise	se laver	to get washed
posséder	to own	se lever	to get up
promener	to walk	se promener	to go for a walk
répéter	to repeat	se rappeler	to remember
sécher	to dry	se reposer	to rest
sécher un cours	to cut class	se réveiller	to wake up
s'amuser	to have fun	se sentir	to feel
s'appeler	to be called	se trouver	to find oneself
s'endormir	to fall asleep		

Adjectifs / Adverbes

bien	well	régulièrement	regularly
davantage	more	tard	late
généralement	generally	tôt	early
grave	serious	vers	toward
hypocondriaque	hypochondriac		

Expressions

aller mieux	to feel better	être en bonne santé	to be in good health
alors	then	être en mauvaise santé	to be in bad health
avoir bonne mine	to look good	faire un régime	to be on a diet
avoir mal à	to hurt	ne pas fermer l'œil	not to sleep a wink
avoir mauvaise mine	to look sick	se faire mal à	to hurt one's…
de la nuit	all night long	se porter bien	to be in good health …
être au régime	to be on a diet		

Les sports

Commençons

Grammaire

Communiquons

Lecture culturelle

Vocabulaire

Dans les Alpes

Objectives

Language

Vocabulary for sports • The sounds / s / and / z / • **-ire** verbs • Demonstrative pronouns • Possessive pronouns

Culture

The **Tour de France** • Sports • **Le snowboard**

Communication

Talking about sports • Expressing ownership • Pointing out something • Expressing precise quantities

Commençons

Chez Ernest à l'heure du Tour de France

WWW

Robert et Jean prennent l'apéritif dans leur café préféré et ils regardent les informations à la télévision. Ils attendent le reportage sur le Tour de France. Ernest, le patron, vient de servir un pastis et lève son verre à leur santé.

ERNEST: A la vôtre, Messieurs!

ROBERT ET JEAN: A la tienne, Nénesse!

JEAN: Oh, regarde, ils vont montrer le film de l'étape d'aujourd'hui.

ROBERT: Celle d'hier était formidable! Le maillot jaune avait encore deux secondes d'avance à cent mètres de l'arrivée, mais il a perdu sa première place.

JEAN: J'ai lu dans *L'Equipe* que son contrôle anti-doping était négatif, et tout le monde dit qu'il va gagner aujourd'hui.

ERNEST: Est-ce que je vous sers un autre pastis? Vos verres sont vides.

ROBERT: Celui de Jean, oui, mais moi, je n'ai pas encore terminé le mien.

JEAN: Non, merci. J'ai soixante kilomètres à faire ce soir et il faut que je me dépêche parce que je n'aime pas conduire la nuit.

Etudions le dialogue

1. Où sont Robert et Jean?
2. Que font-ils?
3. Qu'est-ce que Nénesse leur dit?
4. Qu'est-ce qu'on va montrer à la télévision?
5. Qu'est-ce que le maillot jaune a fait?
6. Que boivent Robert et Jean?
7. Est-ce que Robert veut encore un pastis? Pourquoi pas?
8. Pourquoi est-ce que Jean ne veut plus de pastis?

Mots clés

informations *(f.)*	*the news*	**mètre** *(m.)*	*meter (39.4 inches)*
patron	*owner*	**place**	*place*
pastis	*anise-flavored alcoholic drink*	**lu (lire)**	*read*
verre	*glass*	**contrôle anti-doping**	*drug test*
A la vôtre!	*Here's to you! To your health!*	**négatif**	*negative*
A la tienne!	*Here's to you! To your health!*	**dit (dire)**	*says*
Nénesse	*(diminutive for Ernest)*	**gagner**	*to win*
étape *(f.)*	*stage*	**vide**	*empty*
celle	*that*	**celui**	*that*
maillot	*jersey*	**le mien**	*mine*
d'avance	*ahead*	**kilomètre** *(m.)*	*kilometer (0.62 miles)*

Faisons connaissance

The **Tour de France,** one of the world's major bicycle races, is on the minds of many French people each year during July. The race is a succession of day-long stages called **étapes.** Some are quite long and are run over flat countryside; others are much shorter and take place across steep mountainous terrain. The leader in the race, who wears a yellow jersey (**un maillot jaune**), is determined after each stage of the race by computing who has the lowest total time of all the competitors. The final winner of the Tour de France is the cyclist who has the lowest total time at the end of the race.

L'Equipe is a daily newspaper devoted entirely to sports. True devotees of the **Tour** rely on it for information during the race. In recent years, considerable emphasis has been placed on checking for drugs. As with all major sporting events, any drugs designed to enhance performance are illegal.

French television gives extensive coverage to the race. There are live broadcasts of each day's finish and filmed highlights on the evening news. Many French people go to cafés to watch the coverage with their friends. While there, they might order a **pastis,** a very popular drink, especially in southern France. It has a strong licorice flavor and is high in alcohol content.

Une étape du Tour de France

Enrichissons notre vocabulaire   www

Les sports *(Sports)*

l'alpinisme (m.)

le base-ball

le basketball

le catch

le deltaplane

l'équitation (f.)

le football

le football américain

le golf

la gymnastique

le hockey

le jogging

le patinage

la planche à roulettes

le roller

le ski

le ski nautique

le snowboard

le tennis

le volley-ball

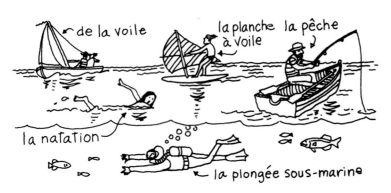

de la voile

la planche à voile

la pêche

la natation

la plongée sous-marine

Pratiquer un sport *(To play a sport)*

faire du, de la, de l'	*to do / play (a sport)*	le champion la championne	*champion*
jouer à	*to play (a sport)*	le championnat	*championship*
		l'équipe *(f.)*	*team*
nager	*to swim*	le joueur	*player*
patiner	*to skate*	sportif (-ive)	*athletic / fond of sports*

—Quels sports **pratiquez-vous?**   *What sports **do you play?***
—Je joue à la **pétanque.**   *I play **lawn bowling.***
—Je fais du **rugby.**   *I play **rugby.***
—Nous allons à la **chasse.**   *We go **hunting.***

—Nous adorons les **courses** *(f.)* de voiture / de bicyclette.

We love car races / bike races.

—Nous ne sommes pas sportifs; nous jouons seulement aux **cartes** *(f.)*!

We aren't athletic; we only play cards!

Prononciation   The sounds / s /, / z /, / sj / and / zj /

A. The distinction between the sounds / s / and / z / is very clear in French. A single letter **s** between two vowels is always pronounced / z /, while a double **s** represents / s /. This permits contrasts between words such as **le désert** and **le dessert.**

Repeat the following pairs of words, which have the same meanings in English and French, but vary between the sounds / s / and / z /.

English	French	English	French
philosophy	la philosophie	disagreeable	désagréable
dessert	le dessert	disobey	désobéir
curiosity	la curiosité	resemble	ressembler

Now repeat the following words, which contain the sound / s /, the sound / z /, or both.

ils choisissent / vous finissez / qu'il désobéisse / Nénesse / nous réussissons / la bise / tu laisses / la phrase / la boisson / la chasse / ennuyeuse / mes amis

B. In French, the sounds / s / and / z / may be followed by the / j / sound, which is very similar to the initial sound in *yes.* In English, equivalent words usually have a / ʃ / sound. In French, it is important to make two distinct sounds, / s / or / z /, then the / j / sound.

Repeat the following pairs of words, which contrast the sounds / s / + / j / and / z / + / j /.

/ sj /	/ zj /	/ sj /	/ zj /
nous passions	nous faisions	traditionnel	vous lisiez
l'expression	la télévision	les sciences	les yeux
une émission	parisien	une description	une allusion

Now, pronounce the following pairs of words, which contrast the / ʃ / sound in English with the / sj / sound in French.

English	French	English	French
patience	la patience	essential	essentiel
pollution	la pollution	national	national
exceptional	exceptionnel	action	l'action

Exercice

Read aloud the following sentences, paying attention to the difference between the / s / and / z / sounds and pronouncing the sound / sj / instead of / ʃ /.

1. Ma cousine a refusé son dessert.
2. Nous allons visiter une église suisse.
3. Les Parisiens préfèrent la conversation à la télévision.
4. Les Tunisiens ont réussi à supporter l'invasion romaine.
5. Il est essentiel que vous annonciez les résultats du championnat d'équitation.
6. Nous excusons son hypocrisie et sa curiosité excessives.

Grammaire

1. -ire verbs

You use verbs to describe actions.

A. Several verbs in French have infinitives that end in **-ire** and have similar conjugations.

écrire *(to write)*	conduire *(to drive)*
j'**écris**	je **conduis**
tu **écris**	tu **conduis**
il / elle / on **écrit**	il / elle / on **conduit**
nous **écrivons**	nous **conduisons**
vous **écrivez**	vous **conduisez**
ils / elles **écrivent**	ils / elles **conduisent**

B. To conjugate these verbs, you must learn which pronounced consonant appears in the plural forms. You then add the same endings used with **-ir** verbs like **servir** (Chapter 7).

Ils écrivent des poèmes.   Nous ne conduisons pas la nuit.

ECRIVEZ LE FRANÇAIS COMME LES FRANÇAIS

GRAM*R*

Détecteur d'erreurs grammaticales, correcteur orthographique & conjugueur

Mots clés   -ire *verbs*

conduire	*to drive*	nous conduisons
se conduire	*to behave*	nous nous conduisons
décrire	*to describe*	nous décrivons
dire	*to say / tell*	nous disons
écrire	*to write*	nous écrivons
lire	*to read*	nous lisons
produire	*to produce*	nous produisons
traduire	*to translate*	nous traduisons

Tout le monde **dit** qu'il va gagner.
Décrivez-moi l'étape d'aujourd'hui.
Ils **lisent** *L'Equipe* tous les jours.

Attention!

1. **Dire** has the irregular form **vous dites.**

2. **Dire** and **écrire** take indirect objects.

   Je vais dire cela **à mes amis.**
   Elle va écrire une lettre **au président.**

3. If a clause follows **dire, écrire,** or **lire,** you must use the conjunction **que** (**qu'**) plus the indicative.

   Elle dit **qu'**elle va faire de la gymnastique.

C. In other tenses (the imperfect and subjunctive), **-ire** verbs follow the normal rules.

   Je **conduisais** déjà quand j'avais quinze ans.
   Elle veut que nous **lisions** ce livre.

D. The past participles of **-ire** verbs vary somewhat.

(se) conduire	**conduit**	lire	**lu**
décrire	**décrit**	produire	**produit**
dire	**dit**	traduire	**traduit**
écrire	**écrit**		

Mots clés   *Words often used with* -ire *verbs*

On écrit et on traduit...

un conte	*tale*	de la poésie	*poetry*
une phrase	*sentence*	un texte	*text*
une pièce	*play*		

On dit...   On lit...

une bêtise / des bêtises	*dumb thing(s)*	un journal / des journaux	*newspaper(s)*
un mensonge	*lie*	un magazine	*magazine*
la vérité	*truth*	une revue	*magazine*

Langue

A. Un voyage en Martinique. Mettez les verbes au temps indiqué entre parenthèses.

1. On produit du sucre ici. *(passé composé)*
2. Ils lisent un bon roman pendant le match de tennis. *(imparfait)*
3. Elles écrivent une carte postale. *(futur proche)*
4. Elles disent qu'elles adorent le ski nautique. *(passé composé)*
5. A l'hôtel nous avons écrit trois lettres. *(présent)*
6. J'ai lu le journal de Fort-de-France. *(imparfait)*
7. Vous me décrivez votre voyage. *(impératif)*
8. Vous avez dit que vous allez retourner en Martinique? *(présent)*

B. De la poésie. Faites des phrases avec les mots donnés, en faisant tous les changements nécessaires.

1. Jacques et Marie / écrire / poèmes
2. Luc / les / lire / hier
3. Je / les / traduire / français
4. Louise / dire / ils / être / bon
5. Il / être / possible / ils / écrire / pièce / aussi
6. Vouloir / vous / écrire / poésie?

Culture   **WWW**

C. Il n'y a pas que le vin! Certaines régions francophones sont connues pour leurs produits. Regardez les listes, et identifiez les régions suivantes avec leur produit.

MODÈLE: En Suisse *En Suisse, on produit du chocolat.*

1. En Bourgogne		a.	lait / crème
2. En Normandie		b.	moutarde
3. En Bretagne		c.	huile d'olive
4. En Provence		d.	fruits de mer
5. En Alsace		e.	bière
6. En Belgique		f.	choucroute

D. La lecture. On a interrogé 1550 étudiants sur leurs lectures au cours des sept derniers jours. Faites des phrases indiquant les résultats.

MODÈLE: dictionnaire / 16%
               Seize pourcent des étudiants ont lu un dictionnaire.

1. un guide pratique		a.	46%
2. des poèmes		b.	44%
3. des magazines		c.	37%
4. un journal		d.	9%
5. un livre d'art		e.	8%
6. un roman		f.	3%

Communication

E. **Des descriptions.** Demandez à un(e) étudiant(e) de vous décrire les choses suivantes.

> MODÈLE: ta maison
>> Etudiant(e) 1: *Décris ta maison.*
>> Etudiant(e) 2: *Ma maison est grande et blanche.*

ta chambre	tes dernières vacances
ton (ta) petit(e) ami(e)	ton sport préféré
ta voiture	ton film préféré
ton professeur	ta pièce préférée

F. **Vos lectures.** Que lisez-vous? Qu'est-ce que vous avez lu récemment? Qu'est-ce que les autres personnes lisent? Donnez des titres *(titles).*

des journaux	des magazines de sport
des romans	un livre de français
des poèmes	des contes de...

1. Moi, je...
2. Mon (Ma) camarade de chambre...
3. En cours, nous...
4. Mes ami(e)s...
5. Mes parents...
6. Mes professeurs...

G. **Questions personnelles.** Vos habitudes.

1. Comment vous conduisiez-vous quand vous étiez petit(e)? Qu'est-ce que vous faisiez de méchant? Quelles bêtises disiez-vous?
2. Avez-vous écrit une lettre à une personne importante? A qui? Pourquoi?
3. Qu'est-ce que vous lisiez quand vous étiez jeune? Qu'est-ce que vous lisez maintenant?
4. Qui a écrit votre roman préféré? Votre chanson préférée?
5. Quel journal lisez-vous? Pourquoi? Quel magazine?
6. Quand avez-vous dit un mensonge?

II. Demonstrative pronouns

> You use demonstrative pronouns to refer to people or things already mentioned in the conversation, often to point them out or to make a distinction.

A. Demonstrative pronouns are similar to demonstrative adjectives (ce, cet, cette, ces) in that they point out something, but demonstrative pronouns *replace nouns.* They have the same number and gender as the nouns they replace.

	singular	*plural*
masculine	**celui**	**ceux**
feminine	**celle**	**celles**

B. Demonstrative pronouns have several equivalents in English, depending on how they are used *(this one, that one, these, those, the one[s])*. These pronouns are usually followed by one of two structures:

1. the suffixes **-ci** or **-là** to indicate degree of closeness.

> Ce livre-**ci** est bon, mais **celui-là** est ennuyeux.
> J'aime **cette** chanson-**ci**, mais je préfère **celle-là**.
> Donnez-moi **celle-ci** et **celle-là**.

2. the preposition **de**, which can show possession.

> —Vos verres sont vides?
> —**Celui de** Jean, oui.
> Ils vont montrer l'étape d'aujourd'hui. **Celle d'**hier était formidable.
> Préférez-vous l'équipe de Lyon ou **celle de** Marseille?

Ce qu'ils disent

When demonstrative pronouns refer to people, they can have a somewhat derogatory meaning.

Oh, **ceux-là,** je ne les aime pas.	*Those guys! I don't like them.*
Celui-là, il n'est jamais à l'heure.	*That character is never on time.*

Langue

A. A la bibliothèque. Dans les phrases suivantes, remplacez les mots en italique avec un pronom démonstratif.

MODÈLES: Donnez-moi *ce livre-là.*
   Donnez-moi celui-là.

   Voilà *les CD* de Berlioz.
   Voilà ceux de Berlioz.

1. Aimez-vous *les pièces* de Molière?
2. Je préfère *les poèmes* de Ronsard.
3. Nous allons traduire *ces phrases-ci.*
4. Avez-vous lu *ce roman-ci?*
5. Voltaire n'a pas écrit *ces lettres-là.*
6. Voulez-vous voir *le journal* de Montréal?
7. Où produit-on *les films* de Bertolucci?
8. Elles n'écoutent jamais *ces cassettes*-ci.

B. Où sont nos affaires? Dans les phrases ci-dessous, remplacez les mots en italique avec un pronom démonstratif pour indiquer la possession.

MODÈLE: Tu as perdu *le stylo* du professeur?
   Tu as perdu celui du professeur?

1. *La bicyclette* de Luc est là.
2. J'ai oublié *le courrier* de Marie.
3. *La planche à roulettes* de Tim n'est pas dans la rue.

4. *Le maillot* de Robert n'est pas dans sa valise.
5. Tu as trouvé *les rollers* de ma sœur?
6. Passez-moi *le verre* de Jacqueline.
7. J'ai laissé *les devoirs* de mon copain chez moi.
8. *Le portefeuille* de Marie est dans son sac.

C. **Faisons du sport.** Refaites les phrases suivantes en remplaçant les noms en italique par des pronoms démonstratifs.

1. *Ce sport-là* n'est pas très difficile.
2. *Les voitures de sport* des Italiens sont formidables!
3. *Ce joueur-là* me semble paresseux.
4. *Les montagnes* de Lyon ne sont pas assez grandes pour faire du ski.
5. *Les vêtements* des Galeries Lafayette sont excellents pour faire du sport.
6. *Ce magazine de catch-ci* est plein de bêtises.
7. Evite *les cigarettes* de mon père si tu veux jouer au football.
8. *Le français* des joueurs québécois est différent du *français* des joueurs marseillais.

Culture

D. **De grands mouvements artistiques.** Les tableaux *(paintings)* des artistes ci-dessous représentent quel mouvement artistique?

MODÈLE: Matisse *Ceux de Matisse représentent le fauvisme.*

1.	David	a.	le cubisme
2.	Delacroix	b.	le pointillisme
3.	Monet	c.	le primitivisme
4.	Seurat	d.	le classicisme
5.	Rousseau	e.	le romantisme
6.	Picasso	f.	l'impressionnisme
7.	Dali	g.	l'expressionnisme
8.	Rouault	h.	le surréalisme

Communication

E. **Conversation interrompue.** Au moment où vous interrompez *(interrupt)* une conversation, vous entendez les phrases suivantes. Imaginez ce que *(what)* le pronom démonstratif peut représenter.

MODÈLE: J'ai trouvé ceux de Marc dans ma voiture.
Il a trouvé les livres / les CD de Marc.

1. Vous avez goûté ceux-ci? Ils sont délicieux!
2. Ceux du professeur sont sur son bureau.
3. Celle-là n'est pas très économique.
4. Moi, je préfère celui-ci.
5. Celle-là n'est pas assez jolie pour aller dîner.
6. Ils ont traduit celles-là en français.

F. **Vos achats.** Qu'est-ce que vous achetez? Vous pouvez commencer la réponse avec «**Moi, j'achète…**».

1. Les chemises de Van Heusen ou les chemises d'Hawaii?
2. Les CD de Hootie ou les CD de Dolly Parton?
3. Les jeans de Calvin Klein ou les jeans de Levi Strauss?
4. Les chaînes stéréo du Japon ou les chaînes stéréo d'Allemagne?
5. Le journal de New York ou le journal de chez vous?
6. Les robes de Coco Chanel ou les robes de Sears?
7. Les ordinateurs d'Apple ou les ordinateurs d'IBM?
8. Les frites de McDonald's ou les frites de Burger King?

G. **Questions personnelles.** Vos préférences.

1. Préférez-vous les cours du matin ou les cours de l'après-midi?
2. Regardez-vous les reportages sportifs d'ABC, de CBS, de NBC, ou d'ESPN?
3. Aimez-vous mieux la musique des années quatre-vingt-dix ou la musique des années cinquante?
4. Vous voudriez avoir les cheveux de Michael Jordan ou les cheveux de Dennis Rodman?
5. Avez-vous envie d'aller aux concerts de Pavarotti ou aux concerts de R.E.M.?
6. Vous aimez recevoir les lettres de votre petit(e) ami(e) ou les lettres d'Ed McMahon?

III. Possessive pronouns

You use possessive pronouns to show ownership of something already mentioned in the conversation.

A. Possessive pronouns replace possessive adjectives and the items possessed.

—**Vos verres** sont vides?
—Non, je n'ai pas encore terminé **le mien**.

	m. sing.	f. sing.	m. pl.	f. pl.	English
1st sing.	le mien	la mienne	les miens	les miennes	mine
2nd sing.	le tien	la tienne	les tiens	les tiennes	yours
3rd sing.	le sien	la sienne	les siens	les siennes	his / hers / its
1st pl.	le nôtre	la nôtre	les nôtres		ours
2nd pl.	le vôtre	la vôtre	les vôtres		yours
3rd pl.	le leur	la leur	les leurs		theirs

Mon sport préféré est la gymnastique; **le sien,** c'est l'équitation.
Elle n'aime pas cette planche à voile. Elle préfère **la sienne.**
Mes parents habitent à Paris. Et **les vôtres?**

B. Remember that possessive adjectives agree in gender and number with the thing possessed, not with the possessor as in English. The same is true of possessive pronouns.

son verre = *his glass or her glass*   **le sien** = *his or hers*

Attention!

1. Note that with all possessive pronouns, *It's . . .* and *They are . . .* translate as **C'est...** and **Ce sont... Ils** and **Elles** are not used, except with the expression of ownership in the **être à** + *noun or pronoun* and **appartenir à** constructions.

—C'est celui de Pierre?
—Oui, **c'est** le sien.

—Est-ce que **ce sont** vos livres ou les leurs?
—Ce sont **les miens.**

—A qui sont ces skis?
—**Ils** sont à moi. / **Ils** m'appartiennent.

2. Don't forget that **le** and **les** combine with any preceding **à** or **de** in the ways you studied in Chapter 4.

As-tu téléphoné **à** tes parents? Moi, je vais téléphoner **aux** miens.
Vous voulez que je parle **de** mon avenir, mais vous ne parlez pas **du** vôtre.
Leur vélo est à côté **des** nôtres.

Langue

A. Nos possessions. Dans les phrases suivantes, remplacez les mots en italique par des pronoms possessifs.

1. Je n'aime pas *tes vêtements.*
2. Veux-tu regarder *mes photos?*
3. *Ses chaussures* sont grandes.
4. *Mes disquettes* sont tombées dans l'eau.
5. Le facteur a oublié *celui de Jacques.*
6. Elle a retrouvé *son journal.*
7. *Vos gâteaux* sont excellents.
8. J'ai perdu *leur parapluie.*

B. Pas de chance! Complétez les phrases suivantes avec un pronom possessif.

1. J'ai fait mes devoirs; tu n'as pas fait _____ !
2. Il n'a pas de voiture; il veut que je lui prête _____ .
3. Ils viennent de recevoir leur courrier, mais nous n'avons pas encore reçu _____ .
4. C'est son verre; donnez-moi _____ .
5. Les Baillard ont vendu leur maison, mais M. Ducharme n'a pas pu vendre _____ .
6. Garçon! Ce n'est pas ma boisson. C'est _____ .

Culture

C. **Comparaison de cultures.** Comparez les phénomènes suivants comme ils existent en France et aux Etats-Unis. Utilisez les adjectifs donnés ou vos propres idées.

MODÈLE: voitures: petit / grand
Les leurs sont petites; les nôtres sont grandes.

1. églises: ancien / moderne
2. nourriture: bon marché *(cheap)* / cher
3. courses de bicyclettes: très apprécié / peu connu
4. conducteurs: prudent / agressif
5. vacances: moins long / plus long
6. billets d'avion: bon marché / cher

Communication

D. **Des descriptions.** Avec un(e) camarade de cours, employez des pronoms possessifs pour décrire les choses suivantes. Indiquez les différences et les similarités aux autres étudiants.

MODÈLE: tes week-ends
Les miens ne sont pas assez longs.

ton équipe de football de lycée
La nôtre perd ses matchs.

1. ta famille
2. ton appartement
3. ton (ta) petit(e) ami(e)
4. tes CD
5. tes vacances
6. tes professeurs de lycée
7. ta résidence
8. tes sports préférés
9. tes magazines préférés
10. tes cours

E. **Nos villes.** Séparez-vous en groupes de deux et comparez les villes où vous êtes né(e)s. Utilisez les suggestions données ou vos propres idées.

MODÈLES: avoir beaucoup / peu de musées
Etudiant(e) 1: *Ma ville a beaucoup de musées.*
Etudiant(e) 2: *La mienne a peu de musées.*

être calme / avoir du bruit
Etudiant(e) 1: *Ma ville est très calme.*
Etudiant(e) 2: *Il y a beaucoup de bruit dans la mienne.*

être petite / grande
être loin / près des montagnes
avoir peu / beaucoup de cinémas
avoir de bons / mauvais
restaurants

avoir beaucoup / peu de
pollution
avoir beaucoup / peu de parcs
être loin / près de la plage
???

F. **Questions personnelles.** Votre université.

1. Comment s'appelait votre lycée? Et celui de votre petit(e) ami(e)?
2. Est-ce que votre université est trop grande ou trop petite?
3. Il y a souvent du bruit dans les résidences, et dans la vôtre?
4. Comment est votre chambre? Petite ou grande? Bien rangée?
5. Est-ce que vos week-ends sont agréables?
6. Est-ce que vos profs sont sympathiques? Qu'est-ce qu'ils n'aiment pas?

Communiquons

Utiliser le système métrique

WWW

To function in most French-speaking countries, you must be familiar with the metric system, the official system of measurement in most of the world. It was first established by the French National Assembly in 1791, and the International Bureau of Weights and Measures is still located in France, just outside Paris in Sèvres. The meter, the basic unit of length, is defined by the wavelength of krypton, whereas the kilogram, the basic unit of weight, is defined by a block of platinum that is housed at the bureau.

The following comparisons will help you do conversions from the U.S. system to the metric system and vice versa.

Expressions

▶ **On exprime le poids** *(weight)*.

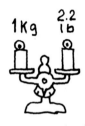

1. Here are some comparisons between metric weights and weights in the American system.

   28 grammes (g) = *1 ounce*   100 grammes = *4 ounces*
   454 grammes = *1 pound*   1 kilogramme (kg) = *2.2 pounds*
   500 grammes = une livre

2. To convert weights from the American system to the metric system and vice versa, use the following calculations as a guide.

   ? grammes = *3 ounces*
   Multipliez 28 par 3. Cela fait 84 grammes.

   50 kilogrammes = *? pounds*
   Multipliez 50 par 2,2. Cela fait 110 *pounds*.

3. The following expressions are used for weight.

   Je pèse quatre-vingts kilos.   *I weigh eighty kilos.*
   Ça coûte vingt francs le kilo.   *That costs twenty francs a kilo.*

▶ **On exprime la longueur** *(length)*.

1. The following are some comparisons between metric lengths and those of the American system.

   2,54 centimètres (cm) = *1 inch*   1 centimètre = *about 0.4 inches*
   30 centimètres = *about 1 foot*   1 mètre = *about 39.4 inches*
   0,94 mètre (m) = *about 1 yard*   1 kilomètre = *about 0.62 miles*
   1,6 kilomètres (km) = *about 1 mile*

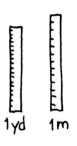

2. To convert lengths from the metric system to the American system and vice versa, use the following calculations as a guide.

? mètres = *5 feet 8 inches*
5 feet 8 inches = 68 *inches.* Multipliez 68 par 2,54.
Cela fait 172,72 centimètres. Divisez par 100. Cela fait 1,73 mètres ou un mètre soixante-treize.

525 kilomètres = *? miles*
Multipliez 525 par 0,62. Cela fait 325,50 ou 325 *miles* et demi.

3. These expressions are used for length or distance in French.

Paris est à 5.000 km d'ici.	*Paris is 5,000 kilometers from here.*
Ils habitent à 50 km de chez nous.	*They live 50 kilometers from our house.*
Jacques fait presque deux mètres.	*Jacques is almost two meters tall.*
Elle mesure un mètre soixante.	*She is one meter sixty centimeters tall.*

▶ On exprime le volume.

1. Here are some comparisons between metric measurements of volume and those of the American system.

0,95 litre (l) = *1 quart*   1 litre = *1.06 quarts*
3,8 litres = *1 gallon*   25 centilitres (cl) = *about 1 cup*

2. To convert measurements of volume from the metric system to the American system and vice versa, refer to the following calculations.

? litres = *20 gallons*
Multipliez 20 par 3,8. Cela fait 76 litres.

0,75 litre = *? quarts*
Multipliez 0,75 par 1,06. Cela fait .795 *quarts.*

3. The following expression is used for miles per gallon.

Ma nouvelle voiture fait du 8 aux 100 km.	*My new car uses 8 liters (of gas) per 100 kilometers.*

▶ On exprime la température.

1. The following are some comparisons between the Celsius and Fahrenheit scales for measuring temperatures.

0° Celsius (C) = *32° Fahrenheit (F)*
100° C = *212° F*

2. To convert temperatures from the Celsius scale to the Fahrenheit scale, use the following formulas as guides.

40° C = ? F
degrés Fahrenheit = 9/5 C + 32
Multipliez 40 par 9 et divisez par 5. Cela fait 72.
   Ajoutez *(Add)* 32. Cela fait 104° F.

? C = 68° F
degrés Celsius = 5/9 (F − 32)
68° moins 32 font 36. Multipliez 36 par 5 et divisez
   par 9. Cela fait 20° C.

3. The following expressions are used with temperatures.

Ma fille a trente-neuf.	*My daughter has a temperature of thirty-nine degrees Celsius.*
Il fait trente degrés aujourd'hui.	*It is thirty degrees Celsius out today.*

(thermomètre)
—50 } Il fait très chaud.
—40
—30 } Il fait chaud.
—20 } Il fait bon. / Il fait frais.
—10
—0 } Il fait froid.

Interaction

Monsieur Gosselin et son fils font des courses à l'hypermarché.

M. GOSSELIN: Va acheter un rosbif pendant que je prends deux kilos de pommes de terre.

SON FILS: Pour nous cinq, quel poids est-ce qu'il faut?

M. GOSSELIN: Oh, entre deux kilos et deux kilos cinq cents.

SON FILS: N'oublie pas non plus un litre de lait et une demi-livre de beurre.

M. GOSSELIN: Tu as raison. Et il nous faut aussi une bouteille de vin d'Alsace et 600 grammes de gruyère.

SON FILS: Chic! Maman va faire aussi une fondue.

Activités

A. Quelle unité de mesure détermine le prix des choses suivantes en France? Choisissez parmi *(among)* les possibilités données.

MODÈLE: du café à l'épicerie   *les 500 grammes*

3 ou 5 centilitres	le kilogramme
le litre	75 centilitres
le kilomètre	100 grammes
25 ou 33 centilitres	25 centilitres

1.	des bananes	7.	du gigot
2.	une bière au café	8.	du fromage
3.	des bonbons	9.	des crevettes
4.	un vin de qualité	10.	de l'essence *(gasoline)*
5.	un vin de table	11.	l'apéritif au café
6.	un pichet de vin au restaurant	12.	un billet de train

B. Répondez aux questions suivantes.

1. Combien pesez-vous en kilos? Combien mesurez-vous?
2. A combien de kilomètres habitez-vous de la maison de vos parents? de l'université?
3. En Amérique, on mesure la consommation d'une voiture en *miles per gallon*. En France, c'est en litres aux 100 kilomètres. Combien est-ce que votre voiture consomme?
4. Quelle est la température normale d'une personne en degrés Celsius? Quelle température avez-vous eue quand vous étiez malade?
5. Est-ce qu'il fait beau aujourd'hui? Combien fait-il en degrés Celsius?

Lecture culturelle

Avant la lecture

WWW

France has a multitude of winter resorts that attract not only French people but also tourists from all over the world. In addition to resorts such as Megève and Courchevel that have been popular for several decades, many new places have shown up on the map in the sixties and seventies. They have been developed to

Le snowboard

accommodate the increasing domestic and foreign demand, and many of them, especially those in the Alps, have been built at high elevations in order to allow for snow sports in the summer. Skiing remains the most popular snow sport, but more and more people are trading in their regular skis for monoskis and snowboards.

Activités

A. In the following reading, you can find names of sports that are the same in French and in English. Prepare a list of other sports you know that are the same in both languages. Point out any spelling differences.

B. Scan the following reading to find the possessive and demonstrative adjectives on the one hand, and the possessive and demonstrative pronouns on the other.

Le snowboard

out a commencé aux USA au début° des années 70. Des pionniers ont pris des planches° en bois°, ont fait un trou° et ont fixé une corde° pour la faire tourner: Le «Snurfer» (*snow* + *surf*) était né!
En Europe, comme aux Etats-Unis, les premières personnes qui ont fait du
5 snowboard ont été des surfeurs et des skateboarders fatigués des hivers rigoureux qui les empêchaient° de pratiquer leurs sports. En 1974 José Fernandès a ramené° le premier snowboard des USA. Il est devenu un des premiers champions professionnels de ce nouveau sport, et aujourd'hui, à 32 ans, il travaille en collaboration avec la fédération internationale de snowboard. Quand il
10 parle des débuts° difficiles de ce sport, il raconte qu'avec ses amis, il donnait des gâteaux et du vin aux employés des stations de ski° pour qu'ils leur permettent de monter en haut des pistes° avec leurs snowboards. Il constate° comment d'un extrême à l'autre, de compétitions° en compétitions, le snowboard a progressé de façon constante. Le nombre d'adeptes est éloquent, et Fernandès pense
15 comme beaucoup d'autres que le siècle° prochain sera celui du snowboard dans les stations de sports d'hiver. Avec d'autres passionnés°, il n'hésite pas à affirmer qu'un jour, il y aura plus de surfeurs que de skieurs, et il pense que cela s'explique parce que les enfants ne veulent pas faire ce que les parents ont fait. Il croit que ceci est une règle° universelle dans le sport comme ailleurs°. Il est
20 également certain que le sport va continuer à se transformer, un peu comme le rock 'n' roll, et que seulement les initiés° vont être capables de suivre tous ces changements.
De façon plus sérieuse, les adeptes du snowboard sont aussi convaincus° que leur sport va bientôt devenir olympique. Ils sont naturellement enchantés de
25 penser qu'il va recevoir cette reconnaissance° officielle internationale, mais ils craignent° aussi qu'elle soit le résultat d'un grand succès économique et que le sport n'ait pas encore eu le temps de trouver sa véritable° identité.
Il serait dommage que le snowboard devienne un sport établi avant d'avoir terminé sa croissance°. Que ce soit° pour le ski, pour le snowboard ou pour un
30 autre sport qui n'a pas encore été inventé, il est clair que les Français s'intéressent de plus en plus aux sports d'hiver qui ne sont pas encore à la portée de toutes les bourses°, mais qui attirent° de plus en plus de familles qui ont besoin de s'évader° une dizaine de jours l'hiver pour se remettre en forme° et échapper° au stress de leur vie quotidienne°.

au... *at the beginning*
boards / en... *wooden /
hole / rope*

prevented
brought back

beginnings
stations... *ski resorts*
en... *to the top of the
slopes / points out /
events*

century
fanatics

rule / elsewhere

fans

convinced

recognition
are afraid
true

growth / Que... *Be it*

pocketbooks / attract
get away / se... *get back in
shape / escape / daily*

Après la lecture

Questions sur le texte

1. Qu'est-ce que les pionniers du snowboard ont utilisé au commencement?
2. Qu'est-ce qu'ils devaient faire pour pouvoir arriver en haut des pistes?
3. Pourquoi est-ce qu'on pense qu'il va y avoir bientôt plus de surfeurs que de skieurs?
4. Pourquoi est-ce que le snowboard va peut-être devenir très rapidement un sport olympique?
5. Pourquoi est-ce que de plus en plus de Français vont aux sports d'hiver?

Activités

A. Préparez une liste des différents sports olympiques d'été et d'hiver.

B. Débat en classe: Les avantages des vacances d'hiver *vs* les avantages des vacances d'été.

C. Mettez-vous en petits groupes et préparez une annonce publicitaire *(ad)* pour votre sport favori. Présentez les résultats à la classe.

Vocabulaire

Noms / Pronoms

alpinisme	mountain climbing	(le) mien	mine
base-ball	baseball	natation	swimming
basket-ball	basketball	(le) nôtre	ours
bêtise	dumb thing	pastis	pastis (licorice-flavored drink)
cartes	cards		
catch	wrestling	patinage	skating
celle	the one	patron	owner
celui	the one	pêche	fishing
ceux	those	pétanque	lawn bowling
champion(ne)	champion	phrase	sentence
championnat	championship	pièce	play
chasse	hunting	place	place
conte	tale	planche à roulettes	skateboarding
contrôle	test	planche à voile	sailboarding
course de bicyclettes	bicycle race	plongée sous-marine	scuba diving
course de voitures	car race	poésie	poetry
deltaplane	hang gliding	revue	review
équipe	team	roller	in-line skating
équitation	horseback riding	rugby	rugby
étape	stage	(le) sien	his / hers
football américain	football	ski	skiing
golf	golf	ski nautique	waterskiing
gymnastique	gymnastics	snowboard	snowboarding
hockey	hockey	tennis	tennis
informations	the news	texte	text
jogging	jogging	(le) tien	yours
joueur	player	Tour de France	Tour de France
journal	TV news	vérité	truth
(le) leur	theirs	verre	glass
magazine	magazine	voile	sailing
maillot	jersey	volley-ball	volleyball
mensonge	lie	(le) vôtre	yours
mètre	meter		

Verbes

conduire	to drive	nager	to swim
décrire	to describe	patiner	to skate
dire	to say / to tell	pratiquer	to practice
écrire	to write	produire	to produce
gagner	to win	se conduire	to behave
jouer à	to play	traduire	to translate
lire	to read		

Adjectifs / Adverbes

négatif	negative
sportif	athletic
vide	empty

Expressions

A la tienne!	Cheers!	contrôle anti-doping	drug testing
A la vôtre!	Cheers!	d'avance	ahead

Chapitre 15

Les arts

Commençons

Grammaire

Communiquons

Lecture culturelle

Vocabulaire

Un peintre amateur

Objectives

Language
Vocabulary for musical instruments and fine arts • Intonation • Verbs followed by infinitives • Verbs followed by nouns • The pronouns y and **en**

Culture
The status of the French language • Movies and **le festival de Cannes**

Communication
Talking about the arts and other activities • Writing letters

Commençons

Le français en péril?   WWW

La revue française L'Express *a consacré un reportage à la question suivante:
«Sait-on encore parler le français?» Dans plusieurs articles, des journalistes ont
critiqué l'état du français parlé et écrit. Quelques semaines après, la revue a
publié la lettre d'un lecteur furieux. En voici un extrait.*

Messieurs:

Qu'est-il arrivé à la langue de Voltaire et de Gide? [...] Moi, je pense
que le mal vient surtout d'un enseignement insuffisant et je dois dire que
les fautes de français entendues à la radio et à la télévision me font souffrir, comme des atteintes à la beauté de notre langue. [...]

Je pense qu'il s'agit d'une volonté de certains milieux de contribuer à
la destruction d'une société par celle de sa langue. Parler et enseigner un
français correct est «bourgeois». Donc,... !

Moi, je dis que nous devons défendre notre langue car elle est vivace,
généreuse, et elle peut servir à toutes sortes d'usages.

Veuillez agréer, Messieurs, l'expression de mes salutations
distinguées.

André Florion

(Adapté du *Débat des lecteurs*, L'Express, numéros 1735 et 1736)

Etudions la lettre

1. De quoi est-ce qu'on parle dans cette lettre à *L'Express?*
2. D'où vient le problème selon le lecteur?
3. Comment est-ce que la radio et la télévision contribuent au problème?
4. Est-ce que le lecteur pense qu'on a tort ou qu'on a raison d'être
   «bourgeois»?
5. Finissez la phrase «Donc,... !».
6. Pourquoi faut-il défendre la langue française?

Mots clés

en péril	*in danger*	**publié (publier)**	*published*
consacré (consacrer)	*devoted*	**lecteur**	*reader*
plusieurs	*several*	**en**	*of it*
articles *(m.)*	*articles*	**extrait** *(m.)*	*excerpt*
critiqué (critiquer)	*criticized*	**arrivé (arriver)**	*happened*
état *(m.)*	*state*	**mal**	*damage*

surtout	*above all*	contribuer	*contribute*
enseignement	*teaching*	destruction	*destruction*
insuffisant	*insufficient*	enseigner	*to teach*
fautes *(f.)*	*mistakes*	correct	*correct*
souffrir	*suffer*	bourgeois	*bourgeois*
atteintes *(f.)*	*affronts*	donc	*therefore*
beauté	*beauty*	défendre	*defend*
il s'agit d'	*it's about / it's a question of*	vivace	*alive*
volonté	*will*	usages	*uses*
milieux *(m.)*	*circles*		

Faisons connaissance WWW

The French language is a constant preoccupation for the people who speak it daily. In France, many feel that their language has deteriorated: there is too much slang; people do not follow grammar rules; and too many words have been borrowed from English. Others think that languages are in a constant state of change and that it is useless to try to stop the process. The majority of the readers responding to that issue of *L'Express* agreed that the situation is deplorable. Yet a move to simplify French spelling, promoted by the government and endorsed by the **Académie française,** has been abandoned.

The French language is also an issue in other countries. Belgium is administratively divided into areas where one of two languages is official—French or Dutch, with the city of Brussels being the only officially bilingual area. A conflict exists between French and Dutch speakers, and it is so intense that it has led to riots in the past.

The province of Quebec in Canada has undergone profound changes. While the country is bilingual, the province has established French as its official language. For example, non-English-speaking immigrants must send their children to schools where classes are taught in French.

In Louisiana, several active groups have been working for years to reestablish the value of using French. The body of poetry, prose, music, and journalism in French is quite significant.

Enrichissons notre vocabulaire

Des instruments de musique *(Musical instruments)*

un orchestre / les instruments *(m.)*

un violon — une guitare — une flûte — un violoncelle — une trompette — le chef d'orchestre — un piano

—De quel instrument **jouez-vous?**	*What instrument do you **play?***
—Je joue **du trombone.**	*I play the trombone.*

Des métiers *(m.)* artistiques *(Careers in the arts)*

Les **musiciens** *(m.)* écrivent des **opéras** *(m.)* et des **symphonies** *(f.)*.	*Musicians write **operas** and **symphonies**.*
Les **écrivains** *(m.)* produisent des **œuvres** *(f.)* **littéraires**.	*Writers produce **literary works**.*
Les **auteurs** *(m.)* **dramatiques** font des **pièces**: des **drames** *(m.)*, des **comédies** *(f.)*, des **tragédies** *(f.)*, et des **comédies musicales**.	*Playwrights write **plays**: **dramas, comedies, tragedies,** and **musicals**.*
Les **danseurs** et les **danseuses** font de la **danse classique** (du **ballet**).	*Dancers perform **ballet**.*
Les **peintres** *(m.)* font des **tableaux** *(m.)*: des **peintures** *(f.)* à l'**huile** *(f.)* et des **aquarelles** *(f.)*.	*Painters make **paintings**: oil **paintings** and **watercolors**.*
Les **sculpteurs** *(m.)* font des **sculptures** *(f.)* en **pierre** *(f.)* et en **bronze** *(m.)*	*Sculptors make **stone** and **bronze sculptures**.*

LE CHANT DU MONDE LDC 278 943
EDITION DAVID OISTRAKH

MENDELSSOHN
TRIOS POUR PIANO, VIOLON ET VIOLONCELLE

Prononciation Intonation

A. Intonation is the change in the pitch of the voice. It enables a speaker to distinguish between sentences such as *She's going to the movies.* and *She's going to the movies?* French intonation is not radically different from that of English. The two basic kinds are rising intonation and falling intonation.

B. With rising intonation the pitch of the voice rises in yes-or-no questions and sentences when you pause for a breath at the end of a group of related words.

Repeat the following yes-or-no questions after your teacher.

Aimez-vous ce tableau? / Est-ce qu'il est parti?

Vous avez un violon?

Repeat the following sentences with pauses after your teacher.

Elle n'est pas venue parce qu'elle est malade.

J'ai acheté un parapluie, mais je l'ai perdu.

Nous sommes allés au cinéma et nous avons dîné après.

C. With falling intonation, the pitch of the voice drops in declarative and imperative sentences and in information questions (those that start with an interrogative adverb or pronoun).

Repeat the following declarative sentences after your teacher.

Il va faire beau. / Marie n'est pas là.

Nous sommes très fatigués.

Repeat the following imperative sentences after your teacher.

Dépêche-toi. / Venez avec nous. / Allons au théâtre.

Repeat the following information questions after your teacher.

Qu'est-ce que vous allez faire? / Comment allez-vous?

Pourquoi fait-il cela?

Exercice

Read the following sentences aloud, paying particular attention to rising and falling intonation.

1. Voulez-vous danser?
2. Passez-moi le sucre.
3. Qui n'a pas pris de dessert?
4. Monique fait de la danse moderne.
5. J'ai lu un livre et j'ai téléphoné à un ami.
6. Couchez-vous plus tôt!

Grammaire

I. Verbs followed by infinitives

Verbs describe actions or states of being.

A. Verbs followed directly by an infinitive

You have learned that it is possible to use two consecutive verbs in a sentence in French. Verbs and verbal expressions you already know that take an infinitive directly after the conjugated verb are as follows.

adorer	devoir	préférer
aimer	espérer	savoir
aimer mieux	il faut	sembler
aller	laisser	souhaiter
désirer	penser	il vaut mieux
détester	pouvoir	vouloir

Je **dois dire** que les fautes me font souffrir.
Sait-on encore **parler** le français?
Je **ne peux pas répondre.**

B. Verbs followed by à and an infinitive

Some verbs that take the preposition à before an infinitive are as follows.

s'amuser à	continuer à
apprendre à	hésiter à *to hesitate*
avoir du mal à *to have a hard time*	inviter à
	réussir à
chercher à *to try*	tenir à
commencer à	

Nous **avons du mal à nous lever** tôt.
Il **ne réussit pas à comprendre** la danse moderne.
Avez-vous **commencé à lire** cette comédie?

C. Verbs followed by de and an infinitive

Here are some examples of verbs that take the preposition **de** before an infinitive.

accepter de	essayer de
avoir besoin de	être + *adjective* + de
avoir envie de	éviter de
avoir peur de	finir de
avoir raison / tort de	oublier de
cesser de *to stop*	refuser de
choisir de	regretter de
décider de	rêver de *to dream*
se dépêcher de	venir de

As-tu **envie d'aller** au théâtre?
Alors, **dépêche-toi de t'habiller!**
J'ai décidé de faire une sculpture.

Attention!

1. If you use object pronouns with two verbs, remember that the pronoun precedes the verb of which it is an object. For example, in the first sentence below, **amis** is the object of **inviter**, and **orchestre** is the object of **écouter**.

   J'ai invité **mes amis** à écouter **cet orchestre**.
   Je **les** ai invités à l'écouter.

   Je vais essayer de téléphoner **aux lecteurs**.
   Je vais essayer de **leur** téléphoner.

2. Note that the prepositions **à** and **de** *do not* combine with the direct object pronouns **le** and **les**.

   Il regrette de vendre **ce tableau**.
   Il regrette **de le** vendre.

   Je n'ai pas encore commencé à faire **mes devoirs**.
   Je n'ai pas encore commencé **à les** faire.

Langue

A. **Vos activités.** Complétez les phrases suivantes avec une préposition, s'il y a lieu *(if necessary)*.

1. Détestez-vous _____ étudier?
2. Elle regrette _____ arriver en retard.
3. Nous continuons _____ regarder la télévision.
4. Je viens _____ terminer le roman.
5. Mes voisins s'amusent _____ jouer de la guitare.
6. Mon père tient _____ écouter cet orchestre.
7. Notre professeur ne nous laisse jamais _____ partir tôt.
8. Ils vont _____ essayer _____ nous téléphoner ce soir.

B. **En famille.** Formez des phrases avec les mots donnés.

1. Mon mari / cesser / travailler / année / dernier
2. Notre fils / adorer / aller à la pêche avec lui
3. En semaine / nous / finir / dîner / huit heures
4. Notre fille / apprendre / jouer du violon
5. Nous / aimer mieux / se coucher / tôt
6. On / aller / visiter / Paris / printemps
7. Je / avoir du mal / décrire / nos vacances
8. Ma sœur / décider / aller voir / nos parents / Canada

Culture   **WWW**

C. **Au lycée.** Formez des phrases complètes avec les mots donnés et dites si la phrase est vraie ou fausse selon la vie des lycéens *(high school students)* français.

1. On / pouvoir / apprendre / conduire / au lycée
2. lycéens / adorer / écouter / musique américaine
3. On / devoir / étudier la religion
4. Ils / rêver / acheter / surtout / voiture
5. lycéens / ne... pas / chercher / travailler / après / classes
6. Parmi *(Among)* les langues étrangères, / ils / préférer / étudier / espagnol
7. Ils / avoir peur / passer le bac
8. La majorité des jeunes / obtenir le bac / et / choisir / aller / université

Communication

D. **Mes activités.** Qu'est-ce que vous préférez faire?

J'aime...	J'accepte...	Je déteste...	Je refuse...
me lever tôt		écrire des lettres	
préparer le petit déjeuner		lire des pièces / des romans	
sortir quand il pleut		conduire vite	
aller en classe en autobus		jouer à / de...	
suivre des cours le matin		???	

E. **L'avenir.** Posez des questions à un(e) camarade de cours sur ses projets pour l'avenir en employant un élément de chaque *(each)* colonne. Ensuite, faites un résumé de ses réponses.

aller	suivre des cours pendant dix ans
tenir	gagner peu / beaucoup d'argent
décider	avoir peu / beaucoup de responsabilités
rêver	faire du cinéma / du théâtre
hésiter	devenir professeur / médecin
espérer	faire du deltaplane
avoir envie	écrire de la poésie
devoir	???

F. **Questions personnelles.** Vos préférences.

1. Préférez-vous aller au cinéma ou au théâtre?
2. Avez-vous choisi d'habiter dans une résidence universitaire ou dans un appartement? Pourquoi?
3. Qu'est-ce que vous voulez apprendre à faire?
4. Qu'est-ce que vous avez du mal à faire?
5. Qu'est-ce que vous avez envie de faire ce week-end?
6. Où pensez-vous aller pour vos vacances?

II. Verbs followed by nouns

Verbs describe actions or states of being.

A. Verbs are either transitive or intransitive. A transitive verb takes a direct object. An intransitive verb has no direct object, or it requires a preposition.

Transitive	Intransitive
Les peintres font **des tableaux.**	Elle est rentrée tôt.
On a critiqué **le président.**	Nous allons **chez** le dentiste.

B. There are a number of verbs that are transitive in French but intransitive in English. The following are some transitive French verbs that you know.

attendre	demander	payer
chercher	écouter	regarder

Ils demandent du gâteau. *They are asking **for** cake.*
J'attends l'autobus. *I'm waiting **for** the bus.*

C. There are also verbs that take **à** before a noun in French. Most of the following verbs are transitive in English.

désobéir à	rendre visite à
échouer à *to fail*	répondre à
entrer à / dans	ressembler à
faire peur à	réussir à
jouer à + *name of a sport*	s'intéresser à *to be interested in*
obéir à	téléphoner à
penser à	tenir à

Ne désobéissez pas **à** vos parents! *Don't disobey your parents!*
Tenez-vous **à** ce vieux violon? *Are you fond of this old violin?*

D. Several verbs in French must take the preposition **à** before a person and **de** before an infinitive.

conseiller à quelqu'un **de** faire quelque chose	*to advise someone to do something*
demander à quelqu'un **de** faire quelque chose	*to ask someone to do something*
dire à quelqu'un **de** faire quelque chose	*to tell someone to do something*
écrire à quelqu'un **de** faire quelque chose	*to write someone to do something*
rappeler à quelqu'un **de** faire quelque chose	*to remind someone to do something*
recommander à quelqu'un **de** faire quelque chose	*to recommend to someone to do something*

Conseillez **aux** étudiants **d'**apprendre à taper.
J'ai demandé à Mme Leblanc **de** jouer de la guitare.

E. Some verbs take the preposition **de** before a noun or a pronoun.

avoir besoin de	il s'agit de
avoir envie de	jouer de + *musical instrument*
avoir peur de	s'inquiéter de
changer de	s'occuper de

Il **s'occupe du** courrier des lecteurs.
Il **s'agit d'**une volonté de certains milieux.

Attention!

1. **Penser** takes the preposition **à** when it means *to have something in mind*. When **penser** means *to have an opinion*, it takes **de** and is almost always used in a question. You answer the question with **penser que...** .

   Je n'aime pas **penser aux** examens.

   —Que **pensez**-vous **de** l'art moderne?
   —Je **pense que** c'est fascinant.

2. When a verb that takes the preposition **de** is followed by a noun, the noun does not take an article if it is used in a general sense.

   Il **change** souvent **de vêtements!**
   Elle **s'occupe d'étudiants** étrangers.

3. **Il s'agit de** cannot take a noun subject. Use a prepositional phrase with **dans** instead.

   Dans ce magazine, **il s'agit de** la langue française. | *This magazine deals with the French language.*

Ce qu'ils disent

Se rappeler takes a direct object, but in daily speech, many French speakers add **de**.

Je ne me rappelle pas cela. → Je ne me rappelle pas **de** cela.

Langue

A. **Faisons attention au professeur.** Complétez les phrases suivantes avec une préposition ou un article, ou avec les deux s'il y a lieu.

1. Pour être professeur, on a besoin _____ patience.
2. Mon professeur a recommandé _____ étudiants _____ bien préparer la leçon.
3. Il a conseillé _____ ses étudiants _____ étudier le latin aussi.
4. Il leur a demandé pourquoi ils ont échoué _____ examen.
5. Moi, je vais réussir _____ examens de l'année prochaine.
6. J'écoute toujours _____ conseils du professeur.

B. **Un agent de police donne des conseils aux touristes.** Formez des phrases complètes avec les mots donnés.

1. Dire / votre / amis / entrer / musée / avant six heures
2. Je / rappeler / gens / obéir / lois
3. Entrer / bureau de poste / pour / téléphoner / votre / famille
4. Je / donner / adresse / du Louvre / étudiants
5. Recommander / amis / regarder / ce / beau / église
6. Je / conseiller / Américains / visiter / musée d'Orsay

C. **Conversation avec votre camarade de chambre.** Répondez aux questions suivantes en utilisant les mots donnés.

1. Est-ce que c'est ton violoncelle?   (Non… appartenir… Marie)
2. Tu pars pour l'université?   (Non… revenir… supermarché)
3. Est-ce que tu as froid?   (Oui… demander… Robert… fermer… fenêtre)
4. Tu veux écouter de la musique?   (Non… préférer… regarder… film)
5. Alors, tu veux aller au cinéma?   (Oui… chercher… journal)
6. Qu'est-ce qu'on va faire après?   (… s'occuper… ménage)

Culture

D. **Au lycée.** Formez des phrases complètes avec les mots donnés et dites si la phrase est vraie ou fausse selon la vie des lycéens français.

1. Quand / deux lycéens / aller au cinéma, / garçon / payer / places
2. lycéens / regarder / souvent / télévision / l'après-midi
3. La majorité / lycéens / échouer / bac
4. On / demander / lycéens / étudier / deux langues étrangères
5. La majorité des lycéens / penser / football / et / penser / jouer / football
6. cours d'anglais / ressembler / cours de français aux Etats-Unis
7. beaucoup de lycéens / chercher / leurs amis / cafés / après les cours
8. Ils / jouer / flûte / et / guitare / comme instruments de musique préférés

Communication

E. **Vos activités.** Racontez vos activités pendant une journée typique. Utilisez les verbes suivants ou vos propres idées.

téléphoner	chercher	revenir
écrire	penser	jouer
regarder	s'occuper	fréquenter
écouter	parler	changer

F. **Mes rêves.** Séparez-vous en petits groupes et complétez les phrases. Ensuite expliquez à la classe les similarités et les différences entre vos réponses.

1. J'ai besoin _____ pour être heureux.
2. Je cherche _____ dans la vie.
3. Je pense souvent _____ .
4. Avec mes amis, je parle _____ .
5. Je tiens beaucoup _____ .
6. Pour l'avenir, je ne demande que _____ .

G. **Questions personnelles.** Décrivez-vous.

1. A quoi vous intéressez-vous?
2. A qui ressemblez-vous?
3. A qui téléphonez-vous souvent? A qui écrivez-vous?
4. A quoi pensez-vous en ce moment?
5. De qui ou de quoi avez-vous peur?
6. Quelle sorte de musique aimez-vous écouter?
7. Quels sports pratiquez-vous?
8. De quel instrument jouez-vous?

LE **BON** MOMENT
—— *la Restauration du Voyage* ——

*La SNCF vous propose de passer un Bon Moment
à bord des trains avec les restaurateurs du voyage,
qu'elle a choisis pour leur savoir-faire
et leurs qualités de service.
Pensez à réserver votre repas en même temps
que votre place en 1ère classe.*

III. The pronouns y and en

Pronouns replace nouns. You use **y** when referring to places and things when the reference is clear, and you use **en** for things and occasionally people.

A. The pronoun y

1. The pronoun **y** replaces prepositional phrases indicating a place. It means *there* and has the same position as the object pronouns you have already learned.

—Il habite **à Paris**?
—Oui, il y habite.

—Ils vont travailler **au cinéma**?
—Oui, ils vont y travailler.

—Sylvie nous invite **chez elle.**
—Allons-y tout de suite!

—Etes-vous allées **en France**?
—Oui, nous y sommes allées.

2. **Y** is also used with verbs taking the preposition **à** whenever the object is *not* a person.

> —Avez-vous répondu **à sa lettre?**
> —Oui, nous **y** avons répondu.

> —Ils ne s'intéressent pas **à la sculpture?**
> —Si, ils **s'y** intéressent.

Drôle de lieu de vacances: les sourires y sont naturels, pas saisonniers.

En Bretagne, les sourires ne naissent pas à Pâques pour s'éteindre en octobre, une fois achevée la saison touristique. En Bretagne, quand on vous gratifie d'un mot aimable, on ne s'y sent jamais forcé. Et quand on commerce avec vous, les raisons en sont rarement commerciales. Vous objecterez que les Bretons ne sourient pas toujours ? Réjouissez-vous-en : c'est parce que, chez eux, la spontanéité n'est pas affaire de saisonnalité. Renseignez-vous à la Maison de la Bretagne tél. : (1) 45.38.78.42

BRETAGNE NOUVELLE VAGUE

Attention!

1. If the object of the preposition **à** is a person, you cannot use **y**; you must use an indirect object pronoun, **lui** or **leur**.

> J'ai répondu **à la question.** → J'**y** ai répondu.
> J'ai répondu **au professeur.** → Je **lui** ai répondu.

2. Two verbs you have learned require **à** plus the stressed pronoun when referring to people: **penser** and **s'intéresser.**

> Elle pense souvent **à son frère.** → Elle pense souvent **à lui.**
> Je m'intéresse **aux musiciens de jazz.** → Je m'intéresse **à eux.**

3. **Y** is used to indicate location. With some verbs, a place name receives the action of the verbs. In these cases, you must use a direct object pronoun.

> Ils ont visité **la France.** → Ils **l'**ont visitée.
> J'adore **le Québec.** → Je **l'**adore.

B. The pronoun en

1. The pronoun **en** replaces any direct object modified by an indefinite or a partitive article. It is the equivalent of the English *some* or, in negative sentences, *any.*

> —Elle va écrire **des lettres?**   —Tu ne bois jamais **de vin?**
> —Non, elle **en** a déjà écrit.   —Non, je n'**en** bois jamais.

2. **En** can replace a noun modified by a number or an adverb of quantity. The number or adverb remains after the verb in the sentence.

—Est-ce qu'elle connaît **beaucoup d'écrivains?**

—Ne donnez pas **trop de devoirs!**

—Oui, elle **en** connaît **beaucoup.**

—Je n'**en** donne jamais **trop.**

—Les Ducharme ont **deux voitures?**

—Non, ils **en** ont **trois.**

3. **En** is also used when the object is preceded by the preposition **de.**

—Tu as besoin **de vacances,** n'est-ce pas?

—Je peux lui parler de **son travail?**

—Oui, j'**en** ai besoin.

—Non, elle n'aime pas **en** parler.

Ce qu'ils disent

If the object of the preposition **de** is a person, you do not use **en**; you must use **de** plus a stressed pronoun (**lui, elle, eux,** etc.). In casual conversation, however, **en** is often used for people.

Des enfants? Oui, il s'occupe **d'eux.**
Mon prof? Je n'**en** ai pas peur.

Attention!

1. There is no agreement between **y** or **en** and a past participle.

Ils ont habité **en Angleterre.** → Ils **y** ont habité.
Il a acheté **des romans.** → Il **en** a acheté.

2. **Liaison** is always obligatory between pronouns and **y** and **en.** The verbs that normally drop the **s** in the **tu** form of the imperative add it back in order to make a liaison possible.

Ils y sont allés l'année dernière.
Elles en ont trouvé au supermarché.
Vas-y. Achètes-en.

3. When **y** and **en** are used with a reflexive verb, they follow the reflexive pronoun.

Elle s'intéresse **à la musique classique.** → Elle s'**y** intéresse.
Il s'occupe **de la vaisselle.** → Il s'**en** occupe.

4. When **en** is used with **il y a,** it follows **y.**

Il y a des stylos dans le bureau. → Il **y en a** dans le bureau.
Y a-t-il des montagnes au Maroc? → **Y en a-t-il** au Maroc?

Langue

A. Quelle bonne élève! Remplacez les mots en italique par les pronoms **y** ou **en**, selon le cas.

1. Elle monte *dans l'autobus.*
2. Elle va *à l'école.*
3. Elle fait *des maths.*
4. Elle suit sept *cours.*
5. Elle s'intéresse *aux sciences.*
6. Elle n'échoue pas *aux examens.*
7. Elle rentre *chez elle* à l'heure.
8. Elle s'occupe *de ses devoirs.*

B. Un voyage à Bruxelles. Dans les phrases suivantes, remplacez les mots en italique par un pronom.

1. Nous sommes allés *en Belgique.*
2. Nous avons visité *la Grand-Place.*
3. Je m'intéresse *à cette architecture.*
4. On a bu trop *de bière.*
5. Laure a perdu *de l'argent.*
6. J'ai prêté cent francs *à Laure.*
7. On a joué *au tennis* dans un parc.
8. Tu veux parler *de tes vacances?*

C. Un week-end à la résidence. Votre camarade de chambre revient après un week-end chez ses parents et il / elle vous pose des questions. Répondez aux questions suivantes en utilisant les mots entre parenthèses et en remplaçant les noms par des pronoms.

1. As-tu répondu à la lettre de ta mère?   (Oui,…)
2. As-tu mangé une pizza?   (Non,…)
3. Tout le monde a obéi aux règles de la résidence?   (Non,… pas du tout…)
4. Tes amis et toi, vous avez écouté mes cassettes?   (Oui,…)
5. As-tu rencontré d'autres étudiants?   (Oui,… trois…)
6. On a pensé à moi?   (Non, personne… !)

Culture

WWW

D. Les sports dans le monde francophone. Certains endroits sont connus pour le sport qu'on y pratique. Identifiez les endroits suivants du monde francophone selon ce sport.

MODÈLE: Chamonix   *On y fait du ski.*

1. Roland-Garros
2. Le Mans
3. le stade Olympique à Montréal
4. Dakar
5. les bayous de Louisiane
6. les Ardennes

a. aller à la pêche
b. jouer au tennis
c. faire des courses de voitures de Formule I
d. aller à la chasse
e. finir une course de voitures
f. jouer au base-ball

E. **Les arts dans le monde francophone.** Répondez aux questions suivantes en employant le pronom **en.**

MODÈLE: Qui a écrit des romans? *Camus en a écrit.*

1. Qui a fait des sculptures?
2. Qui joue de la flûte?
3. Qui a fait des tableaux?
4. Qui a écrit des opéras?
5. Qui a écrit des chansons?
6. Qui joue de l'accordéon?

a. Clifton Chenier
b. Auguste Rodin
c. Jacques Brel
d. Jean-Pierre Rampal
e. Claude Monet
f. Georges Bizet

Communication

F. **Vos activités.** Que faites-vous très souvent? de temps en temps? rarement? jamais?

MODÈLE: dîner au restaurant *J'y dîne souvent. / Je n'y dîne jamais.*

1. boire du champagne
2. manger du caviar
3. aller à la chasse
4. jouer d'un instrument
5. écrire des poèmes
6. échouer aux examens
7. penser aux vacances
8. faire des tableaux

G. **Combien en avez-vous?** Interrogez vos camarades pour trouver qui a le plus grand nombre de...

MODÈLE: frères et sœurs *Marc en a six.*

1. camarades de chambre
2. instruments de musique
3. dollars dans son portefeuille
4. robes / pantalons
5. examens cette semaine
6. disques
7. tableaux
8. petit(e)s ami(e)s

santé magazine

le journal qui fait du bien !

Un problème de beauté, de diététique, d'enfant... il y a des solutions. Un symptôme, une maladie, un traitement...

SANTÉ MAGAZINE en a parlé.

H. **Questions personnelles.** Vos pensées.

1. Vous intéressez-vous à la littérature?
2. Connaissez-vous des auteurs français? Que pensez-vous d'eux?
3. Allez-vous au restaurant universitaire? Qu'est-ce que vous en pensez?
4. Quand pensez-vous à vos parents?
5. Vous avez visité le musée d'art de votre ville? Pourquoi pas?
6. Est-ce que vous réfléchissez souvent à votre avenir? Etes-vous optimiste ou pessimiste?

Communiquons

Ecrire des lettres

The French observe a certain style when writing letters. The two basic types of letters, business and personal, are described below. Business letters are usually typed, but it is acceptable to write by hand if a typewriter is not available. A personal letter, however, should never be typed.

Elle écrit des cartes postales.

▶ On écrit des lettres d'affaires.

1. To start a business letter, write or type your own name and address in the upper left corner. In the upper right corner, put your city and the date. Below them, you write the title and address of the person to whom you are writing. Note that the place of these elements is the reverse in English.

Jean-Michel Boirond
22, rue du Bac
75007 Paris

Paris, le 3 septembre 1997

Monsieur Henri Paulin
56, avenue Wagram
75017 Paris

Monsieur,

2. To begin the letter, use the person's title or simply **Monsieur, Mademoiselle,** or **Madame.** The standard English salutation *Dear* is generally not used in French business letters.

Monsieur le Directeur,	*(Dear) Director,*
Madame la Directrice,	*(Dear) Director,*
Monsieur le Maire,	*(Dear) Mr. Mayor,*
Madame la Présidente,	*(Dear) Madam President,*

3. The first sentence of a business letter is often a form of politeness.

J'ai l'honneur de vous...	*It's my privilege to . . .*
J'ai le plaisir de vous...	*I have the pleasure of . . .*
Je vous serais reconnaissant(e) de...	*I would be grateful if . . .*
Je vous prie de...	*I beg you to . . .*
Je vous remercie pour / de...	*I thank you for . . .*
Je vous suis reconnaissant(e) de...	*I thank you for . . .*

4. The closing sentence is usually a set expression in a very formal style. The person to whom you are writing must be addressed in the same way as in the opening.

Veuillez agréer, Monsieur le Directeur, l'expression de mes sentiments distingués.

Veuillez agréer, Madame la Présidente, l'expression de mes sentiments les meilleurs.

Veuillez agréer, Mademoiselle, l'expression de mes salutations distinguées.

▶ On écrit des lettres personnelles.

1. To begin a personal letter, choose a heading that reflects how well you know the person to whom you are writing and his / her age. The following expressions progress from salutations used with people you do not know well to those used with friends and relatives.

Monsieur, / Madame, / Mademoiselle,	*Sir, / Madam, / Miss,*
Cher Monsieur,	*Dear Sir,*
Chère Madame, / Mademoiselle	*Dear Madam, / Miss,*
Cher Monsieur, Chère Madame,	*Dear Mr. and Mrs. _____ ,*
Cher Jacques, / Cher ami,	*Dear Jacques,*
Chère Maman,	*Dear Mom,*
Chers tous, / tous deux,	*Dear folks,*

2. To conclude a personal letter, you can use a number of closing phrases. The following expressions progress from closures used with people you do not know well to those used with friends and relatives.

Amitiés,	*Fondly,*
Amicalement,	*Sincerely,*
Cordialement,	*Cordially,*
Je t'embrasse, / Je vous embrasse,	*Love,*
Affectueux baisers,	*Hugs and kisses,*
Grosses bises,	*XXX,*

Interaction *Jacqueline écrit une lettre à sa mère.*

> *Toulouse, le 7 juillet, 1998*
>
> Chère Maman,
>   J'espère que tout va bien à la maison. La semaine prochaine, je vais venir passer le pont° du 14 juillet avec vous. Dis à Papa que je voudrais que nous fassions un pique-nique° et que nous invitions les Fromentin.
>   Tout va bien au travail. Mon nouvel appartement est formidable. A bientôt !
>
>   Affectueux baisers,
>   Jacqueline

long weekend

picnic

Activités

A. Comment allez-vous commencer et terminer une lettre dans les situations suivantes?

1. à vos grands-parents: Vous voulez aller les voir.
2. à votre voisin: Il joue de la trompette à minuit.
3. à votre concierge: Vous n'avez pas d'eau.
4. au doyen *(dean)*: Votre prof est formidable.
5. à PBS: Vous aimez leurs émissions.
6. à votre cousin: Vous l'invitez à venir.

B. Ecrivez une des lettres suivantes.

	Destinataire	Sujet
1.	secrétaire général de la faculté	cours pour les étrangers
2.	une organisation charitable	pourquoi vous admirez leur travail
3.	une revue	pourquoi vous n'êtes pas d'accord avec eux
4.	votre journal préféré	leur usage de l'anglais
5.	votre petit(e) ami(e)	vos activités du week-end dernier
6.	vos parents	pourquoi vous avez besoin d'argent

Lecture culturelle

Avant la lecture

For the past twenty years, there has been a crisis in the French film industry. The high cost of tickets, uncomfortable theaters, and long lines at newly released films have been gradually angering and alienating more and more movie-goers. In the mid-eighties, the French film industry reacted by trying to make tickets more affordable, modernizing the theaters, and creating new multi-theater complexes. These efforts resulted in a renewed interest in the movies. Unfortunately, this renaissance did not last, and around 1987 attendance began to decline again. Television and VCRs have been responsible in part for this second decline in movie attendance, but the French film industry must also share the blame. Lately, it has failed to produce many films that arouse the interest of French audiences, who turn more and more to foreign films.

It would be wrong, however, to assume that no one goes to the movies in France. Adolescents and children continue to be avid movie-goers (although they are particularly attracted by the flashy, big-budget American films). Also, in the spring, the international film festival in Cannes overshadows all current events in France and steals the headlines of all French newspapers and magazines.

Activités

A. Try to name five films that won an Oscar for best movie at the Academy Awards in Hollywood.

B. Among the films mentioned in the following reading, you will find *Sexe, mensonges et vidéo*. In this case, you can probably guess that it stands for *Sex, Lies, and Videotape*. In many instances, however, the foreign title of a film does not resemble its original title. Look at the following list of French titles and try to match them with their English titles.

1.	*La Dernière Marche*	a.	*Twelve Monkeys*
2.	*La Folie du roi Georges*	b.	*Dead Man Walking*
3.	*Maudite Aphrodite*	c.	*The Madness of King George*
4.	*Stars et truands*	d.	*Sense and Sensibility*
5.	*Raison et sentiments*	e.	*Mighty Aphrodite*
6.	*L'Armée des 12 singes*	f.	*Get Shorty*

C. List the titles of five French films that you have seen in French or in their English version, or that you have heard of.

Gérard Depardieu au festival de Cannes

Le festival de Cannes   WWW

Tous les ans au mois de mai, l'élite du cinéma mondial° se retrouve° à Cannes pour les deux semaines du Festival international du film.

Créé° en 1946, le festival de Cannes est pour les Français ce que° le festival de Venise est pour les Italiens, et ce que les Oscars d'Hollywood
5 sont pour les Américains. Mais, alors qu'°on décerne° des douzaines d'Oscars chaque année en Californie, la Palme d'Or est la récompense° suprême sur la Côte d'Azur. Elle est réservée aux courts° et aux longs métrages°, et elle peut être attribuée à un film français ou à un film étranger. On se rappelle, par exemple, que dans les dix dernières années, des films comme *Missing* du réalisateur°
10 Costa-Gavras, *Sous le soleil de Satan,* inspiré du roman de Georges Bernanos, et *Sexe, mensonges et vidéo* ont reçu cette prestigieuse récompense.

On attribue aussi d'autres prix° comme le Grand Prix spécial du jury, les Prix d'interprétation masculine et féminine et le Prix de la mise en scène°.

Le palmarès° du festival de Cannes est impressionnant et il ne faut pas
15 oublier que beaucoup de films comme, pour en citer quelques-uns, *Orfeu Negro* de Marcel Camus, *La Dolce Vita* de Federico Fellini, *Blow-Up* de Michelangelo Antonioni, ou *Les Parapluies de Cherbourg* de Jacques Demy, qui ont tous reçu une Palme d'Or, sont maintenant considérés comme des classiques du cinéma international.

20 Le choix des films primés° au festival de Cannes n'est pas facile à faire. Cette tâche° est confiée° à un jury composé de célébrités, pour la plupart°, du monde du cinéma, mais aussi des milieux journalistiques, politiques et artistiques. Pendant deux semaines, les membres du jury se réunissent° tous les jours et assistent° à la projection° d'un nombre considérable de films de toutes sortes.
25 Ils sont épiés° et assaillis° par une meute° de journalistes qui répandent° toutes sortes de rumeurs et qui essayent de prédire quel film va recevoir la Palme d'Or. Le suspense se termine à la clôture° du festival, lors° d'une grande soirée de gala qui se tient° dans le palais des Festivals et des Congrès sur la célèbre° Croisette, le boulevard bordé° de palmiers° qui longe° le bord de mer et où se trouvent les
30 grands hôtels comme le Carlton, qui depuis des années accueillent° des milliardaires du monde entier°.

La soirée de gala et la remise° des prix constituent, bien entendu°, le clou° du festival. Comme à Hollywood, les gens se pressent° autour du Palais des Festivals pour voir arriver leurs acteurs et actrices favoris. Mais, les deux semaines
35 où se fait la délibération° du jury sont aussi passionnantes pour les touristes qui affluent° sur la Côte d'Azur à cette époque. Le festival attire les vedettes° déjà consacrées que les chasseurs d'autographes° assez audacieux poursuivent, soit sur la plage, soit dans la rue, soit dans le hall d'un hôtel, jusqu'à ce qu'ils aient obtenu satisfaction. Il permet également aux acteurs et actrices encore inconnus
40 de se faire remarquer° par les journalistes présents en leur accordant° des interviews sur la Croisette, ou même, quelquefois°, sur la plage.

Avec toutes ses joies, ses déceptions°, ses rivalités, ses scandales, le festival international du film de Cannes continue à exercer la même fascination, et l'intérêt que les gens lui portent° montre bien qu'il est devenu une véritable
45 institution française.

---

international / **se…** *meets*

Created
ce… *what*
alors… *whereas* / *award*
reward
short / *features*

filmmaker

prizes
mise… *directing*
prize list

that receive a prize
task / *entrusted* / **pour…**
   for the most part
se… *meet*
attend / *viewing*
spied upon / *mobbed* /
   swarm / *spread*
closing / *during*
se… *is held* / *famous*
lined / *palm trees* / *borders*
receive
entire
awarding / **bien…** *of course*
   / *peak* / **se…** *huddle*

judging
rush / *stars*
chasseurs… *autograph*
   collectors / *until*

se… *to be noticed* / *granting* / *sometimes*

disappointments

show

Après la lecture

Questions sur le texte

1. Depuis quand est-ce que le festival de Cannes existe?
2. Comment s'appelle le grand prix donné à un film?
3. Est-ce que seuls les films français peuvent gagner un prix?
4. Qui sont les membres du jury?
5. Quand et comment est-ce qu'on apprend la liste des gagnants *(winners)*?
6. Quels acteurs et actrices viennent au festival de Cannes?
7. Pourquoi beaucoup de touristes vont à Cannes pendant le festival?
8. Comment les artistes peu connus peuvent-ils devenir célèbres?

Activités

A. Répondez aux questions suivantes.

1. Quels sont vos acteurs et actrices préférés? Pourquoi?
2. Pourquoi allez-vous au cinéma? Quelles sortes de films préférez-vous?

B. Racontez l'histoire d'un de vos films favoris.

C. Formez deux groupes et organisez un débat sur la censure *(censorship)* au cinéma. Est-il nécessaire de séparer les films avec des lettres comme *G*, *PG*, *R*, and *NC 17* comme aux Etats-Unis?

Vocabulaire

Noms / Pronoms

aquarelle	watercolor	extrait	excerpt
article	article	faute	mistake
atteinte	affront	flûte	flute
auteur dramatique	playwright	guitare	guitar
ballet	ballet	instrument	instrument
beauté	beauty	instrument de musique	musical instrument
bronze	bronze	lecteur	reader
chef d'orchestre	conductor	mal	damage
comédie	comedy	métier	career
comédie musicale	musical	milieu	circle
danse classique	ballet	œuvre	work
danseur	dancer	opéra	opera
destruction	destruction	orchestre	orchestra
drame	drama	peintre	painter
écrivain	writer	peinture à l'huile	oil painting
en	some, of it	piano	piano
enseignement	teaching	pierre	stone
état	state	sculpteur	sculptor

sculpture	sculpture	**usage**	use
symphonie	symphony	**violon**	violin
tableau	painting	**violoncelle**	cello
tragédie	tragedy	**volonté**	will
trombone	trombone	**y**	there / of / to it
trompette	trumpet		

Verbes

accepter (de)	to accept	**inviter (à)**	to invite
apprendre (à)	to learn / to teach	**jouer (à)**	to play (sport)
arriver	to happen	**jouer (de)**	to play (musical instrument)
cesser (de)	to stop		
changer (de)	to change	**oublier (de)**	to forget
chercher (à)	to try	**penser (à)**	to think about / have in mind
choisir (de)	to choose		
commencer (à)	to begin	**penser (de)**	to think of / have an opinion
continuer (à)	to continue		
contribuer	to contribute	**rappeler (à)**	to remind
critiquer	to critique	**recommander (à)**	to recommend
défendre	to forbid	**refuser (de)**	to refuse
demander (à)	to ask	**regretter (de)**	to regret / be sorry
dire (à)	to tell	**réussir (à)**	to succeed
échouer (à)	to fail	**rêver (de)**	to dream
écrire (à)	to write	**souffrir**	to suffer
enseigner	to teach	**s'amuser (à)**	to have a good time
essayer (de)	to try	**s'inquiéter (de)**	to worry
éviter (de)	to avoid	**s'intéresser (à)**	to be interested
finir (de)	to finish	**se dépêcher (de)**	to hurry
hésiter (à)	to hesitate		

Adjectifs / Adverbes

artistique	artistic	**littéraire**	literary
bourgeois	bourgeois	**publié**	published
consacré	devoted	**surtout**	above all
correct	correct	**vivace**	lively
insuffisant	insufficient		

Expressions

avoir du mal à	to have trouble	**donc**	therefore
avoir raison de	to be right	**en péril**	endangered
avoir tort de	to be wrong	**il s'agit de…**	it's about . . .

Chapitres 13 à 15

Révision E

Tous ensemble!

A. **Les vacances de Christine et d'Eric.** Répondez aux questions suivantes en employant les mots entre parenthèses et des pronoms pour les mots en italique.

1. Comment vous appelez-vous?   (… Eric et Christine.)
2. Etes-vous déjà allés *en France*?   (… 1992.)
3. Est-ce que vous avez dû vous occuper de *vos billets d'avion*?   (Oui,…)
4. Christine, t'es-tu promenée *dans Paris*?   (Oui,… déjà…)
5. Eric, tes parents étaient contents quand tu as voyagé?   (Non,… s'inquiéter beaucoup.)
6. Le soir, qu'est-ce que vous aviez envie de faire?   (… se détendre.)
7. Avez-vous fait du roller?   (Oui,… à Paris.)
8. Quand il a plu, qu'est-ce que vous avez fait?   (… lire… magazines et… écrire… lettres.)
9. Quand vous êtes en voyage, vous achetez beaucoup de choses?   (Oui,… acheter des vêtements.)
10. Etes-vous allés *à l'Opéra*?   (Oui,… aller trois fois.)

B. Faites des phrases avec les mots donnés.

La détente

1. Je / avoir / besoin / se détendre
2. Entrer / maison / et / se reposer!
3. Papa, / écouter / maman! / Cesser / travailler / tard!
4. Elles / ne… pas / se dépêcher / parce que / elles / ne… pas / tenir / arriver / à l'heure
5. Nous / venir / se coucher

Au travail!

6. Nous / choisir / faire / métier / artistique
7. Nous / commencer / traduire / poème / hier
8. Elles / écrire / romans / et / contes
9. Je / venir / lire / ce / revue
10. Je / dire / enfants / continuer / étudier / piano

C. **Mes amis écrivains.** Remplacez les mots en italique par des pronoms.

1. Victor et Suzanne passent tout l'été *sur la Côte d'Azur.*
2. *Leur appartement* de Paris est petit, mais *leur maison* de Nice est grande.
3. Avez-vous lu *leurs livres?*
4. J'ai traduit *le poème de* Victor et *les poèmes* de sa femme.
5. Lui, il parle *de la mer;* elle, elle ne parle jamais *de cela.*
6. Voulez-vous que je vous montre *les poèmes* de Suzanne?

7. A Noël, j'ai acheté *le dernier livre* de Victor, et Suzanne m'a offert un *autre livre* pour mon anniversaire.

8. Je ne pense pas qu'ils aient beaucoup *d'argent*.

9. Ils s'intéressent à *la musique classique* aussi.

10. Ils invitent souvent *leurs amis* à écouter *des disques* avec eux.

D. **La matinée d'Anne-Marie.** Complétez le paragraphe suivant avec la forme correcte des verbes donnés et avec des prépositions, s'il y a lieu.

Hier, Anne-Marie _____ (se réveiller) à sept heures et _____ (se lever) quelques minutes après. Elle _____ (se laver) et _____ (aller chercher) le journal. Elle l(e) _____ (lire) rapidement parce qu'il n'y _____ (avoir) rien d'intéressant et elle _____ (se dépêcher) s'habiller. Elle _____ (appeler) un taxi et l' _____ (attendre) pendant vingt minutes. Elle _____ (demander) au chauffeur _____ la conduire au bureau. Dans le taxi elle _____ (écrire) des lettres à ses employés. Quand elle _____ (arriver) au bureau, elle _____ (appeler) sa secrétaire; elle _____ (vouloir) qu'elle _____ (commencer) taper ses lettres. Elle _____ (inviter) son amie Andrée _____ déjeuner avec elle. Elles _____ (décider) _____ finir _____ travailler à 11 h 30 parce qu'elles _____ (avoir) faim.

E. **Réactions personnelles.** Complétez les phrases suivantes de manière logique.

1. J'aime lire...
2. J'espère être...
3. Pour le week-end, nous avons besoin...
4. Mon ami(e) a du mal...
5. Mon / Ma camarade de chambre se dépêche quand...
6. T'inquiètes-tu quand... ?
7. Pour me détendre...
8. Je refuse...

Entre nous!

A. **Ma journée.** Avec un(e) camarade de cours, décrivez une journée typique d'un(e) étudiant(e). Employez les suggestions données et vos propres idées.

se réveiller	lire le journal	rentrer
se lever	commencer	acheter
se laver	s'amuser	changer de vêtements
prendre le petit déjeuner	décider	écrire
s'habiller	jouer à / de	se coucher
partir	se détendre	s'endormir

B. **Mes projets.** Dans un petit groupe de trois ou quatre, parlez de vos projets pour demain, pour ce semestre et pour l'avenir. Parlez aussi des choses que vous n'allez pas faire. Ensuite, informez les autres des résultats de votre discussion.

MODÈLE: *Je tiens à apprendre le français.*
J'ai décidé de devenir médecin.
Je vais éviter de dépenser trop d'argent.

souhaiter	aller	éviter
rêver	commencer	refuser
chercher	avoir envie	choisir
tenir à	avoir peur	s'amuser
il faut que	devoir	vouloir

C. **Ginger ou Mary Ann?** Un(e) camarade de cours et vous, vous vous trouvez sur une île *(island)* déserte. Qu'est-ce qu'il faut que vous ayez pour être heureux (-euse)? De quoi n'avez-vous pas besoin? Quelles personnes préférez-vous avoir avec vous?

MODÈLE: *J'ai besoin d'une radio.*
Nous n'avons pas besoin d'argent.

D. **Que font-ils?** Donnez le nom d'un(e) athlète ou d'un(e) musicien(ne) à votre camarade de cours. Ensuite, demandez-lui quel sport il / elle pratique ou de quel instrument il / elle joue.

MODÈLE: Monica Seles   *Elle joue au tennis.*
             Miles Davis   *Il jouait de la trompette.*
             Hulk Hogan   *Il fait du catch.*

E. **Questions personnelles.** Vos pensées.

1. Que pensez-vous...

MODÈLE: des westerns?   *Je pense qu'ils sont ennuyeux.*

a. des Beatles?
b. du Président des Etats-Unis?
c. des Français?
d. de la télévision?
e. de votre cours de français?
f. ???

2. Quand vous vous trouvez dans les situations suivantes, à quoi ou à qui pensez-vous?

MODÈLE: Vous êtes en cours.
        Quand je suis en cours, je pense à mes vacances.

a. Vous téléphonez à votre petit(e) ami(e).
b. Vous vous reposez.
c. Vous êtes en cours.
d. Vous êtes seul(e).
e. Vous passez un examen.
f. Vous recevez un télégramme.
g. Vous partez en vacances.
h. ???

F. **Jeu de rôles.** Jouez les scènes suivantes avec un(e) camarade de cours.

1. Vous êtes chez le médecin. Expliquez-lui vos problèmes. Le médecin vous donne des conseils.
2. Un journaliste français va vous interviewer. Il veut savoir comment est la journée typique d'un étudiant américain. Décrivez-lui la vôtre.
3. Vous jouez le rôle de votre athlète préféré. Un(e) autre étudiant(e) va vous interviewer après une compétition importante.
4. Vous êtes écrivain. Un(e) camarade de cours est journaliste et va vous interviewer. Parlez de vos créations littéraires.
5. Vous travaillez à la télévision. Faites de la publicité pour une marque *(brand name)* qui a une équipe dans le Tour de France.
6. Vous êtes guide dans un musée. Décrivez vos œuvres d'art *(works of art)* préférées. Un(e) camarade est touriste et va vous poser des questions.

Chapitre 16

Le français aux Etats-Unis

 Commençons

 Grammaire

 Communiquons

 Lecture culturelle

 Vocabulaire

Le Vieux Carré à La
Nouvelle-Orléans

Objectives

Language
Vocabulary for rooms of the house and furniture • Mute **e** • The relative
pronouns **qui, que,** and **où** • The conditional mood • Expressing time with
pendant, depuis, and **il y a**

Culture
Lodging in France • The francophone press • The French language in the
United States

Communication
Finding a place to live • Expressing hypothetical statements • Expressing
continuous and completed actions

Commençons

Réponse à une petite annonce   WWW

Un étudiant américain qui vient de Louisiane et qui s'appelle Daniel est à Lyon depuis une semaine. Il lit les petites annonces dans Le Progrès. *Il a trouvé des chambres à louer qui l'intéressent et il a téléphoné aux propriétaires pendant toute la matinée. Quelqu'un répond enfin.*

DANIEL: Allô, bonjour, Madame. J'ai lu la petite annonce que vous avez placée dans le journal et j'aimerais avoir des renseignements sur la chambre que vous voulez louer.

MME LUCAS: Bien sûr! C'est une grande chambre meublée qui donne sur le parc de la Tête d'Or et que je loue tous les ans à des étudiants étrangers. J'ai trouvé quelqu'un il y a un mois, mais il a dû rentrer chez lui.

DANIEL: Quel est le prix du loyer?

MME LUCAS: Quinze cents francs par mois, charges comprises. Voudriez-vous aller voir la chambre maintenant?

DANIEL: Oui, mais je ne sais pas où elle se trouve. Pourriez-vous m'indiquer le chemin?

MME LUCAS: Connaissez-vous le musée Guimet? C'est juste en face, au numéro vingt et un. C'est au sixième étage, la troisième porte à gauche. Demandez la clé à la concierge.

DANIEL: Très bien, je vais y aller tout de suite et je vais vous rappeler dans la soirée.

Etudions le dialogue

1. Qu'est-ce que Daniel lit? Pourquoi?
2. A qui téléphone-t-il?
3. Décrivez la chambre.
4. Quel est le prix du loyer?
5. Où se trouve la chambre?
6. Est-ce que Daniel la prend tout de suite?

Mots clés

qui	*who*	**donne sur (donner sur)**	*looks out on*
Louisiane	*Louisiana*	**il y a**	*ago*
petites annonces	*classified ads*	**loyer**	*rent*
qui	*that*	**charges comprises**	*utilities included*
intéressent (intéresser)	*interest*	**Voudriez-vous… ? (vouloir)**	*Would you like … ?*
propriétaires *(m. / f.)*	*owners*	**Pourriez-vous… ? (pouvoir)**	*Could you … ?*
enfin	*finally*	**chemin**	*way*
que	*that*	**juste**	*just*
avez placée (placer)	*placed*	**étage**	*floor*
aimerais (aimer)	*would like*	**à gauche**	*on the left*
meublée	*furnished*	**concierge**	*concierge*

Faisons connaissance

Many French families rent rooms to students in their own homes or apartments or in property they own for purely financial reasons. This is particularly true of widows and older couples whose children have left home. They use the rent money to pay taxes and to supplement their incomes. This is a fortunate situation for students because few universities have enough student housing.

A **concierge,** such as the one mentioned in the dialogue at the beginning of the chapter, is usually a woman responsible for distributing mail, helping visitors, and keeping the building clean. **Concierges** are rapidly disappearing, however, as building owners install automatic locks and individual mailboxes.

French people have a different way of counting floors. The first floor is **le rez-de-chaussée,** the second floor, **le premier étage,** and so on. In Quebec, however, people use the word **plancher,** which also means floor, for **étage,** and they count the floors the same way Americans do. Thus, to a person from Quebec or the United States, in the dialogue, the room **au sixième étage** would be on the seventh floor. On the top floor of many apartment buildings (**un immeuble**) there are maids' rooms (**des chambres de bonne**), which are often rented to students.

Un immeuble en
construction

Enrichissons notre vocabulaire

Les pièces de la maison *(The rooms of the house)*

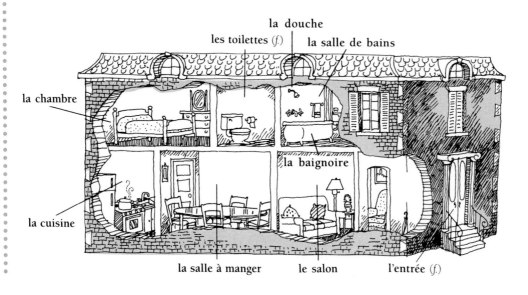

Les meubles et les appareils électro-ménagers
(Furniture and appliances)

WWW

un fauteuil
une lampe
une table

un divan / un canapé

un frigidaire
un évier
un four

un lave-vaisselle   une cuisinière

une armoire
une étagère
une table de nuit
un lit
un tapis
un lavabo

une machine à laver

un sèche-linge

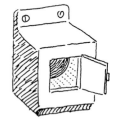

un four à micro-ondes

Prononciation   *Mute* e

A. Mute e may or may not be pronounced, according to its position in the sentence. When pronounced, it is represented by the symbol / ə / and is pronounced as the / ø / of **peu**.

une petite annonce / la petite annonce

B. Mute e is identified in written form by the letter e with no accent mark, and it is never followed by double consonants.

Devoirs and **besoin** both contain mute e.
Derrière has the / ɛ / sound, as indicated by the double **r**.

C. In casual conversation, most French speakers drop as many mute e's as possible, short of creating a string of unpronounceable consonants. One important rule is that mute e is never pronounced before a vowel sound.

quatre heures / votre appartement / un autre étudiant /
notre ami / une table immense / un pauvre homme

D. In general, a mute **e** is also dropped if it is preceded by only one pronounced consonant. For example, **trop de gens** is pronounced / tʁo dʒɑ̃ /. The / ʒ / is preceded by **d**, but **p** is not pronounced.

> beaucoup dé livres / sans cé livre / un kilo dé beurre / dans lé bureau / assez dé travail / Vous lé savez. / pas dé place / Tu né bois pas.

E. If a mute **e** follows two pronounced consonants, however, it is better to keep the sound.

> Il ne sait pas. / Regarde le garçon. / avec le couteau / Elles me connaissent. / Jeanne te voit / une pauvre femme / le gouvernement / quatre semaines de vacances

Exercise

Read the following sentences aloud, dropping as many mute **e**'s as possible.

1. Je ne sais pas si je veux cette table de nuit.
2. Beaucoup de gens se reposent le matin.
3. Elle me donne trop de travail.
4. A quatre heures nous décidons de préparer le dîner.
5. Qu'est-ce que vous allez me montrer?
6. Mon appartement se trouve au rez-de-chaussée près de la cuisine.

Grammaire

I. The relative pronouns qui, que, and où

> You use relative pronouns to connect two sentences or clauses into a single sentence.

A. Uses of relative pronouns

In English, relative pronouns are used to combine two sentences or clauses into a single sentence. The relative pronoun introduces the second clause and refers to a word in the main clause. This word is called the *antecedent*.

> Here is the book. I read the book.
>
>   **antecedent rel. pro.**
>   ↓   ↓
> Here is the *book that* I read.
>
> Did you see the man? The man drove a red car.
>
>   **antecedent rel. pro.**
>   ↓   ↓
> Did you see the *man who* drove a red car?

B. The relative pronoun qui

1. **Qui** *(who, which, that)* may refer to people or things and serves as the subject of the verb that follows it.

> Nous avons demandé des renseignements à **Paul. Paul** connaît bien la ville.
> Nous avons demandé des renseignements à Paul **qui** connaît bien la ville.

> C'est **une grande chambre. La chambre** donne sur un parc.
> C'est une grande chambre **qui** donne sur un parc.

2. The verb following **qui** agrees with the antecedent.

> C'est **moi** qui **suis arrivé** à l'heure.   C'est **elle** qui **est montée**.

C. The relative pronoun que

1. **Que** *(whom, which, that)* also refers to people or things and serves as the direct object of the verb that follows it.

> Je cherche **la chambre.** Vous louez **la chambre.**
> Je cherche la chambre **que** vous louez.

> Elle n'aime pas **l'émission.** Ils regardent **l'émission.**
> Elle n'aime pas l'émission **qu'**ils regardent.

2. **Que** becomes **qu'** before a vowel sound.

> Ma mère lit le roman **qu'**elle a trouvé sur le fauteuil.

L'orthographe

If the clause following **que** is in the **passé composé,** the past participle agrees with the antecedent of **que,** which is the preceding direct object.

> Elle s'intéresse à **la robe** que tu lui as montrée.
> Nous n'avons pas vu **les meubles** qu'ils ont achetés.
> J'ai lu **les petites annonces** que vous avez placées dans le journal.

D. The relative pronoun où

1. **Où** *(where)* is used when the second clause indicates a place.

> Il n'a pas dit **où** il allait.   Voilà la chambre **où** ils dorment.

2. If the antecedent is a place but is the *direct object* of the verb in the second clause, use **que** instead of **où**.

> L'Espagne est un pays **que** nous n'avons jamais visité.
> Le parc de la Tête d'Or est un parc **que** les Lyonnais fréquentent beaucoup.

E. In Chapter 15, you learned that demonstrative pronouns (**celui, celle, ceux, celles**) must be followed by **-ci, -là,** or the preposition **de.** They can also be followed by relative pronouns.

> Elle n'aime pas ceux **que** j'ai achetés.
> Prenez celui **qui** est sur la table.
> Regardez cette maison. C'est celle **où** je suis née.

Ce qu'ils disent

1. French intonation and rhythm do not allow a speaker to emphasize a word in a sentence simply by saying it louder, as we do in English. To emphasize a word, you must put it just before a new clause. Relative pronouns are frequently used in this construction, which you hear very often in casual conversation. In the following examples, the word in boldface in the first sentence is emphasized in the second.

Jean cherche un appartement.	C'est Jean qui cherche un appartement.
Je n'aime pas **tes meubles.**	Ce sont tes meubles que je n'aime pas.
Madeleine travaille **là.**	C'est là où Madeleine travaille.

2. In this construction, stressed pronouns replace subject pronouns, and the verb in the second clause agrees with its subject in the first.

Tu achètes un lave-vaisselle? C'est **toi** qui **achètes** un lave-vaisselle?	Il ne va pas conduire! Ce n'est pas **lui** qui **va** conduire!

Langue

A. Dans notre appartement. Complétez les phrases suivantes avec un pronom relatif.

1. J'adore les appartements _____ il y a beaucoup de fenêtres.
2. Apportez-moi le verre _____ j'ai laissé dans la cuisine.
3. L'appartement _____ ma petite amie habite est derrière celui-ci.
4. Je préfère les salons _____ n'ont pas trop de meubles.
5. Nous n'apprécions pas les voisins _____ font du bruit.
6. Le lit _____ ils veulent me prêter est trop petit.

B. Une promenade en ville. Complétez les phrases suivantes.

1. Nous avons acheté des disques que…
2. Je vous recommande un film qui…
3. J'ai visité une ville où…
4. Le restaurant sert des repas qui…
5. Allez-vous acheter les vêtements que… ?
6. Ils passent leur temps dans un magasin où…

C. **L'appartement de Corinne.** Pour mettre en relief *(to emphasize)* les mots en italique dans les phrases suivantes, refaites les phrases en plaçant les mots en italique au début et en utilisant un pronom relatif. Suivez le modèle.

MODÈLE: Corinne habite *un grand appartement.*
         C'est un grand appartement que Corinne habite.

1. Corinne habite *avec ses deux sœurs.*
2. *Sa sœur Caroline* s'occupe du ménage.
3. Elles dorment *dans cette chambre.*
4. Elles font leurs devoirs *là.*
5. *Leur sœur Claude* n'est pas étudiante.
6. Elle aime se détendre *sur ce canapé.*

Culture

D. **Le français cajun.** Le français parlé en Louisiane a beaucoup de mots qui n'existent pas en France. Quels mots est-ce que les Cajuns utilisent pour les choses suivantes?

MODÈLE: Il est mort.
         «Il est gone» est l'expression que les Cajuns utilisent   **WWW**
           pour «Il est mort.»

1.	maintenant	a.	affreux
2.	un bal *(a dance)*	b.	bleu
3.	un dollar	c.	un grand char
4.	très	d.	asteur
5.	triste	e.	un fais-dodo
6.	un train	f.	une piasse

E. **Où habiter?** Quels sont les facteurs les plus importants quand les Français choisissent un logement? Mettez la liste suivante dans l'ordre du facteur le plus important au moins important en utilisant les pourcentages donnés.

MODÈLE: les commodités *(conveniences)* de l'immeuble / 23%
         23% des Français veulent un logement où il y a des commodités.

1.	de la sécurité	a.	57%
2.	la proximité des écoles	b.	48%
3.	une vue	c.	47%
4.	des espaces verts	d.	43%
5.	l'absence de bruit	e.	35%
6.	la proximité des commerces	f.	33%

Communication

F. **Mes préférences.** Formez des phrases logiques avec un élément de chaque colonne.

J'admire les gens	qui	être intéressant
Je ne peux pas supporter les gens	que	parler trop
J'aime visiter des pays	où	ne pouvoir rien faire
Je déteste les villes		être trop difficile
Je voudrais avoir un métier		donner mal à la tête
Je n'écoute jamais les gens		ne rien apprendre
Les étudiants s'intéressent aux cours		travailler beaucoup
On n'aime pas s'occuper de problèmes		être sincère
???		???

G. **Mes préférences (suite).** Complétez les phrases suivantes logiquement.

1. J'aime les filles / les garçons qui...
2. Je préfère les maisons qui...
3. J'adore les appartements où...
4. Je m'intéresse aux journaux que...
5. J'apprécie les étudiants qui...
6. Je tiens aux meubles que...

H. **Questions personnelles.** Votre logement.

1. Dans quelle sorte de ville habitez-vous?
2. Habitez-vous dans une résidence, dans une maison, ou dans un appartement?
3. Décrivez votre chambre.
4. De quels meubles avez-vous besoin?
5. Vous avez cherché un(e) camarade de chambre? Qu'est-ce que vous avez demandé?
6. Vous aimez quelles sortes de voisins?

II.   The conditional mood

You use the conditional mood to express an occurrence that would exist under certain circumstances or to make a polite request.

A.   Formation of the conditional: Regular verbs

aimer	descendre
j'aimerais	je descendrais
tu aimerais	tu descendrais
il / elle / on aimerait	il / elle / on descendrait
nous aimerions	nous descendrions
vous aimeriez	vous descendriez
ils / elles aimeraient	ils / elles descendraient

choisir	écrire
je choisirais	j'écrirais
tu choisirais	tu écrirais
il / elle / on choisirait	il / elle / on écrirait
nous choisirions	nous écririons
vous choisiriez	vous écririez
ils / elles choisiraient	ils / elles écriraient

J'aimerais avoir des renseignements sur la chambre.

1. You form the conditional mood by adding the endings of the imperfect tense to the infinitive. If the infinitive ends in **-re,** you drop the **e** before adding the endings.

2. If the infinitive ends in **-r,** you pronounce the **r.**

    aimer → **j'aimerais**   louer → **tu louerais**

B. Formation of the conditional: Irregular verbs

1. Several verbs that you already know have irregular conditional stems:

aller	j'**ir**ais	pouvoir	elles **pourr**aient
avoir	tu **aur**ais	recevoir	vous **recevr**iez
devenir	on **deviendr**ait	savoir	elle **saur**ait
devoir	il **devr**ait	tenir	nous **tiendr**ions
être	nous **ser**ions	valoir	il **vaudr**ait (mieux)
faire	vous **fer**iez	venir	il **viendr**ait
falloir	il **faudr**ait	voir	tu **verr**ais
mourir	il **mourr**ait	vouloir	je **voudr**ais
pleuvoir	il **pleuvr**ait		

2. Stem-changing verbs use the **accent grave** or double consonant in the last syllable of the stem to keep the / ɛ / sound. Verbs with an **accent aigu** in the last syllable of the stem keep the / e / sound.

    acheter   →   elle ach**è**terait
    se lever   →   nous nous l**è**verions
    appeler   →   vous appe**ll**eriez

    but: préférer   →   je préf**é**rerais
              répéter   →   tu rép**é**terais

C. Uses of the conditional

1. The conditional mood softens a request or a statement. Use it instead of the present or the imperative when you want to be polite.

    Voudriez-vous aller voir la chambre?
    Vous **devriez** consulter une carte.

2. The conditional mood expresses a possible occurrence that would exist under certain conditions.

    Nous **aimerions** habiter en Louisiane.
    A ce prix-là, ce **serait** trop cher.
    Il ne **viendrait** pas sans son ami.

3. Several expressions are frequently used with the conditional mood to show a condition that does not exist.

à ta / votre / sa place:	A ta place, je **choisirais** un autre divan.
sans / avec cela:	Sans cela, nous ne **finirions** jamais.
si j'étais / si vous étiez:	Si vous étiez riche, vous ne **feriez** pas le ménage.

Langue

A. A la bibliothèque. Formez des phrases plus polies en mettant les phrases suivantes au conditionnel.

1. Pouvez-vous m'indiquer le bureau des renseignements?
2. Je veux savoir où se trouvent les revues.
3. Mon copain aime lire des journaux.
4. Où est-ce qu'on trouve les films?
5. Je suis heureux de pouvoir utiliser un ordinateur.
6. Avez-vous le temps de m'expliquer tout cela?

B. Sans argent. Formez des phrases avec les mots donnés. Mettez les verbes au conditionnel.

1. Sans argent / vous / ne… pas / pouvoir / acheter / fauteuil
2. A votre place, je / ne… pas / entrer / ce / magasin
3. Il / avoir peur / louer / voiture
4. Ce / enfants / ne… pas / pouvoir / aller / cinéma / sans adulte
5. Nous / ne… pas / appeler / médecin
6. Moi, / je / ne… pas / aller / ce / restaurant

C. On invite nos voisins. Répondez aux questions en employant les mots entre parenthèses et en mettant le verbe au conditionnel.

1. Vous voulez quelque chose?   (… vouloir du thé)
2. Que feriez-vous à ma place?   (… acheter un nouveau divan)
3. Est-ce que je peux ouvrir la fenêtre?   (Non,… avoir froid)
4. Est-ce que votre amie aimerait partir?   (Oui, mais… revenir tout de suite)
5. Est-elle en retard?   (Oui,… devoir se dépêcher)
6. Aimeriez-vous rester dîner?   (Non,… préférer rentrer)

Culture

D. La politesse. Si un Français vous invitait à un dîner officiel, que feriez-vous pour être poli(e)? Qu'est-ce que vous ne feriez pas?

MODÈLE: demander aux gens d'allumer la télé
Je ne demanderais pas aux gens d'allumer la télé.

1. apporter des bonbons
2. arriver bien en avance
3. amener un ami
4. faire des bises à tout le monde
5. enlever mes chaussures
6. avoir les mains sous la table
7. demander encore de la viande
8. partir avant 11 heures
9. manger des choses que je n'aime pas
10. placer mes coudes sur la table

Communication

E. Si les choses étaient différentes. Avec les petits changements suivants dans votre vie, que feriez-vous? Finissez les phrases.

1. Avec beaucoup d'argent,…
2. Si j'étais au / en [pays],…
3. Avec une voiture de sport,…
4. Avec de longues vacances,…
5. Sans ma famille,…
6. Sans ce cours,…

F. **Recommençons!** Si vous pouviez refaire votre vie, que feriez-vous de différent? Utilisez les suggestions données ou vos propres idées.

MODÈLE: *J'étudierais beaucoup plus. / J'habiterais en Europe.*

suivre plus / moins de cours de… dépenser moins d'argent
aller à l'université de… être plus / moins sympathique
apprendre à jouer du / de la… louer un appartement
acheter un four à micro-ondes ???

G. **Questions personnelles.** Votre avenir.

1. Sans diplôme, que feriez-vous?
2. Quand est-ce que vous devriez commencer à travailler? Qu'est-ce que vous préféreriez faire?
3. Qu'est-ce que vous n'accepteriez jamais de faire?
4. Qu'est-ce que vous pourriez faire pour trouver une solution à un problème social?
5. Que faudrait-il que vous ayez pour être heureux (-euse)?
6. Avec un tapis volant *(flying carpet)*, où iriez-vous?

III. Expressing time with pendant, depuis, and il y a

> You use time expressions to indicate when an action or a state began and whether or not it is still going on.

A. Pendant

Use **pendant** or no preposition at all to express the amount of time an action or a condition lasts. The English equivalent is *for*.

J'ai téléphoné **pendant** toute la matinée.
or: J'ai téléphoné toute la matinée.

Les élèves attendent l'autobus **pendant** une heure.
or: Les élèves attendent l'autobus une heure.

B. Depuis

1. To describe the duration of an action that started in the past but is still going on, use the *present tense* of the verb and **depuis**. The English equivalent is *has / have been* or *has / have been doing*.

Daniel **est** à Lyon **depuis** une semaine.	*Daniel **has been** in Lyon for a week.*
Il **cherche** une chambre **depuis** longtemps.	*He **has been looking** for a room for a long time.*

2. **Depuis** may also be used with a specific time. In this case, its English equivalent is *since*.

Chirac est président **depuis** 1995.	*Chirac has been president since 1995.*
Elle attend une lettre **depuis** lundi.	*She has been waiting for a letter since Monday.*

3. To express how long it has been since something happened, use a negative, the **passé composé**, and **depuis.**

> Je **n'ai pas fait** la vaisselle **depuis** trois jours.
> Le concierge **n'a rien fait depuis** une semaine.

C. Il y a... que and Voilà... que

Il y a... que and **Voilà... que** also express the duration of an action that started in the past but is still going on. They are used only with amounts of time. These two structures often show more impatience on the part of the speaker than **depuis** and must precede the subject and verb.

Il y a trois jours **qu'**on n'a pas d'eau.	*We haven't had water **for three** days.*
Voilà une heure **que** nous téléphonons au propriétaire.	*We have been phoning the landlord **for an hour.***

D. Il y a

To describe the amount of time that has passed since an action took place, use **il y a** and a verb in a past tense. It may precede or follow the verb. The English equivalent is *ago.*

J'**ai trouvé** un appartement **il y a** un mois.	*I **found** an apartment a month **ago.***
Il y a trois jours, elle **était** encore en Europe.	*Three days **ago**, she **was** still in Europe.*

Attention!

There are two differences between **il y a** meaning *for* and meaning *ago.* When **il y a** means *ago,* a past tense is used and there is no **que.**

Il y a trois minutes, il **était** là.	*He **was** here three minutes **ago.***
Il y a trois minutes **qu'**il **est** là.	*He's **been** here **for** three minutes.*

E. Other useful time expressions

1. **Dès** and **à partir de** *(from . . . on, as of . . . , beginning with . . .)* can be used at the beginning or at the end of the sentence.

> **Dès** maintenant, il faut que vous utilisiez un ordinateur.
> Les Français ont eu des vacances payées **à partir des** années 30.

2. **Pour** *(for)* is used with time only for projection into the future with a verb of motion.

> Il est parti **pour** trois mois en Afrique.
> Elle va sortir **pour** une heure.

3. **Dans** *(in)* describes the amount of time before you do something; **en** *(in)* describes the amount of time it takes to do something.

> Je vais passer un examen **dans** trois jours.
> Je dois passer cet examen **en** 50 minutes.

Langue

A. **Robert utilise les petites annonces.** Complétez les phrases suivantes en traduisant le(s) mot(s) entre parenthèses.

1. Robert achète le journal ici _____ deux ans. *(for)*
2. Il lit les petites annonces _____ quelques minutes. *(in)*
3. _____ trois semaines _____ il cherche une voiture. *(for)*
4. _____ une semaine, il pensait en avoir trouvé une. *(ago)*
5. Il a téléphoné au propriétaire _____ plusieurs jours. *(for)*
6. Sa femme lui a dit qu'il venait de partir _____ une semaine en Angleterre. *(for)*
7. Il peut retéléphoner _____ mardi prochain. *(from Tuesday on)*
8. Il décide de chercher une autre voiture _____ demain. *(as of)*

B. **Ma première année à l'université.** Traduisez les phrases suivantes.

1. I have been here since September.
2. Classes started four weeks ago.
3. Every day, I stay in the lab for one hour.
4. From three o'clock on, I am in the library.
5. I have known my roommate for eight months.
6. I am going to have my last exam in three weeks.

C. **Fin du siècle.** C'est le vendredi 31 décembre 1999 à midi, et vous préparez les festivités pour le Nouvel An. Depuis quand ou depuis combien de temps faites-vous les choses suivantes? Ou bien, vous les avez faites il y a combien de temps?

1. attendre ce jour / des années
2. téléphoner / amis / mardi dernier
3. préparer / plats / huit heures du matin
4. choisir / musique / mois
5. acheter le champagne / semaine dernière
6. répéter «Ce n'est qu'un *au revoir*» / toute la matinée

Culture

WWW

D. **Prenons le train.** Vous êtes à Montréal et vous décidez de prendre le train pour aller à Ottawa. Consultez l'horaire *(schedule)* et répondez aux questions page 413.

Connecting Train No. Correspondance ferroviaire	km			**21** Ex. Sa. Su. Sauf sa. di.	**23**	**23**	
Québec, QC (Gare du Palais)	0	Dp		06 45	11 50	11 50	
Montréal, QC (Central Stn./Gare Centrale)	272	Ar		09 55	15 00	15 00	

	km						
Montréal, QC ET/HE ⁶⁰ (Central Stn./Gare Centrale)	0	Dp	07 20	09 30	13 05	16 30	17 50	19 40
Dorval ³¹ ⁶⁰	19		07 40	09 50	13 26	16 51	18 10	20 01
Coteau, QC	63				F 13 51			F 20 26
Alexandria, ON	100		F 08 32	F 10 35	F 14 16	F 17 36	F 18 55	F 20 58
Maxville	117		F 08 46	F 10 49				F 21 12
Casselman	140				F 14 41			
Ottawa, ON	187	Ar	09 29	11 32	15 22	18 40	19 49	21 58

1. On peut aller de Montréal à Ottawa en combien de temps?
2. Vous êtes dans le train de Montréal de 7 h 20 et vous venez de partir de Maxville. Vous voyagez depuis combien de temps?
3. Vous allez arriver à Ottawa dans combien de temps?
4. A Montréal vous montez dans le train de 13 h 05. Il y a combien de temps que les gens qui sont montés à Québec sont dans le train?
5. Ils ont attendu à la Gare Centrale à Montréal pendant combien de temps?
6. Vous arrivez à la gare de Montréal à huit heures du soir. Le dernier train est parti pour Ottawa il y a combien de temps?

Communication

E. **Mes études.** Complétez les phrases suivantes.

1. J'étudie le français depuis…
2. J'ai reçu mon diplôme de lycée il y a…
3. Il y a… que je suis étudiant(e) à cette université.
4. Je vais rentrer dans…
5. Je vais commencer à chercher du travail dans…
6. J'ai préparé cette leçon pendant…

F. **Questions personnelles.** Votre logement

1. Pendant combien de temps est-ce que votre famille a habité votre maison?
2. Vous êtes parti(e) de chez eux il y a combien de temps?
3. Combien de temps avez-vous passé à chercher votre appartement / votre chambre?
4. Vous êtes là depuis combien de temps?
5. Vous faites le ménage en combien de temps?
6. Dans combien de temps pensez-vous acheter une maison?

Communiquons

Consulter la presse francophone   WWW

In France, most newspapers and news magazines can be associated with major political movements. For example, in Paris *Le Figaro* is rather conservative, but *Libération* is to the political left. One of the most respected dailies, *Le Monde*, has a liberal point of view, while *Le Canard Enchaîné*, a weekly newspaper, specializes in political satire. It uses many puns, innuendos, and allusions that only people who follow the daily political scene understand. Although these and other major Parisian newspapers are available throughout France, each region has its own paper. For example, Lyon has *Le Progrès*, Toulouse *La Dépêche du Midi*, and Rennes *Ouest-France*.

Other francophone countries have their own daily papers in French, such as *Le Devoir*, which is published in Montréal. In many areas, residents have a choice of languages for their papers: French or Dutch in Belgium, French or German in Switzerland, French and English in Quebec.

In addition to daily papers (**les quotidiens**), there are also several types of weekly magazines (**les hebdomadaires**) and monthly publications (**les mensuels**). On a weekly basis, *L'Express, Le Point,* and *Le Nouvel Observateur* cover the news on the national and international scenes, while *Paris-Match,* the most widely read news magazine, provides lighter, general information, emphasizing photographs and gossip about popular figures. Monthly magazines include those for fashion (**les journaux de mode**), such as *Marie-Claire* and *Marie-France,* or publications, such as *Femme,* that represent the feminist point of view. *Elle* and *Femme Actuelle* are magazines for women.

Numerous publications appeal to specific interests (**la presse spécialisée**). You have already learned that *L'Equipe* is a daily newspaper for sports fans and that *Télé 7 Jours* and *TV Magazine* provide information on television programming, and are the most widely read French publications by far. Other types of specialized publications include the Parisian magazines *Pariscope* and *L'Officiel des Spectacles,* which give a complete listing of the current movies, plays, and nightclub acts. In addition, most French hobbyists and sports lovers have publications for their individual interests. There is even a periodical for users of the **Minitel!**

Expressions

▶ **On parle des rubriques d'un journal.**

Les enfants lisent les bandes dessinées.	*Children read the comic strips.*
Je voudrais lire le courrier du cœur.	*I would like to read the advice column.*
Maman regarde l'économie.	*Mom reads the business section.*
Papa préfère l'éditorial.	*Dad prefers the editorial.*
Mon frère lit les faits divers.	*My brother reads human interest stories.*
Ma sœur lit seulement les gros titres.	*My sister reads only the headlines.*
Passe-moi l'horoscope.	*Pass me the horoscope.*
Il y a des mots croisés difficiles.	*There are difficult crossword puzzles.*
Les petites annonces ne m'intéressent pas.	*The classified ads don't interest me.*
J'ai vu le film décrit dans les spectacles.	*I saw the film described in the entertainment section.*
Tout le monde lit les sports.	*Everyone reads the sports section.*
Cette histoire est à la une.	*That story is on the front page.*

▶ On emploie d'autres expressions journalistiques.

Un(e) abonné(e) à *L'Express* a écrit une lettre à la revue.	*A subscriber to* L'Express *wrote a letter to the magazine.*
J'ai un abonnement à *Paris-Match.*	*I have a subscription to* Paris-Match.
Tu t'abonnes à un magazine?	*Do you subscribe to a magazine?*
J'achète le journal au kiosque de journaux.	*I buy the paper at the newspaper stand.*
Le vendeur de journaux y travaille.	*The news dealer works there.*

Interaction   *Monsieur et Madame Legrand lisent le journal.*

M. LEGRAND:	Tu as vu le journal?
MME LEGRAND:	François l'a laissé sur le divan.
M. LEGRAND:	Qu'est-ce qu'il y a d'intéressant à la une?
MME LEGRAND:	Pas grand-chose°. Le président a parlé de l'économie.
M. LEGRAND:	Je veux regarder les sports.
MME LEGRAND:	François a cette page dans la salle à manger. Il cherche aussi une moto dans les petites annonces.
M. LEGRAND:	Dans ce cas°-là, j'espère qu'il trouve du travail aussi!

Pas... *Not much*

case

Activités

A. Quel journal ou quelle revue faut-il acheter dans les situations suivantes en France?

1. Vous voulez aller au cinéma.
2. Vous voulez savoir qui a gagné le match de football.
3. Vous voulez connaître la nouvelle mode.
4. Vous voulez des renseignements sur les événements *(events)* internationaux de la semaine.
5. Vous voulez regarder la télévision.

B. Quelle rubrique faut-il consulter dans les situations suivantes?

1. Vous cherchez un appartement.
2. Vous voulez connaître votre avenir.
3. Vous voulez savoir quelles sortes de problèmes personnels ont les Français.
4. Vous voulez vous détendre.
5. Vous voulez savoir qui a gagné l'étape du Tour de France.
6. Vous avez envie de sortir.

C. **Où on travaille.** Comme aux Etats-Unis, les journaux français se réfèrent aux organisations gouvernementales françaises par le nom du bâtiment *(building)* où elles se trouvent. Trouvez le bâtiment pour chaque organisation.

MODÈLE: (aux Etats-Unis) la Maison-Blanche
    C'est là où le Président travaille.

1. Matignon
2. l'Elysée
3. le palais Bourbon
4. l'Hôtel de Ville
5. le palais du Luxembourg
6. le quai d'Orsay

a. le maire de Paris
b. le ministre des Affaires étrangères
c. le président
d. le Premier ministre
e. l'Assemblée nationale
f. le Sénat

D. Répondez aux questions suivantes.

1. Quel journal lisez-vous? Quelles revues? Depuis quand?
2. Où se trouve votre vendeur de journaux préféré?
3. A quelles revues vous êtes-vous abonné(e)? Pour combien de temps?
4. Aimez-vous faire les mots croisés? Dans quel journal y a-t-il des mots croisés très difficiles? très faciles?
5. Lisez-vous votre horoscope? Souvent? Qu'est-ce que vous en pensez?
6. Avez-vous écrit une lettre au courrier du cœur? Pourquoi?
7. Avez-vous consulté les petites annonces? Que cherchiez-vous?
8. Quelle bande dessinée préférez-vous? Pourquoi? Quel journal a de bonnes bandes dessinées?

Lecture culturelle

Avant la lecture

The fact that French is not really a "foreign" language in the United States, but a second language, is becoming widely known. For example, the cultural renaissance in Louisiana has produced, most noticeably, a popular style of cooking, as exemplified by Paul Prudhomme, and lively music, such as **zydeco**. American poets and novelists of French expression produce a diverse body of literature in their native French language. In the past, however, the French language was not viewed favorably. Earlier in the century, children were punished for speaking French in school. Unfortunately, Hollywood has been guilty of much exaggerated stereotyping and inaccurate portrayals in such films as *Southern Comfort* and *Angel Heart*.

Most Americans of French origin owe their heritage not directly to France but to Canada. Many French speakers were forced to leave Canada after France lost the Seven Years' War (French and Indian War) in 1763. Again in the nineteenth century, economic conditions in Quebec forced many people to emigrate to the United States in search of work. There are still towns in New England where nearly everyone speaks French. Close ties have always existed between Canada and the United States, as evidenced by the fact that we have the longest undefended border in the world.

Bec Doux et ses amis,

*by Ken Meaux
and Earl Comeaux*

© *1980*

Activités

A. Look at a map of Louisiana. Look for Lafayette, the francophone capital of Louisiana. What other names with a French origin can you see?

B. When the British drove the French away from Canada after 1763, why do you think the latter chose to go to Louisiana? What about nineteenth-century Quebec? Why did the people choose New England?

Le français aux Etats-Unis   WWW

Des vagues° successives d'immigration pendant plus de trois cents ans ont contribué à former la population américaine. Parmi° celles-ci, l'apport° français et canadien-français est prédominant par son ancienneté et son importance. Deux étapes principales en marquent
5 l'histoire: l'installation en Louisiane et l'émigration québécoise de 1840 à 1930.

waves
Among
contribution

La Louisiane

Ce grand territoire du sud des Etats-Unis a appartenu à la France de 1699 à 1763, puis° de 1800 à 1802. Pendant cette période, trois mouvements d'immigration y ont constitué une population francophone importante. D'abord, il y a eu les Créoles, comme on appelait les colons° français qui sont arrivés aux
10 dix-septième et dix-huitième siècles°. Puis, les Cajuns (écrit aussi «Cadien»), prononciation locale du mot «Acadien», expulsés d'Acadie en 1755 par les Britanniques, ont trouvé refuge sur les bords° du golfe du Mexique. Enfin, les Créoles noirs, amenés comme esclaves° d'Afrique et des Antilles, ont constitué aussi une partie importante de la population.

then

settlers
centuries

shores
slaves

15   De leur héritage français, les Créoles ont conservé leur religion catholique et ils ont converti une grande partie de la population anglophone, presque toujours à l'occasion d'intermariages. Ils ont développé une riche tradition musicale et théâtrale et, en 1808, ont fondé la première troupe d'opéra aux Etats-Unis. Les Créoles ont donné naissance à une cuisine qui est aujourd'hui une adapta-
20 tion de la cuisine française continentale traditionnelle où on a ajouté° des épices° et des ingrédients de la région. Cette culture a aussi produit une littérature francophone importante qui s'est épanouie° surtout au dix-neuvième siècle.

added / spices

flourished

   Les Cajuns, eux, sont devenus une minorité francophone rurale. Jusque° vers le milieu° des années 60, de plus en plus de jeunes Cajuns refusaient même

Until
middle

25 de continuer à parler français car ils voulaient s'assimiler au plus vite° à la majorité anglo-saxonne. Puis soudain°, les choses ont changé. Comme beaucoup d'autres minorités, les Acadiens ont commencé à proclamer leur héritage, et ils sont maintenant très fiers° de parler français et d'être cajuns.

au... as fast as possible
suddenly

proud

Après la guerre de Sécession°, les noirs francophones de La Nouvelle-
30 Orléans ont formé une société stratifiée avec à sa tête une élite riche et cultivée. La vie sociale de cette élite ressemblait en tous points à celle de l'élite créole blanche. Ils voyageaient beaucoup et envoyaient° fréquemment leurs enfants à l'école en France. Ils parlaient le même français que celui des blancs de La Nouvelle-Orléans, comme le font encore leurs quelques descendants qui parlent
35 encore français.

guerre... Civil War

sent

Aujourd'hui, il n'est pas facile d'estimer l'importance de la population francophone de la Louisiane: en 1980, environ 947.000 personnes déclaraient être d'origine ethnique française, et on estime qu'à peu près 270.000 personnes parlent encore le français. Ces statistiques sont incertaines, mais il est sûr que le
40 français est devenu la principale langue seconde des Louisianais, même anglophones. Ainsi°, chaque° jour, des stations de télévision et de radio offrent plusieurs heures d'émissions en français.

Thus / each

Un million d'expatriés

De 1840 à 1930, près d'un million de Québécois se sont expatriés aux Etats-Unis pour y trouver un emploi. Dans une société surtout agricole, avec une crois-
45 sance° démographique explosive, les jeunes ne trouvaient plus de terres° à cultiver et le chômage hivernal° affectait cruellement les travailleurs agricoles. Deux tiers° de ces immigrants se sont installés en Nouvelle-Angleterre, surtout dans le Massachusetts et dans le Connecticut, et un tiers dans le centre des Etats-Unis, surtout au Michigan. Des chercheurs du Québec ont estimé que, sans cet
50 exode historique, dix millions de personnes habiteraient maintenant le Québec et qu'il y aurait quatre millions de Franco-Québécois de plus.

growth / land
winter
thirds

Dans l'ensemble°, on estime que treize millions d'Américains sont d'origine française et qu'environ un million et demi d'entre eux parlent français à la maison. En plus de la Louisiane et de la Nouvelle-Angleterre, on trouve deux autres

Dans... As a whole

55 concentrations importantes de francophones aux Etats-Unis: l'une en Californie, l'autre en Floride, où plus de 100.000 habitants permanents seraient° des immi- *are thought to be* grés francophones récents. Dans le cas de la Floride, pendant la période hivernale, plus de 400.000 Québécois y séjournent° pour chercher le soleil! *stay*

Après la lecture

Questions sur le texte

1. Quelles sont les deux étapes principales de l'immigration francophone aux Etats-Unis?
2. En quoi consiste la population francophone de Louisiane?
3. Quelles ont été les contributions des Créoles?
4. Où habitent principalement les Cajuns?
5. Quel français parlaient les Créoles noirs?
6. Pourquoi beaucoup de Québécois ont-ils émigré au dix-neuvième siècle? Où se sont-ils installés?
7. Combien d'Américains d'origine française parlent encore le français à la maison?
8. Quelles sont les autres régions où on trouve beaucoup de francophones aux Etats-Unis?

Activités

A. Quels aspects de la culture louisianaise francophone connaissez-vous personnellement? Avez-vous essayé un plat créole ou cajun? Avez-vous regardé une émission télévisée sur la cuisine ou sur la musique de cette région? Quels sont les chanteurs connus de la Louisiane francophone?

B. Quel contact avez-vous eu avec des francophones aux Etats-Unis? Si vous n'avez pas rencontré de gens qui parlent français, peut-être avez-vous été exposé(e) à une culture francophone?

C. Quel est votre héritage? D'où sont venus vos ancêtres? Avez-vous étudié votre arbre généalogique? Jusqu'où? Savez-vous pourquoi vos ancêtres sont venus aux Etats-Unis?

Vocabulaire

Noms / Pronoms

appareil électro-ménager	appliance	concierge	concierge / caretaker
armoire	armoire	cuisine	kitchen
baignoire	bathtub	cuisinière	stove
canapé	sofa	divan	sofa
chambre de bonne	maid's room	douche	shower
charges	utilities	entrée	entrance
chemin	way	étage	floor

étagère	shelf	petites annonces	classified ads
évier	kitchen sink	pièce	room
fauteuil	armchair	plancher	floor
four	oven	propriétaire	owner
four à micro-ondes	microwave oven	que (pron. rel.)	whom / that /which
frigidaire	refrigerator	qui (pron. rel.)	who / that
immeuble	apartment building	rez-de-chaussée	ground floor
lampe	lamp	salle à manger	dining room
lavabo	sink	salle de bains	bathroom
lave-vaisselle	dishwasher	salon	living room
lit	bed	sèche-linge	dryer
Louisiane	Louisiana	table	table
loyer	rent	table de nuit	bedside table
machine à laver	washing machine	tapis	carpet
meubles	furniture	toilettes	bathroom
où (pron. rel.)	where		

Verbes

intéresser	to interest	placer	to place

Adjectifs / Adverbes

compris	included	juste	just
enfin	finally	meublé(e)	furnished

Expressions

à gauche	on the left	en	in (time)
à partir de	starting from	il y a	ago
à ta / votre / sa place	in your / his / her place	il y a... que	it has been . . . that
dans	in (time)	pour	for
dès	from	voilà... que	it has been . . . that
donner sur	to look out on		

Chapitre **17**

Le français au Québec

 Commençons

 Grammaire

 Communiquons

 Lecture culturelle

Vocabulaire

Le Château Frontenac et la Basse Ville à Québec

Objectives

Language

Vocabulary for nature and the environment • **Liaisons** • The future tense • **Si** clauses • **Mettre** and verbs conjugated like **mettre**

Culture

The Quebec poet Robert Mélançon • Hydro-Québec and the environment

Communication

Talking about events in the future • Expressing hypothetical situations • Expressing emotions

Commençons

Neige ▭

Un poète évoque un ballet de couleurs créé par le contact du soleil et de la neige sur la nature québécoise.

Le soleil ondoie sur le blanc,
Jour couché entre les troncs
Que le gel a noircis, délivrés
Des feuilles, des oiseaux, des rumeurs.
Le soleil coule sur la neige
Comme une eau plus vive que l'eau.
Terre lucide d'où jaillit la forêt
Intelligible (colonnes de raison,
Idées dont la rigueur inclut l'écorce,
Que la main touche), la neige méditative
Où passent les reflets du jour rose,
Jaune, bleu, où se dispersent des étoiles
Moins nombrables que la Voie lactée,
La neige incarne la lumière, elle est
Sa seule forme, sa seule matière.

Robert Mélançon

Dans la campagne québécoise

Etudions le poème

1. Comment expliquez-vous le deuxième vers *(line)*: «Jour couché entre les troncs»?
2. Quels sont les mots du poème qui évoquent l'hiver?
3. Que signifie «colonnes de raison» au vers 8?
4. Aux vers 11 et 12, «les reflets du jour rose, / Jaune, bleu…» évoquent quelle heure de la journée?
5. Quelle impression de la nature québécoise est-ce que ce poème vous donne?

Mots clés

poète	*poet*	ondoie	*shines*
évoque	*evokes*	troncs	*trunks*
créé	*created*	gel	*frost*
contact	*contact*	noircis	*blackened*
nature	*nature*	délivrés	*freed*

feuilles	*leaves*	méditative	*pensive*
rumeurs	*rumors*	reflets	*reflexions*
vive	*lively*	rose	*pink*
lucide	*lucid*	se dispersent	*scatter*
jaillit	*springs*	nombrables	*countable*
colonnes	*columns*	Voie lactée	*Milky Way*
raison	*reason*	incarne	*embodies*
dont	*of which*	lumière	*light*
inclut	*includes*	matière	*matter*
écorce	*bark*		

Faisons connaissance   WWW

Robert Mélançon is a Quebec poet born in Montreal in 1947. A professor at the University of Montreal, he spent some time writing literary editorials for the newspaper *Le Devoir*. He also served on the editorial board of the review *Liberté*. His poetry has often been labeled classical. Among his works, one might note a collection of poems, *Inscriptions,* published in 1978, and *Peinture aveugle,* which appeared a year later.

The people of Quebec have always been very proud of their origins, their language, and their customs. Their profound attachment to their land is in evidence throughout their literature. For generations **québécois** poets have sung the beauty of the countryside and of the Quebec soul.

Today, Quebec and the rest of Canada are not just looking backward at their past; they are also oriented toward the future. Two examples of Canadian technological achievements are Hydro-Québec, one of the largest hydroelectric networks in the world, and the robotic arm (**le bras spatial**) used to manipulate objects outside the American space shuttle.

Québec, Montréal, même pays

A Québec, cité-refuge des valeurs francophones, et surtout à Montréal, on est en « presque Amérique ». Mais tout est dans ce « presque ».

Enrichissons notre vocabulaire

Le paysage *(Countryside)*

les montagnes *(f.)*

le lac — la riviére

le fleuve

les arbres *(m.)*

les fleurs *(f.)*

le champ

la pelouse

le jardin

L'environnement *(m.)* *(The environment)*

l'écologie *(f.)* / les écologistes *(m., f.)*	*ecology / ecologists*
l'énergie *(f.)* solaire / nucléaire	*solar / nuclear energy*
les espaces *(m.)* habitables	*livable spaces*
la pluie acide	*acid rain*
La pollution **augmente / diminue.**	*Pollution is increasing / decreasing.*
le recyclage	*recycling*

Le futur *(The future)*

la biotechnologie	*biotechnology*
la lune, les planètes *(f.)*	*the moon, the planets*
la navette spatiale	*the space shuttle*
la station spatiale	*the space station*

Prononciation   Liaisons   [○━○]

A. You learned in Chapter 4 that **liaisons** occur when a normally silent, final written consonant is pronounced because a word starting with a vowel follows. Often, a certain amount of flexibility is allowed when deciding whether or not to pronounce the consonant, but sometimes you must make a **liaison.**

B. **Liaisons** that you must make are called **liaisons obligatoires.** They fall into the following categories:

1. **article + noun / article + adjective + noun**

    mes‿amis / un petit‿homme / des‿efforts /
        mon‿ordinateur / un grand‿appartement /
        deux‿autres‿exemples / un‿habitant /
        de vieilles‿églises / dix‿étudiants

2. **pronoun + verb / verb + pronoun / pronoun + pronoun**

    ils‿habitent / Nous‿en voudrions. / Nous‿y allons. /
        Il va les‿inviter. / Donnez-en. / Vont-ils les‿acheter? /
        On‿en‿a. / Vous‿en‿avez vu. / Elles les‿ont.

    Do not pronounce, however, the **liaison** between subject pronouns and verbs with inversion.

    Sont-ils / arrivés?   Voulez-vous / en acheter?
        Peuvent-elles / ouvrir?

3. **after many one-syllable prepositions and adverbs**

    chez‿eux / trop‿aimable / dans‿un restaurant /
        très‿utile / sous‿un‿arbre / bien‿aimé /

C. Some **liaisons,** called **liaisons facultatives,** are optional. Generally, you should make more of them when speaking in a formal style. Some categories are as follows:

negation

pas‿avec moi	*or*	pas / avec moi
jamais‿au théâtre	*or*	jamais / au théâtre
plus‿à Paris	*or*	plus / à Paris

verbs + verbs / verbs + prepositions / verbs + articles

je dois‿aller	*or*	je dois / aller
il faut‿appeler	*or*	il faut / appeler

But with **est** and present-tense verbs ending in **-ont,** liaison is very frequent:

Il est‿arrivé. / Ils font‿une erreur. /
    Elles‿ont‿un‿appartement.

two-syllable prepositions and adverbs

devant‿une église	*or*	devant / une église
beaucoup‿aimé	*or*	beaucoup / aimé
souvent‿excellent	*or*	souvent / excellent

Exercice

Read the following sentences aloud, making all **liaisons obligatoires**.

1. Ils en ont un.
2. Montrez-en aux enfants.
3. Elles y sont allées sans eux.
4. Je les ai emmenés avec leurs amis.
5. Etes-vous allés en Irlande cet été?
6. Les bons étudiants adorent étudier sous les arbres.

Grammaire

I. The future tense

You use the future tense to talk about events and states that will occur in the future, but with a degree of uncertainty.

A. Forms

1. In French, the most frequent way of expressing a future action in conversation is by using the **futur proche**, but there is also a future tense that uses only one verb form. To conjugate a verb in the future tense, you add the following endings to the stems you learned for the conditional mood.

parler	finir	répondre
je parlerai	je finirai	je répondrai
tu parleras	tu finiras	tu répondras
il / elle / on parlera	il / elle / on finira	il / elle / on répondra
nous parlerons	nous finirons	nous répondrons
vous parlerez	vous finirez	vous répondrez
ils / elles parleront	ils / elles finiront	ils / elles répondront

Nous **construirons** une maison ici. — *We **will build** a house here.*

Tu me **diras** le nom de ce vin? — *Will you **tell** me the name of this wine?*

Ils **apprendront** le recyclage aux enfants. — *They **will teach** recycling to the children.*

> ## L'orthographe
>
> Note that in the preceding examples you drop the **e** from infinitives ending in **-re** before you add the future endings: **répondre** → **ils répondront.**

2. All verbs that have irregular stems in the conditional mood also have the same irregular stems in the future tense. For these irregular stems, refer to the section on the formation of the conditional in Chapter 16.

B. Use

There is a slight difference in meaning between the **futur** and the **futur proche**. The **futur proche** expresses actions that are more certain than those in the **futur**.

Elle va avoir un enfant.	*(She's pregnant.)*
Elle aura un enfant.	*(She hopes to have a child.)*
Je vais écrire un poème.	*(Now!)*
J'écrirai un poème.	*(When I have time.)*

C. Expressions of time

1. French has four expressions that are frequently used to introduce events in the future:

quand / lorsque	*when*
dès que / aussitôt que	*as soon as*

2. When you use these expressions in a sentence with both actions in the future, you must use the **futur** in *both* clauses, even though you would use the present tense in English.

Je lui demanderai **quand il arrivera.**	*I will ask him **when he comes.***
Dès qu'elle partira, nous nous coucherons.	***As soon as she leaves,** we shall go to bed.*

3. An imperative used in the main clause of a sentence with an expression of time implies a future action; therefore, you must use the future tense.

Téléphonez **quand vous aurez le temps!**	*Call **when you have time.***

Langue

A. Une promenade à la campagne. Dans les phrases suivantes, mettez les verbes au futur.

1. Allez-vous faire un voyage?
2. Oui, nous allons partir samedi.
3. Je vais aller à la campagne.
4. Mais, il va pleuvoir!
5. Nos amis vont nous emmener en auto.
6. Nous allons voir de vieilles maisons.

B. **La visite d'une vieille amie.** Dans les phrases suivantes, changez les verbes du passé au futur.

1. Aussitôt que nous avons reçu sa lettre, nous avons su qu'elle revenait.
2. Quand elle a téléphoné de la gare, j'ai commencé à faire le ménage.
3. Dès qu'elle est arrivée, elle a sonné à la porte.
4. Dès que je l'ai vue, je l'ai embrassée.
5. Quand on a fini de parler, elle est allée se reposer.
6. J'ai été malheureux quand elle a dû partir.

C. **Notre avenir.** Formez des phrases complètes avec les mots donnés.

1. Nous / ne... pas / devenir / vieux
2. On / pouvoir / aller / sur la lune
3. Il / ne... plus / y / avoir / cancer
4. Président / recevoir / lettre / d'une autre planète
5. Il / falloir / vous / utiliser / énergie / solaire
6. Il / ne... plus / pleuvoir

Culture

D. **Que faire?** Vous irez en France un jour. Que ferez-vous dans les situations suivantes? Trouvez la meilleure *(best)* solution.

MODÈLE: aller de Paris à Lyon / prendre le TGV
Quand j'irai de Paris à Lyon, je prendrai le TGV.

1. acheter des vêtements
   a. aller chez Chanel   b. aller à un hypermarché
   c. aller à une poissonnerie
2. mourir de soif
   a. entrer dans un café   b. chercher une fontaine
   c. chercher un distributeur de boissons
3. avoir mal à la gorge
   a. aller chez le médecin   b. aller au supermarché
   c. aller à la pharmacie
4. quelqu'un éternue *(sneezes)*
   a. dire «Mon Dieu!»   b. dire «Gesundheit!»
   c. dire «A vos souhaits!»
5. aller à Disneyland Paris   WWW
   a. valoir mieux prendre le R.E.R.   b. le métro   c. l'autobus
6. prendre l'apéritif
   a. demander un coca   b. dire «A la vôtre!»
   c. boire directement la bouteille

Communication

E. **Votre avenir.** Que ferez-vous…

1. aussitôt que le week-end arrivera?
2. quand vous serez en vacances?
3. lorsque vous pourrez avoir un appartement?
4. lorsque vous serez vieux / vieille?
5. dès que ce cours finira?
6. aussitôt que vous aurez beaucoup d'argent?

F. Le futur. Imaginez la vie au vingt et unième siècle. Utilisez les suggestions données ou vos propres idées.

MODÈLE: *On passera le week-end sur la lune.*
Nous ne travaillerons plus.
Les gens resteront jeunes.

ne plus aller chez le dentiste	ne plus avoir besoin de médecins
avoir des robots pour...	voir les gens au téléphone
ne jamais être fatigué(e)	vouloir retourner en 1990
ne plus faire la vaisselle	(le bon vieux temps!)
falloir parler plusieurs langues	???
pouvoir travailler à la maison	

G. Questions personnelles. Votre avenir.

1. Où irez-vous cet été?
2. Quand commencerez-vous à travailler?
3. Quand aurez-vous trente ans?
4. Qu'est-ce que vous ferez ce jour-là?
5. Quand aurez-vous des enfants? Combien?
6. A quelle université iront-ils? A celle-ci?

II. Si clauses

> You use **si** clauses to state the conditions under which things happen, even if only hypothetically.

Both French and English have sentences in which one action depends on a certain condition. In French, there is a sequence of verb tenses used in sentences that state a condition with **si**. At this point, you can construct three types.

A. Use the sequence **si** + *present tense / present tense* with general rules or typical conditions.

S'il **fait beau**, j'**emmène** mes enfants au parc.
Il **fait** ses devoirs s'il n'y **a** rien à la télé.

B. Use the sequence **si** + *present tense / futur* for a specific event.

S'il **fait** beau ce soir, on **regardera** la lune.
Les élèves s'**endormiront** si le prof **est** ennuyeux.

C. Use the sequence **si** + *imperfect / conditional* for hypothetical situations.

S'il **faisait** attention, il **réussirait**.
La pollution **augmenterait** si nous ne l'**arrêtions** pas.

Langue

A. Ce soir... Dans les phrases suivantes, ajoutez l'expression **ce soir** et mettez le verbe en italique au futur.

MODÈLE: Si tu pars, je *viens* avec toi.
        Si tu pars ce soir, je viendrai avec toi.

1. S'il pleut, on *reste* à la maison.
2. Si nos amis veulent entrer, ils *peuvent* sonner.
3. Si on est fatigué, on *se couche* de bonne heure.
4. Si quelqu'un appelle, nous ne *répondons* pas.
5. Si tu ne travailles pas maintenant, *peux*-tu finir à l'heure?
6. Je ne *reviens* pas s'il n'y a pas d'autobus.

B. Mais, ce n'est pas le cas! Faites des phrases hypothétiques en mettant *(by putting)* les verbes à l'imparfait et au conditionnel, selon le cas.

MODÈLE: Si Marie est malade, nous irons sans elle.
        Si Marie était malade, nous irions sans elle.

1. S'il fait beau, ils iront à la montagne.
2. S'il y a des nuages, nous ne verrons pas les étoiles.
3. Nous ne prendrons pas la voiture s'il neige.
4. Tu auras mal à la tête si tu bois trop.
5. Si vous aimez la musique classique, nous irons au concert.
6. Nous n'irons pas dans la forêt si nous prenons ce chemin.

C. Des projets pour ce soir. Faites deux phrases avec chaque groupe de mots.

MODÈLE: Si / nous / finir / ménage / nous / pouvoir / s'occuper / pelouse
        Si nous finissons le ménage, nous pourrons nous occuper de la pelouse.
        Si nous finissions le ménage, nous pourrions nous occuper de la pelouse.

1. Je / lui / écrire / si / je / recevoir / son / lettre
2. Si / elle / nous / poser / question, / nous / ne... pas / savoir / réponse
3. Les autres / ne... pas / vouloir / venir / si / je / inviter / Luc
4. Si / tout le monde / être en retard, / il / falloir / attendre
5. Si / elle / ne... pas / se dépêcher, / elle / ne... jamais / être / à l'heure
6. Si / il / ne... pas / arriver à l'heure, / il / valoir mieux / partir / sans lui

Si le français vous intéresse...
...Le Québec vous passionnera!

Culture

D. Allons au cinéma! *L'Officiel des Spectacles,* comme *Pariscope,* est un magazine qui indique les choses à faire à Paris. Consultez l'extrait suivant à
gauche qui décrit le festival de films pour enfants au cinéma Saint-Lambert
dans le 15ᵉ arrondissement et la liste des abréviations à droite pour répondre aux questions.　　　　　　　　　　　　　　　　　　　　　WWW

1. Si on prend le métro, à quelle station est-ce qu'on descendra?
2. Si on est étudiant, quel jour faudra-t-il y aller pour avoir un tarif
   réduit?
3. Si vous n'aviez qu'un billet de cinquante francs ce jour-là, combien
   recevriez-vous en monnaie?
4. Si vous vouliez voir un dessin animé français, quel film verriez-vous?
5. Quels films pourriez-vous voir, si vous ne pouviez y aller que dimanche
   matin?
6. Si vous étiez là, quel film choisiriez-vous?

SAINT-LAMBERT, 6, rue Péclet, Mᵒ Vaugi-
rard, 45 32 91 68. Pl. 37F. TR. 30F : mer + ET, CV,
FN, CH, MI et - de 15 ans. TU. 20F : groupes (48
28 78 87).
Mer 16h50, sam 13h30, dim 11h (TU. 30F): ♦ **Les
101 dalmatiens** (Dolby stéréo).
Mer, sam 13h30, dim 11h (TU. 30F): ♦ **La belle
au bois dormant, de Walt Disney** (Dolby sté-
réo).
Dim 13h30 : ♦ **Les voyages de Gulliver, de
Dave Fleischer.**
Sam 16h50 : ♦ **L' Indien du placard** (Dolby SR).
Dim 11h : ♦ **Tintin et le temple du soleil** (TU.
30F).
Dim 16h45 : ♦ **Super Noël** (Dolby SR).
Mer, sam 15h05, dim 13h30 : ♦ **Pocahontas**
(Dolby SR).
Mer, sam 15h05, dim 15h : ♦ **Jumanji** (Dolby
SR).
Mer 16h50, sam 13h30, dim 15h : ♦ **Casper**
(Dolby SR).
*Mer 13h30, 15h05, jeu, mar 15h05, ven 15h30,
sam, dim 15h05, 16h50, lun 14h30 :* ♦ **Babe**
(Dolby SR).
Dim 13h30 : ♦ **Astérix chez les Bretons** (Dolby
stéréo).
Mer 13h30, dim 16h45 : ♦ **Un Indien dans la ville**
(Dolby stéréo).
Mer 16h50 : ♦ **Jonathan Livingston, le goé-
land.**
Sam 16h50 : **The mask** (Dolby SR).
Jeu, sam 18h30, lun 21h: **Apollo 13** (Dolby SR).
Sam 18h30 : **Goldeneye** (Dolby SR)

DESIGNATION DES CARTES EN USAGE :
CB : Carte Bancaire acceptée.
CG : Carte Gaumont (170 F - 5 entrées - 2 mois).
CUGC : Carte UGC (130 F - 4 entrées pour 1 pers. ou
195 F - 6 entrées pour 1 ou 2 pers.).
TR : Tarif réduit appliqué aux catégories indiquées,
sauf le vendredi soir, samedi, dimanche, fêtes et veille
de fêtes.
TU : Tarif unique.
CF : Carte fidélité de la salle.　**CE :** Comité d'Entreprise.
CV : Carte Vermeil.　　　　　**FN :** Familles nombreuses.
ET : Etudiants.　　　　　　　**MI :** Militaires appelés.
CH : Chômeurs.　　**GS :** Groupes scolaires sur réserv.

Communication

E. Mes habitudes. Formez des phrases avec **si** pour décrire ce que *(what)* vous
faites en général. Employez **si** et un élément de chaque colonne pour former
des phrases logiques.

je
mes amis
ma famille
mon copain
???

avoir froid / chaud
avoir soif
être fatigué(e)
le prof est absent
faire beau
avoir trop de travail
pleuvoir
échouer à un examen
avoir de l'argent
???

F. **Un peu d'imagination!** En quoi votre vie serait-elle différente…

1. si vous n'alliez pas à l'université?
2. si vous aviez / n'aviez pas de camarade de chambre?
3. si vous aviez une auto? / n'aviez pas d'auto?
4. si vous aviez des cours faciles?
5. si vous ne saviez pas lire?
6. si vous étiez très paresseux (-euse)?

G. **Questions personnelles.** Imaginez!

1. Si vous receviez vos amis, qu'est-ce que vous feriez pour vous amuser?
2. Où habiteriez-vous si vous pouviez choisir?
3. Si vous étiez président, quel serait votre première décision?
4. Si vous alliez prendre votre dernier repas, qu'est-ce que vous préféreriez manger?
5. Si vous pouviez voyager sans payer, où iriez-vous?
6. Si vous pouviez prévoir le futur, qu'est-ce qui vous intéresserait le plus?

III. Mettre / Verbs conjugated like mettre

You use these verbs to describe activities, such as placing something somewhere, putting on clothes, turning on the TV, giving permission, and making promises.

The irregular verb **mettre** means *to put, to put on (clothing), to set the table, to turn on (a TV),* or *to take (an amount of time to do something).*

	mettre	
présent:	je **mets**	nous **mettons**
	tu **mets**	vous **mettez**
	il / elle / on **met**	ils / elles **mettent**
futur et conditionnel:	je **mettrai**	nous **mettrions**
passé composé:	il **a mis**	elles **ont mis**
subjonctif:	que je **mette**	que nous **mettions**
impératif:	**mets**	**mettons** **mettez**

Où est-ce que je peux **mettre** mon parapluie?
Elle **a mis** sa robe neuve.
On ne **met** que trois heures et demie pour aller à Paris en Concorde.

Mots clés	*Verbs conjugated like* **mettre**
permettre	*to permit* *to allow*
promettre	*to promise*
remettre	*to postpone* *to hand in* *to hand back* *to put back*
se mettre à	*to begin*

Une navette nous **permettra** d'aller à une station spatiale.
Il **s'est mis** à pleuvoir.

Attention!

1. **Permettre** and **promettre** take **à** before a person and **de** before an infinitive.

   Elle ne **permet** pas **aux** enfants **de** jouer dans la rue.
   Je **lui** ai **promis d'**acheter des fleurs.

2. To promise *not* to do something, put both parts of the negation (**ne pas, ne plus,** etc.) before the infinitive.

   Ils ont promis de **ne pas augmenter** la pollution.
   On promet de **ne plus contribuer** à la pluie acide.

Langue

A. Faisons la cuisine. Formez des phrases complètes avec les mots donnés.

1. Je / ne… pas / mettre / lait / dans / gâteau
2. Tu / remettre / viande / dans le frigidaire / ce matin?
3. Ils / promettre / ne pas mettre / sel
4. Ne… pas / permettre / enfants / utiliser / cuisinière
5. Elle / se mettre / préparer / dîner
6. Nous / mettre / table / sept heures

B. Habillons-nous. Refaites les phrases suivantes en employant les mots entre parenthèses.

1. Cet automne nous mettrons des vêtements chauds. (L'hiver dernier…)
2. Je n'aimerais pas que mon frère porte mes vêtements. (… permettre… mettre)
3. Tous les magasins vous recommandent d'essayer leurs vêtements. (… permettre…)
4. Si tu mets ton imperméable, il ne pleuvra pas. (… pleuvrait…)
5. Les enfants n'ont pas porté de chaussettes. (… mettre…)
6. Regarde cette jupe; maman m'a promis de l'acheter. (Mettre… permettre…)

Culture

C. **Le code de la route.** Vous préparez un voyage au Canada en voiture et vous avez besoin de connaître les différences entre les lois au Québec et celles des Etats-Unis. Qu'est-ce qu'on vous permet de faire et qu'est-ce qu'on ne vous permet pas?

MODÈLE: conduire à l'âge de seize ans?
On vous permet de conduire à l'âge de seize ans.

1. conduire et boire de l'alcool
2. conduire sans mettre sa ceinture de sécurité
3. transporter un jeune enfant sans siège de bébé
4. rouler à 105 à l'heure *(65 m.p.h.)*
5. tourner à droite à un feu *(light)* rouge
6. entrer dans le pays sans assurance
7. tourner à droite sans signaler
8. utiliser un détecteur de radar

Communication

D. **Tenez-vous vos promesses?** Qu'est-ce que vous avez promis de faire que vous avez fait, et que vous n'avez pas fait? Utilisez un élément de chaque colonne et suivez le modèle.

MODÈLE: *J'ai promis à mon petit ami de lui téléphoner plus souvent.*
(Je le fais.)
J'ai promis au professeur de venir en cours tous les jours.
(Je ne le fais pas.)

à	de
parents	faire moins de bruit
petit(e) ami(e)	écrire toutes les semaines
camarade(s) de chambre	l' / les inviter au restaurant
voisin(e)(s)	être patient(e)
agents de police	rentrer le week-end
???	???

E. **Des enfants dans votre avenir?** Quand vous aurez des enfants, qu'est-ce que vous leur permettrez de faire et qu'est-ce que vous ne leur permettrez pas de faire?

MODÈLE: *Je leur permettrai de faire du vélo.*
Je ne leur permettrai pas de jouer à table.

manger du gâteau	mettre les pieds sur la table
jouer au football	regarder la télévision
sortir le soir	avoir un(e) petit(e) ami(e)
se promener sans vêtements	avoir une voiture
fumer	boire du… / de la…
partir le week-end	???

F. **Questions personnelles.** Chez vous.

1. Quels disques mettez-vous le plus souvent? Et votre camarade de chambre?
2. Permettez-vous aux gens de fumer chez vous?
3. Quand est-ce qu'on met la radio?
4. Remettez-vous toujours une partie du ménage à plus tard?
5. Quels vêtements mettez-vous quand vous êtes seul(e)?
6. Qu'est-ce que vous avez promis de faire cette semaine?

Communiquons

Exprimer des émotions

In conversations, it is often necessary to express emotional reactions to statements or events. The following groups of words will help you express yourself in an authentic manner in French, particularly in informal situations.

Expressions

▶ **On exprime l'étonnement** *(surprise).*

Ça alors!	*I'll be darned!*
C'est pas vrai!	*No?!*
Comment?	*What?*
Quoi?	*What?*
Tiens!	*Hey!*
Nous avons du mal à croire qu'elle a dit cela.	*We have a hard time believing that she said that.*
Je suis étonnée qu'il refuse de le faire.	*I am surprised that he refuses to do it.*
Elle est surprise qu'ils n'en sachent rien.	*She is surprised that they don't know anything about it.*
Il s'étonne que la pluie acide soit si mauvaise.	*He is astonished that the acid rain is so bad.*
Tu ne sais pas que Jean a eu un accident?	*You don't know that John had an accident?*

► On exprime la déception *(disappointment)*.

(Quel) dommage!	*That's too bad! / What a shame!*
Tant pis!	*Too bad!*
Zut alors!	*Darn!*
Nous sommes déçus qu'il n'y ait pas de jardin.	*We are disappointed that there isn't a yard.*
Il est désolé que nous n'allions pas à la rivière.	*He is sorry that we aren't going to the river.*
Je suis navrée que mon mari ne puisse pas venir.	*I'm sorry that my husband can't come.*
Je regrette que le lac soit si loin.	*I'm sorry that the lake is so far away.*

► On exprime la satisfaction.

Bon!	*Good!*
Chouette alors!	*Great!*
Fantastique!	*Fantastic!*
Formidable!	*Great!*
Parfait!	*Perfect!*
Tant mieux!	*Good!*
Terrible!	*Super!*
Ils sont contents que nous nous promenions dans la forêt.	*They are happy we are walking in the forest.*
Vous êtes heureux que vos enfants arrêtent leurs plaintes?	*Are you happy that your children have stopped complaining?*
Je suis ravie que tu sois là!	*I am delighted that you are here!*
Elles sont satisfaites que tu réussisses.	*They are satisfied that you are passing.*

► On exprime la colère *(anger)*.

Arrête!	*Stop!*
Ça suffit!	*Enough!*
Ça va pas, non?	*Are you crazy?*
Fiche-moi la paix! / Laisse-moi!	*Leave me alone!*
J'en ai assez!	*I've had it!*
J'en ai marre! / J'en ai ras le bol!	*I've had it up to here!*
Tu me casses les pieds!	*You really annoy me!*
Il est fâché que tu mentes.	*He is angry that you are lying.*
Elle est furieuse que les enfants jouent sur la pelouse.	*She is furious that the children are playing on the lawn.*

► **On exprime l'indifférence.**

Ça m'est égal. / Je m'en fiche.	*I don't care.*
Ça ne fait rien.	*It doesn't matter.*
Ce n'est pas grand-chose.	*It's no big deal.*
Ce n'est pas grave.	*It's not serious.*
Comme ci, comme ça.	*So-so.*
Et après?	*So what?*
Ça m'est égal si tu fais cela.	*I don't care if you do that.*
Peu m'importe si tu ne viens pas.	*It doesn't matter if you don't come.*

Interaction   *Jean-Paul et Anne-Marie cherchent quelque chose à faire.*

JEAN-PAUL: Qu'est-ce que tu veux faire cet après-midi?

ANNE-MARIE: Ça m'est égal.

JEAN-PAUL: On peut aller au ciné.

ANNE-MARIE: Les films qu'on joue en ce moment ne sont pas terribles.

JEAN-PAUL: Tiens! Les étudiants vont avoir un débat sur l'énergie nucléaire.

ANNE-MARIE: J'en ai assez de la politique!

JEAN-PAUL: Alors, tant pis. Je vais y aller tout seul.

ANNE-MARIE: Chouette alors. Il y a Jean-François qui m'a invitée au café!

Activités

A. Quelqu'un va proposer quelque chose. Indiquez si la deuxième personne veut le faire ou non.

1. MARIE: On va aller au cinéma!
   ROBERT: Chouette!
2. PIERRE: J'ai acheté deux billets pour le concert de Patricia Kaas.   WWW
   YVONNE: Elle est terrible!
3. MARIE-ANNE: Tu veux étudier à la bibliothèque?
   CHANTAL: Ça m'est égal!
4. JEAN-PAUL: On va écouter encore un disque.
   CLAUDE: Moi, j'en ai marre!
5. MME MORIN: Il reste encore un petit gâteau.
   SABINE: Tant mieux!
6. M. GILBERT: Nous avons loué un appartement à la plage et il y a un lit pour toi.
   ÉRIC: Formidable!

B. Que pourriez-vous dire dans les situations suivantes?

1. Votre camarade de chambre met la radio à minuit.
2. Vos ami(e)s veulent aller voir un western.
3. Vous trouvez cent dollars dans la rue.
4. Vous rencontrez un(e) ami(e) que vous n'avez pas vu(e) depuis trois ans.
5. Vous perdez votre Walkman.
6. Vos voisins parlent des problèmes de la pluie acide.
7. Quelqu'un veut que vous parliez de l'énergie solaire.
8. Un ami vous invite à passer le week-end au lac.

Lecture culturelle

Avant la lecture   www

Created in 1944, Hydro-Québec is a publicly owned electric utility with a single shareholder: the Quebec government. It ranks among North America's largest electric utilities. It generates, transmits, and distributes most of the electricity consumed in Quebec, but it also buys and sells power in other Canadian provinces and in the United States. Hydro-Québec's activities extend to energy-related research and promotion, energy transformation and conservation, and other areas connected with energy. The company plays a very important part in the economy of Quebec, being its biggest consumer, and in 1994 alone, spending close to $2.3 billion for operations, research, and expansion. During that same year, its investments represented 17 percent of the total investments in Quebec. It is also a major employer, with about 29,000 people on its payroll and another 22,000 employed by companies directly related to it. Hydro-Québec's eagerness to grow is paralleled by a concern for the environment. For the past twenty-five years it has developed programs to study the impact of its projects on the environment. However, because Hydro-Québec's main business is energy, it is constantly at odds with environmental groups in Quebec and in Canada in general.

Activités

A. Scan the following reading and try to find all the verbs used in the future tense.

B. The following reading contains a certain number of words and expressions dealing with nature. You already know some, but others are new. Try to make a list of all the vocabulary about nature that you can identify.

C. Can you think of major ecological disasters that have occurred in different parts of the world in the past fifteen to twenty years?

Hydro-Québec et le projet Grande-Baleine°

Whale

L e projet Grande-Baleine fait partie° d'un plan à long terme pour   **fait...** *belongs*
l'exploitation du potentiel hydroélectrique de plusieurs rivières du
Nord du Québec qui se jettent° dans la baie James et la baie d'Hud-   *flow into*
son. La première étape du projet a vu la construction, au début des années 1970,
5   d'une centrale électrique° sur La Grande Rivière. Selon Hydro-Québec, une   **centrale...** *power plant*
autre centrale sur la Grande Rivière de la Baleine permettra de répondre aux be-
soins grandissant du Québec en électricité. Mais cette nouvelle installation,
qui aura une puissance° de 3 212 mégawatts, demandera la submersion de 672   *power*
milles carrés° de terre.   **milles...** *square miles*
10   En 1975, le gouvernement du Canada, celui du Québec, les Cris° et les Inuit   *Cree*
de la baie James signent la Convention de la baie James et du Nord québécois
(CBJNQ). Elle est basée sur deux principes: la nécessité pour le Québec d'utiliser
les ressources de son territoire pour le bénéfice de tous ses résidents, et la recon-
naissance° que les peuples autochtones°, les Cris et les Inuits, ont une culture et   *recognition / indigenous*

Un projet
d'Hydro-Québec

15   un mode de vie° différents de ceux des autres Québécois. Elle promet toute une   mode... *way of life*
série d'études de l'impact sur l'environnement et une de ses conclusions est
qu'Hydro-Québec ne pourra pas commencer les travaux avant de démontrer
qu'il existe un besoin réel d'augmenter la puissance° énergétique, et la compag-   *power*
nie d'État devra prouver que toutes les autres solutions ont déjà été examinées.
20   Hydro-Québec devra prendre des mesures relatives à l'impact global du projet
sur tous les éléments de l'écosystème, par exemple la question des oiseaux mi-
grateurs°, et sur les conditions climatiques mondiales. Enfin, le projet respectera   *migratory*
le droit des collectivités locales de déterminer leurs objectifs sociaux futurs.

En août 1993, Hydro-Québec a présenté ses conclusions dans un document
25   de 5 000 pages. En novembre 1994, les comités de la CBJNQ ont conclu que le
rapport était incomplet et ne permettait pas de déterminer vraiment° les consé-   *truly*
quences environnementales. Quant à° la nécessité du projet, ces mêmes comités   Quant... *As for*
ont déclaré ne pas avoir assez de renseignements sur les coûts d'autres sources
d'énergie possibles.

30   Le 18 novembre 1994, le gouvernement du Québec a annoncé qu'il ne con-
sidérait plus le projet Grande-Baleine comme prioritaire pour un proche° avenir   *near*
et la société Hydro-Québec a informé la CBJNQ qu'elle avait décidé de suspendre le projet temporairement. Elle a aussi déclaré son intention de mettre
l'accent° sur l'efficience° et la conservation à l'avenir.   mettre... *emphasize / effi-*
ciency

(Adapté de «Le Projet Grande-Baleine: Fichier.»)

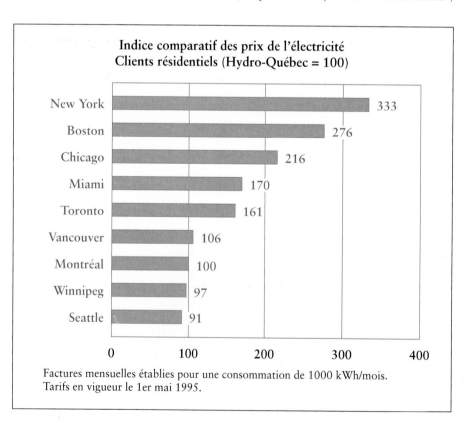

Indice comparatif des prix de l'électricité
Clients résidentiels (Hydro-Québec = 100)

Ville	Indice
New York	333
Boston	276
Chicago	216
Miami	170
Toronto	161
Vancouver	106
Montréal	100
Winnipeg	97
Seattle	91

Factures mensuelles établies pour une consommation de 1000 kWh/mois.
Tarifs en vigueur le 1er mai 1995.

Après la lecture

Questions sur le texte

1. Qu'est-ce que le projet Grande-Baleine?
2. Pourquoi est-ce qu'Hydro-Québec a initié ce projet?
3. Quel est le rôle de la Convention de la baie James et du Nord québécois (CBJNQ)?
4. Qu'est-ce qu'Hydro-Québec doit faire avant de commencer les travaux?
5. Pourquoi les comités de la CBJNQ ont-ils déclarés que le rapport soumis était incomplet?
6. Dans l'avenir, à quoi est-ce qu'Hydro-Québec donnera sa priorité?

Activités

A. Consultez une carte du Québec et trouvez tous les noms géographiques mentionnés dans la lecture.

B. Quels sont aux Etats-Unis les plus grands problèmes qui menacent l'environnement aujourd'hui?

C. Discutez des mérites et des inconvénients respectifs de l'énergie hydroélectrique et de l'énergie nucléaire.

Vocabulaire

Noms / Pronoms

arbre	tree	lumière	light
biotechnologie	biotechnology	lune	moon
champ	field	matière	matter
colonne	column	nature	nature
contrat	contract	navette	shuttle
dont	whose, of which	nature	nature
écologie	ecology	paysage	countryside
écologiste	ecologist	pelouse	lawn
écorce	bark	planète	planet
énergie	energy	pluie acide	acid rain
environnement	environment	poète	poet
espace	space	raison	reason
feuille	leaf	recyclage	recycling
fleur	flower	reflet	reflexion
fleuve	river	rivière	river
forêt	forest	rumeur	rumor
futur	future	station	station
gel	frost	tronc	trunk
jardin	yard / garden	Voie lactée	Milky Way
lac	lake		

Verbes

augmenter	to increase
créer	to create
diminuer	to diminish
évoquer	to evoke
incarner	to embody
inclure	to include
jaillir	to spring
mettre	to put (on) / to set / to turn on / to take (time to do something)

noircir	to blacken
ondoyer	to shine
permettre	to allow
promettre	to promise
remettre	to postpone / to hand in / to put or hand back
se disperser	to scatter
se mettre à	to begin

Adjectifs / Adverbes

délivré	freed
habitable	livable
lucide	lucid
méditatif	pensive
noirci	blackened
nombrable	countable

nucléaire	nuclear
rose	pink
solaire	solar
spatial	space
vif	lively

Expressions

aussitôt que	as soon as
dès que	as soon as

lorsque	when

Les immigrés

Chapitre

18

Commençons

Grammaire

Communiquons

Lecture culturelle

Vocabulaire

Arrivée d'immigrants

Objectives

Language

Vocabulary for animals • **Des mots difficiles** • Adverbs • The French equivalents of *good* and *well, bad* and *badly* • Comparatives and superlatives

Culture

North Africa • Immigrants in France

Communication

Describing the manner in which you do something • Comparing and contrasting people and things • Using colloquial French

Commençons

La Prière du Chacal

Voici un conte populaire du Maghreb.

Un matin, le Chacal voit le Coq qui chante sur une branche. Il s'approche et lui dit: «Que tu chantes bien! Quand je t'ai entendu, j'ai eu envie de devenir bon et de prier Dieu. Je suis venu tout de suite. Descends! Viens faire la prière avec moi.

—Oncle Chacal, répond le Coq, tu vois bien que j'appelle les gens à la prière!

—Oui, je vois, mais maintenant que tu as fini d'appeler, descends faire la prière avec moi!

—D'accord, dit le Coq. Mais j'attends l'imam.

—Qui est votre imam ici? demande le Chacal.

—Tu ne le connais pas? C'est le Chien de chasse.

—Au revoir! Au revoir! dit le Chacal. J'ai oublié de me laver avant la prière. J'y cours.»

(From Jean-Paul Tauvel, *Contes et histoires du Maghreb*. Paris: Hachette)

Etudions la fable

1. A quelle sorte de personne est-ce qu'on pense quand on parle d'un chacal?
2. Comment le Chacal essaye-t-il de devenir ami avec le Coq?
3. Pourquoi est-ce que le Chacal veut que le Coq descende? Pour prier?
4. Qui est-ce que le Coq attend?
5. Pourquoi le Chacal décide-t-il de partir? Quelle raison donne-t-il?
6. Qui est plus intelligent, le Chacal ou le Coq? Pourquoi?

Mots clés

prière	*prayer*	Que	*How*
chacal	*jackal*	prier	*pray*
populaire	*popular*	Dieu	*God*
Maghreb	*North Africa*	imam *(m.)*	*prayer leader*
coq	*rooster*	chien	*dog*
branche	*branch*	cours (courir)	*am running*
s'approche (s'approcher)	*gets closer*		

Faisons connaissance   WWW

Maghreb is an Arabic word meaning *sunset;* it is the name used to refer to the northern part of Africa, the area now occupied by Morocco, Algeria, and Tunisia. In France these countries are also known as **l'Afrique du Nord,** and because they were once French colonies, French is still used, together with Arabic, as an administrative and literary language.

According to statistics released by the French Ministry of the Interior, there are now 4.5 million foreigners residing in France. Approximately one third come from the **Maghreb,** including **Algériens, Marocains,** and **Tunisiens.** Since 1954 the number of new European immigrants has decreased while the number of **Maghrébins** has constantly increased. They bring with them their ways of life and their Islamic religion.

La Prière du Chacal is set in a Muslim context where public prayer is conducted five times a day. The one who calls the faithful to assemble to pray is called the **muezzin,** but the **imam** is the one who leads the prayer.

This popular tale is reminiscent of the animal fables written by Jean de La Fontaine in the seventeenth century. Like those fables, its intent is to teach a lesson using animals as protagonists, a device used in literature since ancient times and featured in the fables of Aesop (ancient Greece), the *Roman de Renard,* popular in the Middle Ages, and more recently, in this country, the stories of Joel Chandler Harris.

Enrichissons notre vocabulaire

Un animal / des animaux *(An animal / animals)*

Prononciation   Des mots difficiles

At this point you have learned all the main features of French pronunciation. There always remain a few individual words that are difficult to pronounce, however. One problem for people learning French is that they rely on spelling too much when they try to determine the correct pronunciation of a word. French spelling, as does English, represents the pronunciation of the language as it was spoken hundreds of years ago. The following words and phrases are among the most difficult to pronounce that you have learned in this book.

Repeat the following verbs after your teacher.

il peut, ils peuvent / je fais, nous faisons / tu achètes, vous achetez / je verrai, je ferai, je serai / que j'aille, que nous allions / qu'il veuille / soyons / choisissez, réussissez / ayez, aie / gagner / elle prend, elles prennent / j'aime

Repeat the following adjectives after your teacher.

un, une / ancien, ancienne / ennuyeux / bon, bonne / utile, inutile / ambitieux

Repeat the following nouns after your teacher.

les gens / un examen / ma sœur / la peur / le pays / mille, ville, fille / juin, juillet, août / un cours, un corps / monsieur, messieurs / une famille tranquille / la faim, la femme / l'Allemagne / la gare, la guerre / la psychologie / l'école / l'hiver, l'automne / un œil, des yeux / la campagne, la montagne / deux heures / Jean, Jeanne / un an, une année / les Etats-Unis / un franc / un œuf, des œufs / vingt-cinq, quatre-vingt-cinq

Exercice

Read the following sentences aloud, taking care to pronounce each word correctly.

1. Monsieur Martin utilise de l'huile et du beurre et sa cuisine est fantastique.
2. Je ne pense pas que Jean veuille gagner le match.
3. Nos familles prennent des vacances magnifiques en juin et en juillet.
4. Il est inutile de chercher un pays où les gens ne sont pas ambitieux.
5. Nous faisons une promenade ennuyeuse entre la gare et l'école.
6. En automne et en hiver ils peuvent suivre un cours de psychologie ou d'anthropologie.

Grammaire

I. Adverbs

You use adverbs to describe actions and to qualify descriptions.

A. Introduction

Adverbs are words that modify verbs, adjectives, or other adverbs. They usually indicate manner or degree and answer the questions *How?*, *How much?*, *When?*, and *Where?*

1. The following adverbs indicate manner or degree.

assez *rather*	**ensemble**	**surtout**
beaucoup	**mal** *badly*	**très**
bien	**mieux** *best*	**trop**
encore	**peu**	**vite** *quickly*
	presque	

Le Coq chante **bien**.   Je l'aime **beaucoup**.

2. The following indications of time and place are also adverbs.

ailleurs *elsewhere*	ici	quelquefois *sometimes*
aujourd'hui	là	souvent
bientôt	là-bas	tard *late*
déjà	longtemps	tôt
demain	maintenant	toujours
hier	partout *everywhere*	tout de suite

Demain il va appeler les gens à la prière.   Il chante **là-bas**.

B. Adverbs created from adjectives

Other adverbs may be created from adjectives by adding the ending **-ment** (/ mã /).

1. Adjectives ending in a written vowel take **-ment** directly.

facile → **facilement**	rapide → **rapidement**
nécessaire → **nécessairement**	rare → **rarement**
probable → **probablement**	vrai → **vraiment**

2. Most adjectives that end in a written consonant add **-ment** to the feminine form.

certain, certaine → **certainement**
complet, complète → **complètement**
général, générale → **généralement**
heureux, heureuse → **heureusement** *fortunately*
lent, lente → **lentement** *slowly*
malheureux, malheureuse → **malheureusement** *unfortunately*
parfait, parfaite → **parfaitement**
seul, seule → **seulement** *only*
sûr, sûre → **sûrement**
tel, telle → **tellement** *so*
traditionnel, traditionnelle → **traditionnellement**

3. Most adjectives ending in **-ent** or **-ant** (/ ã /) change those letters to **em** or **am**, respectively, then add **-ment**. In both cases, / ã / becomes / amã /. The following list shows examples.

-ant	-ent
brillant → **brillamment**	évident → **évidemment**
indépendant → **indépendamment**	fréquent → **fréquemment**
insuffisant → **insuffisamment**	intelligent → **intelligemment**
méchant → **méchamment**	prudent → **prudemment**
suffisant → **suffisamment** *sufficiently*	récent → **récemment**

C. Position of adverbs

1. As a general rule, short, frequently used adverbs precede the words they modify, including past participles and infinitives, while longer adverbs follow the words they modify.

Il est **déjà** parti.	*but*	Elle a conduit **lentement**.
Je vais **vite** sortir.		Je suis venu **tout de suite**.

2. While there are exceptions to the above rule, two other rules always hold true.

    a. In French, a subject and conjugated verb are *never* separated by an adverb, as in English.

        Ils rentrent **souvent** tard.   *They **often** get home late.*
        (s.) (v.)   (adv.)   (s.) (adv.)   (v.)

    b. In French, most adverbs of time and place always precede or follow the subject-verb group. Adverbs of time and place *never* occur between those elements.

        Nous allons commencer **demain**.   **Ici,** il n'y a pas de cafés.
           (s.-v. group)   (adv.)   (adv.)   (s.-v. group)

Langue

A. On dîne chez Christine. Changez les adjectifs entre parenthèses en adverbes, et ajoutez-les aux phrases données.

1. Christine nous a préparé du poisson.   (récent)
2. Il n'était pas bon.   (tel)
3. Tu m'en parles!   (méchant)
4. Vous avez mangé.   (rapide)
5. Nous ne reviendrons pas.   (certain)
6. J'ai d'autres amis.   (heureux)

B. A la résidence. Mettez les phrases suivantes au passé composé et faites attention à la place des adverbes.

1. Mon camarade de chambre parle beaucoup.
2. Nous finissons les cours aujourd'hui.
3. Hélène s'habille rapidement.
4. Jacques étudie peu.
5. Mes copains viennent me voir souvent.
6. Ils arrivent déjà.

Culture   **WWW**

C. La société algérienne change. La vie en Algérie a beaucoup changé depuis un certain temps. Caractérisez ces changements en parlant des choses qu'on fait **traditionnellement** et qu'on fait **aujourd'hui** dans ce pays. Employez les adverbes indiqués.

MODÈLE: boire de l'alcool (quelquefois)
        Traditionnellement on ne buvait pas d'alcool. Aujourd'hui on en
           boit quelquefois.

1. mettre les garçons et les filles ensemble à l'école   (plus)
2. avoir l'enseignement primaire en français / en arabe   (surtout)
3. voir un voile *(veil)* sur toutes les femmes   (moins souvent)
4. rencontrer des femmes avec des responsabilités professionnelles (assez souvent)
5. faire son service militaire obligatoirement   (encore)
6. séparer la politique et la religion   (moins)

Communication

D. **Ces jours-ci.** Comment faites-vous les activités suivantes?

> MODÈLE: étudier   (bien, longuement, rarement, vite)
> *J'étudie vite.*

1. faire le ménage   (souvent, rapidement, mal, fréquemment, demain)
2. faire vos devoirs   (sérieusement, tranquillement, attentivement, vite, bientôt)
3. dormir   (peu, beaucoup, bien, longtemps)
4. s'habiller   (simplement, curieusement, traditionnellement, bien)

Et l'année prochaine?

5. parler français   (bien, mal, fréquemment, rarement)
6. voyager   (souvent, partout, sûrement, longuement)
7. chercher un appartement   (partout, peut-être, certainement, sérieusement, prudemment)
8. faire du sport   (souvent, rarement, sûrement, régulièrement)

E. **Hier.** Comment avez-vous fait ces choses hier?

> MODÈLE: se réveiller
> *Je me suis réveillée lentement.*

1. se lever
2. manger
3. faire vos devoirs
4. conduire votre auto

5. s'habiller
6. lire le journal
7. travailler
8. s'endormir

F. **Questions personnelles.** Votre vie à l'université.

1. Où allez-vous tout de suite après ce cours?
2. A qui avez-vous écrit récemment?
3. Qu'est-ce que vous faites particulièrement bien ou mal ce semestre / trimestre?
4. Allez-vous préparer suffisamment l'examen final?
5. Quelle note *(grade)* allez-vous probablement avoir dans ce cours?
6. Allez-vous étudier régulièrement le semestre / trimestre prochain?

II. The French equivalents of *good* and *well*, *bad* and *badly*

> You use these adjectives and adverbs to make value judgments about people, things, ideas, and activities.

A. When expressing the equivalents of *good / well* and *bad / badly* in French, it is important to distinguish between adjectives and adverbs.

1. The adjectives **bon** and **mauvais** modify only nouns.

C'est un **bon** vin.	*It's a **good** wine.*
Cette bière est **mauvaise**.	*This beer is **bad**.*

2. The adverbs **bien** and **mal** modify verbs or adjectives.

Ce professeur parle **bien**.　　　　*This teacher speaks **well**.*
Mais il s'habille **mal**.　　　　　*But he dresses **badly**.*

Ce qu'ils disent

You learned in Chapter 2 that in conversation, **bien** is used as an adjective to describe a person ("a fine person") or a thing ("a good thing").

Ton copain est **bien**.　　　　Je connais un restaurant très **bien**.

B. To make a comparison, English uses *better* for both the adjective *good* and the adverb *well*. French, however, keeps the distinction between the adjective and the adverb. The comparative of the adjective **bon(ne)(s)** is **meilleur(e)(s)**. The comparative of the adverb **bien** is **mieux**.

C'est un **bon** vin. → C'est un **meilleur** vin.
Il parle **bien**. → Il parle **mieux**.

C. To complete a comparison, use **que** *(than)*.

M. Lebrun est un **très bon** professeur.
M. Ducharme est un **bon** professeur.
M. Lebrun est un **meilleur** professeur **que** M. Ducharme.

Les vins français sont **très bons**.
Les vins de Californie sont **bons**.
Les vins français sont **meilleurs que** les vins de Californie.

J'aime **bien** la viande.
J'aime **aussi** le poisson.
J'aime **mieux** la viande **que** le poisson.

Louise chante **très bien**.
Marc chante **bien**.
Louise chante **mieux que** Marc.

D. French also distinguishes between adjective and adverb forms to express the idea of *worse*. The adjective is **plus mauvais(e)(es)**, the adverb **plus mal**. To complete the comparison, use **que**.

Robert a de **très mauvaises** idées.
Jacqueline a de **mauvaises** idées.
Robert a de **plus mauvaises** idées **que** Jacqueline.

Je dors **très mal**.
Mon camarade de chambre dort **mal**.
Je dors **plus mal que** lui.

E. To form the superlative *(best)*, use **le, la,** or **les** with **meilleur(e)(s)** and **le** with **mieux.** To express the idea of *in,* use **de.**

> Pavarotti est **le meilleur** chanteur **du** monde.
> Non, c'est Domingo qui chante **le mieux.**

Langue

A. Au théâtre. Ajoutez le mot entre parenthèses aux phrases suivantes. Faites attention à l'accord des adjectifs.

1. Michel est un acteur.   (bon)
2. Il a joué hier.   (bien)
3. Il est dans une pièce anglaise.   (mauvais)
4. J'ai entendu les acteurs.   (mal)
5. Moi, j'aime aller au cinéma.   (mieux)
6. J'adore voir des films étrangers.   (bon)

B. Nos devoirs d'anglais. Complétez les phrases suivantes avec la forme correcte de **bon, bien, mauvais, mal, meilleur** ou **mieux,** selon le cas.

1. Je viens de lire un _____ roman pour mon cours d'anglais.
2. L'auteur écrit _____.
3. Mon prof pense qu'il écrit _____ que Hemingway.
4. Certains étudiants ont _____ compris les intentions de l'auteur.
5. C'est le _____ roman du semestre.
6. Je vais faire le _____ de toute la classe au prochain examen!

C. Dînons ensemble. Formez des phrases complètes avec les mots donnés.

1. Nous / s'amuser / bien / hier
2. Je / trouver / bon / restaurant / en ville
3. On / prendre / mon / voiture, / je / conduire / bien / toi
4. Ce / restaurant-là / être / bon / celui-ci
5. On / manger / bien / ici / là-bas
6. Nous / commander / bon / lapin

Culture

D. **Vos impressions.** Qui produit les meilleures choses, la France ou les Etats-Unis? Donnez votre opinion pour les catégories suivantes.

MODÈLE: le café   *Le café français est meilleur que le café américain.*
la bière   *La bière américaine est meilleure.*

1. la musique
2. le vin
3. les voitures
4. les vêtements
5. les films
6. les avions
7. la cuisine
8. les trains
9. les ordinateurs
10. les émissions de télévision

Communication

E. **Etes-vous sexiste?** Pensez-vous qu'il y ait des choses que les hommes font mieux que les femmes, ou vice versa?

MODÈLE: *Les femmes jouent au tennis mieux que les hommes.*
Les hommes font mieux les courses.

conduire
faire la cuisine
jouer au football
réussir aux examens
???

nager
comprendre les mathématiques
apprendre les langues étrangères
retenir les dates
faire des économies

F. **Votre santé.** Est-ce que les choses suivantes sont bonnes ou mauvaises pour la santé?

MODÈLE: l'alcool   *Un peu d'alcool est bon pour la santé.*

les cigarettes
le vin
le sport

le sucre
le sel
les œufs

le café
le poisson
l'eau de votre ville

G. **Questions personnelles.** Vos souvenirs.

1. Quel moment de votre vie vous rappelez-vous le mieux?
2. Que pensez-vous de votre lycée? Vous êtes mieux préparé(e) à l'université que d'autres étudiants?
3. Aimez-vous mieux votre vie au lycée ou votre vie ici?
4. Avez-vous connu un meilleur professeur que le vôtre?
5. Quand avez-vous mal dormi? Pourquoi?
6. Combien de très bons amis / bonnes amies avez-vous eu(e)s?

III. The comparative and superlative

You use the comparative and superlative to rank people, places, things, and activities.

A. Comparative of adjectives and adverbs

1. With the exception of **bon** and **bien,** French adjectives and adverbs form the comparative with the expression **plus... que...** or **moins... que...** .

> Ce chat est **plus gros que** le mien.   *This cat is **bigger than** mine.*
> Ils sortent **plus souvent que** nous.   *They go out **more often than** we do.*
> Je comprends **moins bien que** toi.   *I understand **less well than** you.*

2. To express equality, use **aussi... que** (*as . . . as*) with adjectives and adverbs and **autant... que...** (*as much as . . .*) with verbs.

> Il est **aussi** intelligent **que** sa sœur.
> Elle tape **aussi** mal **que** nous.
> Je travaille **autant que** vous!

B. Comparative of nouns

To compare nouns, you use the following expressions: **plus de... que,** (*more . . . than*), **autant de... que** (*as much / many . . . as*) and **moins de... que** (*less / fewer . . . than*).

> Elle a **plus de** patience **que** lui.   Nous avons **moins d'**argent
> J'ai **autant de** talent **que** Marc.   **qu'**eux.

C. Superlative of adjectives and adverbs

1. To form the superlative, use the *definite article* before **plus** or **moins** followed by the adjective or adverb. Use **de** to express the idea of *in* or *of.*

> Anne-Marie est **la plus**   *Anne-Marie is **the most artistic***
>   **artistique de** sa famille.   *in her family.*
> Pierre est **le moins insupportable**   *Pierre is **the least annoying of***
>   **de** tes amis.   *your friends.*
> Jean-Paul travaille **le plus**   *Jean-Paul works **the most***
>   **régulièrement de** tous mes   ***consistently** of all my*
>   étudiants.   *students.*

2. If an adjective normally follows the noun it modifies, its superlative form uses the definite article twice, keeping the same number and gender.

> J'habite **la** ville **la plus** intéressante de mon pays.
> Ce sont **les** étudiants **les plus** sérieux de l'université.

3. If the adjective precedes the noun, the superlative does also.

> C'est **le plus bel** enfant de la famille.
> Voilà **la plus vieille** église de la ville.

Attention!

1. Note that in comparative constructions, you use **de,** not **que,** with numbers.

> Nous avons moins **d'**une heure pour finir.
> Il faut plus **de** deux cent mille dollars pour acheter cette maison.

2. The superlative of adverbs always takes **le** because adverbs have no number or gender.

> Marie-France répond **le** moins souvent de toute la classe.
> Nous habitons **le** plus loin de l'université de tous nos amis.

Langue

A. Les impressions des touristes. Formez des phrases complètes avec les mots donnés. Les symboles +, − et = représentent **plus, moins** et **aussi,** respectivement.

1. Les voitures / français / être / + petit / nôtre
2. théâtre / être / + cher / cinéma
3. hôtels / être / − grand / aux Etats-Unis
4. agents de police / être / = sympa / nôtre
5. Ce / église / être / + vieux / de la ville
6. pain / français / être / + bon / pain / américain
7. Le Louvre / être / musée / + connu / monde
8. La France / avoir / − McDonald's / Etats-Unis!

B. Deux manières de dire la même chose. Changez l'ordre des comparaisons sans changer le sens *(meaning)* de la phrase.

MODÈLE: Je suis plus riche que Paul.   *Paul est moins riche que moi.*

1. Il parle plus vite qu'eux.
2. Tu as plus de problèmes que les autres.
3. Son français est moins bon que le tien.
4. Robert est aussi ennuyeux que Monique.
5. Jean travaille autant que ses camarades.
6. Son fils est plus laid que le mien.

Culture

C. La France: le pays et ses habitants. Répondez aux questions suivantes sur la France en choisissant la bonne réponse.

1. Quelle est la plus grande montagne?
   a. le pic du Midi   b. le mont Cenis   c. le mont Blanc
2. Quel est le plus long fleuve?
   a. la Loire   b. la Seine   c. le Rhône
3. Quel est le pays d'origine du plus grand nombre d'immigrés?
   a. l'Algérie   b. le Maroc   c. le Portugal
4. Ce sont les Français qui ont le plus grand nombre d(e)_____.
   a. accidents de voiture   b. résidences secondaires   c. enfants
5. Quel est l'animal qu'on trouve le plus souvent dans une maison française?
   a. le chat   b. le chien   c. l'oiseau
6. Quelle est l'activité la plus fréquente des Français quand ils ne travaillent pas?
   a. lire   b. faire une promenade   c. regarder la télévision
7. Quel est le journal qu'on achète le plus?
   a. *L'Equipe*   b. *Le Monde*   c. *Le Figaro*
8. Quel âge avait la plus vieille personne à avoir fait un CD de rap?
   a. 50 ans   b. 60 ans   c. 120 ans   **WWW**

Communication

D. **Des comparaisons.** Séparez-vous en groupes de deux. Comparez-vous en employant les expressions suivantes. Présentez quelques différences importantes aux autres.

MODÈLE: Etudiant(e) 1: *Es-tu aussi grand(e) que moi?*
Etudiant(e) 2: *Je suis plus grand(e) que toi.*

avoir des sœurs / frères	lire des romans
habiter loin de l'université	aller au cinéma
se coucher tard	être sérieux
travailler bien	dépenser de l'argent
conduire vite	???

E. **A votre avis.** Quel(le) est / Qui est, à votre avis,…

1. le plus grand écrivain?
2. la langue la plus difficile?
3. la plus mauvaise voiture?
4. la ville la plus agréable de votre pays?
5. l'homme politique le moins honnête?
6. le cours le plus intéressant de votre université?
7. la profession la plus difficile?
8. la meilleure pizza de votre ville?

F. **Comparez-vous.** Dans votre cours, qui a autant d(e)… que vous?

cousins	cours aujourd'hui
dollars dans son portefeuille	examens finals
chiens	disques compacts
camarades de chambre	petit(e)s ami(e)s

G. **Questions personnelles.** Rêvez un peu.

1. Quel a été le jour le plus fantastique de votre vie?
2. Quelle personne admirez-vous le plus? Qui admirez-vous presque autant qu'elle?
3. Aimeriez-vous avoir autant d'argent que Bill Gates? Qu'est-ce que vous en feriez?
4. Vous voudriez être aussi beau / belle / riche / connu(e) que quelle personnalité?
5. Préféreriez-vous avoir plus d'amis? Quelles qualités font les meilleur(e)s ami(e)s?
6. Quelle est la chose la plus importante que vous avez entendue récemment?

Communiquons

S'exprimer en français familier

Although the **Ce qu'ils disent** sections of this textbook have shown you many ways in which spoken French differs from the formal language, the French you have been studying is the standard variety used in more formal speech. If you go to a francophone country, you are more likely to hear colloquial, or popular,

©1991 Nicole Lambert

French (**le français familier**) in casual conversation. One characteristic of colloquial French is the frequent use of conversational fillers (**des remplisseurs de pause**) similar to words like *well, like,* or *ya know.* French speakers also omit or elide sounds (**élision**), just as English speakers replace *I am going to* with *I'm gonna.* Because so many sounds are dropped, this level of speech is often harder for foreigners to understand. In addition, colloquial French, like English, abounds in popular vocabulary. The following sections will review some features and describe others that characterize rapid, casual speech.

Expressions

> ▶ **On remplit les pauses.**

—Euh	*Uh*
—Ben	*Um*
—M'enfin	*Well*
—M'alors	*So*
—Eh bien / Eh ben	*So*

> ▶ **On fait des élisions.**

1. More mute **e**'s than usual are dropped.

J¢ te verrai d¢main.	*See ya tomorrow.*
C¢la n¢ s¢ fait pas.	*That isn't done.*

2. The **u** of **tu** is dropped.

T'es vraiment stupide.	*You're a dope.*
T'as fini?	*You done?*

3. The **l** of **il** and **ils** is not pronounced before a consonant.

I/s sont partis.	*They left.*
I/ n¢ sait pas.	*He doesn't know.*
but Il‿est bon.	*It's good.*

4. The **ne** of negations is not used.

J¢ peux pas venir.	*I can't come.*
J¢ veux pas m¢ coucher.	*I don't wanna go to bed.*
C'est pas vrai!	*It isn't true!*

5. The consonant group **-re** at the end of words before a word beginning with a consonant is not pronounced.

Donne-moi l'aut⫽¢ stylo.	*Gimme the other pen.*
Il a quat⫽¢ chiens.	*He's got four dogs.*
Le pauv⫽¢ garçon!	*The poor guy!*

▶ **On emploie un vocabulaire familier.**

1. Following are some popular words for common things.

C'est sa bagnole.	C'est son auto.
Il n'aime pas son boulot.	Il n'aime pas son travail / emploi.
De la flotte? J'en bois jamais!	De l'eau? Je n'en bois jamais!
J'ai pas de fric.	Je n'ai pas d'argent.
Où sont mes godasses *(f.)*?	Où sont mes chaussures?
C'est un bon pinard.	C'est un bon vin.

2. There are popular words used to talk about people.

Voilà des flics.	Voilà des agents de police.
T'as vu les gosses?	Tu as vu les enfants?
Elle parle avec un type / mec.	Elle parle avec un homme.
Il sort avec une nana.	Il sort avec une jeune femme.
C'est mon pote.	C'est mon ami.
Son père est toubib.	Son père est médecin.

3. The following expressions describe actions.

Ils bouffent au restau-U.	Ils mangent au restaurant universitaire.
Ta gueule!	Tais-toi! *(Shut up!)* [vulgar]

4. Several popular words are adjectives used to describe people or things.

T'es dingue?!	Tu es fou?! *(Are you nuts?!)*
C'est dégueulasse!	C'est dégoûtant! *(That's disgusting!)* [vulgar]
Il est moche.	Il est laid.

Interaction   *Julie et Etienne sont au restaurant universitaire.*   ◉

JULIE: Qu'est-ce qu'on a à bouffer aujourd'hui?

ÉTIENNE: Ben, les mêmes choses dégueulasses!

JULIE: Tu me cherches de la flotte?

ÉTIENNE: Pas moi! Je vais acheter du pinard.

JULIE: T'es dingue? C'est toi qui as la bagnole!

Activités

A. Mettez les phrases suivantes en français standard.

1. I' veut pas m' donner d' fric.
2. L' pauv' mec peut pas acheter d' bagnole.
3. T' as vu l'aut' nana?
4. Tu vas pas porter ces godasses au boulot?
5. T' es dingue? J'aime pas la flotte!
6. T' as pas encore fini d' bouffer?

B. Dans les phrases suivantes, remplacez autant de mots que possible avec du vocabulaire familier.

1. Les Américains sont fous. Ils mangent dans leur voiture!
2. Mon ami n'a jamais d'argent parce qu'il n'a pas de travail.
3. Qui a mis de l'eau dans mon vin? C'est dégoûtant!
4. Voilà un homme et une femme qui jouent avec leurs enfants.
5. Tais-toi! Tes chaussures sont beaucoup plus laides que les miennes.
6. Les agents de police ont trouvé la voiture de mon ami en ville.

Lecture culturelle

Avant la lecture

Racial tension has been a problem in France for a long time, just as it has been in most other countries. Many French people are concerned with the growing number of foreigners living and working in France.

The efforts to combat racial tension are numerous, and one of the most effective groups doing this work is **S.O.S. Racisme**, which was organized by the descendants of both immigrants and native French people. One group that has traditionally borne the brunt of racism in France is the group of Arabs from the Maghreb. The young now call themselves **Beurs** (a reversal of the syllables in **Arabes**) and have developed a new pride in their heritage.

The following passage not only describes the origin of the group **S.O.S. Racisme,** but it also illustrates another tradition of youth: **l'engagement,** or making a commitment to a cause.

Activités

A. In recent years, the French have borrowed a great deal of vocabulary directly from English. Scan the following reading to find the three examples of **franglais** that it uses.

B. This reading is about **xénophobie,** the fear or hatred of foreigners or anything that is foreign. What other phobias do you know? The words would be the same in French, because they come from ancient Greek. What would **francophobie** mean? What is the opposite?

C. You have learned that one should always use complete sentences (subjects, verbs, and perhaps an object) when writing. Occasionally, a writer will break this rule to achieve a specific effect. Scan the reading, and find four sentences that are not complete.

Touche pas à mon pote!

«Toucher» est un mot important dans la langue française. Surtout parce que c'est un des premiers mots que les petits Français entendent. A travers° des expressions comme «Touche pas», «Il ne faut pas toucher», c'est tout un monde d'interdictions° qui se dresse° devant eux. On
5 ne sera donc° pas surpris qu'un slogan comme «Touche pas à mon pote°» ait obtenu une notoriété immédiate.

Tout remonte° au mois de novembre 1984: Diego, un jeune Sénégalais de la banlieue° parisienne, se trouve dans le métro. Tout à coup°, une jeune femme affolée° se met à crier qu'on lui a volé° son portefeuille. Aussitôt, sans qu'un mot
10 soit prononcé, tous les regards° accusateurs se portent° sur Diego. C'est le seul noir du wagon°! La tension monte. Il n'y a pas de doute, Diego est coupable°. Puis, miracle! Deux stations plus loin, la jeune femme retrouve le portefeuille «volé» au fond° de son sac. Même silence, mais cette fois, c'est un silence gêné°.

Il s'agissait d'une scène de racisme ordinaire, mais ce jour-là, S.O.S.
15 Racisme est né. Après l'incident, Diego est allé retrouver ses copains et copines de fac, Fatima, Thaima, Jean-Pierre, Hervé et Harlem Désir. Immigrés, jeunes de la deuxième génération, Français ou métis° comme Harlem Désir. De père antillais° et de mère alsacienne, étudiant avant de devenir animateur° de centres de loisirs°, Harlem est devenu naturellement le président de l'association qui venait
20 de naître à cause de Diego: S.O.S. Racisme.

A... Through
forbidden things / se... rises
thus / buddy

goes back
suburb / Tout... Suddenly
frantic / stolen
glances / se... converge
car / guilty

au... at the bottom /
embarrassed

mixed race
from the Antilles /
organizer / centres...
community centers

Manifestation contre le racisme.

Une association de plus° contre le racisme? Justement pas. Copains de fac, fréquentant les mêmes cités° tristes de la banlieue nord, Harlem, Fatima, Thaima, Jean-Pierre et Hervé ont déjà participé à la lutte° contre la xénophobie à l'occasion de la manifestation° des Beurs pour l'égalité. Pour eux, la société
25 multiculturelle, ce n'est pas une découverte°. Quand on écoute Michael Jackson et Sade, la symbiose des cultures, ce n'est pas un problème. Conclusion de Harlem, de Fatima et de leurs copains: les jeunes sont mieux équipés que les adultes pour résister à la vague° raciste. S.O.S. Racisme donc. Mais il faut aussi trouver un slogan. Fatima dit que si Diego n'avait pas été seul dans le métro, les
30 choses ne se seraient pas passées comme cela. C'est une idée! Le slogan naît: «Touche pas à mon pote». Fini les slogans comme «Le racisme ne passera pas» ou les discours° sur l'égalité des hommes, mais plutôt° une réaction toute simple: touche pas à mes copains, qu'ils soient noirs, beurs ou portugais.

«Touche pas à mon pote», c'est évidemment un préalable°. Mais ensuite°,
35 s'il faut parler, on parle. Fatima, une Algérienne de la deuxième génération, pourrait passer pour une Française du Midi° de la France. Pourtant, elle porte le badge, une main ouverte avec le slogan inscrit dans la paume°. «Je n'ai pas peur de parler aux racistes. Je connais les mots pour leur répondre», dit-elle. Et Fatima ajoute° qu'elle prend la parole°, en pensant à ses parents algériens qui,
40 «eux, n'ont pas les mots pour se défendre». «Touche pas à mes parents.»

Avait-elle une chance, Fatima? Y avait-il une possibilité pour que cette campagne «Touche pas à mon pote» soit un peu plus qu'un gadget antiraciste sans lendemain°? Autrement dit°, la montée du racisme n'était-elle pas irrésistible dans les lycées comme ailleurs? Pas sûr... Dans de nombreux lycées, des élèves
45 ont fait grève° pour indiquer leur opposition à «un racisme rampant».

Annick Percheron, auteur de nombreuses études sociologiques sur la politique et les jeunes, observe: «Pour s'affirmer, ils n'ont pas trente-six solutions. La plus immédiate: s'emparer° des thèmes délaissés° par les partis politiques. La faim dans le monde, c'est leur truc°. L'altruisme et la générosité sont une
50 manière douce° d'entrer en politique sans singer° les adultes.» Le succès d'organisations comme Médecins sans Frontières auprès° des jeunes est significatif. Quand on a quinze ans, on ne dit plus: «Je voudrais être guérillero ou pilote d'essai°», mais plus souvent, «J'ai envie d'être médecin-sans-frontières».

Ce à quoi° on assiste°, c'est un élan du cœur°. Les organisations charitables
55 sont débordées° par les dons° et les offres de service des jeunes. «Touche pas à mon pote», c'est avant tout un grand mouvement de solidarité de la jeunesse qui a compris qu'elle seule possède la clé aux problèmes que pose une société de plus en plus multiculturelle.

(Adapté d'un article de *L'Express*, no. 1058)

Glossary (right margin):

de... *another*
high-rise projects
fight
protest march
discovery

wave

speeches / rather

preamble / then

South
palm

adds / **prend**... *speaks*

sans... *without a future /* **Autrement**... *In other words /* ont... *went on strike*

s'... *to pick up / abandoned*
thing
gentle / aping
with

pilote... *test pilot*
Ce... *What / witness /* élan... *emotional commitment / overwhelmed / gifts*

Après la lecture

Questions sur le texte

1. Pourquoi le slogan «Touche pas à mon pote» a-t-il eu un succès immédiat?
2. Quel incident a eu lieu dans le métro? A la fin, pourquoi les gens sont-ils gênés?
3. Qui sont les jeunes qui ont fondé S.O.S. Racisme? D'où viennent-ils?

4. Pourquoi ces jeunes gens sont-ils particulièrement bien préparés pour s'occuper d'une association comme S.O.S. Racisme?
5. Quel est, avec le slogan, l'autre symbole de l'association?
6. Selon Annick Percheron, que font les jeunes pour s'affirmer?

Activités

A. Répondez aux questions suivantes.

1. Est-ce qu'on vous a volé quelque chose? Avez-vous accusé quelqu'un? Est-ce que cette personne était coupable? Racontez l'aventure.
2. Avez-vous observé un événement raciste? Décrivez-le. Vous a-t-on accusé de quelque chose à cause de *(because of)* votre race, de votre âge ou de votre sexe? Expliquez.

B. Débats en cours.

1. On a dit que les tensions raciales augmentent sur les campus des Etats-Unis. Qu'en pensez-vous? Quelles solutions à ce problème pourriez-vous proposer?
2. Y a-t-il d'autres problèmes sociaux dans le monde que les jeunes pourraient aider à résoudre *(resolve)*?

Vocabulaire

Noms/Pronoms

Afrique du Nord	North Africa	**Dieu**	God
Algérien	Algerian	**imam**	imam (prayer leader)
animal	animal	**immigré**	immigrant
branche	branch	**Maghreb**	Maghreb
canard	duck	**Maghrébin**	from the Maghreb
chacal	jackal	**Marocain**	Morrocan
chat	cat	muezzin	muezzin
cheval	horse	poule	hen
chien	dog	prière	prayer
cochon	pig	**Tunisien**	Tunisian
coq	rooster	vache	cow

Verbes

courir	to run
prier	to pray
s'approcher	to get closer

Adjectifs / Adverbes

ailleurs	elsewhere	méchamment	out of meanness
algérien	Algerian	meilleur	better
assez	rather	mieux	best
aussi... que	as . . . as	nécessairement	necessarily
autant	as much, as many	parfaitement	perfectly
brillamment	brilliantly	partout	everywhere
brilliant	brilliant	populaire	popular
certainement	certainly	probablement	probably
complet	complete	prudemment	carefully
complètement	completely	que	how, than
évidemment	obviously	quelquefois	sometimes
facilement	easily	rapidement	rapidly
fréquemment	frequently	rarement	rarely
fréquent	frequent	récent	recent
général	general	seulement	only
heureusement	fortunately	suffisamment	sufficiently
indépendamment	independently	suffisant	sufficient
insuffisamment	insufficiently	sûrement	surely
intelligemment	intelligently	tard	late
lent	slow	tel(le)	such / like
lentement	slowly	tellement	so / so much
mal	badly	traditionnel	traditional
malheureusement	unfortunately	traditionnellement	traditionally
marocain	Morrocan	vite	fast

Chapitres 16 à 18

Révision

Tous ensemble!

A. Répondez aux questions suivantes en employant les mots entre parenthèses.

Conversation avec mes parents quand je rentre tard

1. A ta place, est-ce que nous rentrerions après minuit? (Non,... ne... pas faire cela.)
2. Qu'est-ce que vous avez fait ensemble? (Nous... danser... pendant... heures)
3. Qu'est-ce que tu as promis? (... revenir avant minuit.)
4. Vous êtes rentrés lentement? (Non,... vite...)
5. Quand nous téléphoneras-tu? (... aussitôt que... je... savoir quand je... arriver)

Un vieil ami

6. A qui ressemble-t-il? (... tenir... son père.)
7. Depuis quand êtes-vous amis? (... 1987.)
8. Est-ce qu'il sait parler français? (Oui,... + bien... que moi.)
9. Vous allez voyager ensemble pendant les vacances? (Oui,... partir... quinze jours.)
10. Est-ce qu'il est très riche? (Oui,... promettre... payer le voyage!)

B. Parlez-moi de votre chambre. Refaites les phrases suivantes en employant les mots entre parenthèses.

1. Il faut que tu viennes la voir. (Demain... vous...)
2. Je la loue depuis trois mois. (Il y a... que...)
3. Je ne veux pas faire le ménage. (... avoir envie...)
4. Mon frère est arrivé il y a peu de temps. (récemment)
5. On met dix minutes pour aller en ville. (L'année prochaine,...)

C. Connaissez-vous l'amie mystérieuse de Jacques? Combinez les phrases suivantes.

1. Vous ne connaissez pas la jeune femme? La jeune femme sort avec Jacques.
2. Il refuse de me présenter cette femme fascinante. Il vient de décrire la femme.
3. Elle habite un village formidable. Il y a trois ans, j'ai passé mes vacances dans ce village.
4. Elle sait bien faire de la planche à voile. Jacques ne sait pas aussi bien en faire.
5. Elle joue très bien au tennis. Jacques joue moins bien.

D. Robert. Formez des phrases complètes avec les mots donnés. Les symboles = et + représentent **aussi** et **plus**, respectivement.

Allons voir Robert

1. Si / nous / avoir / temps / nous / aller voir / Robert
2. Il / permettre / gens / passer le voir / sans téléphoner
3. Il / ne… pas / être / = / sympa / Jean
4. Son / chien / être / = / méchant / tien

Chez Robert

5. Vouloir / vous / je / mettre / musique?
6. Regarder / divan / je / venir / acheter
7. Si / vous / avoir / faim / je / pouvoir / vous / servir / mouton
8. Dire / moi / quand / vous / avoir envie / partir

E. **Mes opinions.** Complétez les phrases suivantes de manière logique.

1. Je n'aime pas les gens qui…
2. Je pense que…
3. J'aime les animaux qu(e)…
4. Je ne sais pas où…
5. Si j'étais en retard…
6. Je partirai vendredi, dès que…
7. Je ferai mieux si…
8. J'ai plus de talent…

Entre nous!

A. Avec un(e) camarade de cours, comparez des gens que vous connaissez. Employez un élément de chaque colonne, mais n'hésitez pas à utiliser vos propres idées.

je	être	plus	bien	moi
mes amis	avoir	moins	mauvais	vous
mon	conduire	aussi	mal	mes amis
professeur	comprendre	autant	beau	la ville
mes voisins	manger		brillant	l'université
mes parents	jouer		talent	le cours
mon frère /	danser		???	???
ma sœur	???			

B. Interviewez un(e) camarade de cours. Parlez des sujets suivants.

1. la ville où tu habites
2. les cours que tu suis
3. les gens que tu aimes
4. les choses les plus importantes de ta vie
5. le genre de film que tu préfères
6. les endroits où tu vas
7. les animaux que tu as eus
8. les gens qui t'ont influencé(e)

C. En groupe de trois ou quatre étudiants, imaginez votre vie quand vous aurez cent ans.

MODÈLE: se lever à cinq heures du matin
Nous nous lèverons à cinq heures du matin.

ne pas se rappeler les gens	ne pas bien entendre / voir
manger peu	ne plus rien remettre à plus tard
ne pas sortir	se coucher de bonne heure
ne boire que du lait	prendre beaucoup d'aspirine

D. Interrogez vos camarades de cours. Demandez-leur depuis quand ils font les choses suivantes ou pendant combien de temps ils les ont faites.

s'occuper d'un chien / d'un chat
se coucher à huit heures
jouer au docteur
posséder une voiture
habiter la ville où tu es né(e)

être étudiant(e) dans cette
    université
connaître ton / ta meilleur(e)
    ami(e)
savoir nager

E. Avec un(e) camarade de cours, imaginez ce que *(what)* vous feriez si vous étiez de l'autre sexe.

mettre une robe / cravate
(ne plus) jouer au football
(ne plus) faire la cuisine
payer au restaurant
avoir les cheveux plus / moins
    longs

dire aux personnes du sexe opposé
    qu(e)...
trouver... formidable / affreux
    (-euse)
???

F. Dans un petit groupe, décrivez comment vous avez fait les choses le semestre / trimestre dernier.

vite	méchamment	brillamment
souvent	horriblement	le mieux
bien	fréquemment	le plus mal
mal	rarement	???

G. Jeu de rôles. Jouez les scènes suivantes avec un(e) camarade de cours.

1. Vous êtes journaliste pour une revue spécialisée. Choisissez le sujet (sports, mode *[fashion]*, pêche, etc.) et interviewez un(e) camarade qui le connaît mieux que vous.
2. Vous voulez louer un appartement. Téléphonez au / à la propriétaire et posez-lui des questions.
3. Vous venez de gagner 100.000 francs dans un jeu télévisé. Discutez avec votre femme / mari ce que *(what)* vous allez faire avec cet argent.
4. Vous avez besoin d'emprunter de l'argent à un(e) ami(e). Faites beaucoup de compliments.
5. Vous voulez que votre camarade s'engage *(makes a commitment)* pour une cause. Expliquez-lui celle que vous préférez.
6. Vous êtes guide dans un musée de l'avenir. Décrivez la vie qu'on y représente.
7. Essayez d'être plus snob que votre ami(e). Mentionnez toutes les choses que vous achetez qui sont de la meilleure qualité.
8. Vous êtes professeur de français, et vous parlez avec un étudiant qui n'est pas sérieux. Expliquez-lui comment il peut réussir dans votre cours.

Appendices

I. International Phonetic Alphabet

Consonants

/ p /	*P*ierre		/ v /	*v*ous
/ t /	*t*u		/ z /	bi*s*e
/ k /	*c*omme		/ ʒ /	bon*j*our
/ b /	*b*onjour		/ l /	*l*a
/ d /	*d*e		/ ʀ /	ga*r*çon
/ g /	*g*arçon		/ m /	*m*ain
/ f /	*f*ille		/ n /	An*n*e
/ s /	mer*c*i, profe*ss*eur		/ ɲ /	poi*gn*ée
/ ʃ /	*ch*ez			

Vowels

/ i /	b*i*se		/ y /	*u*ne
/ e /	caf*é*		/ ø /	d*e*, p*eu*
/ ɛ /	app*el*le		/ œ /	h*eu*re
/ a /	v*a*		/ ɛ̃ /	bi*en*, *un*, m*ain*
/ ɔ /	c*o*mme		/ ɑ̃ /	connaiss*an*ce
/ o /	*au*		/ ɔ̃ /	fais*on*s
/ u /	v*ou*s			

Semivowels

/ j /	P*i*erre
/ w /	*ou*i
/ ɥ /	n*u*it

Mute e

/ ə /	*j*e, f*e*rai

II. Les Etats-Unis et le Canada

A. Les Etats-Unis

ETAT	in or to	ETAT	in or to
l'Alabama (m.)	dans l'Alabama / en Alabama	le Maine	dans le Maine
l'Alaska (m.)	dans l'Alaska / en Alaska	le Maryland	dans le Maryland
		le Massachusetts	dans le Massachusetts
l'Arizona (m.)	dans l'Arizona / en Arizona	le Michigan	dans le Michigan
		le Minnesota	dans le Minnesota
l'Arkansas (m.)	dans l'Arkansas / en Arkansas	le Mississippi	dans le Mississippi
		le Missouri	dans le Missouri
la Californie	en Californie	le Montana	dans le Montana
la Caroline du Nord	en Caroline du Nord	le Nebraska	dans le Nebraska
la Caroline du Sud	en Caroline du Sud	le Nevada	dans le Nevada
le Colorado	dans le Colorado / au Colorado	le New Hampshire	dans le New Hampshire
		le New Jersey	dans le New Jersey
le Connecticut	dans le Connecticut	l'état de New York	dans l'état de New York
le Dakota du Nord	dans le Dakota du Nord	le Nouveau-Mexique	au Nouveau-Mexique
le Dakota du Sud	dans le Dakota du Sud	l'Ohio (m.)	dans l'Ohio
le Delaware	dans le Delaware	l'Oklahoma (m.)	dans l'Oklahoma
la Floride	en Floride	l'Oregon (m.)	dans l'Oregon
la Géorgie	en Géorgie	la Pennsylvanie	en Pennsylvanie
Hawaii (m.)	à Hawaii / aux îles Hawaii	le Rhode Island	dans le Rhode Island
		le Tennessee	dans le Tennessee
l'Idaho (m.)	dans l'Idaho	le Texas	au Texas
l'Illinois (m.)	dans l'Illinois / en Illinois	l'Utah (m.)	dans l'Utah
		le Vermont	dans le Vermont
l'Indiana (m.)	dans l'Indiana	la Virginie	en Virginie
l'Iowa (m.)	dans l'Iowa	la Virginie-Occidentale	en Virginie-Occidentale
le Kansas	dans le Kansas	l'état de Washington	dans l'état de Washington
le Kentucky	dans le Kentucky	le Wisconsin	dans le Wisconsin
la Louisiane	en Louisiane	le Wyoming	dans le Wyoming

B. Le Canada

PROVINCE	in or to	TERRITOIRE	in or to
l'Alberta	dans l'Alberta	les Territoires du Nord-Ouest	dans les Territoires du Nord-Ouest
la Colombie britannique	en Colombie britannique	le Yukon	au Yukon
l'île du Prince-Edouard	dans l'île du Prince-Edouard		
le Manitoba	au Manitoba		
le Nouveau-Brunswick	au Nouveau-Brunswick		
la Nouvelle-Ecosse	en Nouvelle-Ecosse		
l'Ontario	dans l'Ontario		
le Québec	au Québec		
le Saskatchewan	au Saskatchewan		
Terre-Neuve	à Terre-Neuve		

III. Double Pronoun Objects

A. **If you use two pronoun objects in a sentence or a negative command, you must keep the following order:**

me				
te	le	lui		
se	la	leur	y	en
nous	les			
vous				

Il prête ses livres à ses amis. → Il **les leur** prête.
J'ai donné de l'argent aux enfants. → Je **leur en** ai donné.
Nous allons vendre l'auto à notre voisin. → Nous allons **la lui** vendre.

B. **Object pronouns in the first and third columns above cannot be used together. Use a tonic pronoun instead.**

Il m'a présenté à Robert.   Il m'a présenté à lui.

C. **In affirmative commands, use the following order:**

		moi / m'		
	le	toi / t'		
verb	la	lui	y	en
	les	nous		
		vous		
		leur		

D. **Me and te become moi and toi when they are the final elements of the command. If y or en is included, me and te become m' and t'.**

Donnez-moi trois stylos. → Donnez-**m'en** trois.
Montrez-moi vos photos. → Montrez-**les-moi**

Apportez-nous le journal. → Apportez-**le-nous**.

IV. Le passé simple

A. **This tense may replace the** passé composé **in formal writing. There are three sets of endings:**

-er verbs	-ir verbs	-re verbs
je chantai	je partis	je vendis
tu chantas	tu partis	tu vendis
il chanta → 'a' ending not 'ta'	il partit	il vendit
nous chantâmes	nous partîmes	nous vendîmes
vous chantâtes	vous partîtes	vous vendîtes
ils chantèrent	ils partirent	ils vendirent

B. **Irregular verbs add the following endings to their stems:**

```
-s     - ˆmes
-s     - ˆtes
-t     -rent
```

C. **The irregular stems of the verbs you know are:**

avoir → eu-	être → fu-	prendre → pri-
boire → bu-	faire → fi-	savoir → su-
conduire → conduisi-	lire → lu-	suivre → suivi-
connaître → connu-	mettre → mi-	venir → vin-
devoir → du-	mourir → mouru-	voir → vi-
dire → di-	naître → naqui-	vouloir → voulu-
écrire → écrivi-	pouvoir → pu-	

Annibal **voulut** traverser les Alpes.	Hannibal **wanted** to cross the Alps.
Il **fit** ses devoirs.	He **did** his homework.
Nous **vîmes** un accident.	We **saw an** accident.
Napoléon **naquit** en Corse; il **mourut** à Sainte-Hélène.	Napoleon **was born** in Corsica; he **died** on St. Helena.
Elles ne **dirent** jamais la vérité.	They never **told** the truth.

V. Conjugaison des verbes

Regular Verbs

Infinitif	Indicatif — Présent	Indicatif — Passé Composé	Indicatif — Imparfait	Indicatif — Futur	Impératif	Subjonctif	Conditionnel
-ER chanter							
je / j'	chante	ai chanté	chantais	chanterai		chante	chanterais
tu	chantes	as chanté	chantais	chanteras	chante	chantes	chanterais
il / elle / on	chante	a chanté	chantait	chantera		chante	chanterait
nous	chantons	avons chanté	chantions	chanterons	chantons	chantions	chanterions
vous	chantez	avez chanté	chantiez	chanterez	chantez	chantiez	chanteriez
ils / elles	chantent	ont chanté	chantaient	chanteront		chantent	chanteraient
-IR servir							
je / j'	sers	ai servi	servais	servirai		serve	servirais
tu	sers	as servi	servais	serviras	sers	serves	servirais
il / elle / on	sert	a servi	servait	servira		serve	servirait
nous	servons	avons servi	servions	servirons	servons	servions	servirions
vous	servez	avez servi	serviez	servirez	servez	serviez	serviriez
ils / elles	servent	ont servi	servaient	serviront		servent	serviraient
-IR finir							
je / j'	finis	ai fini	finissais	finirai		finisse	finirais
tu	finis	as fini	finissais	finiras	finis	finisses	finirais
il / elle / on	finit	a fini	finissait	finira		finisse	finirait
nous	finissons	avons fini	finissions	finirons	finissons	finissions	finirions
vous	finissez	avez fini	finissiez	finirez	finissez	finissiez	finiriez
ils / elles	finissent	ont fini	finissaient	finiront		finissent	finiraient

Regular Verbs

Infinitif		Indicatif				Impératif	Subjonctif	Conditionnel
		Présent	Passé Composé	Imparfait	Futur			
-RE vendre								
je / j'		vends	ai vendu	vendais	vendrai		vende	vendrais
tu		vends	as vendu	vendais	vendras	vends	vendes	vendrais
il / elle / on		vend	a vendu	vendait	vendra		vende	vendrait
nous		vendons	avons vendu	vendions	vendrons	vendons	vendions	vendrions
vous		vendez	avez vendu	vendiez	vendrez	vendez	vendiez	vendriez
ils / elles		vendent	ont vendu	vendaient	vendront		vendent	vendraient
-IRE conduire								
je / j'		conduis	ai conduit	conduisais	conduirai		conduise	conduirais
tu		conduis	as conduit	conduisais	conduiras	conduis	conduises	conduirais
il / elle / on		conduit	a conduit	conduisait	conduira		conduise	conduirait
nous		conduisons	avons conduit	conduisions	conduirons	conduisons	conduisions	conduirions
vous		conduisez	avez conduit	conduisiez	conduirez	conduisez	conduisiez	conduiriez
ils / elles		conduisent	ont conduit	conduisaient	conduiront		conduisent	conduiraient
-IRE écrire								
j'		écris	ai écrit	écrivais	écrirai		écrive	écrirais
tu		écris	as écrit	écrivais	écriras	écris	écrives	écrirais
il / elle / on		écrit	a écrit	écrivait	écrira		écrive	écrirait
nous		écrivons	avons écrit	écrivions	écrirons	écrivons	écrivions	écririons
vous		écrivez	avez écrit	écriviez	écrirez	écrivez	écriviez	écririez
ils / elles		écrivent	ont écrit	écrivaient	écriront		écrivent	écriraient

Auxiliary Verbs

Infinitif	Indicatif				Impératif	Subjonctif	Conditionnel
	Présent	Passé Composé	Imparfait	Futur			
avoir							
j'	ai	ai eu	avais	aurai		aie	aurais
tu	as	as eu	avais	auras	aie	aies	aurais
il / elle / on	a	a eu	avait	aura		ait	aurait
nous	avons	avons eu	avions	aurons	ayons	ayons	aurions
vous	avez	avez eu	aviez	aurez	ayez	ayez	auriez
ils / elles	ont	ont eu	avaient	auront		aient	auraient
être							
je / j'	suis	ai été	étais	serai		sois	serais
tu	es	as été	étais	seras	sois	sois	serais
il / elle / on	est	a été	était	sera		soit	serait
nous	sommes	avons été	étions	serons	soyons	soyons	serions
vous	êtes	avez été	étiez	serez	soyez	soyez	seriez
ils / elles	sont	ont été	étaient	seront		soient	seraient

Reflexive Verbs

Infinitif	Indicatif				Impératif	Subjonctif	Conditionnel
	Présent	Passé Composé	Imparfait	Futur			
se laver							
je	me lave	me suis lavé(e)	me lavais	me laverai		me lave	me laverais
tu	te laves	t'es lavé(e)	te lavais	te laveras	lave-toi	te laves	te laverais
il / elle / on	se lave	s'est lavé(e)	se lavait	se lavera		se lave	se laverait
nous	nous lavons	nous sommes lavé(e)s	nous lavions	nous laverons	lavons-nous	nous lavions	nous laverions
vous	vous lavez	vous êtes lavé(e)(s)	vous laviez	vous laverez	lavez-vous	vous laviez	vous laveriez
ils / elles	se lavent	se sont lavé(e)s	se lavaient	se laveront		se lavent	se laveraient

Verbs with Stem Changes

Infinitif		Indicatif				Impératif	Subjonctif	Conditionnel
		Présent	Passé Composé	Imparfait	Futur			
acheter								
	j'	achète	ai acheté	achetais	achèterai		achète	achèterais
	tu	achètes	as acheté	achetais	achèteras	achète	achètes	achèterais
	il / elle / on	achète	a acheté	achetait	achètera		achète	achèterait
	nous	achetons	avons acheté	achetions	achèterons	achetons	achetions	achèterions
	vous	achetez	avez acheté	achetiez	achèterez	achetez	achetiez	achèteriez
	ils / elles	achètent	ont acheté	achetaient	achèteront		achètent	achèteraient
appeler								
	j'	appelle	ai appelé	appelais	appellerai		appelle	appellerais
	tu	appelles	as appelé	appelais	appelleras	appelle	appelles	appellerais
	il / elle / on	appelle	a appelé	appelait	appellera		appelle	appellerait
	nous	appelons	avons appelé	appelions	appellerons	appelons	appelions	appellerions
	vous	appelez	avez appelé	appeliez	appellerez	appelez	appeliez	appelleriez
	ils / elles	appellent	ont appelé	appelaient	appelleront		appellent	appelleraient
posséder								
	je / j'	possède	ai possédé	possédais	posséderai		possède	posséderais
	tu	possèdes	as possédé	possédais	posséderas	possède	possèdes	posséderais
	il / elle / on	possède	a possédé	possédait	possédera		possède	posséderait
	nous	possédons	avons possédé	possédions	posséderons	possédons	possédions	posséderions
	vous	possédez	avez possédé	possédiez	posséderez	possédez	possédiez	posséderiez
	ils / elles	possèdent	ont possédé	possédaient	posséderont		possèdent	posséderaient

Irregular Verbs

Infinitif	Indicatif				Impératif	Subjonctif	Conditionnel
	Présent	Passé Composé	Imparfait	Futur			
aller							
je / j'	vais	suis allé(e)	allais	irai		aille	irais
tu	vas	es allé(e)	allais	iras	va	ailles	irais
il / elle / on	va	est allé(e)	allait	ira		aille	irait
nous	allons	sommes allé(e)s	allions	irons	allons	allions	irions
vous	allez	êtes allé(e)(s)	alliez	irez	allez	alliez	iriez
ils / elles	vont	sont allé(e)s	allaient	iront		aillent	iraient
boire							
je / j'	bois	ai bu	buvais	boirai		boive	boirais
tu	bois	as bu	buvais	boiras	bois	boives	boirais
il / elle / on	boit	a bu	buvait	boira		boive	boirait
nous	buvons	avons bu	buvions	boirons	buvons	buvions	boirions
vous	buvez	avez bu	buviez	boirez	buvez	buviez	boiriez
ils / elles	boivent	ont bu	buvaient	boiront		boivent	boiraient
connaître							
je / j'	connais	ai connu	connaissais	connaîtrai		connaisse	connaîtrais
tu	connais	as connu	connaissais	connaîtras	connais	connaisses	connaîtrais
il / elle / on	connaît	a connu	connaissait	connaîtra		connaisse	connaîtrait
nous	connaissons	avons connu	connaissions	connaîtrons	connaissons	connaissions	connaîtrions
vous	connaissez	avez connu	connaissiez	connaîtrez	connaissez	connaissiez	connaîtriez
ils / elles	connaissent	ont connu	connaissaient	connaîtront		connaissent	connaîtraient

Infinitif		Indicatif					Impératif	Subjonctif	Conditionnel
	Présent	Passé Composé	Imparfait	Futur					
devoir									
je / j'	dois	ai dû	devais	devrai			doive	devrais	
tu	dois	as dû	devais	devras		dois	doives	devrais	
il / elle / on	doit	a dû	devait	devra			doive	devrait	
nous	devons	avons dû	devions	devrons		devons	devions	devrions	
vous	devez	avez dû	deviez	devrez		devez	deviez	devriez	
ils / elles	doivent	ont dû	devaient	devront			doivent	devraient	
dire									
je / j'	dis	ai dit	disais	dirai			dise	dirais	
tu	dis	as dit	disais	diras		dis	dises	dirais	
il / elle / on	dit	a dit	disait	dira			dise	dirait	
nous	disons	avons dit	disions	dirons		disons	disions	dirions	
vous	dites	avez dit	disiez	direz		dites	disiez	diriez	
ils / elles	disent	ont dit	disaient	diront			disent	diraient	
faire									
je / j'	fais	ai fait	faisais	ferai			fasse	ferais	
tu	fais	as fait	faisais	feras		fais	fasses	ferais	
il / elle / on	fait	a fait	faisait	fera			fasse	ferait	
nous	faisons	avons fait	faisions	ferons		faisons	fassions	ferions	
vous	faites	avez fait	faisiez	ferez		faites	fassiez	feriez	
ils / elles	font	ont fait	faisaient	feront			fassent	feraient	

Infinitif		Indicatif				Impératif	Subjonctif	Conditionnel
		Présent	Passé Composé	Imparfait	Futur			
falloir								
il		faut	a fallu	fallait	faudra		faille	faudrait
mettre								
je / j'		mets	ai mis	mettais	mettrai		mette	mettrais
tu		mets	as mis	mettais	mettras	mets	mettes	mettrais
il / elle / on		met	a mis	mettait	mettra		mette	mettrait
nous		mettons	avons mis	mettions	mettrons	mettons	mettions	mettrions
vous		mettez	avez mis	mettiez	mettrez	mettez	mettiez	mettriez
ils / elles		mettent	ont mis	mettaient	mettront		mettent	mettraient
pleuvoir								
il		pleut	a plu	pleuvait	pleuvra		pleuve	pleuvrait

Infinitif	Indicatif Présent	Passé Composé	Imparfait	Futur	Impératif	Subjonctif	Conditionnel
pouvoir							
je / j'	peux	ai pu	pouvais	pourrai		puisse	pourrais
tu	peux	as pu	pouvais	pourras		puisses	pourrais
il / elle / on	peut	a pu	pouvait	pourra		puisse	pourrait
nous	pouvons	avons pu	pouvions	pourrons		puissions	pourrions
vous	pouvez	avez pu	pouviez	pourrez		puissiez	pourriez
ils / elles	peuvent	ont pu	pouvaient	pourront		puissent	pourraient
prendre							
je / j'	prends	ai pris	prenais	prendrai		prenne	prendrais
tu	prends	as pris	prenais	prendras	prends	prennes	prendrais
il / elle / on	prend	a pris	prenait	prendra		prenne	prendrait
nous	prenons	avons pris	prenions	prendrons	prenons	prenions	prendrions
vous	prenez	avez pris	preniez	prendrez	prenez	preniez	prendriez
ils / elles	prennent	ont pris	prenaient	prendront		prennent	prendraient
recevoir							
je / j'	reçois	ai reçu	recevais	recevrai		reçoive	recevrais
tu	reçois	as reçu	recevais	recevras	reçois	reçoives	recevrais
il / elle / on	reçoit	a reçu	recevait	recevra		reçoive	recevrait
nous	recevons	avons reçu	recevions	recevrons	recevons	recevions	recevrions
vous	recevez	avez reçu	receviez	recevrez	recevez	receviez	recevriez
ils / elles	reçoivent	ont reçu	recevaient	recevront		reçoivent	recevraient

Infinitif	Indicatif				Impératif	Subjonctif	Conditionnel
	Présent	Passé Composé	Imparfait	Futur			
savoir							
je / j'	sais	ai su	savais	saurai		sache	saurais
tu	sais	as su	savais	sauras	sache	saches	saurais
il / elle / on	sait	a su	savait	saura		sache	saurait
nous	savons	avons su	savions	saurons	sachons	sachions	saurions
vous	savez	avez su	saviez	saurez	sachez	sachiez	sauriez
ils / elles	savent	ont su	savaient	sauront		sachent	sauraient
suivre							
je / j'	suis	ai suivi	suivais	suivrai		suive	suivrais
tu	suis	as suivi	suivais	suivras	suis	suives	suivrais
il / elle / on	suit	a suivi	suivait	suivra		suive	suivrait
nous	suivons	avons suivi	suivions	suivrons	suivons	suivions	suivrions
vous	suivez	avez suivi	suiviez	suivrez	suivez	suiviez	suivriez
ils / elles	suivent	ont suivi	suivaient	suivront		suivent	suivraient
tenir							
je / j'	tiens	ai tenu	tenais	tiendrai		tienne	tiendrais
tu	tiens	as tenu	tenais	tiendras	tiens	tiennes	tiendrais
il / elle / on	tient	a tenu	tenait	tiendra		tienne	tiendrait
nous	tenons	avons tenu	tenions	tiendrons	tenons	tenions	tiendrions
vous	tenez	avez tenu	teniez	tiendrez	tenez	teniez	tiendriez
ils / elles	tiennent	ont tenu	tenaient	tiendront		tiennent	tiendraient

| Infinitif | Indicatif | | | | Impératif | Subjonctif | Conditionnel |
	Présent	Passé Composé	Imparfait	Futur			
venir							
je	viens	suis venu(e)	venais	viendrai		vienne	viendrais
tu	viens	es venu(e)	venais	viendras	viens	viennes	viendrais
il / elle / on	vient	est venu(e)	venait	viendra		vienne	viendrait
nous	venons	sommes venu(e)s	venions	viendrons	venons	venions	viendrions
vous	venez	êtes venu(e)(s)	veniez	viendrez	venez	veniez	viendriez
ils / elles	viennent	sont venu(e)s	venaient	viendront		viennent	viendraient
voir							
je / j'	vois	ai vu	voyais	verrai		voie	verrais
tu	vois	as vu	voyais	verras	vois	voies	verrais
il / elle / on	voit	a vu	voyait	verra		voie	verrait
nous	voyons	avons vu	voyions	verrons	voyons	voyions	verrions
vous	voyez	avez vu	voyiez	verrez	voyez	voyiez	verriez
ils / elles	voient	ont vu	voyaient	verront		voient	verraient
vouloir							
je / j'	veux	ai voulu	voulais	voudrai		veuille	voudrais
tu	veux	as voulu	voulais	voudras	veuille	veuilles	voudrais
il / elle / on	veut	a voulu	voulait	voudra		veuille	voudrait
nous	voulons	avons voulu	voulions	voudrons	veuillons	voulions	voudrions
vous	voulez	avez voulu	vouliez	voudrez	veuillez	vouliez	voudriez
ils / elles	veulent	ont voulu	voulaient	voudront		veuillent	voudraient

Vocabulaires

Français-anglais

The French-English vocabulary contains all the French words in this text except obvious cognates that are not active vocabulary items.

A number following a definition of a word indicates the chapter in which it first appears as an active vocabulary item. (P) indicates **Chapitre Préliminaire.**

A number-letter combination indicates the appearance of a new word in a chapter's **Lecture culturelle** (L) or **Communiquons** (C) section. Your instructor may or may not require you to include these entries in your active French vocabulary. Passive vocabulary has no chapter reference.

abrév. indicates that the word is the abbreviation of another word.

fam. indicates colloquial language.

Voir followed by a word indicates a reference to another entry.

All nouns have gender markers (*m.* or *f.*). All adjectives appear in the masculine form followed by the feminine ending or feminine form. Plural forms of nouns or adjectives are indicated by the abbreviation *pl.*

Irregular verbs are followed by chapter references indicating when each verb first appears. If the infinitive or a verb form appears in the textbook prior to the presentation of the complete conjugation of the verb, the chapter in which the conjugation of the verb form appears is indicated by the reference forms + chapter number. An asterisk (*) indicates aspirate **h.**

(Compiled by Valérie Boulanger, Ph.D. candidate, University of Georgia.)

A

à at, in, to (1); *contraction avec le, les:* **au, aux** (2)

abonné(e) *m., f.* subscriber (7-L; 16-C)

abonnement *m.* subscription (16-C)

s'abonner (à) to subscribe (to) (16-C)

abord
  d'~ first (7)

absent(e) absent (2)

absolument absolutely (11)

accent *m.* accent
  ~ aigu acute accent
  ~ circonflexe circumflex accent
  ~ grave grave accent
  mettre l'~ sur to emphasize (17-L)

accepter (de) to accept (15)

accident *m.* accident (10)

accord *m.* agreement
  d'~! OK!, (all) right (8-C; 10)
  être d'~ to agree

accorder to grant (15-L)

accusateur (-trice) accusing (18-L)

achat *m.* purchase (5)
  faire des ~s to go shopping, to run errands (5)

acheter to buy (5)

acteur *m.* actor (2)

activité *f.* activity (8-L)
  ~ extra-universitaire *f.* extracurricular activity (1-L)

actrice *f.* actress (2)

actualités *f. pl.* news (11)

addition *f.* check *(in a restaurant)* (9-C)

adepte *m., f.* enthusiast (14-L)

administration *f.* government, administration (5-L)

adorer to adore (1)

adresse *f.* address (8)

adulte *m.* adult (2-C)

aérogramme *m.* air letter (8)

aéroport *m.* airport (10)

affaire *f.* business, affair (7-L)
  ~s *f. pl.* belongings, things (7)

affecter to affect (9-L)

affectueux (-euse) affectionate (2)

affiche *f.* poster (1)

affirmer to proclaim (13-L); to maintain (14-L)

affluer to rush (15-L)

affolé(e) frantic (18-L)

affreux (-euse) horrible (2)

africain(e) African (5-L)

Afrique *f.* Africa (4)
  ~ du Nord North Africa (18)

âge *m.* age (3)
  quel ~ avez-vous? how old are you? (3)

agence de voyages *f.* travel agency (4)

agenda *m.* calendar

agent de police *m.* policeman (2)

agir
  il s'agit de it's about (15)

agneau *m. (pl. -eaux)* lamb (3)

agonie *f.* death throes (10-L)

agréable pleasant (2)

agréer to accept (15-C)

agricole agricultural (16-L)

ah non! oh no! (4)

aide *f.* assistance (13-L)

ailleurs elsewhere (14-L; 18)

aimer to like, to love (1)
  ~ bien to like, to be fond of (2)
  ~ faire to enjoy doing (2)
  ~ mieux to prefer (2)

ainsi thus (5-L)

air *m.*
  avoir l'~ to look, to appear to be (5)

ajouter to add (14-C)

alcool *m.* alcohol (3)

Algérie *f.* Algeria (4)

algérien(ne) Algerian (18)

alimentation *f.* food (12-L)

Allemagne *f.* Germany (4)

allemand(e) German (2)

aller to go; *(+ infin.)* to be going to (4)
  ~ mieux to feel better (13)
  ~ voir to visit (8)
  allez-y! go ahead! (4)
  allons-y! let's go! (4)
  ça va? how are you? (P)
  ça va bien I'm fine (P)
  ça va pas, non? are you crazy? (17-C)
  comment allez-vous? how do you do? (P)
  comment ça va? how are you? (P)
  je vais bien I'm fine. (P)
  on y va? shall we go? (4)
  on y va let's go (4)

vas-y! go ahead! (4)

Allô, j'écoute Hello (7)

allumer to turn on (light, TV) (7)

alors then (1); well (13)
  ~ que while (15-L)
  ça ~! I'll be darned! (17-C)
  m'~ *(fam.)* so (18-C)

alphabet *m.* alphabet (1)

alpinisme *m.* mountain climbing (14)

ambassadeur extraordinaire *m.* ambassador extraordinary (9-L)

ambitieux (-euse) ambitious (2)

amélioration *f.* improvement (2-L)

améliorer to improve (12-L)

amener to bring (13)

américain(e) American (1-L; 2)

Amérique *f.* America (4)
  ~ du Nord North America (4)
  ~ du Sud South America (4)

ami(e) *m., f.* friend (1)

amicalement sincerely (15-C)

amitiés *f. pl.* fondly (15-C)

amour *m.* love (11)

amusant(e) funny (11-C)

s'amuser (à) to have a good time, to play (13)

an *m.* year (3)

analyse *f.* analysis (12-L)

anarchique anarchic (8-L)

ancien(ne) old, former (2)

anesthésiste *m., f.* anesthesiologist (13-L)

anglais *m.* English (language) (1)

anglais(e) English (1)

Angleterre *f.* England (4)

anglophone English-speaking (16-L)

animal *m. (pl. -aux)* animal (18)

animateur *m.* organizer (18-L)

année *f.* year (2-L; 4)
  ~ scolaire school year (8)

anniversaire *m.* birthday
  ~ de mariage wedding anniversary

annonce *f.*
  petite ~ classified ad (16)

annuaire *m.* phone book (7-C)

annulation *f.* cancellation (9-C)

anonyme anonymous (13-L)

anthropologie *f.* anthropology (8)

anti-doping
  contrôle ~ drug testing (14)

Antillais(e) *m., f.* person from the Antilles (8-L)

août *m.* August (9)

apéritif *m.* before-dinner drink (3)

apostrophe *f.* apostrophe

apparaître to appear (11-L)

appareil *m.*
~ **électro-ménager** appliance (16)
à l'~ on the phone (7)
qui est à l'~? who's speaking? (7)

appartement *m.* apartment (4)

appartenir (à) to belong (to) (10)

appel *m.* phone call (8-C)
~ **international** international call (8-C)
~ **interurbain** long-distance call (8-C)
faire un ~ de phares to flash the high beams (10-C)

appeler to call (4-L; 13)
comment vous appelez-vous? what's your name? (1)
je m'appelle my name is (P)
s'~ to be called (13)

application *f.* use (11-L)

apport *m.* contribution (16-L)

apporter to bring (3)

apprécier to appreciate (2)

apprendre (à) to learn, to teach (9)

s'approcher (de) to get closer (to) (18)

après after (1)
et ~? so what? (17-C)

après-midi *m.* afternoon (4)
de l'~ P.M. (6)

aquarelle *f.* watercolor (15)

arabe Arabic (8); Arab (18-L)

arbre *m.* tree (4-L; 17)

architecte *m.* architect (2)

architecture *f.* architecture (8)

argent *m.* money (3); silver (6-L)
~ **de poche** allowance (12-C)

armé(e) armed (13-L)

armoire *f.* armoire (16)

arrêt *m.* stop
~ **d'autobus** bus stop (4)

arrêter to stop (11)

arrière rear, back (10-C)

arrivée *f.* arrival (8)

arriver to arrive (1); to happen (7)

art *m.* art (8)
~ **moderne** modern art (2)

article *m.* (newspaper) article (15)
~ **défini** definite article
~**s de sport** *m. pl.* sporting goods (12)

artiste *m., f.* artist (2)

artistique artistic (15-L)

asiatique *m., f.* Asian (8-L)

Asie *f.* Asia (4)

asperge *f.* asparagus (9)

assaillir to mob (15-L)

assainissement *m.* decontamination (13-L)

assez rather (18)
~ **de** enough (3)
j'en ai ~! I've had it! (17-C)

assiette *f.* plate (9-C)

assimiler to assimilate (16-L)

assis(e) sitting (4-L)

assister (à) to attend (15-L); to witness (18-L)

association *f.* association (13-L)

assurance *f.* insurance (12-L)
~ **tous risques** full collision insurance (10)

assurer to ensure (13-L)

attacher to fasten

atteinte *f.* affront (15)

attendre to wait, to wait for (6)

attention *f.* attention
faire ~ to pay attention (5)

attirance *f.* attraction (6-L)

attirer to attract (8-L)

attribuer to attribute (3-L)

au *voir* à

aucun(e) no, not any (13-L)

audacieux (-euse) audacious (15-L)

audiovisuel(le) audiovisual (11-L)

augmenter to increase (12-L; 17)

aujourd'hui today (4)

auprès with (18-L)

ausculter to examine (13-C)

aussi also, too (2)
~**... que** as . . . as (9-L; 18)

aussitôt que as soon as (17)

autant as much, as many (18)

auteur *m.* author (2)
~ **dramatique** playwright (15)

auto *f.* car (6)

autobus *m.* bus (1)

autocar *m.* intercity bus (6)

autochtone indigenous (17-L)

auto-école *f.* driving school (10-C)

automatique automatic (10)

automne *m.* fall (9)

autonomie *f.* independence (13-L)

autoroute de l'information *f.* information superhighway (11-L)

autour around (15-L)

autre other (4)
~ **chose** something else (12)

autrement dit in other words (18-L)

Autriche *f.* Austria (4)

auxiliaire médical(e) *m., f.* medical auxiliary (13-L)

avance *f.* advance
~ **rapide** fast-forward button (11-L)
d'~ ahead (14)
en ~ early (6)

avant before (6)
avant-poste *m.* outpost (13-L)

avec with (1)

avenir *m.* future (11)
à l'~ in the future (17-L)

avion *m.* airplane (6)

avocat(e) *m., f.* lawyer (2)

avoir to have (3)
~**... an(s)** to be . . . year(s) old (3)
~**... (degrees)** to have a temperature of . . . (14-C)

avril *m.* April (9)

B

bac *abrév. de* baccalauréat

baccalauréat *m.* exam at the end of high school (1-L)

bachot *abrév. de* baccalauréat

bagages *m. pl.* luggage (5)
~ **à main** hand luggage (5)
faire les ~ to pack (5)

bagnole *(fam.)* *f.* car (18-C)

baignoire *f.* bathtub (16)

baiser *m.* kiss (8)

bal *m.* dance

balayer to sweep (4-L)

baleine *f.* whale (17-L)

ballet *m.* ballet (15)

banane *f.* banana (9)

bande dessinée *f.* comic strip (16-C)

banlieue *f.* suburb (9-L)
banque *f.* bank (4)
banquette *f.* seat (6)
baptiser to call (10-L)
bas(se) low
base-ball *m.* baseball (14)
basket-ball *m.* basketball (14)
basque *m.* Basque language
bateau *m.* (*pl.* -eaux) boat (6)
bâtiment *m.* building
bavardage *m.* gossip
beau (bel, belle, beaux, belles)
    handsome, beautiful, nice (9)
  faire ~ to be nice (weather) (5)
beau-père *m.* (*pl.* beaux-pères)
    stepfather, father-in-law (2)
beaucoup much, many, a lot
    of (1)
beauté *f.* beauty (15)
beige beige (6)
Belgique *f.* Belgium (4)
belle *voir* beau (4-L)
belle-mère *f.* (*pl.* belles-mères)
    stepmother, mother-in-law (2)
belligérance *f.* belligerence (13-L)
ben (*fam.*) uh (18-C)
bénévole voluntary (13-L)
besoin *m.* need (17-L)
  avoir ~ (de) to need (10)
bêtise *f.* dumb thing (14)
Beur (*fam.*) child of Arab
    immigrants (18-L)
beurre *m.* butter (3)
bibliothèque *f.* library (4)
bicentenaire *m.* bicentennial (8-L)
bicyclette *f.* bicycle (6)
bidule (*fam.*) *m.* thingamajig
    (11-C)
bien *m.* good
  ~s durables consumer durables
    (12-L)
bien well (P); nice (2)
  ~ entendu of course (15-L)
  ~ sûr of course (5)
bientôt soon (8)
  à ~ see you soon (P)
bière *f.* beer (3)
bifteck *m.* steak (9)
bijouterie *f.* jewelry store (12)
billet *m.* ticket (6)
  ~ de banque bank note (12-C)
biologie *f.* biology (8)
biotechnologie *f.* biotechnology
    (17)

bise *f.* kiss (8)
  faire une ~ à to kiss (*someone*)
    (P)
  grosses ~s hugs and kisses (8)
bistrot *m.* café, restaurant (3)
blanc(he) white (3)
blessé(e) *m., f.* injured person
    (13-L)
bleu(e) blue (4-L; 5)
bœuf *m.* beef (9)
boire to drink (12)
  je, tu bois I, you drink (3)
  il, elle, on boit he, she, one
    drinks (3-L)
  ils, elles boivent they drink
    (3-L)
  vous buvez you drink (3)
bois *m.*
  en ~ wooden (14-L)
boisson *f.* drink (3)
boîte *f.* club (2)
  ~ de nuit nightclub (2)
bon(ne) good (4-L; 5)
  ~ marché cheap (12-C)
  faire ~ to be nice (*temperature*)
    (8)
bonbon *m.* candy (9)
bonheur *m.* happiness (9-L; 11)
bonjour good morning, hello (P);
    (*in Quebec*) bye (1-C)
bonne nuit goodnight (1-C)
bonsoir good evening, good night,
    hello (P)
bord *m.* shore (16-L)
  à ~ de aboard (6-L)
  au ~ de along, by (4)
  ~ de la mer seaside (4)
bordé(e) lined (15-L)
botte *f.* boot (5)
bottin *m.* phone book (7-C)
bouche *f.* mouth (13)
boucher (-ère) *m., f.* butcher (12)
boucherie *f.* butcher shop (12)
bouffer (*fam.*) to eat (18-C)
boulanger (-ère) *m., f.* baker (12)
boulangerie *f.* bakery (12)
boules *f. pl.*
  partie de ~ bowling game (4-L)
boulot (*fam.*) *m.* job (18-C)
bourgeois(e) bourgeois,
    middle-class (15)
Bourgogne *f.* Burgundy
bourse *f.* *voir* portée (14-L)
bout *m.* end (6)

bouteille *f.* bottle (3-C; 12)
boutique *f.* shop (12)
branche *f.* branch (18)
branché(e) (*fam.*) *m., f.* someone
    in the know (7-L)
brancher to plug in, to connect (7)
bras *m.* arm (10-L; 13)
brasserie *f.* café-restaurant (12)
Brésil *m.* Brazil (4)
breton *m.* Breton language
brillamment brilliantly (18)
brillant(e) brilliant, shiny (18)
britannique British (6-L)
bronze *m.* bronze (15)
se brosser to brush (13)
brouillard *m.*
  faire du ~ to be foggy (8)
bruit *m.* noise (11)
  faire du ~ to make noise (11)
brûlé(e) burned
brûler un feu to run a red light
    (10-C)
brun(e) brown (5)
Bruxelles Brussels (4)
budget *m.* budget (12-L)
bulletin météorologique *m.*
    weather report
buraliste *m.* tobacconist (12)
bureau *m.* (*pl.* -eaux) desk, office
    (1)
  ~ de change currency exchange
    (12-C)
  ~ de poste post office (4)
  ~ des objets trouvés lost and
    found (6)
  ~ de tabac tobacco shop (7)

C

ça that, it (9)
cabine *f.* booth (8-C)
  ~ téléphonique phone booth (7)
câble *m.* cable (11)
cadeau *m.* (*pl.* -eaux) gift (1)
cadre *m.* middle manager (11)
  ~ supérieur executive (12-L)
café *m.* café (1); coffee (3)
  ~ au lait *m.* coffee with milk
    (9-C)
cahier *m.* notebook (1)
caisse *f.* cashier's (9-C; 12)
calculatrice *f.* calculator (7)
calculer to calculate
calculette *f.* pocket calculator (7)
calendrier *m.* calendar (9)

camarade *m., f.* friend (2)
~ de chambre roommate (2)
~ de cours classmate (2)
camion *m.* truck (6)
camp de réfugiés *m.* refugee camp (13-L)
campagne *f.* country (8); campaign (18-L)
campus *m.* campus
Canada *m.* Canada (4)
canadien(ne) Canadian (2)
canal *m.* (*pl.* -aux) canal (8-L)
canapé *m.* sofa (16)
canard *m.* duck (18)
capable capable (10-L)
capitale *f.* capital (6-L; 8)
caractère *m.* nature (8-L)
Caraïbes *f. pl.* Caribbean (5-L)
cardiaque cardiac (3-L)
carnet *m.* book (of tickets) (6)
carotte *f.* carrot (9)
~s râpées grated carrots (9)
carré(e) square (17-L)
carrière *f.* career (10-L)
carte *f.* map (1); menu (3); card (14)
à la ~ on request (11-L)
~ de crédit credit card (10)
~ des vins wine list (9-C)
~ orange orange card (6)
~ postale postcard (8)
carter *m.* gearbox casing (10-L)
cas *m.* case (13-L)
casino *m.* casino (4)
casser to break
se ~ le (la, les)... to break one's . . . (13-C)
tu me casses les pieds! you really annoy me! (17-C)
cassette *f.* cassette (7)
cataclysme *m.* cataclysm (13-L)
catalan *m.* Catalan language
catastrophe naturelle *f.* natural disaster (13-L)
catch *m.* wrestling (14)
cause *f.*
à ~ de because of (4-L)
causé(e) caused (3-L)
CD *m.* CD (7)
ce this, that, it (1)
~ qui, que what (15-L)
~ sont they are (1)
c'est it is (1)
c'est à qui? whose turn is it? (6)

c'est-à-dire that is (11-L)
ce (cet, cette) this, that (7)
cédille *f.* cedilla
ceinture *f.* belt (5)
~ de sécurité seat belt (10)
cela this, that, it (1)
célèbre famous (9-L)
célébrité *f.* celebrity (15-L)
celui (celle) the one; this (that) one; that (14)
censure *f.* censorship
cent hundred (4)
centenaire hundred-year-old (8-L)
centime *m.* 1/100th of a franc (12-C)
centimètre (cm) *m.* centimeter (14-C)
centrale électrique *f.* electric power plant (17-L)
centre *m.* center (6-L)
~ commercial *m.* shopping center (4)
~ de loisirs *m.* community center (18-L)
centre-ville *m.* downtown (12)
cependant however (2-L)
cerise *f.* cherry (9)
certain(e) certain, some (2)
certainement certainly (18)
ces these, those (7)
cesser (de) to stop (15)
cet *voir* ce
ceux (celles) these, those; the ones (14)
chacal *m.* jackal (18)
chaîne *f.* channel, station (11)
~ câblée cable station (11)
~ stéréo stereo system (7)
chaise *f.* chair (1)
chaleur *f.* heat (8)
chambre *f.* bedroom (1-L; 4)
~ de bonne maid's bedroom (16)
champ *m.* field (17)
champagne *m.* champagne (9-L)
champion(ne) *m., f.* champion (14)
championnat *m.* championship (14)
chance *f.* luck (6)
quelle ~! how lucky! (6)
changement *m.* change (2-L)
~ d'avis change of mind
changer (de) to change (3-L; 6)

chanson *f.* song (9-L; 10)
chanter to sing (1)
chapeau *m.* (*pl.* -eaux) hat (5)
~ haut de forme top hat (10-L)
chapitre *m.* chapter
chaque each (3-L)
charcuterie *f.* cold cuts (9-C); pork butcher's shop (12)
charcutier (-ère) *m., f.* pork butcher (12)
se charger to be responsible (9-L)
charges *f. pl.* utilities (16)
charmant(e) charming (2)
charte *f.* charter (13-L)
chasse *f.* hunting (14)
chassé(e) de forced out of (5-L)
chasseur d'autographes *m.* autograph collector (15-L)
chat *m.* cat (18)
chaud(e) hot (2)
avoir ~ to be hot (3)
faire ~ to be warm (*weather*) (4-L; 5)
il fait ~ it's hot (1-C)
chauffard *m.* reckless driver (10-C)
chauffeur *m.* driver (10)
chaussette *f.* sock (5)
chaussure *f.* shoe (5)
chef *m.*
~ d'Etat *m.* head of state (5-L)
~ d'orchestre *m.* conductor (15)
chemin *m.* way (16)
chemise *f.* shirt (5)
~ de nuit nightgown (5)
chemisier *m.* blouse (5)
chèque de voyage *m.* traveler's check (12-C)
cher (-ère) dear (8); expensive (4)
chercher to look for (4)
~ à to try (15)
chercheur *m.* researcher (16-L)
chère *f.* food (9-L)
cheval *m.* (*pl.* -aux) horse (18)
à ~ on horseback (6)
cheveux *m. pl.* hair (13)
cheville *f.* ankle (13)
chez at the house of (4)
chien *m.* dog (18)
chimie *f.* chemistry (8)
Chine *f.* China (4)
chinois(e) Chinese (3-L; 8)
chirurgien *m.* surgeon (13-L)

chocolat *m.* chocolate (3)

choisir (de) to choose (7)

choix *m.* choice (11-L)

chômage *m.* unemployment (11)

chose *f.* thing (11)

choucroute garnie *f.* sauerkraut and assorted meat (12)

chouette alors! great! (17-C)

ci-dessous below

ciel *m.* sky (4-L; 8)

cinéma *m.* cinema, movie theater (4)

cinq five (1)

cinquante fifty (2)

cinquième fifth (2)

circulation *f.* traffic (10)

cité *f.* high-rise project (18-L)

clair(e) clear (14-L)

classe *f.* classroom (1)

classique classical (2)

clavier *m.* keyboard (8)

~ à touches keyboard (7-L)

clé *f.* key (1)

client(e) *m., f.* customer (12-C)

cligner des yeux to blink (4-L)

clignotant *m.* car signal (10-L)

clôture *f.* closing (15-L)

clou *m.* climax (15-L)

club *m.* club *(association)* (2)

coca *m.* Coca-Cola (3)

cochon *m.* pig (18)

code *m.* code (7-L)

~ de la route *m.* traffic regulations (10-C)

cœur *m.* heart (6-L)

coexister to coexist (7-L)

coffre *m.* trunk (10)

coiffeur *m.* hairdresser (12-L)

coin *m.* corner, area (9)

au ~ de at the corner of (4)

colère *f.* anger (17-C)

colis *m.* package (8)

collectivité territoriale *f.* overseas region of France (P-L)

colline *f.* hill (4-L)

colon *m.* settler (16-L)

colonne *f.* column (17)

combien how many, how much (1)

c'est ~? how much is it? (5-C)

~ de how many, how much (6)

~ de temps? how long?

~ font... ? how much is . . . ? (1)

comédie *f.* comedy (15)

~ musicale musical (15)

commande *f.* order (10-L; 12)

commander to order (3)

comme as, like (3); how (9) since (10-L)

~ ci, ~ ça so-so (P)

tout ~ like (9)

commencer (à) to begin (to) (1)

comment how (6)

~? what? (17-C)

~ dit-on... ? how do you say . . . ? (1)

~ est-il? what is it like? (6)

commerçant(e) *m., f.* shopkeeper (12)

commercialisé(e) marketed (10-L)

communication *f.* phone call (7-C)

communiquer communicate (2-L)

compagnie de location *f.* rental agency (10)

compagnon *m.* companion (7-L)

compétent(e) competent (2)

compétition *f.* event (14-L)

complet (-ète) complete, full (1-L; 18)

complètement completely (18)

compliqué(e) complicated (2)

composer to make up (13-L)

~ un numéro de téléphone to dial a number (7-C)

comprendre to understand (9)

compris(e) included (16)

compte en banque *m.* bank account (7-L; 11)

compter to plan on (10-C); to count

conception *f.* conception (2-L)

concert *m.* concert (6)

concevoir to devise (10-L)

concierge *m., f.* concierge, caretaker (16)

concombre *m.* cucumber (9)

condition *f.* condition (6-L)

conduire to drive (10; 14)

se ~ to behave (14)

confier to entrust (15-L)

confiture *f.* jam (3)

conflit *m.* conflict (13-L)

confort *m.* comfort (6-L)

confrérie *f.* brotherhood (9-L)

connaissance *f.* acquaintance (1-C; 2); knowledge (13-L)

faire la ~ de to meet (2-C)

connaître to know (8-L; 10)

consacré(e) devoted (15)

consacrer to devote (9-L)

conseil *m.* piece of advice (11)

conseiller to advise (12)

conserver to keep, to preserve (5-L)

conserves *f. pl.* canned foods (12)

consommer to consume (3)

~ du... litres aux cent to use . . . liters per 100 kilometers (10-L)

constant(e) constant (14-L)

constater to notice (14-L)

constituer to form (2-L)

construit(e) built (8-L)

consulter to consult (7-L; 11)

contact *m.* contact (6-L; 17)

conte *m.* tale (14)

contemporain(e) contemporary (11)

contenir to include, to contain (10)

content(e) happy (2)

continent *m.* continent (4)

continuer (à) to continue (1)

contraction *f.* blend (7-L)

contravention *f.* traffic ticket

contre against (18-L)

contribuer (à) to contribute (15)

contrôle *m.* test (14)

~ anti-doping drug test (14)

contrôler to control (11-L)

convaincu(e) convinced (14-L)

convenu

c'est ~ all right (9-C)

conversation *f.* conversation (1-C)

converser to have a conversation (7-L)

convertir to convert (16-L)

copain *m.* friend *(male)* (2)

copieux (-euse) copious, hearty (6-L)

copine *f.* friend *(female)* (2)

coq *m.* rooster (18)

corde *f.* rope (14-L)

cordialement cordially (15-C)

corps *m.* body (13)

correct(e) correct (15)

correspondance *f.* connection (6)

correspondant(e) *m., f.*   person one is calling (7-L)
corriger   to correct
Corse *f.*   Corsica (4)
corse *m.*   Corsican language
costume *m.*   suit (5)
Côte d'Azur *f.*   Riviera (4)
Côte d'Ivoire *f.*   Côte d'Ivoire (4)
côté *m.*   aspect (8-L)
  à ~ de   next to (4)
côtelette *f.*   chop (9)
cou *m.*   neck (13)
se coucher   to go to bed (13)
coude *m.*   elbow (13)
couleur *f.*   color (4-L; 5)
coupable   guilty (18-L)
couper   to hang up, to disconnect (7)
courageux (-euse)   courageous (2)
courant(-e)   widespread (12-L)
courir   to run (18)
couronné(e)   crowned
courrier *m.*   mail (8)
  ~ du cœur   advice column (16-C)
  ~ électronique   e-mail (8)
cours *m.*   class, course (1)
  en ~   in class (1)
course *f.*   errand (5); race (14)
  ~ de bicyclettes   bicycle race (14)
  ~ de voitures   car race (14)
  faire des ~s   to shop (5)
court(e)   short (6-L)
couscous *m.*   couscous (3)
cousin(e) *m., f.*   cousin (2)
coût *m.*   cost (17-L)
couteau *m.* (*pl.* -eaux)   knife (9-C)
coûter   to cost (5)
  ~... le kilo   to cost . . . a kilo (14-C)
couture *f.*
  haute ~   designer clothes (9-L)
couvert *m.*   table setting (9-C)
  mettre le ~   to set the table (9-C)
couvert(e)   overcast (8)
  le ciel est ~   it's cloudy (8)
craie *f.*   chalk (1)
craindre   to fear, to be afraid of (14-L)
cravate *f.*   tie (5)
crayon *m.*   pencil (1)
créateur (-trice) *m.*   designer (7-L)

crédit *m.*   credit (12-L)
créer   to create (13-L; 17)
crème *f.*   cream (3)
crémerie *f.*   dairy store (12)
créole *m.*   Creole (5)
crêpe *f.*   crepe (5)
crevette *f.*   shrimp (9)
criminalité *f.*   crime (11)
crise *f.*   crisis (12-L)
  ~ de foie   liver attack (13-C)
  ~ économique   economic crisis (12-L)
critère *m.*   criterion (13-L)
critique   critical (13-L)
critiquer   to critique (15)
croire   to believe (14-C)
croissance *f.*   growth (14-L)
Croix Rouge *f.*   Red Cross (13-L)
croix verte *f.*   green cross (drug store sign) (13)
crucial(e) (*pl.* -aux, -ales)   crucial (13-L)
crudités *f. pl.*   raw vegetables (9)
cuillère *f.*   spoon (9-C)
  petite ~   teaspoon (9-C)
cuisine *f.*   cooking, cuisine (3); kitchen (16)
  ~ fine   refined cuisine (3-L)
  ~ minceur   low-calorie cuisine (3-L)
  faire la ~   to cook (5)
cuisinier (-ère) *m., f.*   chef, cook (9-L)
cuisinière *f.*   stove (16)
cuisse *f.*   thigh (13)
culminer   to reach its highest point (10-L)
cultivé(e)   cultivated (16-L)
cure *f.*
  faire une ~   to go to a health spa (13-C)
curiste *m., f.*   person going to a health spa (13-C)
cyprès *m.*   cypress (4-L)

D

d'abord   *voir* abord
d'accord   *voir* accord
dame *f.*   lady (8)
Danemark *m.*   Denmark (4)
dangereux (-euse)   dangerous (2)
dans   in (P-L; 3); in (*time*) (16)
danse classique *f.*   ballet (15)
danser   to dance (1)

danseur (-euse) *m., f.*   dancer (15)
date *f.*   date (9)
davantage   more (13)
de   of, from, about (1); any (3); *contraction avec* le, les: du, des (3)
  ~ la (l')   some (3)
débordé(e)   overwhelmed (18-L)
début *m.*   beginning (6)
décalage horaire *m.*   time difference (6-L)
décembre *m.*   December (9)
déception *f.*   disappointment (15-L; 17-C)
décerner   to award (15-L)
décider (de)   to decide (to) (6)
déclarer   to declare (16-L)
découverte *f.*   discovery (18-L)
découvrir   to discover
décrire   to describe (9-L; 14)
décrocher   to pick up (the phone) (7-C)
déçu(e)   disappointed (17-C)
dedans   inside (10-L)
défaut *m.*   fault
défendre   to forbid (15)
défense *f.*   prohibition (10-C)
degré *m.*   degree (14-C)
dégueulasse (*fam.*)   disgusting (18-C)
déjà   already (5)
déjeuner   to have lunch (3)
déjeuner *m.*   lunch (3-L; 9)
délaissé(e)   abandoned (18-L)
délicieux (-euse)   delicious (3)
délinquance *f.*   delinquency (11)
délivré(e)   freed (17)
deltaplane *m.*   hang gliding (14)
demain   tomorrow (4)
  à ~   see you tomorrow (1-C)
  ~ matin   tomorrow morning (4)
  ~ soir   tomorrow evening, tomorrow night (4)
demande *f.*
  à la ~   on request (11-L)
demander (à)   to ask for (1)
  ~ son chemin   to ask for directions (4-C)
démarrer   to start (car) (10)
demi(e)   half (6)
démolir   to demolish (8-L)
démontrer   to demonstrate (17-L)
dent *f.*   tooth (13)
dentiste *m., f.*   dentist (13)

dépanner to repair (10-L)

département *m.* administrative division of France (5)

se dépêcher (de) to hurry (8-L; 13)

dépense *f.* spending (12-L)

dépenser to spend (8)

depuis since, for (3-L; 6)

dernier (-ère) last (5)

   le ~ the latest (2)

derrière behind (4)

des *voir* de; some (3)

dès from . . . on, as of (10-L; 16)

   ~ que as soon as (17)

désagréable unpleasant (2)

désastre *m.* disaster (11)

descendant(e) *m., f.* descendant (5-L)

descendre to get off, to go down, to come down (6)

description *f.* description

désert *m.* desert (10-L)

se déshabiller to undress (13)

désintéressé(e) neutral, unselfish (13-L)

désirer to desire, to wish (2)

désobéir to disobey (7)

désolé(e) sorry (7)

dessin animé *m.* cartoon (11)

destruction *f.* destruction (15)

détaillé(e) detailed (12-L)

se détendre to relax (13)

détente *f.* relaxation

détester to hate (2)

   ~ faire to hate doing (2)

détresse *f.* distress (13-L)

deux two (1)

deuxième second (2)

devant in front of (2)

développement *m.* spreading (2-L); development (6-L)

développer to develop (2-L)

devenir to become (10)

   qu'est-ce que tu deviens? what are you up to? (1-C)

deviens *voir* devenir

deviner to guess

devoir to have to, to owe (12)

devoir *m.* duty (9-L)

   ~s homework (1)

   ~s écrits written work (8)

   faire ses ~s to do one's homework (5)

dialogue *m.* dialogue (1)

diététique *f.* nutrition (9-L)

Dieu *m.* God (18)

différent(e) different (2-L; 9)

difficile difficult (2)

diffuser to broadcast (11-L)

diffusion *f.* broadcast (11-L)

dimanche *m.* Sunday (9)

diminuer to decrease, to diminish (12-L; 17)

dîner to have dinner (3)

dîner *m.* dinner (3-L; 9)

dingue *(fam.)* nuts (18-C)

diplomate *m.* diplomat (2)

diplôme *m.* degree (13-L)

dire to tell, to say (14)

   cela veut ~ it means (1)

   ce qu'ils disent what people say

   on dit you say (1)

   pourriez-vous me ~. . . (1)?

     could you tell me . . . ? (4-C)

   qu'est-ce que. . . veut ~? what does . . . mean? (1)

directement directly

dis donc! say! (1-C)

discours *m.* speech (18-L)

discrimination *f.* discrimination (13-L)

discuter to have a chat (4-L); to discuss (11)

disent *voir* dire

disquette *f.* diskette (8)

disparaître to disappear (6-L)

disparition *f.* disappearance, removal (8-L)

se disperser to scatter (17)

disque *m.* record (1)

   ~ compact *m.* compact disk (7)

distance *f.* distance (6-L)

distinction *f.* distinction (12-L)

distingué(e) distinguished (15-C)

distinguer to distinguish (13-L)

distraction *f.* entertainment (2)

dit *voir* dire

divan *m.* sofa (16)

divers(e) various (13-L)

diversifier to diversify (13-L)

divisé(e) divided (1)

diviser to divide (14-C)

divorce *m.* divorce (2-L)

dix ten (1)

dix-huit eighteen (1)

dix-neuf nineteen (1)

dix-sept seventeen (1)

dix-septième seventeenth (2)

doigt *m.* finger (13)

doivent (devoir) must (8-L)

DOM (départements d'outre-mer) *m. pl.* overseas regions of France (P-L)

domaine *m.* area (11-L)

dommage *m.* damage, harm (11)

   il est ~ (que) it's too bad (that) (11)

   quel ~! what a shame! (17-C)

don *m.* donation, gift (13-L)

donc therefore (15)

donner to give (1)

   ~ sur to look out on (16)

   ~ un coup de téléphone to make a phone call (8-C)

dont whose, which (17)

dormir to sleep (7)

dos *m.* back (13)

douane *f.* customs

doubler to pass *(in traffic)* (10-C)

douche *f.* shower (16)

douter to doubt (11)

doux (-ouce) gentle (18-L)

douzaine dozen (15-L)

douze twelve (1)

doyen *m.* dean

drame *m.* drama (15)

se dresser to rise (18-L)

drogue *f.* illegal drug (11)

droit *m.* law (8)

   tout droit straight ahead (4-C)

   à ~e right, to the right (4-C)

du *voir* de

durer to last (6-L)

E

eau *f.* water (3)

   ~ minérale *f.* mineral water (3)

   ~ naturelle *f.* tap water (3-L)

échanger to exchange (7-L)

échapper to escape (14-L)

écharpe *f.* scarf (5)

échouer (à) to fail (1-L; 15)

éclair *m.* lightning (8)

éclater to break, to explode (13-L)

école *f.* school (3)

   ~ secondaire *f.* high school (1-L; 3)

écologie *f.* ecology (17)

écologique ecological (11)

écologiste *m., f.* ecologist (17)

économies *f. pl.*

   faire des ~ to save money (8)

économique economical (5-L)

économiser   to save (12-C)
économiste *m., f.*   economist (2)
écorce *f.*   bark (17)
écouter   to listen (1)
écran *m.*   screen (7-L)
écrevisse *f.*   crayfish
écrire (à)   to write (to) (14)
écrit(e)   written (7-L; 8)
écrivain(e) *m., f.*   writer (2)
éditorial *m.*   editorial (16-C)
éducation *f.*   upbringing (2-L);
    education (11-L)
  ~ physique *f.*   physical
    education (8)
éduquer   to educate (13-L)
effet *m.*   consequence, result (3-L)
efficience *f.*   efficiency (17-L)
égal(e)
  ça m'est ~   I don't care (17-C)
également   also (14-L)
égalité *f.*   equality (11)
église *f.*   church (4)
eh ben *(fam.)*   so (18-C)
eh bien   well then (1)
élan du cœur *m.*   emotional
    commitment (18-L)
électronique   electronic (11-C)
élève *m., f.*   pupil (1-L; 3)
élevé(e)   high
éliminer   to eliminate (3-L)
élision *f.*   elision (18-C)
élite *f.*   elite (15-L)
elle   she, it (1); her (5)
elles   they (1); them (5)
éloquent(e)
  être ~   to speak for itself (14-L)
élu(e)   elected
embêter   to bother (11)
embourgeoisé(e)   gentrified,
    adopting a middle-class
    outlook (10-L)
embouteillage *m.*   traffic jam (10)
embrasser   to kiss (2)
émission *f.*   program, show (11)
emmener   to take (someone)
    (6-L; 13)
s'emparer   to pick up, to take
    possession (18-L)
empêcher (de)   to prevent (14-L)
emploi *m.*   job (11)
  ~ du temps   schedule
employé(e) *m., f.*   employee,
    clerk (6)
employer   to use (5-L)

emporter   to take (5)
emprunter   to borrow (8)
en   to, in (4); some, any
    (11-C; 15); of it (15); in
    (time) (16)
enchanté(e)   delighted (2)
encore   still, again (2-L; 6); more
    (9-C)
  ne... pas ~   not yet (8)
s'endormir   to fall asleep (13)
endroit *m.*   place (4)
énergie *f.*   energy (17)
enfance *f.*   childhood
enfant *m., f.*   child (1)
enfin   at last, finally (4-L; 16)
  m'~ *(fam.)*   well (18-C)
engagement *m.*   commitment
    (18-L)
engin *(fam.) m.*   thingamajig
    (11-C)
enlever   to remove (13)
ennuyeux (-euse)   boring (2)
enrayer   to stop, to check (13-L)
enrichissement *m.*   improvement
    (9-L)
enseignement *m.*   teaching,
    education (15)
enseigner   to teach (15)
ensemble   together (1)
  dans l'~   as a whole (16-L)
ensuite   then (4-C)
entendre   to hear (4-L; 6)
enterrer   to bury (10-L)
entier (-ère)   whole (10-L)
entre   between (4)
entrée *f.*   entrance, hall (16)
entreprise *f.*   company (7-L)
entrer (à, dans)   to enter, to go in
    (1-L; 2)
entretenir *m.*   to maintain (10-C)
enveloppe *f.*   envelope (8)
envie *f.*
  avoir ~ de   to feel like (11)
environnement *m.*   environment
    (17)
envoyer   to send (8-C)
s'épanouir   to flourish (16-L)
épargner   to save (12-L)
épaule *f.*   shoulder (13)
éphémère   short-lived (12-L)
épice *m.*   spice (16-L)
épicerie *f.*   grocery store (12)
épicier (-ère) *m., f.*   grocer (12)
épidémie *f.*   epidemic (13-L)

épier   to watch, to spy on (15-L)
épinards *m. pl.*   spinach (9)
époque *f.*   era (10-L)
équipe *f.*   team (13-L; 14)
équipement ménager *m.*
    household appliances (12-L)
équitation *f.*   horseback riding
    (14)
erreur *f.*   mistake, wrong
    number (7)
éruption volcanique *f.*   volcanic
    eruption (13-L)
escalope *f.*   cutlet (9)
esclave *m., f.*   slave (5-L)
espace *m.*   space (17)
  ~ vert *m.*   park (8-L)
Espagne *f.*   Spain (4)
espagnol(e)   Spanish (2)
espérer   to hope (9)
espoir *m.*   hope (8-L)
essayer (de)   to try (12)
essence *f.*   gas (10-C)
essentiel(le)   essential (2-L)
est *m.*   east (4-C)
est-ce que... ?   *question phrase*
    (1)
estimer   to believe, to think (16-L)
et   and (P)
établi(e)   established (14-L)
étage *m.*   floor (16)
étagère *f.*   shelf (16)
étape *f.*   stage (14)
état *m.*   state (15)
Etats-Unis *m. pl.*   United States (4)
été *m.*   summer (4-L; 5)
éternuer   to sneeze
éthique *f.*   ethics (13-L)
éthylotest *m.*   blood-alcohol test
    (10-C)
étoile *f.*   star (9-L)
étonné(e)   amazed (11)
étonnement *m.*   surprise (17-C)
s'étonner   to be astonished, to
    wonder (17-C)
étranger (-ère) *m., f.*   foreigner
    (8-L; 10)
étranger (-ère)   foreign (3-L; 8)
être   to be (2)
  ça y est   that's it (5)
  ~ à   to belong to (5)
  ~ à... km. de   to be . . .
    (kilometers) from (14-C)
étudiant(e) *m., f.*   student (1)
étudier   to study (1)

euh uh (18-C)
Europe *f.* Europe (4)
européen(ne) European (10)
Eurotunnel *m.* Channel Tunnel (6-L)
eux they, them (5)
s'évader to get away, to escape (14-L)
événement *m.* event (13-L)
évidemment obviously (18)
évident(e) obvious (11)
évier *m.* kitchen sink (16)
éviter (de) to avoid (11)
évolution *f.* evolution (12-L)
évoquer to evoke (17)
exactement exactly (8)
examen *m.* exam (1)
examiner to examine (12-L; 13)
excusez-moi pardon me (1-C)
exemplaire *m.* unit (10-L)
exemple *m.* example
  par ~ for example (8-L)
exercice *m.* exercise (1)
  faire de l'~ to exercise (13)
exister to exist (1-L)
exotique exotic (8-L)
s'expatrier to move to a foreign country (16-L)
expédier to mail (8)
expérience *f.* experience (13-L)
expérimenter to try (7-L)
expliquer to explain (1)
explorateur *m.* explorer
expression *f.* expression (18-L)
exprimer to express (14-C)
  s'~ to express oneself (9-L)
expulsé(e) expelled (16-L)
extérieur(e) outside (2-L)
  à l'~ outside (5)
extrait *m.* excerpt (15)
extrême extreme (14-L)

F
fabriquer to manufacture (10-L)
fac *abrév. de* faculté
face *f.*
  en ~ de across from (4)
fâché(e) angry (17-C)
se fâcher to get angry (4-L)
facile easy (2)
facilement easily (2-L; 18)
façon *f.* way (14-L)
facteur *m.* mail carrier (8)
faculté *f.* university, school (1)

faim *f.*
  avoir ~ to be hungry (3)
faire to do, to make (5)
  ~... mètres to be . . . meters tall (14-C)
  ~... degrés to be . . . degrees *(weather)* (14-C)
  ~ du, de la, de l', des to study (8); to play *(sport)* (14)
  ~ du... kilomètres à l'heure to go . . . kilometers per hour (10-C)
  ~ du... aux 100 kilomètres to use . . . *(liters of gas)* per 100 kilometers (14-C)
  faites... ! do . . . ! (1)
faites *voir* faire
faits divers *m. pl.* human interest stories (16-C)
falloir must (10-L; 12)
  il faut it's necessary (4)
fallu *participe passé de* falloir
familier (-ère) colloquial (18-C)
famille *f.* family (1-L; 2)
  en ~ as a family (1-L); at home (5-L)
fantastique fantastic (2)
farine *f.* flour (3)
fascinant(e) fascinating (2)
fatigué(e) tired (2)
faut *voir* falloir
faute *f.* mistake (15)
fauteuil *m.* armchair (16)
faux (fausse) false (11)
  ~ ami *m.* false cognate
favori(te) favorite (2)
favorisé(e) favored (13-L)
fédération *f.* federation (14-L)
féminin(e) feminine (2)
femme *f.* woman (1); wife (2)
fenêtre *f.* window (1)
fermé(e) closed (2)
fermer to shut, to close (1)
  ne pas ~ l'œil not to sleep a wink (13)
festival *m.* festival (15-L)
fête *f.* holiday (9)
  ~ des Mères Mother's Day
  ~ du Travail Labor Day (9)
  ~ nationale Independence Day (9)
feu rouge *m.* red light
feuille *f.* leaf (17)
feuilleton *m.* series (11)

février *m.* February (9)
ficher
  fiche-moi la paix! leave me alone! (17-C)
  je m'en fiche! I don't care! (17-C)
fier (-ère) proud (4-L)
fièvre *f.* fever (13)
filet *m.* filet (9)
fille *f.* girl, daughter (2)
film *m.* film (2)
fils *m.* son (2)
fin *f.* end (1-L)
  en ~ de at the end of (4-L)
finalement finally (10-L)
financement *m.* financing (13-L)
financier (-ère) financial (13-L)
fini(e) finished (6-L)
finir (de) to finish (7)
Finlande *f.* Finland (4)
fixer to fasten (14-L)
fleur *f.* flower (9-C; 17)
fleuriste *m., f.* florist (12)
fleuve *m.* river (17)
flic *m. (fam.)* policeman (18-C)
flotte *f. (fam.)* water (18-C)
flûte *f.* flute (15)
fois *f.* time (10-L)
  une ~ once (11-L)
fond *m.*
  au ~ in the back (5-C); at the bottom (18-L)
fonder to found (16-L)
fondue *f.* cheese fondue
football *m.* soccer (2)
  ~ américain football (1-L; 14)
forcer to force (12-L)
forêt *f.* forest (17)
forme *f.* form (11-L)
  en ~ in shape (14-L)
former to train (13-L); to make up (16-L)
formidable sensational, terrific (2)
fort strongly (4-L)
fou (folle) crazy (4-L)
se fouler le (la)... to sprain one's . . . (13-C)
four *m.* oven (16)
  ~ à micro-ondes microwave oven (16)
fourchette *f.* fork (9-C)
fournir to provide (13-L)
frais *m.* cost (10)

frais (-aîche) cool
  faire ~ to be cool (8)
fraise *f.* strawberry (9)
franc *m.* franc (12)
français(e) French (1)
  en ~ in French (1)
Français(e) *m., f.* French person
  (2)
France *f.* France (4)
franchise *f.* frankness (11)
francophone French-speaking
  (P-L)
francophonie *f.* French-speaking
  communities (P-L)
frein *m.* brake (10)
freiner to brake (10)
fréquemment frequently
  (16-L; 18)
fréquent(e) frequent (18)
fréquenter to go to, to go out
  with (2)
frère *m.* brother (2)
fric *m. (fam.)* money (18-C)
frigidaire *m.* refrigerator (16)
frites *f. pl.* French fries (3)
froid(e) cold (2)
  avoir ~ to be cold (3)
  faire ~ to be cold *(weather)* (5)
  il fait ~ it's cold (1-C)
fromage *m.* cheese (3)
frontière *f.* border (6-L)
fruit *m.* fruit (3)
  ~s de mer shellfish (9)
fumer to smoke (1)
furieux (-euse) furious (11)
futur *m.* future (9-L; 17)

G

gagnant *m.* winner
gagner to earn (8); to win (14)
galet *m.* smooth stone (4)
gant *m.* glove (5)
garagiste *m.* mechanic (10-C)
garantie *f.* guarantee (13-L)
garçon *m.* boy (2); waiter (3)
garder to keep (8-L)
gare *f.* train station (4)
garer to park (2)
gaspiller to waste (12-C)
gastronomie *f.* gastronomy
  (3-L)
gâteau *m. (pl.* -eaux) cake (3)
gauche
  à ~ on the left (4-C; 16)

gel *m.* frost (17)
geler to freeze (10-L)
gendarme *m.* policeman (10)
gêné(e) embarrassed (18-L)
général(e) (*pl.* -aux, -ales) general
  (18)
  en ~ in general (1)
généralement generally (1-L; 13)
génération *f.* generation (2-L)
généreux (-euse) generous (2)
Genève Geneva (4)
genou *m.* (*pl.* -oux) knee (13)
gens *m. pl.* people (7-L; 10)
gentil(le) nice (4-L)
géographie *f.* geography (8)
géologie *f.* geology (8)
gestion *f.* management (8)
gigot *m.* leg of lamb (9)
glace *f.* ice cream (3)
glissant(e) slippery (10-C)
globe *m.* globe (13-L)
gloire *f.* glory (10-L)
godasse *f. (fam.)* shoe (18-C)
golf *m.* golf (14)
gorge *f.* throat (13)
gosse *m. (fam.)* child (18-C)
goûter to taste, to have an
  afternoon snack (3)
grâce à thanks to (12-L)
gramme *m.* gram (12)
grand(e) large, big, tall (4-L; 9)
  ~es vacances summer vacation
  (10)
  ~ magasin department store
  (11)
  ~ standing deluxe (8-L)
grand-chose
  pas ~ ! not much! (5-C)
  ce n'est pas ~ it's no big deal
  (17-C)
Grande-Bretagne *f.*
  Great Britain (4)
grandir to grow up (8-L)
grandissant(e) growing (17-L)
grand-mère *f.* (*pl.* grands-mères)
  grandmother (2)
grand-père *m.* (*pl.* grands-pères)
  grandfather (2)
grands-parents *m. pl.*
  grandparents (2)
grave serious (13)
  ce n'est pas ~ it's not serious
  (17-C)
grec (grecque) Greek (8)

Grèce *f.* Greece (4)
grève *f.*
  faire ~ to go on strike (18-L)
grippe *f.* flu (13-C)
gris(e) gray (5)
gros(se) large, big (6)
  ~ titre *m.* headline (16-C)
gruyère *m.* Swiss cheese
guerre *f.* war
  ~ de Sécession Civil War (16-L)
  ~ mondiale world war (10-L)
  ~ nucléaire nuclear war (11)
guillemets *m. pl.* quotation marks
guitare *f.* guitar (15)
Guyane *f.* French Guyana (5-L)
gymnastique *f.* gymnastics (14)

H

s'habiller to get dressed (13)
habitable livable (17)
habiter to live (1)
habitude *f.* habit, custom
  (3-L; 10)
*hamburger *m.* hamburger (3)
*haricot vert *m.* green bean (9)
*haut(e) high
  en ~ at the top of (14-L)
Havane (La) *f.* Havana (4)
hebdomadaire *m.* weekly
  publication (16-C)
hésiter (à) to hesitate (14-L; 15)
heure *f.* hour, time (6)
  à l'~ on time (6)
  à quelle ~? at what time? (5-C)
  à tout à l'~ see you later (P)
  de bonne ~ early (12)
  ~ conventionnelle conventional
  time (6-C)
  ~ officielle official time (6-C)
  quelle ~ est-il? what time is it?
  (5-C; 6)
heureusement fortunately (6)
heureux (-euse) happy (2)
hier yesterday (5)
histoire *f.* history (8); story (10-L)
  ~ de l'art art history (8)
hiver *m.* winter (5)
hivernal(e) winter (16-L)
*hockey *m.* hockey (14)
*Hollande *f.* Holland (4)
homme *m.* man (1)
  ~ d'affaires businessman (12-L)
  ~ politique politician (9-L)
honneur *m.* honor (15-C)

horoscope *m.*   horoscope
    (7-L; 16-C)
*hors-d'œuvre *m.*   appetizer (3)
hostile   hostile (13-L)
hôte *m.*   guest (9-L)
hôtel *m.*   hotel (1)
hôtesse *f.*   hostess (4)
huile *f.*   oil (3)
*huit   eight (1)
humanisme *m.*   humanism (9-L)
hygiène *f.*   hygiene (13-L)
hypermarché *m.*   giant
    supermarket (12)
hypocondriaque   hypochondriac
    (13)
hypocrisie *f.*   hypocrisy (2)
hypocrite   hypocritical (2)

I

ici   here (1)
idée *f.*   idea (5)
identité *f.*   identity (14-L)
il   he, it (1)
    ~ y a   there is, there are (3);
        since, ago (16)
    ~ y a... que   it has been . . . that
        (16)
île *f.*   island (6-L)
ils   they (1)
imaginer   to imagine (7-L)
imam *m.*   imam (prayer leader)
    (18)
immédiat(e)   immediate (10-L)
immédiatement   immediately (7-L)
immeuble *m.*   apartment building
    (8-L; 16)
immigré(e)   immigrant (18)
imparfait *m.*   imperfect tense (10)
imper *m.*   raincoat (6)
imperméable *m.*   raincoat (5)
impoli(e)   impolite (2)
importance *f.*   importance (11)
important(e)   important (2-L; 11)
impossible   impossible (2)
impôt *m.*   tax (12-L)
imprécision *f.*   imprecision (11-C)
impression *f.*   impression
    avoir l'~   to have a feeling
        (12-L)
impressionnant(e)   impressive (8)
imprimante *f.*   printer (8)
incarner   to embody (17)
incertain(e)   uncertain (16-L)

incertitude *f.*   uncertainty (11)
inclure   to include (17)
incompétent(e)   incompetent (2)
inconnu(e) *m., f.*   stranger (1-C)
inconnu(e)   unknown (4-L)
inconvénient *m.*   annoyance (11)
incrédule   incredulous
indépendamment   independently
    (18)
indépendance *f.*   independence
    (13-L)
indépendant(e)   independent (2)
indifférence *f.*   indifference (17-C)
indiquer   to indicate (4-C; 9)
    pourriez-vous m'~... ?   could
        you show me . . . ? (4-C)
indispensable   indispensable
    (7-L; 10)
individuel(le)   individual (13-L)
infirmière *f.*   nurse (13-L)
inflation *f.*   inflation (11)
influence *f.*   influence (2-L)
informations *f. pl.*   news (14)
informatique *f.*   computer science
    (8)
informatisé(e)   computerized (7-L)
ingénieur *m.*   engineer (2)
initié(e) *m., f.*   fan (14-L)
injuste   unfair (11)
inondation *f.*   flood (13-L)
inoubliable   unforgettable
inquiéter   to worry (13)
    s'~ (de)   to be worried (13); to
        worry (15)
inspirer   to inspire (15-L)
installation *f.*   settlement (16-L)
installer   to install (7-L)
    s'~   to settle (16-L)
instant *m.*   moment (7-C)
instantanément   instantly (11-L)
instrument *m.*   instrument
    (12-L; 15)
    ~ de musique   musical
        instrument (15)
insuffisamment   insufficiently (18)
insuffisant(e)   insufficient (15)
insupportable   unbearable (8)
intelligemment   intelligently (18)
intelligent(e)   intelligent (2)
interdiction *f.*   forbidden thing
    (18-L)
interdit(e)   forbidden (10-C)
intéressant(e)   interesting (2)

intéresser   to interest (16)
    s'~ (à)   to be interested (in) (15)
intermariage *m.*   mixed marriage
    (16-L)
international(e)   international
    (14-L)
interprétation *f.*   acting (15-L)
interroger   to ask questions
interrompre   to interrupt
interrompu(e)   interrupted
intervenir   to intervene (13-L)
intervention *f.*   intervention (13-L)
interview *f.*   interview (9-L; 11)
intolérance *f.*   intolerance (2)
inutile   useless (2)
s'investir   to put effort (11-L)
invité(e) *m., f.*   guest
inviter   to invite (1)
Irlande *f.*   Ireland (4)
isolation *f.*   isolation (6-L)
Italie *f.*   Italy (4)
italien(ne)   Italian (2)
ivre   drunk

J

jaillir   to spring (17)
jalousie *f.*   jealousy
jamais   never (8)
jambe *f.*   leg (13)
jambon *m.*   ham (3)
janvier *m.*   January (9)
Japon *m.*   Japan (4)
japonais(e)   Japanese (8)
jardin *m.*   yard, garden (17)
jaune   yellow (5)
jazz *m.*   jazz (2)
je, j'   I (1)
jean *m.*   jeans (5)
se jeter dans   to flow into (17-L)
jeu *m.* (*pl.* -eux)   game (7-L)
    ~ télévisé   game show (11)
jeudi *m.*   Thursday (9)
jeune   young (9)
    ~s gens *m. pl.*   young people (2)
jeunes *m. pl.*   young people (9-L)
jeunesse *f.*   youth (10-L)
jogging *m.*   jogging (14)
joli(e)   pretty (9)
jouer   to play (1)
    ~ à   to play (*game, sport*) (14)
    ~ de   to play (*musical
        instrument*) (15)
    ~ un rôle   to play a part (2-L)

joueur *m.* player (14)

jour *m.* day (3-L; 9)

journal *m.* (*pl.* -aux) newspaper (7-L); TV news (11)

~ **de mode** fashion magazine (16-C)

~ **télévisé** TV news (11-L)

journalisme *m.* journalism (8)

journaliste *m., f.* journalist (2)

journée *f.* day (4-L; 13)

juillet *m.* July (9)

juin *m.* June (1-L; 9)

jupe *f.* skirt (5)

jus de fruit *m.* fruit juice (3)

jusqu'à until (4-C; 6)

~ **ce que** until (15-L)

jusque until (16-L)

juste fair (11); just (16)

~ **avant** just before (8)

~ **un peu** just a little (1)

justement as a matter of fact (6)

justice *f.* justice (11)

K

kilogramme (kilo, kg) *m.* kilogram (2.2 pounds) (3-C)

kilomètre (km) *m.* kilometer (10)

à… ~s de . . . kilometers away (14-C)

~s/heure kilometers per hour (6-L)

kiosque (de journaux) *m.* newspaper stand (16-C)

klaxon *m.* horn (car) (10)

klaxonner to honk

L

la *voir* le

là there (2)

là-bas over there (4)

laborantin(e) *m., f.* lab technician (13-L)

laboratoire *m.* laboratory (4)

lac *m.* lake (17)

laid(e) ugly (2)

laisser to leave, to allow (6)

lait *m.* milk (3)

lampe *f.* lamp (16)

langue *f.* language (5-L; 8)

lapin *m.* rabbit (9)

latin *m.* Latin (8)

lavabo *m.* sink (16)

lavande *f.* lavender (4-L)

se laver to wash, to bathe (13)

lave-vaisselle *m.* dishwasher (12-L; 16)

le (la, l', les) the (1); him, her, it, them (8)

~ **plus** the most (2-L; 11)

leçon *f.* lesson (1)

lecteur (-trice) *m., f.* reader (15)

lecteur de disquettes disk drive (8)

lecteur de disques compacts CD player (7)

légumes *m. pl.* vegetables (3)

lendemain *m.*

sans ~ without a future (18-L)

lent(e) slow (12-L; 18)

lentement slowly (8-L; 18)

lequel (laquelle, lesquels, lesquelles) which (11-L)

les *voir* le

lessive *f.*

faire la ~ to do laundry (5)

lettre *f.* letter (8)

leur to them (9)

leur (le, la, leurs (les) theirs (14)

leur(s) their (2-L; 5)

lever to raise (13)

se ~ to get up (13)

librairie *f.* bookstore (4)

libre free (7)

ligne *f.* line (6)

limiter to restrict (8-L)

lire to read (14)

lisez! read! (1)

Lisbonne Lisbon (4)

liste *f.* list (4)

lit *m.* bed (16)

litre (l) *m.* liter (3-C)

littéraire literary (5-L; 15)

littérature *f.* literature (8)

livraison *f.* delivery (10-L)

livre *m.* book (1)

livre *f.* pound (3-C)

local(e) (*pl.* -aux, -ales) local (11-L)

localité *f.* town, city (7-L)

location *f.* rental (10)

logement *m.* housing (12-L)

logiciel *m.* software (8)

loi *f.* law (10)

loin de far from (4)

loisirs *m. pl.* free time (12-L)

Londres London (4)

longer to border (15-L)

longtemps a long time (6)

lors de during (15-L)

lorsque when (17)

louer to rent (1-L; 10)

Louisiane *f.* Louisiana (5-L; 16)

loyer *m.* rent (16)

lucide lucid (17)

lui to him, to her, to it (2, 9)

lumière *f.* light (4-L; 17)

lundi *m.* Monday (9)

lune *f.* moon (17)

lunettes de soleil *f. pl.* sunglasses (5)

lutte *f.* fight (18-L)

luxe *m.* luxury

lycée *m.* high school (4)

lycéen(ne) *m., f.* high school student

M

ma my (5)

machin *m.* (*fam.*) thingamajig (11-C)

Machin-Chouette what's-his-name (11-C)

machine à laver *f.* washing machine (12-L; 16)

Madame *f.* (*pl.* Mesdames) Mrs., Ms., ma'am (P)

~ **Unetelle** Mrs. So-and-So (11-C)

Mademoiselle *f.* (*pl.* Mesdemoiselles) Miss, Ms. (P)

magasin *m.* store (4)

grand ~ department store (11)

magazine *m.* magazine (14)

Maghreb *m.* Maghreb (18)

Maghrébin(e) *m., f.* person from the Maghreb (18)

magnétophone *m.* tape recorder (7)

magnétoscope *m.* VCR (7)

magnifique magnificent (2)

mai *m.* May (1-L; 9)

maillot *m.* jersey (14)

~ **de bain** bathing suit (5)

main *f.* hand (13)

maintenant now (4)

maintenir to maintain (12-L)

maire *m.* mayor (15-C)

mais but (1)

maison *f.* house (4)
maître d'hôtel *m.* maitre d' (9-C)
majorité *f.* majority (2-L)
mal *m.* damage (15)
  avoir du ~ à to have trouble (15)
  avoir ~ à to have a sore . . . (13)
  pas ~ not bad (P)
  se faire ~ à to hurt one's . . . (13)
mal badly (5)
malade sick (2)
maladie *f.* illness (13)
malgré despite (2-L)
malheureusement unfortunately (18)
malheureux (-euse) unhappy (2)
mandat *m.* money order (8)
manger to eat (1)
manière *f.* way (13-L)
manifestation *f.* protest march (18-L)
manquer to miss (7-L)
manteau *m.* (*pl.* -eaux) coat (5)
manufacturé(e) manufactured (12-L)
marchand(e) *m., f.* merchant (9)
marchander to bargain (12-C)
marché *m.* market (9)
  ~ en plein air open-air market (9)
marcher to work, to function (7)
mardi *m.* Tuesday (9)
mari *m.* husband (2)
maritime maritime (6-L)
Maroc *m.* Morocco (4)
marocain(e) Moroccan (18)
marquer to mark (10-L)
marre
  j'en ai ~ ! I've had it up to here! (17-C)
mars *m.* March (9)
masculin(e) masculine (2)
masse *f.* mass (7-L)
massif (-ive) massive (13-L)
match *m.* match (2)
  ~ de football soccer game (2)
matérialiste materialistic (11)
matériel *m.* hardware (8)
maternel(le)
  langue ~le mother tongue (5-L)
mathématiques (maths) *f. pl.* mathematics (8)

matière *f.* subject (8); matter (17)
matin *m.* morning (4)
  du ~ A.M. (6)
matinée *f.* morning (9)
  faire la grasse ~ to sleep late (5)
mauvais(e) bad (2)
  faire ~ to be bad (weather) (5)
mec *m.* (*fam.*) guy (18-C)
mécanicien *m.* mechanic (10-C)
méchamment out of meanness (18)
méchant(e) mean, bad (2)
médecin *m.* doctor (2)
médecine *f.* medicine (8)
médias *m. pl.* mass media (2-L)
médical(e) medical (13-L)
médicalisé(e) medicalized (13-L)
médico-chirurgical(e) medico-surgical (13-L)
méditatif (-ive) pensive (17)
meilleur(e) better (18)
  le ~, la ~e, les ~(e)s the best
melon *m.* cantaloupe (4-L)
membre *m.* member (15-L)
même self (5); same (7-L); even (5-L)
ménage *m.*
  faire le ~ to do housework (5)
mensonge *m.* lie (14)
mensuel *m.* monthly publication (16-C)
menthe *f.* mint (4-L)
mentir to lie (7)
menu *m.* menu, fixed price meal (3)
mer *f.* sea (4)
merci thank you (P)
  ~ mille fois thanks a million (4)
mercredi *m.* Wednesday (9)
mère *f.* mother (2)
merguez *f.* North African spicy red sausage (3)
mes my (5)
Mesdames *f. pl.* ladies (1-C)
Mesdemoiselles *f. pl.* ladies (1-C; 12)
message *m.* message (7)
messagerie rose *f.* adult message service (7-L)
Messieurs *m. pl.* Gentlemen (4)
mesure *f.* measurement
  être en ~ de to be in a position to (13-L)

mesurer to evaluate (13-L); to be . . . tall (14-C)
météo *f.* weather forecast (7-L; 8)
métier *m.* occupation, career (9-L; 15)
  ~ artistique career in the arts (15)
métis *m.* person of mixed race (18-L)
métrage *m.*
  court ~ short feature (15-L)
  long ~ full-length feature (15-L)
mètre *m.* meter (14)
métro *m.* subway (6)
mettre to put (on), to set, to turn on, to take (*time to do something*) (17)
  se ~ à to begin (17)
meublé(e) furnished (16)
meubles *m. pl.* furniture (12-L; 16)
meute *f.* herd (15-L)
mexicain(e) Mexican (2)
Mexico Mexico City (4)
Mexique *m.* Mexico (4)
midi *m.* noon (6)
Midi *m.* south of France (18-L)
mien (le), mienne (la), mien(ne)s (les), mine (14)
mieux better (18)
  le ~ the best (18)
migrateur migratory (17-L)
milieu *m.* circle (15); middle (16-L)
mille thousand (4)
milliard *m.* billion (4)
million *m.* million (4)
mine *f.*
  avoir bonne ~ to look good, healthy (13)
  avoir mauvaise ~ to look sick (13)
Ministère *m.* department (11-L)
Minitel *m.* telephone computer (7-C)
minuit *m.* midnight (6)
minute *f.* minute (4)
mise en scène *f.* directing (15-L)
mission *f.* mission (10-L)
mobilisation *f.* mobilization (13-L)
moche (*fam.*) ugly (18-C)
mode de vie *m.* lifestyle (12-L); way of life (17-L)

modem *m.* modem (8)

moi me, I (2; 9)

moins less (1)
 de ~ en ~ less and less (12-L)

mois *m.* month (5)

moitié *f.* half (10-L)

moment *m.* time (10-L)

mon (ma, mes) my (5)

monde *m.* world (P-L; 11)

mondial(e) worldwide (9-L); international (15-L)

moniteur *m.* monitor (8)

monnaie *f.* change (12-C)

Monsieur *m.* (*pl.* Messieurs) Mr., sir (P)
 ~ Untel Mr. So-and-So (11-C)

montagne *f.* mountain (11)

montant *m.* cost

montée *f.* rise (18-L)

monter to get on, to go up (6)

montrer to show (1)

monument *m.* monument (8)

moral(e) (*pl.* -aux, -ales) moral (13-L)

morceau *m.* (*pl.* -eaux) piece (3-C)

Moscou Moscow (4)

mot *m.* word (4-L)
 ~ clé key word
 ~s croisés crossword puzzle (16-C)

moto *f.* motorcycle (6)

mourir to die (10)

moutarde *f.* mustard (3)

mouton *m.* mutton (3); sheep (18)

moyen *m.* means (11-L)

Moyen Age *m.* Middle Ages

Mozambique *m.* Mozambique (4)

muezzin *m.* muezzin (18)

multimédia multimedia (11-L)

multiplié(e) (par) multiplied (1)

multiplier to multiply (14-C)

mur *m.* wall (3)

musée *m.* museum (4)

musicien(ne) *m.*, *f.* musician (2)

musique *f.* music (2)
 ~ classique classical music (2)

mutuel(le) mutual (6-L)

N

nager to swim (14)

naissance *f.* birth (2-L)

naître to be born (6)

nana *f.* (*fam.*) girl (18-C)

natation *f.* swimming (14)

nationalité *f.* nationality (2)

nature *f.* nature (17)

naturel(le) natural (13-L)

naturellement naturally (14-L)

navette *f.* shuttle (17)

navré(e) sorry (17-C)

ne (n') (negation) (2)
 ~... jamais never (8)
 ~... pas not (1-L; 2)
 ~... pas encore not yet (8)
 ~... personne nobody (12)
 ~... plus no more (1-L; 12)
 ~... que only (12)
 ~... rien nothing (12)

né(e) born (6)

nécessaire necessary (7)

nécessairement necessarily (18)

négatif (-ve) negative (14)

neige *f.* snow (8)

neiger to snow (8)

n'est-ce pas? isn't it so? (1)

neuf nine (1)

neuf (neuve) new (10)

neuvième ninth (2)

neveu *m.* nephew (2)

nez *m.* nose (13)

nièce *f.* niece (2)

niveau de vie *m.* standard of living (12-L)

Noël Christmas

noir(e) black (5)

noirci(e) blackened (17)

noircir to blacken (17)

nom *m.* name (7-L; 9)

nombrable countable (17)

nombre *m.* number (2-L; 11)

nombreux (-euse) numerous (1-L)

non no (1)
 ~ plus neither (7-L)

nord *m.* north (4-C)

nord-africain(e) North African (3-L)

Norvège *f.* Norway (4)

nos our (5)

note *f.* note (8)

noté
 c'est ~ I've got it (9-C)

notoriété *f.* publicity (18-L)

notre our (5)

nôtre (le, la), nôtres (les) ours (14)

nourriture *f.* food (3)

nous we (1); us (11)

nouveau (nouvel), nouvelle, nouveaux, nouvelles new (6-L; 9)

Nouvelle-Angleterre *f.* New England (5-L)

Nouvelle-Orléans (La) *f.* New Orleans (4)

nouvelles *f. pl.* news (7-L; 8)
 donnez-moi de vos ~ let me hear from you (8)

novembre *m.* November (9)

nuage *m.* cloud (4-L; 8)

nucléaire nuclear (11)

nuit *f.* night (7-L; 13)

numéro *m.* number (8-C)
 ~ de téléphone *m.* phone number (7-C; 10)

O

obéir (à) to obey (7)

objet *m.* thing
 ~s trouvés lost and found (6)

obligatoire compulsory (10)

observer watch (2-L)

obtenir to obtain (10)

occasion *f.* opportunity (7-L)
 à l'~ on the occasion (11-L)
 d'~ used (10)

occupant(e) *m.*, *f.* passenger (10-C)

occupé(e) busy (7-C)

s'occuper de to take care of (13)

octobre *m.* October (1-L; 9)

œil *m.* (*pl.* yeux) eye (13)

œuf *m.* egg (9)

œuvre *f.* work (15)

officiel(le) official (5-L)

offrir to offer (7-L)

oiseau *m.* (*pl.* -eaux) bird (17)

olive *f.* olive (9)

olivier *m.* olive tree (4-L)

olympique olympic (14-L)

ombre *f.* shade (4-L)

omelette *f.* omelet (5)

on one, we, they (1)

oncle *m.* uncle (2)

ondoyer to shine (17)

onze eleven (1)

onzième eleventh (2)

opéra *m.* opera (8-L; 15)

opinion *f.* opinion (11)

opposé à against, opposed to (8-L)

s'opposer à to oppose (6-L)

optimiste optimistic (2)

orage *m.*

  faire de l'~ to storm (8)

orange *f.* orange (9)

orchestre *m.* orchestra (15)

ordinateur *m.* computer (8)

oreille *f.* ear (13)

organisation *f.* organization (13-L)

organisé(e) organized (11-L)

orienté(e) directed toward (9-L)

originalité *f.* originality (8-L)

origine *f.*

  à l'~ originally (10-L)

orthographe *f.* spelling

ou or (1)

où where (9-L; 16)

  ~? where? (2)

  ~ ça? whereabout? (4)

oublier (de) to forget (5)

ouest *m.* west (4-C)

oui yes (P)

ouvert(e) open (2)

ouverture *f.* opening time (6-L)

ouvreuse *f.* usher

ouvrez votre livre! open your book! (1)

P

page *f.* page (1)

pain *m.* bread (3)

paix *f.* peace (11)

palmarès *m.* prize list (15-L)

Palme d'or *f.* Golden Palm (15-L)

palmier *m.* palm tree (15-L)

panneau routier *m.* (*pl.* -eaux) road sign (10-C)

pantalon *m.* pants (5)

papeterie *f.* stationery store (12)

papetier *m.* stationer (12-C)

papier *m.* paper (7-L)

  ~ à lettres stationery (8)

  ~s documents (10)

paquet *m.* parcel (8)

par by (1)

paradis *m.* heaven (7-L)

parapluie *m.* umbrella (5)

parc *m.* park (4)

parce que because (4)

pardon excuse me (1-C)

pardonnez-moi excuse me (1-C)

pare-brise *m.* windshield (10)

parents *m. pl.* parents (2)

paresseux (-euse) lazy (2)

parfait(e) perfect (5)

parfaitement perfectly (18)

parfois sometimes (4-L)

parfum *m.* perfume, smell (8-L)

parisien(ne) Parisian (2)

parking *m.* parking lot (4)

parlé(e) spoken (5-L)

parler to speak (1)

parmi among (11-L)

part *f.* proportion (12-L)

  c'est de la ~ de qui? may I say who's calling? (7-C)

participer to participate (7-L)

particularité *f.* characteristic (11-L)

partie *f.* game (4-L); part (9-L; 13)

  faire ~ to belong (17-L)

partir to leave (7)

  à ~ de starting from (16)

partout everywhere (10-L; 13-C; 18)

pas not (2)

  ne... ~ not (1-L; 2)

  ~ du tout not at all (4)

  ~ encore not yet (5)

passage *m.* way (4-L)

  de ~ passing (4-L)

passager (-ère) *m., f.* passenger (10-C)

passant(e) passerby

passé *m.* past

  ~ composé compound past tense

passer to take (*an exam*) (1-L); to spend (*time*) (2); to be displayed (*on screen*), to pass (9-C)

  ~ un coup de fil (*téléphone*) to make a phone call (7-C)

  ~ par to pass by (10)

  se ~ to happen (7)

passionnant(e) exciting (15-L)

passionné(e) *m., f.* fanatic (14-L)

pastis *m.* pastis (licorice-flavored drink) (14)

pâté *m.* pâté (9)

  ~ de foie liver pâté (12)

pâtes *f. pl.* noodles (5)

patience *f.* patience (3)

  avoir de la ~ to be patient (3)

patinage *m.* skating (14)

patiner to skate (14)

pâtisserie *f.* pastry shop (12)

pâtissier (-ère) *m., f.* pastry maker (12)

patron *m.* boss (14)

patte *f.* leg (animal) (9)

paume *f.* palm (18-L)

pause *f.* pause (11-L)

pauvre poor (2)

payer to pay (8-C; 10)

pays *m.* country (4)

paysage *m.* landscape, countryside (4-L; 17)

Pays-Bas *m. pl.* the Netherlands (4)

pêche *f.* peach (9); fishing (14)

peine *f.* trouble (7)

  ~ capitale capital punishment

  ce n'est pas la ~ it's not worth the trouble (7)

peintre *m.* painter (4-L; 15)

peinture *f.* painting (15)

  ~ à l'huile oil painting (15)

pelouse *f.* lawn (17)

pendant during, for (8)

penser to think (5)

  ~ à to think about, to have in mind (5)

  ~ de to think of, to have an opinion about (15)

perdre to lose (6)

  ~ patience to lose patience (6)

père *m.* father (2)

Père Noël Santa Claus

péril *m.* danger (13-L)

  en ~ endangered (15)

permettre to allow (2-C; 17)

permis de conduire *m.* driver's license (10)

personne *f.* person (7-L)

  ne... ~ nobody (12)

  ~ ne nobody (4-L)

personnel(le) private, personal (7-L)

peser to weigh (14-C)

pessimiste pessimistic (2)

pétanque *f.* lawn bowling (14)

petit(e) small, little (7-L; 9)

  ~ déjeuner *m.* breakfast (3-L; 9)

  ~ gâteau *m.* (*pl.* -eaux) cookie (3-L)

  ~ pois *m.* pea (9)

  ~(e) ami(e) *m., f.* boyfriend, girlfriend (2)

  ~e annonce *f.* classified ad (16)

Petites Antilles *f. pl.* Lesser Antilles (5)

petits-enfants *m. pl.* grand-children (2)

peu little, few (3)

~ **m'importe** it doesn't matter (17-C)

un ~ **de** a little, a few (3)

peuple *m.* people (17-L)

peur *f.* fear

avoir ~ **de** to be afraid of (11)

faire ~ to scare (11)

peut-être maybe (9-C; 12)

phare *m.* headlight (10)

pharmacie *f.* drugstore (4)

~ **de garde** emergency drugstore (13)

~ **de nuit** all-night drugstore (13)

philosophie (philo) *f.* philosophy (2)

photo *f.* photo (3)

phrase *f.* sentence (14)

physique *f.* physics (8)

piano *m.* piano (15)

pichet *m.* pitcher (3)

pièce *f.* coin (12-C); play (14); room (16)

~ **d'identité** *f.* ID (8-C)

pied *m.* foot (13)

à ~ on foot (6)

pierre *f.* stone (6-L; 15)

pile *f.* battery (7)

pilote d'essai *m.* test pilot (18-L)

pinard *m. (fam.)* wine (18-C)

pionnier (-ère) *m., f.* pioneer (14-L)

pique-nique *m.* picnic

piscine *f.* swimming pool (4)

piste *f.* (ski) slope (14-L)

pizza *f.* pizza (3)

place *f.* square (9); seat (10); place (14)

à ta (votre, sa) ~ in your (his, her) place (16)

de la ~ room (4)

~ **du marché** *f.* market square (9)

placer to place (16); to put (8-L)

plage *f.* beach (4)

plaire

ça vous plaît? do you like it?

s'il te plaît please (3)

s'il vous plaît please (3)

plaisir *m.* pleasure (15-C)

plaît *voir* **plaire**

planche *f.* board (14-L)

~ **à roulettes** skateboarding (14)

~ **à voile** sailboarding (14)

plancher *m.* floor *(Quebec)* (16)

planète *f.* planet (17)

plat *m.* dish (3)

~ **cuisiné** prepared dish (12)

~ **du jour** special of the day (9-C)

~ **principal** main course (3)

platane *m.* plane tree (4-L)

plein *m.*

faire le ~ to fill up (10-C)

plein(e) full (4)

~ **air** outdoor (9)

pleuvoir to rain (8)

plongée sous-marine *f.* scuba diving (14)

pluie *f.* rain (8)

~ **acide** acid rain (17)

plupart *f.*

la ~ **de...** most . . . (12-L)

pour la ~ for the most part (15-L)

pluriel *m.* plural

plus more (1); no longer (2-L)

de ~ furthermore (2-L); another (18-L)

de ~ **en** ~ more and more (8-L)

en ~ in addition (10)

le ~ **de** the most (5-L; 11)

ne... ~ no more (1-L; 12)

~ **de** more than (5-L)

~ **tard** later (7)

plusieurs several (3-C; 15)

plutôt rather (18-L)

pneu *m.* tire (10)

poche *f.* pocket (5)

poème *m.* poem (10)

poésie *f.* poetry (14)

poète *m.* poet (17)

poids *m.* weight (14-C)

poignée de main *f.* handshake (P)

point *m.* period

pointe *f.*

à la ~ on the cutting edge (11-L)

poire *f.* pear (9)

poisson *m.* fish (3)

poissonnerie *f.* fish market (12)

poissonnier (-ère) *m., f.* fishmonger (12)

poli(e) polite (2)

politesse *f.* politeness

politique political (5-L)

politique *f.* politics (11)

pollution *f.* pollution (11)

polo *m.* polo shirt (5)

Pologne *f.* Poland (4)

pomme *f.* apple (9)

~ **de terre** potato (9)

pont *m.* long weekend

populaire popular (18)

porc *m.* pork (9)

portable *m.* cellular phone (7)

porte *f.* door (1)

portée *f.* reach (7-L)

à la ~ **de toutes les bourses** within everyone's reach (14-L)

portefeuille *m.* wallet (7)

porter to wear (5); to bear, to show (15-L)

se ~ to converge (18-L)

se ~ **bien** to be in good health (13)

portière *f.* car door (10)

Portugal *m.* Portugal (4)

poser to put (9); to set down (11-C)

~ **une question** to ask a question (9)

positif (-ve) positive (3-L)

posséder to own (12-L; 13)

possession *f.* belonging

possibilité *f.* possibility (11)

possible possible (2)

poste *m.* extension *(phone)* (7-C); position (13-L)

poste restante *f.* general delivery (8-C)

pot *m.* drink (6)

pote *m. (fam.)* friend, buddy (18-C)

poule *f.* hen (18)

poulet *m.* chicken (3)

pour to, in order to (4); for (16)

~ **rien** for nothing (6)

pourboire *m.* tip (9-C)

pourcentage *m.* percentage (12-L)

pourquoi why (4)

poursuivre to follow, to chase (15-L)

pouvoir to be able to (7)

il se peut que it's likely that (11)

pratiquer to practice (14)

préalable *m.*   preamble (18-L)
précieux (-euse)   precious (6-L)
prédire   to predict (15-L)
préférable   preferable (11)
préféré(e)   favorite (3)
préférence *f.*   preference
   de ~   preferably
préférer   to prefer (13)
premier (-ère)   first (2)
Premier ministre *m.*   prime
   minister (6-L)
prendre   to take, to have (3); to
   have (meal) (9)
   ~ la parole   to speak (18-L)
   ~ le volant   to get behind the
      wheel (10-C)
   ~ un pot   to have a drink (6)
prenez   *voir* prendre (3)
préoccuper   to preoccupy (11)
préparer   to prepare (3)
préposé(e) *m., f.*   employee (8-C)
près de   near (4)
présent(e)   present (2)
présenter   to introduce (2-C; 9)
président *m.*   president (2)
presque   almost (3-L; 10)
presse spécialisée *f.*   specialized
   publications (16-C)
se presser   to huddle (15-L)
prestigieux (-euse)   prestigious
   (15-L)
prêt(e)   ready (5)
prêter   to lend (8)
prévoir   to predict, to foresee (8);
   to plan (10-L)
prier   to beg (15-C); to pray (18)
   je vous en prie   don't mention it
prière *f.*   prayer (18)
primé(e)   awarded a prize (15-L)
principal(e)   main (5-L)
principalement   mainly (3-L)
principe *m.*   principle (17-L)
printemps *m.*   spring (9)
priorité *f.*   priority
   ~ à droite   right of way on the
      right (10)
prise de sang *f.*   blood test (13)
privilège *m.*   privilege (12-L)
prix *m.*   price (3); prize (15-L)
   ~ fixe   menu (3)
probable   probable (11)
   il est ~   it is likely (11)
   il est peu ~   it is unlikely (11)
probablement   probably (18)

problème *m.*   problem (3-L; 6)
procès *m.*   trial
prochain(e)   next (4)
   à la ~e   see you next time (1-C)
proche   near (17-L)
proclamer   to proclaim (16-L)
production *f.*   production (10-L)
produire   to produce (14)
produit *m.*   product (11-L; 12)
   ~ surgelé   frozen food (12)
prof *m., f.*   *abrev. de* professeur
professeur *m.*   professor,
   teacher (1)
profession *f.*   profession (2)
professionnel(le)   professional
   (13-L)
profiter (de)   to take advantage
   of (8)
profond(e)   deep (9-L)
programme *m.*   program (7-L; 11)
programmeur (-euse) *m., f.*
   computer programmer (2)
progresser   to progress (14-L)
projection *f.*   viewing (15-L)
projet *m.*   plan, project (6-L)
prolifération *f.*   proliferation (8-L)
promenade *f.*
   faire une ~   to go for a walk (5)
promener   to walk (13)
   se ~   to go for a walk (13)
promettre   to promise (17)
proposé(e)   offered (11-L)
propre   clean; own (9)
propriétaire *m., f.*   owner
   (12-L; 16)
prouver   prove (6-L)
provençal(e) (*pl.* -aux, -ales)   from
   Provence (4-L; 9)
province *f.*   province (4-L)
provincial(e)   provincial (4-L)
provisions *f. pl.*   grocery shopping
   faire ses ~   to do one's
      shopping (9)
provenir   to come from (13-L)
prudemment   carefully (18)
prudent(e)   careful (2)
pseudonyme *m.*   pseudonym (7-L)
psychiatre *m.*   psychiatrist (7-L)
psychologie *f.*   psychology (8)
public *m.*   public (10-L)
public (-ique)   public (7-L)
publicité *f.*   ads (11)
publié(e)   published (15)
publier   to publish (9-L)

puis   then (16-L)
puisque   since (8)
puissance *f.*   power (17-L)
pull *m.*   sweater (5)
punir   to punish (7)
pyjama *m.*   pajamas (5)

Q

qualité *f.*   quality (11)
quand   when (1-L; 2)
quant à   as for (17-L)
quantité *f.*   quantity (3-L)
quarante   forty (2)
quart *m.*   quarter (6)
quartier *m.*   neighborhood (8-L)
quatorze   fourteen (1)
quatre   four (1)
quatre-quatre *f.*   four-wheel drive
   vehicle (10-L)
quatre-vingt dix   ninety (2-L)
quatre-vingts   eighty (2-L)
quatrième   fourth (2)
que   than (3-L; 18); *(pron. rel.)*
   that, which, whom (3-L; 16);
   what, which (7); how (18)
   ne... que   only (12)
   ~ ce soit   be it (14-L)
   ~ veut dire... ?   what does . . .
      mean? (5-C)
québécois(e)   from Quebec (P-L; 5)
quel(le)   what, which (5)
quelque   some (2)
   ~ chose   something (5)
   ~ part   somewhere (11-C)
quelquefois   sometimes (15-L; 18)
quelqu'un   someone (9-L; 10)
qu'est-ce que   what (7)
   ~ c'est?   what is it? (1)
   ~... veut dire?   what does . . .
      mean? (1)
   qu'est-ce qu'il y a?   what's the
      matter? (5-C)
qu'est-ce qui   what (7)
   ~ ne va pas?   what's wrong?
      (5-C)
   ~ se passe?   what's going on?
      (5-C)
   ~ s'est passé?   what happened?
      (5-C)
question *f.*   question (1)
queue *f.*
   faire la ~   to stand in line (5)
qui   who (3-L; 7); *(pron. rel.)*
   who, that (16)

à ~ to whom? (7)

~ est-ce que whom (7)

~ est-ce qui who (7)

quinze fifteen (1)

quitter to leave (6-L)

Ne quittez pas! Hold on! (7)

quoi what (7)

ce à ~ what (18-L)

il n'y a pas de ~ don't mention it, you're welcome (1)

~ de neuf? what's new? (P)

quotidien(ne) daily (14-L)

R

raccourcir to shorten (6-L)

raccrocher to hang up (the phone) (7-C)

race *f.* race (13-L)

raconter to tell (4-L)

radio *f.* radio (1)

raisin *m.* grape (9)

raison *f.* reason (17)

avoir ~ (de) to be right (3)

raisonnable moderate, reasonable (3-L)

ramener to bring back (14-L)

ranger to put away, to clean up (7)

rapide fast (2)

rapidement rapidly (3-L; 18)

rappeler to call back (7)

~ (à) to remind (15)

se ~ to remember (13)

rapport *m.* relationship

rapporter to bring back (6)

rare rare (11)

rarement rarely (18)

ras le bol

j'en ai ~! I've had it up to here! (17-C)

ravi(e) delighted (17-C)

rayer to cross out

rayon *m.* department (12)

raz-de-marée *m.* tidal wave (13-L)

réalisateur *m.* (film) director (15-L)

récemment recently (5)

récent(e) recent (18)

recette *f.* recipe

recevoir to receive (8-C; 12)

réclamer to demand (13-L)

recommandé(e) registered (8)

recommander (à) to recommend (to) (3)

récompense *f.* award (15-L)

reconnaissance *f.* recognition (14-L)

reconnaissant(e) grateful (15-C)

reconnaître to recognize (10)

record *m.* record (10-L)

recrutement *m.* recruitment (13-L)

recueillir to receive (15-L)

recyclage *m.* recycling (17)

redevance *f.* fees, tax (11-L)

réduction *f.* reduction (2-L)

réduire to reduce (3-L)

réel(le) real (17-L)

réfléchir to think about (7)

reflet *m.* reflection (17)

refuge *m.* refuge (2-L)

trouver ~ to find refuge (16-L)

réfugié(e) *m., f.* refugee (13-L)

refuser (de) to refuse (15)

regard *m.* glance (18-L)

regarder to look at (1)

régime *m.* diet (13); regime (13-L)

être au ~ to be on a diet (13)

faire un ~ to be on a diet (5)

région *f.* region, area (4-L)

régional(e) (*pl.* -aux, -ales) regional (3-L)

règle *f.* rule (10)

régler to pay (10); to solve

regret *m.* regret (8-L)

regretter (de) to regret, to be sorry (11)

régulièrement regularly (5-L; 13)

relation *f.* relationship (2-L)

~ d'affaires *f.* business acquaintance (2)

relevable folding (10-L)

religion *f.* religion (13-L)

remarquer to notice (3-L)

remercier to thank (11)

remettre to put on, to hand in, to hand back, to postpone (14-L; 17)

remise *f.* discount (12); awarding (15-L)

remonter to go back (18-L)

remplacer to replace (7-L)

remplir to fill (8-L)

remplisseur de pause *m.* conversational filler (18-C)

rencontrer to meet (8)

rendre to return (something), to give back (6); to make (11)

~ visite à to visit (*a person*) (6)

renommé(e) famous (4-L)

renseignement *m.* piece of information (4)

se renseigner to obtain information (11-L)

rentrée *f.* beginning of the school year (8)

rentrer to go in, to come back (3-L; 4)

répandre to spread (15-L)

réparation *f.* repair (12-L)

réparer to repair (10)

repas *m.* meal (3-L; 9)

repasser to retake (a test) (1-L)

répéter to repeat (13)

répétez! repeat! (1)

répondeur *m.* answering machine (7)

répondre to answer (6)

répondez à... ! answer . . . (1)

réponse *f.* answer (10)

reportage *m.* report (11)

se reposer to rest (13)

réputation *f.* reputation (9-L)

requis(e) required (13-L)

réseau Internet *m.* Internet (8)

réservation *f.* reservation

faire une ~ to book a seat

réserver to reserve (10)

résidence *f.* residence (4)

~ universitaire university dorm (4)

résident(e) *m., f.* resident (8-L)

résister to resist (8-L)

résoudre to resolve

respectabilité *f.* respectability (8-L)

responsable responsible (9-L)

ressembler à to resemble, to look like (1-L; 9)

ressource *f.* resource (11-L)

restaurant *m.* restaurant (3)

restau-U *m.* university cafeteria (4)

rester to stay (4); to remain (3-L; 7)

résultat *m.* result (2-L)

retard *m.*

en ~ late (2)

retenir to hold back; to remember (10)

retour *m.* return

~ en arrière rewind button (11-L)

retourner to return (10)

retrouver to find again, to meet (6); to encounter (4-L)
  se ~ to meet (4-L)
réunion *f.* meeting (5-L)
se réunir to meet (15-L)
réussir (à) to succeed, to pass (*a test*) (7)
se réveiller to wake up (13)
revenir to come back (10)
revenu *m.* income (12-L)
rêver (de) to dream (8-L; 15)
revoir to see again (8)
  au ~ good-bye (P)
révolution *f.* revolution (8-L)
revue *f.* magazine (14)
rez-de-chaussée *m.* ground floor (16)
riche rich (2)
rien nothing (5)
  ça (cela) ne fait ~ it doesn't matter (12-C)
  de ~ you're welcome (1)
  ne... ~ nothing (12)
  ~ d'important nothing much (5-C)
rigoureux (-euse) harsh (14-L)
risque *m.* risk (13-L)
rivalité *f.* rivalry (15-L)
rivière *f.* river (17)
riz *m.* rice (9)
robe *f.* dress (5)
  ~ de chambre robe (5)
rock *m.* rock (2)
rôle *m.* part (2-L)
roller *m.* in-line skating (14)
roman *m.* novel (10)
romarin *m.* rosemary (4-L)
rosbif *m.* roast beef (9)
rose pink (17)
rôti *m.* roast (9)
rouge red (3)
rougir to blush (7)
rouler à... km à l'heure to go . . . kilometers per hour (10)
route *f.* road
rubrique *f.* section of a newspaper (16-C)
rudimentaire rudimentary (13-L)
rue *f.* street (4)
rugby *m.* rugby (14)
rumeur *f.* rumor (15-L; 17)
russe Russian (8)
Russie *f.* Russia (4)

S

sa his, her, its (5)
sac *m.* bag (7)
  ~ à dos backpack (1)
sage-femme *f.* midwife (13-L)
Saint-Valentin *f.* Valentine's Day (9)
sais *voir* **savoir**
saison *f.* season (9)
salade *f.* salad (3)
salle *f.* room
  ~ à manger dining room (16)
  ~ de bains bathroom (16)
  ~ de classe classroom (1)
  ~ d'opération operating room (13-L)
salon *m.* living room (16)
salut hi (P); so long (1-C)
salutation *f.* greeting (15-C)
samedi *m.* Saturday (9)
sandwich *m.* sandwich (5)
sanitaire sanitary (13-L)
sans without (2)
  ~ lendemain without a future (18-L)
sans-abri *m.* homeless (11)
sans-logis *m.* homeless (11)
sans-papiers *m.* undocumented aliens (11)
santé *f.* health (3-L; 11)
  être en bonne ~ to be in good health (13)
  être en mauvaise ~ to be in bad health (13)
satisfaction *f.* satisfaction (13-L; 17-C)
satisfait(e) satisfied (17-C)
saucisson *m.* hard salami (9)
savoir to know (10)
  je ne sais pas I don't know (1)
savoir-faire *m.* know-how (9-L)
sciences éco(nomiques) *f. pl.* economics (8)
sciences po(litiques) *f. pl.* political science (8)
sculpteur *m.* sculptor (15)
sculpture *f.* sculpture (15)
SDF (*abrév. de* sans domicile fixe) homeless (11)
sec (sèche) dry (12)
sèche-linge *m.* dryer (16)
sécher to dry (13)
  ~ un cours to cut class (13)
second(e) second (2)

secours *m.* help (13-L)
secrétaire *m., f.* secretary (2)
sécurité *f.* security (11)
seize sixteen (1)
séjour *m.* stay (8)
séjourner to stay (16-L)
sel *m.* salt (3)
sélectionné(e) selected (11-L)
selon according to (11)
semaine *f.* week (4)
sembler to seem (3-L; 11)
  il semble (que) it appears (that) (11)
semestre *m.* semester (8)
semoule *f.* semolina (3)
Sénégal *m.* Senegal (4)
sénégalais(e) Senegalese (8)
sens interdit do not enter (10-C)
sens unique one way (10-C)
sentiment *m.* feeling (15-C)
sentir to smell (4-L); to feel (7)
  se ~ to feel (13)
séparer to separate
sept seven (1)
septembre *m.* September (1-L; 9)
séquence *f.* sequence (11-L)
série *f.* series (2-L; 11)
sérieux (-euse) serious (2)
serti(e) set (stone) (6-L)
serveuse *f.* waitress (9-C)
service *m.* service (7-L)
  ~ compris tip included (3)
serviette *f.* napkin (9-C)
servir to be used for (7)
ses his, her, its (5)
seul(e) alone (2); only (5-L)
seulement only (9-L; 18)
sexologue *m., f.* sexologist (7-L)
short *m.* shorts (5)
si yes, of course (2); if (4)
sida *m.* AIDS (11)
siècle *m.* century (5-L)
siège *m.* seat (10)
  ~ arrière back seat (10)
  ~ avant front seat (10)
sien (le), sienne (la), sien(ne)s (les) his, hers, its (14)
sieste *f.*
  faire la ~ to take a nap (4-L)
signaler to indicate (2-L)
signer to sign (10)
signification *f.* meaning
similaire similar (5-L)
simple simple (2)

sincère   sincere (2)
sincérité f.   sincerity (2)
singer   to ape (18-L)
singulier m.   singular
sinon   if not
situation f.   situation (13-L)
six   six (1)
skateboardeur (-euse) m., f.
   skateboarder (14-L)
ski m.   skiing (14)
   ~ nautique   waterskiing (14)
skieur (-euse) m., f.   skier (14-L)
snowboard m.   snowboarding (14)
social(e) (pl. -aux, -ales)   social
   (11)
société f.   society (11)
sociologie f.   sociology (8)
sœur f.   sister (2)
soif f.
   avoir ~   to be thirsty (3)
soigner   to treat (13-L)
soin m.   care (13-L)
soir m.   evening (3)
   ce ~   tonight (1)
   du ~   P.M. (6)
   à ce ~   see you this evening (1-C)
soirée f.   evening (2)
   ~ de gala   gala (15-L)
soixante   sixty (2)
solaire   solar (17)
soldat m.   soldier
solde m.   sale (12)
   en ~   on sale (12)
sole m.   sole (9)
soleil m.   sun
   faire du ~   to be sunny (8)
solution f.   solution (12-L)
son   his, her, its (5)
sondage m.   poll (11)
   ~ d'opinion   opinion poll (11)
sonner   to ring (6-L; 7)
sorte f.   sort, kind (15-L)
   quelle ~ de   what kind of (3)
sortir   to go out (7)
soudain   suddenly (16-L)
souffler   blow (4-L)
souffrir   to suffer (15)
souhait m.   wish
   à tes (vos) ~s!   bless you! (13-C)
souhaiter   to wish (11)
soupe f.   soup (3)
sous   under (4)
souterrain(e)   underground (8-L)
souvent   often (2)

spatial(e) (pl. -aux, -ales)   space
   (17)
spécial(e) (pl. -aux, -ales)   special
   (7-L)
spécialiste m., f.   specialist (3-L)
spécialité f.   specialty (3-L)
spécifique   specific (13-L)
spectacle m.   performance, show
   (11-L)
   ~s   entertainment section (of a
   newspaper) (16-C)
splendide   splendid (6-L)
sport m.   sport (2)
   faire du ~   to play sports (5)
sportif (-ve)   athletic (14)
stade m.   stadium (4)
standard   standard (5-L)
station f.   stop (6); station
   (16-L; 17)
   ~ de ski   ski resort (14-L)
   ~ service   gas station (10-C)
   ~ spatiale   space station (17)
   ~ thermale   health spa (13-C)
stationnement interdit   no parking
   (10-C)
stationner   to park (10)
stop m.
   faire du ~   to hitchhike (6)
stress m.   stress (14-L)
studieux (-euse)   studious (2)
stupide   stupid (2)
stylo m.   pen (1)
succès m.   success (10-L; 11)
sucre m.   sugar (3)
sud m.   south (4-C)
Suède f.   Sweden (4)
suffire
   ça suffit!   enough! (17-C)
suffisamment   sufficiently (18)
suffisant(e)   sufficient (18)
Suisse f.   Switzerland (4)
suivant(e)   following (15)
suivre   to follow; to take
   (courses) (8)
super   super (5)
super m.   premium (gas) (10-C)
supermarché m.   supermarket (12)
supporter   to tolerate (11)
suprême   supreme (15-L)
sur   on (1-L; 4)
sûr(e)   certain (11)
sûrement   surely (18)
surfeur (-euse) m., f.   surfer (14-L)
surgelé(e)   frozen (12)

surpris(e)   surprised (11)
surtaxe f.   fee (8-C)
surtout   above all (2-L; 15)
sus
   en ~   extra (9-C)
suspendre   to suspend (17-L)
symbole m.   symbol (9-L)
sympathique   nice (2)
symphonie f.   symphony (15)
Syndicat d'Initiative m.   tourist
   information bureau (4)
système m.   system (11-L)

T

ta   your (5)
table f.   table (16)
   à ~   food is ready (9-C)
   ~ de nuit   bedside table (16)
   ~ ronde   round table
   (discussion) (11)
tableau m. (pl. -eaux)   chalkboard
   (1); painting (4-L; 15)
tableur m.   spreadsheet (8)
tâche f.   task (15-L)
taille f.   size
talent m.   talent (3)
   avoir du ~   to have talent (3)
tant mieux!   good! (17-C)
tant pis!   too bad! (17-C)
tante f.   aunt (2)
taper   to type (7-L; 8)
tapis m.   carpet (16)
   ~ volant   flying carpet
tard   late (13)
   à plus ~   see you later (P)
tarte f.   pie (3)
tasse f.   cup (3-C)
taux m.   rate (12-C)
   ~ de change   exchange rate
   (12-C)
taxi m.   taxi (6)
Tchad m.   Chad (4)
technologie f.   technology (11-L)
tee-shirt m.   T-shirt (5)
teinturerie f.   dry cleaner's (12)
tel(le)   such, like (18)
télé f.   TV (2)
télécarte f.   pay phone card (7-C)
télécommande f.   remote control
   (11-L)
télégramme m.   telegram (8)
télématique   tele-computing
   (7-L)
téléphone m.   telephone (7)

téléphoner (à)   to telephone, to call (7)

~ avec préavis   to make a person-to-person call (8-C)

~ en P.C.V.   to call collect (8-C)

téléspectateur (-trice) *m.*, *f.*   TV viewer (11-L)

téléviseur *m.*   TV set (7)

télévision (télé) *f.*   television (1)

tellement   so; so much (18)

température *f.*   temperature (13-C)

temps *m.*   weather (6); time (6)

de ~ en ~   from time to time

il est ~   it's time (11)

quel ~ fait-il?   what's the weather like? (5)

tendre le bras   to extend one's arm (10-L)

tenir   to hold (10)

se ~   to be held (15-L)

~ à   to be fond of; to be anxious to (10)

~ de   to take after (10)

tennis *m.*   tennis (14); *pl.* tennis shoes (5)

terminal *m.*   terminal (7-L)

terminale *f.*   senior year of high school

terminé(e)   finished (8-L)

terminer   to end (1)

terrain *m.*

sur le ~   in the field (13-L)

terre *f.*   land (16-L)

terrible   terrible (13-L); super (17-C)

tes   your (5)

tête *f.*   head (9)

texte *m.*   text (14)

T.G.V. *m.*   high-speed train (6-L)

thalassothérapie *f.*   seawater therapy (13-C)

thé *m.*   tea (3)

théâtre *m.*   theater (4)

ticket *m.*   ticket (6)

tien (le), tienne (la), tien(ne)s (les)   yours (14)

à la ~ne   cheers, to your health (14)

tiens!   hey! (1-C; 2)

tiers *m.*   third (16-L)

timbre *m.*   stamp (8)

timide   shy (2)

titre *m.*   title

toi   you (P)

et ~   and you (P)

toile *f.*   canvas (10-L)

toilettes *f. pl.*   restroom (16)

toit *m.*   roof (9-L)

TOM (territoires d'outre-mer) *m. pl.*   overseas regions of France (P-L)

tomate *f.*   tomato (4-L; 9)

tomber   to fall (10)

~ en panne   to break down (car) (10)

ton   your (2)

tonnerre *m.*   thunder (8)

tort *m.*

avoir ~ (de)   to be wrong (3)

tôt   early (13)

toubib *m. (fam.)*   doctor (18-C)

toucher   to touch (18-L)

toujours   always (2); still (2-L)

tour *m.*

faire un ~   to go for a walk (5)

tourisme *m.*   tourism (6-L)

touriste *m.*, *f.*   tourist (4-L; 5)

touristique   touristic (4-L)

tourner   to turn (4-C)

tout(e), tout(e)s   all, every; each (4)

~ les ans   every year (5)

~ les jours   every day (4)

~ le monde   everybody (6-L; 12)

~ le temps   all the time (8)

tout   all; completely (4-L; 8)

~ à coup   suddenly (18-L)

~ de suite   immediately (3)

~ droit   straight ahead (4-C)

tradition *f.*   tradition (3-L)

traditionnel(le)   traditional (18)

traditionnellement   traditionally (18)

traduire   to translate (14)

trafic *m.*   (drug) traffic (11)

tragédie *f.*   tragedy (15)

train *m.*   train (6)

trait d'union *m.*   hyphen

traitement *m.*   treatment (13-L)

~ de texte *m.*   word processor (8)

tranche *f.*   slice (3-C)

transformation *f.*   transformation (8-L)

transformer   to transform (14-L)

transistor *m.*   transistor radio (7)

transmettre   to hand down (9-L)

transport *m.*   transportation (6)

transporter   to carry (10-L)

travail *m.*   work (5-L; 11)

travailler   to work (1)

travailleur (-euse) *m.*, *f.*   worker (16-L)

travers

à ~   through (18-L)

traversée *f.*   crossing (6-L)

traverser   to cross (4-C)

treize   thirteen (1)

tréma *m.*   diaeresis

tremblement de terre *m.*   earthquake (13-L)

trente   thirty (2)

trentième   thirtieth (2)

très   very (P)

~ bien   very well (P)

trimestre *m.*   quarter (8)

triste   sad (11)

trois   three (1)

troisième   third (2)

trombone *m.*   trombone (15)

trompette *f.*   trumpet (15)

tronc *m.*   trunk (17)

trop   too much, too many (3)

trou *m.*   hole (14-L)

trouver   to find (3)

comment trouvez-vous... ?   how do you like . . . ? (3)

où se trouve... ?   where is . . . located? (4-C)

se ~   to be located (4-C; 9-L); to find oneself (13)

truc *m. (fam.)*   thingamajig (11-C); thing (18-L)

truite *f.*   trout (9)

tu   you (1)

Tunisie *f.*   Tunisia (4)

tunisien(ne)   Tunisian (3)

tunnel *m.*   tunnel (6-L)

T.V.A. *f.*   value-added tax (10)

type *m. (fam.)*   guy (18-C)

typique   typical (4-L)

U

un(e)   a, an, one (1), (3)

à la ~e   on the front page (16-C)

union libre *f.*   living together (2-L)

unir   to unite (6-L)

unité *f.*   unit (10-L)

universel(le) universal (14-L)
universitaire university *(adj.)* (1-L)
université *f.* university (1)
urgence *f.* emergency (13-L)
usage *m.* use, usage (5-L; 15)
usine *f.* factory (4)
utile useful
utiliser to use (3-L; 8)
utilitaire utilitarian (7-L)

V

va *voir* aller
vacances *f. pl.* vacation (9)
  grandes ~ summer vacation
    (10)
vache *f.* cow (18)
vague *f.* wave (16-L)
vais *voir* aller
vaisselle *f.*
  faire la ~ to do the dishes (5)
valise *f.* suitcase (5)
  faire les ~s to pack the suitcases
    (5)
valoir to be worth
  il vaut mieux it's better (11)
vantard *m.* braggart
varier to vary (13-L)
variété *f.* variety (5-L; 9)
  ~s variety show (11)
Varsovie Warsaw (4)
vas-y! go ahead! (4)
veau *m.* (*pl.* -eaux) veal, calf (9)
vedette *f.* star (9-L)
végétarien(ne) vegetarian (9)
vélo *m.* bicycle (6)
vendeur (-euse) *m., f.* salesperson
    (12)
  ~ de journaux news dealer
    (16-C)
vendre to sell (6)
vendredi *m.* Friday (9)
venir to come (10)
  ~ de to have just (8-L; 10)
vent *m.* wind (4-L)
  faire du ~ to be windy (8)
ventre *m.* stomach (13)
vérifier to check (10-C)
véritable true (9-L)

vérité *f.* truth (14)
verre *m.* glass (3-C; 14)
vers toward, about, around
    (6-L; 13)
vert(e) green (5)
veste *f.* jacket (5)
veston *m.* coat (5)
vêtements *m. pl.* clothes (5)
vétérinaire *m.* veterinarian (7-L)
veut *voir* vouloir
viande *f.* meat (3)
victime *f.* victim (13-L)
vide empty (14)
vidéo *f.* video (11-L)
vie *f.* life (1-L; 11)
  ~ familiale *f.* family life (2-L)
vietnamien(ne) Vietnamese (3-L)
vieux (vieil, vieille[s], vieux) old
    (7-L; 9)
vif (-ive) lively (17)
vigne *f.* vineyard (4-L)
vignette *f.* annual tax on
    automobile (10-L)
vilain(e) ugly (10-L)
village *m.* village (4-L)
ville *f.* city, town (1-L; 4)
  en ~ in town, downtown (1-L; 4)
vin *m.* wine (3)
vingt twenty (1)
  ~ et unième twenty-first (2)
vingtième twentieth (2)
violet(te) violet (4-L)
violon *m.* violin (15)
violoncelle *m.* cello (15)
virgule *f.* comma
visiter to visit *(a place)* (4)
visiteur *m.* visitor (8-L)
vite quickly (18)
  au plus ~ as fast as possible
    (16-L)
vitesse *f.* speed (10-C)
vitre *f.* window (10-L)
vivace vivacious (15)
voici here is, here are (1)
Voie lactée *f.* Milky Way (17)
voilà there is, there are (1)
  ~... que it has been . . . that
    (16)

voile *f.* sailing (14)
voile *m.* veil
voir to see (7)
voisin(e) *m., f.* neighbor (11)
voiture *f.* car (2)
  ~ d'occasion used car (10)
  ~ neuve new car (10)
voix *f.* voice (7)
volant *m.* steering wheel (10)
voler to steal (18-L)
volley-ball *m.* volleyball (14)
volonté *f.* will (15)
vos your (1)
votre your (1)
vôtre (le, la), vôtres (les) yours (14)
  à la ~! cheers, to your health
    (14)
voudrais *voir* vouloir
vouloir to want to (7)
  ~ bien to be willing (7)
  je voudrais I would like (2-C; 3)
  qu'est-ce que... veut dire? what
    does . . . mean? (1)
vous you (P)
  et ~ and you (P)
voyage *m.* trip (4)
  ~ organisé tour (5)
  faire un ~ to take a trip (5)
voyager to travel (4)
voyons! let's see! come on! (8)
vrai(e) true (2)
  c'est pas ~! no?! (17-C)
vraiment really, truly (9)

W

wagon *m.* train car (18-L)
Walkman *m.* Walkman (7)
week-end *m.* weekend (4)

Y

y there, of it, to it (15)
yeux *m. pl.* eyes (13)

Z

Zaïre *m.* Zaire (4)
zéro zero (1)
zut alors! darn! (17-C)
zydeco Louisiana music (16-L)

Anglais-français

The English-French Vocabulary contains only active vocabulary.

A

a un, une (3)
about
  it's ~ il s'agit de (15)
above all surtout (15)
absent absent(e) (2)
absolutely absolument (11)
to accept accepter (de) (15)
accident accident m. (10)
according to selon (11)
acquaintance connaissance f. (2)
across from en face de (4)
actor acteur m. (2)
actress actrice f. (2)
ad publicité f. (11)
  classified ~ petite annonce f. (16)
addition
  in ~ en plus (10)
address adresse f. (8)
to adore adorer (1)
advantage
  to take ~ profiter (de) (8)
advice conseil m. (11)
to advise conseiller (12)
affectionate affectueux (-euse) (2)
affront atteinte f. (15)
afraid
  to be ~ avoir peur (11)
Africa Afrique f. (4)
after après (1)
afternoon après-midi m. (4)
age âge m. (3)
ago il y a (16)
ahead d'avance (14)
AIDS sida m. (11)
air letter aérogramme m. (8)
airplane avion m. (6)
airport aéroport m. (10)
alcohol alcool m. (3)
Algeria Algérie f. (4)
Algerian algérien(ne) m., f. (18)
all tous, toutes (4)
  ~ right d'accord (10)
to allow permettre (17)
almost presque (10)
alone seul(e) (2)
along au bord de (4)

alphabet alphabet m. (1)
already déjà (5)
also aussi (2)
always toujours (2)
A.M. du matin (6)
amazed étonné(e) (11)
ambitious ambitieux (-euse) (2)
American américain(e) (2)
an un, une (3)
and et (P)
  ~ you et toi, et vous (P)
animal animal m. (pl. -aux) (18)
ankle cheville f. (13)
annoyance inconvénient m. (11)
answer réponse f. (10)
to answer répondre (à) (6)
  answer! répondez! (1)
answering machine répondeur m. (7)
anthropology anthropologie f. (8)
apartment appartement m. (4)
to appear
  it appears (that) il semble (que) (11)
appetizer *hors-d'œuvre m. (3)
apple pomme f. (9)
appliance appareil électroménager m. (16)
to appreciate apprécier (2)
April avril m. (9)
Arabic arabe m. (8)
architect architecte m. (2)
architecture architecture f. (8)
area coin m. (9)
arm bras m. (13)
armchair fauteuil m. (16)
armoire armoire f. (16)
arrival arrivée f. (8)
to arrive arriver (1)
art art m. (8)
  ~ history histoire de l'art f. (8)
article article m. (15)
artist artiste m., f. (2)
as . . . as aussi… que (18)
Asia Asie f. (4)
to ask demander (à) (15)
  ~ for demander (1)

  ~ a question poser une question (9)
asleep
  to fall ~ s'endormir (13)
asparagus asperges f. pl. (9)
at à (1); au (2); chez (4)
athletic sportif (-ive) (14)
attention
  to pay ~ faire attention (5)
August août m. (9)
aunt tante f. (2)
Australia Australie f. (4)
Austria Autriche f. (4)
author auteur m. (2)
automatic automatique (10)
to avoid éviter (de) (11)

B

back dos m. (13)
backpack sac à dos m. (1)
bad mauvais(e), méchant(e) (2)
  it is too ~ (that) il est dommage (que) (11)
  to be ~ (weather) faire mauvais (5)
badly mal (18)
baker boulanger (-ère) m., f. (12)
bakery boulangerie f. (12)
ballet ballet m.; danse classique f. (15)
banana banane f. (9)
bank banque f. (4)
  ~ account compte en banque m. (11)
bark écorce f. (17)
baseball base-ball m. (14)
basketball basket-ball m. (14)
bathing suit maillot de bain m. (5)
bathroom salle de bains f.; toilettes f. pl. (16)
bathtub baignoire f. (16)
battery pile f. (7)
to be être (2)
  it is c'est (1)
  they are ce sont (1)
beach plage f. (4)

beautiful   beau (bel), belle, beaux, belles (9)
beauty   beauté *f.* (15)
because   parce que (4)
to become   devenir (10)
bed   lit *m.* (16)
   to go to ~   se coucher (13)
bedroom   chambre *f.* (4)
beef   bœuf *m.* (9)
beer   bière *f.* (3)
before   avant (6)
   just ~   juste avant (8)
to begin   commencer (à) (1); se mettre à (17)
beginning   début *m.* (6)
to behave   se conduire (14)
behind   derrière (4)
beige   beige (6)
Belgium   Belgique *f.* (4)
to belong to   être à (5); appartenir à (10)
belt   ceinture *f.* (5)
best   le mieux; le meilleur, la meilleure, les meilleur(e)s (18)
better   meilleur(e) (18)
   it's ~ (that)   il vaut mieux (que) (11)
between   entre (4)
bicycle   bicyclette *f.*; vélo *m.* (6)
big   gros(se) (6); grand(e) (9)
billion   milliard *m.* (4)
biology   biologie *f.* (8)
biotechnology   biotechnologie *f.* (17)
bird   oiseau *m.* (*pl.* -eaux) (17)
black   noir(e) (5)
to blacken   noircir (17)
blackened   noirci(e) (17)
blood test   prise de sang *f.* (13)
blouse   chemisier *m.* (5)
blue   bleu(e) (5)
to blush   rougir (7)
board   tableau *m.* (*pl.* -aux) (1)
boat   bateau *m.* (*pl.* -eaux) (6)
body   corps *m.* (13)
book   livre *m.* (1)
   ~ of tickets   carnet *m.* (6)
bookstore   librairie *f.* (4)
boot   botte *f.* (5)
boring   ennuyeux (-euse) (2)
born
   to be ~   naître (6)
to borrow   emprunter (8)
to bother   embêter (11)

bottle   bouteille *f.* (12)
bourgeois   bourgeois(e) (15)
bowling
   lawn ~   pétanque *f.* (14)
boy   garçon *m.* (2)
boyfriend   copain *m.*; petit ami *m.* (2)
brake   frein *m.* (10)
to brake   freiner (10)
branch   branche *f.* (18)
Brazil   Brésil *m.* (4)
bread   pain *m.* (3)
to break down   tomber en panne (10)
breakfast   petit déjeuner *m.* (9)
brilliant   brillant(e) (18)
brilliantly   brillamment (18)
to bring   apporter (3); amener (13)
   ~ back   rapporter (6)
bronze   bronze *m.* (15)
brother   frère *m.* (2)
brown   brun(e) (5)
to brush   (se) brosser (13)
Brussels   Bruxelles (4)
building
   apartment ~   immeuble *m.* (16)
bus   autobus *m.* (1); bus *m.* (6)
   ~ stop   arrêt d'autobus (4)
business acquaintance   relation d'affaires *f.* (2)
but   mais (1)
butcher   boucher (-ère) *m., f.* (12)
   ~ shop   boucherie *f.* (12)
butter   beurre *m.* (3)
to buy   acheter (5)
by   par (1); au bord de (4)

C

cable   câble *m.* (11)
café   café *m.* (1); bistrot *m.* (3)
café-restaurant   brasserie *f.* (12)
cake   gâteau *m.* (*pl.* -eaux) (3)
calculator   calculatrice *f.* (7)
   pocket ~   calculette *f.* (7)
calendar   calendrier *m.* (9)
to call   appeler (13)
   ~ back   rappeler (7)
   to be ~ed   s'appeler (13)
can   pouvoir (7)
Canada   Canada *m.* (4)
Canadian   canadien(ne) (2)
candy   bonbon *m.* (9)
canned food   conserves *f. pl.* (12)
capital   capitale *f.* (8)

car   voiture *f.* (2); auto *f.* (6)
   new ~   voiture neuve *f.* (10)
   used ~   voiture d'occasion *f.* (10)
card   carte *f.* (14)
   orange ~   carte orange *f.* (6)
care
   to take ~ of   s'occuper de (13)
career   métier *m.* (15)
   ~ in the arts   métier artistique (15)
careful   prudent(e) (2)
carefully   prudemment (18)
caretaker   concierge *m., f.* (16)
carpet   tapis *m.* (16)
carrots
   grated ~   carottes râpées *f. pl.* (9)
cartoon   dessin animé *m.* (11)
cashier's   caisse *f.* (12)
casino   casino *m.* (4)
cassette   cassette *f.* (7)
cat   chat *m.* (18)
CD   CD *m.* (7)
   ~ player   lecteur de disques compacts *m.* (7)
cello   violoncelle *m.* (15)
cellular phone   portable *m.* (7)
certain   certain(e) (2); sûr(e) (11)
certainly   certainement (18)
Chad   Tchad *m.* (4)
chair   chaise *f.* (1)
chalk   craie *f.* (1)
champion   champion(ne) *m., f.* (14)
championship   championnat *m.* (14)
to change   changer (de) (6)
charming   charmant(e) (2)
cheers!   à la tienne!, à la vôtre! (14)
cheese   fromage *m.* (3)
chemistry   chimie *f.* (8)
cherry   cerise *f.* (9)
chicken   poulet *m.* (3)
child   enfant *m., f.* (1)
China   Chine *f.* (4)
Chinese   chinois(e) (8)
chocolate   chocolat *m.* (3)
to choose   choisir (de) (7)
chop   côtelette *f.* (9)
church   église *f.* (4)
cinema   cinéma *m.* (4)
circle   milieu *m.* (15)

city   ville *f.* (4)
class   cours *m.* (1)
  in ~   en cours (1)
classical   classique (2)
classmate   camarade de cours *m.*, *f.* (2)
classroom   classe *f.*; salle de classe *f.* (1)
clean   propre (9)
to clean   faire le ménage (5)
  ~ up   ranger (7)
clerk   employé(e) *m.*, *f.* (8)
to close   fermer (1)
closed   fermé(e) (2)
clothes   vêtements *m. pl.* (5)
cloud   nuage *m.* (8)
club   boîte *f.*, club *m.* (2)
coat   manteau *m.* (*pl.* -eaux); veste *f.*; veston *m.* (5)
coffee   café *m.* (3)
cola   coca *m.* (3)
cold   froid(e) (2)
  to be ~   avoir froid (3); faire froid (5)
color   couleur *f.* (5)
column   colonne *f.* (17)
to come   venir (10)
  ~ back   revenir (10)
  ~ down   descendre (de) (6)
  come on!   voyons! (8)
comedy   comédie *f.* (15)
compact disk   disque compact *m.*, CD *m.* (7)
competent   compétent(e) (2)
complete   complet (-ète) (18)
completely   complètement (18)
complicated   compliqué(e) (2)
compulsory   obligatoire (10)
computer   ordinateur *m.* (8)
  ~ progammer   programmeur (-euse) *m.*, *f.* (2)
  ~ science   informatique *f.* (8)
concert   concert *m.* (6)
concierge   concierge *m.*, *f.* (16)
conductor   chef d'orchestre *m.* (15)
connection   correspondance *f.* (6)
to consult   consulter (11)
to consume   consommer (3)
contact   contact *m.* (17)
to contain   contenir (10)
contemporary   contemporain(e) (11)
continent   continent *m.* (4)
to continue   continuer (à) (1)

to contribute   contribuer (à) (15)
to cook   faire la cuisine (5)
cooking   cuisine *f.* (3)
cool
  to be ~   faire frais (8)
corner   coin *m.* (9)
  at the ~ of   au coin de (4)
correct   correct(e) (15)
Corsica   Corse *f.* (4)
to cost   coûter (5)
Côte d'Ivoire   Côte d'Ivoire *f.* (4)
countable   nombrable (17)
country   pays *m.* (4); campagne *f.* (8)
countryside   paysage *m.* (17)
courageous   courageux (-euse) (2)
course   cours *m.* (1)
couscous   couscous *m.* (3)
cousin   cousin(e) *m.*, *f.* (2)
cow   vache *f.* (18)
cream   crème *f.* (3)
to create   créer (17)
credit card   carte de crédit *f.* (10)
Creole   créole *m.* (5)
crepe   crêpe *f.* (5)
crime   criminalité *f.* (11)
to critique   critiquer (15)
cross
  green ~   croix verte *f.* (13)
cucumber   concombre *m.* (9)
cuisine   cuisine *f.* (3)
to cut class   sécher un cours (13)
cutlet   escalope *f.* (9)

D
dairy store   crémerie *f.* (12)
damage   mal *m.* (15)
to dance   danser (1)
dancer   danseur (-euse) *m.*, *f.* (15)
dangerous   dangereux (-euse) (2)
date   date *f.* (*calendar*) (9)
daughter   fille *f.* (2)
day   jour *m.* (9); journée *f.* (13)
dear   cher (-ère) (8)
December   décembre *m.* (9)
to decide   décider (6)
delicious   délicieux (-euse) (3)
delighted   enchanté(e) (2)
delinquency   délinquance *f.* (11)
Denmark   Danemark *m.* (4)
dentist   dentiste *m.*, *f.* (13)
department   département *m.* (5); rayon *m.* (12)
  ~ store   grand magasin *m.* (11)

to describe   décrire (14)
to desire   désirer (2)
desk   bureau *m.* (*pl.* -eaux) (1)
destruction   destruction *f.* (15)
devoted   consacré(e) (15)
dialogue   dialogue *m.* (1)
to die   mourir (10)
diet
  to be on a ~   faire un régime (5); être au régime (13)
different   différent(e) (9)
difficult   difficile (2)
to diminish   diminuer (17)
dining room   salle à manger *f.* (16)
dinner   dîner *m.* (9)
  to have ~   dîner (3)
diplomat   diplomate *m.* (2)
disaster   désastre *m.* (11)
to disconnect   couper (7)
discount   remise *f.* (12)
to discuss   discuter (11)
dish   plat *m.* (3)
  prepared ~   plat cuisiné (12)
  to do the ~es   faire la vaisselle (5)
dishwasher   lave-vaisselle *m.* (16)
disk drive   lecteur de disquettes *m.* (8)
diskette   disquette *f.* (8)
to disobey   désobéir (à) (7)
divided   divisé (par) (1)
to do   faire (5)
doctor   médecin *m.* (2)
documents   papiers *m. pl.* (10)
dog   chien *m.* (18)
door   porte *f.* (1); (of a car) portière *f.* (10)
dorm   résidence universitaire *f.* (4)
to doubt   douter (11)
downtown   en ville (4) centre-ville *m.* (12)
drama   drame *m.* (15)
to dream   rêver (de) (15)
dress   robe *f.* (5)
to dress
  to get dressed   s'habiller (13)
drink   pot *m.* (6)
  before-dinner ~   apéritif *m.* (3)
  to have a ~   prendre un pot (6)
to drink   boire (12)
  I drink   je bois (3)
  you drink   tu bois; vous buvez (3)
to drive   conduire (10; 14)

driver chauffeur *m.* (10)
~'s license permis de conduire *m.* (10)
drug drogue *f.* (11)
~ testing contrôle anti-doping *m.* (14)
drugstore pharmacie *f.* (4)
all-night ~ pharmacie de nuit (13)
emergency ~ pharmacie de garde (13)
dry sec (sèche) (12)
~ cleaner's teinturerie *f.* (12)
to dry sécher (13)
dryer sèche-linge *m.* (16)
duck canard *m.* (18)
during pendant (8)

E
ear oreille *f.* (13)
early en avance (6); de bonne heure (12); tôt (13)
to earn gagner (8)
easily facilement (18)
easy facile (2)
to eat manger (1)
ecological écologique (11)
ecologist écologiste *m., f.* (17)
ecology écologie *f.* (17)
economics sciences éco(nomiques) *f. pl.* (8)
economist économiste *m., f.* (2)
education enseignement *m.* (15)
egg œuf *m.* (9)
eight huit (1)
eighteen dix-huit (1)
elbow coude *m.* (13)
eleven onze (1)
eleventh onzième (2)
elsewhere ailleurs (18)
e-mail courrier électronique *m.* (8)
to embody incarner (17)
employee employé(e) *m., f.* (6)
empty vide (14)
end bout *m.* (6)
to end terminer (1)
endangered en péril (15)
energy énergie *f.* (17)
engineer ingénieur *m.* (2)
England Angleterre *f.* (4)
English anglais(e) (1)
English (language) anglais *m.* (1)
to enjoy
~ doing aimer faire (2)

enough assez (de) (3)
to enter entrer (2)
entertainment distraction *f.* (2)
entrance entrée *f.* (16)
envelope enveloppe *f.* (8)
environment environnement *m.* (17)
equality égalité *f.* (11)
equipment matériel *m.* (8)
errands courses *f. pl.* (5)
to run ~ faire des courses (5)
Europe Europe *f.* (4)
European européen(ne) (10)
evening soirée *f.* (2); soir *m.* (3)
every tout(e) (8)
~ day tous les jours (4)
~ year tous les ans (5)
everybody tout le monde (12)
everywhere partout (18)
to evoke évoquer (17)
exactly exactement (8)
exam examen *m.* (1)
to examine examiner (13)
excerpt extrait *m.* (15)
exercise exercice *m.* (1)
to exercise faire de l'exercice (13)
expenses frais *m. pl.* (10)
expensive cher (-ère) (4)
to explain expliquer (1)
expression expression *f.* (7)
eye œil *m.* (*pl.* yeux) (13)

F
factory usine *f.* (4)
to fail échouer (à) (15)
fair juste (11)
fall automne *m.* (9)
to fall tomber (10)
false faux (fausse) (11)
family famille *f.* (2)
fantastic fantastique (2)
far from loin de (4)
fascinating fascinant(e) (2)
fast rapide (2); vite (18)
father père *m.* (2)
father-in-law beau-père *m.* (*pl.* beaux-pères) (2)
favorite favori(te) (2); préféré(e) (3)
February février *m.* (9)
to feel sentir (7); se sentir (13)
~ better aller mieux (13)
~ like avoir envie (11)
feminine féminin(e) (2)

fever fièvre *f.* (13)
field champ *m.* (17)
fifteen quinze (1)
fifth cinquième (2)
fifty cinquante (2)
filet filet *m.* (9)
film film *m.* (2)
finally enfin (16)
to find trouver (3)
~ again retrouver (6)
~ oneself se trouver (13)
fine
I'm ~ ça va bien, je vais bien (P)
finger doigt *m.* (13)
to finish finir (de) (7)
Finland Finlande *f.* (4)
first premier (-ère) (2); d'abord (7)
fish poisson *m.* (3)
~ market poissonnerie *f.* (12)
~monger poissonnier (-ère) *m., f.* (12)
fishing pêche *f.* (14)
five cinq (1)
floor étage *m.* (16); *(in Quebec)* plancher *m.* (16)
ground ~ rez-de-chaussée *m.* (16)
florist fleuriste *m., f.* (12)
flour farine *f.* (3)
flower fleur *f.* (17)
flute flûte *f.* (15)
foggy
to be ~ faire du brouillard (8)
to follow suivre (8)
following suivant(e) (15)
fond
to be ~ of aimer bien (2); tenir à (10)
food nourriture *f.* (3)
foot *(of animal)* patte *f.* (9); pied *m.* (13)
on ~ à pied (6)
football football américain *m.* (14)
for pendant (8); pour (16)
to forbid défendre (15)
foreign étranger (-ère) (8)
foreigner étranger (-ère) *m., f.* (10)
to foresee prévoir (8)
forest forêt *f.* (17)
to forget oublier (de) (5)
former ancien(ne) (2)

fortunately heureusement (6)
forty quarante (2)
four quatre (1)
fourteen quatorze (1)
fourth quatrième (2)
franc franc *m.* (12)
France France *f.* (4)
frankness franchise *f.* (11)
free libre (7)
freed délivré(e) (17)
French (language) français *m.* (1)
   in ~ en français (1)
French français(e) (1)
   ~ fries frites *f. pl.* (3)
frequent fréquent(e) (18)
frequently fréquemment (18)
Friday vendredi *m.* (9)
friend ami(e) *m., f.* (1); copain *m.,*
   copine *f.* (2)
from de (1); dès (16)
front
   in ~ of devant (2)
frost gel *m.* (17)
frozen surgelé(e) (12)
fruit fruit *m.* (3)
   ~ juice jus de fruit *m.* (3)
full plein(e) (4)
fun
   to have ~ s'amuser (à) (13)
to function marcher (7)
furious furieux (-euse) (11)
furnished meublé(e) (16)
furniture meubles *m. pl.* (16)
future avenir *m.* (11); futur *m.*
   (17)

G

game show jeu télévisé *m.* (11)
garden jardin *m.* (17)
general général(e) (18)
   in ~ en général (1)
generally généralement (13)
generous généreux (-euse) (2)
Geneva Genève (4)
gentlemen Messieurs (4)
geography géographie *f.* (8)
geology géologie *f.* (8)
German allemand(e) (2)
Germany Allemagne *f.* (4)
to get
   ~ closer s'approcher (18)
   ~ off descendre (de) (6)
   ~ on monter (dans) (6)
   ~ up se lever (13)

girl fille *f.* (2)
girlfriend copine *f.*; petite amie *f.*
   (2)
to give donner (1)
   ~ back rendre (6)
glass verre *m.* (14)
glove gant *m.* (5)
to go aller (4)
   go ahead! allez-y!; vas-y! (4)
   ~ back rentrer (4)
   ~ down descendre (de) (6)
   ~ in entrer (2)
   ~ . . . kilometers per hour
     rouler à… km à l'heure
     (10)
   ~ out sortir (7)
   ~ out with sortir avec (7)
   ~ to fréquenter (2)
   ~ up monter (dans) (6)
   let's go! allons-y! (4)
   shall we go? on y va? (4)
God Dieu *m.* (18)
golf golf *m.* (14)
good bon(ne) (5)
   ~ evening bonsoir (P)
   ~ morning bonjour (P)
good-bye au revoir (P)
gram gramme *m.* (12)
grandchildren petits-enfants *m. pl.*
   (2)
grandfather grand-père *m.*
   (*pl.* **grands-pères**) (2)
grandmother grand-mère *f.*
   (*pl.* **grands-mères**) (2)
grandparents grands-parents *m.*
   pl. (2)
grape raisin *m.* (9)
gray gris(e) (5)
Great Britain Grande-Bretagne *f.*
   (4)
Greece Grèce *f.* (4)
Greek (language) grec *m.* (8)
green vert(e) (5)
   ~ beans *haricots verts *m. pl.*
     (9)
grocer épicier (-ère) *m., f.* (12)
grocery shop épicerie *f.* (12)
guitar guitare *f.* (15)
gymnastics gymnastique *f.* (14)

H

habit habitude *f.* (10)
hair cheveux *m. pl.* (13)
half demi(e) (6)

ham jambon *m.* (3)
hamburger *hamburger *m.* (3)
hand main *f.* (13)
to hand back/in remettre (17)
handshake poignée de main *f.* (P)
hang gliding deltaplane *m.* (14)
to hang up
   don't hang up! ne coupe(z) pas!
     (7)
to happen se passer, arriver (7)
happiness bonheur *m.* (11)
happy content(e), heureux (-euse)
   (2)
hat chapeau *m.* (*pl.* -eaux) (5)
to hate détester (2)
   ~ doing détester faire (2)
Havana La Havane (4)
to have avoir (3); prendre (9)
   it has been . . . that il y a…
     que, voilà… que (16)
   ~ a sore . . . avoir mal à… (13)
he il (1)
head tête *f.* (9)
headlight phare *m.* (10)
health santé *f.* (11)
   to be in bad ~ être en mauvaise
     santé (13)
   to be in good ~ être en bonne
     santé (13); se porter bien
     (13)
to hear entendre (6)
heat chaleur *f.* (8)
hello bonjour, bonsoir (P); *(on
   telephone)* allô, j'écoute (7)
hen poule *f.* (18)
her elle; son, sa, ses (5); la (l') (8);
   lui (9)
here ici (1)
   ~ is voici, voilà (1)
hers le sien, la sienne, les sien(ne)s
   (14)
to hesitate hésiter (à) (15)
hey! tiens! (2)
hi salut (P)
high school lycée *m.* (4)
him lui (2); le (l') (8); lui (9)
his son, sa, ses (5); le sien, la
   sienne, les sien(ne)s (14)
history histoire *f.* (8)
to hitchhike faire du stop (6)
hockey *hockey *m.* (14)
to hold tenir (10)
   ~ back retenir (10)
   hold on! ne quittez pas! (7)

Holland *Hollande f. (4)
home
  at the ~ of chez (4)
homeless sans-abris *m.*, sans-logis *m.*, SDF *m.* (11)
homework devoirs *m. pl.* (1)
  to do ~ faire (ses) devoirs (5)
to hope espérer (9)
horn klaxon *m.* (10)
horrible affreux (-euse) (2)
horse cheval *m.* (*pl.* -aux) (18)
horseback
  ~ riding équitation *f.* (14)
  on ~ à cheval (6)
hostess hôtesse *f.* (4)
hot chaud(e) (2)
  to be ~ avoir chaud (3); faire chaud (5)
hotel hôtel *m.* (1)
hour heure *f.* (6)
house maison *f.* (4)
how comment (6); que (18)
  ~ are you? ça va?, comment ça va? (P)
  ~ do you do? comment allez-vous? (P)
  ~ many? combien (de) (6)
  ~ much? combien? (1); combien de? (6)
  ~ much is . . . ? combien font... ? (1)
hundred cent (4)
hungry
  to be ~ avoir faim (3)
hunting chasse *f.* (13)
to hurry se dépêcher (de) (13)
to hurt one's . . . se faire mal à... (13)
husband mari *m.* (2)
hypochondriac hypocondriaque (13)
hypocrisy hypocrisie *f.* (2)
hypocritical hypocrite (2)

I
I je (1); moi (2)
ice cream glace *f.* (3)
idea idée *f.* (5)
if si (4)
illness maladie *f.* (13)
imam imam *m.* (18)
immigrant immigré(e) *m., f.* (18)
impolite impoli(e) (2)
importance importance *f.* (11)

important important(e) (11)
impossible impossible (2)
impressive impressionnant(e) (8)
in à (1); dans (3); en (4); *(time)* dans, en (16)
to include inclure (17)
included compris(e) (16)
incompetent incompétent(e) (2)
to increase augmenter (17)
Independence Day Fête nationale *f.* (9)
independent indépendant(e) (2)
independently indépendamment (18)
to indicate indiquer (9)
indispensable indispensable (10)
inflation inflation *f.* (11)
information renseignement *m.* (4)
instrument intrument *m.* (15)
  musical ~ instrument de musique (15)
insufficient insuffisant(e) (15)
insufficiently insuffisamment (18)
insurance
  full collision ~ assurance tous risques *f.* (10)
intelligent intelligent(e) (2)
intelligently intelligemment (18)
to interest intéresser (16)
interested
  to be ~ s'intéresser (à) (15)
interesting intéressant(e) (2)
Internet réseau Internet *m.* (8)
interview interview *f.* (11)
intolerance intolérance *f.* (2)
to introduce présenter (9)
to invite inviter (à) (1)
Ireland Irlande *f.* (4)
isn't it so? n'est-ce pas? (1)
it il (1); le (l'), la (l') (8)
  of ~ en (15)
Italian italien(ne) (2)
Italy Italie *f.* (4)
its son, sa, ses (5)

J
jackal chacal *m.* (18)
jacket veste *f.* (5)
jam confiture *f.* (3)
January janvier *m.* (9)
Japan Japon *m.* (4)
Japanese japonais *m.* (8)
jazz jazz *m.* (2)

jeans jean *m.* (5)
jersey maillot *m.* (14)
jewelry store bijouterie *f.* (12)
job emploi *m.* (11)
jogging jogging *m.* (14)
journalism journalisme *m.* (8)
journalist journaliste *m., f.* (2)
July juillet *m.* (9)
June juin *m.* (9)
just juste (1)
  to have ~ venir de (10)
justice justice *f.* (11)

K
key clé (1)
keyboard clavier *m.* (8)
kilometer kilomètre *m.* (10)
kiss baiser *m.*, bise *f.* (8)
to kiss faire une bise à (P); embrasser (2)
kitchen cuisine *f.* (16)
knee genou *m.* (*pl.* -oux) (13)
to know savoir; connaître (10)
  I don't ~ je ne sais pas (1)

L
Labor Day Fête du Travail *f.* (9)
laboratory laboratoire *m.* (4)
ladies Mesdemoiselles *f. pl.* (12); Mesdames *f. pl.*
lake lac *m.* (17)
lamb agneau *m.* (*pl.* -eaux) (3)
  leg of ~ gigot *m.* (9)
lamp lampe *f.* (16)
landscape paysage *m.* (17)
language langue *f.* (8)
last dernier (-ère) (5)
late en retard (2); tard (13)
later plus tard (7)
latest dernier (-ère) (2)
Latin latin *m.* (8)
laundry
  to do the ~ faire la lessive (5)
law droit *m.* (8); loi *f.* (10)
lawn pelouse *f.* (17)
lawyer avocat(e) *m., f.* (2)
lazy paresseux (-euse) (2)
leaf feuille *f.* (17)
to learn apprendre (à) (9)
to leave laisser (6); partir (7)
left
  on the ~ à gauche (16)
leg jambe *f.* (13)
to lend prêter (8)

less moins (1)
Lesser Antilles Petites Antilles *f. pl.* (5)
lesson leçon *f.* (1)
let's see! voyons! (8)
letter lettre *f.* (8)
library bibliothèque *f.* (4)
lie mensonge *m.* (14)
to lie mentir (7)
life vie *f.* (11)
light lumière *f.* (17)
lightning éclair *m.* (8)
like comme (3); tout comme (9); tel(le) (18)
to like aimer (1); aimer bien (2)
  how do you ~ . . . ? comment trouvez-vous… ? (3)
  I would like je voudrais (3)
likely probable (11)
  it's ~ (that) il est probable (que); il se peut (que) (11)
line ligne *f.* (6)
  to stand in ~ faire la queue (5)
Lisbon Lisbonne (4)
list liste *f.* (4)
to listen écouter (1)
literary littéraire (15)
literature littérature *f.* (8)
little peu (3)
  just a ~ juste un peu (1)
livable habitable (17)
to live habiter (1)
lively vivace (15); vif (-ive) (17)
living room salon *m.* (16)
London Londres (4)
to look
  ~ at regarder (1)
  ~ for chercher (4)
  ~ good avoir bonne mine (13)
  ~ like avoir l'air (5); ressembler (à) (9)
  ~ out on donner sur (16)
  ~ sick avoir mauvaise mine (13)
to lose perdre (6)
  ~ patience perdre patience (6)
lost and found bureau des objets trouvés *m.* (6)
Louisiana Louisiane *f.* (16)
love *(to conclude a letter)* affectueux baisers *m. pl.* (8); amour *m.* (11)
to love aimer (1)
lucid lucide (17)

luck chance *f.* (6)
  what ~! quelle chance! (6)
luggage bagages *m. pl.* (5)
  hand ~ bagages à main *m. pl.* (5)
lunch déjeuner *m.* (9)
  to have ~ déjeuner (3)

M

ma'am madame *f.* (P)
magazine magazine *m.* (14)
Maghreb Maghreb *m.* (18)
  person from the ~ Maghrébin(e) *m., f.*
magnificent magnifique (2)
maid's room chambre de bonne *f.* (16)
mail courrier *m.* (8)
to mail expédier (8)
mailman facteur *m.* (8)
main course plat principal *m.* (3)
to make faire (5); rendre (11)
man homme *m.* (1)
management gestion *f.* (8)
manager
  middle-level ~ cadre *m.* (11)
many beaucoup (1)
  as ~ autant (18)
map carte *f.* (1)
March mars *m.* (9)
market
  ~ square place du marché *f.* (9)
  open-air ~ marché en plein air *m.* (9)
masculine masculin(e) (2)
match match *m.* (2)
materialistic matérialiste (11)
math mathématiques (maths) *f. pl.* (8)
matter matière *f.* (17)
  as a ~ of fact justement (6)
may pouvoir (7)
May mai *m.* (9)
maybe peut-être (12)
me moi (2)
meal repas *m.* (9)
mean méchant(e) (2)
to mean vouloir dire
  it ~s cela veut dire (1)
  what does . . . ~? qu'est-ce que… veut dire? (1)
meanness
  out of ~ méchamment (18)
meat viande *f.* (3)

medicine médecine *(science) f.* (8)
to meet rencontrer (8)
to mention
  don't ~ it il n'y a pas de quoi (1)
menu carte *f.*; menu *m.* (3)
merchant marchand(e) *m., f.* (9)
merguez sausage merguez *f.* (3)
message message *m.* (7)
meter mètre *m.* (14)
Mexican mexicain(e) (2)
Mexico Mexique *m.* (4)
Mexico City Mexico (4)
midnight minuit *m.* (6)
milk lait *m.* (3)
Milky Way Voie lactée *f.* (17)
million million *m.* (4)
mind
  to have in ~ penser (à) (15)
mine le mien, la mienne, les mien(ne)s (14)
mineral water eau minérale *f.* (3)
minute minute *f.* (4)
Miss Mademoiselle *f.* (P)
mistake faute *f.* (15)
modem modem *m.* (8)
modern art art moderne *m.* (2)
Monday lundi *m.* (9)
money argent *m.* (3)
  ~ order mandat *m.* (8)
monitor moniteur *m.* (8)
month mois *m.* (5)
monument monument *m.* (8)
moon lune *f.* (17)
more plus (1); davantage (13)
morning matin *m.* (4); matinée *f.* (9)
Moroccan marocain(e) *m., f.* (18)
Morocco Maroc *m.* (4)
Moscow Moscou (4)
most le plus (11)
mother mère *f.* (2)
mother-in-law belle-mère *f.* (*pl.* belles-mères) (2)
motorcycle moto *f.* (6)
mountain montagne *f.* (11)
  ~ climbing alpinisme *m.* (14)
mouth bouche *f.* (13)
Mozambique Mozambique *m.* (4)
Mr. Monsieur *m.* (P)
Mrs. Madame *f.* (P)
Ms. Madame *f.*, Mademoiselle *f.* (P)

much   beaucoup (1)
  as ~   autant (18)
muezzin   muezzin *m.* (18)
multiplied   multiplié (par) (1)
museum   musée *m.* (4)
music   musique *f.* (2)
musical   comédie musicale *f.* (15)
musician   musicien(ne) *m., f.* (2)
must   devoir, falloir (12)
mustard   moutarde *f.* (3)
mutton   mouton *m.* (3)
my   mon, ma, mes (5)

N

name   nom *m.* (9)
  what's your ~?   comment vous
    appelez-vous?, comment
    t'appelles-tu? (1)
  my ~ is . . .   je m'appelle… (P)
nationality   nationalité *f.* (2)
nature   nature *f.* (17)
near   près de (4)
necessarily   nécessairement (18)
necessary   nécessaire (7)
  it is ~ (that)   il faut (que) (4); il
    est nécessaire (que) (11)
neck   cou *m.* (12)
to need   avoir besoin (de) (10)
negative   négatif (-ive) (14)
neighbor   voisin(e) *m., f.* (11)
nephew   neveu *m.* (2)
Netherlands   Pays-Bas *m. pl.* (4)
neuvième   ninth (2)
never   ne… jamais (8)
new   nouveau (nouvel), nouvelle,
    nouveaux, nouvelles (9); neuf
    (neuve) (10)
  what's ~?   quoi de neuf? (P)
New Orleans   La Nouvelle-Orléans
    (4)
news   nouvelles *f. pl.* (8); actualités
    f. pl. (11); informations *f. pl.*
    (14)
next   prochain(e) (4)
next to   à côté de (4)
nice   bien; sympathique (2); beau
    (bel), belle, beaux, belles (9)
  to be ~ (weather)   faire beau
    (5); faire bon (8)
niece   nièce *f.* (2)
night   nuit *f.* (13)
  all ~ long   de la nuit (13)
nightclub   boîte de nuit *f.* (2)
nightgown   chemise de nuit *f.* (5)

nine   neuf (1)
nineteen   dix-neuf (1)
no   non (1)
  ~ more   ne… plus (12)
nobody   ne… personne (12)
noise   bruit *m.* (11)
  to make ~   faire du bruit (11)
noodles   pâtes *f. pl.* (5)
noon   midi *m.* (6)
North Africa   Afrique du Nord *f.*
    (18)
North America   Amérique du
    Nord *f.* (4)
Norway   Norvège *f.* (4)
nose   nez *m.* (13)
not   ne… pas (2)
  ~ at all   de rien (1); pas du tout
    (4)
  ~ bad   pas mal (P)
  ~ yet   pas encore (5); ne… pas
    encore (8)
note   note *f.* (8)
notebook   cahier *m.* (1)
nothing   rien (5); ne… rien (12)
  for ~   pour rien (6)
novel   roman *m.* (10)
November   novembre *m.* (9)
now   maintenant (4)
nuclear   nucléaire (11)
number   nombre *m.* (11)
  wrong ~   erreur *f.* (7)

O

to obey   obéir (à) (7)
to obtain   obtenir (10)
obvious   évident(e) (11)
obviously   évidemment (18)
October   octobre *m.* (9)
of   de (1)
  ~ course   bien sûr (5)
  ~ it   y (15)
office   bureau *m.* (*pl.* -eaux) (1)
often   souvent (2)
oh no!   ah non! (4)
oil   huile *f.* (3)
old   ancien(ne) (2); vieux (vieil),
    vieille, vieux, vieilles (9)
  how ~ are you?   quel âge
    avez-vous (as-tu)? (3)
  to be . . . years ~   avoir… an(s)
    (3)
olive   olive *f.* (9)
omelet   omelette *f.* (5)
on   sur (4)

one   on *m.* (1)
one   un(e) (1)
  the ~   celui, celle (14)
  the ~s   ceux, celles (14)
only   ne… que (12); seulement
    (18)
open   ouvert(e) (2)
to open   ouvrir (1)
  open your book!   ouvrez votre
    livre! (1)
opera   opéra *m.* (15)
opinion   opinion *f.* (11)
  ~ poll   sondage d'opinion *m.*
    (11)
  to have an ~   penser (de) (15)
optimistic   optimiste (2)
or   ou (1)
orange   orange *f.* (9)
orchestra   orchestre *m.* (15)
order   commande *f.* (12)
  in ~ to   pour (4)
to order   commander (3)
other   autre (4)
our   notre, nos (5)
ours   le (la) nôtre, les nôtres (14)
outside   à l'extérieur (5)
oven   four *m.* (16)
  microwave ~   four à
    micro-ondes *m.* (16)
over there   là-bas (4)
overcast   couvert(e) (8)
own   propre (9)
to own   posséder (13)
owner   patron(ne) *m., f.* (14);
    propriétaire *m., f.* (16)

P

to pack   faire les bagages (5)
  ~ the suitcases   faire les valises
    (5)
package   colis *m.* (8)
page   page *f.* (1)
painter   peintre *m.* (15)
painting   peinture *f.*, tableau *m.*
    (*pl.* -eaux) (15)
  oil ~   peinture à l'huile *f.* (15)
pajamas   pyjama *m.* (5)
pants   pantalon *m.* (5)
parcel   paquet *m.* (8)
parents   parents *m. pl.* (2)
Parisian   parisien(ne) (2)
park   parc *m.* (4)
to park   garer (2); stationner (10)
parking lot   parking *m.* (4)

part partie *f.* (13)
to pass *(an exam)* réussir (à) (7)
　~ by passer par (10)
pastis pastis *m.* (14)
pastry maker pâtissier (-ère) *m., f.* (12)
pastry shop pâtisserie *f.* (12)
pâté pâté *m.* (9)
　liver ~ pâté de foie *m.* (12)
patient
　to be ~ avoir de la patience (3)
to pay payer, régler (10)
peace paix *f.* (11)
peach pêche *f.* (9)
pear poire *f.* (9)
peas petits pois *m. pl.* (9)
pen stylo *m.* (1)
pencil crayon *m.* (1)
pensive méditatif (-ive) (17)
people gens *m. pl.* (10)
perfect parfait(e) (5)
perfectly parfaitement (18)
pessimistic pessimiste (2)
philosophy philo(sophie) *f.* (2)
phone
　cellular ~ portable *m.* (7)
　~ booth cabine téléphonique *f.* (7)
　~ number numéro de téléphone *m.* (10)
photo photo *f.* (3)
physical education éducation physique *f.* (8)
physics physique *f.* (8)
piano piano *m.* (15)
pig cochon *m.* (18)
pink rose (17)
pitcher pichet *m.* (3)
pizza pizza *f.* (3)
place endroit *m.* (4); place *f.* (14)
　in your (his, her) ~ à votre (ta, sa) place (16)
to place placer (16)
planet planète *f.* (17)
play pièce *f.* (14)
to play jouer (1); *(sports)* jouer (à) (14); *(musical instrument)* jouer (de) (15)
　~ sports faire du sport (5)
player joueur (-euse) *m., f.* (14)
playwright auteur dramatique *m.* (15)
pleasant agréable (2)

please s'il te plaît; s'il vous plaît (3)
to plug in brancher (7)
P.M. de l'après-midi, du soir (6)
pocket poche *f.* (5)
poem poème *m.* (10)
poet poète *m.* (17)
poetry poésie *f.* (14)
Poland Pologne *f.* (4)
policeman agent de police *m.* (2); gendarme *m.* (10)
polite poli(e) (2)
political science sciences po(litiques) *f. pl.* (8)
politics politique *f.* (11)
pollution pollution *f.* (11)
polo shirt polo *m.* (5)
poor pauvre (2)
popular populaire (18)
pork porc *m.* (9)
　~ butcher charcutier (-ère) *m., f.* (12)
　~ butcher's shop charcuterie *f.* (12)
Portugal Portugal *m.* (4)
possessions affaires *f. pl.* (7)
possibility possibilité *f.* (11)
possible possible (2)
post office bureau de poste *m.* (4)
postcard carte postale *f.* (8)
poster affiche *f.* (1)
to postpone remettre (17)
potato pomme de terre *f.* (9)
to practice pratiquer (14)
to pray prier (18)
prayer prière *f.* (18)
to prefer aimer mieux (2); préférer (13)
preferable préférable (11)
to preoccupy préoccuper (11)
to prepare préparer (3)
present cadeau *m.* (*pl.* -eaux) (1)
present présent(e) (2)
president président *m.* (2)
pretty joli(e) (9)
price
　fixed ~ *(menu)* prix fixe *m.* (3)
printer imprimante *f.* (8)
probably probablement (18)
problem problème *m.* (6)
to produce produire (14)
product produit *m.* (12)
profession profession *f.* (2)
professor professeur *m.*; prof *m., f.* (1)

program émission *f.*; programme *m.* (11)
to promise promettre (17)
Provence Provence *f.*
　from ~ provençal(e) (*pl.* -aux, -ales) (9)
psychology psycho(logie) *f.* (8)
published publié(e) (15)
pullover pull *m.* (5)
to punish punir (7)
pupil élève *m., f.* (3)
purchase achat *m.* (5)
purse sac *m.* (7)
to put mettre (17)
　~ away ranger (7)
　~ on mettre, remettre (17)

Q

quality qualité *f.* (11)
quarter quart *m.* (6); trimestre *m.* (8)
Quebec Québec *m.*
　from ~ québécois(e) (5)
question question *f.* (1)

R

rabbit lapin *m.* (9)
race course *f.* (14)
　bicycle ~ course de bicyclettes *f.* (14)
　car ~ course de voitures *f.* (14)
radio radio *f.* (1)
rain pluie *f.* (8)
　acid ~ pluie acide *f.* (17)
to rain pleuvoir (8)
raincoat imperméable *m.* (5); imper *m.* (6)
to raise lever (13)
rapidly rapidement (18)
rare rare (11)
rarely rarement (18)
rather assez (18)
to read lire (14)
　read! lisez! (1)
reader lecteur (-trice) *m., f.* (15)
ready prêt(e) (5)
reason raison *f.* (17)
to receive recevoir (12)
recent récent(e) (18)
recently récemment (5)
to recognize reconnaître (10)
to recommend recommander (3)
record disque *m.* (1)

recycling   recyclage *m.* (17)
red   rouge (3)
reflection   reflet *m.* (17)
refrigerator   frigidaire *m.* (16)
to refuse   refuser (de) (15)
registered   recommandé(e) (8)
to regret   regretter (de) (11)
regularly   régulièrement (13)
to relax   se détendre (13)
to remain   rester (4)
to remember   retenir (10); se rappeler (13)
to remind   rappeler (à) (15)
to remove   enlever (13)
rent   loyer *m.* (16)
to rent   louer (10)
rental   location *f.* (10)
   ~ agency   compagnie de location *f.* (10)
to repair   réparer (10)
to repeat   répéter (1; 13)
report   reportage *m.* (11)
to reserve   réserver (10)
to rest   se reposer (13)
restaurant   bistrot *m.*; restaurant *m.* (3)
to return   rentrer (4); retourner (10)
   ~ (something)   rendre (6)
review   revue *f.* (14)
rice   riz *m.* (9)
rich   riche (2)
right
   ~ away   tout de suite (3)
   ~ of way on the right   priorité à droite (10)
   to be ~   avoir raison (de) (3)
to ring   sonner (7)
river   fleuve *m.*, rivière *f.* (17)
Riviera   Côte d'Azur *f.* (4)
roast   rôti *m.* (9)
   ~ beef   rosbif *m.* (9)
robe   robe de chambre *f.* (5)
rock   rock *m.* (2)
room   place *f.* (4); pièce *f.* (16)
roommate   camarade de chambre *m., f.* (2)
rooster   coq *m.* (18)
rugby   rugby *m.* (14)
rule   règle *f.* (10)
rumor   rumeur *f.* (17)
to run   courir (18)
Russia   Russie *f.* (4)
Russian   russe *m.* (8)

S

sad   triste (11)
sailboarding   planche à voile *f.* (14)
sailing   voile *f.* (14)
salad   salade *f.* (3)
salami   saucisson *m.* (9)
sale
   on ~   en solde (12)
   ~s   soldes *f. pl.* (12)
salesperson   vendeur (-euse) *m., f.* (12)
salt   sel *m.* (3)
same   même (5)
sandwich   sandwich *m.* (5)
Saturday   samedi *m.* (9)
sauerkraut and assorted meat   choucroute garnie *f.* (12)
to save   faire des économies (8)
to say   dire (14)
   how do you ~ . . . ?   comment dit-on… ? (1)
to scare   faire peur (à) (11)
scarf   écharpe *f.* (5)
to scatter   se disperser (17)
school   fac(ulté) *f.* (1); école (3)
   secondary ~   école secondaire *f.* (3)
school year   année scolaire (8)
   beginning of the ~   rentrée *f.* (8)
scuba diving   plongée sous-marine *f.* (14)
sculptor   sculpteur *m.* (15)
sculpture   sculpture *f.* (15)
sea   mer *f.* (4)
seafood   fruits de mer *m. pl.* (9)
season   saison *f.* (9)
seat   banquette *f.* (6)
   back ~   siège arrière *m.* (10)
   front ~   siège avant *m.* (10)
   ~ belt   ceinture de sécurité *f.* (10)
   ~s   places *f. pl.* (10)
second   deuxième, second(e) (2)
secretary   secrétaire *m., f.* (2)
security   sécurité *f.* (11)
to see   voir (7; 8)
   ~ again   revoir (8)
   see you later   à plus tard, à tout à l'heure (P)
   see you soon   à bientôt (P)
to seem   sembler (11)
to sell   vendre (6)
semester   semestre *m.* (8)

semolina   semoule *f.* (3)
Senegal   Sénégal *m.* (4)
Senegalese   sénégalais(e) (8)
sensational   formidable (2)
sentence   phrase *f.* (14)
September   septembre *m.* (9)
series   feuilleton *m.*; série *f.* (11)
serious   sérieux (-euse) (2); grave (13)
to set   mettre (17)
seven   sept (1)
seventeen   dix-sept (1)
seventeenth   dix-septième (2)
several   plusieurs (15)
she   elle (1)
sheep   mouton *m.* (18)
shelf   étagère *f.* (16)
to shine   ondoyer (17)
shirt   chemise *f.* (5)
shoe   chaussure *f.* (5)
shop   boutique *f.* (12)
shopkeeper   commerçant(e) *m., f.* (12)
shopping
   to do one's ~   faire ses provisions (9)
   ~ center   centre commercial *m.* (4)
shorts   short *m.* (5)
shoulder   épaule *f.* (13)
to show   montrer (1)
shower   douche *f.* (16)
shrimp   crevette *f.* (9)
shuttle   navette *f.* (17)
shy   timide (2)
sick   malade (2)
to sign   signer (10)
simple   simple (2)
since   depuis (6); puisque (8)
sincére   sincère (2)
sincerity   sincérité *f.* (2)
to sing   chanter (1)
sink   lavabo *m.* (16)
   kitchen ~   évier *m.* (16)
sir   monsieur *m.* (P)
sister   sœur *f.* (2)
six   six (1)
sixteen   seize (1)
sixty   soixante (2)
to skate   patiner (14)
skateboarding   planche à roulettes *f.* (14)
skating   patinage *m.* (14)
   in-line ~   roller *m.* (14)

skiing   ski *m.* (14)
  water ~   ski nautique (14)
skirt   jupe *f.* (5)
sky   ciel *m.* (8)
to sleep   dormir (7)
  not ~ a wink   ne pas fermer
     l'œil (13)
  ~ late   faire la grasse matinée
     (5)
slow   lent(e) (18)
slowly   lentement (18)
small   petit(e) (9)
to smoke   fumer (1)
snack
  to have an afternoon ~   goûter
     (3)
snow   neige *f.* (8)
to snow   neiger (8)
snowboarding   snowboard *m.* (14)
so   tellement (18)
  ~ much   tellement (18)
soccer   football *m.* (2)
social   social(e) (*pl.* -aux, -ales)
  (11)
society   société *f.* (11)
sociology   socio(logie) *f.* (8)
sock   chaussette *f.* (5)
sofa   canapé *m.*, divan *m.* (16)
software   logiciel *m.* (8)
solar   solaire (17)
sole   sole *f.* (9)
some   certain(e), quelque (2);
  en (15)
somebody   quelqu'un (10)
someone   quelqu'un (10)
something   quelque chose (5)
  ~ else   autre chose (12)
sometimes   quelquefois (18)
son   fils *m.* (2)
song   chanson *f.* (10)
soon   bientôt (8)
  as ~ as   aussitôt que, dès que
    (17)
sorry   désolé(e) (7)
  to be ~   regretter (de) (11)
so-so   comme ci, comme ça (P)
soup   soupe *f.* (3)
South America   Amérique du Sud
  f. (4)
space   espace *m.* (17)
space   spatial(e) (*pl.* -aux, -ales)
  (17)
Spain   Espagne *f.* (4)
Spanish   espagnol(e) (2)

to speak   parler (1)
to spend   dépenser (8)
  ~ (time)   passer (2)
spinach   épinards *m. pl.* (9)
sporting goods   articles de sport
  m. pl. (12)
sports   sports *m. pl* (2)
  to play ~   faire du sport (5)
spreadsheet   tableur *m.* (8)
spring   printemps *m.* (9)
to spring   jaillir (17)
square   place *f.* (9)
stadium   stade *m.* (4)
stage   étape *f.* (14)
stamp   timbre *m.* (8)
to start   démarrer (10)
starting from   à partir de (16)
state   état *m.* (15)
station   chaîne *f.* (11); station *f.*
  (17)
  cable ~   chaîne câblée *f.* (11)
  space ~   station spatiale *f.* (17)
stationer's   papeterie *f.* (12)
stationery   papier à lettres *m.* (8)
stay   séjour *m.* (8)
to stay   rester (4)
steak   bifteck *m.* (9)
stepfather   beau-père *m.*
  (*pl.* beaux-pères) (2)
stepmother   belle-mère *f.*
  (*pl.* belles-mères) (2)
stereo system   chaîne stéréo *f.* (7)
still   encore (6)
stomach   ventre *m.* (13)
stone   pierre *f.* (15)
  smooth ~   galet *m.* (4)
stop   station *f.* (6)
to stop   arrêter (11); cesser (de)
  (15)
store   magasin *m.* (4)
stormy
  to be ~   faire de l'orage (8)
stove   cuisinière *f.* (16)
strawberry   fraise *f.* (9)
street   rue *f.* (4)
student   étudiant(e) *m., f.* (1)
studious   studieux (-euse) (2)
to study   étudier (1)
stupid   stupide (2)
subject   matière *f.* (8)
subway   métro *m.* (6)
to succeed   réussir, réussir (à) (7)
success   succès *m.* (11)
such   tel(le) (18)

to suffer   souffrir (15)
sufficient   suffisant(e) (18)
sufficiently   suffisamment (18)
sugar   sucre *m.* (3)
suit   costume *m.* (5)
suitcase   valise *f.* (5)
summer   été *m.* (5)
Sunday   dimanche *m.* (9)
sunglasses   lunettes de soleil *f. pl.*
  (5)
sunny
  to be ~   faire du soleil (8)
super   super (5)
supermarket   supermarché *m.* (12)
  giant ~   hypermarché *m.* (12)
surely   sûrement (18)
surprised   surpris(e) (11)
Sweden   Suède *f.* (4)
to swim   nager (14)
swimming   natation *f.* (14)
  ~ pool   piscine *f.* (4)
Switzerland   Suisse *f.* (4)
symphony   symphonie *f.* (15)

T

table   table *f.* (16)
  bedside ~   table de nuit *f.* (16)
  round ~   table ronde *f.* (11)
to take   emporter (5); *(courses)*
  suivre (8); prendre (9);
  emmener (13); *(time to do*
  something) mettre (17)
  ~ after   tenir de (10)
tale   conte *m.* (14)
talent
  to have ~   avoir du talent (3)
to talk   parler (1)
tall   grand(e) (9)
tape recorder   magnétophone *m.*
  (7)
tart   tarte *f.* (3)
taxi   taxi *m.* (6)
tea   thé *m.* (3)
to teach   apprendre (à) (9);
  enseigner (15)
teacher   professeur *m.*; prof *m., f.*
  (1)
teaching   enseignement *m.* (15)
team   équipe *f.* (13)
telegram   télégramme *m.* (8)
telephone   téléphone *m.* (7)
to telephone   téléphoner (à) (7)
television   télé(vision) *f.* (1)
to tell   dire (à) (14)

ten dix (1)
tennis tennis *m.* (5)
terrific formidable (2)
test contrôle (14)
   blood ~ prise de sang *f.* (13)
text texte *m.* (14)
than que (18)
to thank remercier (11)
thank you merci (P)
thanks a million merci mille fois (4)
that ce (cet), cette (7); ça (9); que *(pron. rel.)* (16)
   ~'s it! ça y est! (5)
the le, la, l', les (1)
theater théâtre *m.* (4)
their leur(s) (5)
theirs le leur, la leur, les leurs (14)
them eux, elles (5); les (8); leur (9)
then alors (1)
there là (2); y (15)
   ~ are il y a (3)
   ~ is voilà (1); il y a (3)
therefore donc (15)
these ces (7)
they ils, elles; on (1)
thigh cuisse *f.* (13)
thing chose *f.* (11)
   dumb ~ bêtise *f.* (14)
to think penser (5); réfléchir (à) (7)
   ~ about penser à (15)
   ~ of penser de (15)
third troisième (2)
thirsty
   to be ~ avoir soif (3)
thirteen treize (1)
thirtieth trentième (2)
thirty trente (2)
this cela (1); ce (cet), cette (7)
those ces (7)
thousand mille (4)
three trois (1)
throat gorge *f.* (13)
thunder tonnerre *m.* (8)
Thursday jeudi *m.* (9)
ticket billet *m.*, ticket *m.* (6)
tie cravate *f.* (5)
time heure *f.*, temps *m.* (6)
   all the ~ tout le temps (8)
   for a long ~ longtemps (6)
   on ~ à l'heure (6)
   to have ~ avoir le temps (8)

to have a good ~ s'amuser (à) (13)
tip included service compris (3)
tire pneu *m.* (10)
tired fatigué(e) (2)
to à (1); pour (4)
   ~ it y (15)
tobacco shop bureau de tabac *m.* (7)
tobacconist buraliste *m.*, *f.* (12)
today aujourd'hui (4)
together ensemble (1)
to tolerate supporter (11)
tomato tomate *f.* (9)
tomorrow demain (4)
   ~ evening demain soir (4)
   ~ morning demain matin (4)
   ~ night demain soir (4)
tonight ce soir (1)
too
   ~ many trop (3)
   ~ much trop (3)
tour voyage organisé *m.* (5)
tourist touriste *m.*, *f.* (5)
   ~ office Syndicat d'Initiative *m.* (4)
tooth dent *f.* (13)
Tour de France Tour de France *m.* (14)
toward vers (13)
town ville *f.* (4)
traditional traditionnel(le) (18)
traditionally traditionnellement (18)
traffic circulation *f.* (10); *(drugs)* trafic *m.* (11)
   ~ jam embouteillage *m.* (10)
tragedy tragédie *f.* (15)
train train *m.* (6)
   ~ station gare *f.* (4)
to translate traduire (14)
transportation transport *m.* (6)
to travel voyager (4)
travel agency agence de voyages *f.* (4)
tree arbre *m.* (17)
trip voyage *m.* (4)
   to take a ~ faire un voyage (5)
trombone trombone *m.* (15)
trouble
   to have ~ avoir du mal à (15)
trout truite *f.* (9)
truck camion *m.* (6)
true vrai(e) (2)

truly vraiment (9)
trumpet trompette *f.* (15)
trunk coffre *m.* (10); tronc *m.* (17)
truth vérité *f.* (14)
to try essayer (de) (12); chercher (à) (15)
T-shirt tee-shirt *m.* (5)
Tuesday mardi *m.* (9)
Tunisia Tunisie *f.* (4)
Tunisian tunisien(ne) (3)
to turn on allumer (7); mettre (17)
TV télé (2)
   ~ news journal *m.* (*pl.* -aux) (11)
   ~ set téléviseur *m.* (7)
twelve douze (1)
twentieth vingtième (2)
twenty vingt (1)
twenty-first vingt et unième (2)
two deux (1)
to type taper (8)

U

ugly laid(e) (2)
umbrella parapluie *m.* (5)
unbearable insupportable (8)
uncertainty incertitude *f.* (11)
uncle oncle *m.* (2)
under sous (4)
to understand comprendre (9)
undocumented aliens sans-papiers *m.* (11)
undressed
   to get ~ se déshabiller (13)
unemployment chômage *m.* (11)
unfair injuste (11)
unfortunately malheureusement (18)
unhappy malheureux (2)
United States Etats-Unis *m. pl.* (4)
university fac(ulté) *f.*, université (1)
   ~ cafeteria restau-U *m.* (4)
unlikely peu probable (11)
unpleasant désagréable (2)
until jusqu'à (6)
use usage *m.* (15)
to use utiliser (8)
used d'occasion (10)
   to be ~ for servir (à) (7)
useful utile (2)
useless inutile (2)
utilities charges *f. pl.* (16)

V

vacation vacances *f. pl.* (9)
  summer ~ grandes vacances *f. pl.* (10)
Valentine's Day Saint-Valentin *f.* (9)
variety variété *f.* (9)
  ~ **show** variétés *f. pl.* (11)
V.A.T. (value-added tax) T.V.A. *f.* (10)
VCR magnétoscope *m.* (7)
veal veau *m.* (9)
vegetables légumes *m. pl.* (3)
  raw ~ crudités *f. pl.* (9)
vegetarian végétarien(ne) (9)
very très (P)
  ~ **well** très bien (P)
violin violon *m.* (15)
to visit
  ~ **(a place)** visiter (4)
  ~ **(people)** rendre visite à (6); aller voir (8)
voice voix *f.* (7)
volleyball volley-ball *m.* (14)

W

to wait (for) attendre (6)
waiter garçon *m.* (3)
to wake up se réveiller (13)
walk
  to go for a ~ faire un tour, faire une promenade (5); se promener (13)
to walk promener (13)
Walkman Walkman *m.* (7)
wall mur *m.* (3)
wallet portefeuille *m.* (7)
to want vouloir (7)
war
  nuclear ~ guerre nucléaire *f.* (11)
Warsaw Varsovie (4)
washed
  to get ~ se laver (13)
washing machine machine à laver *f.* (16)

water eau *f.* (3)
watercolor aquarelle *f.* (15)
way chemin *m.* (16)
we nous; on (1)
to wear porter (5)
weather temps *m.* (6)
  ~ **forecast** météo *f.* (8)
Wednesday mercredi *m.* (9)
week semaine *f.* (4)
weekend week-end *m.* (4)
welcome
  you're ~ il n'y a pas de quoi (1)
well bien (P); alors (13)
  ~ **then** eh bien (1)
what quel(le) (5; 7); qu'est-ce qui?, qu'est-ce que?, quoi? (7)
  ~ **is it?** qu'est-ce que c'est? (1)
  ~ **kind of** quelle sorte de (3)
wheel volant *m.* (10)
when lorsque (17)
  ~? quand? (2)
where où (2)
whereabout? où ça?
which quel(le) (5; 7) que qui *(pron. rel.)* (16)
of ~ dont (17)
white blanc(he) (3)
who qui, qui est-ce qui (7); qui *(pron. rel.)* (16)
  ~'**s speaking?** qui est à l'appareil? (7)
whom qui est-ce que (7); que *(pron. rel.)* (16)
  to ~? à qui? (7)
whose dont (17)
  ~ **turn is it?** c'est à qui? (6)
why pourquoi (4)
wife femme *f.* (2)
will volonté *f.* (15)
willing
  to be willing vouloir bien (7)
to win gagner (14)
window fenêtre *f.* (1)
windshield pare-brise *m.* (10)
windy
  to be ~ faire du vent (8)

wine vin *m.* (3)
winter hiver *m.* (5)
to wish désirer (2); souhaiter (11)
with avec (1)
without sans (2)
woman femme *f.* (1)
word processor traitement de texte *m.* (8)
work travail *m.* (11); œuvre *f.* (15)
to work travailler (1); marcher (7)
world monde *m.* (11)
worried
  to be worried s'inquiéter (13)
to worry inquiéter (13); s'inquiéter (de) (15)
worth
  it's not ~ **the trouble** ce n'est pas la peine (7)
wrestling catch *m.* (14)
to write écrire (à) (14)
writer écrivain(e) *m., f.* (2)
written écrit(e) (8)
wrong
  to be ~ avoir tort (de) (3)

Y

yard jardin *m.* (17)
year an *m.* (3); année *f.* (4)
  school ~ année scolaire *f.* (8)
yellow jaune (5)
yes oui (P); si (2)
yesterday hier (5)
you toi, vous (P); tu (1)
young jeune (9)
  ~ **people** jeunes gens *m. pl.* (2)
your votre, vos (1; 2); ta, ton, tes (5)
yours le tien, la tienne, les tien(ne)s; le (la) vôtre, les vôtres (14)

Z

Zaire Zaïre *m.* (4)
zero zéro (1)

Index

Credits

Text and Illustrations

p. 39, Puigro cartoon from *Le Français dans le monde*, #105, June 1974, p. 8.

p. 77, Recipe and illustrations from «Quiche Lorraine» from *La Pâtisserie est un jeu d'enfant* by Michel Oliver. Used by permission of Librarie Plon.

p. 140, Map of «Le Métropolitain» used by permission of la Régie Autonome des Transports Parisiens.

p. 166, Advertisement appearing in brochure entitled, "Passeport: Voyage du Cœur."

pp. 185–186, Adapté de l'article «Le Minitel», Vol. 9, No. 5 du *Journal Français d'Amérique*. Reprinted by permission.

pp. 212–213, Adapté de l'article «Paris», Vol. 13, No. 10 du *Journal Français d'Amérique*. Reprinted by permission.

pp. 267–268, Adapté de l'article «Paris», Vol. 12, No. 17 du *Journal Français d'Amérique*. Reprinted by permission.

p. 292, Reprinted by permission of TF1.

pp. 317–318, Adapted from articles «Bonheur» and «Dépenses» from *Francoscopie 1987*. Reprinted by permission of Francoscopie, Larousse.

pp. 343–345, Adapté d'une annonce de presse de Médecins sans Frontières.

p. 368, Copy of "Sports et environnement" souvenir sheet issued by the United Nations Postal Administration. Designed by LeRoy Neiman, U.S.A.

p. 373, Copyright by *L'Express*. Distributed by the New York Times Special Features.

p. 417, © 1980 by Ken Meaux and Earl Comeaux.

p. 438, Reprinted from the Hydro-Quebec page on the World Wide Web.

p. 442, Robert Mélançon, «Neige» de *Peinture aveugle*, (Montréal: VLB Éditeur, 1980). Copyright © by Robert Mélançon. Reprinted by permission.

p. 457, «Les Triplés» by Nicole Lambert, originally published in *Figaro Madame*, March 9, 1991, by Nicole Lambert. Reprinted by permission.

pp. 460–461, Adapted from «Touche pas à mon pote» from *L'Express* No. 1058, February 15, 1985. Copyright 1985, *L'Express*. Distributed by the New York Times Special Features.

pp. 103, 193, 228, 292, 438, and 440 illustrations by Network Graphics.

All other illustrations by George M. Ulrich.

Photographs

p. 1, M. Antman/The Image Works; *p. 3*, David Simson/ Stock Boston; *p. 5*, William Stevens/Gamma Liaison; *p. 7*, Ulrike Welsch/Photo Edit; *p. 9*, M. Antman/The Image Works; *p. 27*, Owen Franken/Stock Boston; Judy Poe; *pp. 33, 49*, R. Lucas/The Image Works; *p. 51*, Photo Researchers; *p. 55*, Andrew Brillant; *p. 57*, B & J McGrath/Picture Cube; *p. 76*, R. Lucas/The Image Works; *p. 84*, David Simmons/Stock Boston; *p. 87*, Kip Brundage/Gamma Liaison; *p. 104*, Spencer Grant/Picture Cube; *p. 107*, Topham/The Image Works; *p. 111*, David Simson/Stock Boston; *p. 130*, Ray Scott/The Image Works; *p. 137*, Alain Nogues/Sygma; *p. 156*, Bassignac/ Deville/Gamma Liaison; *p. 163*, C. Fansworth/The Image Works; *p. 165*, P. Gontier/The Image Works; *p. 184*, Peter Menzel/Stock Boston; *p. 190*, Dale Boyer /Photo Researchers; *p. 210*, IPA/The Image Works; *p. 213*, P. Gontier/The Image Works; *p. 216*, Christian Petit/Photo Researchers; *p. 219*, Steven Rothfield/Tony Stone Images; *p. 235*, Joseph Nettis/Stock Boston; *p. 239*, Courtesy of Paul Bocuse; *p. 238*, Courtesy of Paul Bocuse; *p. 245*, Bernard Bakalian/Gamma Liaison; *p. 248*, F. Hildago/The Image Bank; *p. 265*, R. Lucas/The Image Works; *p. 268*, Chris Hackett/The Image Bank; *p. 271*, J. M. Turpin/Gamma Liaison; *p. 296*, Ray Scott/ The Image Works; *p. 297*, C. Snider/The Image Works; *p. 313*, Mikki Ansin/Picture Cube; *p. 324*, Claude Aion/Gamma Liaison; *p. 327*, Matt Jacob/The Image Works; *p. 334*, Ulrike Welsch/Photo Researchers; *p. 344*, Anita Jensen/Gamma Liaison; *p. 348*, Peter Menzel, Stock Boston; *p. 351*, A. Gyori/Sygma; *p. 366*, Philippe Poulet/Gamma Sport; *p. 371*, Thibault/Photo Researchers; *p. 387*, Peter Menzel/Stock Boston; *p. 391*, E. Robert/Sygma; *p. 398*, Wolfgang Kaehler/Gamma Liaison; *p. 401*, Robert Fried/Stock Boston; *p. 421*, M. Antman/The Image Works; *p. 422*, Jocelyn Boutin/ The Picture Cube; *p. 439*, J. P. Laffont/Sygma; *p. 443*, Owen Franken/Stock Boston; *p. 460*, P. Gontier/The Image Works.

EUROPE

Le français est la langue officielle

Le français est une des langues officielles

0   250   500 milles

0   250   500 kilomètres

ISLANDE

NORVÈGE

SUÈDE

FINLANDE

ESTONIE

RUSSIE

LETTONIE

GRANDE-BRETAGNE

IRLANDE

Mer du Nord

DANEMARK

RUSSIE

LITUANIE

BIÉLORUSSIE

PAYS-BAS

BELGIQUE

ALLEMAGNE

POLOGNE

LUXEMBOURG

OCÉAN ATLANTIQUE

RÉPUBLIQUE TCHÈQUE

UKRAINE

SLOVAQUIE

FRANCE

SUISSE

AUTRICHE

HONGRIE

MOLDAVIE

SLOVÉNIE

CROATIE

ROUMANIE

PORTUGAL

ANDORRE

BOSNIE-HERZÉGOVINE

YOUGOSLAVIE

ITALIE

ESPAGNE

BULGARIE

MACÉDOINE

ALBANIE

GRÈCE

TURQUIE

Mer Méditerranée

CHYPRE